# CURRENT ADVANCEMENTS IN STEREO VISION

Edited by **Asim Bhatti**

**Biomedical Engineering – Technical Applications in Medicine**
http://dx.doi.org/10.5772/2608
Edited by Radovan Hudak, Marek Penhaker and Jaroslav Majernik

**Contributors**

Marcin Pisarek, Agata Roguska, Lionel Marcon, Mariusz Andrzejczuk, Luana Marotta Reis de Vasconcellos, Yasmin Rodarte Carvalho, Renata Falchete do Prado, Luis Gustavo Oliveira de Vasconcellos, Mário Lima de Alencastro Graça, Carlos Alberto Alves Cairo, Shabnam Hosseini, Balaprasad Ankamwar, L. Syam Sundar, Ranjit Hawaldar, Elby Titus, Jose Gracio, Manoj Kumar Singh, David Sebastiao Cabral, Robson Luiz Moreno, Tales Cleber Pimenta, Leonardo Breseghello Zoccal, Paulo Cesar Crepaldi, Alireza Zabihian, M.H. Maghami, Farzad Asgarian, Amir M. Sodagar, Ernesto Suaste Gómez, Anabel S. Sánchez Sánchez, Jeremy (Zheng) Li, Radovan Hudák, Jozef Živčák, Richard L. Magin, Dimitris Tsiokos, George T. Kanellos, George Papaioannou, Stavros Pissadakis, Adriana Fontes, Rafael Bezerra de Lira, Maria Aparecida Barreto Lopes Seabra, Thiago Gomes da Silva, Antônio Gomes de Castro Neto, Beate Saegesser Santos, Alvaro Camilo Dias Faria, Karla Kristine Dames da Silva, Gerusa Marítmo da Costa, Agnaldo José Lopes, Pedro Lopes de Melo, Rômulo Mota Volpato, Paul Jansz, Steven Richardson, Graham Wild, Steven Hinckley, Chin-Lung Yang, Yu-Lin Yang, Chun-Chih Lo, Odilon Dutra, Gustavo Della Colletta

**Published by InTech**
Janeza Trdine 9, 51000 Rijeka, Croatia



**Publishing Process Manager** Masa Vidovic
**Technical Editor** InTech DTP team
**Cover** InTech Design team

Additional hard copies can be obtained from orders@intechopen.com

Biomedical Engineering – Technical Applications in Medicine, Edited by Radovan Hudak, Marek Penhaker and Jaroslav Majernik
p. cm.
ISBN 978-953-51-0733-0

For EU product safety concerns:
IN TECH d.o.o., Prolaz Marije Krucifikse Kozulić 3, 51000 Rijeka, Croatia,
info@intechopen.com or visit our website at intechopen.com.

# Meet the editor

Dr Bhatti is affiliated with Centre for Intelligent Systems Research (CISR), Deakin University, Australia and has participated in research and development activities spanning the areas of computer vision, haptics, robotics, human machine interfaces and nanotechnology systems. Dr Bhatti has participated in a number of successful research grants including ARC discovery and linkage, International science linkage, RESS, CRGS and other industrial and government grants that have resulted in accumulative income of over $1.75M of dollars. He has published over 60 research papers, authored 2 and edited 3 books, published over 11 peer reviewed technical reports. Dr Bhatti has been awarded a worldwide patent on haptics applications and has received numerous awards including 2011 Australian Endeavour fellowship.

# Contents

# Preface

Where the possibilities of a man reached the end, especially from the point of view of technical solutions, the nature took over and formed our environment according to its needs. Nowadays technical and engineering activities have a significantly greater impact on the natural laws and rules once considered as changeless. Nonetheless we have been approaching the same pattern that we followed in the past – we get inspired by the nature. We imitate shapes, functions or we deal with combinations of the two. We play with nanomaterials and nanotechnologies, molecules and atoms, biosensors and multisensoric systems measure the required biological parameters and processes with a relatively high accuracy, the electronic systems and computers create artificial intelligence that is integrated into diagnostic, measuring or control systems.

A specific area where these technologies „touch" with a man is the area of biomedical engineering. On the basis of new applications of technics, mathematics and physics into medicine, biomedical engineering has been gradually formed and it is defined as an interdisciplinary science discipline that uses knowledge from science and technology in order to study biological subjects and materials and to transform them to devices or systems designed for diagnostics, analysis, measurement, therapy or rehabilitation.

Based on the interconnection between various scientific areas, disciplines such as biomechanics, biophysics, biocybernetics, bioinformatics, biosensorics, biomaterials and the like have been formed. Thus at present, biomedical engineering is a wide area moving from nano up to macrosphere, applying technical laws and systems also to human body as a whole and it is considered from both points of view of qualitative evaluation and also obtaining of quantitative outputs. Moreover, from the systematic aspect human body largely enables these approaches but on the other side it creates a formula with many unknown quantities.

Let me present you a book that includes chosen results of a recent research and development categorized in the area of biomedical engineering focusing on technical solutions. The book content is relatively wide. It represents material research with an objective of biocompatibility improvement, invasiveness minimizing and integration of the solutions that form nanomedicine. Nevertheless, there are also tissue engineering and genomics that are very often considered as representatives of a future for biomedical engineering by many scientists. Further on it contains relatively wide area of bioelectronics and electrotechnics and there is a significant position for a research in the area of image processing, modeling and simulations. Telemedicine also represents future of diagnostics as well as therapies where the information technologies using database and expert systems may bring interesting results. Also in medicine there has been a need for miniaturization and energetic effectivity. The chosen chapters solve exactly these problems.

I believe that the findings and knowledge presented in the book will enable the readers to complete at least one missing unknown quantity in the metaphoric formula in their research and thus will gain new valuable information.

I wish you a pleasant and inspiring reading.

**Ing. Radovan Hudak, PhD.,**
Head of Biomedical Engineering Division
Technical University of Kosice,
Slovakia

Section 1

# Biomaterials

Chapter 1

# Biomimetic and Electrodeposited Calcium-Phosphates Coatings on Ti – Formation, Surface Characterization, Biological Response

Marcin Pisarek, Agata Roguska, Lionel Marcon and Mariusz Andrzejczuk

Additional information is available at the end of the chapter

http://dx.doi.org/10.5772/48693

## 1. Introduction

Engineering of materials (metals and their alloys) with a controlled and surface morphology in nanoscale is important due to their potential applications in biomedicine and catalysis. Titanium dioxide ($TiO_2$) has attracted the attention of scientists and engineers for its unique properties and has also been considered in above mentioned applications [1]. $TiO_2$ nanostructures offer encouraging implications for the development and optimization of novel substrates for biological research [2,3] and spectroscopic (SERS: Surface Enhanced Raman Spectroscopy) investigations: absorbate-adsorbate systems [4-6]. Titanium oxide layers with controlled morphology have been reported to stimulate apatite formation in the living environment in vitro or simulated body fluid to a greater extent than smooth native oxide layers on titanium [7]. In addition, $TiO_2$ nanostructures can act as an anchor of ceramic top coating and improve mechanical interlocking between the coating and the substrate [2]. However, only a few studies have reported modifications to the surface roughness as well as the chemistry at the nanometer scale in a reproducible and cost effective manner [8-11].

In recent years, there has been increasing interest in the formation of porous bioactive surface layers on titanium substrates, which would contribute to an increase of the surface roughness and the specific surface area provided for the subsequent coating deposition via biomimetic methods (prolonged soaking in simulated body fluid, e.g. Hanks'solution, under physiological conditions) [7,12-14]. Since the heterogeneous nucleation ability of calcium and phosphate ions is directly dependent on a proper "activation" of metal surface, different Ti pretreatments such as alkali treatment [14-18], acid treatment [7,9,10,14], $H_2O_2$ treatment [11,19], and anodic oxidation treatment in a solution containing fluoride ions have been investigated to form bioactive porous oxide layers on Ti [2,3,20-22]. The purpose of those pretreatments is mainly to modify the surface topography, the chemical composition and structure of the oxide layer, and to form a new surface layer. Electrochemical processes are also commonly applied for modifying surfaces of Ti to increase its biocompatibility through direct electrodeposition from Hanks' solution [23,24]. The resulting chemical composition is close to that of hydroxyapatite, one of the few materials that support bone ingrowth and osseointegration when used in orthopedic or dental applications [25,26]. Both biomimetically and electrochemically deposited calcium phosphate coatings are considered as promising alternatives to conventional plasma spraying hydroxyapatite [25,27].

The nucleation and growth of calcium phosphates on titanium oxides has been extensively investigated because of their relevance to orthopedic applications. It is well known that Ca-P coatings have led to better clinical success rates in long term than uncoated titanium implants. These advantages are due to superior initial rate of osseointegration. The apatite coatings deposited on different biomaterials (metals and their alloys, polymers) can reduce fibrous encapsulation, promote bone growth, enhance direct bone contact and has also been shown to promote differentiation of bone marrow stromal cells along osteogenic lineage [28]. The design of novel Ca-P coatings involves also addition of small amount of metal or metal oxides nanoparticles exhibiting antibacterial activity. Such nanoparticle incorporated to Ca-P coatings may impart antibacterial property, which makes them promising to be applied in hard tissue replacement against postoperative infections. However, it is worth to mention, that the size and amount of such nanoparticles should be properly chosen, in order to prevent their toxic effect to living cells [29].

In this chapter a two-step procedure, based on chemical and electrochemical methods aimed at activating titanium surface for subsequent deposition of calcium phosphate coatings, is presented. The combined effects of surface topography and chemistry of Ti substrate on calcium phosphate formation are discussed. The calcium phosphate coatings produced by both biomimetic as well as electrochemical methods are compared with respect to their physicochemical characteristics and biological evaluation.

## 2. Body (problem statement, application area, research course, method used, status, results, further research)

To date, studies of modified Ti surfaces for biomedical purposes have focused on characterization of their morphology and physicochemical properties. Interest in those properties stems from the fact that such materials display high corrosion resistance through a wide pH range as well as in solutions containing aggressive ions in comparison with metallic materials not based on Ti. Data in the literature indicate that many centers in the world try to highlight the chemical composition of oxide layers based on titanium: on defining the chemical state of the elements of which such layers are composed, and defining varieties of the polymorphic forms of titanium dioxide which constitutes the main component of such layers (structural research) [19,30].

The basic factors characterizing a material's surface and significantly affecting the biological processes occurring at the material-cell/tissue interface include its surface topography, chemical and phase composition, and physicochemical properties (e.g. wettability). In spite of intensive studies worldwide, no definitive criteria have yet been established to describe the optimal topographical/morphological features of a biomaterial in relation to particular cell lines. It is known, however, that titanium oxides materials having a relatively highly developed surface should show improved integration with bone tissue. It has also been observed that a titanium surface having a well-developed morphology and high porosity accelerates collagen synthesis and supports bone mineralization. The application of appropriate methods of modifying the surface of the biomaterial has a significant impact on adhesion and the rate of cell growth [31,32]. It must be considered, however, that the cells present at the tissue/material interface will react differently to the particular properties of the implant surface. Contact between the biomaterial and cells, tissues and body fluids results in extra-cellular matrix proteins being spontaneously deposited on the surface, forming a biofilm. Cells adhere through integrin receptors and a specific arrangement of extra-cellular matrix proteins. The resulting complex determines cell behavior including their ability to proliferate and migrate. The distribution and thickness of the biofilm depends on the surface properties of the biomaterial, and mainly on its chemical composition and morphology [33].

Chemical processes for modifying surfaces of Ti and its alloys are widely employed to increase the biocompatibility of those materials. Such methods as Ti etching in alkaline solutions (e.g. NaOH [9,14-18,30,32,34]), acidic solutions (e.g. $H_2SO_4$, $H_3PO_4$ [9,14,32]) or hydrogen peroxide ($H_2O_2$ [11,19]) at high temperatures, combined with subsequent prolonged soaking of samples in artificial physiological solutions (SBF- Simulated Body Fluid, Hanks solution) at pH~7, make it possible to obtain porous oxide layers with built-in ions of calcium and phosphorous [12,14,16,18,22,35]. The chemical composition of the coatings obtained in this way is close to that of hydroxyapatite, one of the most effective materials for increasing biocompatibility. The anodic oxidation of Ti and its alloys in acidic or neutral solutions containing fluorides is a typical electrochemical method for obtaining oxidized layers of different thicknesses, uniform chemical composition and refined nanoporosity [2,3,5,20-22,36]. The addition of an electrolyte of suitable fluoride concentration can ensure that a porous morphology is obtained, in the form of 'honeycomb' titanium oxide nanotubes[20-22]. Such structures can provide very promising substrates which increase biological tolerance, because they allow to precisely control the thickness of layers (by the end voltage of the anodic polarization) and surface morphology (porosity). Further chemical treatment is made to introduce other factors increasing biotolerance, in the form of ions of calcium and phosphorus, by immersing the oxide layers in artificial physiological solutions [22,37-40] or by electro-deposition from the same solutions [41,43]. Such surface modification of titanium may play an additional role providing protection against the action of the biological environment and thus restricting the penetration of metal ions into the organism. This is particularly important because of the increasing frequency of titanium allergies, even though titanium was long considered biologically inert.

One unfortunate phenomenon associated with implant surgery is the high risk of post-operative infections. The adherence of bacteria to the biomaterial causes surgical complications, and poses a particularly serious threat to patients with long-term implants. It is true that modern, effective methods of sterilization now exist which reduce the risk of complications from infection, yet in the case of the early onset of corrosion of the implant, problems with bacterial habitats do arise [43,44]. Post-operative infections can be counteracted by silver nanoparticles on the surface of the biomaterial, since their antibacterial properties are well demonstrated [45,46]. The bactericidal properties of silver nanoparticles largely result from the size of the particles, which allows such structures to penetrate easily through biological membranes to the interior of microorganisms. At the same time, studies indicate that silver has no toxic effect on human cells (limphocytes, fibroblasts and osteoblasts) [29] if the concentration of silver ions in the body fluids is below 10 mg/l [47].

The following materials and methods were used for preparation and characterization of biomimetic coatings:

- Material substrate: 0.25 mm-thick Ti foil (99.5% purity, Alfa Aesar, USA), all samples before any treatment were ultrasonically cleaned with deionized (DI) water, rinsed with acetone and ethanol and dried in air.
- Chemical pretreatment: the samples were soaked in a 3 M NaOH aqueous solution at 70°C for 24 h, or in an $H_3PO_4$ + $H_2O_2$ mixture (with a volume ratio of 1:1) at room temperature for 24 h.
- Electrochemical pretreatment: titanium oxide nanotube layers were fabricated by anodic oxidation of Ti in an optimized electrolyte of $NH_4F$ (0.86 wt.%) + DI water (47.14 wt.%) + glycerol (52 wt.%) at room temperature, applied voltage $V_{max}$ from 10 V up to 25 V. After anodization, the samples were annealed in air at 600°C for 1 or 2 h.
- The annealed nanotubes were covered with a thin Ag layer by the sputter deposition technique in a vacuum ($p = 3 \times 10^{-3}$ Pa), using a JEE-4X JEOL device, in a configuration perpendicular to the surface of the samples. Ag of spectral purity was used. The average amount of the metal deposited per $cm^2$ was estimated from the mass gain of the samples. Both the true average and local amount of the metal deposits may actually vary substantially due to the highly-developed specific surface area of the $TiO_2$ nanotube/Ti substrate.
- Mechanical properties: nano-hardhness, Young's modulus, of anodic oxide layers and Ca-P coatings on a Ti before and after heat treatment were measured using the Hysitron Nanoindenter device equipped with a Berkowich intender. The indentation parameters were as follows: a loading rate of 0.1 mN/s to a maximum load of 1 mN for period of constant load of 2 s. From the measurements, nano-hardness, H, and reduced Young's modulus, Er, were determined according to the standard procedures [48]. Average values were calculated from 8 to 12 measurements for each sample.
- Deposition of biomimetic calcium phosphate coatings on Ti oxide or Ti substrate. The samples were exposed to a stagnant Hanks' solution in a plastic vessel and kept in a glass thermostat at 37°C for 6 h up to 7 days. All samples were washed with distilled water and eventually dried in air at 250°C for 1 h. The direct electrodeposition of

calcium phosphates was performed at laboratory temperature for 2h 15 min in a conventional cell fitted with an Ag/AgCl (3 M KCl) electrode maintaining the cathodic potential of – 1.5 V vs OCP potential (10 min). Titanium substrates were used as cathodes for electrodeposition. The cathodic polarization process was performed using an AutoLab PGSTAT 302N (Ecochemie) potentiostat/galvanostat.

- The Hanks' solution was prepared by dissolving reagent-grade (g/L): NaCl 8.00, KCl 0.40, $Na_2HPO_4{\cdot}2H_2O$ 0.06, $KH_2PO_4$ 0.06, $MgSO_4{\cdot}7H_2O$ 0.20, $NaHCO_3$ 0.35, $CaCl_2$ 0.14 into distilled water and buffering at pH = 7.4.
- For the morphological characterization of the samples top-view and cross-sectional examinations were carried out with a high resolution scanning electron microscope (Hitachi S-5500). A Thermo Noran spectrometer coupled with a Hitachi S-5500 scanning electron microscope was used for local EDS analysis.
- The surface topography of the chemically treated samples was examined by AFM (MultiMode V, Veeco). AFM images were recorded in contact mode using silicon cantilevers with a resonance frequency of 250–300 kHz. The investigated surfaces were scanned within the area of 1 $\mu m^2$. The estimation of the surface roughness parameters, the average roughness (Ra), root-mean-square deviation ($R_q$), the mean roughness depth (Rz) and maximum roughness depth $R_{max}$, was done using the Nanoscope 7.2 software (Veeco).
- A single focused ion beam (FIB) Hitachi FB-2100 system (Hitachi High Technologies Corporation, Japan) was used for TEM specimen preparation. A gallium source ion beam with applied accelerating voltage 40 kV during FIB milling, and 10 kV for final thinning, was used. This system allowed for lift-out sample preparation technique to be used in order to obtain a thin TEM lamella. The thickness of the lamella, as measured by cross-section observations in FIB, was less than 100 nm. The samples prepared by FIB milling were examined with a high resolution scanning transmission electron microscope (Hitachi HD- 2700, Hitachi High-Technology Co., Tokyo) operating at an accelerating voltage of 200 kV and with transmission electron microscope (TEM Jeol 1200) operating at an accelerating voltage 120V.
- The chemical composition of the surface of the samples, with and without the calcium phosphate coatings and after adsorption of the proteins, was characterized by Auger electron spectroscopy and X-ray photoelectron spectroscopy (Microlab 350). For XPS used $Al_{K\alpha}$ non-monochromated radiation (1486.6 eV; 300 W) as the exciting source. The pressure during the analysis was $5.0{\times}10^{-9}$ mbar. The binding energy of the target elements (Ti 2p, O 1s, C 1s, Ca 2p, P 2p, Cl 2p, Mg 1s, Na 1s, N1s) was determined at a pass energy of 40 eV, with a resolution of 0.83 eV, using the binding energy of carbon (C 1s: 285 eV) as the reference. A linear or Shirley background subtraction was applied to obtain XPS signal intensity. The peaks were fitted using an asymmetric Gaussian/Lorentzian mixed function. Fourier transform infrared spectroscopy (FT-IR; Nicolet 6700, Thermo Electron Corporation) was used to analyze the phase composition of the calcium phosphate coatings after incubation in Hanks' solution and adsorption of the proteins. Measurements were made using the attenuated total reflectance (ATR) technique. Each sample was scanned 64 times at a resolution of 4 $cm^{-1}$ over a frequency range of 400–4000 $cm^{-1}$.

- The crystal structure of the substrate materials was determined from the XRD patterns using a Philips PW 1830 X-ray diffractometer equipped with a Cu source ($K\alpha$ line 0.1541837 nm) and X-Pert goniometer. The accelerating voltage was 40 kV, the current 30 mA, and the range of scattering angle $2\theta$ - from 35 up to 100 deg.
- Protein adsorption. Bovine serum albumin (BSA) (Sigma, purity of 99.8%) was used as a model protein in this study. Phosphate buffered saline (PBS, pH = 7.4) was used to prepare the protein solution (10 mg protein / 1 ml PBS), 100 μl of which were pipetted onto the samples' surface coating in a cell culture plate. The plate was then placed in an incubator at 37°C for 20 min. All the samples (before and after immersion in Hanks' solution) were examined immediately after termination of the preparation procedure.
- Living cells attachment. Human osteosarcoma U2OS cells were used to evaluate the biocompatibility of the Ca-P coatings under study. Dulbecco's modified eagle's medium (DMEM, Invitrogen) supplemented with 10% fetal bovine serum (Invitrogen) and 1% of a penicillin/streptomycin mixture was used as a cell culture medium. Cells were seeded on the sample surfaces at $1.0 \times 10^4$ cells/cm$^2$ and cultured at 37°C in a humidified atmosphere containing $CO_2$ for 24, 48, 72 and 120 h. Afterwards, double fluorescent labeling of the cell nuclei and membranes was performed. The cell nuclei were stained with Hoechst 33342 (Invitrogen), and the cell membranes were stained with Vybrant DiI (Molecular Probes) according to the manufacturers' instructions. Morphology of the cells was examined using a fluorescence microscope (Eclipse 80i, Nikon Instruments, Tempe, AZ). All samples were sterilized by autoclaving at 121°C for 20 min prior to the cell culture experiments [49,50].
- The silver ion release from Ag/$TiO_2$ nanotube/Ti samples was measured by inductively coupled plasma mass spectrometry (ICP-MS, Elan 9000 Perkin Elmer). The samples were incubated in 10 ml of deionized water or 0.9% NaCl solution at room temperature without stirring. The amounts of released silver were determined by analyzing the resulting solution.

- **Titanium oxides as potential substrates for deposition of Ca-P coatings: fabrication methods and physicochemical characteristics**
  a. **Formation of nanoporous $TiO_2$ layers on Ti by chemical etching or electrochemical methods**
  b. **Surface and structure characterization**
  c. **Surface roughness and wettability**

The biocompatibility of titanium as an implant material is attributed to the surface oxides spontaneously formed in air [51,52] and/or physiological fluids [33]. It is known that the protective and stable oxides on titanium are favorable for osseointegration [53]. Stability of the oxide depends strongly on its composition, structure and thickness. Among various methods aimed at improving the interfacial properties and lifetime of Ti-based implants [54], anodization and chemical etching methods have attracted considerable attention because of their simplicity and their controllable, reproducible results [7,55].

Fig. 1 shows SEM images of surface morphology of Ti foil (0.25 mm in thickness).

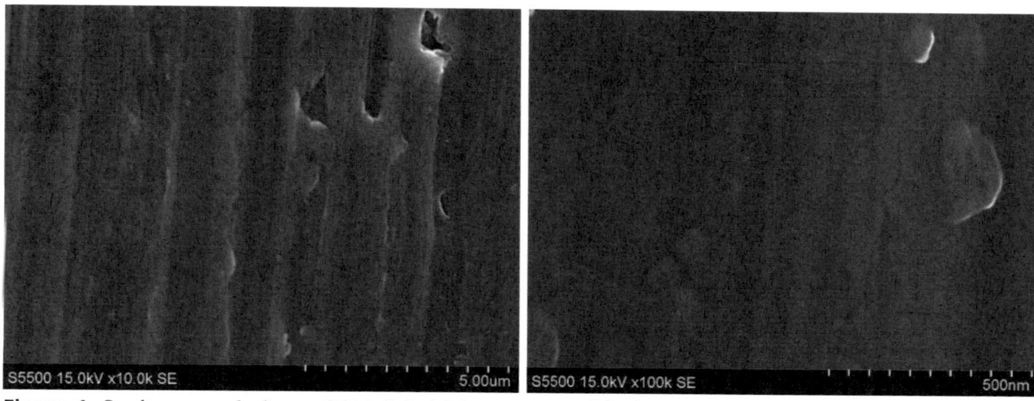


**Figure 1.** Surface morphology of Ti foil (initial sate, unmodified Ti).

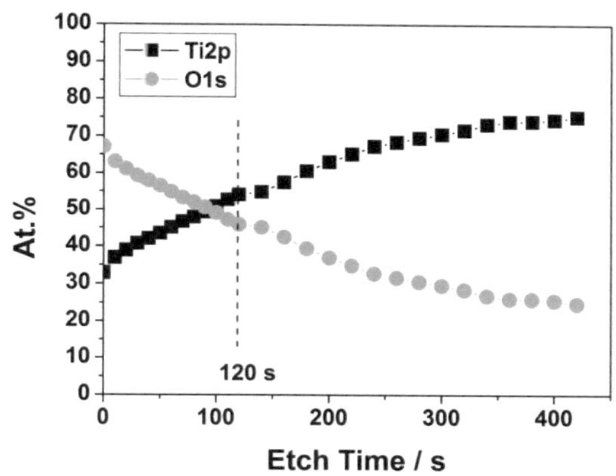


**Figure 2.** Normalized XPS profile for native oxide layer on Ti.

| etch time | Ti2p3/2 / eV | chemical state | atomic fraction / % |
|---|---|---|---|
| 0s | 454.2 | $Ti^0$ (metal) | 7 |
| | 456.1 | $Ti^{2+}$ (TiO) | 6 |
| | 457.3 | $Ti^{3+}$ ($Ti_2O_3$) | 8 |
| | 458.9 | $Ti^{4+}$ ($TiO_2$) | 79 |
| 120s | 454.2 | $Ti^0$ (metal) | 51 |
| | 455.7 | $Ti^{2+}$ (TiO) | 15 |
| | 456.7 | $Ti^{3+}$ ($Ti_2O_3$) | 20 |
| | 458.4 | $Ti^{4+}$ ($TiO_2$) | 14 |

**Table 1.** $Ti2p_{3/2}$ binding energies as measured with XPS and suggested surface chemical species for native oxide layer on Ti before and after 120 s of $Ar^+$ sputtering.

In order to get an insight into the chemical state of titanium in the native oxide layer, XPS measurements were performed. The normalized XPS chemical composition profile is shown in Fig. 2. Table 1 presents binding energies of $Ti2p_{3/2}$ electrons for native oxide layer on Ti. The results show that $TiO_2$ is the main component of the passive layer (native oxide film).

However, some lower Ti-oxides are also present [51]. After 120 h of $Ar^+$ sputtering metallic Ti becomes the main component. In addition, the atomic fraction of the lower Ti oxides is higher than before sputtering. This could be a result of a $TiO_2$ reduction effects during sputtering, as already reported elsewhere [51].

Fig. 3 presents the schematic illustration of native oxide layer on Ti. Such kind of layer is spontanously formed in air on Ti surface and effectively protect metal surface against corrosion.

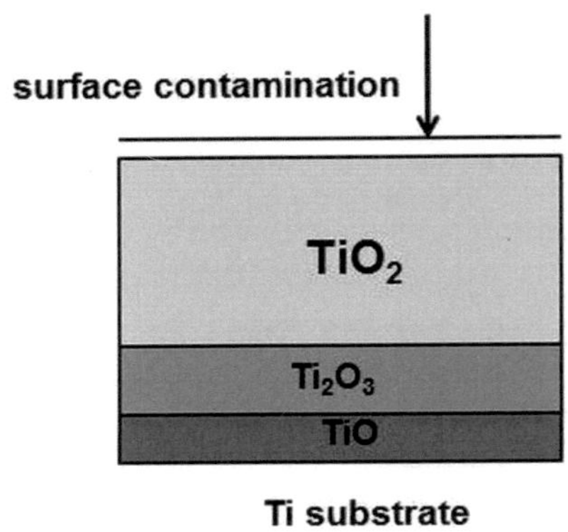


**Figure 3.** Schematic illustration of native oxide layer on Ti.

Results of accelerated corrosion resistance tests – called potentio-dynamic curves - (Fig. 4a, 4b) revealed that Ti exhibits a full resistance to local corrosion in the environment of 0.9% NaCl and artificial physiological solution (Hanks' solution) at pH ~ 7.0 [52]. An increase of current density on the polarization curves, within the region of the corrosion potential ~ 0.0 V up to 2 V, is not related to breakdown of the native oxide film but probably is due to growth

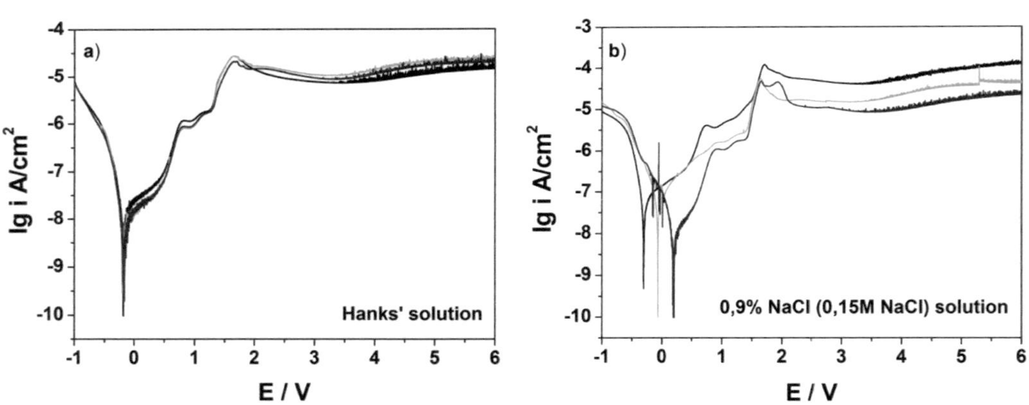


**Figure 4.** Potentiodynamic polarization curves of Ti (initial state) in Hanks' (a) and 0.9% saline solution. The curves were recorded at room temperature (25°C). An AutoLab PGSTAT 302N potentiostat/galvanostat were used in the standard 3-electrode configuration. A normal silver chloride electrode (Ag/AgCl (3M KCl)) and a platinum wire electrode were used as reference and counter electrodes, respectively. A slow potential sweep rate of 1 V/h was applied.

of an oxide layer. This involves also a simultaneous evolution of oxygen during polarization and anodic dissolution of titanium to $Ti^{4+}$ ions [56]. At voltages higher than 2 V a stable oxide layer is formed (plateau in the range of 2 to 6V), in agreement with the analysis of thermodynamic equilibrium diagrams potential - pH for Ti (so-called Pourbaix diagrams [57]).

Preliminary corrosion tests of as-received Ti revealed that the material is resistant to corrosion in environments simulating physiological body fluids in a wide range of potentials. Further data indicate that the native oxide films on Ti allows for bone ingrowth to titanium implant surface REF. Such oxide films increase the biocompatibility of implanted elements reducing the activation of inflammatory reactions in the contact zone between metallic materials and living cells. In addition, a thin layer of protein, which covers the Ti surface, may significantly contribute to improvement of the biocompatibility of Ti [58]. This was confirmed in cell culture experiments (osteoblasts, U2OS). Fig. 5 shows fixed U2OS cells on the Ti substrate. It can be seen that the adsorption of albumin on the Ti surface significantly affects cell proliferation. Careful inspection of the living cells morphology revealed that the osteoblasts have well-developed nuclei (blue staining). The red staining corresponds to the cell membrane which exhibits the "dendritic structure". The characteristic shape of the cells and the presence of filopodia filaments suggest good cell adhesion to the Ti surface. Uniform distribution of the cells may ensure a good contact of the surrounding tissue with Ti implant [53,54].

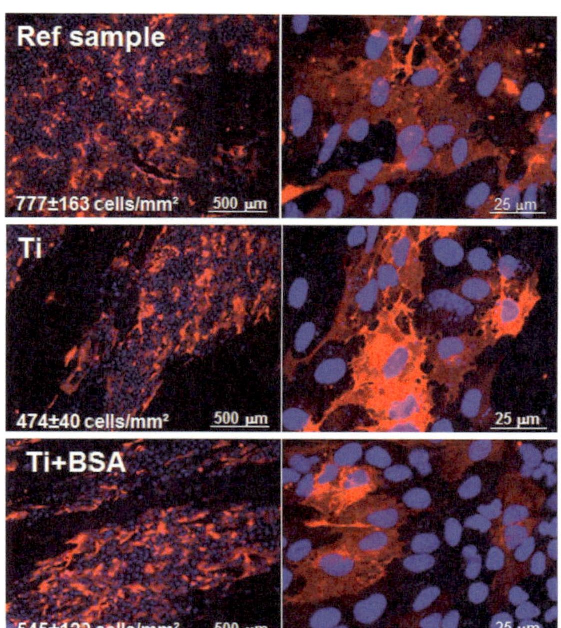


**Figure 5.** Fluorescent microscopy images of U2OS cells cultured for 48 h on pure Ti surface before and after albumin adsorption.

In the following step modification of Ti surface was performed in order to increase its biocompatibility. A two-step procedure (chemical etching or anodic oxidation of Ti followed by soaking in simulated body fluid or direct electrodeposition from Hanks' solution) was applied resulting in a fabrication of composite coatings on Ti which consist of porous titanium oxide layers and calcium phosphate phases.

At first porous titanium oxide layers with high specific surface area were fabricated.

Fig. 6 shows SEM images of a typical morphology of the Ti after chemical/electrochemical pre-treatment in different solutions. The SEM observation revealed that immersion in 3 M NaOH at 70°C for 24 h results in the formation of a 'coral-like' topography (Fig. 6a). The surface layer exhibits a developed, rough morphology characterized by a network of sharp-edged pores of various shapes. After pre-treatment in $H_2O_2$ + $H_3PO_4$ at room temperature, the morphology is quite different, and seems to be less developed (with shallower 'valleys') than that produced during NaOH pre-treatment. Fig. 6b suggests that Ti treated in $H_2O_2$ + $H_3PO_4$ exhibits sponge-like porosity. A distinct texture with round nano-sized pores is clearly seen. The nanopores are uniformly distributed across the surface [14]. The optimized anodization conditions applied resulted in the formation of $TiO_2$ nanotubes (hollow cylinders), at final voltage = 20 V for 2h, arranged perpendicularly to the substrate and separated from each other, Fig. 6c. The final voltage $V_{max}$ has a strong impact on the diameter of the nanotubes, which changes from ~ 40 ± 10 nm at 10 V to almost 110 ± 10 nm at 25 V [22]. A detailed, mechanism of the formation and growth of self-organized $TiO_2$ nanotubes in electrolytes containing fluorides was recently proposed by Macak et al. [21,59] and Petukhov et al. [60]. Thermodynamic aspect of formation such kind of oxide layers was given by Wang et al. [61].

Atomic Force Microscopy - AFM was used to estimate the surface roughness of the samples under investigation [62]. As AFM resolution is limited by the radius of the tip, the AFM tip shape may result in a distorted representation of the actual surface micro-geometry. The parameters calculated from AFM data given in Table 2 may give an idea about the height of the 'hills' and the depth of the 'valleys' formed on the samples after the various surface treatments applied. The average roughness difference is evidenced by the $R_q$ parameter. It should be noticed, however, that the roughness values reported in this paper are based on 1 μm × 1 μm AFM images, Fig.7. Before etching, the sample shows $R_q$ of ~4.7 nm, whereas this parameter slightly increases up to ~5.1 nm for Ti($H_2O_2$ + $H_3PO_4$) and to ~6.3 nm for Ti(NaOH), respectively. The differences in $R_a$ are small, with all values being in the range from 3.8 to 4.8. The $R_z$ and $R_{max}$ values, however, demonstrate a clear difference between the untreated and chemically pre-treated Ti samples. The highest values of those parameters are observed for Ti(NaOH) and indicate the presence of deep valleys, compare Fig 6a.

The as-grown porous anodic layers exhibited poor adhesion to the Ti substrate, so all the samples were annealed in air at 600°C for 2 h to improve their mechanical stability. After anodization process the samples have an amorphous structure. Fig.8 shows an SEM micrograph of $TiO_2$ nanotubes formed by anodic oxidation of Ti, after subsequent annealing. One can see that the heat treatment did not cause any distinct changes in the diameter of the nanotubes (see Fig.6c), but did modify the thickness of the oxide layer. Three distinct

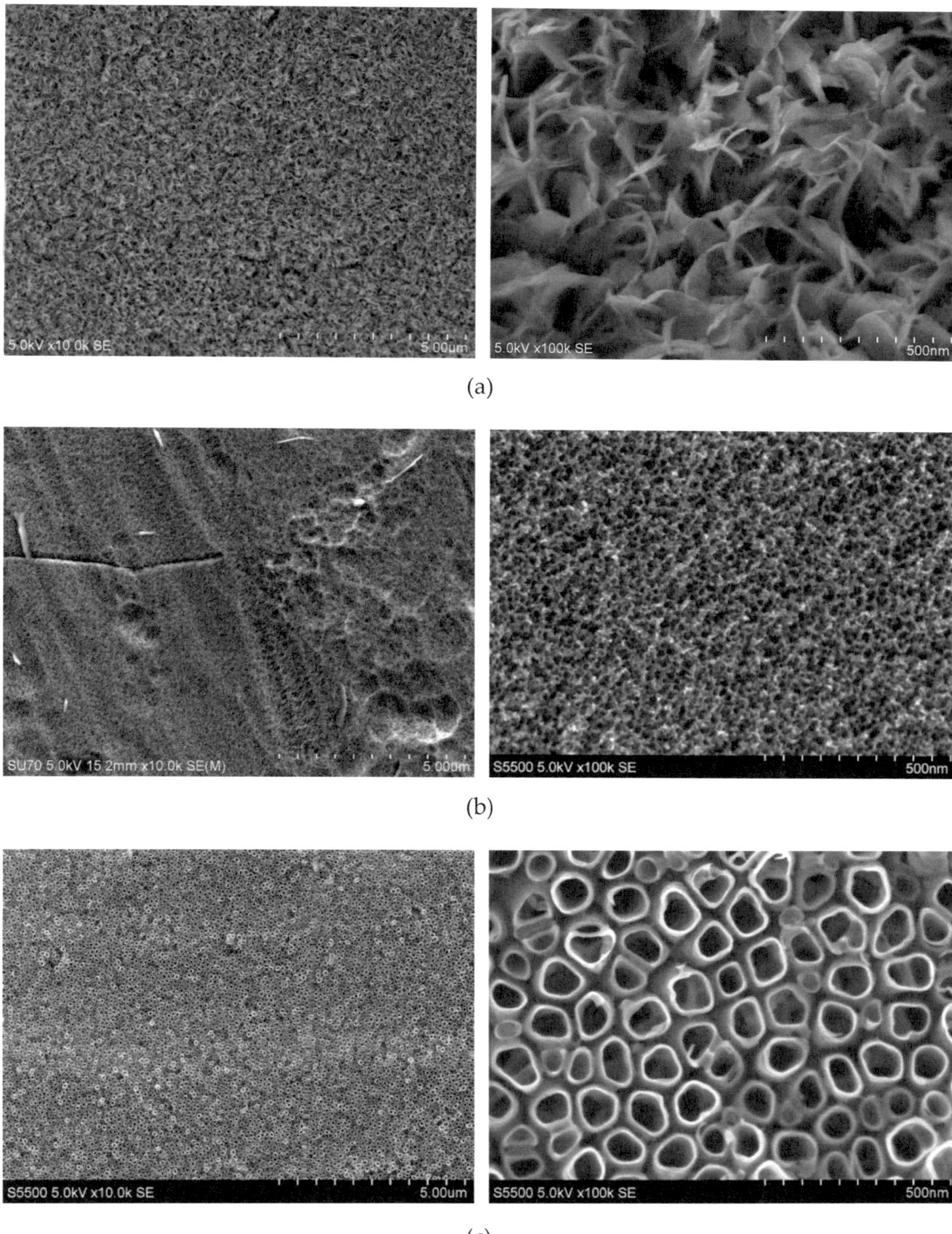


**Figure 6.** SEM images of chemically treated Ti in NaOH (a), $H_3PO_4$+$H_2O_2$ (b) solution and electrochemically treated in $NH_4F$+glycerol+water electrolyte (c).

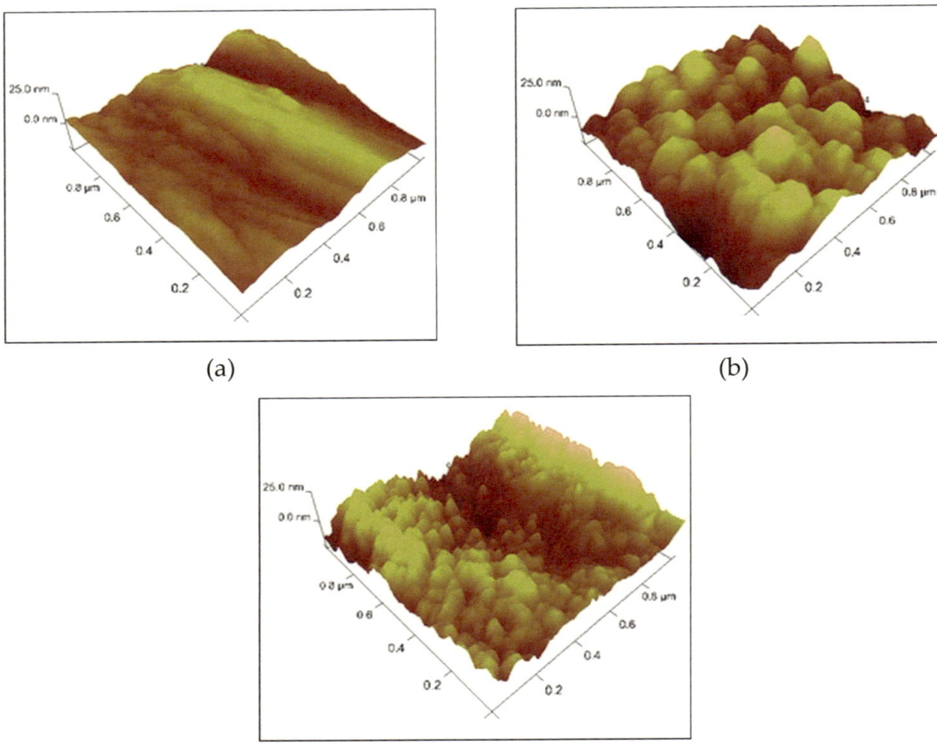


**Figure 7.** AFM images of untreated Ti (a) and chemically treated in NaOH solution (b), $H_3PO_4$+$H_2O_2$ solution (c)

| samples | area | $R_a$ (nm) | $R_q$ (nm) | $R_z$ (nm) | $R_{max}$ (nm) |
|---|---|---|---|---|---|
| **Ti (initial state)** | 1 x 1 µm | 3,8 | 4,7 | 8,7 | 16,9 |
| **Ti (NaOH)** | 1 x 1 µm | 4,8 | 6,3 | 14,1 | 26,2 |
| **Ti($H_3PO_4$+$H_2O_2$)** | 1 x 1 µm | 4,1 | 5,1 | 10,3 | 20,1 |

**Table 2.** Roughness parameter values for the Ti reference and Ti after chemical treatment in NaOH and $H_3PO_4$ + $H_2O_2$.

domains can be distinguished within the cross-section (Fig. 9): titanium dioxide nanotubes, an interphase region (a compact $TiO_2$ layer), and the titanium substrate [22]. TEM examinations revealed that the thickness of the whole oxide layer after heat treatment is about 1.3 µm (before annealing process ~0.8 µm) . The growth of the interphase region due to annealing causes an increase of thickhness of oxide layer, to ~0.5 µm. The intermediate zone is about three times thinner than the nanotube layer. This probably results from an additional oxidation of the Ti substrate and from a consolidation effect due to sintering of the nanotubes with the substrate due to the heat treatment in air [22, 63,64]. Fig.9 shows a high resolution STEM images of the intermediate zone (interphase region - compact $TiO_2$ layer) and single titanium dioxide nanotube after annealing at 600°C for 2 h.

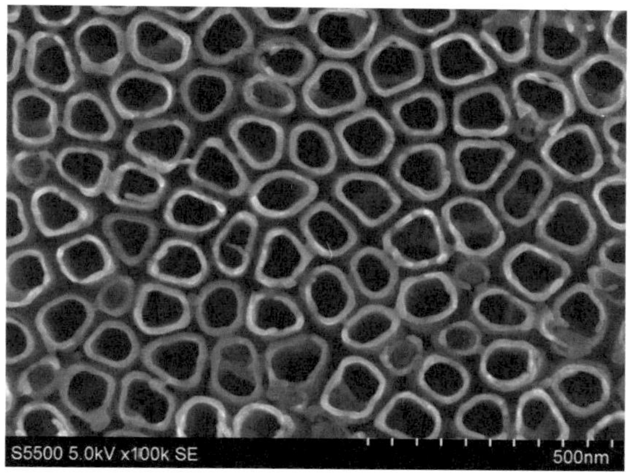


**Figure 8.** SEM image of the $TiO_2$ nanotubes after annealing in air at 600°C for 2 hours

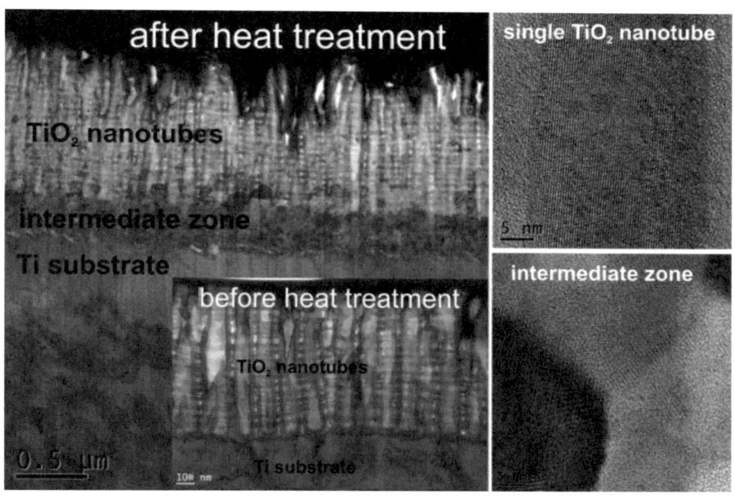


**Figure 9.** TEM image of a cross-section of the porous structure before and after heat treatment in air at 600°C, 2 h. High-resolution STEM images of the intermediate zone (interphase region) and singel $TiO_2$ nanotube.

The crystalline nature of the interphase region and the $TiO_2$ nanotubes is well visible. The lattice spacing for the nanotubes was measured to be circa 0.35 nm, which corresponds to the anatase phase (1 0 1) plane, where d = 0.352 nm (00-021-1272 JCPDS card number) [22]. XRD investigations of the sample annealed at 600°C showed a small amount of rutile phase, which may suggest the occurrence of a phase transition of anatase to rutile at this temperature [64,65], Fig.10. Our findings are in close agreement with those of J. Yu et al., and those of A. Jaroenworaluck et al. [63,65]. The authors suggest that the nucleation of the rutile phase takes place preferentially at the interface between the Ti substrate and the nanotube layer, which in turn suggests that the nanotubes maintain a stable tubular structure above the interfacial layer upon crystallization [64,65].

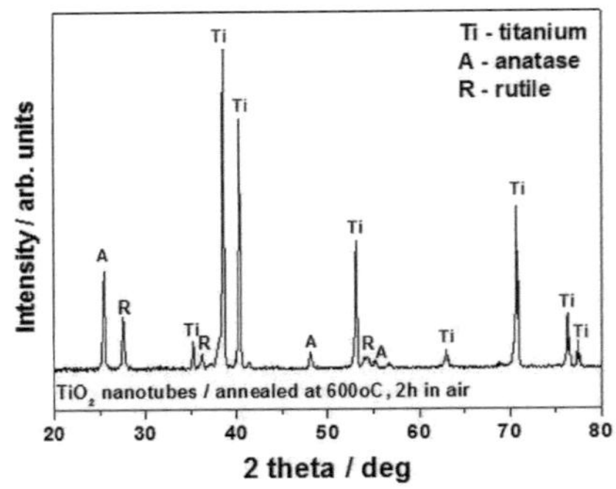


**Figure 10.** XRD spectrum of $TiO_2$ nanotubes formed on a Ti substrate after heat treatment.

Nanoindentation was conducted to probe the mechanical properties such as Young's modulus (Er) and nano-hardness (H) of nanoporous $TiO_2$ layer on a Ti substrate before and after annealing process. However, one should take into account that the parameters Er and H reflect not only the properties of the coating (below 1 μm thick), but are also influenced by the substrate. In addition the mechanism of interaction between indenter and the porous structure is not well understood. Crawford et al. have suggested that during indentation under loading the densification of nanotubes occurs as a result of heavy deformation [66]. In the same work the authors notice that an increased thickness of the porous layer may retard the build-up of stress needed to cause delamination during the loading cycle. This proposed mechanism seems to be also operative in our system.

The results show that the nano-hardness (H) of the annealed anodic porous layer is distinctly different from that of pure Ti and Ti after anodization process (as-received). Reduced elastic modulus Er and nanohardness H are higher for annealed nanotubes than for as-received ones. The nanotubes become hard and brittle due to annealing at 600°C in air, see Table 3. The observed changes of the mechanical properties relate to the effects of transition of the $TiO_2$ nanotubes structure from an amorphous to a crystalline phase (see, Fig. 11) and the formation of interphase region between oxide layer and Ti substrate due to heat treatment at 600°C in air. However, one should mention that after annealing at 600°C the $TiO_2$ nanotubes hardness is even lower than that of Ti metal, see Table 3. Our measurements for pure Ti are in good agreement with data presented by F.K.Mante et al. [67]. This interfacial zone detected by TEM (Fig.9) is probably responsible for the good adhesion of the $TiO_2$ nanotubes to the Ti substrate.

| sample | $E_R$ (GPa) ± $\Delta E_R$ | H (GPa) ± ΔH |
|---|---|---|
| $TiO_2$ nanotubes after anodization (as-received) | 57.0 ± 3 | 1.3 ± 0.1 |
| $TiO_2$ nanotubes annealed at 600°C in air for 1h | 72 ± 5 | 1.8 ± 0.2 |
| Ti foil, initial state | 128 ± 4 | 3.0 ± 0.2 |

**Table 3.** Reduced Young modulus "Er" and nano-hardness "H"

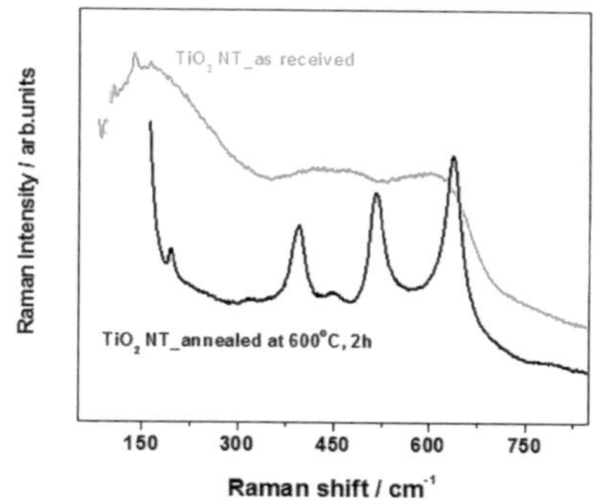


**Figure 11.** Normal Raman spectra of $TiO_2$ nanotubes: as-received and annealed at 600°C. In as-received state we can observed only a broad spectrum from amorphous $TiO_2$ structure. At 600°C the NR spectrum shows peaks around 635, 520, 390 cm$^{-1}$, which correspond to anatase phase. Our measurements for annealed $TiO_2$ nanotubes are in good agreement with data presented in the works [68,69].

$TiO_2$ nanotube structure offers a specific substrate for the development and optimisation of novel orthopedics-related treatments, with precise control over desired cell and bone growth behavior. As far as the effect of the diameter of the $TiO_2$ nanotubes is concerned, it was found that there were distinct size regimes for precisely controlling cell adhesion, cell morphology and/or the alkaline phosphatase (ALP) activity [2, 70]. It turns out that ~100 nm $TiO_2$ nanotubes, which induced the highest biochemical ALP activity of osteoblast cells, hold the most promise for the successful integration of orthopedic implant materials with the surrounding bone [2,70]. Considering the above discussion and Ref. [22],$TiO_2$ nanotube diameter was limited to 75±10 nm (20 V) or 110± 10 nm (25 V) for the purpose of our present studies.

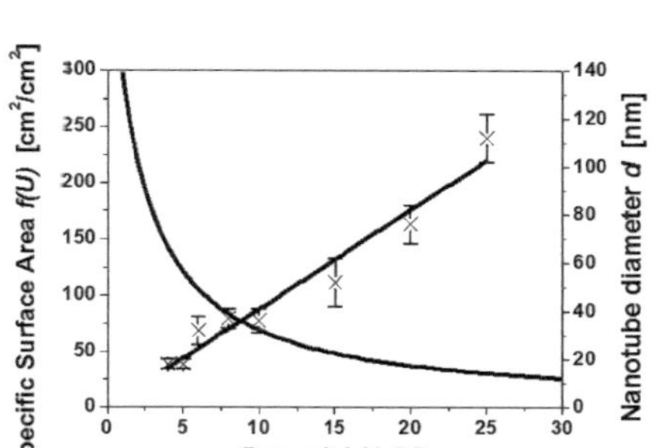


**Figure 12.** The relationship between the diameter of the titania nanotubes and the resulting specific surface area as calculated from the proposed geometric model (more details is given [71]).

The estimated surface area for $TiO_2$ nanotubes with an internal nanotube diameter of ~ 75 nm is ~150 cm$^2$/cm$^2$, while that for ~ 110 nm is about 250 cm$^2$/cm$^2$, see Fig. 12 As the calculations show, the specific surface area of a nanotubular structure increase with the nanotube diameter. In this context, the size of specific surface area for larger nanotubes is more promising for adhesion of proteins and living cells attachment. Higher specific surface area probably offers by higher population of active sites for nucleation of calcium phosphate coatings.

- **Deposition of Ca-P coatings by chemical or electrochemical methods from Hanks' solution**

The nucleation and growth of calcium phosphates (Ca–P) on titanium oxides has been extensively investigated because of its relevance to orthopedic applications [35,72]. A titanium surface can achieve direct bonding with bone tissue (osseointegration) through a very thin calcium phosphate layer. In recent years, intensive investigations have been conducted on the properties of both naturally and artificially formed titanium oxide layers to understand the positive effect of titanium oxide on bone bonding [11,33,53]. However, the mechanism is still not fully understood. Calcium phosphate bioceramics are considered to be more biocompatible than some other materials used for hard tissue replacement, because they more closely resemble living tissue in terms of composition.

For an artificial material to bond to a living bone, one requirement is the formation of a bonelike apatite layer on its surface in the body environment. The bone matrix into which implants are placed possesses its own intrinsic nanotopography. In particular, hydroxyapatite and collagen, which are the major building blocks of bone, expose to osteoblasts an extracellular matrix surface with a high roughness. The implant surface topography has been recently shown to influence the formation of calcium phosphate in simulated body fluid [73]. This phenomenon is related to the charge density and the topographical matching of the titania surface and the size of the Ca–P crystals found in bone [74]. However, it is to be expected that both the surface topography and the physicochemical properties of the surface have a cooperative influence on any surface precipitation reactions. Very few studies have been carried out where the combined effect of these parameters has been studied systematically [74-76]. The functional properties of titanium, especially its bone-binding ability can be improved through surface modification. Traditionally, hydroxyapatite has been used as a coating on the metal substrate to enhance bioactivity. Many coating techniques have been employed for the deposition of thin film coatings of hydroxyapatite, such as plasma spraying [27,77], electrophoretic deposition [78], sol–gel deposition [79] and electrochemical deposition [23,80]. In recent years, there has been increasing interest in the formation of a bioactive surface layer directly on the titanium substrate, which will induce apatite formation in the living environment or simulated body fluid (SBF) [81].

In our investigations, we attempted to use Ti oxides supports to provide a three-dimensional control over nucleation. Moreover, we were able to control the morphology and porosity - the size and number of the nucleation sites by using various methods of Ti oxidation (chemical etching, anodic poarization). The titanium oxide surface is predominantly negative in simulated biological environments (pH 7.4) and is consenquently electrostatically capable of attracting positively charged ions such as calcium. Cationic $Ca^{2+}$ reacts then with negatively-charged $PO_4^{3-}$ and $CO_3^{2-}$ to form a Ca–P containing surface layer which eventually crystallizes to bone-like apatite [11]. Because this reaction takes place in an environment similar to that of natural apatite, it has been suggested [11] that such coatings may provide greater bone-bonding capability than those made by a conventional technique such as plasma spraying. One of the great advantages of a biomimetic method for coating metal implants with bone-like apatite layers over the commonly used plasma-spraying one is that it imitates the mode in which hydroxyapatite bone crystals are formed in the body. The coatings thereby obtained are composed of small crystal units, which are more readily degraded by osteoblasts than are the large ceramic particles produced by plasma spraying [25].

In vitro mineralization studies are usually performed using simulated body fluids (SBFs) of similar composition to blood plasma. Among the most often used fluids are Hanks' balanced salt solution (HBSS) and Kokubo's (SBF). The main differences between HBSS and SBF are the degree of supersaturation in calcium and phosphate (lower in HBSS) and the presence of tris(hydroxymethyl)aminomethane (TRIS) buffer in SBF. Although SBF has a greater similarity with blood in terms of ionic concentration, the presence of TRIS buffer which forms soluble complexes with calcium ions, may be considered a disadvantage [82].

It is generally accepted that rough and porous surfaces could stimulate nucleation and growth of calcium phosphates. The surface topography is also known to strongly influence the wetting properties of materials [83,84]. The hydrophobicity of the surface plays an important role in the deposition of calcium–phosphate coatings from SBF or Hanks' solution. A hydrophilic surface is more favorable for initiating the formation of Ca–P [85]. The values of water contact angle for all the surfaces investigated are given in Table 4.

All morphologies obtained as a result of the chemical/electrochemical pre-treatments applied in this study, followed by simple immersion of the pretreated samples in a solution such as Hanks' medium (which is supersaturated with respect to the apatite), may be promising substrates for nucleation and the growth of calcium–phosphate coatings. Thus, this is the first step, which should be performed prior to the formation of a calcium phosphate layer on the modified Ti substrate.

| samples | contact angle |
|---|---|
| Ti | 77 ± 5 |
| Ti($H_3PO_4$+$H_2O_2$) | 57 ± 5 |
| Ti(NaOH) | 27 ± 3 |
| $TiO_2$ NT (HT) | 3 ± 1 |

**Table 4.** Water contact angle values for surfaces under investigation

The nucleation and growth of apatite on chemically/electrochemically pre-treated Ti depends not only on surface characteristics such as topography/morphology, but also on the chemical composition and chemical state of the elements present on the surface. In order to get an insight into the chemical state of titanium before and after the chemical treatments applied, XPS measurements were performed.

Table 5 provides the binding energies of Ti $2p_{3/2}$ and O 1s electrons for all the samples investigated. In all cases, the pre-treated Ti surfaces exhibited a clear O 1s signal at 530.1–530.5 eV, ascribed to the Ti–O bond due to the presence of titanium oxide at its surface. The results confirm that $TiO_2$ is the main component of the chemically/electrochemically pre-treated Ti surface. Deconvolution of the Ti 2p signals suggests that some lower Ti-oxides are also present for the chemically pre-treated samples (see Table 5). Our XPS investigations do not suggest the presence of Ti–OH bonds on the Ti reference, Ti(NaOH), Ti($H_3PO_4$ + $H_2O_2$) or $TiO_2$ NT substrates [14,22]. Some authors have reported [13] that the presence of hydroxyl groups on the surface is crucial for calcium titanate formation, which then incorporates $PO_4^{-3}$ groups and converts into apatite. The authors believe that the Ti–OH containing species, notably unstable $Ti(OH)_4$, may only be formed in situ, in simulated body fluid, or in vivo, in the presence of blood plasma [13]. Recently, it was found that titanium metal and its alloys, when subjected to successive NaOH aqueous solution and heat treatment, show apatite-forming ability and integrate with the living bone after implantation. This apatite-forming ability is attributed to the amorphous sodium titanate formed during the treatments [15,17]. Interestingly, the $H_2O_2$ + $H_3PO_4$ pre-treated sample produced an oxide film which also contains phosphate ions (see Table 5). A possible incorporation of phosphate ions into the oxide film may provide a compositional basis facilitating the formation of calcium phosphates – primary inorganic phases of bone – which have osteoinductive properties in physiological fluids [14].

| | **Ti2p3 / eV** | **P2p3 / eV** | **O1s / eV** | **chemical state** |
|---|---|---|---|---|
| Ti(NaOH) | **459.0**<br>457.6 | | **530.5** | **$TiO_2$ (major component)**<br>$Ti_2O_3$ (minor component) |
| Ti($H_3PO_4$+$H_2O_2$) | 458.6<br>456.5<br> | <br><br>133.0 | 530.1<br><br>531.7 | **$TiO_2$ (major component)**<br>TiO (minor component)<br>phosphate, $PO_4^{3-}$ |
| $TiO_2$ nanotubes | 458.9 | | 530.4 | **$TiO_2$ (major component)** |

*Ti in $TiO_2$ – 458.8 eV, Phosphates (132.0 – 133.0 eV), Handbook of X-ray Photoelectron Spectroscopy, A Reference Book of Standard Spectra for Identification and Interpretation of XPS Data, Edited by Jill Chastain, Roger C. King, Jr, Physical Electronics, Inc., USA, 1995

**Table 5.** Ti $2p_{3/2}$, O 1s and P $2p_{3/2}$ binding energies as measured from corrected XPS spectra before and after chemical/electrochemicall pre-treatment, and surface compounds evaluated using a deconvolution procedure.

- **Morphology, structure and chemical composition of deposited Ca-P coatings (HR-SEM, AES, XPS, FTIR)**

Having obtained stable Ti oxide substrates we further attempted to functionalize them by means of a calcium phosphate overlayer. The results are discussed below.

As the SEM investigations show, soaking chemically pre-treated Ti surfaces in Hanks' solution at 37°C for 7 days produced calcium phosphate coatings of similar morphology (Fig. 13 a and b). Individual and clustered ball-like particles on top of a compact Ca–P layer containing numerous submicron features are well visible. This type of developed morphology is similar to that reported in the literature [12,14, 18, 22, 80]. After immersion for 7 days, the $TiO_2$ nanotubes are coated with a denser layer which is composed of spheroidal particles tightly packed together. Some single and clustered ball-like particles of about 0.5–1.0 μm in diameter are also present on the surface. The higher magnification micrographs indicate that those features have a cauliflower-like structure composed of

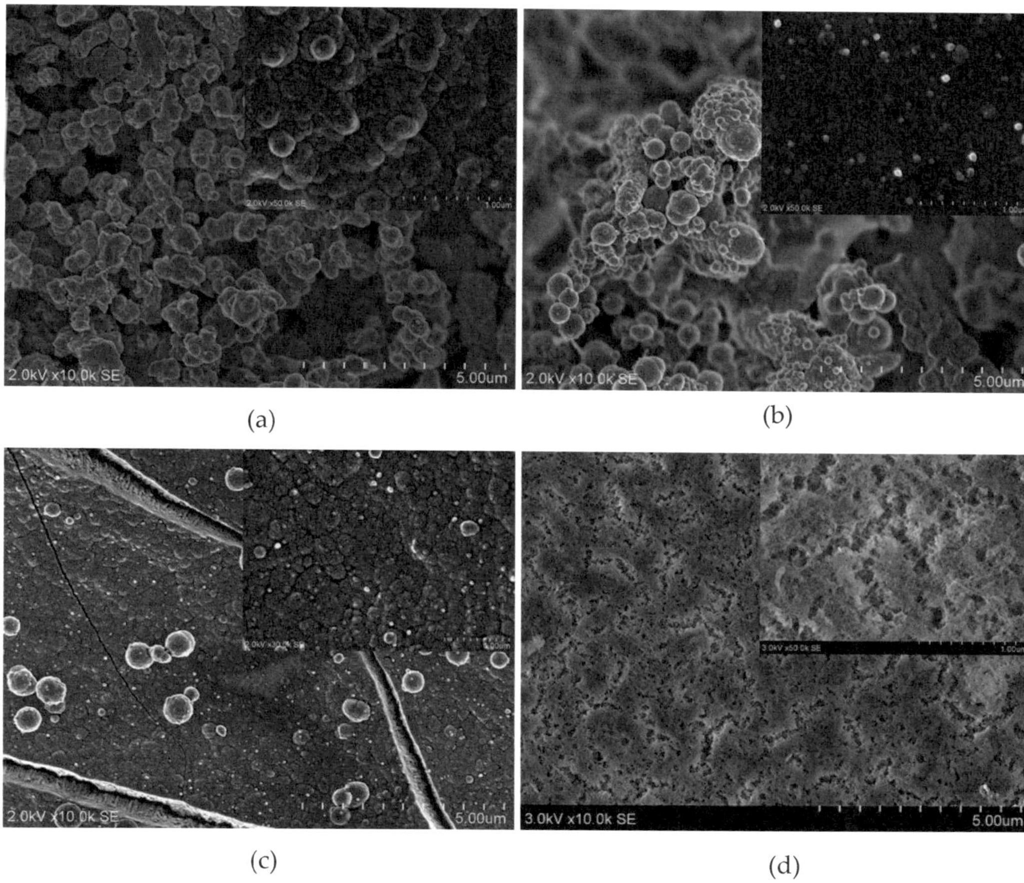


**Figure 13.** SEM images (top view) of Ti after chemical/electrochemical treatment and after subsequent immersion in Hanks' solution – 7 days, temperature 37°C : a – NaOH, b – $H_3PO_4$+$H_2O_2$, c – $TiO_2$ nanotubes. SEM image of the electrodeposited Ca-P coating on a Ti from Hanks' solution (d).

many small crystallites, as shown in Fig. 13c. The Ca-P coating formed on $TiO_2$ nanotubes seems to be better crystallized than on Ti chemically pretreated in alkali and acidic solutions. Our SEM examinations reveald that electrodeposited calcium phosphate coating exhibits a completely different morphology characterized by a network of longitudinal pores of different shapes (Fig. 13d).

Fig. 14 shows a cross-sectional view of the calcium phosphate coating on Ti(NaOH) and $TiO_2$ NT samples. The Ca–P coating on etched Ti is well integrated within the porous $TiO_2$ layer (in fact a Ca–P/Ti oxides/Ti composite is formed), which may improve the bonding of the coating to the pre-treated Ti substrate, Fig. 14a. Fig.14b clearly indicates that Hanks' solution penetrates the interior of the nanotubes and the spaces between individual $TiO_2$ nanotubes. Deposition of the calcium phosphate coating on the surface of the nanotubes by soaking leads to the formation of a specific composite-like layer. An intermediate zone is thus formed with $TiO_2$ nanotubes and phosphates mutually "permeating" each other. The vertically aligned $TiO_2$ nanotubes on Ti substrate act as an intermediate layer for improving the binding between apatite coating and Ti substrate, and for providing a mechanical stability of the whole composite. One may anticipate that a Ca–P deposit on a $TiO_2$ porous layer may promote early bone apposition and implant fixation by enhancing the chemical bonding between the new bone and the surface of those materials [14,22].

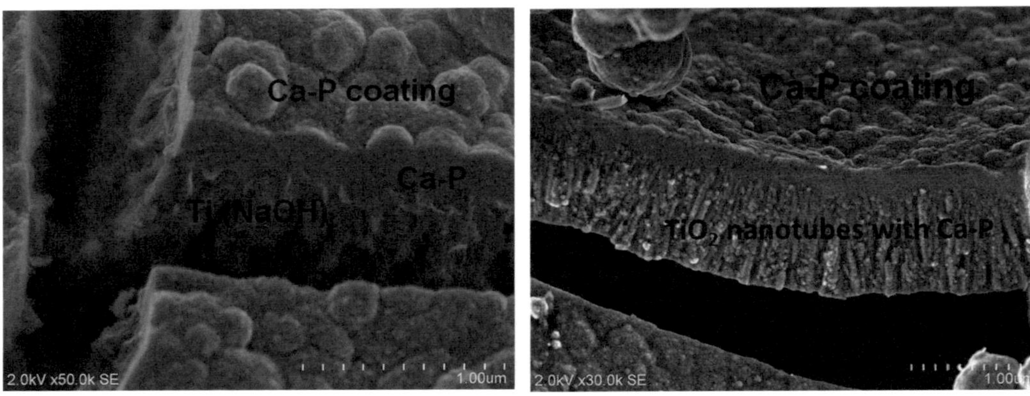


**Figure 14.** SEM images of a cross-section of the titanium oxide porous structure with a deposited calcium phosphate coating.

Fig. 15 shows a STEM cross-sectional view of the Ca-P layer after electrodeposition process. The thickness of the electrodeposited layer is about 200 nm. The high resolution STEM images of the Ca-P coatings suggest that electrodeposition from Hanks' solution at the potential – 1.5V vs OCP leads to the formation of homogenous layer with good adhesion to the substrate.The high resolution STEM image shows a subtle porosity of the Ca-P layer. Well visible nanopores are uniformly distributed across the "sponge like structure" with a

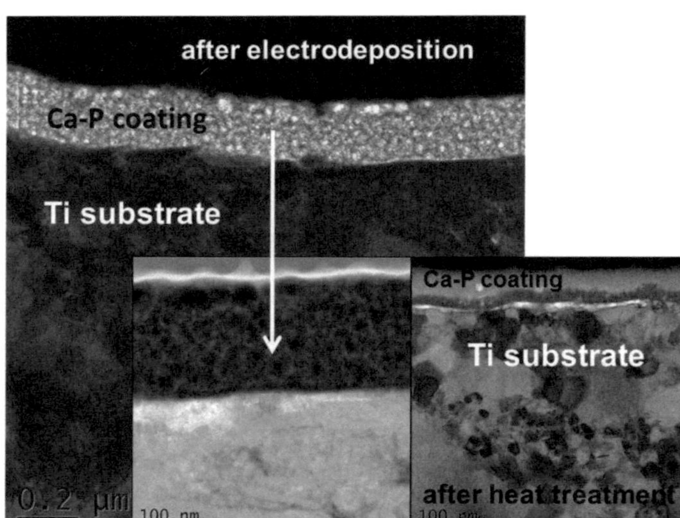


**Figure 15.** STEM images of the electrodeposited Ca-P coatings before and after heat treatment.

gradual change of the pore size with depth. Larger pores within the uppermost layer may assure better integration with bone. Nanoindentation technique allowed the coating's hardness and reduced Young's modulus to be measured with a load of indenter - 1 mN.

Such a low load did not cause the breakdown of the Ca-P layer by the indenter. The hardness of the coating was determined at the level of ~ 0.2 GPa, see Table 6. Thermal treatment was applied to increase the hardness of the electrodeposited coating and to check the influence of temperature on the size of the pores present in the layer. TEM revealed that the thickness of the Ca-P coating after heat treatment is about four times lower than that obtained for the sample after direct electrodeposition (without heat treatment). Three distinct domains can be distinguished within the cross-section (Fig. 15): Ca-P coatings, an interphase region (gray layer), and the titanium substrate. An increase of the hardness of about 6 GPa and Young's modulus to ~ 143 GPa was observed after heat treatment in 700°C for 1 h in air. The values obtained are comparable to the hardness of the layers fabricated by pulse laser deposition method [86]. Such increase is probably related to the change of the structure of electrodeposited layer (solid homogeneous Ca-P layer was formed separated from the Ti substrate with a thin transition zone), and internal structure of the substrate during heat treatment. Ti grains of size below 100 nm could be observed after heat treatment, see Fig.15. The grain size reduction is probably related to recrystallization process during annealing. The change of the electrodeposited Ca-P coating structure also contributes to the increase of the mechanical properties of the investigated system (even in relation to the unmodified Ti). Such phenomenon was not observed for anodically polarized layers subsequently annealed at 600°C in air, see Table 3.

| sample | $E_R$ (GPa) ± $\Delta E_R$ | H (GPa) ± ΔH |
|---|---|---|
| Ti (initial state), Ti foil | 127.8 ± 5.5 | 4.7 ± 0.5 |
| Ti with electrodeposited Ca-P coating | 25.4 ± 2.7 | 0.17 ± 0.03 |
| Ti with electrodeposited Ca-P coating after annealing at 700°C, 1h in air | 143.1 ± 6.1 | 6.4 ± 0.4 |

**Table 6.** Reduced Young modulus "Er" and nano-hardness "H" for electrodeposited Ca-P coatings before and after heat treatment.

Auger electron spectroscopy (AES) technique was used to control the local chemical composition of the Ca-P coatings. AES analysis revealed the presence of P, Ca, O, Mg, and C in the layer. Qualitatively, similar chemical composition of the Ca-P coatings was obtained using chemical/electrochemical methods, see Fig.16.

XPS analysis revealed that the surface is enriched in calcium and phosphorous, with Ca/P molar ratios of 1.08 (NaOH solution), 1.09 ($H_2O_2$ + $H_3PO_4$), 1.10 (electrodeposited layer) and 1.37 ($TiO_2$ nanotubes), Fig. 17. This is less than the stoichiometric hydoxyapatite ratio of 1.67. However, our EDS results show that the atomic concentration ratio of Ca/P is higher for the all samples. In case of bulk sample the EDS technique provides information with a lateral resolution of ~ 1 μm and depth resolution of ~ 2-3 μm. It is noteworthy that XPS measurements provide surface information from the few uppermost nanometers of the samples. This suggests that a

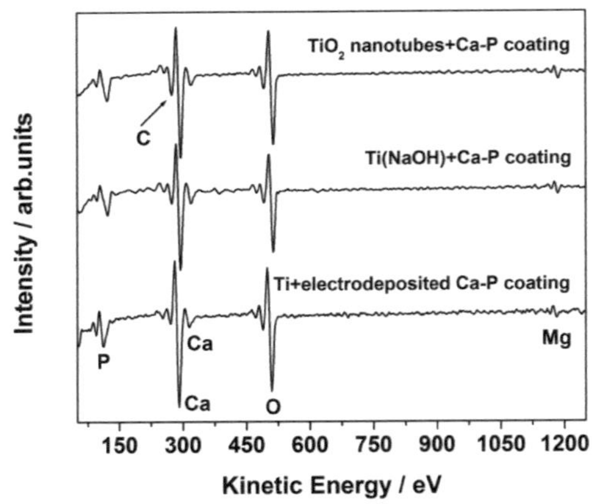


**Figure 16.** AES survey spectra recorded on the surface of Ca-P coatings obtained from Hanks' solution.

nucleation of calcium phosphates phases with lower Ca/P ratio is limited to the outermost surface only. This observation does not concern calcium phosphate layers obtained on $TiO_2$ nanotubes (Ca/P = 1.37). The differences in the morphology and crystallinity of the titanium oxide layers fabricated by chemical etching and anodic polarization are likely to play a role here [14, 22, 87]. The differences in the molar Ca/P ratio may result from different formation stages within the bulk comparing to those in the outermost layer of the coating. Some authors suggest that amorphous calcium phosphate (ACP ($Ca_x(PO_4)_y{\cdot}nH_2O$), Ca/P=1.2–2.2 [35]) is transformed in vitro into octacalcium phosphate (OCP ($Ca_8(HPO_4)_2(PO_4)_4{\cdot}5H_2O$), Ca/P=1.33 [35]) which, in turn, evolves into hydroxyapatite; at lower pH values, the intermediate phase seems to be dehydrated dicalcium phosphate (DCPC ($CaHPO_4{\cdot}2H_2O$), Ca/P=1) [35]. Our results bolster this suggestion. The estimated molar Ca/P ratio by EDS measurements suggest formation of octacalcium phosphate (OCP, Ca/P = 1.33), and probably some intermediate Ca–P phases [88]. The OCP compound is thought to be a precursor for the crystallization of bone-like apatite/hydroxyapatite [89].

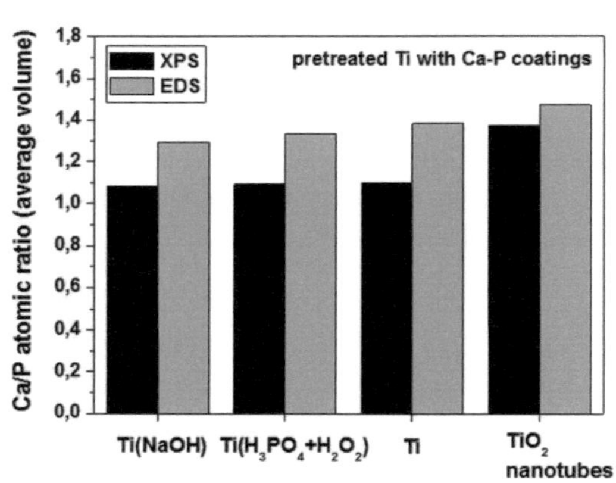


**Figure 17.** Results of the XPS and local EDS analysis (Ca/P atomic ratio) of calcium phosphate coatings electrodeposited on pure Ti or deposited on chemically/electrochemically treated Ti.

Careful inspection of the chemical composition near the uppermost layer revealed that Ca/P molar ratio changed within the Ca-P coating depth. Fig.18 presents partial compositional profile (the relative Ca/P atomic concentration) of electrodeposited layer on Ti, as measured using XPS combined with ion sputtering. As seen from the results presented in Fig.17, the Ca/P concentration ratio is distinctly higher within the layer than at the surface. After 300 s of etching (which corresponds to a thickness of about 12 nm, based on a sputtering rate 0.04 nm/s) the Ca/P atomic ratio is close to 1.43. This later finding correlates with the results of EDS measurements (1.38, see Fig 16). After 600 s of sputtering the Ca/P atomic ratio remains on the same level; apparently the chemical composition does not change further with depth. The differences in the molar Ca/P ratio between the bulk and the outermost layer of the coating, is distinct.

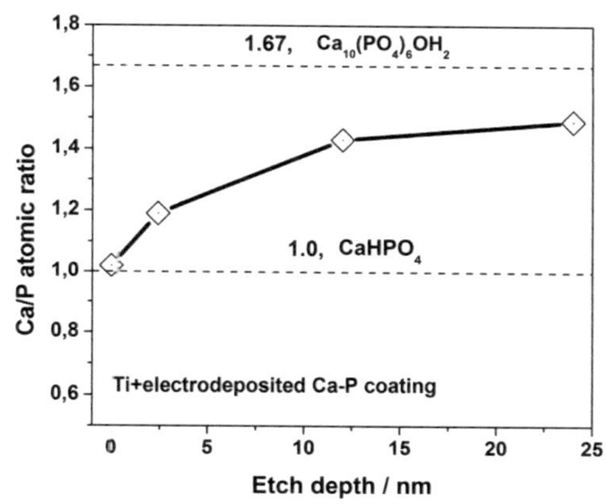


**Figure 18.** Composition of Ca/P concentration ratio vs. sputtering depth for a coating electrodeposited on Ti.

Table 7 shows the binding energies of the O 1s, Ca $2p_{3/2}$, and P $2p_{3/2}$ signals, and the suggested chemical composition of the biomimetic coatings. Position of the main peak of P $2p_{3/2}$ may change within a range of 132.6-133.4 eV for all coatings. The spectral data for Ca suggest the presence of calcium phosphate groups (Ca $2p_{3/2}$: 347.5 - 347.9 eV). The main component of the O 1s peak at BE = 531.1 - 531.6 eV is attributed to $PO_4^{3-}$ groups. The results show that all coatings containing calcium phosphates groups, which are formed on the chemically/electrochemically treated Ti substrate [14, 22].

Fourier transform infrared (FTIR) spectroscopy was used to obtain additional information on the chemical composition of the Ca–P coatings. Hydroxyapatite, the main mineral component of biological bone, absorbs IR radiation due to the vibrational modes from the phosphate and hydroxyl groups. In biological apatites, some $PO_4^{3-}$ ions are substituted by $CO_3^{2-}$ ions, and the IR technique is very sensitive to these carbonate substitutions, so even a small amount of carbonate can be detected [90]. Table 8 shows the results of the FTIR investigations for calcium phosphate coatings formed on chemically/electrochemically treated Ti or on a pure Ti. The $\nu_4$ bending vibrations of $PO_4^{3-}$ are detected circa 560 $cm^{-1}$, although the spectra are dominated by the $\nu_3$ stretching $PO_4^{3-}$ vibration mode in the 1000–1100 $cm^{-1}$ range. Bands for

| Ti surface modification | $Ca2p_{3/2}$ / eV | $P2p_{3/2}$ / eV | O1s / eV |
|---|---|---|---|
| NaOH pretreatment + immersion in Hanks' solution 7 days | 347.5 – 347.9 / $Ca^{2+}$ | 132.6 – 133.4 / $PO_4^{3-}$ | 531.1 – 531.6 / $O_2^-$ |
| $H_3PO_4$ + $H_2O_2$ + immersion in Hanks' solution 7 days | | | |
| after direct electrodeposition in Hanks' solution (- 1.5 V vs. OCP) | | | |
| anodic oxidation pretreatment (20 V) + immersion in Hanks' solution 7 days | | | |

*on the measured surfaces we also detected: $CaCO_3$, $HPO_4^{2-}$, $CaCl_2$

**Table 7.** Ca $2p_{3/2}$, P $2p_{3/2}$ and O1s binding energies as determined from corrected XPS for Ca-P biomimetic coatings, and surface compounds evaluated using a deconvolution procedure.

$\nu_3$ vibrations of C–O mode appear, along with a well-defined bands at 870 – 875 $cm^{-1}$ ($\nu_2$ vibrations of C–O) known to be specific for a carbonated apatite in which $PO_4^{3-}$ ions are substituted by $CO_3^{2-}$ ions [91]. However, the characteristic peaks at the range 870 – 875 $cm^{-1}$ and 959 $cm^{-1}$ suggest the presence of $HPO_4^{2-}$ as well [92]. The OH bands at about 630 $cm^{-1}$ and at about 3570 $cm^{-1}$ are absent for the all coatings. Some authors have attributed these missing OH modes to a perturbation of the hydroxyl stretching and bending modes on the apatite surface by the hydrogen bonding of water molecules to the surface $OH^-$ ions [93]. The absence of the $OH^-$ vibration at 3570 $cm^{-1}$ may also suggest that carbonate substitutes for $OH^-$. However, there is no

| Ti surface modification | $\nu_4$, $PO_4^{3-}$ | $\nu_3$, $PO_4^{3-}$ | $HPO_4^{2-}$ | $\nu_3$, C-O | $\nu_2$, C-O, $CO_3^{2-}$ |
|---|---|---|---|---|---|
| NaOH pretreatment + immersion in Hanks' solution 7 days | 560 – 562 $cm^{-1}$ | 1000 – 1100 $cm^{-1}$ | 870 – 875 $cm^{-1}$, 959 $cm^{-1}$ | 1460 – 1490 $cm^{-1}$ 1420 $cm^{-1}$ | 870 – 875 $cm^{-1}$ |
| $H_3PO_4$ + $H_2O_2$ + immersion in Hanks' solution 7 days | | | | | |
| after direct electrodeposition in Hanks' solution (- 1.5 V vs. OCP) | | | | | |
| anodic oxidation pretreatment (20 V) + immersion in Hanks' solution 7 days | | | | | |

*$H_2O$ (3000 – 3500, 1630 – 1650 $cm^{-1}$)

**Table 8.** Results of the FTIR investigations. Identification of the chemical compounds.

evidence that $CO_3^{2-}$ substitutes for $OH^-$, since the characteristic absorption band at 1545 $cm^{-1}$ associated with this type of substitution was not observed. The above discussion suggests that chemically pre-treated surfaces are a favorable substrate for the deposition of an apatite-like coating [14, 22].

- **Biological response**
  a. Protein adsorption (BSA)
  b. Cell culture experiments (U2OS)

Hydroxyapatite (HA) and calcium phosphate coatings (Ca–P) have been used primarily to alter implant surfaces, on the assumption that the osteointegration of the implants can be improved. However, the processes occurring at the bone/implant interface are still not fully understood; in particular, the role of biomolecules and their influence on initial bioadhesion and coating dissolution has received little attention. When a biomaterial is implanted into the body, its surface is immediately covered with blood and serum proteins. The presence of an adsorbed protein layer mediates cellular responses to the implants [94]. It is expected that, as proteins from biological fluids come in contact with biomimetic surfaces, cellular adhesion, differentiation and extracellular matrix production may be affected. Cell adhesive proteins, found at high concentration in blood, can provide attachment sites for osteoblast precursors binding to the implant, which then leads to faster in-growth of bone and stabilization of the implant. Elsewhere, the surface properties and structures of the materials play an important role in the adsorption of proteins. Surface chemistry and topography are the most important parameters affecting biological reactions [54,95]. The effects of surface topography on protein adsorption and cell adhesion have been extensively investigated by other authors [54,83,96]. The chemical composition of the substrate surface strongly affects the protein adsorption process, as has been documented [53,97].

To evaluate the potential application of our materials for biomedical implants, we examined protein adsorption on the surfaces studied. Serum albumin (SA) was used as a model in this study, as it is the most abundant protein in blood.

Typical XPS spectrum of the Ca-P coating after 20 min incubation in PBS solution containing BSA at 37°C revealed the presence at the surface of Ca, P, O, C and weak signal for Mg and Na. After protein adsorption, a new XPS peak around 400 eV appeared which corresponds to nitrogen, Fig.19. This signal was attributed inter alia to amide groups in albumin molecules. In contrast, the signals from Ca and P are not well visible, suggesting that the surface is completely covered by the protein layer.

Table 9 presents the binding energies of the C1s and N1s XPS signals and the suggested chemical state of the detected elements after protein adsorption on the Ca-P coatings. The XPS reference data for pure BSA are also given. The N1s high-resolution XPS spectrum indicates the presence of N-C=O, C-N, and N-H characteristic protein functional groups at ~ 400.0, ~ 398.0 and ~ 402.0 eV, respectively [22,95,98,99]. XPS signals from the carbon species expected from the bases (C backbone) included the main hydrocarbon, carbon bound to nitrogen or oxygen, amide carbon and carbon double bounded to oxygen [14, 22,95,98,99]. This suggests that the protein molecules are adsorbed on the calcium phosphate coatings.

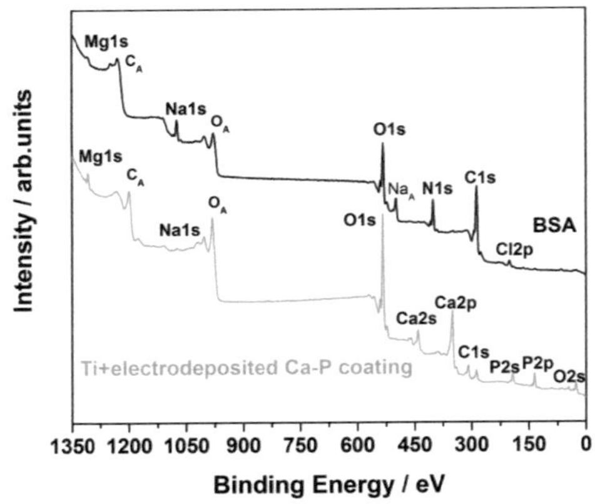


**Figure 19.** XPS survey spectra before and after adsorption of BSA protein on electrodeposited Ca-P coating on a Ti.

| | C1s / eV | N1s / eV | type of bonds |
|---|---|---|---|
| Albumina, ref sample | 288.2<br><br><br><br>285.0<br>286.6<br>290.0 | 400.2<br>398.6<br>402.1 | N - C=O<br>C – N<br>N – H<br><br>C-C / C-H<br>C-O / C-N<br>C=O |
| | | | |
| NaOH pretreatment + immersion in Hanks' solution 7 days | 288.1 – 289.2 | 399.9 – 400.2 | N - C=O |
| $H_3PO_4$ + $H_2O_2$ + immersion in Hanks' solution 7 days | | 398.1 – 398.5<br>401.9 – 402.0 | C – N<br>N – H |
| anodic oxidation pretreatment (20 V) + immersion in Hanks' solution 7 days | 285.0 | | C-C / C-H |
| after direct electrodeposition in Hanks' solution (- 1.5 V vs. OCP) | 286.2 – 287.4<br>289.9* | | C-O / C-N<br>C=O* |

*Only for electrodeposited sample

**Table 9.** C1s and N1s binding energies as measured with XPS and suggested surface chemical species for all samples after protein adsorption.

FTIR results of BSA adsorbed on the calcium phosphate coatings are presented in Table 10. BSA was found to interact with the surfaces studied. The main bands in the range 1650 – 1655 and 1520 – 1540 $cm^{-1}$ have been assigned to amides I and II, respectively [14, 100,101]. Our findings are in good agreement with the measurement for the pure albumin, used as reference sample (Fig. 20) and confirm previous results obtained by XPS method.

<table>
<tr><th></th><th>Amide I (C=O)</th><th>Amide II (N-H)</th></tr>
<tr><td>Albumin, ref sample</td><td>1655 cm$^{-1}$</td><td>1535 cm$^{-1}$</td></tr>
<tr><td>NaOH pretreatment + immersion in Hanks' solution 7 days</td><td rowspan="4">1650 – 1655 cm$^{-1}$</td><td rowspan="4">1520 – 1540 cm$^{-1}$</td></tr>
<tr><td>$H_3PO_4$ + $H_2O_2$ + immersion in Hanks' solution 7 days</td></tr>
<tr><td>anodic oxidation pretreatment (20 V) + immersion in Hanks' solution 7 days</td></tr>
<tr><td>after direct electrodeposition in Hanks' solution (-1.5 V vs. OCP)</td></tr>
</table>

*Resolution 4 cm$^{-1}$

**Table 10.** Position of the main bands: Amide I and Amide II for serum albumin adsorbed on the biomimetic Ca-P coatings.

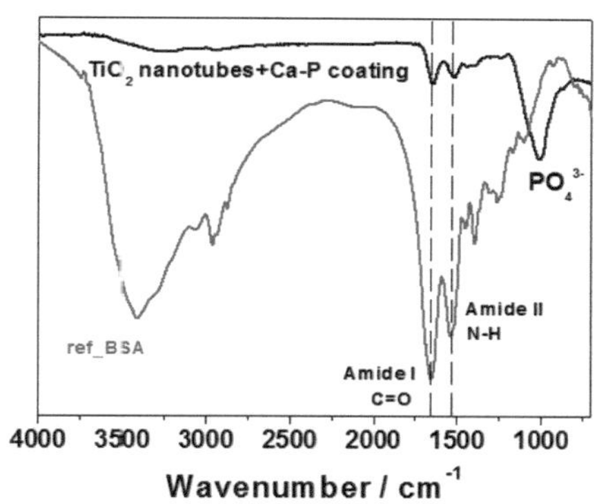


**Figure 20.** FTIR spectrum of $TiO_2$ nanotubes coated with calcium phosphate (Ca–P) after 7 days' immersion in Hanks' solution. Reference spectrum for pure albumin is also given.

Data reported [102,103] in the literature suggested that BSA may have a specific binding interaction with apatite/ hydroxyapatite and thus result in an improvement in the bioactivity for osteoblast cells with regards to their adhesion and proliferation. These findings, taken in relation to present results, suggest that it might be possible to develop better Ca–P-based biomaterials through an incorporation of albumin into the mineral matrix to improve cell adhesion and proliferation [102-104]. Our preliminary results of the response of human osteosarcoma U2OS cells to the surfaces investigated are in qualitative agreement with the protein adsorption measurements. Fig. 21 shows the cells on Ti with electrodeposited Ca-P coatings before and after adsorption of BSA proteins. Fluorescence microscopy observations revealed that the amount of U2OS cells after 72 h of incubation is distinctly higher on the Ca-P coating with adsorbed albumin than for the sample without proteins. A series of investigations performed by Yamaguchi and coworkers have suggested that albumin is released by osteoblast cells present in fracture healing sites and this excess albumin increases proliferation of the surrounding cells. In our study, the surface modification with BSA led to significant improvement in osteoblast-like cells binding to an electrodeposited Ca-P coating. Similar observation, but for MC3T3-E1 cells were reported by other authors [102-104], who have found that adsorption of BSA to the surface of conventional and nanophase ceramic (including hydroxyapatite) influences the activity of adherent cells. After 120 h of incubation, however, the increase in cell number is observed only for surface without BSA. Such a result could be expected. Usually a longer time of incubation increase probability of proliferation of living cells. The adsorption of BSA probably affects positively the kinetics of proliferation of the attached cells. Our fluorescence microscopy observations for both coatings at higher magnifications revealed that the cells are well extended and exhibit an elongated morphology, similar to those on the reference sample (culture dish). The nuclei are clearly shaped, but the cell membranes form a dendritic structure. After 120h of incubation the cells on both coatings (with and without albumin) exhibited cytoplasmic links, as shown in Fig.20. After this time, the cells were well attached on the surface of the electrodeposited Ca-P coating with extending cytoplasmic process [54,105,106].

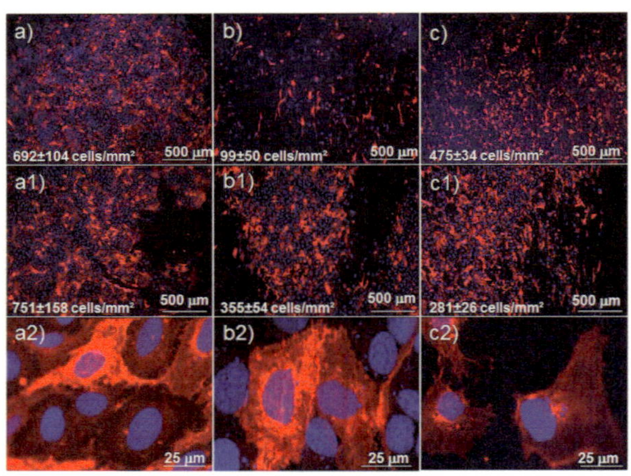


**Figure 21.** Fluorescence microscopy images of U2OS cells cultivated for 72 (a, b, c) and 120 h (a1, b1, c1, a2, b2, c2) on the electrodeposited Ca-P coatings on Ti without and with BSA proteins. Cell density was calculated by averaging 6 images taken randomly from the same surface. a) reference sample, culture dish; b) Ti/Ca-P: -1.5 V vs. OCP after sterilization in autoclave; c) Ti/Ca-P: -1.5 V vs. OCP after sterilization in autoclave + BSA proteins

Similar relations was observed for Ca-P coatings deposited on chemically pre-treated Ti surfaces via soaking in Hanks' solution at 37°C for 7 days. After 48 h of cell culture, cell morphology suggests good adhesion to the substrate, Fig.22. to the substrate, Fig.22., and also we can observed growth of U2OS cells on the Ca-P after 44 h of incubation was observed an increase of U2OS cells on the Ca-P coatings in relation to oxidized and unmodified Ti, see Fig.23.

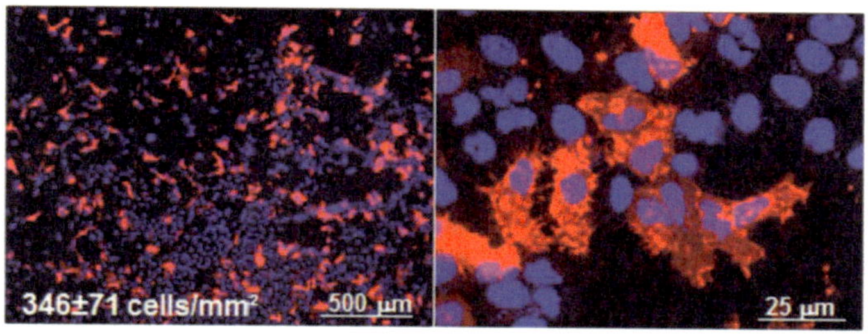


**Figure 22.** Fluorescence microscopy images of U2OS cells cultivated for 48 h on the Ca-P coatings deposited on $TiO_2$ nanotubes.

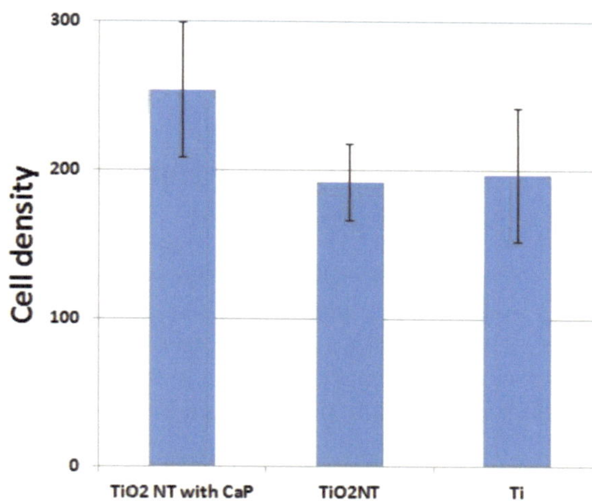


**Figure 23.** Cell density of the U2OS cells cultivated for 44 h on the: Ca-P coating deposited on $TiO_2$ nanotubes, $TiO_2$ nanotubes (20 V) and pure Ti (as-received state).

The ALP activity of the U2OS cells cultured on the various specimens is shown in Fig. 24 (Ca-P coatings, $TiO_2$ nanotubes and pure Ti). ALP test is widely used for the early stage of cell differentiation. ALP enzyme produced by osteoblasts stimulates their activity, which is responsible for the mineralization of bone tissue. After 6 days of cell culture (point 0 h), an increase of ALP activity for cells cultured on pure and modified Ti was observed. After 24 and 48 h the ALP activity is strongly associated with the cell adhesion and proliferation speed, and thus may explain the differences between cultured samples. The highest concentration of the ALP enzyme was observed for $TiO_2$ nanotubes. The specific morphology of the $TiO_2$ nanotubes probably increases the potential of differentiating cells toward osteogenesis process (the formation of new bone material by cells called osteoblasts), as also observed by other authors [70]. The accelerated growth of osteoblast cells observed on vertically aligned nanotubes and Ca-P coatings surfaces may be of importance for biomedical applications, as it could accelerate cell proliferation of other cells line. It was demonstrated that the adhesion/propagation of the osteoblasts cells is significantly improved by the morphology, chemical composition and properties of the investigated surfaces (see Fig. 21, 22) [2,107,108].

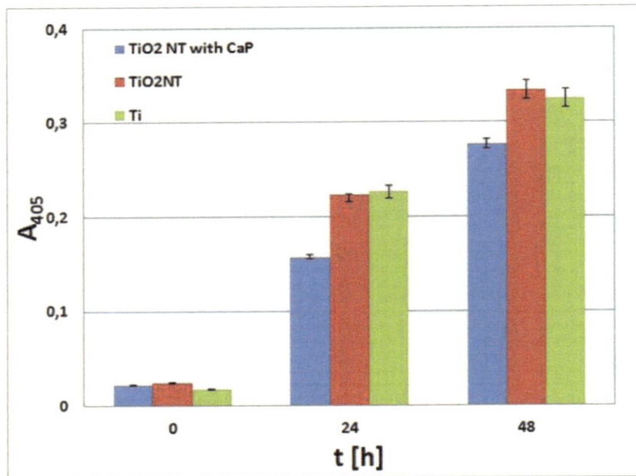


**Figure 24.** ALP activity of U2OS osteoblasts cells cultured on $TiO_2$ nanotubes, Ca-P and pure Ti.

## 3. Modification of Ca-P coating with silver nanoparticles: biocompatibility and antibacterial properties.

The adherence of bacteria to the biomaterial causes serious surgical complications, and poses a threat to patients with long-term implants [44,109]. Although, current methods of sterilization exist, yet in the case of the early onset of corrosion of the implant, problems with bacterial habitats still do arise. A promising method to tackle this issue is the fabrication of materials that retain biocompatibility and prevent infections. Current strategies aimed at minimizing the incidence of biomaterials associated infection involve the addition of antibacterial agents (e.g., antibiotics, specific polymers, toxic metal ions) onto the surface of implantable devices [110-113]. The primary advantage of these antibacterial coatings is the release of the bactericidal agent at the site of implantation, minimizing the risk of reaching concentrations that can cause harmful side reactions to other parts of the body.

SEM image of $TiO_2$ nanotube layer (top-view, before treatment) formed at $V_{max} = 20$ V and loaded with 0.01 mg/cm$^2$ of silver is shown in Figure 24. The sputter-deposited Ag formed spherical nanoparticles that are located on the top edges of the nanotubes and on their inner and outer side walls. It can be seen that the silver particles are distributed homogenously in the $TiO_2$ nanotube layer. Moreover, Fig. 25 shows the Ag-loaded $TiO_2$ nanotubes surface after soaking in Hanks' solution at 37°C for 6 and 24 h. One can see an early stage of Ca-P layer formation on the top of the nanotubes after 6h immersion in Hanks' solution. Nevertheless, the Ag nanoparticles are still present at the nanotubes' edges. After immersion for 24 h, the layer become denser and better integrated with nanoporous substrate. Our previous experiments clearly indicated that Hanks' solution penetrates the interior of the $TiO_2$ nanotubes and the spaces between them [22], see Fig.14. The deposition of the calcium phosphate coating on the surface of the nanotubes leads to the formation of a specific composite-like layer. The vertically aligned $TiO_2$ nanotubes on Ti substrate act as an intermediate layer providing both the apatite-Ti binding and a mechanical stability of the composite. Also, incorporation of silver nanoparticles into apatite increases the strength and toughness of the composite as well as provides antibacterial properties [45] Thus, the composite layer investigated in this study, nano-Ag/Ca-P coating/$TiO_2$ nanotubes, seems to be promising for advanced biomedical applications [114].

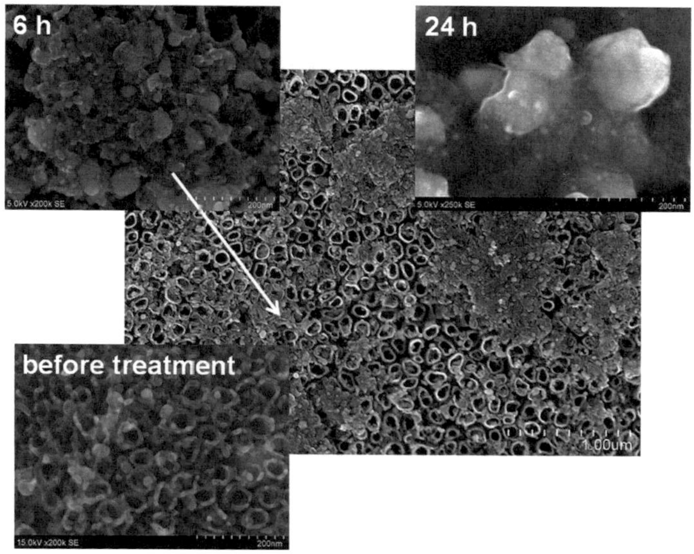


**Figure 25.** SEM image of typical $TiO_2$ nanotube layer (before treatment) formed at $V_{max}$ = 20 V and loaded with 0.01 mg Ag/cm$^2$ and SEM images of $TiO_2$ NT with the same amount of Ag after immersion in Hanks' solution for 6 h and 24 h.

The enrichment of the coating with Ca and P in the present case confirmed the EDS results for the calcium phosphate coatings formed on Ag/$TiO_2$ nanotubes layer. The average concentrations of Ca and P increase with time of exposure to Hanks' solution. The atomic concentration ratio Ca/P for soaked samples is close to 0.73 for 6 h immersion and reaches 1.54 after 24 h, Fig.26. These results suggest that the calcium phosphate layer formed during immersion procedure tends to incorporate more Ca with time. EDS analysis revealed that the silver content in the composite layer decrease with time of immersion in Hanks' solution from ~3.5 to about 1.7 at.%. Such result could be expected, as longer exposition time of samples in simulated physiological solution leads to a partial coverage of silver nanoparticles with a layer of calcium phosphate [114].

Existing literature data show that the antibacterial action of silver is not fully understood, yet [109,115,116]. Some authors argued that the antibacterial action of Ag nanoparticles depends on the availability of silver ions [114]. Silver cations $Ag^+$ can bind to bacterial cell wall membrane (slightly negative) and damage it thus altering its functionality. However, other studies have shown that the cytotoxicity of Ag nanoparticles is primarily the result of the oxidative stress and is independent of the toxicity of silver ions [116]. Silver forms insoluble AgCl in $Cl^-$ containing solution. Thus any contact with simulated body fluids would therefore prevent a release of $Ag^+$ from the metal phase. Nevertheless, the release of $Ag^+$ from Ag nanoparticles in water may provide an insight into the stability of the nanoparticles. In our study the release kinetics of $Ag^+$ was confirmed by ICP-MS (inductively coupled plasma mass spectrometry) measurements [114].

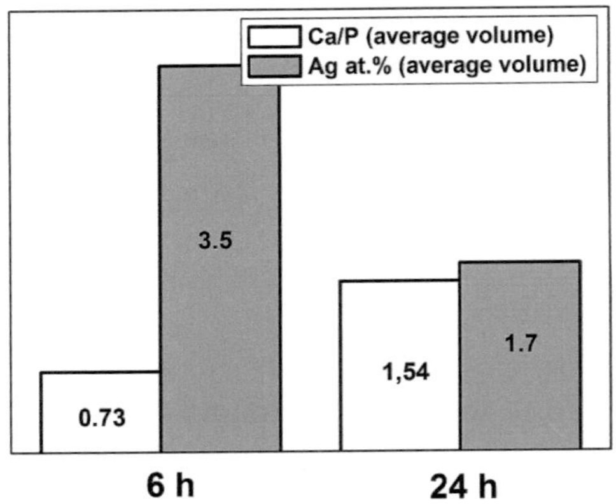


**Figure 26.** Results of EDS analysis Ca/P atomic ratio and silver concentration (average volume) of calcium phosphate coatings deposited on $TiO_2$ nanotubes loaded with 0.01 mg/cm$^2$ of Ag after various immersion times in Hanks' solution: 6 h, 24 h.

Fig. 27 shows the amount of silver ions released in deionized water and 0.9% NaCl solution in function of time. Silver was obviously released faster in NaCl environment than in water solution. After 3 days of incubation the release of the silver ions proceeds relatively slower in water and is stabilized below 170 μg/L. Process occurs much faster in NaCl solution, as a plateau indicating a stabilization of the release of silver ions which was not observed like for water environment. Phenomenon of rapid release of silver ions in NaCl solution may be due to the formation of AgCl during the experiment. After 7 days, less than 550 μg/L of $Ag^+$ were found in 0.9% NaCl solution, indicating that leaching of $Ag^+$ from the nanoparticles is still relatively low. Vik et al. [47] pointed out that the maximum silver concentration released in vitro should be no more than 10 mg/L. Silver becomes toxic to human cells at higher amount. Over this experiment, the silver released from Ag/$TiO_2$ nanotubes/Ti sample is less than the maximum cytotoxic concentration. Thus, our Ag loaded $TiO_2$ nanotube composite layer on Ti proved to be a promising implant material [114].

Recent studies evidenced that silver nanoparticles are more active and reactive than the bulk metallic counterpart, first of all because of their larger specific surface area [115,117]. Morones et al. [118] reported that silver particles with a preferential diameter of about 1–10 nm had direct interactions with bacteria, while larger particles did not. In view of this, the Ag/$TiO_2$ NT composite layer developed here with 0.01 mg/cm$^2$ of Ag are expected to have a great potential for biomedical applications. The well dispersed Ag nanoparticles homogeneously distributed over the $TiO_2$ nanotube layer are very likely to maintain a steady antibacterial effect, as long as Ag nanoparticles remain their metallic state [114].

The antibacterial activity of the Ag/$TiO_2$ nanotube composite layers was examined by bacterial counting method using *Staphylococcus epidermidis* (*S. epidermidis*, ATCC 12228), Fig.28. *S. epidermidis* is the most frequently isolated coagulase-negative staphylococci from implant-associated infections and have been found to be more antibiotic resistant than *S. aureus* [119]. The obtained results revealed that the deposition of Ag nanoparticles significantly reduced the *S. epidermidis* cell adhesion and biofilm formation on modified surface. Interestingly, the $TiO_2$ nanotube layer (pore diameter ~75 nm) also exhibits some antibacterial properties, as reported previously [120,121]. For Ag loaded surface the amount of bacterial cell per surface area unit is about nine times lower than for pure Ti and for $TiO_2$ nanotubes without Ag the amount of bacterial cells is about 3 times lower comparing to pure Ti. Thus, the Ag/$TiO_2$ nanotube composite layers may be promising for combating post-operative infection for applications in hard tissue replacement procedures.

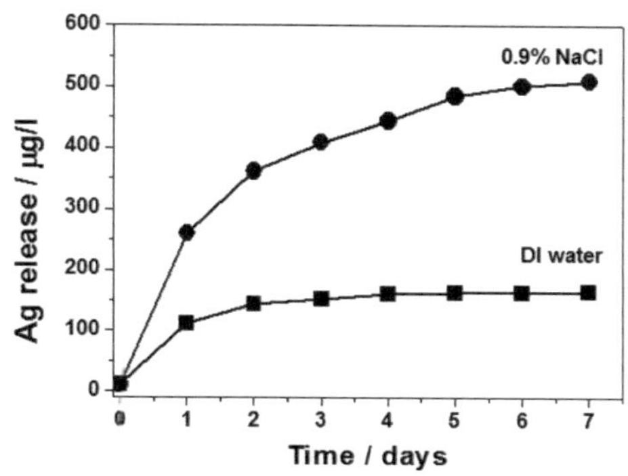


**Figure 27.** Amount of silver released from $TiO_2$ nanotubes loaded with 0.01 mg/cm² of Ag.

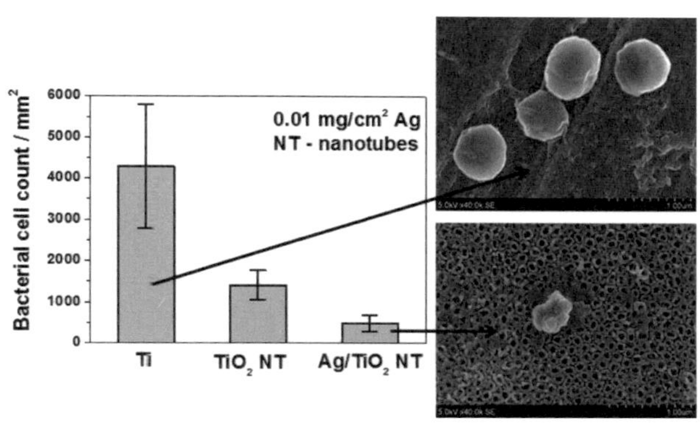


**Figure 28.** *S. epidermidis* cell adhesion on Ti, $TiO_2$ nanotubes and Ag loaded $TiO_2$ nanotubes.

It is noteworthy that this type of composite material has attracted the attention of material scientists and biochemists only recently. It turns out that, depending on the surface properties of the titanium substrate, the deposited biomimetic apatite layer can vary in both surface chemistry and crystallinity [122]. These subtle differences in the local microenvironment can result in significant differences in cell behavior [122].

## 4. Summary and conclusions

Our surface analytical and physico-chemical investigations confirmed that, the chemical treatment of a Ti surface, in both an alkaline (NaOH) and an acidic ($H_2O_2$ + $H_3PO_4$) solution, resulted in significant changes in topography/morphology, with a characteristic feature exhibiting the presence of micro- and nano-porosities. The chemical composition of the treated surfaces did not differ significantly – Ti-oxides (mostly $TiO_2$) were formed at the surface as a result of both treatments. However, the new Ti($H_2O_2$ + $H_3PO_4$) treatment led to the incorporation of some phosphates into the oxide film, which may enhance biocompatibility.

Titanium oxide nanotubes were grown on Ti in fluoride containing electrolytes with an optimum concentration of 0.86 wt.% $NH_4F$ at a constant voltage from 10 V up to 25 V. Self-organized porous structures (nanotubes) with diameters from about ~40 up to ~110 nm and a length of ~800 μm were formed. Annealing at 600°C resulted in crystallization of the nanotube material into anatase and - what is important - in a mechanical stabilization of the nanoporous layer on a Ti substrate.

The present investigations confirm that calcium phosphate coatings of porous apatite-like structure and a specific morphology can be grown on pure titanium by electrodeposition at -1.5 V vs. OCP from the Hanks' solution. A porous Ca-P layer with a pore size gradient is formed with a compact thin overlayer. Our investigations suggest also that calcium phosphate coatings of apatite-like structure (probably B-type) and a developed morphology can be uniformly grown on a chemically/electrochemically pre-treated titanium surface already covered with a highly porous oxide layer by immersion of samples in Hanks' solution [123]. Such porous oxide layers significantly stimulate the formation of calcium phosphate phases in physiological body solution, an in vitro environment: from thermodynamically unstable phases ACP [124], which transform to crystalline calcium orthophosphates, mainly to carbonated apatites, which are of a great biological relevance [125]. Our EDS and XPS results suggest that different phosphates may be formed at the surface and in the bulk of the Ca-P coatings. The nucleation of calcium phosphate crystals on porous $TiO_2$ could provide better adhesion of the coating to the substrate possibly due to the interlocking of the Ca–P crystals within the pores [126,127].

Our results of XPS and FTIR investigations show that bovine serum albumin (BSA) adsorbed readily on a calcium phosphate coating prepared by chemical or electrochemical methods. The presence of adsorbed protein on the Ca–P surface enhances cell attachment and proliferation, which is favorable for achieving better biocompatibility. Thus, one may anticipate that a Ca–P coating on a porous oxide layer may promote early bone apposition and implant fixation by enhancing the chemical binding between new bone and the surface of implant materials. In the case of Ca–P coatings, surface chemistry is probably the dominant factor in the protein adsorption process and living cells adhesion.

A serious problem common to all biomaterials, namely the risk of infection, can be alleviated by incorporating Ag nanoparticles into the biomaterial surface. Our results have shown that Ag nanoparticles can be incorporated in a versatile manner, suitable for fabrication of new types of bactericidal materials and efficient in reducing the number of bacteria present at the surface. To this end silver was sputtered homogenously onto the $TiO_2$ nanotubes layer. The silver nanoparticles deposited guaranteed a sustained release in deionized water and 0.9% NaCl solution at a level below a possible toxicity. Further improvement of bio-functionality of the composite layers was obtained by soaking in Hanks' solution. The present results suggest that the Ag/Ca-P/$TiO_2$ nanotubes composite layers may impart antibacterial property, which makes them promising to be applied in hard tissue replacement against postoperative infections.

## Author details

Marcin Pisarek[1*], Agata Roguska[1,2], Lionel Marcon[3] and Mariusz Andrzejczuk[2]
[1]*Institute of Physical Chemistry, Polish Academy of Sciences, Kasprzaka, Warsaw, Poland*
[2]*Faculty of Materials Science and Engineering, Warsaw University of Technology, Woloska, Warsaw, Poland*
[3]*Interdisciplinary Research Institute, USR CNRS 3078 Parc de la Haute Borne, Villeneuve d'Ascq, France*

## Acknowledgement

We are most grateful to dr Anna Belcarz from Department of Biochemistry and Biotechnology at Medical University of Lublin (Poland) and dr Maciej Spychalski from Faculty of Materials Science and Engineering at Warsaw University of Technology (Poland) for helpful discussions and to all the co-authors who contributed their knowledge and experience to the joint papers quoted in this chapter. This work was financially supported by the Polish Ministry of Science and Higher Education (Grant no. N N507 355035, IP2010 035070), the National Science Center (decision No. DEC-2011/01/B/ST5/06257) and by the Institute of Physical Chemistry PAS (Warsaw, Poland) and Interdisciplinary Research Institute (Lille, France). Surface characterizations (AES, XPS) were performed using a Microlab 350 located at the Physical Chemistry of Materials Center of the Institute of Physical Chemistry, PAS and of the Faculty of Materials Science and Engineering, WUT.

## Abbreviations

HR-SEM (High Resolution – Scanning Electron Microscopy), AFM (Atomic Force Microscopy), AES (Auger Electron Spectroscopy), XPS (X-ray Photoelectron Spectroscopy), FTIR (Fourier Transform Infrared Spectroscopy), FIB (Focused Ion Beam), TEM (Transmission Electron Microscopy), BSA (Bovine Serum Albumin), Ca-P (calcium phosphate coating), SERS (Surface Enhanced Raman Spectroscopy), REF (reference substrate), $R_a$ (average roughness), $R_q$ (root-mean-square deviation), $R_z$ (roughness depth), $R_{max}$ (maximum roughness depth), SEM (Scanning Electron Microscopy), STEM (Scanning Transmission Electron Microscopy), EDS (Energy Dispersive Spectroscopy), ICP-MS (Inductively Coupled Plasma Mass Spectrometry), ACP (Amorphous Calcium Phosphate),

* Corresponding Author

DCP (Dicalcium Phosphate), OCP (Octacalcium Phosphate), ALP (Alkaline Phosphatase Test), U2OS (human osteosarcoma cell line)

## 5. References

[1] Diebold U. (2003) The surface science of titanium dioxide. Surf. sci. r 48:53-229.

[2] Oh S, Daraio C, Chen LH, Pisanic TR, Finones RR, Jin S. (2006) Significantly accelerated osteoblast cell growth on aligned $TiO_2$ nanotubes. J biomed. mater. res a. 78:97–103.

[3] Park J, Bauer S, von der Mark K, Schmuki P (2007) Nanosize and Vitality: $TiO_2$ nanotube diameter directs cell fate. Nano lett., 7(6):1686-1691

[4] Roguska A, Kudelski A, Pisarek M, Lewandowska M, Dolata M, Janik-Czachor M (2009) Raman investigations of $TiO_2$ nanotube substrates covered with thin Ag or Cu deposits. J. raman spectrosc. 40(11):1652-1656.

[5] Roguska A, Kudelski A, Pisarek M, Opara M, Janik-Czachor M (2011) Raman investigations of SERS activity of Ag nanoclusters on a $TiO_2$-nanotubes/Ti substrate. Vibr. spectr. 55:38–43.

[6] Roguska A, Kudelski A, Pisarek M, Opara M, Janik-Czachor M (2011) Surface-enhanced Raman scattering (SERS) activity of Ag, Au and Cu nanoclusters on $TiO_2$-nanotubes/Ti substrate. Appl. surf. sci. 257:8182-8189.

[7] Liu X, Chu PK, Ding Ch (2004) Surface modification of titanium, titanium alloys, and related materials for biomedical applications. Mater. sci. eng. r. 47:49-121.

[8] Liu X, Chu PK, Ding Ch (2010) Surface nano-functionalization of biomaterials. Mater. sci. eng. r. 70:275–302.

[9] Pisarek M, Lewandowska M, Roguska A, Kurzydłowski KJ, Janik-Czachor M (2007) SEM, Scanning Auger and XPS characterization of chemically pretreated Ti surfaces intended for biomedical applications. Mater. chem. phys. 104:93-97.

[10] Chen Y, Lee Chi-Y, Yeng M-Y, Chin H.T (2003) Preparing titanium oxide with various morphologies. Mater. chem. phys. 81:39-43.

[11] Wang XX, Hayakawa S, Tsuru K, Osaka A (2002) Bioactive titania gel layers formed by chemical treatment of Ti substrate with a $H_2O_2$/HCl solution. Biomaterials. 23:1353-1357.

[12] Kokubo T, Kim H-M, Miyaji F, Takadama H, Miyazaki T (1999) Ceramic–metal and ceramic–polymer composites prepared by a biomimetic process. Composites a. 30:405–409.

[13] Kokubo T (1998) Apatite formation on surfaces of ceramics, metals and polymers in body environment. Acta Mater. 46(7):2519–2527.

[14] Pisarek M, Roguska A, Andrzejczuk M, Marcon L, Szunerits S, Lewandowska M, Janik-Czachor M (2011) Effect of two-step functionalization of Ti by chemical processes on protein adsorption. Appl. surf. sci. 257:8196-8204.

Pisarek M, Roguska A, Marcon L, Andrzejczuk M (2012) Biomimetic Ca-P coatings obtained by chemical/electrochemical methods from Hanks' solution on a Ti surface. Eng. biomaterials. Accepted for publication.

[15] Nishiguchi S, Kato H, Fujita H, Ok M, Kim HM, Kokubo T, Nakamura T (2001) Titanium metals form direct bonding to bone after alkali and heat treatments. Biomaterials. 22:2525–2533.

[16] Takadama H, Kim H.-M, Kokubo T, Nakamura T (2001) XPS study of the process of apatite formation on bioactive Ti-6Al-4V alloy in simulated body fluid. Sci. technol. adv. mater. 2:389-396.

[17] Wei M, Kim HM, Kokubo T, Evans JH (2002) Optimizing the bioactivity of alkali treated titanium alloy. Mater. sci. eng. C. 20:125–134.

[18] Liang F, Zhou L, Wang K (2003) Apatite formation on porous titanium by alkali and heat treatment. Surf. coat. technol. 165:133–139.

[19] Park Ji-H, Lee Y.-K, Kim K.-M, Kim K.-N (2005) Bioactive calcium phosphate prepared on $H_2O_2$-treated titanium substrate by electrodeposition. Surf. coat. technol. 195:252-257.

[20] Zhao J, Wang X, Chen R, Li L (2005) Fabrication of titanium oxide nanotube arrays by anodic oxidation. Solid state commun. 134:705-710.

[21] Macak JM, Tsuchiya H, Ghicov A, Yasuda K, Hahn R, Bauer S, Schmuki P (2007) $TiO_2$ nanotubes: Self-organized electrochemical formation, properties and applications. Curr. opinion solid state mater. sci. 11:3-18.

[22] Roguska A, Pisarek M, Andrzejczuk M, Dolata M, Lewandowska M, Janik-Czachor M (2011) Characterization of a calcium phosphate -$TiO_2$ nanotube composite layer for biomedical applications. Mater. sci. eng c. 31:906-914.

[23] Wang H, Eliaz N, Hobbs LW (2011) The nanostructure of an electrochemically hydroxyapatite coating. Mater. lett. 65:2455-2457.

[24] Park Ji-H, Lee D-Y, Oh K-T, Lee Y-K, Kim K-M, Kim K-N (2006) Bioactivity of calcium phosphate coatings prepared by electrodeposition in a modified simulated body fluid. Mater. lett. 60:2573-2577.

[25] de Bruijn JD, van Blitterswijk CA (1998) New developments in implant coatings: biomimetics and tissue engineering. In: Walenkamp G, editor. Biomaterials in Surgery. Stuttgart, Germany: Georg Thieme Verlag; 1998. p 77–82.

[26] Royer P, Rey Ch (1991) Calcium phosphate coatings for orthopaedic prosthesis. Surf. coat. technol. 45(1-3): 171-177.

[27] Wang H, Eliaz N, Xiang Z, Hsu HP, Spector M, Hobbs LW (2006) Early bone apposition in vivo on plasma-spryed and electrochemically deposited hydroxyapatite on titanium alloy. Biomaterials. 27:4192-4203.

[28] Hanawa T, Ota M (1991) Calcium phosphate naturally formed on titanium in electrolyte solution. Biomaterials. 12(8): 767-774.

[29] Bosetti M, Masse A, Tobin E, Cannas M (2002) Silver coated material for external fixation devices; in vitro biocompatibility and genotoxicity. Biomaterials. 23:887–892.

[30] Jonasova L, Muller FA, Helebrant A, Strand J, Greil P (2004) Biomimetic apatite formation on chemically treated titanium. Biomaterials. 25:1187-1194.

[31] Wang J, Layrolle P, Stigter M, de Groot K (2004) Biomimetic and electrolytic calcium phosphate coatings on titanium alloy: physicochemical characteristics and cell attachment. Biomaterials 25:583-592.

[32] Lewandowska M, Roguska A, Pisarek M, Polak B, Janik-Czachor M, Kurzydłowski KJ (2007) Morphology and chemical characterization of Ti surfaces for biomedical applications. Biomol. Eng. 24:438-442.

[33] Kasemo B (1983) Biocompatibility of titanium implants: surface science aspects. J. prosthetic dentistry. 49:832-837.

[34] Lee B.-H, Kim YD, Lee KH (2003) XPS study of bioactive graded layer in Ti-In-Nb-Ta alloy prepared by alkali and heat treatments. Biomaterials. 24:2257-2266.

[35] Vallet-Regi M, Gonzalez-Callet JM (2004) Calcium phosphates as substitution of bone tissues. Prog. solid state chem. 32:1-31.

[36] Tsuchiya H, Macak JM, Taveira L, Balaur E, Ghicov A, Sirotna K, Schmuki P (2005) Self-organized $TiO_2$ nanotubes prepared in ammonium fluoride containing acetic acid electrolytes. Electrochem. commun. 7:576–580.

[37] Kodama A, Bauer S, Komatsu A, Asoh H, Ono S, Schmuki P (2009) Bioactivation of titanium surfaces using coatings of $TiO_2$ nanotubes rapidly pre-loaded with synthetic hydroxyapatite. Acta Biomater. 5:2322–2330.

[38] Oh S, Finones RR, Daraio Ch, Chen LH, Jin S (2005) Growth of nano-scale hydroxyapatite using chemically treated titanium oxide nanotubes. Biomaterials. 26:4938–4943.

[39] Raja KS, Misra M, Paramguru K (2005) Deposition of calcium phosphate coating on nanotubular anodized titanium. Mater. lett. 59:2137–2141.

[40] Kunze J, Muller L, Macak JM, Greil P, Schmuki P, Muller FA (2008) Time-dependent growth of biomimetic apatite on anodic $TiO_2$ nanotubes. Electrochim. acta. 53:6995–7003.

[41] Kar A, Raja KS, Misra M (2006) Electrodeposition of hydroxyapatite onto nanotubular $TiO_2$ for implant applications. Surf. coat. technol. 201:3723-3731.

[42] Wang Y-q, Tao J, Wang L, He P-t, Wang T (2008) HA coating on titanium with nanotubular TiO2 intermediate layer via electrodeposition. Trans. nonferrous met. soc. china. 18:631-635.

[43] Gristina AG, Costerton JW (1985) Bacterial adhesion to biomaterials and tissue. J. Bone Joint Surgery 67A:264-273n

[44] Gristina AG (1994) Implant failure and the immuno-incomponent fibro-inflammatory zone. Clinical orthopaedics related research. 298:106-118.

[45] Sygnatowicz M, Keyshar K, Tiwari A (2010) Antimicrobial properties of silver-doped hydroxyapatite nano-powders and thin films. JOM. 62(7):65-70.

[46] Rai M, Yadav A, Gade A (2009) Silver nanoparticles as a new generation of antimicrobials. Biotechnol. adv. 27:76-83.

[47] Vik H, Andersen KJ, Julshamn K, Todnem K (1985) Neuropathy caused by silver adsorption from arthroplasty cement. Lancet. 1:872.

[48] Fischer-Crips AC (2002) Nanoindentation. Sprinter-Verlag, New York.

[49] Dorozhkin SV, Schmitt M, Bouler JM, Daculsi G (2000) Chemical transformation of some biologically relevant calcium phosphates in aqueous media during steam sterilization. J. mater. sci. mater. med. 11:779-786.

[50] Morejon-Alonso L, Garcia Carrodeguas R, Delgado Garcia-Menocal JA, Alonso Perez JA, Martinez Manent S (2007) Effect of sterilization on the properties CDHA-OCP-β-TCP biomaterial. Mater. res. 10(1):15-20.

[51] McCafferty E, Wightman JP (1999) An X-ray photoelectron spectroscopy sputter profile study of the native air-formed oxide film on titanium. Appl. surf. sci. 143:92-100.

[52] Garbacz H, Pisarek M, Kurzydłowski KJ (2007) Corrosion resistance of nanostructured titanium. Biomole. eng. 24:559-563.

[53] Feng B, Weng J, Yang BC, Qu SX, Zhang XD (2003) Characterization of surface oxide films on titanium and adhesion of osteoblast. Biomaterials. 24:4663-4670

[54] Zhu X, Chen J, Scheideler L, Reichl R, Geis-Gerstorfer J (2004) Effects of topography and composition of titanium surface oxides on osteoblast responses. Biomaterials. 25:4087–4103.

[55] Yang B, Uchida M, Kim HM, Zhang X, Kokubo T (2004) Preparation of bioactive titanium metal via anodic oxidation treatment. Biomaterials. 25:1003–1010.

[56] Kuphasuk Ch, Oshida Y, Andres CJ, Hovijitra ST, Barco MT, Brown DT (2001) Electrochemical corrosion of Ti and titanium based alloys. J. prosthetic dentistry. 85(2):195-202

[57] Schenk R. (2001) The corrosoin properties of titanium and titanium alloys. chapter 6, pp.145-170 in "Titanium in Medicine" Eds. Brunette DM, Tengvall P, Textor M Thomsen P. Springer-Verlag.

[58] Roguska A, Hiromoto S, Yamamoto A, Woźniak MJ, Pisarek M, Lewandowska M (2011) Collagen immobilization on 316L stainless steel surface with cathodic deposition of calcium phosphate. Appl. surf. sci. 257:5037-5045.

[59] Macak JM, Hildebrand H, Marten-Jahns U, Schmuki P (2008) Mechanistic aspects and growth of large diameter self-organized $TiO_2$ nanotubes. J. electroanal. chem. 621:254-266.

[60] Petukhov DI, Eliseev AA, Kolesnik IV, Napolskii KS, Lukashin AV, Tretyakov YD, Griegoriev SV, Gregorieva NA, Eckerlebe H (2008) Microporous mesoporous mater. 114:440-447.

[61] Wang M, Liu Y, Yang H (2012) A unified thermodynamic theory for the formation of anodized metal oxide structures. Electrochem. acta. 62:424-432.

[62] Peltonen J, Jarn M, Areva S, Linden M, Rosenholm JB (2004) Topographical parameters for specifying a three-dimensional surface. Langmuir. 20:9428–9431.

[63] Jaroenworaluck A, Regonini D, Bowen CR, Stevens R (2010) A microscopy study of the effect of heat treatment on the structure and properties of anodised $TiO_2$ nanotubes. Appl. surf. sci. 256:2672-2679.

[64] Fang D, Luo Z, Huang K, Lagoudas DC (2011) Effect of heat treatment on morphology, crystalline structure and photocatalysis properties of $TiO_2$ nanotubes on Ti substrate and freestanding membrane. Appl. surf. sci. 257:6451-6461.

[65] Yu J, Wang B. (2010) Effect of calcination temperature on morphology and photoelectrochemical properties of anodized titanium dioxide nanotube arrays. Appl. catal. b-environ. 94:295-302.

[66] Crawford GA, Chawla N, Das K, Bose S, Bandyopadhyay A (2007) Microstructure and deformation behavior of biocompatible $TiO_2$ nanotubes on titanium substrate. Acta biomater. 3:359–367.

[67] Mante FK, Baran GR, Lucas B (1999) Nanoindentation studies of titanium single crystals. Biomaterials. 20:1051-1055.

[68] Wang J, Lin Z (2009) Anodic formation of ordered $TiO_2$ nanotube arrays: effects of electrolyte temperature and anodization potential. J. phys. chem. c. 113:4026-4030.

[69] Qian L, Du Z-L, Yang S-Y, Jin Z-S (2005) Raman study of titania nanotube by soft chemical process. J. mol. struct. 749:103-107.

[70] Brammer KS, Oh S, Frandsen ChJ, Jin S. (2010) $TiO_2$ nanotubes structures for enhanced cell and biological functionality. JOM. 62(4):50.

[71] A.Kudelski, A.Roguska, M.Pisarek, M.Hołdyński, M.Janik-Czachor (2012) Surface-enhanced Raman scattering (SERS) investigations on silver nanopartcles deposited on alumina and titania nanotubes: influence of the substrate material on SERS activity of Ag nanoparticles. J. raman spectrosc. accepted for publication.

[72] Barrere F, Snel MME, van Blitterswijk CA, de Groot K, Layrolle P. Nano-scale study of the nucleation and growth of calcium phosphate coating on titanium implants. Biomaterials. 25:2901-2910.

[73] Bigi A, Boanini E, Bracci B, Facchini A, Panzavolta S, Segatti F, Sturba L (2005) Nanocrystalline hydroxyapatite coatings on titanium: a new fast biomimetic method. Biomaterials. 26:4085–4089.

[74] Peltola T, Jokinen M, Rahiala H, Pätsi M, Heikkilä J, Kangasniemi I, Yli-Urpo A (2000) Effect of aging time of sol on structure and in vitro calcium phosphate formation of sol–gel derived titania films. J. biomed. mater. res. 51:200–208.

[75] Jarn M, Areva S, Pore V, Peltonen J, Linden M (2006) Topography and surface energy dependent calcium phosphate formation on sol–gel derived $TiO_2$ coatings. Langmuir. 22:8206–8213.

[76] Kim YH, Cho CS, Kang IK, Kim SY, Kwon OH (2007) Mechanism study of calcium phosphate deposition on a titanium surface in simulated body fluid. Key eng. mater. 342–343:693–696.

[77] Kaciulis S, Mattogno G, Napoli A, Bemporad E, Ferrari F, Montenero A, Gnappi G (1998) Surface analysis of biocompatible coatings on titanium. J. electron. spectrosc. relat. phenom. 95:61–69.

[78] Stoch A, Brozek A, Kmita G, Stoch K, Jastrzebski W, Rakowska A (2001) Electrophoretic coating of hydroxyapatite on titanium implants. J. mol. struct. 596:191–200.

[79] Kaciulis S, Mattogno G, Pandolfi L, Cavalli M, Gnappi G, Montenero A (1999) XPS study of apatite-based coatings prepared by sol–gel technique. Appl. surf. sci. 151:1–5.

[80] Zhang Q, Leng Y (2005) Electrochemical activation of titanium for biomimetic coating of calcium phosphate. Biomaterials. 26:3853–3859.

[81] Forsgren J, Svahn F, Jarmar T, Engqvist H (2007) Formation and adhesion of biomimetic hydroxyapatite deposited on titanium substrates. Acta Biomater. 3:980–984.

[82] Serro AP, Saramago B (2003) Influence of sterilization on the mineralization of titanium implants induced by incubation in various biological model fluids. Biomaterials. 24:4749-4760.

[83] Ponsonnet L, Reybier K, Jaffrezic N, Comte V, Lagneau C, Lissac M, Martelet C (2003) Relationship between surface properties (roughness, wettability) of titanium and titanium alloys and cell behavior. Mater. sci. eng. c. 23:551–560.

[84] de Gennes PG (1985) Wetting statics and dynamics. Rev. mod. phys. 57:289–324.

[85] Paital SR, Dahotre NB (2009) Wettability and kinetics of hydroxyapatite precipitation on a laser-textured Ca–P bioceramic coating. Acta Biomater. 5:2763–2772.

[86] Paital SR, Balani K, Agarwal A, Dahotre NB (2009) Fabrication and evaluation of a pulse laser-induced Ca–P coating on a Ti alloy for bioapplication. Biomed. mater. 4:015009 (10pp).

[87] Uchida M, Kim H-M, Kokubo T, Fujibayashi S, Nakamura T (2003) Structural dependence of apatite formation on titania gels in a simulated body fluid. J. biomed. mater. res. a. 64A:164–170.

[88] Lu HB, Campbell CT, Graham DJ, Ratner BD (2000) Surface characterization of hydroxyapatite and related calcium phosphates by XPS and TOF-SIMS. Anal. chem. 72:2886–2894.

[89] Dorozhkin SV (2007) Calcium orthophosphates. J. mater. sci. 42:1061–1095.

[90] Stoch A, Jastrzebski W, Brozek A, Trybalska B, Cichocinska M, Szarawara E (1999) FTIR monitoring of the growth of carbonate containing apatite layers from simulated and natural body fluids. J. mol. struct. 511–512:287–294.

[91] Muller L, Conforto E, Caillard D, Muller FA (2007) Biomimetic apatite coatings – Carbonate substitution and preferred growth orientation. Biomol. eng. 24:462–466.

[92] Koutsopoulos S (2002) Synthesis and characterization of hydroxyapatite crystals: a review study on the analytical methods. J. biomed. mater. res. 62:600–612.

[93] Nriagu JO, Moore BP (Eds.) (1984) Phosphate Minerals. Springer, Berlin.

[94] Bender SA, Bumgardner JD, Roach MD, Bessho K, Ong JL (2000) Effect of protein on the dissolution of HA coatings. Biomaterials. 21:299–305.

[95] Cai K, Bossert J, Jandt KD (2006) Does the nanometre scale topography of titanium influence protein adsorption and cell proliferation? Colloid. surf. b-biointerfaces. 49-136-144.
[96] Cai K, Frant M, Bossert J, Hildebrand G, Liefeith K, Jandt KD (2006) Surface functionalized titanium thin films: Zeta-potential, protein adsorption and cell proliferation. Colloid. surf. b-biointerfaces. 50:1–8.
[97] Feng B, Weng J, Yang BC, Qu SX, Zhang XD (2004) Characterization of titanium surfaces with calcium and phosphate and osteoblast adhesion. Biomaterials. 25:3421–3428.
[98] Deligianni DD, Katsala N, Lada S, Sotiropoulou D, Amedee J, Missirlis YF (2001) Effect of surface roughness of the titanium alloy Ti-6Al-4V on human bone marrow cell response and on protein adsorption. Biomaterials.22:1241-1251.
[99] Ahmed MH, Keyes TE, Byrne JA, Blackledge CW, Hamilton JW (2011) Adsorption and photocatalytic degradation of human serum albumin on $TiO_2$ and Ag-$TiO_2$ films. JPPA. 222: 123-131.
[100] Twardowski J, Anzenbacher P (1994) Raman and IR spectroscopy in biology and biochemistry. Warsaw: Polish Scientific Publishers PWN Ltd.
[101] Zeng H, Chittur KK, Lacefield WR (1999) Analysis of bovine serum albumin adsorption on calcium phosphate and titanium surfaces. Biomaterials. 20:377-384.
[102] Bernards MT, Qin Ch, Jiang S (2008) MC3T3-E1 cell adhesion to hydroxyapatite with adsorbed bone sialoprotein, bone osteopontin, and bovine serum albumin. Colloid. surf. b-biointerfaces. 64:236-247.
[103] Yamaguchi M, Igarashi A, Misawa H, Tsurusaki Y (2003) Enhancement of albumin expression in bone tissues with healing rat fractures. J cell biochem. 89(2): 356-363.
[104] Ishida K, Yamaguchi M Role of albumin in osteoblastic cells: Enhancement of cell proliferation and suppression of alkaline phosphatase activity (2004) Inter. j. mol. med. 14(6): 1077-1081.
[105] Park JH, Lee Y-K, Kim K-M, Kim K-N (2005) Transformation of electrodeposited calcium phosphate coatings in simulated body fluid and in culture medium. Eng. mater. 284-286:473-476.
[106] ter Brugge PJ, Dieudonne S, Jansen JA (2002) Initial interaction of U2OS cells with noncoated and calcium phosphate coated titanium substrates. J. biomed. mater. res. a. 61: 399-407.
[107] Anselme K, Linez P, Bigerelle M, Le Maguer D, Le Maguer A, Hardouin P, Hildebrand HF, Iost A, Leroy JM (2000) The relative influence of the topography and chemistry of Ti6Al4V surfaces on osteoblastic cell behaviour. Biomaterials 21:1567-1577.
[108] von Wilmowsky C, Bauer S, Roedl S, Neukam FW, Schmuki P, Schlegel KA (2012) The diameter of anodic $TiO_2$ nanotubes affects bone formation and correlates with the bone morphogenetic protein-2 expression in vivo. Clinical oral impl. res. 23(3):359–366.
[109] Hanssen AD, Rand JA (1998) Evaluation and treatment of infection at the site of a total hip or knee arthroplasty. J. bone joint surg. 80A:910–922.

[110] Popat CK, Eltgroth M, La Tempa JT, Grimes AC, Desai AT (2007) Decreased Staphylococcus epidermis adhesion and increased osteoblast functionality on antibiotic-loaded titania nanotubes. Biomaterials. 228:4880–4888.

[111] Chua PH, Neoh KG, Kang ET, Wang W (2008) Surface functionalization of titanium with hyaluronic acid/chitosan polyelectrolyte multilayers and RGD for promoting osteoblast functions and inhibiting bacterial adhesion. Biomaterials. 29:1412–142.

[112] Wan YZ, Xiong GY, Liang H, Raman S, He F, Huang Y (2007) Modification of medical metals by ion implantation of copper. Appl. surf. sc.i 253:9426–9429.

[113] Monteiro DR, Gorup LF, Takamiya AS, Ruvollo-Filho AC, de Camargo ER, Barros Barbosa D (2009) The growing importance of materials that prevent microbial adhesion: Antimicrobial effect of medical devices containing silver. Int. j. antimicrob. agents. 34: 103–110.

[114] Roguska A, Pisarek M, Andrzejczuk M, Lewandowska M, Kurzydłowski KJ, Janik-Czachor M (2012) Surface characterization of Ca-P/Ag/$TiO_2$ nanotube composite layers on Ti intended for biomedical applications. J biomed. res. a. Accepted for publication.

[115] Chen X, Schluesener HJ (2007) Nanosilver: A nanoproduct in medical application. Toxicol. let. 176:1–12.

[116] Lok CN, Ho CM, Chen R, He QY, Yu WY, Sun H, Tam PK, Chiu J-F, Che C-M (2007) Silver nanoparticles: Partial oxidation and antibacterial activities. J. boil. Inorg. Chem. 12:527–534.

[117] Kim JS, Kuk E, Yu KN, Kim JH, Park SJ, Lee HJ, Kim SH, Park YK, Park YH, Hwang CY, Kim YK, Lee YS, Jeong DH, Cho MH (2007) Antimicrobial effects of silver nanoparticles. Nanomed. nanotechnol. biol. mned. 3:95–101.

[118] Morones JR, Elechiguerra JL, Camacho A, Holt K, Kouri JB, Ramirez JT, Yacamen MJ (2005) The bactericidal effect of silver nanoparticles. Nanotechnology. 16:2346–2353.

[119] Necula BS, Fratila-Apachitei LE, Zaat SAJ, Apachitei I, Duszczyk J (2009) In vitro antibacterial activity of porous $TiO_2$–Ag composite layers against methicillin-resistant Staphylococcus aureus. Acta biomater. 5:3573–3580.

[120] von Wilmowsky C, Bauer S, Lutz R, Meisel M, Neukam FW, Toyoshima T, Schmuki P, Nkenke E, Schlegel KA (2009) In vivo evaluation of anodic $TiO_2$ nanotubes: An experimental study in the pig. Biomed. mater. res. b appl. biomater. 89:165-171.

[121] Zhao L, Chu PK, Zhang Y, Wu Z (2009) Antibacterial coatings on titanium implants. J. Biomed. Mater. Res. B. 91B(1):470-480

[122] Adams CS, Mansfield K, Perlot RL, Shapiro IM (2001) Matrix regulation of skeletal cell apoptosis – the role of calcium and phosphate ions. J. biol. chem. 276:20316–20322.

[123] Rey C, Combes C, Drouet C, Sfihi H, Barroug A (2007) Physico-chemical properties of nanocrystalline apatites: Implications for biominerals and biomaterials. Mater. sci. eng. c. 27:198-205.

[124] Dorozhkin SV (2010) Amorphous calcium (ortho)phosphates. Acta biomater. 6:4457-4475.

[125] Suzuki O (2010) Octacalcium phosphate: Osteoconductivity and a crystal chemistry. Acta biomater. 6:3379–3387.

[126] Pittrof A, Bauer S, Schmuki P (2011) Micropatterned $TiO_2$ nanotube surfaces for site-selective nucleation of hydroxyapatite from simulated body fluid. Acta biomater. 7(1):424-431.

[127] Dey T, Roy P, Fabry B, Schmuki P (2011) Anodic mesoporous $TiO_2$ layer on Ti for enhanced formation of biomimetic hydroxyapatite. Acta biomater. 7:1873-1879.

Chapter 2

# Porous Titanium by Powder Metallurgy for Biomedical Application: Characterization, Cell Citotoxity and *in vivo* Tests of Osseointegration

Luana Marotta Reis de Vasconcellos, Yasmin Rodarte Carvalho, Renata Falchete do Prado, Luis Gustavo Oliveira de Vasconcellos, Mário Lima de Alencastro Graça and Carlos Alberto Alves Cairo

Additional information is available at the end of the chapter

http://dx.doi.org/10.5772/47816

## 1. Introduction

Surgical implants are used to replace lost body structures and due to the increased life expectancy of the world population, they have become one of the most promising fields for improving the quality of life of these individuals [1]. The biological process of osseointegration or calcified bone matrix apposition on the surface of a synthetic implanted material constitutes one of the most important discoveries of clinical practice of the 20th century. However, there are areas of knowledge that are not fully understood, particularly involving the biochemistry of bone formation, cellular response and the regulatory mechanisms of osteogenesis and bone resorption. Currently, implant dentistry focuses on studies that address and enable more rapid osseointegration of implants for orthopedic and dental use, in an attempt to reduce or even eliminate the period of bone healing free from functional load [2]. Among the various lines of research oriented toward this purpose, the topographical characteristics of the implant surface at the bone-implant interface are considered relevant due to the strong influence on the quality of osseointegration achieved [3-8], together with the characteristics of the biomaterial from which the implant is produced [3,9-11].

Metals are the most commonly used biocompatible materials in commercial manufacturing of surgical implants, while titanium (Ti) and its alloys are the most commonly used metals in the field of biomedicine [3-10,12], due to their excellent physical and chemical properties. Titanium has proven biocompatibility and an extraordinary combination of properties, since it exhibits high tensile strength (200-700 MPa), low specific weight (density = 4.5 g/cm$^3$ at

25°C), a high melting point (1688°C), a modulus of elasticity compatible with calcified body tissues (110 GPa), Vickers hardness between 80 and 105 that varies depending on the purity of Ti, thermal conductivity of 0.2 J/cm.K and thermal expansion of 9:6x10$^{-7}$ K$^{-1}$ [13].

The main limitation of Ti is its chemical reactivity with other materials, at high temperatures. However, at room temperature, when in contact with air, Ti loses this reactivity, becoming extremely inactive. This phenomenon, denominated passive, results in the formation of a very thin oxide film that is highly adherent to the metal surface, which serves as a protective barrier to further corrosion [13]. This thin layer is formed mainly by titanium dioxide ($TiO_2$), which appears amorphous, insoluble and very stable and can form again when removed mechanically. Besides this limitation, Ti exhibits another drawback to its use in clinical practice, orthopedics and dentistry, which is the difference between the modulus of elasticity of the metallic implant of Ti (110GPa) and the modulus of elasticity of bone tissue (10-30GPa) [14]. However, this drawback can be controlled with the fabrication of pores in the structure of Ti implants [9,15] or with new Ti allows of low modulus of elasticity [16].

Regardless of the surface topography of Ti, the bioactivity of this surface is not sufficient to induce the growth of bone tissue in a short period. Several studies have demonstrated greater osteoconductivity of Ti implants that were subjected to thermal and chemical treatments. These treatments, called biomimetics, are specific processes capable of forming in vitro on the implant surface by ion precipitation using calcium phosphates, such as hydroxyapatite ($Ca_5(PO_4)_3(OH)$) [17-21].

Biomimetic methods for HA coating on Ti are based on the nucleation and growth of calcium phosphate in simulated body fluid following preheat treatment [17]. This treatment aims to produce an apatite layer on the surface of Ti implants, increasing their osteoconductivity, consequently favoring osseointegration. Bioactive coating on the porous surface is an attractive method to improve the quality of the bone-implant interface, particularly in the initial stages of healing [21].

Implant topography and surface chemical structure are two aspects considered important for osseointegration, since topography is related to fibrin clot retention and osteoprogenitor cell migration, while the chemical structure influences the surface adsorption of proteins that promote adhesion and the activation of osteoprogenitor cells [20].

Porosity can be defined as the percentage of void spaces in a solid. The osseointegration obtained with porous Ti is achieved by bone growth into the pores, called "bone ingrowth", which improves micromechanical interlocking, the interlacing of bone tissue within the implant, preventing mobility.

Numerous studies have shown that implant porosity promotes positive results in bone neoformation in vivo [4,5,8-10,22,23], since it increases the contact area between the biomaterials and bone tissue [4,22], resulting in improved implant stability over time, as well as accelerating the process of osseointegration [24]. Concomitantly, various studies have shown that the implant surface can alter the metabolism and phenotypic expression of osteoblastic cells [22,23,25].

A porous surface with interconnected pores results in significant improvement in the rate of bone formation and in better fixation of the implant to the bone [20,21]. The porous structure must be produced with high porosity to provide sufficient space for cell adhesion and subsequent formation of new bone that permits the transport of body fluids and the proliferation of new vasculature, while providing adequate mechanical properties to withstand stresses during implantation and use [4-8,12,22]. However, although increased porosity and pore size favors new bone growth, this increase can diminish the mechanical properties of the implant [6-8,26].

Xue et al. [27] showed that effects like increased cell attachment, cell differentiation, alkaline phosphatase expression occur when using porous Ti samples with pores larger than 200μm. Osteoblasts respond differently depending on the pore size. In pores smaller than 100μm, the cells spread directly on top of the pore by filopodia, while in pores larger than 200μm, osteoblasts do not spread over the pore, growth within the pores is observed. In an extensive review, Karageorgiou and Kaplan [28] considered that the minimum pore size should be 100μm due to cell size and the characteristics of cell migration and transport. However, pores of 300μm are considered ideal, since they facilitate the formation of capillaries. It is also possible to correlate this data with the size of Haversian channels of approximately 100-200μm in diameter. Small pores could favor hypoxia, which can result in the formation of osteocartilaginous tissue, while large richly vascularized pores permit direct osteogenesis. The authors conclude by recommending the development of technologies that can produce a gradient of pore sizes, resulting in an improved bone-implant interface.

Osteoblasts in culture were capable of covering distances of 600μm in diameter to populate a channel in a Ti sample, forming cell bridges [24]. In channels 300μm in diameter, a single cell was capable of creating extensions side to side by filopodia. The capacity to quickly cellularize a channel is inversely proportional to cell differentiation. Once attached to the wall of the channel a cells begins its differentiation, increasing the expression of molecules such as osteocalcin, osteopontin, fibronectin, collagen I and III. From a morphological point of view, in this study, a diameter of 600μm was favorable to cell response. Lamellar bone formation occurs within pores of 100, 200 and 300μm. However, it has been reported that for implants with pores of 100μm, the bone formation rate was lower and for 300μm, it was initially slower than for a pore size of 200μm. Thus, the optimal size for surface structuration of Ti implants was 200μm [29].

High porosity facilitates the transport of body fluids, benefits the spread of cells into the implant and promotes the proliferation of bone tissue, since it increases the contact area [4,5] however, equilibrium between the rate of porosity and mechanical properties of the material should be maintained.

Some researchers have reported that the percentage of pores suitable for Ti samples is between 25 and 66% [30,31]. Takemoto et al. [32] suggested that porous Ti with 40% porosity could be an alternative for clinical use. However, samples of 5 and 80% porosity have also shown bone formation [33]. Increased porosity permits the growth of tissue into the pores and, subsequently, mineralization [30]; however, maintaining the mechanical properties of the implant is fundamental. The ideal microtopography for commercial porous implants remains undetermined.

Currently, researchers are attempting to develop implants based on a multifactorial vision, since it is necessary to consider the mechanical properties of the biomaterial, such as corrosion resistance, passivity levels and bone adherence potential, together with mechanical properties that include the deformation behavior of the porous material and its relation to the bone in which it is implanted, in order to withstand the conditions of daily loading. Finally, parameters involving diameter, shape and the distribution of pores that will enhance the fatigue strength and proliferation of bone tissue should also be considered [34].

In order to promote optimal tissue integration with the surgical implant, interactions at the biomaterial-host tissue interface should be optimized. Thus, researchers are strongly committed to modify the surface of Ti implants to improve and accelerate the cellular response [35], since cells interact with the outermost layer of the implant, thus conferring an important role to the implant surface in the initial response of the patient [36]. These interactions occur at the cellular level and, therefore, it is necessary to develop new biomaterials with controlled surface characteristics that are able to directly influence cells.

## 2. Biomimetic treatment

Surface modifications of Ti that have been described in the literature have greatly improved surface contact at the bone-implant interface and reduced repair time. This result is attributed to increased osteoblastic activity on the surface of the implants [37]. However the cellular mechanisms have not been fully elucidated [38].

Studies have reported that topography can determine the adsorption of biomolecules and their orientation on the surface of the implant, immediately following installation of the same in the surgical cavity. Furthermore, it may influence the early formation of fibrin clots, platelet activation and the production of growth factors related to bone tissue, thereby interfering directly in cell recruitment, adhesion, proliferation and differentiation [24]. Evidence suggests that the mechanism by which the topography of Ti influences the differentiation of osteoblasts is related to the pathways of phospholipase A2, protein kinase A and integrin. Cells growing on roughened Ti surfaces present increased expression of TGF-β1 and interleukin Iβ and a prostaglandin-mediated response, which leads to decreased proliferation and favors cell differentiation with an increase in alkaline phosphatase activity and increased expression of molecules, such as osteocalcin [39,40].

Hydroxyapatite corresponds to the main mineral component of human bone tissue. However, its poor mechanical properties limit its practical applications as implants subjected to loading. More recently, implants based on Ti coated with bioinert apatite or hydroxyapatite have attracted a lot of attention because these coatings result in a biomaterial that combines the advantageous mechanical properties of Ti with the biological affinity of bone to hydroxyapatite [41].

Therefore calcium phosphate coatings have been widely investigated due to their chemical similarity with the bone mineral portion. Several chemical and physical techniques have been developed to deposit thin coatings on metals in order to form a bioactive surface layer capable of chemically binding to bone that also accelerates the process of bone apposition, particularly during the initial period of healing.

Among the methods of applying calcium phosphate, thermal blasting by plasma spraying has been the most widely used technique commercially. This technique consists of pulverizing ceramic particles on the implant surface from a plasma spray at high temperature. Although this provides a highly osteoconductive surface [42], researchers have reported that this technique does not permit precise control of the chemical composition and crystal structure of calcium phosphate formed on the metal [43], which could provoke a mechanically and chemically unstable and weak bond between the metal substrate and bone. It is difficult to achieve uniform thickness of the deposited layer and difficult to use on implants with complex geometries [44].

In 1996, Kokubo et al. published studies showing a chemical treatment method for Ti that promotes the deposition of apatite on its surface, in order to induce bioactivity for use in endosseous implants. Heating in alkali was performed to form sodium titanate on the surface, followed by immersing the specimens in a simulated body fluid (liquid ionic conditions simulating blood plasma), resulting in the formation of an apatite layer on the samples. The term biomimetic treatment is attributed to this type of process. According to the authors, bioactive Ti and its alloys could be used as bone substitute materials, even in conditions requiring mechanical loads. According to Chen et al. [41], Ti implants coated with apatite or hydroxyapatite combine the advantages of the biomechanical strength of the metal with the biological affinity between hydroxyapatite and the underlying bone.

Biomimetic methods of hydroxyapatite coating on Ti are based on the nucleation and growth of calcium phosphate on the surface of implants immersed in simulated body fluid at 37°C. Chemically, the changes occurring on the surface of biomimetic Ti that is subjected to this treatment can be summarized as follows. When subjected to alkaline treatment with NaOH, a hydrogel layer of sodium titanate is formed, which, following the heat treatment, constitutes an amorphous and/or crystalline layer of sodium titanate. Subsequently, during immersion in simulated body fluid, the apatite layer is formed due to the initial precipitation of $Ca^{2+}$ ions that attract phosphate ions $PO_4^{3-}$ [19].

Porous Ti implants subjected to biomimetic treatment were inserted into rabbit tibia in a study by Machado et al. [45]. Observation verified that the mean percentage of bone neoformation in the treated implants, for each of the experimental periods, was higher compared with untreated implants; bone repair showed a statistically significant difference within 15 days. The mechanical test showed that displacement of the coated implants occurred at greater tension values. According to the author, biomimetic treated implants performed better than untreated implants.

According to Nishiguchi et al. [21], the low cost and the effects achieved, including minimizing implant irregularities, make the biomimetic process a better technique than plasma spraying. Furthermore, the authors observed that treatment did not reduce the porosity space available for bone growth, because it causes very little change in the implant surface morphology, affecting approximately 1μm of the surface. Controlling the composition and growth of the apatite film by altering the composition of the simulated body fluid, the incorporation of protein without altering its functions and without the need for heat treatment, are additional advantages of this promising technique [46].

## 3. Titanium implants obtained by powder metallurgy technique

Titanium is widely used for the production of dental or orthopedic implants because direct contact occurs between bones and implant surfaces [25]. Titanium is biocompatible, highly corrosion resistant and durable. Moreover, it is easily prepared in many different shapes and textures without affecting its biocompatibility [47]. However, most titanium implants consist of dense components, which lead to problems such as bone resorption and implant loosening due to biomechanical mismatch of the elastic modulus [48]. To overcome these problems, porous structures are being investigated extensively, since a reduction in elastic modulus can be coupled with bone integration through tissue ingrowth into pores [49]. The interaction between mechanical behavior and biological processes in cells and tissue is studied in mechanobiology.

Several factors are important for promoting cell growth, such as pore shape and size, as well as their interconnectivity and spatial distribution throughout the implant. Implant architecture is crucial for allowing vascularization and the supply of nutrients to the developing tissue. Studies have shown that the optimum pore size required for implants fixation remains undefined, the consensus is that in order to optimize mineralized bone ingrowth, pore sizes between 100 and 500μm are required [4,5,22]. These porous structures have many applications ranging from spinal fixation to acetabular hip prostheses, dental implants, permanent osteosynthesis plates, and intervertebral discs [50]. In general, porous-surfaced Ti-based implants can be manufactured by one of the following techniques: plasma-spraying [50], anodic dissolution, and grit blasting [33], but these techniques produce only cavities or craters and not interconnected pores. However, there are few efficient techniques for manufacturing these complex shapes with interconnected pores without the need for machining steps [51] such as powder metallurgy (P/M) [4,5,22], the multiple coating technique [52], and powder sintering techniques [53].

The powder metallurgy technique seems to be particularly advantageous because of its processing route and cost [51]. In powder metallurgy, pores can originate from the particle compacting arrangement or from changes in this arrangement, when decomposition of spacer particles causes increasing porosity, and from solid-state diffusion in the sintering step [26]. Finally, the porous structure must also present adequate mechanical strength, since large pores have a deleterious effect on the implant's mechanical properties. The gradient of maximum porosity must be adjusted adequately with respect to porosity and pore size, in order to ensure the implant's suitable mechanical strength [51,54].

### 3.1. The powder metallurgy technique

The P/M technique aims to transform metallic powders, using pressure and heat, by means of a thermal treatment (sintering) that substitutes the classic melting and that is carried out below the melting point of the most important metal. The use of the P/M in the biomedical area is recent and its great advantage is the production of prosthesis near to the final format (near net shapes), dense or with controlled porosity and generally less expensive than the conventional processes [4,6].

Titanium powder with different particle sizes can be obtained commercially or by the hydride-dehydride technique (HDH). Hydriding is carried out at 770 K (500°C), in a vertical furnace, for 3 hours, under a positive hydrogen pressure. After cooling to room temperature, the friable hydride is milled in a titanium or niobium container for nearly 30 minutes with argon protecting atmosphere. The dehydriding stage is carried out at 770 K (500°C) in dynamic vacuum conditions.

Porous titanium implants can be manufactured by mixing, in a rolling container for nearly an hour, titanium powder and urea particles as spacer material. Then the powders are uniaxially pressed at 100 MPa into a stainless steel mold and isostatically pressed, using silicone pipe moulds top sealed with plugs, at 200 - 250 MPa. The porous cylindrical samples are heat treated at 453 – 473 K (180 – 200ºC) for 2 h in air to burn out the spacer particles. Sintering is done at 1473 K (1200ºC) for 1 h, under vacuum ($10^{-4}$ Pa ($10^{-7}$ torr)) and free cooling in furnace. Pore size and distribution in the finished implant can be controlled by the particle size and quantity of urea added to the titanium powder.

Dense implants can be obtained by the utilization of powder with optimized size particle distribution which allows better packing during the pressing before sintering. Dense packing of particles is based on selecting particles in such sizes and fractions that voids between larger particles are occupied by successively smaller particles. The remaining porosity is then composed of interstices created by the non-existence of smallest particles in the distribution. Particle size distribution, particle shape, shape factor, surface roughness are some factors that determine final properties of the consolidated powder.

Working with titanium powder obtained by HDH process, starting from titanium sponge, the best densification results after sintering at 1673 K (1400ºC) with 99.8% mean relative density) was obtained for powder milled in a rotative ball mill under vacuum for 36h, that presents a trimodal distribution with higher frequencies for sizes 15 μm, 5 μm and 0.8 μm (Fig. 1). The irregular shape of particles produce an irregular array of voids with the small particles filling voids between the great ones, that enhancing compaction [55].

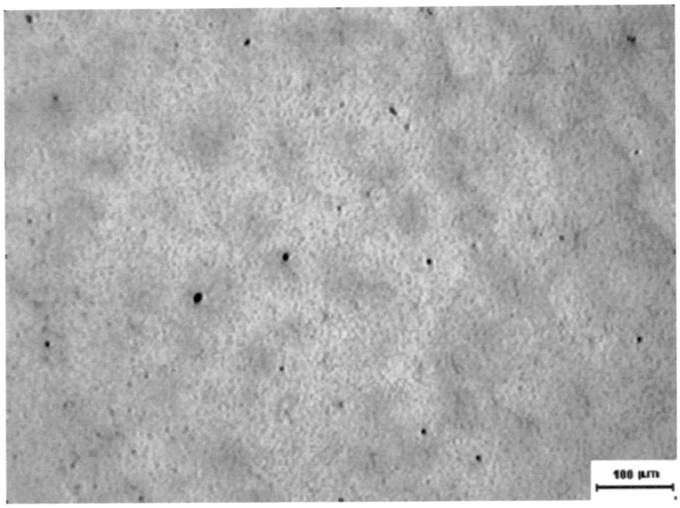


**Figure 1.** SEM micrography of Ti sample, milled for 36 hours, after sintering at 1673 K (1400ºC), dark points are porous.

## 3.2. Rough and entirely porous implants

The porous and rough cylindrical implants are fabricated using the powder metallurgy technique. The materials used to manufacture the implants are commercially pure titanium powder with mean particles size of around 80µm, and urea particles around 250 a 350µm in size as spacer material. Titanium/urea powder mixture, in the ratio of 80% weight to 20% weight, respectively, are used to manufacture the porous cylindrical implants and only pure titanium powders are used to manufacture the rough cylindrical implants (Fig. 2). The final implants dimensions are 3.0 mm in diameter and 6.0 mm long [4,5,22].

**Figure 2.** Cylinders of dense and porous titanium, respectively.

### 3.3. Surgical procedures

Male New Zealand albino rabbits, aged 6-8 months-old and weighing between 3.5 and 4.0 kg, were used in the studies. The rabbits were provided by the Animal Center of the São José dos Campos School of Dentistry, maintained in individual cages and fed commercial pet food (Coelhil R, Socil) and water ad libitum. These studies were approved by the Research Ethics Committee (044-2002) of the Graduate School of Dentistry of São José dos Campos of São Paulo State University (UNESP).

The implants were cleaned, wrapped and sterilized in autoclave at 393 K (120°C) for 15 min. Prior to surgery, the rabbits were weighed and anesthetized intramuscularly with a mixture of 13 mg/kg of aqueous solution of 2% hydrochloride of 2-(2,6-xylidine)-5,6-dihydro-4H-1,3-thiazine (Rompun®, Bayer, São Paulo, Brazil), an analgesic, sedative and muscular relaxant, and 33 mg/kg of ketamine (Dopalen®, Agibrands do Brazil Ltda., São Paulo, Brazil), a general anesthetic.

The procedures were performed under standard usual sterile conditions. After trichotomy, shaving, and disinfection a straight 3 cm skin incision was made over the medial portion tibiae. a 3 cm longitudinal incision was made over the medial portion of the tibiae, in the proximal cortical bone. The periosteum was carefully detached from the cortical bone and the implantation sites were carefully prepared using an electric surgical drill (AEU707Av2, Aseptico, Washington, USA). The equidistant perforations were made bilaterally and during drilling, the hole was continuously cooled with saline. Just before insertion of the implants, the hole was irrigated with saline to remove any bone shards. The sample was placed in the perforation and pressed into the surgical cavity until it was fixed to the cortical bone. The muscle tissue and skin were sutured with mononylon 4-0 surgical thread (Johnson & Johnson, São José dos Campos, São Paulo, Brazil). Next, all of the rabbits received one dose of antibiotics, 0.35 mg/kg (Pentabiotico®, Fort Dodge Saúde Animal, São Paulo, Brazil). The rabbits were inspected daily for clinical signs of complications or adverse reactions.

The rabbits were sacrificed using an anesthetic overdose administered intramuscularly. Following euthanasia, the surgical segments with the implants were removed and the implants were tested for mobility using a clinical clamp and prepared for histology. The specimens were fixed in 10% formalin. Next, the fragments were embedded in methyl metacrylate (Sigma-Aldrich Chemistry St Louis, MO, USA). Three nondecalcified sections measuring approximately 700μm in thickness were obtained using a diamond saw in a cutting machine for hard tissues (Labcut 1010, Extec, USA). The sections polished (Labpol 8-12, Extec, USA) to a final thickness of approximately 80μm and stained with toluidine blue and histomorphometric analysis was performed using a light microscope (Axioplan 2, Carls Zeiss, Germany) combined with a Sony digital camera (DSC-S85, Cyber-shot). The interfaces were also evaluated by scanning electron microscope (SEM) to characterize the microtopography, morphology and porous interconnection.

The bone formation was evaluated by a blinded investigator, using two different images of both sides of each section of the bone-implant interface, with three sections obtained from each sample taken from each of the rabbits. Thus, numerous images were analyzed, since six fields from each sample were digitized (100x). New bone formation and bone ingrowth into the interior of the pores were calculated using Image J software (NIH, USA). All the quantitative data are expressed as the mean ± standard deviation (SD). Statistical analyses were performed on the histomorphometric results of bone ingrowth depth using a randomized block design ANOVA, with a post-hoc Tukey test ($p=0.05$), to determine the differences between sample conditions.

After each sacrifice period, the bone fragments of rabbits, containing the implant were preserved in distilled water in a freezer at 253 K (-20ºC) until the mechanical testing, which was performed at room temperature. For the push-out test, each specimen was mounted on a special platform with a central circular opening. This jig was designed to maintain the pushing load parallel to the long axis of the implant. The pushing load was applied to the end of the implant using a universal testing machine (Instron 2301) at a cross-head speed of 0.5 mm/min until the peak load was obtained.

It is necessary to determine the area to which the force was applied to determine the shear stress needed to displace the implant. Therefore, the cortical thickness of each specimen was measured at three locations for each push-out sample. The mean thickness was calculated and used to determine the contact area according to the following formula: mean area (Am) = $2\pi r$ x mean cortical thickness, where $r$ = implant radius. Next, the shear stress was calculated using the equation: $\tau = F/Am$, where $\tau$ = shear stress; and $F$ = peak load at failure. Statistical analyses was performed on the values obtain in the push-out test by a randomized block design ANOVA, with a post-hoc Tukey test ($p<0.05$), to determine the differences between sample conditions. Cylindrical implants with porous surface were compared to cylindrical implants with rough surface regarding the quantity and quality of new bone formation on the implant-bone interface after implantation in rabbit tibiae.

As results, all animals presented satisfactory postoperative results, without any evidence of inflammation or infection in the surgical site. No adverse reaction was observed during the procedure. During the clinical evaluation, the implants were not loose manually. The appearance of the surrounding tissue and healing in the implantation site were examined, and any mobility of the sample or other abnormalities were noted.

The results showed that all implants were well tolerated and osseointegration was observed in both groups with no difference of new bone quality. However, when the quantity of bone neoformation at implant-bone interface was evaluated, a larger formation of bone tissue was observed for the porous-surface implants, and this difference was statistically significant. This results point out that the cylindrical porous-surface implants yielded greater bone neoformation than the cylindrical rough-surface implants because of their larger area in contact with the bone tissue and the presence of an intercommunicating porous structure that allowed the formation of a three dimensional osseointegration network.

The micrography of the porous cylindrical implants showed different types of pores, interconnected pores and few isolated pores. The average interconnected pore diameter was about 480μm (± 210), and 37% (± 2.0) total porosity. The micrography of the rough cylindrical implants showed only isolated smaller pores, with average pore diameter of about 180μm (± 80) and 3% (± 0.8) total porosity. The rough cylindrical implants presented an average surface roughness of Ra 5.30μm.

At 4 and 8 weeks, new bone was observed at the implant–bone interface, regardless of the type of implant, leading to an osseointegration (Fig. 3), and in the porous implants new bone was also noticed into the pores. This new bone was similar in the two periods of sacrifice; it was constituted of mature bone trabeculae that presented lamellar arrangement and of different size medullar spaces. There was, especially in the rabbits sacrificed in the 4 weeks period, a distinct border between newly formed bone and preexisting bone (Fig. 4), emphasizing the biocompatibility of the material and the adequate surface to new bone proliferation.

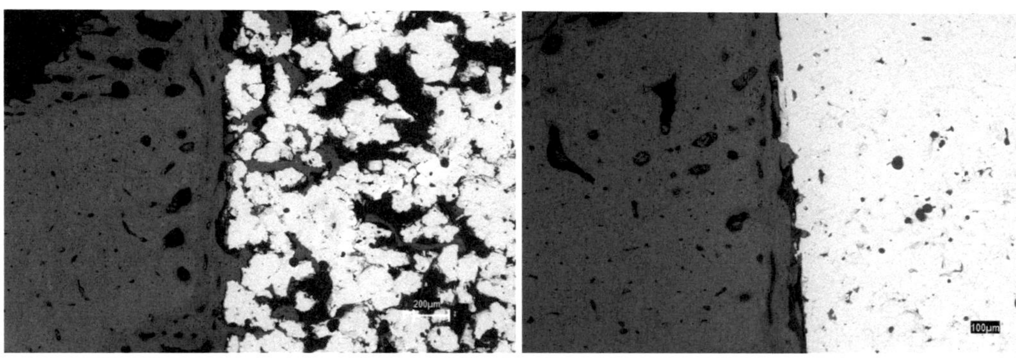


**Figure 3.** SEM micrography of (left)porous implants with bone ingrowth and (right) rough implant. Both 4 weeks after surgery, note a distinct border between new bone and preexisting bone (arrow)

Bone ingrowth was observed in all animals that received porous implants. Regardless of the sacrifice period, bone ingrowth into the pores was observed, even into more internal pores. In general, for both periods the small pores were totally filled with bone, whereas in the 4-week period bigger pores presented partial filling, and in the 8-week period bigger pores were total filling. New bone was also observed above the implants and in the inferior region of the implants and the pores of these areas also presented new bone (Fig. 4). No fibrous tissue was observed on the interface regardless of the implant type or sacrifice period.

The mean values obtained for the percentage of implant–bone contact in the porous versus the rough cylindrical implants were, respectively, 57% (0.7%) vs. 46% (0.9%) after 4 weeks, and 59% (1.3%) vs. 50% (0.8%) after 8 weeks.

Additionally, in this study, the shear strengths of porous and rough implants 4 weeks postsurgery were 14 MPa (1.1 MPa) and 4 MPa (1.8 MPa), respectively. At 8 weeks, the shear strength was greater, 20 MPa (2.3 MPa) for porous implants and 13 MPa (0.95 MPa) for rough implants. Observation also verified that, regardless of the implant type, shear strength increased as the experimental period increased. The porous implants of the rabbits euthanized at 8 weeks of bone repair exhibited the greatest shear strength values. Therefore, bone ingrowth into pores provides a more effective fixation of porous implant to bone, due to the development of resistant areas to shear strength. These resistant areas were directly related to the quantity of open pores in the surface. Thus, in order to occur the dislodging of porous implant, the fracture of bone that proliferated into pores was necessary.

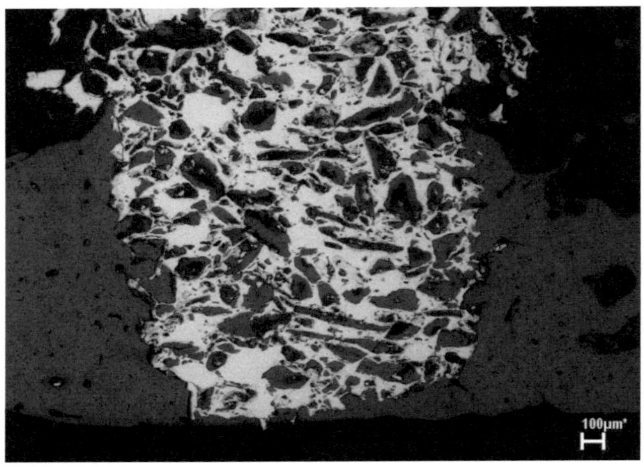


**Figure 4.** SEM micrography of porous titanium scaffold 4 week period showing new bone growth in the region above the implant and in the inferior region and pores.

The powder metallurgy technique was efficient in producing porous titanium implants and dense titanium samples for biomedical applications. This technique allows for the preparation of implants with interconnected pores resembling a three-dimensional network and the control of pore size and porosity, through the selection of appropriate spacers, providing excellent implants for bone ingrowth.

Finally, an important prospective clinical use for porous implants is the manufacture of short implants for clinical situations such as cases of limited available bone height, poor quality bone [56,57], or orthodontic loading [58]. The small segment of porous implant allowed an effective osseointegration, due to increased contact area provided by its surface configuration. The porous implants of this study were manufactured with dimensions that could be used in these dental clinical situations, since they presented small diameter and height, and exhibited threedimensional bone ingrowth and mechanical interlocking.

## 3.4. Dense implants with a porous coating

Porous structures were produced by powder metallurgy techniques. The pure titanium grade 2 powder (Micron Metals, EUA) by HDH process coatings were placed over rod substrates of Ti-6Al-7Nb (Fig. 5) with 5.8 μm medium roughness (Ra), produced by powder metallurgy. Titanium powders were mixed with different quantities of urea as a binder, in order to produce a high porosity level. Both titanium and urea powders were separated in narrow particle size range in order to control de medium pore sizes and total porosity. The powder ranges were 144 – 177μm for titanium and 500 a 590μm for urea. A size range of < 840μm for urea was also used for comparison. Coatings specified as C1, C2 and C3 were processed from titanium powders, mixed with 30%, 40% and 50% weight of urea respectively [59].

**Figure 5.** (a) Macrophotography of the Ti-6Al-7Nb substrate and a coating on substrate sample; (b) and (c) SEM surface topographic images for the coating-substrate samples C1-30% urea and C3-50% urea, respectively

Cold isostatic compaction (CIP) was performed using silicone pipe moulds top sealed with plugs. For the coatings samples, the substrates were centered in the mould and the mixtures were then tapered. Compaction pressure was 250 MPa for all samples. The compacted samples were heat-treated in a muffle for complete elimination of the binder. Then they were sintered in a high vacuum furnace ($10^{-3}$ Pa ($10^{-6}$ torr)), one hour step at 1473K (1200ºC) and free cooling in furnace.

All samples exhibits open macroporosity in the range of 100 – 800μm and closed microporosity in the range of 1 – 50 μm. The macropores were originated from the binder evaporation while the micropores can be related with the porous nature of the titanium powder and the low compaction pressure used (250 MPa) which doesn't lead to a high densification after sintering. Measured coating thickness was in the range of 750 – 955μm.

The influence of the binder parameters in the sample porosity was succeeded. Pore volume fractions ranges where coherent with the percent binder additions, for both types of samples. Foam samples exhibited less volume fraction of pores than the coatings made with the same binder additions. The coatings presented many regions linked with the substrate, indicating a qualitatively strong bond of the coating. The similarity of the pore size distribution for coatings and foams samples indicates a good reproducibility of the porous structures [59].

### 3.5. Dense core implants with an integrated porous surface

Several porous coating fabrication methods have been proposed, including sintering uniform-sized beads, fibers by isostatic press sintering, sintering loosely packed powders, the atomization process and powder metallurgy on a dense core. Materials produced by these methods present an interface between the dense core and porous coating [8,60-63]. To overcome this problem a new method to produce titanium samples was to develop, that exhibit a dense core with an integrated porous surface, reducing the problems of displacing a porous coating [6,7,64].

Titanium samples were produced with a dense core and porous surface in one step, using a purpose-designed stainless steel mold. The porous surface titanium samples were prepared using pure Ti powders developed in the General Command of Aerospace Technology (CTA), Institute of Air and Space (IAE), Division of Material (AMR), Brazil (purity ≥ 99.5%, particle size ≤ 8μm), which were formed by HDH process. An organic additive (urea) was used as a space holder. The weight ratio of Ti powder to space-holder was calculated to obtain defined porosities of 30 and 40% in the sintered compact samples. The powder Ti and space particles were mixed in a rolling container for an hour. By controlling the quantity and size of the spacer particles, we fabricated three different porous surfaces with different porosities and pore sizes: Group 1 - 30% pores with an average pore diameter of 180μm; Group 2 - 30% pores with an average diameter of 300μm, and Group 3 - 40% pores with an average diameter of 180μm.

All the samples used in this study were fabricated through cold compaction using a manually operated uniaxial press. Initially, the Ti powder was compacted into a central tube of purpose-designed stainless steel mold. Then, the mixture was inserted around the central tube and strongly compacted. Previously to uniaxial press, the central tube was removed, and the stainless steel mold was uniaxially pressed at 500 MPa. Green samples were obtained by cold isostatic pressing at 300 MPa and heat-treated on a stove to eliminate urea. The sintering process consisted of two steps and it was performed on a vacuum furnace ($10^{-4}$ Pa ($10^{-7}$ torr)). The first step included heating stage at 1473 K (1200ºC) with heating rate of 293 K (20ºC)/min. In the second step the samples were maintained at 1473 K for 1 h. After sintering, the samples presented 4 mm diameter and 6 mm long (Fig. 6).

The surface morphology and porous structures were evaluated by optical quantitative metallography and the Image Tool software. The cylindrical samples were previously divided into 5 sections, and 4 images of each section were captured, totaling 20 images of each sample, which were taken at 100X magnification. Porous surface microstructure and topography were characterized by scanning electron microscopy (SEM). Prior to implantation, porous surface titanium samples were cleaned by ultrasonic action for 30 min in a 1% (v/v) detergent/distilled water ($dH_2O$) solution, and then rinsed 3 times in $dH_2O$. Following cleaning, the samples were packaged in sterilizable pouches and sterilized in an autoclave at 394 K (121ºC) for 15 min.

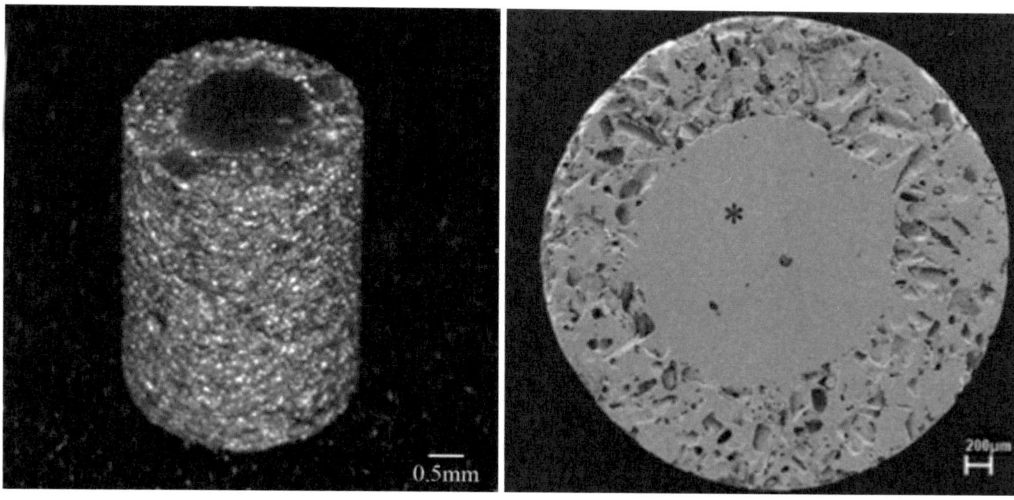


**Figure 6.** Figure 6- Visual aspect of titanium sample, and cross section, with a dense core with an integrated porous surface, fabricated by a powder metallurgy technique.

The implants were surgically inserted into thirty rabbits, that received a total of 6 porous surface titanium samples in the cortical bone beds of the proximal left and right tibia, so each tibia received 3 samples, with one of each group (G1, G2, G3). All animals were given a dose of antibiotic and were monitored until sacrifice at 8 and 12 weeks after implantation. Following euthanasia, the six rabbits surgical segments with the implants were removed and submitted to histological and histomorphometric analysis.

Osseointegration was evaluated by a blinded investigator, using 2 different images of both sides of each section of the bone-implant interface, with three sections obtained from each sample taken on each of six different rabbits. Thus, 72 pictures were analyzed, since six fields of each sample were digitized (100X), and each animal received two samples of each group (G1, G2, G3). New bone formation and bone ingrowth into the interior of the pores were calculated using Image J software (NIH). Shear mechanical tests (push out) were performed to evaluate the implant removal resistance.

All quantitative data were expressed as a mean ± standard deviation (SD). Statistical analyses were performed on compression test values, on histomorphometrical results of bone ingrowth depth and on values of the push-out test by a randomized block design ANOVA with a post hoc Tukey test (5%) to determine differences between samples conditions.

The structure of the sample observed by SEM is presented in Fig. 7, and it was not observed line fracture or any discontinuity in the transition region of the different structures of Ti (porous/dense). The porous structure exhibited different types of pores, with interconnected macro and micropores.

The bone ingrowth percentages are presented in Table 1. All of the rabbits presented satisfactory postoperative results. There were no surgical complications and all implants were firmly attached to the bone. No macroscopic or microscopic signs of infection were found, and during clinical evaluation, the implants could not be loosened manually. New bone was observed at the implant-bone interface (Fig. 8), regardless of the type of sample, leading to osseointegration, and new bone was also observed growing into the pores (Fig. 9). This new bone consisted of mature bone trabeculae that presented lamellar arrangement and different-sized medullary spaces. Regardless of the sacrifice period, bone ingrowth into the pores was observed in all implants, even deep inside the more internal pores (Fig. 9). In general, the smaller pores were totally filled with bone, whereas bigger pores were partially filled. No fibrous tissue was observed at the interface, regardless of the sample type or sacrifice period.

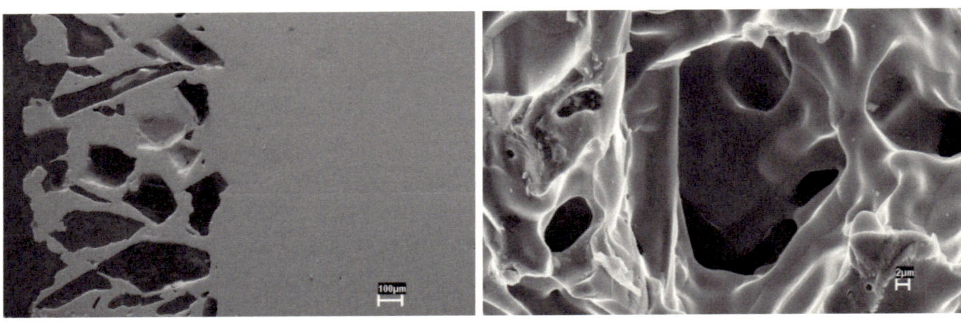


**Figure 7.** Scanning electron images of a longitudinal section showing a dense core with an integrated porous surface and interconnected pores, micropores and macropores.

| SP (weeks)[a] | Implants | | |
|---|---|---|---|
| | G1 | G2 | G3 |
| 8 | 59,460 ± 7,980 | 72,814 ± 8,936 | 72,146 ± 6,430 |
| 12 | 60,540 ± 8,310 | 73,006 ± 9,760 | 72,714 ± 7,020 |

[a] Sacrifice period

**Table 1.** Average bone ingrowth (%)

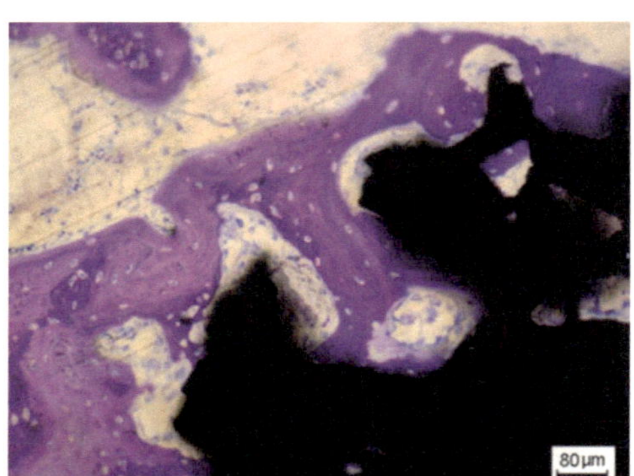


**Figure 8.** Histological optical image stained with toluidine blue: osteocytes in the lacunae, new bone proliferation, osteoid matrix, and osteoblasts.

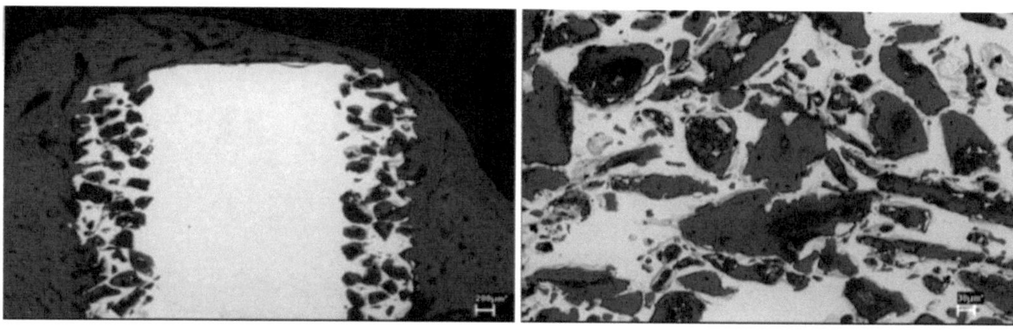

**Figure 9.** SEM micrograph of the bone-sample interface: osseointegration and new bone ingrowth into a porous surface as far as the more internal pores near to the dense core.

The values obtained for the percentage of bone ingrowth into the available space inside the implants with different pores and porosities were not significantly different at 8 and 12 weeks post-implantation. However, statistically significant differences were determined among the implant types ($p<0.01$), with group 1 (30% pores/180 μm) presenting the lowest quantities of new bone and group 2 (30% pores/300 μm) showing the greatest quantity of new bone. The mean value for bone-implant contact percentage was 72.43% (±6.89) for group 3 (40% pores/180 μm) and 72.91% (±9.62) for group 2. These values were lower in group 1, which demonstrated bone ingrowth of 60% (±8.54) into the available space inside the implants.

The shear strengths of all groups exhibited statistically significant differences when the implant type ($P<0.05$), sacrifice period ($P<0.001$) and interaction effect ($P<0.05$) were analyzed. Group 2 presented the lowest shear strength at 8 weeks (9.05 MPa), while group 3 presented the greatest shear strength at 12 weeks (16.63 MPa) (Table 2).

| SP (weeks)[a] | Implants | | |
|---|---|---|---|
| | G1 | G2 | G3 |
| 8 | 11.67 ± 1.941 | 9.05 ± 2.940 | 10.34 ± 3.270 |
| 12 | 11.18 ± 3.600 | 11.66 ± 4.020 | 16.63 ± 5.110 |

[a] Sacrifice period

**Table 2.** Average shear strength (MPa)

Not surprisingly, in this current experiment, the observations revealed the smallest amount of bone neoformation at the bone-implant interface in Group 1 samples when compared with the other groups. This phenomenon was attributed to the association of porosity percentage with pore areas, since this combination in G2 and G3 groups permitted greater vascularization and subsequent differentiation, improving bone ingrowth.

Increasing both area and complexity of the surface improves the mechanical interlocking and can increase the implant stability. This provides a mechanical interlocking, a mechanism that is not observed on flat or rough surfaces.

Mechanical shear testing verified that Group 2 samples showed the least resistance to displacement (9.05 MPa) at 8 weeks, probably because of their larger pore size, which were not entirely filled by bone at 8 weeks, and their lower porosity. In contrast, At 12 weeks, while Groups 1 and 2 showed similar resistance, Group 3 implants showed the greatest resistance to displacement (16.63 MPa), probably due to their structure with high porosity. Its high porosity provided more area for bone ingrowth at the interface, since the rupture of the bone ligaments grown into the interface pores are the main resistance source to the shear stresses generated in the push out test.

Titanium sample exhibiting a dense core with an integrated porous surface developed and characterized in this current study is unique and different of standard structures used in orthopedic or dentistry implants. The porous surfaces were fabricated using a powder metallurgy technique in one step, using a purpose-designed stainless steel mold, instead of produced by sintered beads on a dense core. This new method reduces the problems of displacement of the porous coating. Three types of porous surface titanium implants with varying pore diameters and porosities were fabricated by powder metallurgy in one step and all specimens presented an interconnected, complex porous structure and dense core. Bone ingrowth into the pores was observed in all implants, even deep inside the more internal pores.

## 3.6. Porous implants with biomimetic coating

Titanium implants can also be bioactivated by a biomimetic precipitation process which is an alternative for other coatings methods. The biomimetic process is employed both to identify the material ability to form calcium phosphate *in vitro* (biocompatibility evaluation) and to obtain calcium phosphate coatings on metallic substrates. The process advantages compared to other process are: the low temperature, which is usable to any heat sensitive material, formation of bonelike apatite crystals with high bioactivity, deposition on and into porous surfaces without changing the pore morphology, good adhesion to the substrate and the possibility of bone growth stimulating factors incorporation [65].

Chemical composition and surface topography are important parameters influencing the mechanical bond between bone and implant. The biomimetic process promotes a Calcium phosphate (CaP) film deposition by immersion of the porous titanium part in a simulated body fluid [19,65]. CaP coatings onto metallic biomaterials have gained great interest, due to the chemical interactions between the coated surface and the biological tissues. CaP coatings also enhance biocompatibility, associated to the good mechanical properties of the metallic substrate, stimulating osseointegration [66-68].

Porous titanium cylindrical samples (8mm diameter x 5mm length) were prepared using a titanium powder grade 2 with particle size range of 149 - 177μm and manufactured by HDH-hydrogenation-dehydrogenation process. Urea with 250 - 297μm was used as an organic additive for pore formation. The powders were mixed in a proportion of 70% and 30% respectively, encapsulated in silicone molds which were tapered and sealed. Thereafter, cold isostatic pressing was performed at 300 MPa. For the elimination of the organic additive, the samples were heat treated on a stove at 473 K (200°C) for 2 hours. Compacted samples were sintered in a vacuum furnace ($10^{-4}$ Pa ($10^{-7}$ Torr)) at 1473 K (1200°C) for 1 hour and later were cleaned with deionized water [45].

Samples were submitted to biomimetic treatment, beginning with alkali treatment of the samples in NaOH (10M) at 403 K (130°C) in an autoclave (Fanem (London - SP) for 1h, followed by heat treatment at 473 K (200°C) for 1 hour and immersion in a solution of modified simulated body fluid (mSBF) at 37°C. The mSBF solution used to accomplish the biomimetic process was: $[Na^-]$ = 142.0 mM; $[K^-]$ = 5.000 mM; $[Mg^{-2}]$ = 1.500 mM; $[Ca^{-2}]$ = 2.500 mM; $[Cl^-]$ = 147.8 mM; $[HCO_3^-]$ = 4.200 mM; $[HPO_4^{-2}]$ = 1.000 mM and $[SO_4^{-2}]$ = 0.050 mM; a modification proposed by Andrade et al. The pretreated samples were immersed in mSBF solution with pH 7.4 at 310 K (37 °C) for 14 days. The solution was renewed every two days. After the immersion period, the samples were cleaned with deionized water, dried in air sterilized by ionizing radiation 20KGF prior to use. No treated implants were used as controls.

The implants were surgically inserted into thirty rabbits, with three coated implants in the left tibia and three untreated/control implants in the right tibia. All animals were given penicillin and were monitored until sacrifice 15, 30 and 45 days after surgery. After euthanasia, the surgical segments with the implants were removed and submitted to histological and histomorphometric analysis. Shear mechanical tests (push out) were performed to evaluate the implant removal resistance.

Microstructural analyses were performed by Scanning Electron Microscopy (SEM), Electron Dispersive X-Ray Spectroscopy (EDS) and Raman Spectroscopy. Evaluation of the bone tissue neoformation was conducted by SEM and optical microscopy (OM), by comparison between coated and uncoated implants.

SEM analysis has shown an implant surface without treatments with small closed micropores (< 50 μm) and interconnected macropores from 100 – 500 μm (Fig. 10a, 10b). Figure 14c shows a pretreated sample, which exhibited needle-like sodium titanate ($Na_2TiO_3$) crystals (Fig. 10c). After fourteen days under biomimetic treatment, samples presented globular formations, associated with the deposition of a CaP film (Fig 10d).

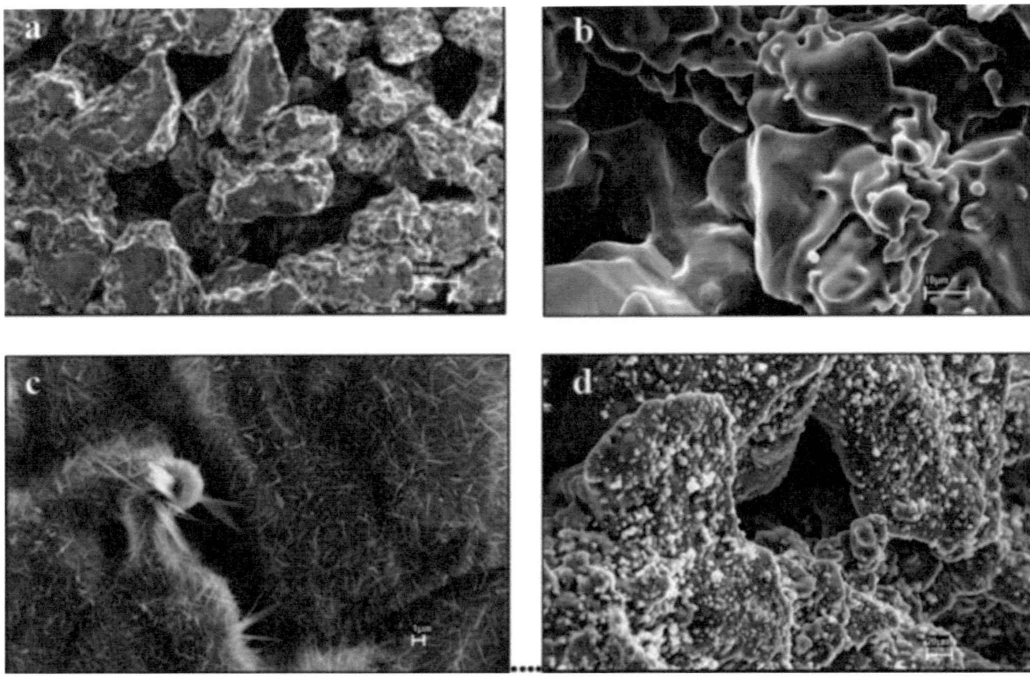


**Figure 10.** SEM images of a control implant, without treatments (a, b), after treatments (c) and with biomimetic coating (d).

EDS analysis showed high peaks of Ca and P at the surface of the implants (Fig. 11 left), while Raman spectra evidenced a 960 cm-1 peak, characteristic of hydroxyapatite (Fig. 11 right).

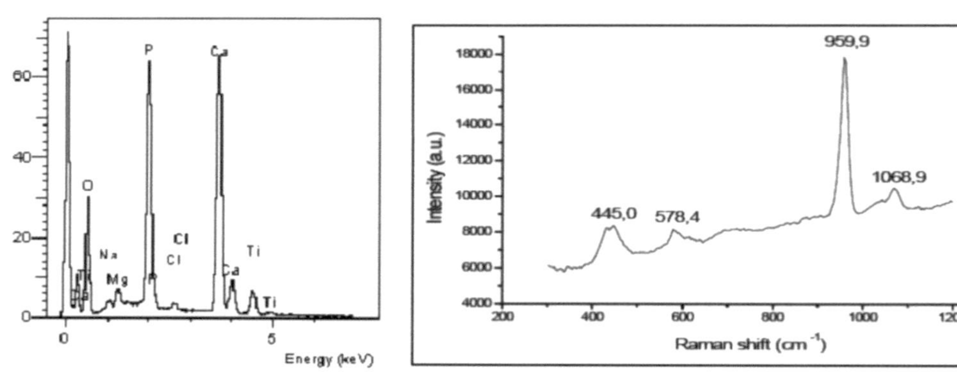


**Figure 11.** EDS (left) and Raman (right) spectra after biomimetic treatment

SEM images and optical micrographs (Fig. 12) revealed the bone tissue neoformation at the bone-implant interface which was also detected inside the pores, including internal ones. This result evidenced the osseointegration of the designed CaP-coated titanium implant.

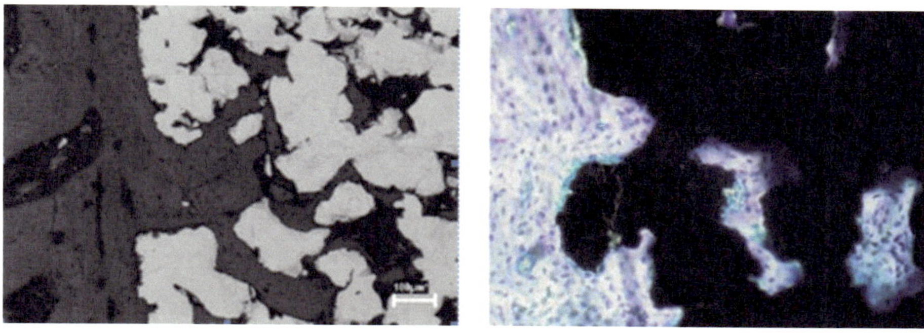

**Figure 12.** SEM image of tibiae sample evidencing the bone ingrowth into the surface pores and an optical micrograph of tibiae sample evidencing the bone-implant interface and bone ingrowth into de pores.

Table 3 lists the bone neoformation in rabbits'tibiae measured at 15, 30 and 45 days.

| Time (days) | Test group (%) | Control group (%) |
|---|---|---|
| 15 | 37.45 ±2.26 | 32.26 ±3.18 |
| 30 | 37.91±5.44 | 37.13±3.57 |
| 45 | 38.37±6.32 | 37.18±6.05 |

**Table 3.** Mean bone neoformation in rabbits'tibiae.

Displacement resistance values of the implants from bone of the test and control groups, are listed in Table 4.

| Time (days) | Test group (MPa) | Control group (MPa) |
|---|---|---|
| 15 | 7.30 ±1.63 | 6.36 ±3.48 |
| 30 | 19.24±2.89 | 12.88±2.51 |
| 45 | 19.48±3.35 | 15.65±3.32 |

**Table 4.** Shear test results: displacement resistance (MPa) of the implants from bone.

The biomimetic coating treatment induced the formation of hydroxyapatite on the porous Ti implant surfaces. The coated implants presented better osseointegration than the implants without coating, being bone neoformation enhanced in the period of 15 days after surgery.

The biomimetic process can be considered as an experimentally simple and viable alternative to obtain osseoconductive coatings of calcium phosphate onto metallic substrates, especially titanium.

### 3.7. Human osteoblast response to porous titanium with biomimetic coating

*In vitro* evaluation of osteoblast response is widely used to explain the phenomena of osseointegration to Ti. Papers describe osteoblast-like MG-63 cultures [39,40]. One of the main criticisms of these studies is the use of immortal osteosarcoma cells.

To conduct research involving human cell cultures, approval is required from the institute's Ethics Committee on Human Research and must include donor signatures on a term of free, informed consent.

During different surgical procedures on the maxillary bones that require drilling, regularization of the alveolar interradicular and/or interdental crests, the dental surgeon removes bone fragments that are discarded. Instead of disposing of these, such fragments can be prepared as described below to obtain osteoblast cell cultures.

The osteogenic cells are isolated by enzymatic digestion of tissue fragments of human alveolar type II collagenase (Gibco-Life). Cells and explants are cultured for up to 14 days in Minimum Essential Medium alpha modification ($\alpha$-MEM), supplemented as previously described (Rosa et al. 2009) at 37°C in a humid atmosphere containing 5% $CO_2$. Titanium samples biocompatibility may be analyzed with these cells.

Titanium disks were fabricated by powder metallurgy, using a 12mm diameter, 5mm thick matrix. The porosities were determined by mixing proportions of 80% Ti and 20% urea and 70% Ti and 30% urea, the organic additive used as a spacer. Each porous sample used 1 g of the mixture, which was fabricated, by powder metallurgy, as described above. Urea particle size determined a pore diameter of 300$\mu$m.

Six experimental groups were outlined: a) control, a dense Ti sample; b) a lower porosity Ti sample; c) a higher porosity Ti sample; d) a dense Ti sample + biomimetic treatment; e) a lower porosity Ti sample + biomimetic treatment; and f) a higher porosity Ti sample + biomimetic treatment.

Dense Ti sample density was determined first, following measurements of mass, diameter, height, using the density formula. The density obtained (4.40 g/cm$^3$) was similar to that classically described in the literature (4.50 g/cm$^3$). Next, the porous Ti samples were subjected to the same measurements and porosity percentage was determined, considering all the void space as pores. The lower porosity group presented 33±1.69% and the higher porosity group presented 41.4±1.93% porosity. Half of the samples were submitted to biomimetic treatment as described previously. The presence of calcium phosphate in the biomimetically treated samples was observed in the form of whitish granules or flakes on the surface of the pores. Analysis was also performed by X-ray diffraction, which detected the crystal structure of the hydroxyapatite (calcium phosphate) layer.

The results of cell adhesion, alkaline phosphatase activity, total protein content and cell growth or cell viability *in vitro* obtained in this study are shown in Figure 13.

ANOVA and Tukey tests verified that the percentage of adherent cells and alkaline phosphatase activity were similar in all the Ti samples, independent of porosity and the presence of biomimetic coating (Fig. 13). However, phosphate hydroxide deposition in samples with biomimetic treatment reduced the total protein content and viability of the cells tested. Analyzing cell behavior based on the results obtained in this study, we conclude that the biomimetic treatment impaired Ti biocompatibility. Mammalis et al [69] also found that chemical modification decreases cell attachment and proliferation. It is possible that the physical presence of calcium phosphate granules damages cells in culture. This has not occurred *in vivo*, most likely due to the fibrin network, and our group has reported good results with biomimetic coating [45].

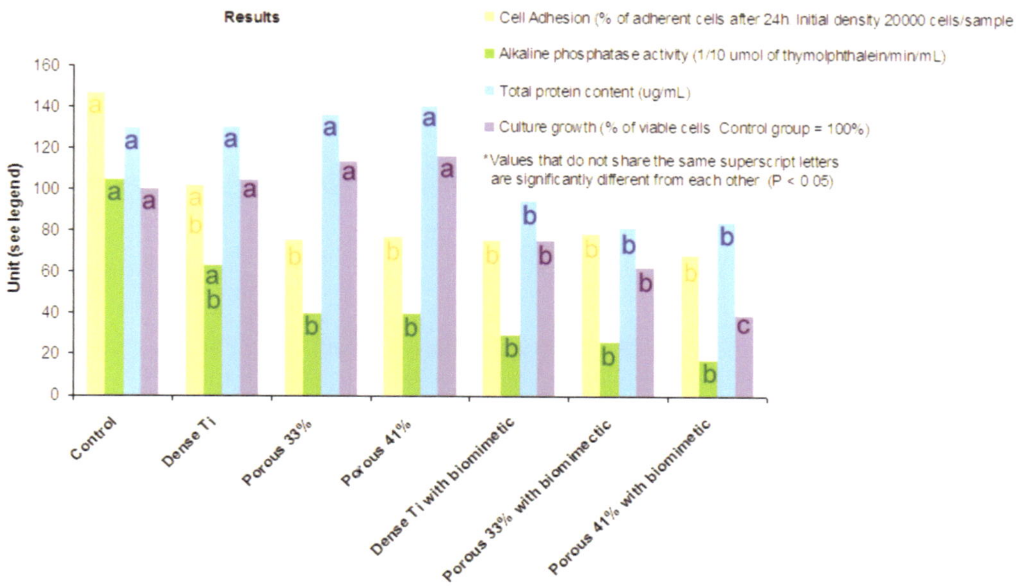


**Figure 13.** *In vitro* effects of porosity and biomimetic treatment in titanium samples

## 4. Conclusion

Titanium porous implants with interconnected porous structure were successfully prepared by powder metallurgy techniques by using grounded HDH titanium powder. Porous size and porosity can be controlled by space material characteristics prior to powder mixture. The porous structure enhances the bone formation, ingrowth and the implant displacement resistance. Dense core with integrated porous surface titanium implants were manufactured by one step compacting method seems to be a promising approach for bone tissue engineering. The implant porous region behaviors like a titanium/bone composite in order to accommodate the tensions due the mismatch of elastic modulus. Despite the conflicting results, the hydroxyapatite coating through biomimetic treatment merits further study because of the improved osseointegration obtained *in vivo*.

## Author details

Luana Marotta Reis de Vasconcellos and Yasmin Rodarte Carvalho
*Department of Bioscience and Oral Diagnosis,*
*São Jose dos Campos School of Dentistry Univ. Estadual Paulista (UNESP), Brazil*

Renata Falchete do Prado, Mário Lima de Alencastro Graça and Carlos Alberto Alves Cairo
*Department of Materials – Aeronautical and Space Institute,*
*Aerospace Science and Technology Department, Brazil*

Luis Gustavo Oliveira de Vasconcellos
*Department of Prosthodontics and Dental Materials, São Jose dos Campos,*
*School of Dentistry, Univ. Estadual Paulista (UNESP), Brazil*

## Acknowledgement

The authors would like to thank the São Paulo Research Foundation (FAPESP) for the grants required to complete this work.

## 5. References

[1] Park JB, Lakes RS (1980) Biomaterials: an introduction. New York: Plenum Press. 561p.

[2] Teixeira E.R. (2004) Superfície dos implantes: o estágio atual. In: Implantes Osseointegrados: cirurgia e prótese. Dinato JC, Polido WD. São Paulo:Artes Médicas. pp. 63-80.

[3] Bhattarai SR, Khalil KA, Dewidar M, Hwang PH, Yi HK, Kim HY. (2008) Novel production method and in-vitro cell compatibility of porous Ti-6Al-4V alloy disk for hard tissue engineering. J. biomed. mat. res. A. 86: 289-299.

[4] Vasconcellos LM, Oliveira MV, Graça ML, Vasconcellos LG, Cairo CAA, Carvalho YR. (2008(a)) Design of dental implants, influence on the osteogenesis and fixation. J. mat. sci.: mat. med. 19: 2851-2857.

[5] Vasconcellos LM, Oliveira MV, Graça MLA, Vasconcellos LGO, Cairo CAA, Carvalho YR. (2008(b)) Porous titanium scaffolds produced by powder metallurgy for biomedical applications. Mat. res. 11: 275-280.

[6] Vasconcellos LM, Leite DO, Nascimento FO, Vasconcellos LGO, Graça MLA, Carvalho YR, Cairo CAA. (2010(a)) Porous titanium for biomedical applications - An experimental study on rabbits. Med. oral patol. oral cir. bucal. 2: E407-412.

[7] Vasconcellos LM, Leite DO, Nascimento FO, Carvalho YR, Cairo CAA. (2010(b)) Evaluation of bone ingrowth into porous titanium implant: histomorphometric analysis in rabbits. Braz. oral res. 24: 399-405.

[8] Wazen RM, Lefevre L-P, Baril E, Nanci A (2010) Initial evaluation of bone ingrowth into a novel porous titanium coating. J. biomed. mat. res. B: applied biomat. 94: 64-71.

[9] Bottino MC, Coelho PG, Henriques VA, Higa OZ, Bressiani AH, Bressiani JC (2009) Processing, characterization, and in vitro/in vivo evaluations of powder metallurgy processed Ti-13Nb-13Zr alloys. J. biomed. mater. res. A. 88: 689-696.

[10] Bottino MC, Coelho PG, Yoshimoto M, König Jr B, Henriques VAR, Bressiani AHA, et al. (2008) Histomorphologic evaluation of Ti-13Nb-13Zr alloys processed via powder metallurgy. A study in rabbits. Mat. sci. engin. C. 28: 223-227.

[11] Santos DR, Pereira MS, Cairo CAA, Graça MLA, Henriques VAR (2008) Isochronal sintering of the blended Elemental Ti-35Nb alloy. Mat. sci. eng. A. 472: 193-197.

[12] Rosa AL, Crippa GE, Oliveira PT, Taba MJ, Lefebvre LP, Beloti MM. (2009) Human alveolar bone cell proliferation, expression of osteoblastic phenotype, and matrix mineralization on porous titanium produced by powder metallurgy. Clin. oral implant res. 20: 472–481.

[13] Callister WD (2007). Propriedades mecânicas dos metais. In: Callister WD, Willian D. Ciência e Engenharia de Materiais: uma introdução. Rio de Janeiro: LTC. pp. 131-168.

[14] Dewidar M., Yoon HC, Lim JK. (2006) Mechanical properties of metals for biomedical applications using powder metallurgy process. Met mat int. 12: 193-206.

[15] Laheurte P, Prima F, Eberhardt A, Goriant T, Wary M, Pattor E. (2010) Mechanical properties of low modulus beta titanium alloys designed from the electronic approach. J. mec. behav. biomed. mat. 3: 565-573.

[16] Santos DR, Henriques VAR, Cairo CAA, Pereira MS. (2005) Production of a low young modulus titanium alloy by powder metallurgy. Mat. res. 8: 439-442.

[17] Andrade MC, Sader MS, Filgueiras MR, Ogasawara T. (2000) Microstructure of ceramic coating on titanium surface as a result of hydrothermal treatment. J. mat. sci. mat. med. 11: 751-755.

[18] Kim HM, Kokubo T, Fujibayashi S, Nishiguchi S. Nakamura T. (2000) Bioactive macroporous titanium surface layer on titanium substrate. J. biomed. mat. res. 52: 553-557.

[19] Kokubo T, Miyaji F, Kim HM, Nakamura T. (1996) spontaneous formation of bonelike apatite layer on chemically treated titanium metals. J. am. ceram. soc. 79:1127-1129.

[20] Nguyen HQ, Deporter DA, Pilliar RM, Valiquette N, Yakubovich R (2004) The effect of sol-gel formed calcium phosphate coatings on bone ingrowth and osteoconductivity of porous-surfaced Ti alloy implants. Biomaterials. 25: 865-876.

[21] Nishiguchi S, Kato H, Neo M, Oka M, Kim HM, Kokubo T, Nakamura T. (2001) Alkali- and heat-treated porous titanium for orthopedic implants. J. biomed. mat res. 54: 198-208.

[22] Brentel AS, Vasconcellos LM, Oliveira MV, Graça ML, Vasconcellos LG, Cairo CA, Carvalho, YC. (2006) Histomorphometric analysis of pure titanium implants with porous surface versus rough surface. J. appl. oral sci. 14: 213-218.

[23] Faria PEP, Carvalho AL, Felipucci DNB, Wen C, Sennerby L, Salata LA. (2010) Bone formation following implantation of titanium sponge rods into humeral osteotomies in dogs: a histological and histometrical study. Clin. implant dent. rel. res. 12: 72-79.

[24] Frosch KH, Barvencik F, Lohmann CH, Viereck V, Siggelkow H, Breme J, Dresing K, Stürmer KM. (2002) Migration, matrix production and lamellar bone formation of human osteoblast-like cells in porous titanium implants. Cell tis. org. 170: 214-227.

[25] Branemark PI. (1983) Osseointegration and its experimental background. J. Prosth. Dent. 50: 399-410.

[26] Ryan G, Pandit A, Apatsidis DP. (2006) Fabrication methods of porous metals for use in orthopaedic applications. Biomaterials. 27: 2651-70.

[27] Xue W, Krishna BV, Bandyopadhyay A, Bose S. (2007) Processing and biocompatibility evaluation of laser processed porous titanium. Acta biomater. 3: 1007-1018.

[28] Karageorgiou V, Kaplan D (2005) Porosity of 3D biomaterial scaffolds and osteogenesis. Biomaterials. 26: 5474-5491.

[29] Götz HE, Müller M, Emmel A, Holzwarth U, Erben RG, Stangl R. (2004) Effect of surface finish on the osseointegration of laser-treated titanium alloy implants. Biomaterials. 25: 4057-4064.

[30] Liu YL, Schoenaers J, Groot K, Wijn JR, Schepers E. (2000) Bone healing in porous implants: a histological and histometrical comparative study on sheep. J mat. sci mat. med. 11: 711-717.

[31] Kujala S, Ryhänen J, Danilov A, Tuukkanen J. (2003) Effect of porosity on the osteointegration and bone ingrowth of a weight-bearing nickel-titanium bone graft substitute. Biomaterials. 24: 4691-4697.

[32] Takemoto M, Fujibayashi S, Neo M, Suzuki J, Kokubo T, Nakamura T. (2005) Mechanical properties and osteoconductivity of porous bioactive titanium. Biomaterials. 26: 6014-6023.

[33] Wen CE, Yamada Y, Shimojima K, Chino Y, Asahina T, Mabuchi M. (2002) Processing and mechanical properties of autogenous titanium implant materials. J. mat. sci. mat. med. 13: 397-401.

[34] Thelen S, Barthelat F, Brinson LC. (2004) Mechanics considerations for microporous titanium as an orthopedic implant material. J. biomed. mat. res. A. 69: 601-610.

[35] Oliveira PT, Nanci A. (2004) Nanotexturing of titanium-based surfaces upregulates expression of bone sialoprotein and osteopontin by curtured osteogenic cells. Biomaterials. 25: 403-413.

[36] Borsari V, Giavaresi G, Fini M, Torricelli P, Tschon M, Chiesa R, Chiusoli L, Salito A, Volpert A, Giardino R. (2005) Comparative in vitro study on a ultra-high roughess and dense titanium coating. Biomaterials. 26: 4948-4955.

[37] Mendonça G, Mendonça DB, Simões LG, Araújo AL, Leite ER, Duarte WR, et al. (2009) (b) Nanostructured alumina-coated implant surface: effect on osteoblast-related gene expression and bone-to-implant contact in vivo. Int. j. oral maxillofac. implants. 24: 205–215.

[38] Mendonça G, Mendonça DB, Simões LG, Araújo AL, Leite ER, Duarte WR, et al. (2009) (a) The effects of implant surface nanoscale features on osteoblastspecific gene expression. Biomaterials. 30: 4053–4062.

[39] Schwartz Z, Lohmann CH, Sisk M, Cochran DL, Sylvia VL, Simpson J, et al. (2001) (a) Local factor production by MG63 osteoblast-like cells in response to surface roughness and 1,25-(OH)2D3 is mediated via protein kinase C- and protein kinase A-dependent pathways. Biomaterials. 22: 731-741.

[40] Schwartz Z, Lohmann CH, Vocke AK, Sylvia VL, Cochran DL, Dean DD, et al. (2001) (b) Osteoblast response to titanium surface roughness and 1a,25-(OH)2D3 is mediated through the mitogen-activated protein kinase pathway. J. biomed. mater. res. 56: 417–426.

[41] Chen XB, Li YC, Du Plessis J, Hodgson PD, Wen C. (2009) Influence of calcium ion deposition on apatite-inducing ability of porous titanium for biomedical applications. Acta biomater. 5: 1808-1820.

[42] Roy M, Bandyopadhyay A, Bose S. (2011) Induction plasma sprayed nano hydroxyapatite coatings on titanium for orthopaedic and dental implants. Surf. coat. techn. 205: 2785-2792.

[43] Zaffe D. (2005) Some considerations on biomaterials and bone. Micron. 36: 583-592.

[44] Barrère F, van der Valk CM, Meijer G, Dalmeijer RA, de Groot K, Layrolle P. (2003) Osteointegration of biomimetic apatite coating applied onto dense and porous metal implants in femurs of goats. J. biomed. mat. res. B: Appl. Biomat. 67: 655-665.

[45] Machado ACP, Oliveira MV, Pereira RP, Carvalho YR, Cairo CAA. (2009) In vivo evaluation of porous titanium implants with biomimetic coating. Key eng. mat. 396-398: 179-182.

[46] Ohtsuki C, Kamitakahara M, Miyazaki T. (2007) Coating bone-like apatite onto organic substrates using solutions mimicking body fluid. J. tiss. eng. reg. med. 1: 33-38.

[47] Kasemo B, Lausmaa J. (1988) Biomaterial and implant surfaces: a surface science approach. Int. j. oral maxillofac. implant 3: 247-59.

[48] Rak ZS, Walter J. (2005) Porous titanium foil by tape casting technique. J. mat. proc. techn. 175: 755-758.

[49] Spoerke ED, Murray NG, Li H, Brinson LC, Dunand DC, Stupp SI. (2005) A bioactive titanium foam implant for bone repair. Acta biomater. 1: 523-33.

[50] Likibi F, Assad M, Coillard C, Chabot G, Rivard CH. (2005) Bone integration and apposition of porous and non porous metallic orthopaedic biomaterials. Ann. Chirur. 130: 235-41.

[51] Li JP, Li SH, Van Blitterswijk CA, De Groot K. (2006) Cancellous bone from porous Ti6Al4V by multiple coating technique. J. mat. sci. mat. med. 17: 179-85.

[52] Svehla M, Morberg P, Zicat B, Bruce W, Sonnabend D, Walsh WR. (2000) Morphometric and mechanical evaluation of titanium implant integration: comparison of five surface structures. J biomed. mat. res. 51: 15-22.

[53] Zinger O, Zhao G, Schwartz Z, Simpson J, Wieland M, Landolt D, Boyan B. (2005) Differential regulation of osteoblasts by substrate microstructural features. Biomaterials. 26:1837-47.

[54] Sepulveda P, Bressiani AH, Bressiani JC, Meseguer L, König BJ. (2002) In vivo evaluation of hydroxyapatite foams. J. biomed. mat res. 62: 587-92.

[55] Ueta MCC, Fracote CA, Henriques VAR, Graça MLA, Cairo CAA. Densification study of titanium powder compacts. Mat. sci. forum. 2005; 498-499:211-216.

[56] Deporter DA, Todescan R, Riley N. (2002) Porous-surfaced dental implants in the partially edentulous maxilla: assessment for subclinical mobility. Int. j period. rest. dent. 22: 184-192.

[57] Pilliar RM, Deporter DA, Watson PA, Todescan R. (1998) The endopore implant-enhanced osseointegration with a sintered porous-surfaced design. Oral health, 88: 61-64.

[58] Oyonarte R, Pilliar RM, Deporter D, Woodside DG. (2005) Peri-implant bone response to orthodontic loading: Part 1. A histomorphometric study of the effects of implant surface design. Am. j. orthod. dentofacial orthop. 128: 173-81.
[59] Oliveira MV, Pereira LC, Cairo CAA. (2005) Titanium powder processing with binder addition for biomedical applications. Mat. sci. forum, 498-499: 173-178.
[60] An YB, Lee WH. (2006) Synthesis of porous titanium implants by environmental-electro-discharge-sintering process. Mat. chem. phys. 95: 242-247.
[61] Deporter DA, Watson PA, Pilliar RM, Pharoah M, Smith DC, Chipman M, Locker D, Rydall A. (1996) A prospective clinical study in humans of an endosseous dental implant partially covered with a powder-sintered porous coating: 3- to 4-year results. Int. J. oral maxillofac. impl. 11: 87-95.
[62] Pilliar DA (1998) Overview of surface variability of metallic endosseous dental implants: textured and porous surface-structured designs. Impl. dent. 7: 305-312.
[63] Oliveira MV, Pereira LC, Cairo CAA. (2002) Porous structure characterization in titanium coating for surgical implants. Mat. res. 5: 269–273.
[64] Vasconcellos LM, Oliveira FN, Leite DO, Vasconcellos LGO, Prado RF, Ramos CJ, Graça ML, Cairo CAA, Carvalho YR. (2012) Novel production method of porous surface Ti samples for biomedical application. J. mat. sci. mat. med. 23: 357-364.
[65] Medeiros WS, Oliveira MV, Pereira LC, Cairo CAA, Calixto MA. (2006) Study of calcium phosphate deposition on porous titanium samples. Mat. Sci. Forum. 530-531: 569-574.
[66] Eisenbarth E, Velten D, Breme J. (2007) Biomimetic implant coatings. Biomol. eng. 24: 27-32.
[67] Rigo ECS, Boschi AO, Yoshimoto M, Allegrini JS, Konig JB, Carbonari MJ. (2004) Evaluation in vitro and in vivo of biomimetic hydroxyapatite coated on titanium dental implants. Mat sci eng C. 24: 647-651.
[68] Nishiguchi S, Nakamura T, Kobayashi M, Kim HM, Miyaji F, Kokubo T. (1999) The effect of heat treatment on bone-bonding ability of alkali-treated titanium. Biomaterials. 20: 491-500.
[69] Mamalis AA, Silvestros SS. (2011) Analysis of osteoblastic gene expression in the early human mesenchymal cell response to a chemically modified implant surface: an in vitro study. Clin. oral implants res. 22: 530-7.

Chapter 3

# Fatigue of Ti-6Al-4V

Shabnam Hosseini

Additional information is available at the end of the chapter

http://dx.doi.org/10.5772/45753

## 1. Introduction

Metallic biomaterials have essentially three fields of use; these are the artificial hip joints, screw, plates and nails for internal fixation of fractures, and dental implants. Any of these devices must support high mechanical load and resistance of material against breakage is essential. High mechanical properties are needed for structural efficiency of surgical and dental implants. But their volume is restricted by anatomic realities what require good yield and fatigue strengths of metal [1].

The use of titanium alloys is due to their excellent corrosion resistance. Also, that is because of their tensile strength, a high strength to weight ratio and low elastic modulus. Titanium continues to be widely used in biomedical applications. Ti-6Al-4V alloy is the most frequently used these days [2].

Fatigue fracture and wear have been identified as some of the major problems associated with implant loosening, stress-shielding and ultimate implant failure. Although wear is commonly reported in orthopedic applications such as knee and hip joint prostheses, it is also a serious and often fatal experience in mechanical heart valves. Fig.1 illustrates some examples of fatigue fracture of implant devices in the hip prosthesis and a mechanical heart valve. It can be seen that fatigue-wear interaction plays a significant role in ultimate failure of these medical devices [3]. In orthopedic implants design, it is unavoidable the presence of geometrical fillets such as notches which cause stress locally. It's necessary to pay attention these notches, because they affect on fatigue resistance [4]. In addition about fatigue ratio, fatigue notch factor, notch sensitivity and effect of ultimate strength and notch size on the fatigue strength of Ti-6Al-4V will be discussed.

### 1.1. Orthopedic metal alloys

The main goal of design and fabrication of an orthopedic biomaterial is to restore the function and mobility of the native tissue that is considered to be replaced. In order to select an ideal biomaterial for orthopedic and dental applications specific property requirements must be fulfilled. The ideal materials for hard tissue replacement should be biocompatible and bioadhesive, possess adequate mechanical properties to tolerate the applied physiological load, be corrosion/wear resistant and finally show good bioactivity to ensure sufficient bonding at the material/bone interface. The materials used in orthopedic surgery can be divided into five major classes of metals, polymers, ceramics, composites, and natural materials [5].

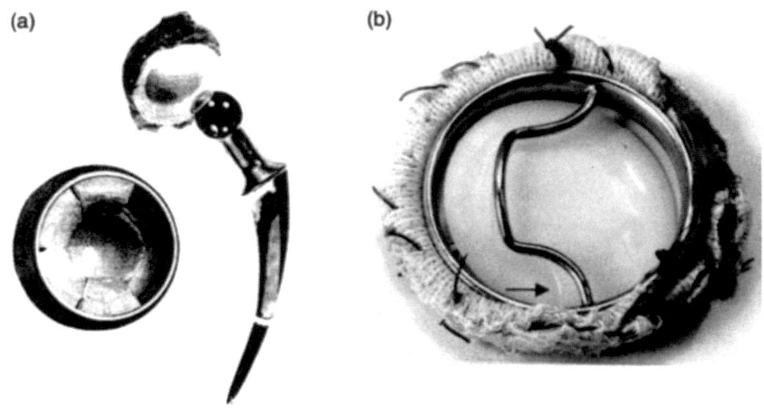


**Figure 1.** Some examples of fatigue failure of medical devices: (a) hip prosthesis; (b) explanted Bjo¨rk–Shiley polyacetal disc mechanical heart valve(arrow indicates fatigue-wear mark)[1].

Compared to other biomaterials like ceramics and polymers, the metallic biomaterials offer a wider range of mechanical properties such as high strength, ductility, fracture toughness, hardness, formability, as well as corrosion resistance, and biocompatibility. These are the required properties for most load-bearing applications in fracture fixation and bone replacement (total joint arthroplasty) [5].

Standard metallic orthopedic materials include stainless steels, cobalt-base alloys, and titanium base alloys (table 1), with an increasing number of devices being made of titanium and titanium alloys. The latter alloys are generally preferred to stainless steel and Co-alloys because of their lower modulus, superior biocompatibility and corrosion resistance [6].

## 1.2. Titanium and its alloy as orthopedic biomaterials

The need to find more reliable materials to replace broken or deteriorating parts of the human body is increasing with the increase in number of both younger and older recipients. Modern surgery and dentistry need metals and alloys of extreme chemical inertness and adequate mechanical strength. Metals and alloys in use include stainless steel, Co-Ni-Cr alloy, cast and wrought Co-Cr-Mo alloy, commercially pure titanium, Ti-6Al-4V alloy and other titanium alloys [7]. Recently, new titanium alloy compositions, specifically tailored for biomedical applications, have been developed. These first generation orthopedic alloys included Ti-6Al-7Nb and Ti-5Al-2.5Fe. Two alloys with properties similar to Ti-6Al-4V that were developed in response to concerns relating V to potential cytotoxicity and adverse reaction with body tissues. Further, biocompatibility enhancement and lower modulus has been achieved through the introduction of second generation titanium orthopedic alloys including Ti-12Mo-6Zr-2Fe (TMFZ), Ti-15MO-5Zr-3Al, Ti-15Mo-3Nb-3O, Ti-15Zr-4Nb-2Ta-0.2Pd and Ti-15Sn-4Nb-2Ta-0.2Pd alloys, as well as the completely biocompatible Ti-13Nb-13Zr alloy [6]. Commercially pure titanium is a material of choice as an implant because of its biocompatibility resulting in no allergic reaction with the surrounding tissue and also no thrombotic reaction with the blood of human body. The average yield strength of commercially pure titanium is approximately 480 MPa. If a higher strength of the implant is necessary, for example, in hip prosthesis, titanium alloys have to be used. The most widely used alloy, Ti-6Al-4V, reaches yield strength almost double the yield strength of commercially pure titanium [7].

| | Stainless steels | Cobalt-base alloys | Ti & Ti-base alloys |
|---|---|---|---|
| Designation | ASTM F-138<br>(316 LDVM) | ASTM F-75<br>ASTM F-799<br>ASTM F-1537<br>(Cast and wrought) | ASTM F-67(ISO 5832/II)<br>ASTM F-136(ISO 5832/II)<br>ASTM F-1295<br>(Cast and wrought) |
| Principal alloying Elements (wt%) | Fe(bal.)<br>Cr(17-20)<br>Ni(12-14)<br>Mo(2-4) | Co(bal.)<br>Cr(19-30)<br>Mo(0-10)<br>Ni(0-37) | Ti(bal.)<br>Al(6)<br>V(4)<br>Nb(7) |
| Advantages | Cost, availability processing | Wear resistance<br>Corrosion resistance<br>Fatigue strength | Biocompatibility<br>Corrosion<br>Minimum modulus<br>Fatigue strength |
| Disadvantages | Long term behavior<br>High modulus | High modulus<br>Biocompatibility | Power wear resistance<br>Low shear strength |
| Primary utilizations | Temporary devices (fracture plates, screws, hip nails)<br>Used for THRs stems<br>In UK (high Nitrogen) | Dentistry castings<br>Prostheses stems<br>Load-bearing components<br>In TJR(wrought alloys) | Used in THRs with modular (CoCrMo or ceramic) femoral heads long-term, permanent devices (nails, pacemakers) |

**Table 1.** Some characteristics of orthopedic metallic implant materials [6]

Titanium is a transition metal with an incomplete shell in its electronic structure enables it to form solid solution with most substitutional elements having a size factor within ±20%. In its elemental form titanium has a high melting point (1678°C), exhibiting a hexagonal close packed crystal structure (hcp) $\alpha$ up to the beta (882.5°C), transforming to a body centered cubic structure(bcc) $\beta$ above this temperature.

Titanium alloys may be classified as either $\alpha$, near-$\alpha$, $\alpha+\beta$, metastable $\beta$ or stable $\beta$ depending upon their room temperature microstructure. IN this regard alloying elements for titanium fall into three categories: $\alpha$-stabilizers, such as Al, O, N, C, $\beta$-stabilizer such as Mo, V, Nb, Ta, Fe, W, Cr, Si, Ni, Co, Mn, H and neutral, such as Zr. A and near-$\alpha$ titanium alloys exhibit superior corrosion resistance with their utility as biomedical materials being principally limited by their low ambient temperature strength. In contrast, $\alpha+\beta$ alloys exhibit higher strength due to the presence of both $\alpha$ and $\beta$ phases. Their properties depend upon composition, the relative proportions of the $\alpha/\beta$ phases, and the alloy's prior thermal treatment and thermo-mechanical processing conditions. $\beta$ alloys(metastable or stable) are titanium alloys with high strength, good formability and high hardenability. $\beta$ alloys also offer the unique possibility of combined low elastic modulus and superior corrosion resistance[8].

Ti alloys were first used in orthopedics in the mid-1940s and have continued to gain attention because of their unique properties, including high specific strength, light weight, excellent corrosion resistance and biocompatibility. Due to the aforementioned properties, this class of materials exhibits tremendous clinical advantages in terms of reduced recovery time and rehabilitation, and improved comfort for patients. However, for bone replacement components, the strength of pure Ti is not sufficient and Ti alloys are preferred due to their superior mechanical properties. In general, alloying elements would lead to an improvement in the properties of Ti for orthopedic applications. Ti-6Al-4V ELI and NiTi shape memory alloys (SMA) are the most commonly used Ti alloys in orthopedic applications because of their good combination of mechanical properties and corrosion resistance. However, the possible release of toxic ions from aluminum (Al), vanadium (V) and nickel (Ni) during in vivo corrosion of the implant remains the matter of concern. Al for exceeding content of 7% at low temperature would lead to possible embrittlement and it may also cause severe neurological, *e.g.* Alzheimer's disease and metabolic bone diseases, *e.g.* osteomalacia. Similarly, V can alter the kinetics of the enzyme activity associated with the cells and results in potential cytotoxic effects and adverse tissue reactions. Moreover, the oxide layer of $Al_2O_3$ and $VO_2$ are less thermodynamically stable than that of $TiO_2$, as their harmful debris may take place in living organism. Evident cytotoxic and allergic responses of Ni have also been reported. Thus, it is necessary to develop new Ti alloys that contain non-toxic elements [5]. New titanium alloys are being introduced to change the chemical composition and the mechanical properties. Some titanium alloys that are in use today or are being considered for use as implant materials are listed in table 1 along with their mechanical properties. The properties in table 2 result from specific heat treatments and will vary depending on their processing parameters. Information in this table permits a comparison of mechanical properties of pure titanium, some alpha/beta titanium alloys and some beta titanium alloys [7].

| Type, Alloy, Nominal wt.% | E GPa | UTS MPa | YS(0.2%) MPa | % E1 | %Red Area |
|---|---|---|---|---|---|
| Alpha Ti | 105 | 240-617 | 165-520 | 12-27 | |
| Alpha/Beta | | | | | |
| Ti-6a1-4V | 88-116 | 990-1184 | 789-1013 | 2-30 | 2-41 |
| Ti-5A1-2.5Fe | 110 | 943-1050 | 818-892 | 13-16 | 33-42 |
| Ti-6A1-7Nb | 108 | 900-1100 | 910-970 | 11-14 | |
| Beta | | | | | |
| Ti-13Nb-13Zr | 79 | 550-1035 | 345-932 | 8-15 | 15-30 |
| Ti-11.5Mo-6zr-2Fe | 74-85 | 1060-1100 | 910-970 | 18-22 | 46-73 |
| Ti-15Mo-5Zr-3Al | 15-113 | 882-1312 | 870-1284 | 11-20 | 43-83 |
| Ti-15Mo-3Nb | 79 | 1035 | 993 | 15 | 60 |

**Table 2.** Mechanical properties of selected titanium alloys [7]

The biocompatibility performance of a metallic alloy is closely associated with its corrosion resistance and the biocompatibility of its corrosion products. Corrosion data show excellent resistance for titanium and its alloys though some precautions should be taken in order to optimize their composition [9].

Alloy design and thermo-mechanical processing control of titanium alloys has allowed the production of implant materials with enhanced properties. Titanium and its alloys areused in orthopedic surgery as implants in the shape of wires, nails, plates and screws for fixation and stabilization of fracture or in the form of artificial joints for the replacement of joints of the human body. Some implants are used for short time duration in the human body whereas others remain in place providing a continuous and trouble free function for decades. To avoid a reoperation caused by the implant material, the material must meet certain chemical and mechanical requirements. As previously mentioned, chemical requirement include high biocompatibility without altering the environment of the surrounding tissue even under deformation and sterilization. Mechanical property requirement relate to specific strength, modulus, fatigue, creep and fracture toughness which, in turn, relate to microstructures. The direct relation of the microstructure to properties and performance makes it necessary that the microstructural condition be part of the specification for a finished device [7].

In general, most of the Ti alloys offer appropriate mechanical properties for orthopedic applications. The modulus of Ti alloys is closer to those of bone and theoretically provides less stress shielding than those of stainless steel and Co-Cr alloys. Figure 2 present elastic moduli of some important materials used in bone tissue engineering. The Young's moduli of 316L stainless steel and Co–Cr–Mo alloy are much greater than that of cortical bone. The Young's moduli of biomaterials have been said to be desirable to be equal to that of cortical bone because if the Young's moduli of biomaterials are much greater than that of cortical bone, bone resorption occurs. The Young's modulus of $\alpha + \beta$ type titanium alloy, Ti–6Al–4V that is the most widely used titanium alloy for biomedical applications, is much lower than those of stainless steel and Co based alloy. However, its Young's modulus is still much greater than that of cortical bone [10].

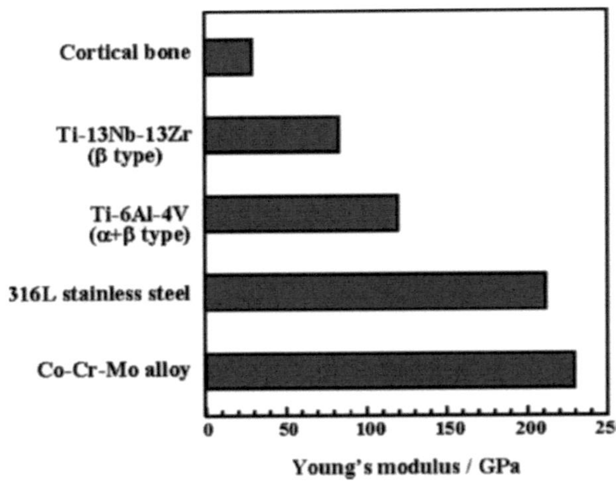


**Figure 2.** Comparison of Young's modulus of cortical bone, $\beta$ type Ti–13Nb–13Zr, $\alpha + \beta$ type Ti–6Al–4V, 316L stainless steel and Co–Cr–Mo alloy for biomedical applications [10]

## 2. Fatigue of biomaterials

Safety is of concern for any biomaterial and its mechanical aspect, breakdown of a metallic implant, is a major complication. High mechanical properties are needed for structural efficiency of surgical and dental implants. But their volume is restricted by anatomic realities what require good yield and fatigue strengths of the metal. The yield strength fixes the forces above which a bone screw and a bone plate lose their shape and will no more fulfill a given function. The fatigue strength, less than yield in size, fixes the admissible load for any implant. On the other hand, an implant bridges the forces in bone, i.e. it may reduce the normal physiological level of forces, and effect an unwanted stress shielding. This would give advantage to a less-rigid bone plate, hip prosthesis or dental implant. Frequently this suggestion is associated with a low elastic modulus, near to that of bone. The conjecture is misplaced and convincing clinical evidence for it lacks. Flexible structure cannot guide and transport forces. But Young's modulus is connected to the ratio yield strength/Young's modulus, or fatigue limit/Young's modulus. The engineer calls this ratio the admissible strain; it is a design criterion. It equal 0.67% for human cortical bone and only titanium alloys can match this figure. Another concern of the engineer is damage tolerance [2].

Cyclic loading is applied to orthopedic implants during body motion, resulting in alternating plastic deformation of microscopically small zone of stress concentration produced by notches or microstructural inhomogeneteies. The interdependency between factors such as implant shape, material, processing and type of cyclic loading, makes the determination of the fatigue resistance of a component an intricate, but critical, task. Since testing an actual implant under simulated implantation and load conditions is a difficult and expensive process, standardized fatigue tests have been selected for initial screening of orthopedic material candidates, joint simulator trials being generally reserved for a later stage in the implant development process. Standard fatigue tests include tension/compression, bending, torsion, and rotating bending fatigue (RBF) testing, the latter, a relatively simple test, being widely used to evaluate orthopedic metallic materials. Unfortunately, no standard for fatigue evaluation of biomaterials testing has yet been established, a variety of testing conditions being encountered in reported fatigue studies of orthopedic materials [6].

One of the main reasons for concern about fatigue of biomaterials arises from the adverse host-tissue response to wear debris generated by the fatigue process. This appears to be a natural defence mechanism of the body. The wear debris often invokes an inflammatory and immunological response. This in turn causes blood clotting processes, leukocytes, macrophages and, for severe cases, giant cells to move in on the foreign wear particles resulting in interfacial problems between the implant and the host tissue. Numerous biochemical activities occur at this stage. These include a change in the local environment to a highly acidic one (pH less than 3) [1].

Metal fatigue has been extensively studied [1,2,11]. The fatigue strengths of common metallic implant alloys used in hip replacements such as stainless steel, cobalt chrome and titanium, and their relationship to their microstructures, surface and corrosion properties have been reported [1].

Fig. 3 shows the fatigue strength (in air) of some common implant alloys using the S/N approach. It is of interest to note the importance of post processing treatment such as forging, which introduces compressive surface stresses. It can be seen that forged 316L stainless steel and forged cobalt–chromium have significant fatigue strengths over the cast components. The use of hot isostatic pressing (HIP) which introduces fine microstructures also has a pronounced improvement. The strength of the leg and arm bones is in the range of 100–200 MPa, the skull is about 97 MPa and that of the vertebral bodies is 1–10

MPa. It can be seen that the majority of these alloys (especially the HIP cobalt–chromium and titanium alloys) have fatigue strengths in excess of 500 MPa (in air) and hence have been deemed to be good for orthopedic implant applications such as those for the leg and arms [1].

The S/N approach has been used in a simulated body fluid environment with electrochemical and fretting devices incorporated. The combined mechanical and chemical processes play a vital role in crack initiation. The inability to repassivate quickly causes the electrochemical breakdown of the surface layers. Fig. 4 shows schematically how the formation of slip planes can break through the protective oxide film during fatigue [1].

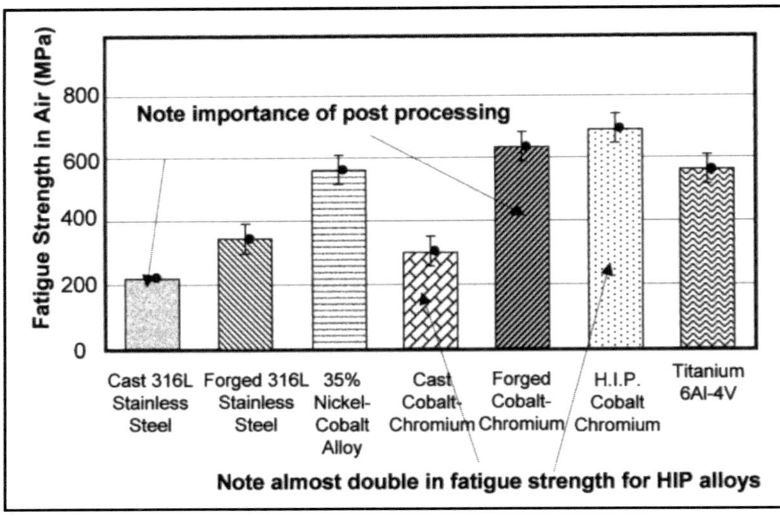


**Figure 3.** Fatigue strength of some common implant alloys [1]

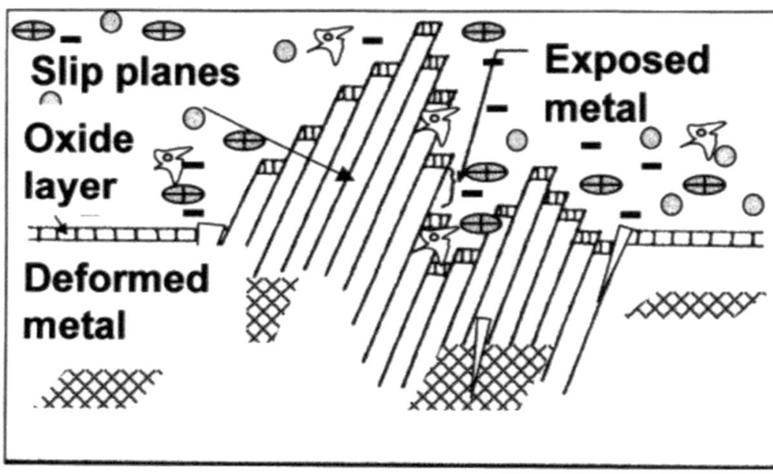


**Figure 4.** Schematic illustration of the formation of fresh slip planes in a body fluid environment during fatigue, exposing unprotected regions to electrochemical and biological activities [1].

Fretting fatigue of implant alloys based on the S/N approach has been studied [12]. In titanium implants, wear debris has given rise to blackening of surrounding tissue. Wear particles also cause implant loosening giving rise to severe 3 body wear. Fretting fatigue is essentially a micromotion phenomenon and often occurs at interfaces such as between the metal and the cement in the case of a hip prosthesis. This can result in a drastic reduction in fatigue strength. The fretting fatigue experiment in simulated body fluid is illustrated in Fig.5 for Ti-6Al-4V. The plain fatigue performance in air at 20 Hz and in pseudo-body fluid (PBS) at 2 Hz seems to be same. This is understood to be due to the ability of the titanium alloy to undergo rapid passivation. However, when fretting is carried out (artificially removing the oxide layer faster than repassivation can occur), a drastic drop of more than 150 MPa in the fatigue endurance stress limit is noted [12].

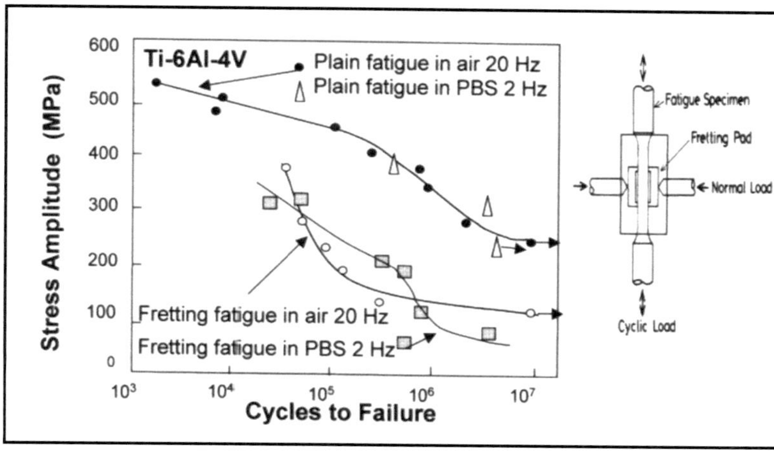


**Figure 5.** Fretting fatigue in PBS environment of Ti-6Al-4V [12]

## 2.1. Fatigue behavior of Ti-6Al-4V

Ti-6Al-4V is generally considered as a standard material when evaluating the fatigue resistance of new orthopedic titanium alloys. The mechanical response of Ti-6Al-4V alloy is, however, extremely sensitive to prior thermo-mechanical processing history, e.g., prior β grain size, the ratio of primary α to transformed β, the α grain size and the α/β morphologies, all impacting performance, particularly high-cycle fatigue lifetime (HCF). For example, maximum fracture toughness and fatigue crack growth resistance is achieved with Widmanstätten microstructures resulting from a β recrystallization anneal. However, this microstructure results in inferior HCF performance, the development of a bi-modal primary α plus transformed β microstructure being preferred to prevent fatigue crack initiation. Indeed, the transition to fine equiaxed, fine lamellar, coarse equiaxed, and coarse lamellar leads to progressive reductions in lifetime [6].

Further enhancement of the HCF resistance of Ti-6Al-4V may be achieved, under careful control, by shot peening. Shot peening is a cold working process in which the surface is bombarded with small, typically spherical media plastically deforming the surface. The resulting compressive residual stresses may provide increased part life when surface related failure mechanisms, such as fatigue or corrosion, are involved. While shot peening may increase the fatigue limit, a balance between the high compressive surface residual stresses and the increased surface roughness produced during shot peening is required for optimal fatigue performance. Shot peening prior to grit blasting can increase by 10% the fatigue strength of Ti-6Al-4V over grit blasting alone [13].

Table 3 illustrates the effect of surface finishing techniques on the fatigue strength of α and α/β titanium alloys [6].

| Titanium alloy | Test conditions | Fatigue limit(MPa) | $K_f$ |
|---|---|---|---|
| cpTi | Mechanically polished | 234 | - |
| | Electrolytically polished | 200 | 0.9 |
| Ti-6A1-4V | Gentle surface grinding | 427 | - |
| | Gentle chemical machining | 90 | 0.8 |
| | Abusive chemical machining | 352 | 0.8 |
| | Abusive surface grinding | 310 | 0.2 |
| | Polished (320-600 alumina grit) | 596 | - |
| | Belted and glass bead blasted | 610 | 1.0 |
| | Belted,beaded,shot-peened, and grit | 505 | 0.9 |
| | blasted | 555 | 0.8 |
| | Belted, beaded, and grit blasted | | |
| Ti-5A1-2.5Sn | Ultrasonic machined | 676 | - |
| | Shot peened | 531 | 0.8 |
| | Ground | 359 | 0.5 |
| | Electrical-discharge machined | 145 | 0.2 |

**Table 3.** Effect of surface preparation on the fatigue of $\alpha$ and $\alpha/\beta$ titanium alloys [6]

### *2.1.1. High cycle Fatigue of Ti-6Al-4V*

Because of cyclic loading while moving body, the most important reason for implants alloys is fracture of fatigue. The division of fatigue into low cycle and high cycle regions has been used for decades. Originally, the low cycle region was considered to be related to plastic strain fatigue and the high cycle region to elastic strain fatigue. As the fatigue process is always conditioned by cyclic plastic deformation, this division lost its basis, but nevertheless remained as a useful convention [14]. Orthopedic implants are often applied in HCF condition but when the stress rate is high they are used in LCF condition. A high percentage of failures now involved HCF. Most of the HCF data collected thus far for titanium alloys has been performed at low stress ratio and low frequencies. The reason why most testing has been done at low stress ratios and low frequency can be traced to lack of equipment necessary to achieve high loads at high frequencies [15].

The fatigue properties of Ti-6Al-4V alloy are so notable. Titanium and its alloys have the similar properties of fatigue with steel alloys [16]. The alpha phase tends to control the mechanical properties of this alloy when used at low temperature. In addition to alpha grain size, the fatigue life of Ti-6Al-4V components is influenced by the amount of age hardening, oxygen content, and grain morphology [17]. High cycle fatigue tests performed on Ti-6Al-4V showed that by decreasing alpha grain size, fatigue properties of both smooth and notched ($K_t$=1.8) specimens, can be improved [18].

The fatigue limit of Ti-6Al-4V substantially improved by increasing the UTS values, for the specimens with the same composition can be increased by reducing their grain size [4]. In a different research performed by Lucas and Konieczny [16] on the effect of UTS on fatigue behavior of steel alloys, was shown that the fatigue limit can be changed by varying UTS of these alloys. Fatigue strength to tensile strength ratio in steel alloys is 0.5. In the presence of notch, this ratio will be decreased. It can be said, the reasons for increasing tensile strength can be increase fatigue strength. This increasing and effect of ultimate strength on fatigue ratio ($\sigma_e/\sigma_u$) is shown in figure 6. So that it seems, the factors cause an increase in ultimate strength. Due to limited number of slip system in HCF of Ti alloys, i.e. (1000)<1120> the chance of slip and moving mobile dislocations in favorite planes has been substantially reduced, so that probability of formation of intrusions and extrusions which are the prime cause of crack nucleation has been decreased. So, this means the fatigue crack nucleation process which apparently determines the maximum fatigue life for ductile materials is delayed [4].

Using the fatigue limits in both HCF and LCF, reduction percents of fatigue strength were obtained. *Fatigue reduction percent* is defined as:

$$\text{Fatigue reduction percent} = \frac{\sigma_e(smooth) - \sigma_e(notched)}{\sigma_e(smooth)} \times 100 \tag{1}$$

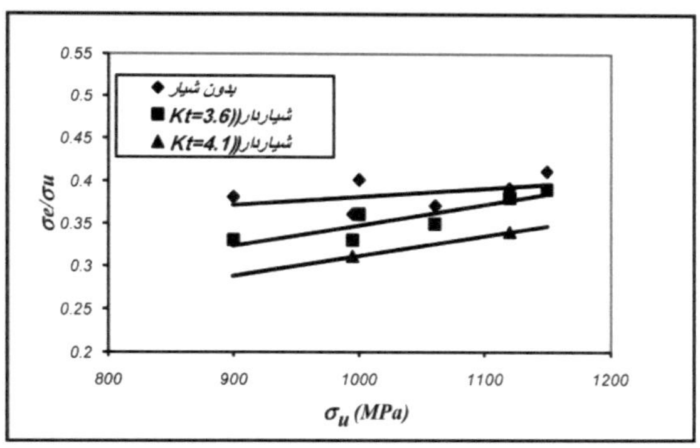


**Figure 6.** Effect of tensile strength on fatigue ratio in Ti-6Al-4V [4]

Fig. 7 shows fatigue reduction percent for LCF and HCF for various tensile strength, but for constant stress concentration factor ($K_t$=3.6). According to this figure, the fatigue reduction percent decrease with increasing tensile strength.

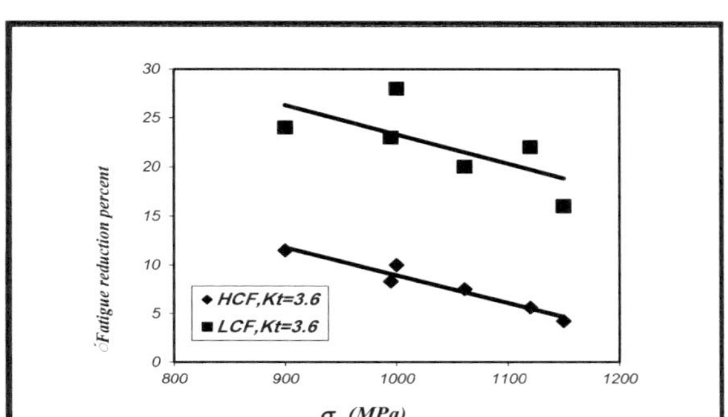


**Figure 7.** Effect of tensile strength on fatigue reduction in Ti-6Al-4V [4]

### *2.1.2. Fatigue notch factor and notch sensitivity*

In orthopedic implants design, it is unavoidable the presence of geometrical fillets such as notches which cause stress locally. It's necessary to pay attention these notches, because they affect on fatigue resistance [6]. Because of rarely non-smooth surface in implants, the notch sensitivity of this material is important [7]. Geometric discontinuities that are unavoidable in design, such as holes, fillets, grooves and keyways cause the stress to be locally elevated and so are called *stress raisers*. Stress raisers, generically termed *notches* for brevity, require special attention as their presence reduces the resistance of a component to fatigue failure. This is simply a consequence of the locally higher stresses causing fatigue cracks to start at such locations [19]. As it mentioned before, geometrical fillets such as notch or porosity in a material will caused the nonmonotone (local) stress distribution around the fillets. Stress distribution around notch is more than its mean. Therefore, each fillet is called *stress concentration* area or *stress raiser* [20]. Stress concentration factor not only depends upon the geometry of the notch but also the mode of loading. This factor is defined by maximum local stress ($\sigma_{max}$) to nominal stress ($\sigma_{nom}$) ratio [20]:

$$k_t = \frac{\sigma_{\max}}{\sigma_{nom}} \tag{2}$$

The commonly used equation for obtaining $K_t$ :

$$K_t = 1 + 2\frac{b}{a} \tag{3}$$

a and b as were shown are in figure 8 Notch radius( ϱ) equals to [21]:

$$\rho = \frac{a^2}{b} \tag{4}$$

So the above equation can be written as the following way:

$$K_t = 1 + 2\sqrt{b/\rho} \tag{5}$$

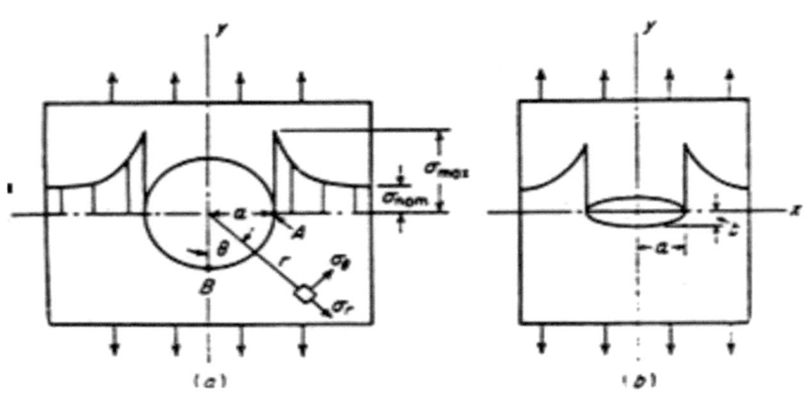

**Figure 8.** Schematic of distribution around a crack perpendicular to applied stress [20]

The actual reduction factor at long fatigue lives, specifically at $N_f = 10^6$ to $10^7$ cycles or greater, is called the *fatigue notch factor* and is denoted $K_f$ [19].

$$K_f = \frac{unnotched\ fatigue\ limit}{notched\ fatigue\ limit} \tag{6}$$

When $K_f = 1$, there is no degradation in the component due to the notch. If the notch has a large radius (ϱ) at its tip, $K_f$ may be essentially equal to $K_t$ and the notch produces the full theoretical reduction in the fatigue limit. However, for small ϱ, the above noted discrepancy may be quite large, so that $K_f$ is considerably smaller than $K_t$. Some values of $K_f$ illustrating this variation with ϱ for notched bars of mild steel are shown in Fig.9. Due to the complexity involved, empirical estimates are generally used to obtain $K_f$ values for use in design [19].

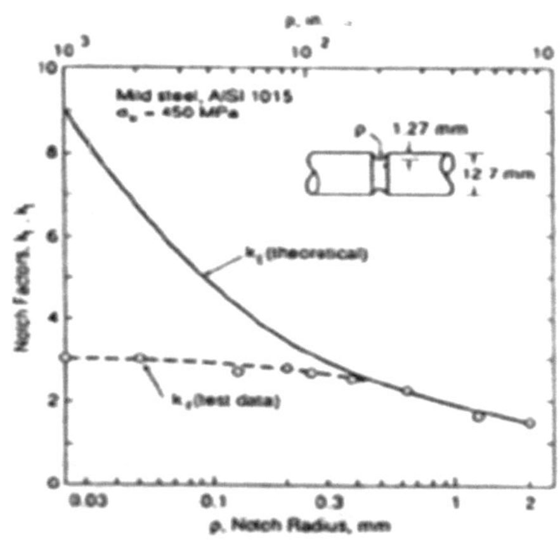


**Figure 9.** Fatigue notch factors for various notch radii based on fatigue limits from rotating bending of mild steel [19]

Figure 10 shows the effect of tensile strength on fatigue notch factor in HCF ($K_f$) and LCF ($K'_f$). This figure illustrates that the presence of notch, doesn't affect noticeably the changes in fatigue notch factor, which is a measure of sensitivity of a material to the presence of a notch. That is to say, since the slopes of $K_f$ and $K'_f$ lines in fig.10 did not change and two lines which represent fatigue notch factors for HCF and LCF are nearly parallel, it seems, the presence of notch has not affected the fatigue behavior of the alloy subjected to various fatigue condition and this material has a very low sensitivity to notch.

Therefore, one may say that the small rate of fatigue notch factor reduction due to increase of tensile strength, is a good indication of non sensitivity of this material to notch. This means that Ti-6Al-4V is an ideal alloy for complex shape device which can be used as body components [4].

The mechanism of crack nucleation in deformable materials is said [20] to be usually the formation of intrusion and extrusion in HCF process. However, in LCF process this is not the case. Crack nucleates in the LCF by bulk plastic deformations [22]. So, due to the presence of this huge plastic area, the plastic deformation due to notch is not practically effective. Therefore, sensitivity of the material subjected to LCF is nearly independent of the presence of notch. On the other hand, the rate of changes of $K_f$ with tensile strength in HCF is similar to that of LCF. This indicates that, the fatigue crack growth of this alloy under the condition of HCF is similar to that of LCF. Hence it is non-sensitive to notch under HCF conditions. Thus, this alloy can be used under HCF conditions with acceptable amount of safety, even if the surface conditions of component is not to be smooth [4].

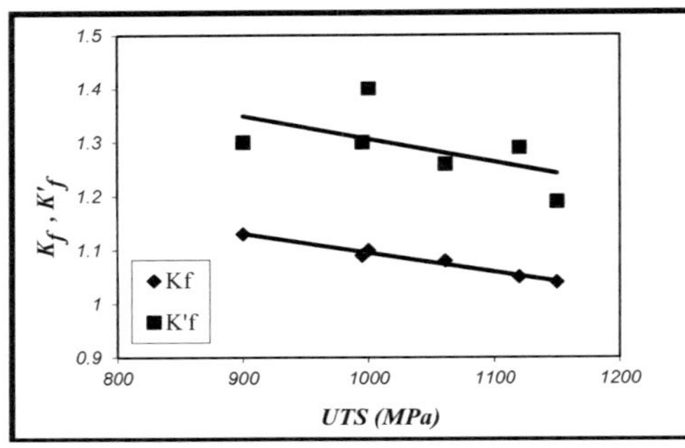


**Figure 10.** Effect of tensile strength on $K_f$ and $K'_f$ [4]

*Cause of the $K_f < K_t$ effect*

The stress in a notched member decreases rapidly with increasing distance from the notch as illustrated in fig.11. The slope $d\sigma/dx$ of the stress distribution is called the *stress gradient*, and the magnitude of this quantity is especially large near sharp notches. It is generally agreed that the $K_f < K_t$ effect is associated with this stress gradient.

One argument based on stress gradients is that the material is not sensitive to the peak stress, but rather to the average stress that acts over a region of small but finite size. In other words, some finite volume of material must be involved for the fatigue damage process to proceed. The size of the active region can be characterized by a dimension δ, called the *process zone size*, as illustrated in fig.10. Thus, the stress that controls the initiation of fatigue damage is not the highest stress at $x$=0, but rather the somewhat lower value that is average out to distance $x$=δ.

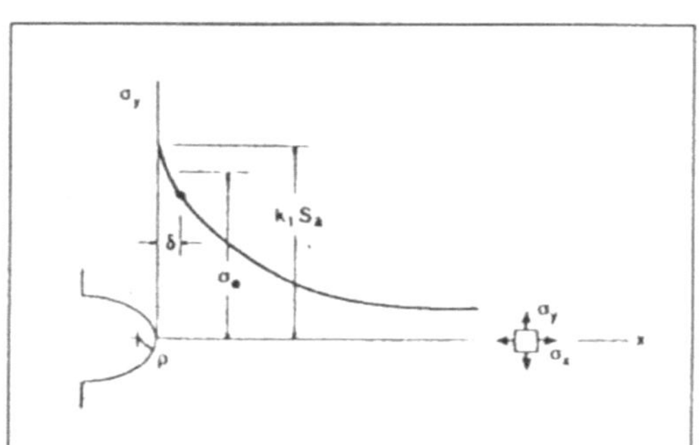

**Figure 11.** Interpretation of the fatigue limit as the average stress over a finite distance δ ahead of the notch [19]

Another possible stress gradient effect involves a weakest link argument based on statistics. Recall that the fatigue damage process may initiate in a crystal grain that has an unfavorable orientation of its slip planes relative to the planes of applied shear stresses, or in other cases at an inclusion, void, or other microstructure stress raiser. Many potential damage initiation sites occur within the volume of a smooth specimen. However, at a sharp notch, there is a possibility that no such damage initiation site occur in the small region where the stress is near its peak value. Hence, on the average, the notched member will be more resistant to fatigue if the comparison is made on the basis of the local notch stress.

A third possible effect is related to the fact that a crack may start at a sharp notch but then be unable to grow to failure. Finally, if there is *reversed yielding* at the notch during each loading cycle, plastic strains occur and the actual stress amplitude is less than it with $K_t$. This is simply a consequence of the fact that the calculation based on assuming elastic behavior is not valid if yielding occurs. Such an effect occurs at high stress levels corresponding to short fatigue lives in most engineering metals, and it occurs even at long lives in a few very ductile metals. However, there is little or no yielding at long lives, say around $10^6$ or $10^7$ cycles, for most engineering metals, so that this explanation alone is insufficient.

Cracks that have failed to grow in long life fatigue tests, called *nonpropagating cracks*, are commonly found at sharp notches. Analysis of these indicates that the presence of cracks is probably a major cause of the $K_f < K_t$ effect. Reversed yielding is clearly also a factor at short lives, and the process zone and weakest link effects may play a further role [19].

*Notch sensitivity*

The fatigue notch factor is dependent not only upon the component geometry, but also on the material properties and the mode of loading. The degree of difference between $K_f$ and $K_t$ is of practical interest to engineers, and is frequently expressed using the *notch sensitivity (q)* given by [21]:

$$q = \frac{K_f - 1}{K_t - 1} \tag{7}$$

Where, in general, $0 \leq q \leq 1$ When the theoretical stress concentration factor equals the fatigue notch factor, q=1 and if notch has no adverse effect on the fatigue limit, q=0 [19].

Notch sensitivity of Ti-6Al-4V for various round bars with different strength is presented in table 4 and figure 12. These values show that notch sensitivity reduces with increasing UTS.As it was noted before, Slip happens more difficult in stronger materials. Therefore, under HCF conditions the chance of formation of intrusion and extrusion in a high strength material is reduced substantially. Thus, crack nucleation in this type of material experience a delay which results to higher fatigue life of the component.

| Tensile strength (MPa) | | 900 | 995 | 1000 | 1061 | 1120 | 1150 |
|---|---|---|---|---|---|---|---|
| q | $K_t = 3.6$ | 0.05 | 0.035 | 0.038 | 0.03 | 0.02 | 0.015 |
| | $K_t = 4.1$ | ---- | 0.05 | ---- | ---- | 0.045 | ---- |

**Table 4.** Notch Sensitivity of Ti-6Al-4V [2]

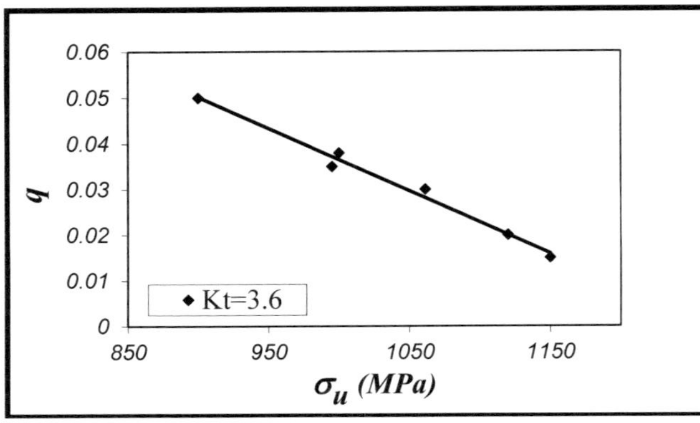


**Figure 12.** Effect of tensile strength on notch sensitivity of Ti-6Al-4V [2]

Notch sensitivity can be obtained for steel by Peterson equation. In the same condition (same tensile strength (1000MPa) and same notch radius (0.144mm) that for Ti-6Al-4V alloys are mentioned above (the samples that were tested by writer) [4], the notch sensitivity of steel can be obtained by the following equation(Peterson equation)[19]:

$$q = \frac{1}{1+\frac{\alpha}{\rho}} \Rightarrow q = 0.59 \qquad (8)$$

While this value for Titanium alloy is:

$$q = \frac{K_f - 1}{K_t - 1} = \frac{1.1 - 1}{3.6 - 1} = 0.038$$

So, it is clear that notch sensitivity for Ti-6Al-4V alloy is less than steels. As it was mention above, reason of this subject is due to hcp structure of Ti-6Al-4V alloy.

## 3. Summary

Titanium continues to be widely used for implant and biomedical applications. Titanium alloys have a high strength to weight ratio with a density approximately 60% that of steel. Their excellent corrosion resistance in many environments is due to the formation of a stable oxide surface layer. The most commonly used titanium alloy is Ti-6Al-4V, an alpha-beta alloy which at room temperature is around 90% alpha phase by volume. High cycle fatigue tests performed on Ti-6Al-4V alloy showed that by decreasing alpha grain size, fatigue properties of both smooth and notched ($K_t$=1.8) specimens, can be improved.

The fatigue limit of Ti-6Al-4V is improved by increasing the tensile strength. So that it seems, the factors cause an increase in tensile strength, will also increase the fatigue strength.

Presence of notch in Ti-6Al-4V alloy, doesn't affect the fatigue crack growth behavior, under the condition of HCF and LCF. Therefore this alloy with high strength is the most suitable for parts that are used in HCF conditions.

Notch sensitivity of Ti-6Al-4V alloy reduces with increasing tensile strength for a constant concentration factor ($K_t$), and this value is less than steel alloys in the same condition.

## Author details

Shabnam Hosseini
*Department of Metallurgy, Ayatollah Amoli Branch, Islamic Azad University, Amol, Iran*

## 4. References

[1] S.H.Teoh, "Fatigue of biomaterials: a revie"", International journal of fatigue, 22, 2000, 825-837.
[2] Shabnam Hosseini, M.B.Limooei,"Investigation of fatigue behavior and notch sensitivity of Ti-6Al-4V", Applied Mechanics and Materials, 80-81, 7, 2001.
[3] S.G.Steinemann, "Fatigue of biomaterials", Fatigue 96,1793-1798.
[4] Shabnam Hosseini, H. Arabi, M. Tamizifar and A. Zeyaei, "Effect of tensile strength on behavior and notch sensitivity of Ti-6Al-4V", Iranian journal of materials science and engineering, Vol.3, Winter & Spring 2006, PP.12-16.
[5] Alireza Nouri, Peter D.Hodgson and Cui'e Wen, "Biomimetic Porous Titanium Scaffolds for Orthopedic and Dental Applications", InTech. pp.415-450.
[6] Marc Long, H.J.Rack, "Titanium Alloys in Total Joint Replacement- A Materials Science Perspective", Biomaterials 19 (1998) 1621-1639.
[7] M.Ashraf Imam and A.C.Fraker, "Titanium alloys as implant materials", Medical application of titanium and it's alloy: The material and biological Issues, ASTM STP 1272,1996, 1-16.
[8] I.J.Polmear,"Light Alloys",ASM,1989, pp.211-271.
[9] Steinemann SG, "Corrosion of Titanium and Titanium Alloys for Surgical Implants", Titanium 84 Science and Technology, Vol.2, Munich, Germany, 1985, 2, 1373-9.
[10] Mitsuo Niinomi, "Recent research and development in titanium alloys for biomedical applications and healthcare goods", Science and Technology of Advanced Materials 4 (2003) 445–454.
[11] S.Suresh, "Fatigue of Material", New York, Cambridge University Press, 1998.
[12] A.Yamamoto, T. Kobayashi, N. Maryama, K. Nakazawa , M.Sumita, "Fretting Fatigue Properties of Ti–6Al–4V Alloy in Pseudo body Fluid and Evaluation of Biocompatibility by Cell Culture Method". J Japan Inst Metals 1995, 59, 463–70.
[13] AW.Eberhardt, BS.Kim, ED.Rigney, GL.Kutner, CR. Harte, "Effect of Precoating Surface Temperatures on Fatigue of Ti-6Al-4V", J Appl Biomat, 1995, 6,171-4.
[14] Mirko Klesnil, Petr LUKÁŠ, "Fatigue of Metallic Materials", Elsevier Scientific Publishing Company", Amsterdam, Oxsford,New York, 1980.
[15] R.J.Morrissey, D.L.McDowell, T.Nicholas, "Frequency and stress ratio effects in high cycle fatigue of Ti-6Al-4V", International of Fatigue, 21,1999, 679-685.
[16] J.J.Lucas, P.P. Konieczny, "Relation between Alpha Grain Size and Crack Initiation on Fatigue Strength in Ti-6Al-4V", Metal Trans., 1971, 2 (March).

[17] ASM Metals Handbook, "Fatigue and Fracture", 1996.
[18] D.B.Lanning, G.K.Haritos, T.Nicholas, "Influence of Stress State in HCF of Notched Ti-6Al-4V Specimens", Int.J.of Fatige, Vol.21, 1999, S87-S95.
[19] N.E. Dowling, "Mechanical Behavior of Material, Engineering Method for Deformation, Fracture and Fatigue", Prentice hall, 1999, PP. 397-449.
[20] G. E. Dieter, "Mechanical Metallurgy", Mc Grow-Hill, 1976.
[21] G.K. Haritos, T. Nicholas, D.B. Lanning, "Notch Size Effect in HCF Behaviour of Ti-6Al-4V", Int. J. of Fatigue, 21, 1999, PP. 643-652.
[22] Shabnam Hosseini, "Effect of Mechanical Parameter on Fatigue Behavior of Ti-6Al-4V", Master of Science Theseis, Fall 2002.

Chapter 4

# Size and Shape Effect on Biomedical Applications of Nanomaterials

Balaprasad Ankamwar

Additional information is available at the end of the chapter

http://dx.doi.org/10.5772/46121

## 1. Introduction

Fundamental properties of nanomaterials are strong function of their size and shapes. Surfactants are also equally important, since not only it stabilizes the nanoparticles but also makes nanoparticles compatible for various biomedical applications. The different size and shapes of the nanoparticles certainly have an influence and important place in clinical applications.

Earlier, we studied [1] the I-V response of electron transport within the plain and normal to the film surface of gold nanotriangles formed using the crude lemongrass extract. The I-V plot was fairly linear for the out-of-plane measurement while considerably higher across the film surface (681 kΩ) than within the plane of the film (32 kΩ). This could be due to the field-enhancement effects (FEE) near the sharp vertices of the nanotriangles considerably higher when the electric field was applied parallel to the film surface than when applied normal to the film surface. The FEE near sharp vertices of single crystalline triangular gold nanoprisms (Figure 1A) would be more as compare to truncated (1B) triangular gold nanoprisms. Costa and Dmitriev observed the better field confinement and enhancement in the plane $xy$ for the triangular disk in comparison with the circular disk and circular disk in comparison with the sphere [2]. The FEE could have important application in the use of the sharp vertices biogenic gold nanotriangle as conductive tips in scanning tunneling microscope for studying biological samples. The size of the nanotriangles (thickness: 8-18 nm) makes manipulation on to cantilevers feasible for detection of cancer cells by antibody-antigen mechanism.

Ankamwar *et al.* [3] reported the synthesis of flat and thin sharp vertices single crystalline triangular gold nanoprisms (Figure 1A; thickness: 20-40 nm) using aqueous chloroauric acid solution and tamarind leaf extract and their applications in vapor sensing. Nevertheless, these triangular gold nanoprisms (TGNs) could be used in the biosensing also.

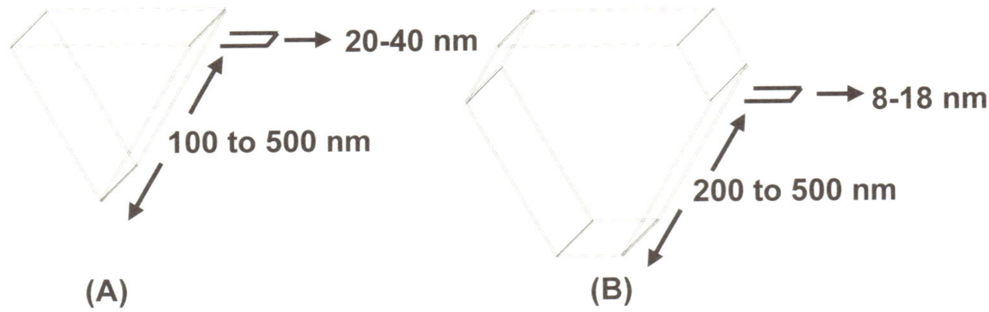


**Figure 1.** Schematic diagram of sharp vertices (A) and truncated ( B) triangular gold nanoprisms.

Gold nanotriangles have potential applications in hyperthermia of tumors. Triangular gold nanoprisms functionalized by suitable antibody can be delivered by intra-venous injection and preferentially associate with cancerous cells as an effect of strong affection of antibody for corresponding antigens of cancerous cells.

We can selectively kill cancerous cells by focusing IR radiation using laser (850-1100 nm) to heat up cancerous cells associated with functionalized TGNs, thus hyperthermia of tumors could be exploited for practical purposes. Ankamwar *et al.* [4] studied the biocompatibility of $Fe_3O_4$ nanoparticles evaluated by *in-vitro* cytotoxicity assays using normal, glia and breast cancer cells and observed that in all types of cells, nanoparticles were preferentially either adhered to cell membrane or internalized into the cells. The cytotoxic effects seems to be associated principally with an oxidative stress and this stress can result from the generation of reactive oxygen species with the interplay of oxygen with reduced iron species($Fe^{3+}/Fe^{2+}$) or from the disturbance of the electronic and/or ionic transport chains due to the strong affinity of the nanoparticles for the cell membrane.

**Figure 2.** Schematic diagram of spherical (A) and rod (B) shaped gold nanoparticles.

The spherical (Figure 2 A) biogenic gold nanoparticles synthesized using *Terminalia catappa* leaf extract [5] could be exploited in the use of cancer therapy due to the anticancer [6], antibacterial [7] and antioxidant [8] properties of *Terminalia catappa* leaf extract. The size of the nanoparticles being in the range 10-35 nm with average size of 21.9 nm makes their circulation into blood vessels feasible [5].

Intrinsic properties such as Surface Plasmon Resonance (SPR) of Ag, Au metallic nanoparticles (NPs) can be exploited for biosensing, drug delivery, bioimaging; fluorescence and luminescence of semiconductor CdS, CdSe NPs for immunoassays, bioimaging, biosensing; magnetism of magnetic $Fe_3O_4$ for MRI, drug delivery; electronic, mechanical and conductivity of carbon nanotubes (CNTs), and fullerene for drug, gene delivery, therapy and biosensing [9].

Gold nanoparticles, including rods (Figure 2B), enter cells by a non-specific process of endocytosis and concentrate in endosomes [10]. Chithrani *et al.* [11] studied the effects of size, shape, concentration, and incubation time on kinetics of uptake of nanorods and nanospheres of different sizes into mammalian (HeLa) cells and observed that, the fastest uptake in the case of spheres was for comparatively large particles of 50 nm diameter. Actually, a similar conclusion was drawn by Osaki *et al.* [12] for semiconductor nanoparticles, where once again it was the larger particles that more readily entered cells by receptor-mediated endocytosis. Intracellular uptake of gold nanoparticles into cells has been confirmed by imaging in a TEM. This showed that gold nanoparticles in the range of 14 to 100 nm were located inside cells and trapped in vesicles inside the cytoplasm, and external to the nucleus. Furthermore, the balance of evidence so far is that there is no cytotoxicity associated with the presence of the gold nanoparticles [10]. The change in the shape of the gold nanoparticles from spherical to rod-shaped enables the optical tuning of the SPR to Near Infrared (NIR) biological window region in which biological tissue has high transmitivity. This enables the gold nanorods for *in- vivo* imaging and therapy, making them highly promising for clinical applications [13]. However, mere spherical and anisotropic structured gold nanoparticles won't be able to solve the problem of target drug delivery. Nevertheless, different combinations of size and shapes with surface properties of nanomaterials need to be considered and implemented. One of the options could be iron oxide@Au spherical Figure 3A and rod Figure 3B shaped core-shell nanoparticles. Researchers are making efforts to find best possible option for cancer treatment using various combinations of nanoparticles by exploiting size and shapes effect of nanomaterials on their properties. As a result promising results are obtained. Hence, a revolution in nanotechnology is growing interest, however it is important to understand the how nanomaterials interact with biological systems especially for biomedical applications. Brief outline of biomedical applications of various nanomaterials with their different size and shapes is presented in this article.

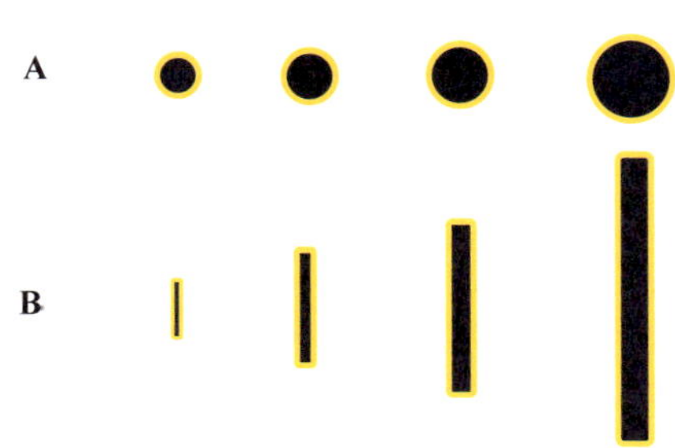


**Figure 3.** Schematic diagram of spherical (A) and rod (B) shaped iron@Au core-shell nanoparticles.

# 2. Application area

## 2.1. Role of size and shape of nanomaterials in biomedical applications

The role of proper size and shape of nanomaterials is un-debatable in biomedical applications. Moreover, multifaceted aspects of size and shapes of nanomaterials always remain inspiration to many researchers in this domain. Nevertheless, classification of particles is inevitable in this context.

Particles can be classified according their size, in terms of diameter; coarse particles in a range between 10,000 and 2,500 nm, fine particles, 2,500 and 100 nm and ultrafine particles or nanoparticles 100 and 1 nm [14].

## 2.2. Nanoparticles selection based on size, shape and surface

Selection of nanoparticles is indispensable step prior its application and it should be based on their earlier reported effects and potential effects with consideration of size, shape and surface.

### *2.2.1. Size*

Size determines the surface to volume ratio, and can strongly affect the material uptake and biodistribution, e.g. drug loaded nanoparticles can be used for site specific drug delivery only when uptake and blood circulation could be feasible. Blood Brain Barrier (BBB) and Blood Retina Barrier (BRB) like problems are still challenging task for site specific drug delivery due to size problem.

### *2.2.2. Shape*

Shape is critical parameter which effects cell uptake and/or the rate and site specific drug delivery from the system. Preferential interaction with specific proteins could be achieved on proper shape selection of nanomaterials.

### *2.2.3. Surface*

Surface and/or functionalized surface of nanomaterial has a special significance, since surface molecules determine the particles hydrophobic or hydrophillic, lipophobic or lipophillic, nature of particles and the extent to which they will interact with other molecules or trigger an immune response [15].

Non linear optical properties of nanostructured materials [16-18] can be useful in optoelectronics. Size and shape dependent properties of noble nanomaterials are resulting in the strong scattering and absorption of light [19-21] due to large optical field enhancement, however in semiconductors, due to the confinement of the electronic motion to a length scale that is comparable to or smaller than the length scale characterizing the electronic motion in bulk semiconducting material [22-24]. In case of noble metals, as the size is reduced to tens of nanometers scale, a new very strong absorption is observed, due to the collective oscillation of the electrons in the conduction band from one surface of the particle to the other [25, 26].

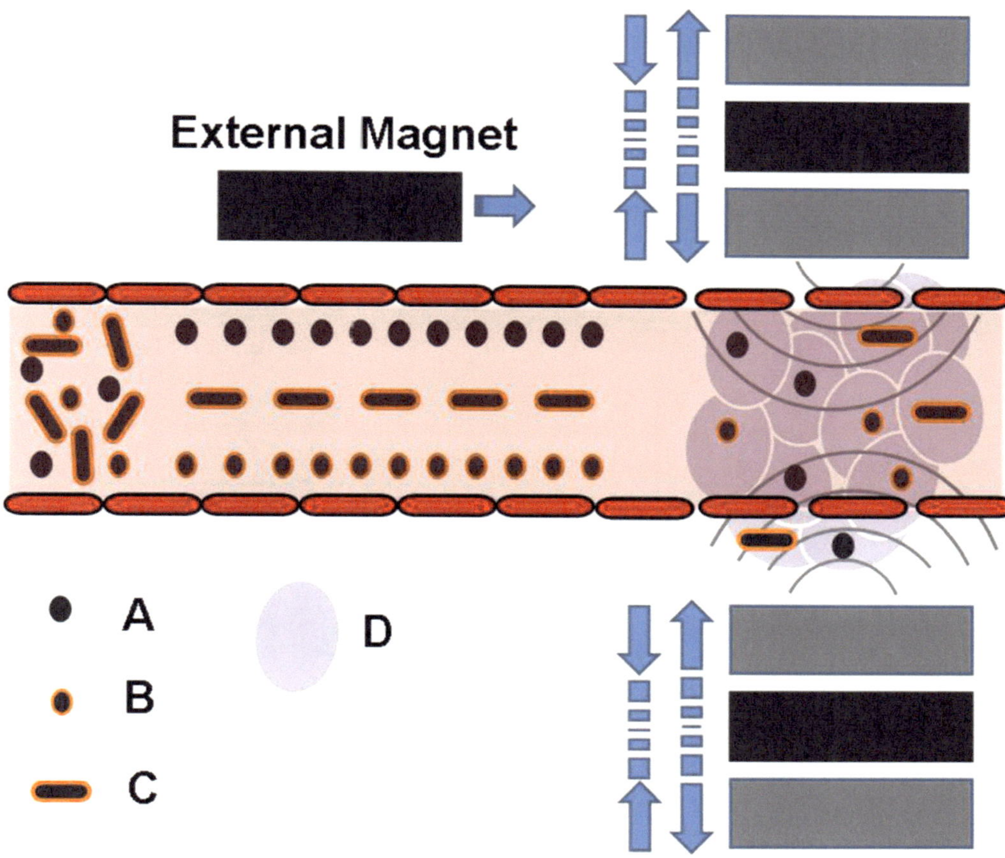


**Figure 4.** Schematic diagram of cell target delivery and hyperthermia of tumors under the influence of alternating magnetic field: iron nanospheres (A), iron@Au core-shell nanosphere (B), iron@Au core-shell nanorods (C) and cancer cells (D).

## 2.3. Targeted drug delivery by nanoparticles

Targeted drug delivery, is to confine, target and have a protected drug interaction with the diseased tissue. The advantages of the targeted release system are the less number of dosages to the patient, whereas the disadvantage of the high cost may not be affordable by the patient. Cost reduction without affecting drug efficiency against the diseased tissue is prime demand of the society. Due to high surface to volume ratio and less cost as compare to bulk materials, nanoparticles could be the best option in this regard.

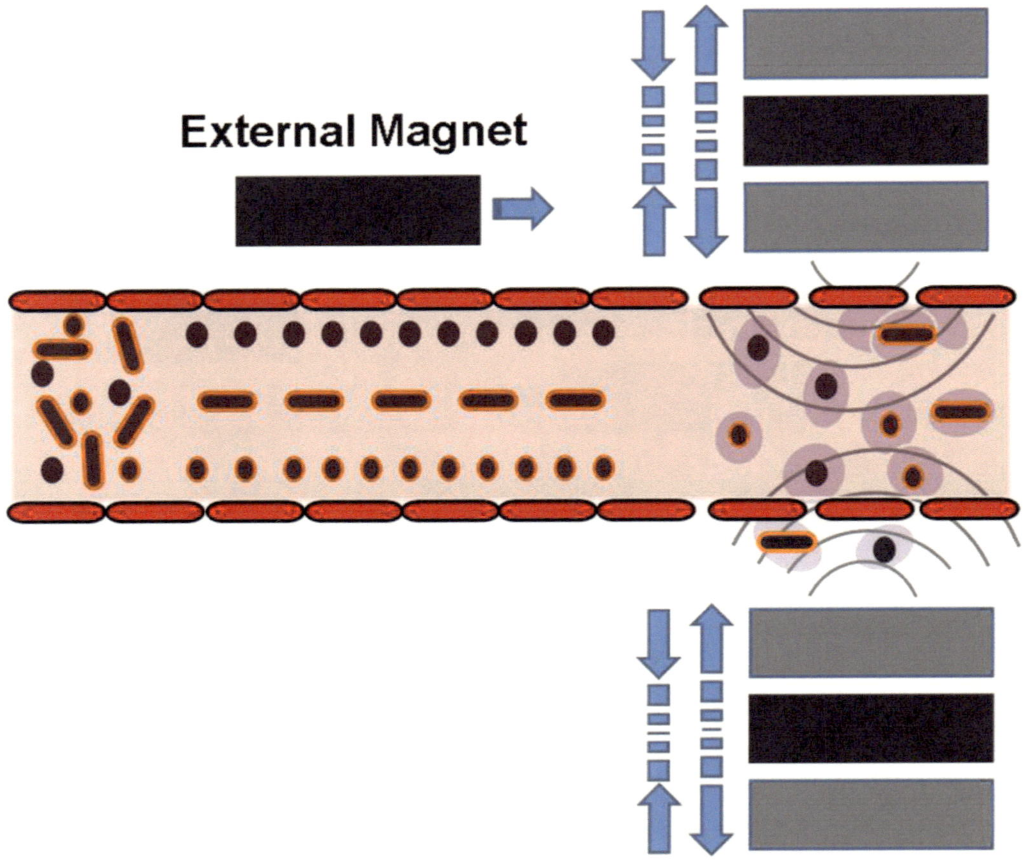


**Figure 5.** Schematic diagram depicting cell contraction under the influence of alternating magnetic field.

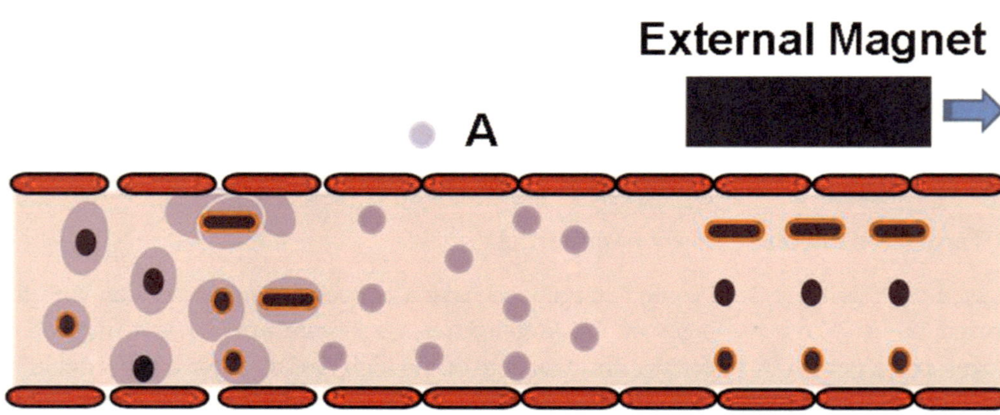


**Figure 6.** Schematic diagram depicting cell death (A) and excretory organ delivery of nanoparticles under the influence of external magnetic field.

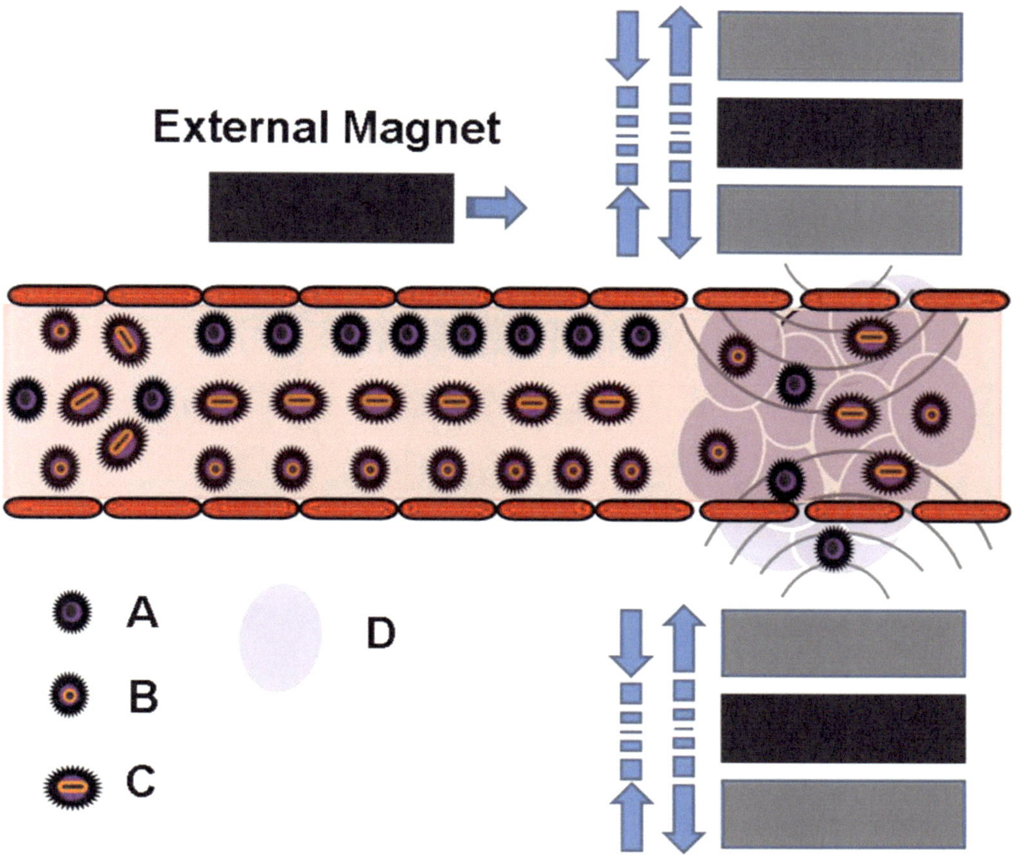


**Figure 7.** Schematic diagram of cell target drug delivery and hyperthermia of tumors under the influence of alternating magnetic field: iron@drug (A), iron@Au@drug core-shell nanosphere (B), iron@Au@drug core-shell nanorods (C) and cancer cells (D).

**Figure 4-9**: shows intravenous injection of nanoparticles

## 2.4. The role of blood vessel

The blood vessels are the part of the circulatory system that transports blood throughout the body. Hence, it is frequently adopted for delivery of the drug for a sustained period of time to target diseased area. Frankly speaking, the drug delivery system requires various disciplines, such as chemists, biologist and engineers, to join forces to optimize this system [27]. In case of anticancer drug to effective in cancer treatment they should be able to reach the desired tumor with minimal loss of their volume and activity in the blood circulation. Moreover, after reaching the tumor tissue, they should have selectivity in killing tumor cells without affecting normal cells. Here, the number of doses can be reduced with extra benefit of fewer side effects of extra doses of drug in existing methodology. Nanoparticles of appropriate size and shape can be used as effective drug carrier.

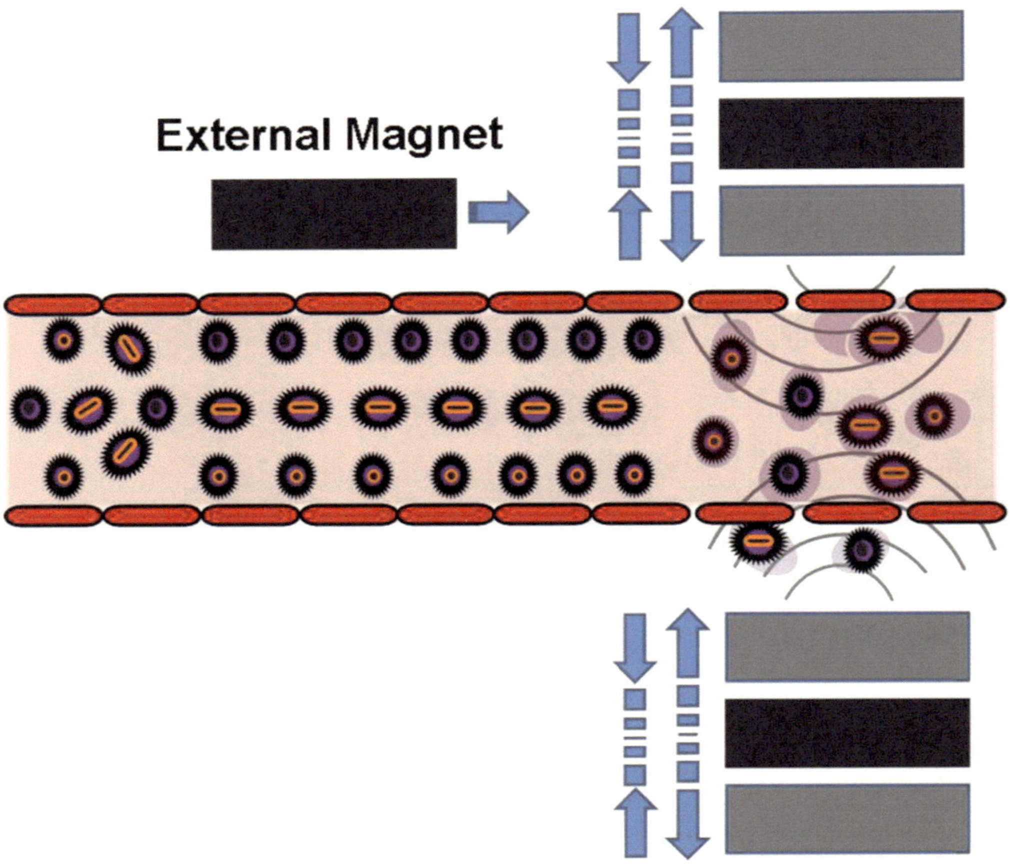


**Figure 8.** Schematic diagram depicting cell contraction under the combine effect of drug and hyperthermia of tumors due to the alternating magnetic field.

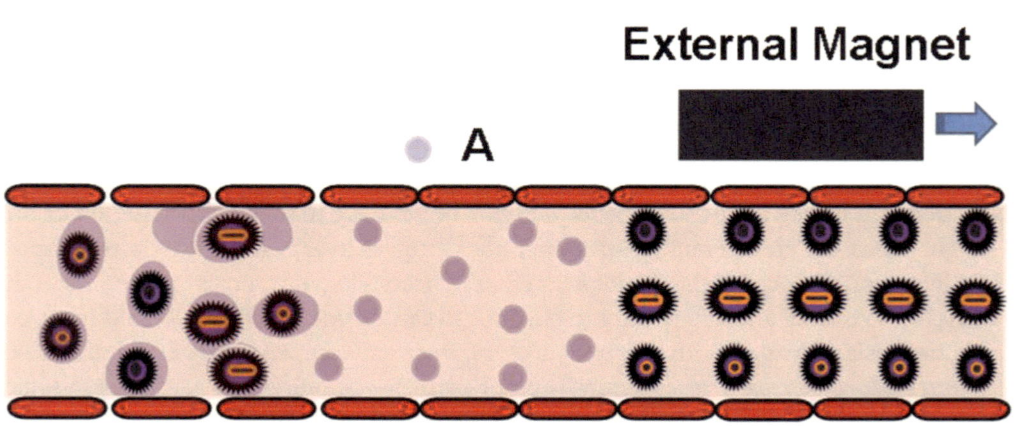


**Figure 9.** Schematic diagram depicting cell death (A) and excretory organ delivery of nanoparticles under the influence of external magnetic field.

## 2.5. The significance of size, shape and surface characteristics of nanoparticles in biomedical applications

Drug loaded nanoparticles should remain sufficient period in blood stream to interact with an active site of the drug with the tumor. Conventional surface non reformed nanoparticles are usually trapped in the circulation by the reticulo endothelial system, such as the liver and the spleen, reliant on their size and surface characteristics [28]. Hence, size, shape and surface characteristics play significant role in tumor targeted drug delivery.

Lia [29] presented a thermodynamic approach to elucidate the effects of the size and shape of nanoparticles on endocytosis. It was found that endocytosis needs to surmount a thermodynamic energy barrier and has a minimum radius of nanoparticles for endocytosis. Through referring to the concept of "diffusion length of receptors," he obtained a simple and analytical expression for the optimal size of nanoparticles and suggested that the spherical nanoparticles with the optimal radius about 25 nm have the fastest endocytosis speed. Pan *et al.* [30] reported that the cytotoxicity of $Ph_2PC_6H_4SO_3Na$ (TPPMS) and tris-sulfonatedtriphenylphosphine $P(C_6H_4SO_3Na)_3$TPPTS-modified gold nanoparticles depended primarily on their size and not on ligand chemistry. Particles of 1–2 nm in size were highly toxic and both smaller gold compounds (Tauredon) and larger 15-nm gold colloids were comparatively nontoxic.

### 2.5.1. *Significance of size*

Small size of nanoparticles are preferred, since after drug loading overall diameter should be more than enough to circulate though out the blood circulatory network for sustained period of time. Ankamwar *et al.* [4] reported synthesis of ~5 nm $Fe_3O_4$ nanoparticles using modified earlier reported protocol [31] and studied their biocompatibility with breast and brain cancer cells. These nanoparticles could be the one of the best option to use it as drug carrier. The size of the sinusoid in the spleen and fenestra of the Kuffer cells in the liver varies from 150 to 200 nm [32] and the size of gap confluence between endothelial cells of the leaky tumor vasculature may vary from 100 to 600 nm [33]. This suggests that, the size of nanoparticles should not be above 100 nm to reach tumor tissues by passing through these two particular vascular structures. However, Elsabahy and Wooley [34] suggested that intermediate sizes (20–200 nm) have the highest potential for *in-vivo* applications.

### 2.5.2. *Significance of shape*

Shape of nanoparticles is also equally important in sustained drug delivery as good as their size. Spherical nanoparticles are good option for drug delivery; however anisotropic structures could be the best option due to their large surface area e.g. dendrimer. This kind of structures can make good seating and binding arrangements for the drug which can be useful for sustained drug delivery. However, sharp edges of anisotropic structures can be responsible for injury of blood vessels [35].

The mechanism that allows nanoparticles to cross the cell membrane has been the subject of much recent research because the understanding and control of such uptake processes is important for the development of nanomedicine [35, 36]. Cellular uptake through endocytosis is crucial for drug delivery and nanomedicine. However, the conditions under which passive endocytosis (i.e. not ATP driven) takes place are not well understood. We report MD simulations of the passive uptake of ligand-coated nanoparticles with varying size, shape, coverage, and membrane-binding strength. They found that the efficiency of passive endocytosis was higher for spherocylindrical particles than for spheres and that endocytosis was suppressed for particles with sharp edges.

### *2.5.3. Significance of surface characteristics of nanoparticles*

In addition to their size and shape, the surface characteristics of nanoparticles are also an indispensable factor determining their life span, fate during circulation, drug binding and site specific release. Nanoparticles should ideally have a hydrophilic surface to escape macrophage capture [37]. This can be achieved in two ways: coating the surface of nanoparticles with a hydrophilic polymer, such as PEG, protects them from plasma proteins; alternatively, nanoparticles can be formed from block copolymers with hydrophilic and hydrophobic domains [38, 39].

However, Elsabahy and Wooley [34] suggested that the surface chemistry of the nanomaterials greatly impact their toxicity, immunogenicity, biodistribution and excess positive charge results in rapid opsonization and clearance with possible blood vessels and capillary occlusion.

### *2.5.4. Significance of nanoshells*

When the nanoshells are used for the drug delivery these shells wrap the tumor cells. When external field of infrared light is applied the tumor cells gets destroyed and the normal cells are left unaffected. Nanoshells tuned to absorb NIR radiation are particularly useful as mediators of photo thermal cancer therapy because they efficiently convert absorbed radiation into heat, and are thermally stable at therapeutic temperatures. The inert gold surface of nanoshells provides several advantages, including biocompatibility, non cytotoxicity, and it also facilitates conjugation to monoclonal antibodies or other biomolecules for both active tumor targeting and biosensing applications.

Nanoshells exhibit unique properties because their interaction with the electromagnetic field is greatly intensified by a phenomenon known as Localized Surface Plasmon Resonance (LSPR). This resonance effect arises from the collective oscillation of the conduction electrons in the gold shell, which efficiently couple to the incident electromagnetic field, and propagate along the surface [40].

## 2.6. Comparison between nanorods and nanospheres

The use of spherical gold nanoparticles are common practice for drug delivery, however the use of gold nanorods, have the promising feature in this regard. The nanorods of different lengths absorb different frequencies of infrared radiation. It is shown that gold nanorods absorb infrared much more efficiently than spherical gold nanoparticles. Therefore gold nanorods do a better job of absorbing infrared light and heating up the tumor than spherical nanoparticles do [41]. Hence, could be the best option in hyperthermia of tumors. Mere absorption of infrared light to maximum extent does not solve destruction of tumor problem. Magnetic nanoparticles such as spherical and rod shaped $Fe_3O_4$ coated with gold could be the better option, since magnetic $Fe_3O_4$ nanoparticles can be utilized for site specific drug delivery under the influence of applied external magnetic field and gold coating for hyperthermic destruction of tumors. Obviously, triangular gold nanoprisms would be the best option than rod shaped nanoparticles and rod shaped nanoparticles would be better option than spherical nanoparticles.

## 2.7. Thermotherapy or hyperthermia of tumors

Hyperthermia is one of the many treatment options that may be used in treating cancer. Hyperthermia therapy is a type of medical treatment in which body tissue is exposed to slightly higher temperatures to damage and kill cancer cells or to make cancer cells more sensitive to the effects of radiation and certain anti-cancer drugs [42, 43]. When combined with radiation therapy, it is called thermoradiotherapy. The preferential killing of cancer cells without damaging normal cells has been a desired goal in cancer therapy for many years. However, the various procedures used to date, including chemotherapy, radiotherapy or surgery, can fall short of this aim [44]. The potential of hyperthermia as a treatment for cancer was first predicted following observations that several types of cancer cells were more sensitive to temperatures in excess of 41°C than their normal counterparts [45, 46]. In the past external means of heat delivery were used such as ultrasonic or microwave treatments, but more recently research has focused on the injection of magnetic fluids directly into the tumour body, or into an artery supplying the tumour. The magnetic fluids used are preferably suspensions of super paramagnetic particles, prepared much as described for MRI contrast agents, as these produce more heat per unit mass than larger particles [47]. The level heating is simply controlled by the materials Marie Curie temperature, that is, the temperature above which materials loses their magnetic properties and thus their ability to heat [48]. There are two approaches, the first is called magnetic hyperthermia and involves the generation of temperatures up to 45–47°C by the particles. This treatment is currently adopted in conjunction with chemotherapy or radiotherapy, as it also renders the cells more sensitive [49]. The second technique is called magnetic thermoblation, and uses temperatures of 43–55°C that have strong cytotoxic effects on both tumour and normal cells [45, 50]. The reason for this use of increased temperatures is due to the fact that about 50% of tumours regress temporarily after hyperthermic treatment with temperatures of up to 44°C, therefore authors prefer to use temperatures up to 55°C [50]. On the basis of recent studies, tumours with volumes of approximately 300mm$^3$ can be heated and no potential problems were expected with larger tissue volumes (e.g. >1000mm$^3$) if there is proper regulation of the magnetic mass used and the intra-tumoural particle distribution [50]. The frequency should be greater than that sufficient to cause any neuromuscular response, and less than that capable of causing any detrimental heating of healthy tissue, ideally in the range of 100–1000 kHz [51, 52]). If suitable frequencies and field strength combinations are used, no interaction is observed between the human body and the field.

Various different types of nanocrystallites such as iron nanospheres Figure 4 (A), iron@Au core-shell nanosphere (B), iron@Au core-shell nanorods (C) may be injected intravenously. These nanoparticles are randomly oriented at the point of injection; however under the influence of magnetic field, they can be oriented in proper direction. External magnet can be used for proper orientation and site target delivery of magnetic nanoparticles as shown in Figure 4 alternating magnets generate heat to kill cancer cells. The method relies on the theory that any metallic objects when placed in an alternating magnetic field will have induced currents flowing within them. The amount of current is proportional to the size of the magnetic field and the size of the object [44]. As these currents flow within the metal, the metal resists the flow of current and thereby heats, a process termed inductive heating. If the metal is magnetic, such as iron, the phenomenon is greatly enhanced. Therefore, when a magnetic fluid is exposed to an alternating magnetic field the particles become powerful heat sources, destroying the tumour cells [51, 52] (Figure 5). The proper disposal of dead tumor cells and magnetic particles is also equally important. External magnetic field can be utilized to direct magnetic particles towards excretory organ as shown in Figure 6. Superparamagnetic iron oxide nanoparticles have been used for many years as Magnetic Resonance Imaging (MRI) contrast agents [53], receptor-mediated targeting of magnetic nanoparticles using insulin as a surface ligand to prevent endocytosis. However, gold coated spherical or rod iron nanoparticles can be better option for their scattering properties for imaging and laser therapy both combine together along with magnetic properties of iron nanoparticles. Gold coated iron nanorods could be the best option for thermotherapy in addition to imaging and laser therapy, since gold nanorods absorb infrared radiation better than spherical gold particles.

Tissue and cell-specific drug targeting by superparamagnetic iron oxide nanoparticles can be achieved by employing nanoparticles coatings or carrier-drug conjugates that contain a ligand recognized by a receptor on the target cell. In this study, superparamagnetic iron oxide nanoparticles with specific shape and size have been prepared and coupled to insulin for their targeting to cell expressed surface receptors and thereby preventing the endocytosis [53]. Figure 7 depicts a schematic diagram of cell target drug delivery and hyperthermia of tumors under the influence of alternating magnetic field: iron@drug (A), iron@Au@drug core-shell nanosphere (B), iron@Au@drug core-shell nanorods (C) and cancer cells (D). Figure 8 shows tumor cell death and Figure 9 the proper disposal of dead tumor cells and magnetic particles towards excretory organs. Here magnetic particles are intended to use for tumor specific site delivery under the influence of external magnetic field and hyperthermia of tumors. However, gold coating can be used to loading drug and imaging due to scattering properties of gold nanoshell. Obviously, gold coated nanorods would be best option due to infrared absorption properties of gold nanorods, which in turn can be used for laser therapy.

The best combination of various therapies such as chemotherapy by tumor specific drug delivery, thermotherapy (hyperthermia) and laser therapy would be the most suitable option to solve cancer problem to maximum extent as depicted in Figure 7-9. Many oncologists agree with multi therapy rather than any single therapy for cancer treatment. Since in many type of cancer cells single therapy did not show 100% cure.

## 2.8. Advantages of nanorods over nanospheres

By combining the delivery of rods with drugs, tumor death is triggered with minimizing toxicity by a combination of chemotherapy and external laser beam stimulation. Apart from an initial laser cost, the combination of these two drugs would be relatively noninvasive and inexpensive [54].

We also note that silica nanospheres with a nanoscale overcoat of gold ("nanoshells") also have tunable absorption in the visible and NIR, and these materials are the subject of another recent review [55].

| **Author** | **Size (nm)** | **Shape** | **Surface group** | **Cell line** | **Toxicity results** |
|---|---|---|---|---|---|
| Ankamwar *et al.* [4] | ~5nm | Sphere | COOH, $NH_2$ | U-251 Glia cancer cells | 75.4 ± 7.2 cell viability after being exposed to 100μM$Fe_3O_4$ nanoparticles for 72 h. |
| Ankamwar *et al.* [4] | ~5nm | Sphere | COOH, $NH_2$ | T47D Breast cancer cells | 81.8 ± 7.6 cell viability after being exposed to 100μM$Fe_3O_4$ nanoparticles for 72 h. |
| Jie Pan *et al.* [56] | 280–300 nm | Sphere | TPGS-COOH, PEG | MCF-7 breast cancer cells and NIH 3T3 cells | In vitro cell viability of MCF-7 cells treated with free QDs is 80%, QDs-loaded 11.1% (tri-noctylphosphine oxide (TOPO)-capped QDs) TC NPs is 95% and QDs-loaded 11.1% (folate-decorated) FD NPs is 82% at the same 0.63 nMQDs concentration after 4 h and 24 h. In vitro cell viability of NIH 3T3 cells treated with free QDs is 87 %, QDs-loaded 11.1% TC NPs is 90% and QDs-loaded 11.1% FD NPs 89% at the same 0.63 nMQDs concentration after 4 h and 24 h. |
| Niidome *et al.* [57] | 65 nm | Rod | CTAB, PEG | HeLa cells | 80% cell death with 0.05 mMCTAB-coated nanorods, only 10% of cell death at 0.5 mM PEG coated nanorods. |
| Takahashi *et al.* [58] | 65 nm | Rod | Phospatidyl choline | HeLa cells | Phosphatidylcholine modified gold nanorods were much less |

| **Author** | **Size (nm)** | **Shape** | **Surface group** | **Cell line** | **Toxicity results** |
|---|---|---|---|---|---|
| | | | | | toxic than C-TAB coated nanorods. |
| Sun *et al.* [59] | --- | --- | --- | Sarcoma 180 mouse tumor cell line (S180) and SGC-7901 human gastric carcinoma cell line (SGC-7901) | The concentration of the gold complexes is 32 μM. Sarcoma 180 mouse tumor cell line S180cell human gastric carcinoma cell line SGC-7901cell. ClAuTCPPNa treated with S180 cell and SGC-7901 cell shows cell viability 66.63% and 57.93% respectively. ClAuTPPCOONa treated with S180 cell and SGC-7901 cell shows cell viability 16.46% and 50.47% respectively. The result showed that the anti-tumor activity of ligandTCPPNa is lower than its gold(III) complex. |
| Temminka *et al.* [60] | --- | --- | --- | WiDr and H630 | The cell viability of WiDr cells treated with TFTc at 2 nM shows 95% after 72 hrs. The cell viability of H630 cells treated with TFTc at 0.5 nM shows 95% after 72 hrs. |
| Wei *et al.* [61] | 10–30 nm | Sphere | MAA-coated nanoparticles | CBRH7919 liver cancer cells | CdS-based QDs was prepared and cellular imaging was conducted. The (QDs) CdS–MAA–PEI–FA has highly photostable and very excellent water-dispersibility and bioimaging. By use of confocal microscopy, demonstrated the internalization of QD–MAA–PEI–FA in FRs (folate receptors) over expressing tumor cells such as CBRH7919livercancer cell and their receptor-mediated uptake is confirmed by the rapid uptake (in less than 3 h). |
| Abbasalipourkabir *et al.* [62] | 145.00 ±3.39 | Sphere | 30% lecithin and 1 % oleyl alcohol | MCF-7 and MDA-MB231 | Cell viability of MCF-7 MDA-MB231 and cells treated with SLN-03 for 72hr is 45 and 50% respectively. |
| Pourgholami *et al.* [63] | --- | --- | ABZ–CD + citric acid (CA) | human ovarian cystadenocarcinoma | The cell viability of human heptocytes cells treated with |

| Author | Size (nm) | Shape | Surface group | Cell line | Toxicity results |
|---|---|---|---|---|---|
| | | | | cancer cell lines 1A9, OVCAR-3 and SKOV-3 | ABZCD+CA(albendazole β-cyclodextrins + citric acid) at 1 μM shows 90% after 3 days. |
| Yong *et al.* [64] | ---- | Rods | CTA3 | Pancreatic cancer cell lines | The cell viability of Panc-1 treated with anti-claudin 4 and drug conjugated QDs with ADM at 1.1 μM shows 66% for 24 h. |
| Glazer *et al.* [65] | ------ | Sphere | PEG | Panc-1 or Cama-1 cells | Cell viability greater than 92% CdSe quantum dot toxicity has been reported at concentrations greater than 0.8 μM. 26 indium based quantum dots InGaPhosphide (i.e., eFluorNC700) are ten times less toxic. |
| Das et al. [66] | 8 nm | Sphere | poloxamers,poloxamines or polyethylene glycol (PEG) derivatives | human cervical HeLa cancer cells, | The cell viability of HeLa cells treated with folate conjugated magnetite NPs at 200 μg/ml of magnetite NPs is 97%. No significant reduction in cellular viability was observed, the survival rate being higher than 90%, even at the highest nanoparticle concentration. |
| Gupta *et al.* [53] | 550 nm | --- | Insulin | Infinity telomerase-immortalized primary human fibroblasts (hTERT-BJ1, Clonetech Laboratories, Inc., Hampshire, U.K.) | Insulin-coated nanoparticles revealed no cytotoxic effects to cells, and they remained more than 100% viable relative to control at concentration as high as 1mg/ml. Incubation with uncoated plain magnetic particles, the fibroblasts showed significant loss in viability of about 25%-50% observed at concentrations 250 g/ml. |
| Ahrens *et al.* [67] | ~50 nm | Sphere | Polysaccharide | Bone marrow myeloid progenitor cells from NOD mice ,myeloid progenitor cell | The result demonstrate that RME (receptor-mediated endocytosis) of magnetic nanoparticles effectively labels DCs in vitro, the labeling procedure does not harm the cell's immunological function and labeled cells can be visualized in vivo in a longitudinal fashion. |

**Table 1.** Summary of selected cytotoxicity and bio-imaging for various nanoparticles, 2003-2012.

## 2.9. Biomedical applications of quantum dots

Quantum dots with their extensive excitation spectra, sharp emission spectra, and easily tunable emission properties are hypothetical candidates for replacing conventional fluorescent markers in biodetection assays. Having already shown considerable promise as intracellular imaging and tracking agents [68] quantum dots made of CdSe and ZnS, with few exceptions [69] have not been widely investigated as materials for biodetection assays. The first example of chemically modifying CdSe quantum dots with DNA involved ligand exchange coupled with particle surface engineering [70]. Recent studies employed quantum dots as labels imbedded in polymeric structures [71].

## 2.10. Electrical detection using nanowire and nanotubes

Nanotubes and nanowires are being reconnoitered as new signal transduction motifs in the electrical detection of DNA as they have for the detection of gases [72], small molecules [73] and proteins. For example, Lieber and colleagues demonstrated that silicon nanowires functionalized with PNA can be used for real-time, label-free detection of DNA at concentrations as low as 10 fM [74].

## 2.11. Biomedical applications of carbon nanotubes

CNTs have very interesting physicochemical properties, such as ordered structure with high aspect ratio, ultra-light weight, high mechanical strength, high electrical conductivity, high thermal conductivity, metallic or semi-metallic behaviour and high surface area. The combination of these characteristics makes CNTs unique materials with the potential for diverse applications [75, 76]. Cui *et al.* examined the influence of single-walled carbon nanotubes (SWCNTs) on human HEK293 kidney cells with the aim to explore SWCNT biocompatibility [77].

## 2.12. Biomedical application of silver nanoparticles

Silver nanoparticles are being used increasingly in wound dressing, catheters and various household products due to their antimicrobial activity. AshaRani et al. [78] reported that silver nanoparticles are cytotoxic, genotoxic and antiproliferative. As a general rule, the DNA damaging agents have the potential to cause genome instability, which is predisposing factor carcinogenesis. Future applications of Ag nanoparticles as an antiproliferative agent could be limited by the fact that it is equally toxic to normal cells [78]. Nevertheless, Sanpui *et al.* [79] reported, induction of appotosis in cancer cells at low silver nanoparticles concentration using chitosan nanocarrier. They used chitosan coated silver nanoparticles for successful delivery of silver nanoparticles to human colon cancer cells, HT 29 adenocarcinoma cells and demonstrated that the concentration of Ag nanoparticles required to reduce the viability of HT 29 cells by 50% was 0.33 $\mu g\ mL^{-1}$ , much less than in previously reported data. These reports indicate that though silver nanoparticles are harmful to normal cells, their use at low concentration could be exploited for biomedical applications.

## 2.13. Future prospects

Lot of work on *in-vitro* diagnostics has been carried out and related to specific detection, imaging, and therapy for very particular target cells. Various size and shaped nanoparticles of different materials have specific applications; e.g. spherical gold nanoparticles can be used for drug delivery, however for site specific drug delivery we need to use viable mechanism such as antibody-antigene mechanism. Here, rod shaped nanoparticles could be the best option, due to its more infrared absorption property as compare to spherical gold nanoparticles. Gold nanorods would be better option for drug delivery and phototherapy. However, rod shaped magnetic nanoparticles such as iron oxide coated by gold shells can be better option for hyperthermia and phototherapy. Moreover, the combination of iron oxide@Au@drug composite would be best option for hyperthermia, site specific drug delivery and chemotherapy. Nowadays, researchers in cancer therapy are realizing that instead of single therapy, multi-therapy would be the best option. It has great future in cancer therapy, if drug would be loaded on the surface of iron oxide@Au nanoparticles and make it iron oxide@Au@drug nanomaterials. Rod shaped magnetic nanoparticles coated by gold nanoshell are an attractive alternative to traditional organic fluorescent dyes in that they do no photo bleach, they can absorb throughout the visible and NIR, and they can be nontoxic under certain experimental conditions. In the next 5-10 years, intensive research activity should be focused on *in-vivo* uses of rod shaped gold nanoparticles, rod shaped iron oxide@Au core-shell nanoparticles and drug loaded rod shaped iron oxide@Au core-shell nanomaterials. Most of the cytotoxicity studies are in progress for every size shape and type of nanomaterials along with surfactants in *in-vitro* and few of them in *in-vivo*. This should be continued along with study of their side effects.

The majority of commercial nanoparticles applications in medicine are geared towards drug delivery. There are some developments in directing and remotely controlling the functions of nano-probes, for example driving magnetic nanoparticles to the tumour and then making them either to release the drug load or just heating them in order to destroy the surrounding tissue [80]. However, multi-therapy in cancer treatment is advocated by many researchers, which also suggests that experts from various discipline should come together to kill cancer problem before it will be too late. These also suggest that there is no place for compartmentalized treatment to the knowledge in their own box rather tailoring together is and would be the only and lonely solution and need of the time.

# 3. Conclusion

Size, shape and surface coating of nanomaterials are critical parameter which effects cell uptake and/or the rate and site specific drug delivery from the system. Shapes of nanomaterials are also play important role in infrared absorption, which has special significance in phototherapy. Anisotropic nanoparticles such as rod and triangular shaped gold nanoparticles strongly absorb in visible and NIR region. This special property of gold anisotropic nanoparticles could be exploited in hyperthermia of tumors. For site specific drug delivery magnetic particles such iron oxide could be the best option under the influence of alternating magnetic field. However, mere iron oxide nanoparticles did not prove the best option for cancer therapy. Nevertheless, iron oxide nanoparticles coated by gold shell along with loaded anticancer drug would be the best option for hyperthermia, phototherapy and chemotherapy together. In conclusive remark, I could not resist mentioning, one should not forget that the main reason of any kind of diseases is our life style, which includes our food style, regular sufficient sleep/rest and foremost important key point is our thinking or will power.

## Author details

Balaprasad Ankamwar
*Bio-Inspired Materials Science Laboratory, Department of Chemistry, University of Pune, Ganeshkhind, Pune, India*

## Acknowledgement

The author grateful to Prof. Ru-Shi Liu, National Taiwan University and Prof. Michael Hsiao, Genomics Research Center, Academia Sinica, Taipei, Taiwan for biocompatibility studies of $Fe_3O_4$ nanoparticles evaluated by *in-vitro* cytotoxicity assays using normal, glia and breast cancer cells, supported by the grants from National Science Council of Taiwan (NSC 97-2113-M-002-012-MY3). The author also thanks his project students Ms. Farah Surti and Annsi Jose I. for help in refining schematic diagrams.

## 4. References

[1] Shiv Shankar S, Rai A, Ankamwar B, Singh A, Ahmad A, Sastry M (2004) Biological Synthesis of Triangular Gold Nanoprisms. Nat. Mate. 3: 482-488.

[2] Da Costa K, Dmitriev V(2010) Comparative Analysis of Circular and Triangular Gold Nanodisks for Field Enhancement Applications. J. Microw. Optoelectron. Electromagn. Appl. 2: 123-130.

[3] Ankamwar B, Chaudhary M, Sastry M (2005) Gold Nanotriangles Biologically Synthesized using Tamarind Leaf Extract and Potential Applications in Vapor Sensing. Syn. React. Inorg. Metal Org. Nano-Metal Chem. 35: 19-26.

[4] Ankamwar B, Lai T, Huang J, Liu R, Hsiao M, Chen C, Hwu Y (2010) Biocompatibility of $Fe_3O_4$ Nanoparticles Evaluated by in vitro Cytotoxicity Assays using Normal, Glia and Breast Cancer Cells. Nanotechnology 21: 075102 (9pp).

[5] Ankamwar B (2010) Biosynthesis of Gold Nanoparticles (Green-gold) using Leaf Extract of *Terminalia catappa*. E-J.Chem. 7 (4): 1334-1339.

[6] Kandil F, Soliman A, Skodack S, Mabry T (1999) A new Anticancer Tannin and Known Tannins from *Terminalia catappa*. Asian J. Chem. 11: 1001-1004.

[7] Pawar S, Pal S (2002) Antimicrobial Activity of Extracts of *Terminalia catappa* Root. Indian J. Med. Sci. 56(6): 276-278.
[8] Lin C, Hsu Y, Lin T (2001) Modifying Effects of *Terminalia catappa* on Azoxymethane-Induced Colon Carcinogenesis in Male F344 Rats. Anticancer Res. 21: 237-243.
[9] Wang X, Liu L, Ramströ O, Yan M (2009) Engineering Nanomaterial Surfaces for Biomedical Applications Exp. Biol. Med. 234: 1128-1139.
[10] Pissuwani D, Valenzuela S, Cortie M (2008) Prospects for Gold Nanorod Particles in Diagnostic and Therapeutic Applications. Biotechnol. Genet. Eng. Rev. 25: 93-112.
[11] Chithrani B, Ghazani A, Chan W (2006) Determing the Size and Shape Dependence of Gold Nanoparticle Uptake into Mammalian Cells. Nano Lett. 6: 662-668.
[12] Osaki F, Kanamori T, Sando S Sera T, Aoyama Y (2004) J. Am. Chem. Soc. 126: 6250-1.
[13] Huang X, Jain P, El-Sayed I, El-Sayed M (2007) Special Focus: Nanoparticles for Cancer Diagnosis and Therapeutics – Review. Nanomedicine 2: 681-693.
[14] Granqvist C, Buhrman C, Wyns J, Sievers A (1976) Far-Infrared Absorption in Ultrafine Al Particles. Phys. Rev. Lett. 37: 625–629.
[15] Guidelines for Nanotoxicology Researchers using Nanocomposix Materials February 2012, v 1.0, Nanocomposix.com
[16] Chandra M, Indi S, Das P (2007) J. Phys. Chem. C. 111: 1065.
[17] Segets D, Tomalino L, Gradl J, Peukert W (2009) J. Phys. Chem. C. 113: 11995.
[18] Boyd R. Nonlinear Optics. San Diego, CA: Academic Press; 1992.
[19] Griffin J, Singh A, Senapati D, Rhodes P, Mitchell K, Robinson B, Yu E, Ray P (2009) Size- and Distance-Dependent Nanoparticle Surface-Energy Transfer (NSET) Method for Selective Sensing of Hepatitis C Virus RNA. Chem. Eur. J. 15: 342.
[20] Liu J, Cao Z, Lu Y (2009) Functional Nucleic Acid Sensors. Chem. Rev. 109: 1948.
[21] Li D, Song S, Fan C (2010) Target-responsive Structures for Nucleic Acid Sensors. Acc. Chem. Res. 43: 631-641.
[22] Zhang H, Banfield J (2009) Identification and Growth Mechanism of ZnS Nanoparticles with Mixed Cubic and Hexagonal Stacking J. Phys. Chem. C. 113: 9681-9687.
[23] Rodriguez E, Cid B, Antonio M, Ivanenko V, Lipovskii A (2009) Chem. Phys. Lett. 467: 335.
[24] Duboisset I, Russier-Antoine E, Benichou G, Jonin B, Brevet P. (2009) Single Metallic Nanoparticle Sensitivity with Hyper Rayleigh Scattering. J. Phys. Chem. C. 113: 13477.
[25] Singh A, Senapati D, Wang S, Griffin J, Neely A, Candice P, Naylor K, Varisli B, Kalluri J, Ray P (2009) Gold Nanorod Based Selective Identification of *Escherichia coli* Bacteria Using Two-Photon Rayleigh Scattering Spectroscopy. ACS Nano. 3: 1906.
[26] Ray P (2010) Size and Shape Dependent Second Order Nonlinear Optical Properties of Nanomaterials and Its Application in Biological and Chemical Sensing. Chem. Rev. 110: 5332–5365.
[27] Muller R, Keck C (2004) Challenges and Solutions for the Delivery of Biotech Drugs – A Review of Drug Nanocrystal Technology and Lipid Nanoparticles. J. Biotech. 113: 151–170.
[28] Moghimi S, Hunter A, Murray J (2001) Long-circulating and Target-specific Nanoparticles: Theory to Practice. Pharmacol. Rev. 53: 283–318.

[29] Lia X (2012) J. Appl. Phys. 111: 024702.
[30] Pan Y, Neuss S, Leifert A, Fischler M, Wen F, Simon U, Schmid G, Brandau W, Jahnen-Dechent W (2007) Size-Dependent Cytotoxicity of Gold Nanoparticles. Small 3: 1941 – 1949.
[31] Sun S, Zeng H, Robinson D, Raoux S, Rice P, Wang S, Li G (2004) J. Am. Chem. Soc.126: 273–9.
[32] Wisse E, Braet F, Luo D, De Zanger R, Jans D, Crabbé E, Vermoesen A (1999) Structure and Function of Sinusoidal Lining Cells in the Liver. Toxicol. Pathol. 24: 100–11.
[33] Yuan F, Dellian M, Fukumura D, Leunig M, Berk D, Torchilin V, Jain R (1995) Vascular Permeability in a Human Tumor Xenograft: Molecular Size Dependence and Cutoff Size. Cancer Res. 55: 3752–6.
[34] Elsabahy M, Wooley K (2012) Chem. Soc. Rev. 41: 2545–2561.
[35] Vacha R, Martinez-Veracoechea F, Frenkel D (2011) Nano Lett. 11: 5391–5395.
[36] Reynwar B, Illya G, Harmandaris V, Muller M, Kremer K, Deserno M (2007) Nature 447: 461–4.
[37] Yang K, Ma Y (2010) Nat. Nanotechnol. 5: 579-583.
[38] Harris J, Martin N, Modi M. (2001) A Novel Process for Modifying Pharmacokinetics. Clin. Pharmacokinet. 40: 539–51.
[39] Adams M, Lavasanifar A, Kwon G (2003) Amphiphilic Block Copolymers for Drug Delivery. J. Pharm. Sci. 92: 1343–55.
[40] Chien, W, Szkopek T (2008)) Multiple- Multipole Simulation of Optical Near Fields in Discrete Metal Nanospheres Assemblies. OpEx. 16: 1820 – 1835.
[41] http://www.understandingnano.com/nanomedicine-nanorod-targeted-drug-delivery.html
[42] van der Zee J. (2002) Annals of Oncology 13: 1173–1184.
[43] Wust P, Hildebrandt B, Sreenivasa G *et al.* (2002) Lancet Oncology. 3(8): 487–497.
[44] Berry C, Curtis A (2003) Funtionalisation of Magnetic Nanoparticles for Applications in Biomedicine. J. Phys. D: Appl. Phys. 36: R198–R206.
[45] Jordan A Wust P, Scholz R, Tesche B, Fahling H, Mitrovics T, Vogl T, Cervos-Navarro J, Felix R (1996) Cellular Uptake of Magnetic Fluid Particles and theirEffects on Human Adenocarcinoma Cells Exposed to AC Magnetic Fields *in-vitro*. Int. J. Hyperthermia 12: 705-22.
[46] Neilsen O , Horsman M, Overgaard J (2001) E. J. Cancer. 37: 1587–1589.
[47] Mitsumori M, Hiraoki M, Shibata T, Okuno Y, Nagata Y, Nishimura Y, Abe M, Hasegawa M, Nagae H, Ebisawa Y (1996) Targeted Hyperthermia Using Dextran Magnetite Complwe: A New Treatment Modality for Liver Tumors. Hepato-Gastroenterology 43: 1431-1437.
[48] Rehman J, Landman J, Tucker R, Bostwick D, Sundaram C, Clayman R (2002) Ferromagnetic Self-Regulating Reheatable Thermal Rd Implants for *in-situ* Tssue Ablation. J. Endourol. 16: 523-531.
[49] Hilger I, Fruhauf K, Andra W, Hiergeist R, Hergt R and Kaiser W A (2002) Acad. Radiol. 9: 198-202.

[50] Hilger I, Andra W, Hergt R, Hiergeist R, Schubert H, Kaiser W A (2001) Electromagnetic Heating of Breast Tumours in Interventional Radiology: *in-vitro* and *in-vivo* Studies in Human Cadavers and Mice. Radiology 218: 570-575.

[51] Babinkova M, Leszczynska D, Sourivong P, Babinec P (2000) Med. Hypoth. 54: 177-179.

[52] Babinkova M Sourivong P, Leszczynska D, Babinec P (2000) Blood-Specific Whole-Body Electromagnetic Hyperthermia. Med. Hypoth. 55: 459-460.

[53] Gupta A, Berry C, Gupta M, Curtis A (2003) Receptor –Mediated Targeting of Magnetic Nanoparticles Using Insulin as a Surface Ligand to Prevent Endocytosis. IEEE Transactions on NanoBioscience 2: 255-261.

[54] http://www.ibridgenetwork.org/utah/targeted-combination-drug-delivery-and-photothermal-therapy-f_1

[55] Hirsch L, Gobin A, Lowery A, Tam F, Drezek R, Halas N, West J (2006) Ann. Biomed. Eng. 34: 15–22.

[56] Pan J, Fen S (2009) Targeting and Imaging Cancer Cells by Folate-Decorated Quantum Dots (QDs)- Loaded Nanoparticles of Biodegradable Polymers. Biomaterials 30: 1176–1183.

[57] Niidome T, Yamagata M, Okamoto Y, Akiyama Y, Takahashi H, Kawano T, Katayama Y, Niidome Y (2006) PEG-Modified Gold Nanorods with a Stealth Character for in vivo Applications. J. Control. Release. 114: 343-347.

[58] Takahashi H, Niidome Y, Niidome T, Kaneko K, Kawasaki H, Yamada S (2006) Modification of Gold Nanorods Using Phosphatidylcholine to Reduce Cytotoxicity. Langmuir 22: 2-5.

[59] Liang S, Chen H , Zhang Z, Yang Q , Tong H , Xu A , Wang C (2012) J. Inorg. Biochem. 108: 47-52.

[60] Temminka O, Hoebea E, Fukushim M, Peters G (2007) Irinotecan-Induced Cytotoxicity to Colon Cancer Cells *in-vitro* is Stimulated by Pre-Incubation with Trifluorothymidine. E. J. Cancer 43: 175-183.

[61] Wei G, Yan M, Ma L, Zhang H (2012) The Synthesis of Highly Water-Dispersible and Targeted CdS Quantum Dots and it is used for Bioimaging by Confocal Microscopy. Spectrochim. Acta Part A 85: 288-292.

[62] Abbasalipourkabir R, Abdullah A (2011) Cytotoxicity Effect of Solid Lipid Nanoparticles on Human Breast Cancer Cell Lines. Biotech. 10: 528-533.

[63] Pourgholami M, Wangoo K, Morris D (2008) Albendazole-Cyclodextrin Complex: Enhanced Cytotoxicity in Ovarian Cancer Cells. Anticancer Research 28: 2775-2780.

[64] Yong K, Indrajit Roy I, Swihart M,Prasad P(2009) Multifunctional Nanoparticles as Biocompatible Targeted Probes for Human Cancer Diagnosis and Therapy. J. Mater. Chem. 19: 4655–4672.

[65] Glazer E, Steven A. Curley S, (2010) Radiofrequency Field-Induced Thermal Cytotoxicity in Cancer Cells Treated with Fluorescent Nanoparicles. Cancer 116: 3285-3293.

[66] Das M, Mishra D, Maiti T, Basak A, Pramanik P (2008) Bio-Functionalization of Magnetite Nanoparticles Using an Aminophosphonic Acid Coupling Agent: New,

Ultradispersed, Iron-Oxide FlateNanoconjugates for Cancer-Specific Targeting. Nanotechnology 19: 415101 (14pp).

[67] Ahrens E, Feili-Hariri M, Xu H, Genoye G, Morel P (2003) Mag. Reso. Med. 49: 1006-13.

[68] Gao X, Cui Y, Levenson R, Chung L, Nie, S. (2004) In-vivo Cancer Targeting and Imaging with Semiconductor Quantum Dots. Nat. Biotechnol. 22: 969.

[69] Gerion D, Chen F, Kannan B, Fu A Parak W, Chen D, Majumdar A, Alivisatos A (2003) Anal. Chem. 75: 4766

[70] Mitchell, G. P.; Mirkin, C. A.; Letsinger, R. L. (1999) J. Am. Chem. Soc. 121: 8122.

[71] Han M, Gao X, Su J, Nie S (2001) Nat. Biotechnol. 19: 631.

[72] Patolsky F, Zheng G, Hayden O, Lakadamyali M, Zhuang X, Lieber C (2004) Electrical Detection of Single Viruses. Proc. Natl. Acad. Sci. 101: 14017.

[73] Wang J, Musameh M (2003) Enzyme-Dispersed Carbon-Nanotube Electrodes: A Needle Microsensor for Monitoring Glucose. Analyst 128: 1382.

[74] Hahm J, Lieber C (2004) Direct Ultrasensitive Electrical Detection of DNA and DNA Sequence Variations Using Nanowire Nanosensors. Nano Lett. 4: 51.

[75] Klumpp C, Kostarelos K, Prato M, Bianco A (2006) Functionalized Carbon Nanotubes as Emerging Nanovectors for the Delivery of Therapeutics. Biochim. Biophys. Acta-Biomembr. 1758: 404–12.

[76] Kostarelos K et al (2007) Cellular Uptake of Functionalized Carbon nanotubes is Independent of functional Group and Cell Type. Nat. Nanotechnol. 2: 108–113.

[77] Cui D, Tian F, Ozkan C, Wang M, Gao H (2005) Effect ofSingle Wall Carbon Nanotubes on Human HEK293 Cells. Toxicol. Lett. 155: 73–85.

[78] AshaRani A, Mun G, Hande M, Valiyaveettil S (2009) Cytotoxicity and Genotoxicity of Silver Nanoparticles in Human Cells. ACS Nano. 2: 279-290.

[79] Sanpui P, Chattopadhyay A, Ghosh S (2011) Induction of Apoptosis in Cancer Cells at Low Silver Nanoparticle Concentrations using Chitosan Nanocarrier ACS Appl. Mater Interfaces. 3: 218-228.

[80] Salata O (2004) Applications of Nanoparticles in Biology and Medicine. J. Nanobiotech. 2: 1-6.

Chapter 5

# Integrated Biomimemic Carbon Nanotube Composites for Biomedical Applications

L. Syam Sundar, Ranjit Hawaldar, Elby Titus,
Jose Gracio and Manoj Kumar Singh

Additional information is available at the end of the chapter

http://dx.doi.org/10.5772/48385

## 1. Introduction

In recent years Nanotechnology form a fascinating interdisciplinary area that brings together biology, material science, and nanoelectronics. Moreover, mainly three different applications of nanotechnology particularly suited to biomedicine: diagnostic techniques, drugs, and prostheses and implants. Interest is booming in biomedical applications for use outside the body, such as diagnostic sensors and "labon- a-chip" techniques, which are suitable for analyzing blood and other samples, and for inclusion in analytical instruments for R&D on new drugs. For inside the body, many companies are developing nanotechnology applications for anticancer drugs, implanted insulin pumps, and gene therapy. Nanotechnology also has applications in the tissue engineering field, helping people who are in need of new bones, teeth, or other body tissues by replacing damaged or missing tissue with an equivalent material. The biological material is introduced into a mould to produce a body part with a characteristic shape, a bone for example. There is a long list of these devices such as orthopedic joint prostheses cardio vascular aids and dental implants; however the theme prepared aims only the first one; orthopedic joint prostheses, with particular emphasis on hip and knee ortheoplasty. Survival of the arthroplasty depends among others on the age of the patient. In patients over 65, failure rate after ten years is about 7 %. In younger patients (<60 year) failure rates are significantly higher (>15%). As the number of arthroplasties will grow due to the ageing of our population, a considerable percentage of this increase will consist of revision arthroplasties. Because results of revisions are worse than those of primary arthoplasties, improved procedures for placement of joint prostheses have to be found. Therefore, an implant made of a mechanically strong material that can support and even enhance the integration of orthopedic implants will increase the clinical effectiveness of bone implants and will make it less likely that the implants will wear out and need to be replaced. The worldwide emergence of nano scale science and engineering will make viable the production of enhanced biomaterials with high compatibility of interacting with the human biological systems.

Of significant biological importance when utilizing this technology is to exercise control over mechanical properties at the material-biological interface (Discher et al., 2005). Manipulation of mechanical properties within these systems can dictate cell response and affect many physiological responses (LeDuc and Robinson, 2007; LeDuc and Bellin, 2006). CNTs have already been employed in the mechanics of materials domain for decades because of their high strength, which makes them ideal for a variety of applications including polymeric composite systems. Their successes *in vivo* though have been inhibited by physiological challenges as the promise of introducing pristine nonfunctionalized CNTs in polymer matrixes has been limited because this type of nanomaterial is practically insoluble and can accumulate in cells, organs, and tissues with dangerous effects (Zanello et al., 2006; Lam et al., 2004). This problem has been overcome, however, by chemically modifying the surfaces of the CNTs, which addresses the solubility challenges in most solvents and polymers (Colvin, 2003; Ajayan and Tour, 2007; Coleman et al., 2006).

However, current joint implants last only 10 to 15 years before failing. Because of this, many patients have to go through a revision surgery due to the failure of bone implants. The main reason for implant failure is aseptic loosening of the implant from juxtaposed bone. In this light, polymethyl methacrylate (PMMA) has been used widely in orthopedics to improve the bonding between the implant and bone. In total hip replacement procedures, PMMA cement is located at the bone-implant interface and plays an important role in inhibiting the aseptic loosening processes. PMMA cement is associated with several drawbacks that limit its efficacy (such as strong exothermic reactions, weak radiopacity and poor fatigue strength; all leading to insufficient bonding to bone). With an expectation of increased revision surgeries and patients receiving orthopaedic implants in the coming years, the emphasis of joint replacement research needs to be focused on improving the mechanical and biocompatibility properties of bone cements. As nanotechnology has been extensively used to improve mechanical and surface properties of implant materials, it certainly provides a unique opportunity to modify the material properties of currently used bone cements in a more precise manner.

For developing a biologically inspired composite system, there are numerous available composite materials. One particular area that has shown promise is in using bone cements such as PMMA. PMMA has been extensively used in orthopaedic surgery as a biomaterial that fixes artificial joints to bone and fills bone defects, as well as a drug-delivery system (Rimessi et al., 2009). One well documented issue with bone cements is that the fixation strength of PMMA cement to bone is primarily dependent on mechanical characteristics. To address this, a complementary material, hydroxyapatite (HA) (Singh et al., 2008), has been used with PMMA. HA is a prime constituent of bone cements and is particularly useful for a diversity of reasons including its ability to bond chemically with living bone tissues as well as its chemical and crystalline similarity to human skeletal apatite. These systems alone though exhibit intrinsic brittleness and poor strength, thus restricting its clinical applications under load-bearing conditions (Curtin and Sheldon, 2004; Vallo et al., 2004; McGee et al., 2000; Stevens, 2008).

In the present chapter we will review the previous bone cements, future prospects and application of carbon nanotubes based nanocomposites for the development of next generation active bone cement for biomedical applications, which have been particularly relevant in our research group at TEMA.

## 2. Polymethylmethacrylate (PMMA) or bone cement

Polymethylmethacrylate (PMMA), a clear plastic, is a pretty versatile material. Plexiglas windows are made from PMMA. Acrylic paints contain PMMA. It also remains one of the most enduring materials in orthopedic surgery where it has a central role in the success of total joint replacement. Being part of a group of medical materials called 'bone cement', its use includes the fixation of biomaterials such as artificial joints to bone, the filling of bone defects and, also, as a drug-delivery system. Beginning in the 1970s, many successful results have been reported for total hip replacement using PMMA cement; however, failures of fixation have also occurred. The fixation strength of PMMA cement to bone is mainly dependent on mechanical interlocking, but it is known that a fibrous tissue layer intervenes between cement and bone - PMMA cement never bonds directly to the bone. One of the problems associated with the conventional types of bone cement used is their unsatisfactory mechanical and exothermic reaction properties. Other problems with PMMA cement include the biological response, leakage of the monomer of methylmethacrylate and a high curing temperature, which can damage cell activity. Ideally, a bone cement material must functionally match the mechanical behavior of the tissue to be replaced, it must be able to form a stable interface with the surrounding natural tissue and be effective in guided tissue regenerative procedures, it should be easy to handle, biologically compatible, non-supporting of microbial growth, and non-allergenic.

## 3. Hydroxyapatite (HA)

Hydroxyapatite (HA) is another key constituent of bone cements because of its ability to bond chemically with living bone tissues; this is due to its similar chemical composition and crystal structure to apatite in the human skeletal system. However, the intrinsic brittleness and poor strength of sintered HA restricts its clinical applications under load-bearing conditions.

## 4. Carbon nanotubes

Carbon nanotubes (CNTs) are allotropes of carbon with a cylindrical nanostructure. Nanotubes have been constructed with length-to-diameter ratio of up to 132,000,000:1 (Dai, 2002) significantly larger than for any other material. These cylindrical carbon molecules have unusual properties, which are valuable for nanotechnology, electronics, optics and other fields of materials science and technology.

Carbon nanotubes are the strongest and stiffest materials yet discovered in terms of tensile strength and elastic modulus respectively. This strength results from the covalent $sp^2$ bonds formed between the individual carbon atoms. In 2000, a multi-walled carbon nanotube was tested to have a tensile strength of 63 giga pascals (Gpa) (Yu et al., 2000). Further studies, conducted in 2008, revealed that individual CNT shells have strengths of up to ~100 GPa, which is in good agreement with quantum/atomistic models (Peng et al., 2008). Since carbon nanotubes have a low density for a solid of 1.3 to 1.4 g/cm$^3$ (Collins, 2000) its specific strength of up to 48,000 kN-m/kg is the best of known materials, compared to high-carbon steel's 154 kN-m/kg. Standard single-walled carbon nanotubes can withstand a pressure up to 24 GPa without deformation. They then undergo a transformation to super hard phase nanotubes. Maximum pressures measured using current experimental techniques are around 55GPa. The bulk modulus of superhard phase nanotubes is 462 to 546 GPa, even higher than that of diamond (420) GPa for single diamond crystal) (Popov, 2003).

### 4.1. Dispersion of functionalized carbon nanotubes in the water

Commercially available (purity >95%, Nanocyl-3150) multi-walled carbon nanotubes with lengths of 1-5 μm and diameters of 5-10 nm were suspended in 3:1 mixture of concentrated $H_2SO_4$ (18.4 M)/$HNO_3$(16M) and sonicated in a water bath for 24 hours. The resulting suspension was then diluted with water, and the MWCNTs were collected on a 100-nm-pore membrane filter and washed with deionized water. The resultant functionalized MWCNTs (MWCNTs-COOH) were investigated by FTIR (Nicolet AVATAR-360 FT-IR spectrophotometer) and visible micro-Raman spectra (Jobyin Ivon T64000, $\lambda$=514.5 nm). IR spectra of COOH functionalized MWCNTs shows carbonyl stretching at 1729 cm$^{-1}$ but in Raman spectra this signal is inactive. In Raman spectra a band centred at 1300 cm$^{-1}$ is attributed to $sp^3$-hybridized carbon in the hexagonal framework of the nanotube walls. This disorder mode band is enhanced, as functional groups are attached to the side walls of the nanotubes (Ying et al., 2003; Dyke and Tour, 2003; Georgakilas et al., 2002; Dyke and Tour, 204; Wang and Tseng, 2007). Acid-base titrations (Zho and Stoddart, 2009; Tsang et al., 1994) were performed to determine the concentration of COOH groups for acid-treated MWCNTs. The result indicates that around 3% Carbon atoms are functionalized with COOH groups.

To obtain a homogeneous dispersion of MWCNTs-COOH in water, it was used an aqueous dispersant "NanoSperse AQ" (http://www.nano-lab.com/dispersant-suspensions.html) a surfactant, which consists mainly of poly (oxy-1,2-ethanediyl), tertramethyl-5-decyne-4,7-diol and butoxyethanol, respectively. The typical procedure involves mixing of 100 mg of MWCNTs-COOH in 100 ml of distilled water with 4 ml of dispersant, and then keeping the mixture in a ultrasonication bath for one hour. The final product presents a black colour with no settling of MWCNTs (Figure 1).

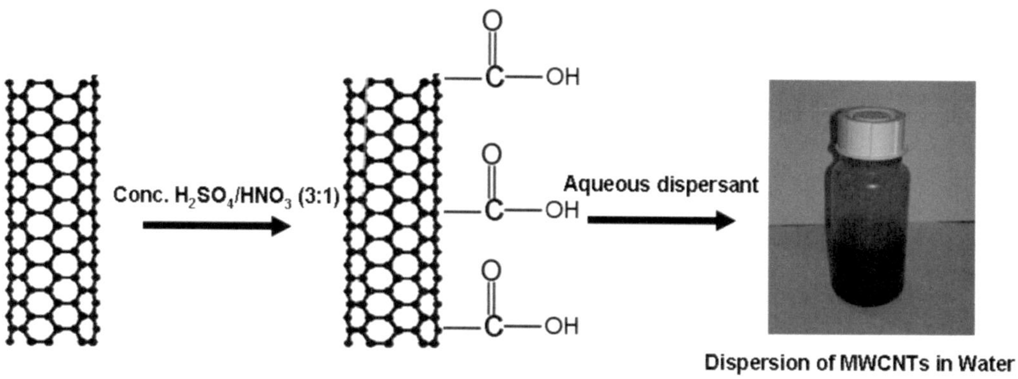


**Figure 1.** Schematic diagram for chemical fictionalization of MWCNTs and their dispersion in water

## 5. Carbon nanotube-reinforced poly (methyl methacrylate) nanocomposite for bone cement application

Carbon nanotubes, due to their small dimensions and high aspect ratio, exhibit exceptional physical and chemical properties (Iijima, 1991; Baughman et al., 2002; Usui et al., 2008). No other material can compete with their outstanding combination of mechanical, thermal and electronic properties, which makes them an outstanding reinforcement material for composites (Goller et al., 2003; Cholpek et al., 2006; Price et al., 2003; Peigney, 2003). The ideal reinforcement material would impart mechanical integrity to the composite at high loadings, without diminishing its bioactivity. Hydroxyapatite (HA) is the prime constituent of bone cements, because of its ability to bond chemically with living bone tissues due to its similar chemical composition and crystal structure to apatite in the human skeletal system. However, the intrinsic brittleness and poor strength of sintered HA restricts its clinical applications under load-bearing conditions (Dimitrievska et al., 2008; White and Best, 2007). The polymethyl methacrylate is another material commonly used as bone cement; however, its low mechanical strength makes the use of PMMA problematic. In the present work, a novel nanocomposite material was synthesized comprising MWCNTs, PMMA and HA, which promises to be a superior material for biomedical applications. The selection of PMMA was made for two main reasons: (i) PMMA is already used as bone cement, and it is highly compatible with HA, and (ii) MWCNTs are highly stable in its original form and PMMA can act as a functionalizing and linking material with HA.

There are two main goals when preparing the MWCNTs/PMMA/HA nanocomposite, namely: (i) to obtain homogenous dispersion of the MWCNTs, ensuring uniform properties throughout the composite, and (ii) to enhance the interaction between the MWCNTs and mixing material to achieve an appropriate level of interfacial stress transfer. The dispersion of the MWCNTs is probably the most pressing issue. The MWCNTs should be uniformly dispersed to guarantee that they are individually coated with PMMA-modified HA composite, which is imperative in order to have an efficient load transfer to the MWCNTs network. This also results in a more uniform stress distribution and minimizes the presence of loci of high stress concentration. To this purpose the percentage of MWCNTs in the nanocomposite material should be controlled – a large amount of MWCNTs cause them to bundle up in weakly interacting tubes as a result of the van der Waals attraction (Kis et al., 2004), and, moreover, it will decrease the interfacial interaction between the mixing material and the MWCNTs.

### 5.1. Freeze-granulation technique to produce the nanocomposite of PMMA and HA with dispersed MWCNTs

The well dispersed MWCNTs mixture in water was obtained for four different weight percentages of MWCNTs, namely 0.01%, 0.1%, 0.5% and 1% MWCNTs, respectively. Each solution was mixed with a composite of commercially available PMMA (high viscosity bone cement purity >99%, Johnson and Johnson Co.) and HA (particle size 2-3 μm with purity >98%, Agoramat-Advanced Materials) in 1:2 weight percentage. The homogenous mixture of HA powders and PMMA were prepared by ball-milling (Satish Kumar et al., 1996; Tsang et al., 1994; Chen et al., 2005; Walker et al., 2007; Poudyal et al., 2004). There is no effect on HA powder size distribution during ball milling it restricts agglomeration of HA powder during mixing of PMMA with HA.

The *freeze-granulation technique* (Power Pro Freeze-granulator L5-2, Sweden) was performed with the objective of drying the nanocomposite of MWCNTs-reinforced PMMA/HA powder to preserve the material homogeneity and enhance the dispersion of the nanoparticles in the composite matrix. Figure 2 shows the schematic diagram for the step-by-step procedure, which yields the synthesis of MWCNTs-reinforced PMMA/HA nanocomposite using the *freeze-granulation technique*. Granules with no cavities can be performed and no migration of small particles will give a high degree of granule homogeneity, while mild drying avoids oxidation of the powder. Also, lower granule density and the aid of evenly distributed low concentration MWCNTs will give softer granules with a wide granule size distribution. The freeze dried nano-particles were then collected and finally dried in vacuum for 3 days. In order to dry any remaining liquid the nano-composite was kept for 24 hours in the oven set at 40°C.

### 5.2. Surface characterization and mechanical properties

Field-Emission Scanning Electron Microscopy (Hitachi S-800, and SU-70, 30 keV) was performed to study the dispersion and distribution of the MWCNTs in PMMA modified HA matrix. The phase composition and purity of the samples were investigated by using the Philips Xpert-MPD X-ray powder diffractometer with Co K$\alpha$ radiation at 45 kV and 40 mA. Room temperature micro-Raman studies were also performed to study the integration of MWCNTs with the PMMA-HA nanocomposite material. Figures 3-6 show the surface morphology of the MWCNTs-reinforced samples for 0.00%, 0.01%, 0.1% and 1.0% of MWCNTs, respectively. From the SEM observations for different concentrations of MWCNTs reinforced samples, it is clearly observed the concentration of 0.1% of MWCNTs yields the best reinforcement for the PMMA/HA nanocomposite (Figures 5 a,b). For 0.1%

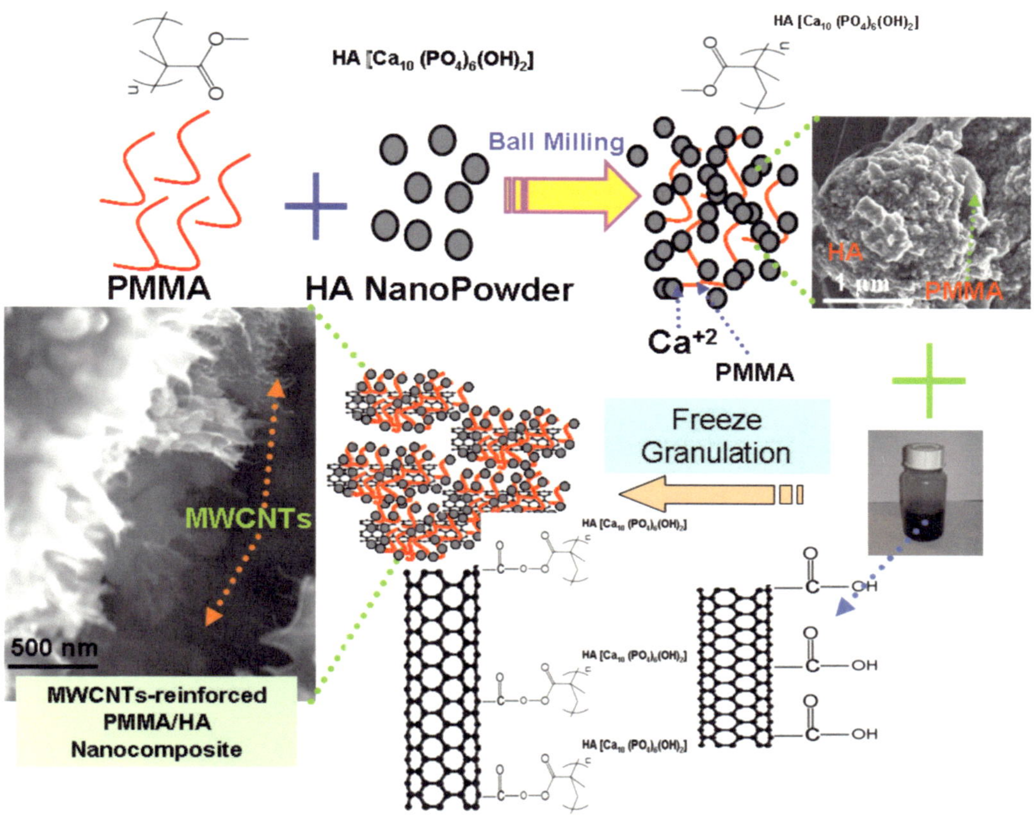


**Figure 2.** Schematic diagram for the formation of MWCNTs-reinforced PMMA/HA nanocomposite by the freeze-granulation technique

oncentration of MWCNTs, an intercalation of the PMMA/HA composite inside the MWCNTs distribution does occur (Figures 6 a,b), leading to an increase in the MWCNTs dispersion. Below this concentration, the mutual interaction between two adjacent MWCNTs is practically non-existent, which tends to decreases the homogeneity of the nanotubes inside the PMMA/HA matrix. Figure 2 depicts the surface morphology of the 0.01% MWCNTs -PMMA/HA nanocomposite. At higher nanotube concentrations, because less PMMA/HA is available to intercalate into the MWCNTs distribution may lead to weak bonding between the PMMA/HA and MWCNTs, making the composite weak in strength. The SEM image of 1% MWCNTs -PMMA/HA composite shows agglomeration of MWCNTs into bundles. This indicates that the PMMA/HA did not intercalate into the bundles. Only the outside nanotubes of a bundle can be bonded to the composite (Figure 5.6).

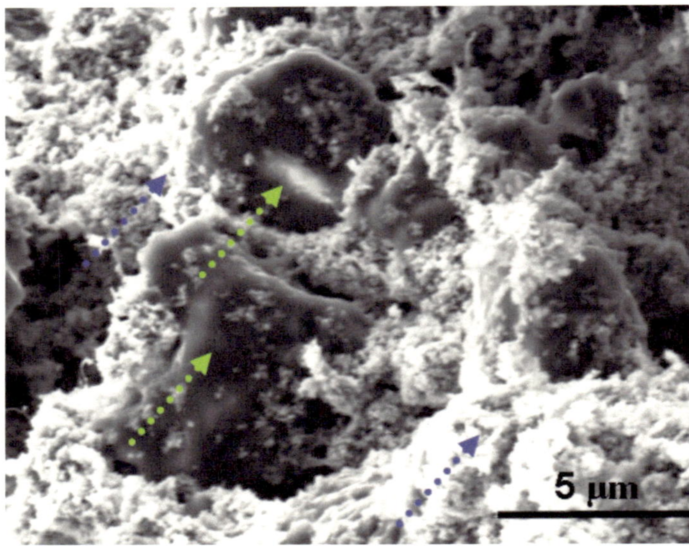


**Figure 3.** FE-SEM image showing the surface morphology of 0.00% MWCNTs-PMMA/HA nanocomposite, prepared by ball milling. The blue and green dotted arrows indicate HA and PMMA phases in the PMMA/HA composite.

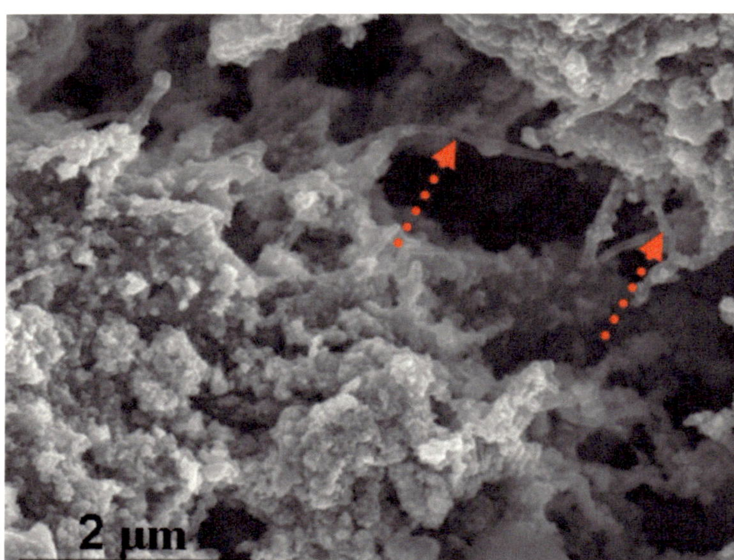


**Figure 4.** FE-SEM image showing the surface morphology for 0.01% MWCNTs -PMMA/HA nanocomposite, prepared by *freeze-granulation technique*. From this image (indicated by a red dotted arrow), it can be observed that some MWCNTs sheathed with the PMMA/HA nanocomposite.

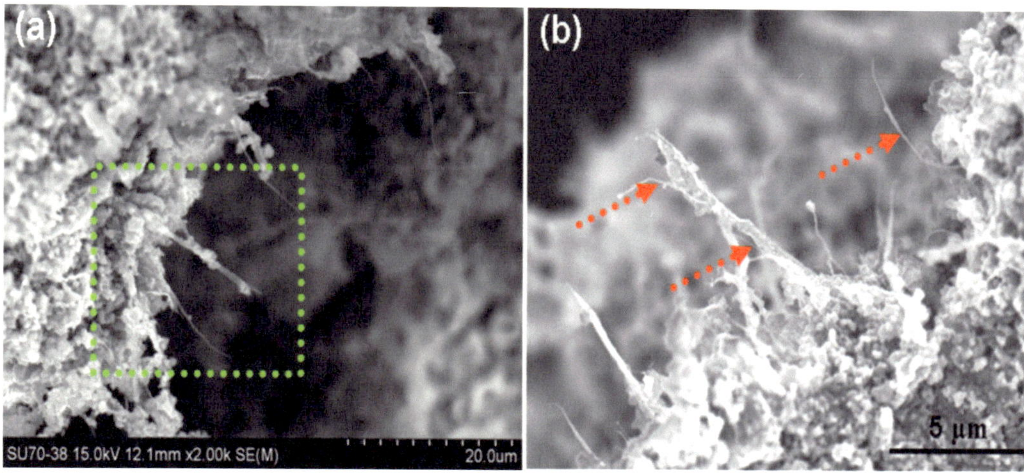


**Figure 5.** (a) FE-SEM image showing the surface morphology of 0.1% MWCNTs-PMMA/HA nanocomposite. (b) Shows the highly magnified SEM image of the area denoted by a green dotted square in (a) and the red dotted arrows point to isolated MWCNTs, which are completely covered by the PMMA/HA matrix.

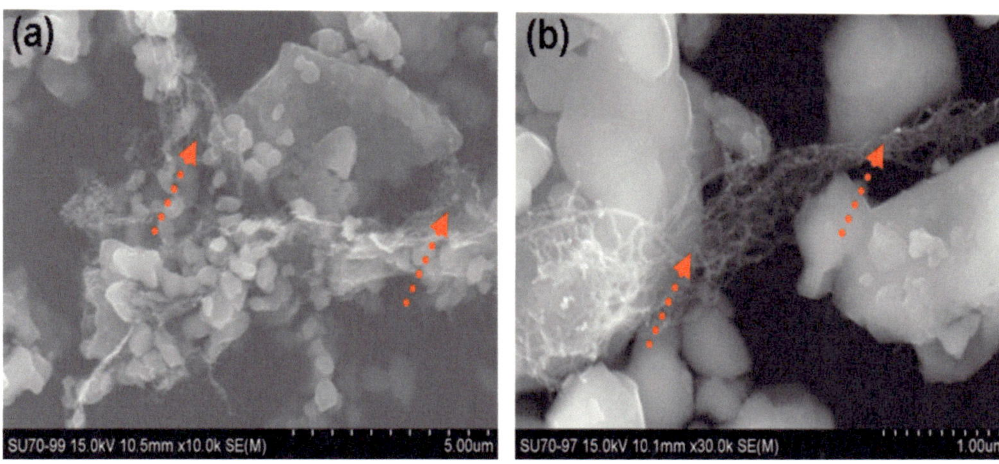


**Figure 6.** (a,b) FE-SEM images performed at various locations of the 1% MWCNTs -PMMA/HA composite sample shows agglomeration of MWCNTs networks (denoted by the red dotted arrows). This indicates that PMMA/HA did not intercalate into the networks; therefore, only the outside nanotubes of a network can bind to the composite.

Figure 7 illustrates the X-ray diffraction (XRD) patterns of PMMA, HA and 0.1% MWCNTs-PMMA/HA, respectively. It is clearly shown the main constituent phases of the composite are crystalline HA (Haque et al., 2007; Bouyer et al., 2000) (JCPDS 09-0432). No MWCNTs peaks were found in the XRD pattern of the 0.1% MWCNTs-PMMA/HA composite, most likely because for small percentages of MWCNTs detection is not possible within the sensitivity limit of XRD. Miller indices of the diffraction peaks are given in parentheses. PMMA, which is an amorphous polymer (Meneghetti et al., 2004), shows a broad peak at $2\theta$

value of 13°. The shape of the most intense broad peak reflects the ordered packing of polymer chains (Ryu et al., 2004).

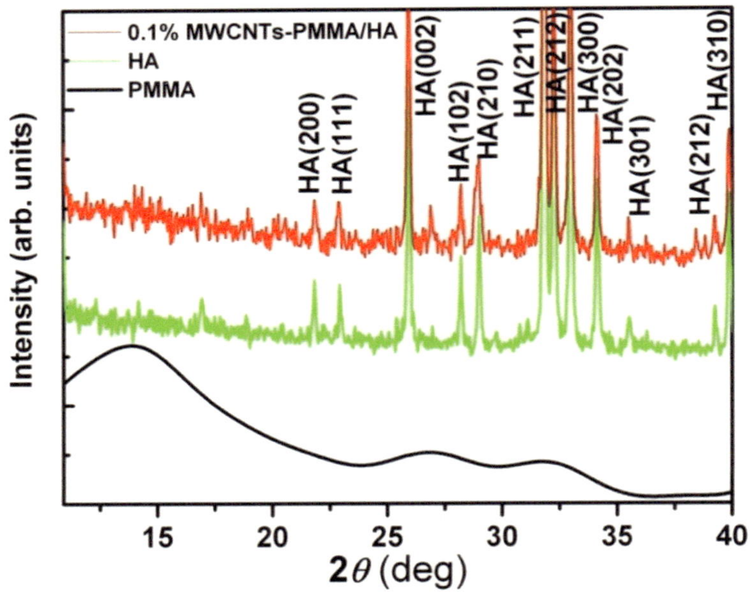


**Figure 7.** XRD results of PMMA, HA and 0.1% MWCNTs-PMMA/HA, respectively, in the composite. PMMA presents a broad amorphous peak at $2\theta$ value of 13°.

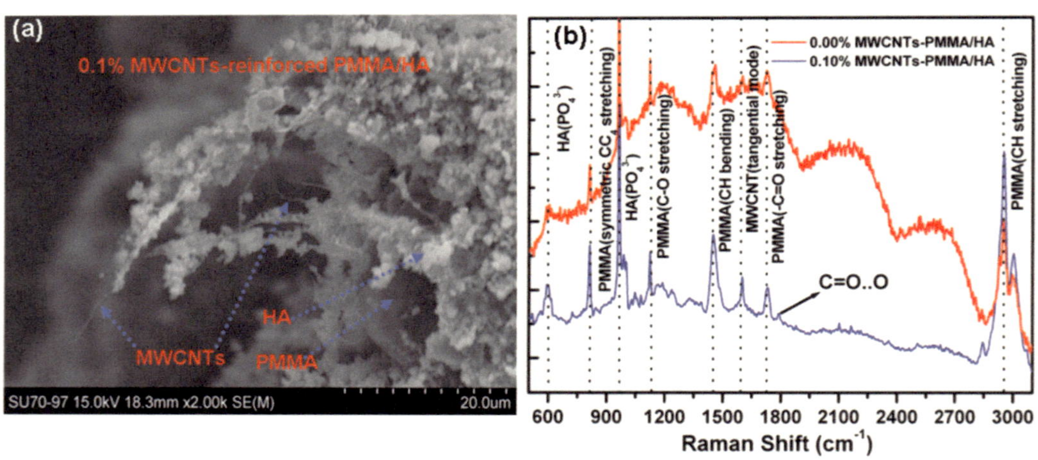


**Figure 8.** (a) FE-SEM image of 0.1% MWCNTs-reinforced PMMA/HA sample prepared by *freeze-granulation technique* (b) Raman spectra (denoted by the blue line) collected from a 0.1% MWCNTs-reinforced PMMA/HA sample shown in (a).

The visible Raman spectra collected from the 0.1% MWCNTs-reinforced PMMA/HA sample (Figure 8a) denoted by a blue line in Figure 8b, shows several distinct features. The feature near 1773 $cm^{-1}$ is attributed to C=O. O bonded and indicates that $COO^-$ functional groups in functionalized MWCNTs interact with C=O of PMMA (Velasco-Santos et al., 2003; Velasco-Santos et al. 2002; Hong et al., 2002). Also, it can be observed several other peaks at 602 ($PO_4^{3-}$), 962 ($PO_4^{3-}$), 1592 (tangential mode) and 814 (symmetric $CC_4$ stretching), 1452 (CH bending), 1123 (C-O stretching), 1724 (-C=O stretching), 2952 (CH stretching) $cm^{-1}$ which are due to the HA, MWCNTs and PMMA, respectively (Paillet et al., 2004; de Mul et al., 1986; Suzuki et al., 1991; Kim et al., 2004; Matsushite et al., 2000).

Nanoindentation tests were performed using a MTS Nano Indenter XP with a Berkovich diamond tip. Hardness and elastic modulus of the PMMA/HA nano-composite with different percentage of MWCNTs were measured as a function of the indentation depth using a continuous stiffness measurement (CSM) method. The typical nanoindentation test consists of seven subsequent steps: approaching the nanocomposite surface; determining the contact point; loading to peak load; holding the tip for 10 s at the peak load; unloading 90% of peak load; holding the tip for 100 s at 10% of the peak load for thermal drift correction; and finally, unloading completely. The hardness and elastic modulus were obtained from the curves using the Oliver-Pharr method (Suzuki et al. 1991).

In the present work the nanoidentation technique is employed to study the variation of the mechanical properties of MWCNTs-reinforced PMMA/HA composite with different concentrations of MWCNTs. Figure 9 displays the typical load-displacement curves at a peak indentation load of 10 mN on the MWCNTs-reinforced PMMA/HA composite; it clearly demonstrates that no cracks were formed during indentation. A considerable amount of creep strain at the peak load was found for all the samples. The holding segment at the peak load is necessary for the dissipation of creep displacement; most polymeric biomaterials and tissues often exhibit this type of time-dependent or viscoelastic behaviour (Li and Bhushan, 2002; Bhushan, 2003).

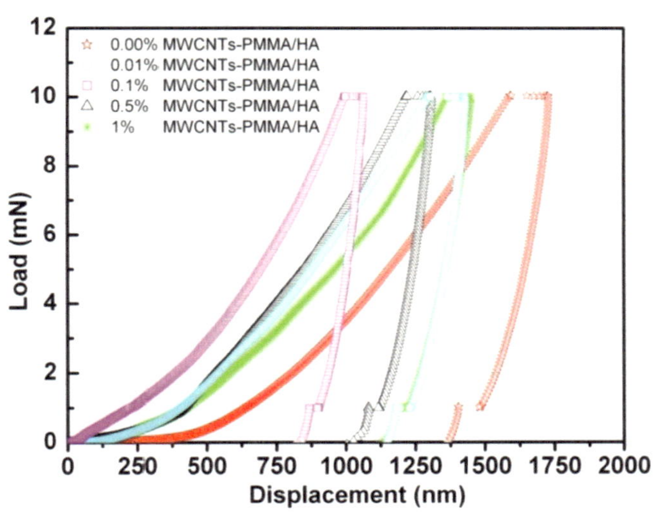


**Figure 9.** Typical load-displacement curves of indentations made at a peak indentation load of 10 mN on the PMMA/HA nanocomposite and its MWCNTs-reinforced samples.

To study the effect of dispersion of nanotubes in the PMMA/HA composite, hardness and elastic modulus values are needed for both small and large indentation depths. Thirty two nanoindentation tests were carried out on each sample, and the experimental errors are ±0.60 GPa for the elastic modulus and ±0.05 GPa for the hardness. The hardness and elastic modulus values as a function of the indentation depth for PMMA/HA and its MWCNTs reinforced samples are presented in Figure 10 and the average hardness and elastic modulus for these composites are listed in Table I. It can be observed the hardness and elastic modulus of these composites increase with increasing MWCNTs content up to 0.1%. Beyond this value, as it can be noted from Figure 8a, an increase in MWCNTs content yields a considerable decrease of the hardness.

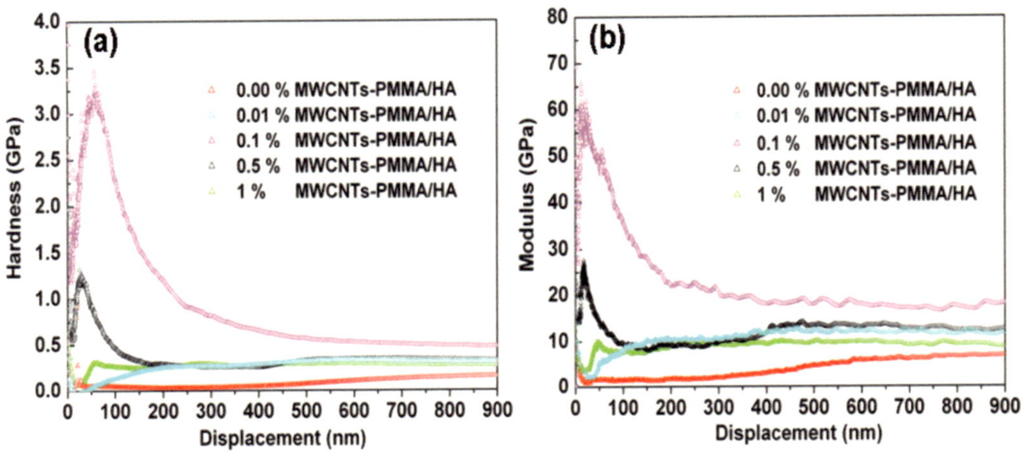


**Figure 10.** Hardness (a) and elastic modulus values (b) as a function of the indentation depth.

| | 0.00% MWCNTs-PMMA/HA | 0.01% MWCNTs-PMMA/HA | 0.1% MWCNTs-PMMA/HA | 0.5% MWCNTs-PMMA/HA | 1% MWCNTs-PMMA/HA |
|---|---|---|---|---|---|
| H (GPa) | 0.288 | 0.510 | 3.460 | 1.321 | 0.624 |
| E (GPa) | 5.949 | 14.022 | 69.528 | 28.08 | 10.56 |

**Table 1.** Average values of hardness and elastic modulus for different concentrations of MWCNTs in the PMMA/HA composite.

In a previous publication (Shokuhfar et al., 2007), the authors demonstrated that there are several key requirements for an optimal fibre-reinforced, polymer-based, composite system, namely: (a) The fibres should be long enough so that the stress developed within them is significantly larger than the nominal stress on the composite; (b) The cross-sectional area of the fibre should be as small as possible - the strength of the fibre is inversely proportional to the square root of its maximum flaw size; therefore for smaller cross-sectional areas the appearance of flaws is reduced; (c) The spatial arrangement of the fibres in the matrix has to be of a significant order to ensure a unidirectional, maximal reinforcement. Also self-consistent calculations lead to the conclusion that an isotropic arrangement of the fibres will result in the dilution of the reinforcement effect within the polymer matrix. Previously, the law of volumetric mixtures was used to analyse the mechanical behaviour of a continuous media of PMMA/HA with a blend of carbon nanotubes distributed in the matrix. According to the numerical calculations (Shokuhfar et al., 2007) carried out the Young Modulus of the composite increases with increasing MWCNTs concentration up to a concentration around 10 %. The present experimental results show that after a concentration of MWCNTs of 0.1 % a noticeable decrease of the Young Modulus is clearly identified (Figure 10b). This discrepancy may be due to the fact the modelling did not take into account two physical phenomena, which, in view of the experiments, are important, namely: 1) the interaction between nanotubes and 2) the character of the interface between the MWCNTs and the matrix. Increasing the MWCNT's concentration up to a certain level promotes a mutual interaction between a crossed pair and a coarse mesh of nanotubes (Figure 11).

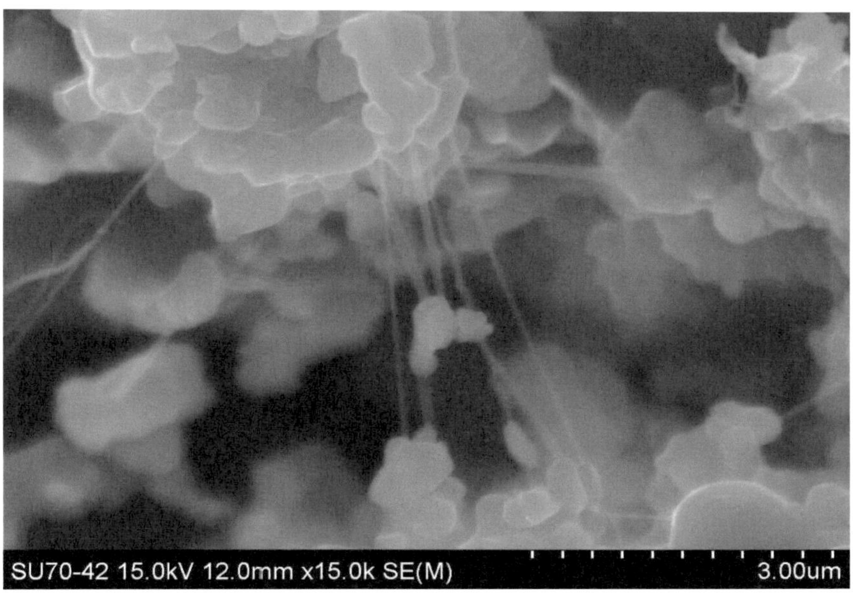


**Figure 11.** FE-SEM image showing mutual interactions between crossed pair of nanotubes.

Consequently, the set of nanotubes can act as a deformation lock, either in extensional or shear mode, giving rise to improved mechanical properties. An identical behaviour was noticed by analysing the effect of the MWCNTs concentration on a PMMA matrix (Akiskalos, 2004). It should be mentioned the SEM images clearly show that after a concentration of 0.1% for the MWCNTs, a drop of homogeneity in the nanotubes-matrix contact occurs, giving rise to the formation of voids and internal cavities with the eventual reduction in the mechanical performance of the composite. In fact, most likely, these defects act as nucleation for internal crack tips and mutual link-up modes, with a fast degradation of the structure integrity and eventual breakdown. Fatigue tests were performed in artificial bones to confirm this analysis (Figure 12). In the tests, after one million of cycles the nanocomposite with 0.1% of MWCNTs-PMMA/HA does not present any signal of crack propagation and delamination (Figures 12 a,b). But when we performed the same type of fatigue tests for only PMMA nanocomposite we can clearly observed the delamination and cracks in Figures 12c and d, respectively.

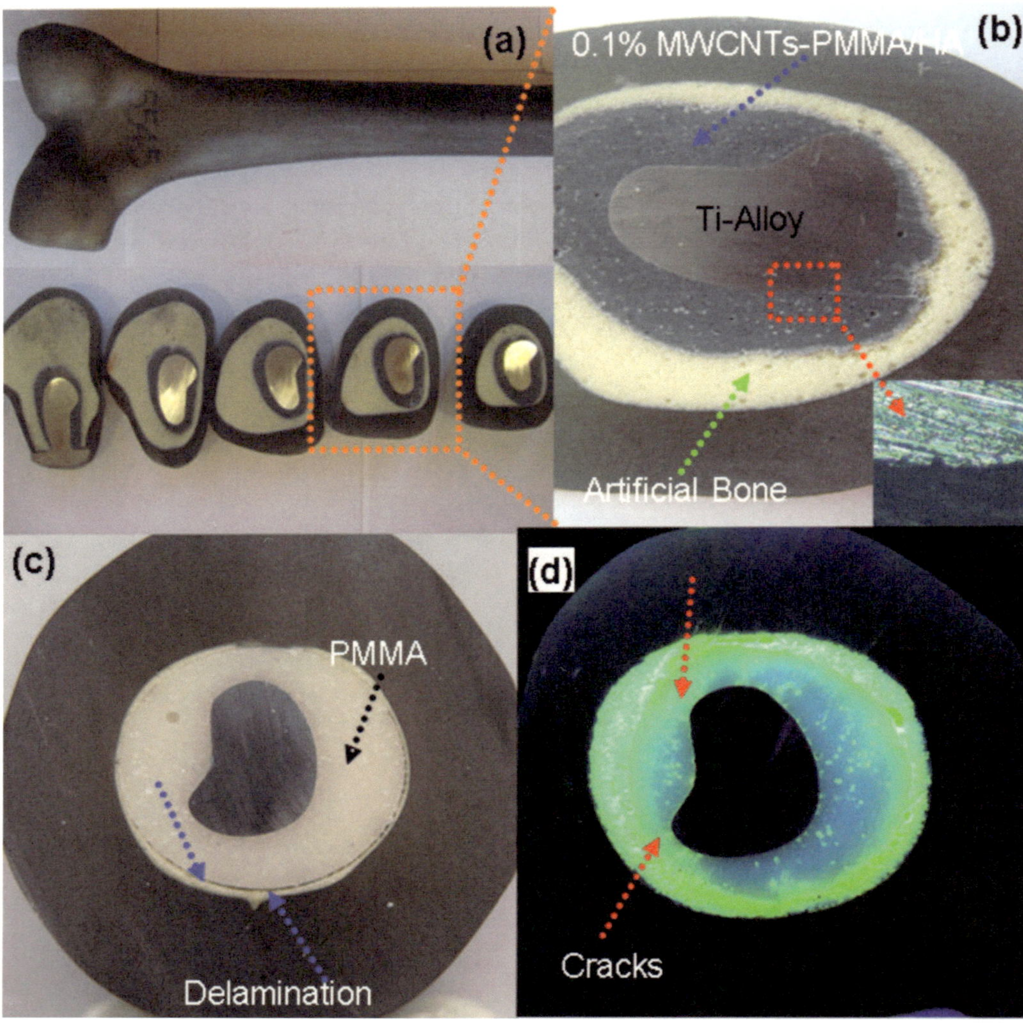


**Figure 12.** (a,b) Optical microscopic observation of the 0.1% MWCNTs-PMMA/HA nanocomposite at the interface with titanium prosthesis after a fatigue test for one million of cycles. (c,d) Optical microscopic image shows delamination and cracks after same type of fatigue test for only PMMA nanocomposite.

## 6. *In Vivo* studies of carbon nanotube-based nanocomposites

### 6.1. *In Vivo* methods

*Animal Model:* Following the experimental protocol approved by the National Ethics Committee for Laboratory Animals (Portugal) (Dias et al., 2008), two healthy, adult male sheep with average weight of 45 kg, were used for the *in-vivo* implantation. The sheep were permanently housed indoors in group housing and were kept under a constant photoperiod cycle (light: from 07:00 to 19:00 hours; dark: from 07:00 to 19:00 hours), temperature (20 ± 2 °C) and humidity (50 ± 10%). Food was withdrawn 36 hours, and water 6 hours prior to anaesthesia.

*Anesthetic and Surgical Method:* Surgery was performed under general anaesthesia, which was induced with pentobarbital through intravenous injection; the animals had been previously premedicated with xilazine and buprenorphine. The anaesthesia was maintained through using isoflurane administered with an endotracheal tube and spontaneous ventilation. An electrocardiogram (ECG) monitor and a pulsioximeter were used to monitor the condition of the animals. The antibiotherapy was initiated during surgery with amoxicillin (Clamoxyl) and these therapies were maintained for one week. The site of the surgery was prepped with a solution of Betadine (povidone-iodine) and alcohol (Dura-Prep; 3M Health Care, St. Paul, MN) after the animals were locally shaved. For the implantation of the bioactive bone cement in the tibia, the animals were placed in a dorsal recumbency position and a longitudinal incision was made on the frontal surface of the left and right tibia. After exposure of the tibial bone, the periosteum was reflected and a 2.5 mm diameter pilot hole was made with a surgical drill and then enlarged with low speed drilling to a 3.0 mm diameter. During the process, the bone was continuously perfused with a sterile saline solution. Three holes were drilled on each tibia as shown in Fig. 13a and then the holes were filled with the bioactive bone cement paste (Fig. 13b). The surgery field was covered with subcutaneous tissue and the skin was closed using absorbable Surgicryl ® 2–0 sutures.

An *in vivo* paste was prepared by thoroughly mixing a monomer solution of bioactive bone cement (Johnson and Johnson Co.) with our dry powder containing the COOH-MWCNTs-reinforced PMMA/HA nanocomposite. These components were mixed together just before the *in vivo* procedure; the resultant mixture was used as a viscous paste. This biocomposite was implanted into a sheep model system, in a similar manner to previous protocols (Dias et al., 2008; Henriksen et al., 2009). For the implantation, three holes were drilled in each tibia (Figure 13a) and then the holes were filled with the bioactive bone cement paste (Figure 13b). The field of the surgical procedure was covered with subcutaneous tissue, and the skin was closed using absorbable sutures. Post-operative X-ray tests were conducted to ensure that proper filling of the holes in the bone had occurred (Fig. 14i). Twelve weeks after implantation, the animals were sacrificed following the experimental protocol approved by the National Ethics Committee for Laboratory Animals (Portugal). The implanted material and the surrounding tissue were removed.

*Radiological and Histological Studies:* Post-operative X-ray tests were performed with a Mammodiagnost UC system (Philips) with 28 kV, 25 mA, using coarse focus and Kodak Min-R Screen film. Twelve weeks after implantation, the animals were sacrificed with an intravenous dose of sodium pentobarbital (Eutasil®). The implanted materials and the surrounding tissue was removed The bone specimens for the histological evaluation were fixed in 4% buffered formaldehyde, dehydrated in graded alcohols and embedded in methyl methacrylate (Merck Supplier Part: 8.00590.1000). After polymerization, non-decalcified 30 μm sections were obtained in the transversal direction using a saw microtome (Leica 1600) and then ground with silicon carbide powder. Thin sections were prepared of each specimen for evaluation by light microscopy (Eclipse 600, Nikon Japan). The bone sections were stained with toluidine blue (Brancroft and Stevens, 1996; Schipper et al., 2008).

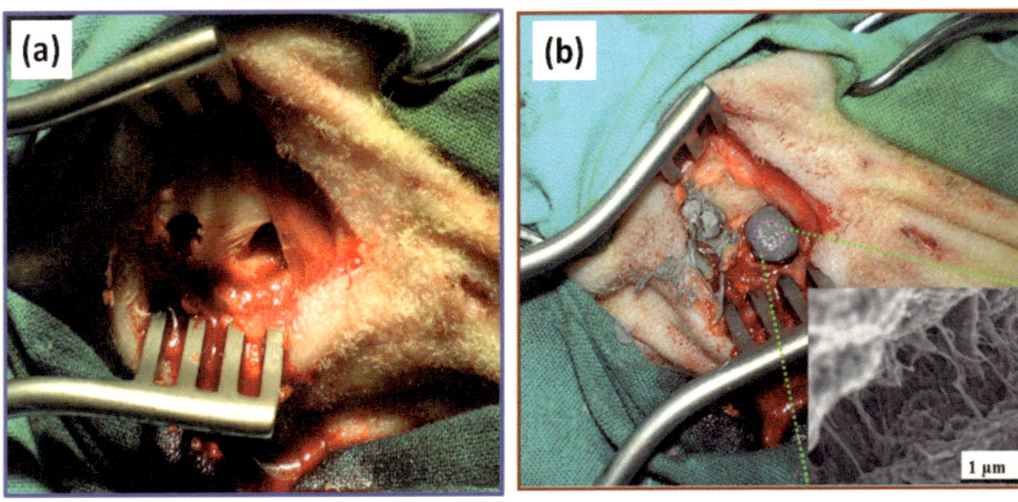


**Figure 13.** (a) Optical image of three holes drilled in tibial bone of a sheep before implantation (b) Digital image of filling the bone during the surgical procedure with the bioactive bone cement paste in three holes of a sheep tibia.

To examine the *in vivo* response with the nanocomposites, x-ray tests were performed. After twelve weeks the inflammatory reactions in the surrounding tissues were examined. X-rays of the left tibia were captured immediately after surgery (Fig. 14i) and then after 12 weeks (Fig. 14ii). The drilled cavities, as indicated by an asterisk in Figures 14(i) and (ii), had been invaded by the marrow region. Also, there were no signs of periosteal or bone negative reactions twelve weeks after implantation. Figures 14(iii-vi) provided a histological evaluation of the stained specimens obtained twelve weeks after implantation. The periosteum covering the outer surface of the implant and the cortical bone at the interface did not show any adverse reaction to the implants (Fig. 14iii,iv). Furthermore, the contact between the cement and the bone showed no fibrous tissues or inflammatory cells as observed in Figure 14(iii). Osteocytes (denoted by red dotted circle in Fig. 14iii) were clearly observed. At higher magnifications, a favourable interface between bone and the cement was observed (Fig. 14iv). However, in the areas where there was no direct contact between

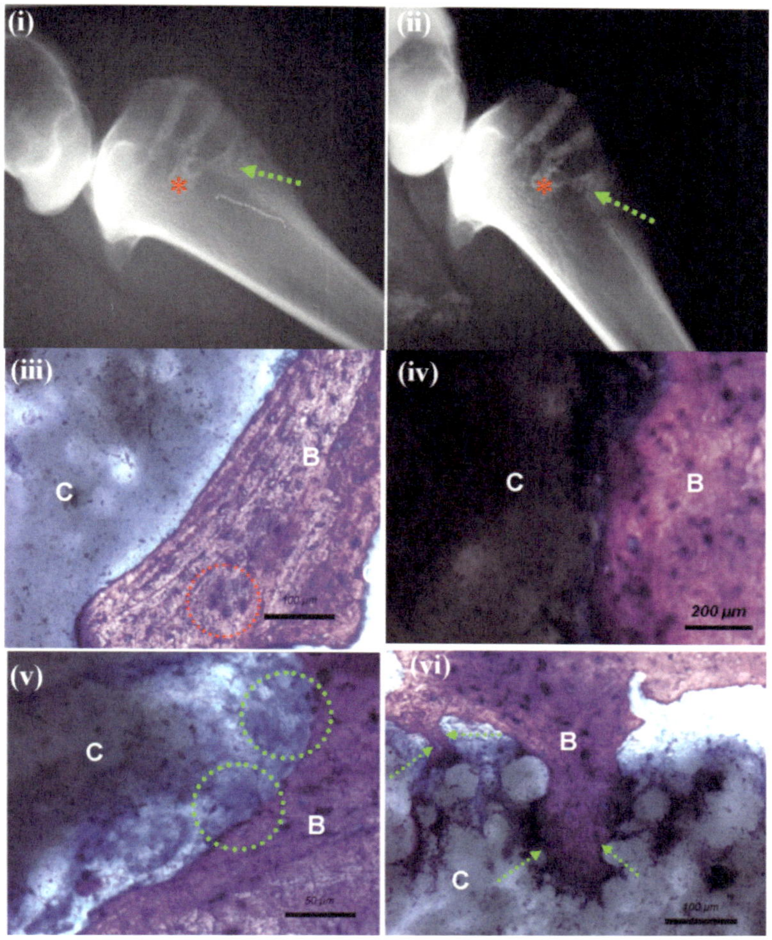


**Figure 14.** *In-vivo* response with the nanocomposite bone cement in sheep. (i) X-rays (left tibia) immediately after surgery and (ii) after 12 weeks. Invasion of the marrow region (indicated by the asterisk) and restoration of the cavities is observed. There are no inflammatory reactions in the surrounding tissues after 12 weeks. (iii) An image of Giemsa surface staining of the specimens at 12 weeks after implantation shows excellent contact between the nanocomposite PMMA-HA-CNT bioactive-bone cement (C) and the bone tissue (B) with no fibrous tissues and no inflammatory cell infiltration. Oteocytes, which are indicated by the red dotted circle regions, are observed (iv) An image of Giemsa surface staining focusing on the interface between the nanocomposite bioactive-bone cement and the tissue (C) and the bone tissue (B), which is very favourable. (v) An image of Giemsa surface staining focusing revealing multinuclear osteoclast-like cells covering the surface of the bone cement, as indicated by the green dotted circles; there was no direct contact between bioactive-bone cement (C) and bone tissue (B) generally observed. (vi) An image of Giemsa surface staining focusing showing that the new bone (B) clearly enters into the pores of the bone cement (C), as indicated by the green dotted arrow.

the bone and the implant, osteoclast-like-cell (Yavropoulou and Yovos, 2008) appeared on the cement surface (indicated by the green dotted circle in Fig. 14v). Furthermore, in our specimens (Fig. 14vi), new bone (B) clearly penetrated the pores of the bone cement (C), as indicated by the green dotted arrow. The biocompatibility and osteoconductivity are critical factors as foreign material reside *in-vivo*. A post-mortem examination of the tibias revealed that the implants were completely covered by the periosteum. This finding was determined by fixing the regional lymph nodes with 4% formaldehyde, embedding them in paraphin, and then cutting them into 30 μm sections with a microtome (Leica, Jung RM 2045). The specimens were stained with hematoxylin/eosin to examine the biocompatibility and osteoconductivity responses. The histological response of the regional lymph nodes revealed no significant morphologic changes in the regional lymph nodes between the control and test groups. The histological evaluations demonstrate that the CNT-reinforced composite with the bioactive-bone cement responded favourably as a tibial bone implant based on its osteoconductivity and biocompatibility results. This biocompatibility has been demonstrated for an extended time period of 12 week post-operation for our 0.1% MWCNTs-PMMA/HAp nanocomposites.

## 7. Conclusions

Herein, we demonstrate a *freeze-granulation technique* to synthesis a novel nanocomposite of carbon nanotube reinforced PMMA/HA for next generation biomedical applications. By using this method it is possible to increase material homogeneity and also optimize the % of MWCNTs in the PMMA/HA matrix. We shows that the concentration of 0.1% of MWCNTs performs the best reinforcement for the PMMA/HA nanocomposites. The hardness and elastic modulus of MWCNTs-reinforced PMMA/HA nanocomposites increase with the increasing concentration of nanotubes up to around 0.1% in weight. Beyond this limit, further addition of MWCNTs in PMMA/HA matrix yields a considerable decrease of these mechanical properties. This can be explained in terms of the nanotube-matrix contact homogeneity – a further increase of the nanotubes may lead to the formation of voids and internal cavities, which can negatively impact the mechanical performance of the composite.

In addition to this, we have found that the use of COOH-functionalized MWCNTs reinforced with PMMA/HA will provide tremendous advancements in the field of regenerative medicine. Of singular importance is the mechano-physical advantage this nanocomposite, which provides for bearing mechanical loads and promoting osteointegration with surrounding bone tissues. These are features not observed with previous materials. Our *in vivo* animal studies shows, new bone extended into the bioactive bone cement. These results confirm that this novel bionanocomposite will be an excellent candidate for bone integration due to its osteoconductivity and biocompatibility. We believe that these results will have applications in a diversity of areas including nanotechnology, biomaterials, and regenerative medicine.

## Author details

Manoj Kumar Singh*, L. Syam Sundar, Ranjit Hawaldar, Elby Titus, Jose Gracio
*Centre for Mechanical Technology and Automation (TEMA), University of Aveiro, 3810-193 Aveiro, Portugal*

* Corresponding Author

## Acknowledgement

The author Manoj Kumar Singh would like to thank FCT, Portuguese Foundation of Science and Technology, Project under Ciencia 2007 Fellowship Program (http://www.fct.mces.pt/ciencia2007/in dexEN.asp)

## 8. References

D.E. Discher, P. Janmey, Y. Wang, Tissue Cells Feel and Respond to the Stiffness of Their Substrate, Science, 2005, 310, 1139-1143.

P.R. LeDuc, D.R. Robinson, Using lessons from cellular and molecular structures for future materials, Adv. Mater., 2007, 19(22), 3761–3770.

P.R. LeDuc, R.R. Bellin, Nanoscale intracellular organization and functional architecture mediating cellular behaviour, Ann. Biomed Eng., 2006, 34 (1), 102-13.

L.P. Zanello, B. Zhao, H. Hu, R.C. Haddon, Bone cell proliferation on carbon nanotubes, Nano Letters, 2006, 6, 562.

C.-W. Lam, J.T. James, R. McCluskey, R.L. Hunter, ulmonary toxicity of single-wall carbon nanotubes in mice 7 and 90 days after intratracheal instillation, Toxicological Sciences, 2004, 77, 126.

V.L. Colvin, The potential environmental impact of engineered nanomaterials, Nat. Biotechnology, 2003, 21, 1166-1170.

P.M. Ajayan, J.M. Tour, Nanotube composites, Nature, 2007, 447, 1066-1068.

J.N. Coleman, U. Khan, Y.K. Gun'ko, Mechanical Reinforcement of Polymers Using Carbon Nanotubes, Adv. Mater., 2006, 18, 689–706.

P. Rimessi, P. Sabatelli, M. Fabris, P. Braghetta, E. Bassi, P. Spitali, G. Vattemi, G. Tomelleri, L. Mari, D. Perrone, A. Medici, M. Neri, M. Bovolenta, E. Martoni, N.M. Maraldi, F. Gualandi, L. Merlini, M. Ballestri, L. Tondelli, K. Sparnacci, P. Bonaldo, A. Caputo, M. Laus, A. Ferlini, Cationic PMMA Nanoparticles Bind and Deliver Antisense Oligoribonucleotides Allowing Restoration of Dystrophin Expression in the mdx Mouse, Molecular Therapy, 2009, 175, 820-827.

M.K. Singh, T. Shokuhfar, J. Gracio, A.C.M. Sousa, J. Fereira, H. Garmestani, S. Ahzi, Hydroxyapatite Modified with Carbon-Nanotube-Reinforced Poly(methyl methacrylate): A Nanocomposite Material for Biomedical Applications, Adv. Funct. Mater., 2008, 18, 694-700.

W.A. Curtin, B.W. Sheldon, CNT-reinforced ceramics and metals, Mater. Today, 2004, 7, 44.

C.I. Vallo, G.A. Abraham, T.R. Cuadrado, J.S. Roman, Influence of cross-linked PMMA beads on the mechanical behavior of self-curing acrylic cements, J. Biomed Mater Res. B, 2004, 70, 407-416.

M.A. McGee, D.W. Howie, K. Costi, D.R. Haynes, C.I. Wildenauer, M.J. Pearcy, J.D. McLean, Implant retrieval studies of the wear and loosening of prosthetic joints: a review, Wear, 2000, 241, 158-165.

M.M. Stevens, Biomaterials for bone tissue engineering, Mater. Today 2008, 11, 18-25.

H. Dai, Carbon nanotubes: opportunities and challenges, Surf Sci., 2002, 500, 218.

Min-Feng Yu, Oleg Lourie, Mark J. Dyer, Katerina Moloni, Thomas F. Kelly, Rodney S. Ruoff, Strength and Breaking Mechanism of Multiwalled Carbon Nanotubes Under Tensile Load, Science, 2000, 287 (5453) 637–640.

Bei Peng, Mark Locascio, Peter Zapol, Shuyou Li, Steven L. Mielke, George C. Schatz, Horacio D. Espinosa, Measurements of near-ultimate strength for multiwalled carbon nanotubes and irradiation-induced crosslinking improvements, Nature Nanotechnology, 2008, 3 (10) 626–631.

P.G. Collins, They are stronger than steel, but the most important uses for these threadlike macromolecules may be in faster, more efficient and more durable electronic devices, Scientific American, 2000, 67–69.

M. Popov, Superhard phase composed of single-wall carbon nanotubes, Physical Review B, 2003, 65 (3), 033408.

Y. Ying, R. K. Saini, F. Liang, A. K. Sadana and W. E. Billups, Functionalization of Carbon Nanotubes by Free Radicals, Org. Lett., 2003, 5, 1471.

C. A. Dyke, J. M. Tour, Solvent-Free Functionalization of Carbon Nanotubes, J. Am. Chem. Soc., 2003, 125, 1156.

V. Georgakilas, D. Voulgaris, E. Vazquez, M. Prato, D. M. Guldi,A. Kukovecz, H. Kuzmany, Purification of HiPCO Carbon Nanotubes via Organic Functionalization, J. Am. Chem. Soc., 2002, 124, 14318.

C. A. Dyke, J. M. Tour, Overcoming the Insolubility of Carbon Nanotubes Through High Degrees of Sidewall Functionalization, Chem. Eur. J., 2004, 10, 812.

T. Wang, C. Tseng, Polymeric carbon nanocomposites from multiwalled carbon nanotubes functionalized with segmented polyurethane, Journal of Applied Polymer Science, 2007, 105, 1642.

Y. Zho, F. Stoddart, Noncovalent Functionalization of Single-Walled Carbon Nanotubes. Accounts of Chemical Research, 2009, 42 (8), 1161-1171

S. C. Tsang, Y. K. Chen, P. J. F. Harris, M. L. H. Green, A simple chemical method of opening and filling carbon nanotubes, Nature, 1994, 372, 159.

S. Iijima, Helical microtubules of graphitic carbon, Nature, 1991, 354, 56.

R. H. Baughman, A. A. Zakhidov, W. A. de Heer, Carbon Nanotubes--the Route Toward Applications, Science, 2002, 787, 297.

Y. Usui, Y.K. Aoki, N. Narita, N. Murakami, I. Nakamura, K. Nakamura, N. Ishigaki, H. Yamazaki, H. Horiuchi, H. Kato, S. Taruta, Y.A. Kim, M. Endo, N. Saito, Carbon Nanotubes with High Bone-Tissue Compatibility and Bone-Formation Acceleration Effects. Small, 2008, 4, 240.

G. Goller, H. Demirkiran, F. N. Oktar, E. Demirkesen, Processing and characterization of bioglass reinforced hydroxyapatite composites, Ceram. Int., 2003, 29, 721

J. Cholpek, B. Czajkowska, B. Szaraniec, F. Beguin, In vitro studies of carbon nanotubes biocompatibility, Carbon, 2006, 44, 1106.

R. L. Price, M. C. Waid, K. M. Haberstroh, T. J. Webster, Selective bone cell adhesion on formulations containing carbon nanofibers, Biomaterials, 2003, 24, 1877

A. Peigney, Composite materials: Tougher ceramics with nanotubes, Nat. Mater., 2003, 2, 15.

S. Dimitrievska, J. Whitfield, S.A. Hacking, M.N. Bureau, Novel carbon fiber composite for hip replacement with improved in vitro and in vivo osseointegration. J Biomed Mater Res A, 2008, 91 (1) 37-51

A. A. White, S. M. Best, Hydroxyapatite–carbon nanotube composites for biomedical applications: a review, Int. J. Appl. Ceram. Technol., 2007, 4, 1.

A. Kis, G. Csanyi, J. -P. Salvetat, T. -N. Lee, E. Couteau, A. J. Kulik, W. Benoit, J. Brugger, L. Forro, Reinforcement of single-walled carbon nanotube bundles by intertube bridging, Nat. Mater., 2004, 3, 153.

B. C. Satishkumar, A. Govindaraj, J. Mofokeng, G. N. Subbanna, C. N. R. Rao, Novel experiments with carbon nanotubes: opening, filling, closing and functionalizing nanotubes, J. Phys. B, 1996, 29, 4925.

S. C. Tsang, Y. K. Chen, P. J. F. Harris, M. L. H. Green, Nature, 1994, 372, 159.

Y. Chen, C. H. Gan, T. H. Zhang, G. Yu, P. Bai and A. Kaplan, Laser-surface-alloyed carbon nanotubes reinforced hydroxyapatite composite coatings, Appl. Phys. Lett., 2005, 86, 251905.

A. M. Walker, Y. Tao, J. M. Torkelson, Polyethylene/starch blends with enhanced oxygen barrier and mechanical properties: Effect of granule morphology damage by solid-state shear pulverization, Polymer, 2007, 48, 1066.

N. Poudyal, B. Altuncevahir, V. Chakka, K. Chen, T. D. Black, J. Liu, Y. Ding, Z. L. Wang, Field-ball milling induced anisotropy in magnetic particles , J. Phys. D: Appl. Phys., 2004, 37, L45.

S. Haque, I. Rehman, J. A. Darr, Synthesis and characterization of grafted nanohydroxyapatites using functionalized surface agents, Langmuir 2007, 23, 6671.

E. Bouyer, F. Gitzhofer, M. I. Boulos, Journal of Materials Science: Materials in Medicine, 2000, 11, 523.

P. Meneghetti, S. Quantubuddin, S. Webber, Synthesis of polymer gel electrolyte with high molecular weight poly(methyl methacrylate)–clay nanocomposite, Electrochim Acta, 2004, 49, 4923

J. G. Ryu, S. W. Park, H. Kim, J. W. Lee, Power ultrasound effects for in situ compatibilization of polymer-clay nanocomposites, Materials Science and Engineering C, 2004, 24, 285.

C. Velasco-Santos, A. L. Martìnez-Hernández, F. T. Fisher, R. Ruoff, V. M. Castaño, Improvement of Thermal and Mechanical Properties of Carbon Nanotube Composites through Chemical Functionalization, Chem. Mater., 2003, 15, 4470.

C. Velasco-Santos, A. L. Martìnez-Hernández, M. Lozada-Cassou, A. Alvarez-Castillo, V. M. Castaño, Chemical functionalization of carbon nanotubes through an organosilane, Nanotechnology, 2002, 13, 495.

P. P. Hong, F. J. Boerio, S. D. Smith, Surface segregation in blends of polystyrene and deuterated polystyrene, Macromolecules, 2002, 35, 5140.

M. Paillet, V. Jourdain, P. Poncharal J. Sauvajol, J. C. Meyer, B. Chaudret, Versatile Synthesis of Individual Single-Walled Carbon Nanotubes from Nickel Nanoparticles for the Study of Their Physical Properties, J. Phys. Chem. B, 2004, 108, 17112.

F. F. M. de Mul, M. H. J. Hottenhuis, P. Bouter, J. Greve, J. Arends, J. J. Ten Bosch, Micro-Raman line broadening in synthetic carbonated hydroxyapatite, J. Dent Res., 1986, 65, 437.

M. Suzuki, H. Kato, S. Wakumoto, Vibrational Analysis by Raman Spectroscopy of the Interface Between Dental Adhesive Resin and Dentin, J. Dent Res., 1991, 70, 1092.

S.B. Kim, Y.J. Kim, T.L. Yoon, S.A. Park, I.H. Cho, J.K. Eun, I.A. Kim, J. Shin, The characteristics of a hydroxyapatite-chitosan-PMMA bone cement. Biomaterials, 2004, 25, 5715-5723.

A. Matsushita, Y. Ren, K. Matsukawa, H. Inoue, Y. Minami, I. Noda, Y. Ozaki, Two-dimensional Fourier-transform Raman and near-infrared correlation spectroscopy studies of poly (methyl methacrylate) blends: 1. Immiscible blends of poly(methyl methacrylate) and atactic polystyrene, Vibrational Spectroscopy, 2000, 24, 171.

X. Li, B. Bhushan, A review of nanoindentation continuous stiffness measurement technique and its applications, Mater. Charact. 2002, 48, 11.

B. Bhushan, X. Li, Nanotribology and nanomechanics in nano/biotechnology, Int. Mater. Rev. 2003, 48, 125.

T. Shokuhfar, E. Titus, G. Cabral, A. C. M. Sousa, J. Gracio, W. Ahmed, T. I. T. Okpalugo, A. Makradi, S. Ahzi, On the mechanical properties of nanocomposite hydroxypatite (HA)/PMMA/CNT , International Journal of Nanomanufacturing, vol. 1, no. 2, pp. 107-115, 2007

T. Shokuhfar, A. Makradi, E. Titus, G. Cabral, S. Ahzi, A. C. M. Sousa, S. Belouettar, J. Gracio, Hydroxyapatite Modified with Carbon-Nanotube-Reinforced Poly(methyl methacrylate): A Nanocomposite Material for Biomedical Applications, Journal of Nanoscience and Nanotechnology 2007 in press.

T. Akiskalos, MSc Thesis, Department of Mechanical Engineering, Massachusetts Institute of Technology (MIT) 2004.

I.R. Dias, C.A. Viagas, J.T. Azevedo, E.M. Costa, P. Lourenco, A. Rodrigues, A.S. Cabrita, Assessment of markers of bone formation under controlled environmental factors and their correlation with serum minerals in adult sheep as a model for orthopaedic research, Laboratory Animals, 2008, 42, 465-472.

K. Henriksen, A.V. Neutzsky-Wulff, L.F. Bonewald, M.A. Karsdal, Local communication on and within bone controls bone remodeling, Bone, 2009, 44, 1026-1033.

J.D. Brancroft, A. Stevens, Theory and practice of histological techniques, Edinburgh: Churchill Livingstone, 1996, 99-211.

M.L. Schipper, N. Nakayama-Ratchford, C.R. Davis, N.W.S. Kam, P. Chu, Z. Liu, X. Sun, H. Dai, S.S. Gambhir, A pilot toxicology study of single-walled carbon nanotubes in a small sample of mice., Nature Nanotechnology, 2008, 3, 216-221.

M.P. Yavropoulou, J.G. Yovos, Osteoclastogenesis-Current knowledge and future perspectives, J. Musculoskelet Neuron

Section 2

# Biomedical Devices and Instrumentation

Chapter 6

# Implementation of Schottky Barrier Diodes (SBD) in Standard CMOS Process for Biomedical Applications

David Sebastiao Cabral, Robson Luiz Moreno,
Tales Cleber Pimenta, Leonardo Breseghello Zoccal and Paulo Cesar Crepaldi

Additional information is available at the end of the chapter

http://dx.doi.org/10.5772/48434

## 1. Introduction

Cost, size, lifetime and safety are important parameters when designing an RFID based biomedical system, especially if the receiver is an implanted device.

For size reduction and extended lifetime, the receiver can be implemented without batteries, thus characterizing a passive tag. Therefore, it is necessary an RF link to make the communication path between the base unit and the transponder. Through the link and a proper protocol, information can be exchanged and energy can be delivered to the implant for its activation. Fig. 1 shows a typical RFID topology applied to biomedical applications (Brandl et al, 2005).

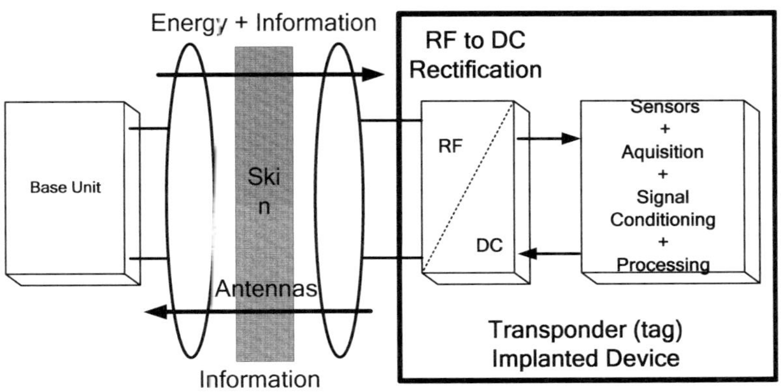


**Figure 1.** Typical RFID System.

As it can be observed, the energy is transmitted by a pair of coupled coils. For patient safety it is important to keep the induced electromagnetic fields at lower levels, to avoid tissues damages by raising the local temperature. The Specific Absorption Rate (SAR) represents direct measurements of the electric field (indirect measurement of the magnetic field) and induced current density over the human tissue at the implant location. The temperature variation over the time indicates the local heating factor. Both relations are given by (Pradier et al, 2005):

$$SAR = \frac{\sigma |E|^2}{\rho} \quad \left[ W/_{Kg} \right] \tag{1}$$

$$\frac{dT}{dt} = \frac{SAR}{c} \quad \left[ {}^{0}C/_{s} \right] \tag{2}$$

where σ, ϱ and c represent the conductivity, the human tissue mass density and specific heat capacity, respectively, at the implant location. *E* is the incident electric field intensity (RMS). Based on equations (1) and (2), a safe value for the power transferred by the RF link is $10mW/cm^2$.

Besides cost and size reduction, microelectronics also allows the implementation of the transponder circuits into a single die. The lowest prices can be achieved by using low cost standard CMOS technology.

Transponder front-end circuits include a rectifier to make the AC-DC conversion to provide unregulated power supply to the tag. In CMOS technology, NMOS and PMOS (more often than one of each type) transistors are used in different topologies to implement the rectifier circuit. These devices, however, have the disadvantage of presenting a turn on threshold voltage (Vth) that may require larger induced voltage in the receiver coil. Although the CMOS technology has been minimizing the transistors geometries, the Vth voltage does not scale down at the same rate. The use of a Schottky Barrier Diode – SBD is an alternative way to design the rectifier circuit in order to improve its efficiency. A more efficient rectifier will reduce the voltage drop between the tag input and the rest of the circuitry, thus reducing the power demand from the transmitter. For low currents levels, typically found in this kind of application, the SBD voltage drop can be lower than a CMOS Vth voltage.

The SBD is not readily implemented on a standard CMOS technology but after a few adjustments in the masking process, it can be implemented. In this work, a mask sequence is presented to implement SBDs in CMOS processes and a simple model for this device is discussed.

## 2. Conventional rectifier circuits

Basically, RFID systems can be divided into three major groups: active, semi-passive and passive tags. An active tag includes embedded batteries as their main energy source for autonomous operation. Semi-passive tags are also dependent on a battery for the start-up, however the required energy for the communication link is provided by the reader. A passive tag, on the other hand, extracts the full power from the signal transmitted by the reader, thus there is no need of an on-board power supply. This autonomous capability of passive tags offers some interesting features such as low production cost, increased reliability and a longer maintenance-free lifetime. The last one is very important considering inherent surgical procedures related to an implanted device.

A passive tag requires a circuit block to obtain the power transmitted from the base unit (known as reader) by the RF signal. This kind of circuit is a RF-DC converter or, simply, rectifier circuit.

Mainly for passive tags, it is important to have a highly efficient RF to DC conversion (the RF energy received at the tag decreases rapidly as a function of distance from the reader) and it is also desired a stable power supply at the rectifier output.

The available power at the tag antenna ($P_{AVAIL}$) can be expressed by (Kotani and Takashi, 2009):

$$P_{AVAIL} = \left(\frac{\lambda}{4\pi d}\right)^2 P_{EIRP} G_{TAG} \qquad (3)$$

where $\lambda$ is the wavelength of the RF link, $d$ is the distance between the base unit and the tag, $P_{EIRP}$ is the effective isotropic radiation power of the base unit transmitter, and $G_{TAG}$ is the tag antenna gain. The effective isotropic radiation power is determined by regulations, for instance, 4W for electronic product code (EPC) protocol in North America.

The tag antenna gain is manly determined by its area. Typically, $G_{TAG}$ is about 1.64 for a $\lambda/2$ dipole type.

In this scenario, the performance of the rectifier circuit, evaluated in terms of power conversion efficiency (PCE) should be as large as possible. The PCE can be expressed as:

$$PCE_{rect} = \frac{P_{out}}{P_{in}} \qquad (4)$$

where $P_{out}$ is the output DC power circuit and $P_{in}$ is the received RF input power.

By combining eq. (3) and (4), and considering the presence of impedance matching, it is possible to state the achievable power of an RFID tag:

$$P_{tag} = P_{EIRP} G_{TAG} PCE_{rect} \left(\frac{\lambda}{4\pi d}\right)^2 \qquad (5)$$

By analysing eq. (5) it is clear that the PCE is the most interesting variable to manipulate as a way to obtain, for instance, an increase in the communication range $d$.

In a typical RF-to-DC rectifier, PCE is mainly degraded as a result of two distinct mechanisms: forward voltage drop in the switches (closed related to the finite on-resistance of this switches) and their leakage currents.

Although typical RF-to-DC implementations also exhibit parasitic elements that contribute to lower the rectifier efficiency, they play a second-order effect.

Rectifier circuits for RFID tags are usually Dickson based rectifiers and designed using CMOS transistors. It must be clear that RFID applications are cost and area sensitive and the tag circuitry is often implemented in CMOS technologies that offer a high level of integration and relative low cost.

The voltage drop of a diode-connected transistor is approximately the threshold voltage ($V_{th}$) of the MOS transistor. The literature presents few proposals to reduce the threshold voltage, known as "$V_{th}$ cancelation". One of then, the external-$V_{th}$-cancelation (EVC), was proposed to for a semi-passive tag and depends on a gate bias voltage that is generated by a switched-capacitor circuit. Since the operation is switched, it requires an external power supply and clocking circuitry, and cannot be applied to passive-type RFIDs.

The internal-$V_{th}$-cancelation (IVC) was also proposed. In this case, gate bias voltage is generated internally from the output DC voltage by a bias generation circuit. This circuit works well under large input power conditions, but not otherwise since the gate bias voltages are generated by a voltage division mechanism. Regarding the efficiency, the IVC circuit dissipates an additional power due to the DC current, resulting in slightly degradation in PCE.

The self-$V_{th}$-cancelation (SVC) has the same topology of diode-connected CMOS rectifier circuit except that gates of the nMOS transistor and PMOS transistor are connected to the output and ground terminal, respectively. This connection boosts the gate source voltage of NMOS and PMOS transistors as much as possible, in other words, the threshold voltages are decreased by the same amount as the output DC voltage. The SVC provides better PCE than EVC and IVC implementations (Hashemi et al, 2012).

Fig. 2 and 3 shows examples of a conventional CMOS diode-connected rectifier and self-$V_{th}$-cancelation CMOS rectifier.

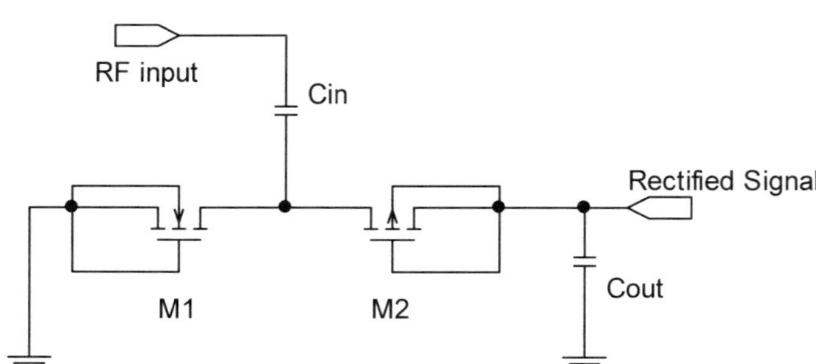


**Figure 2.** Conventional CMOS Type Rectifier Circuit.

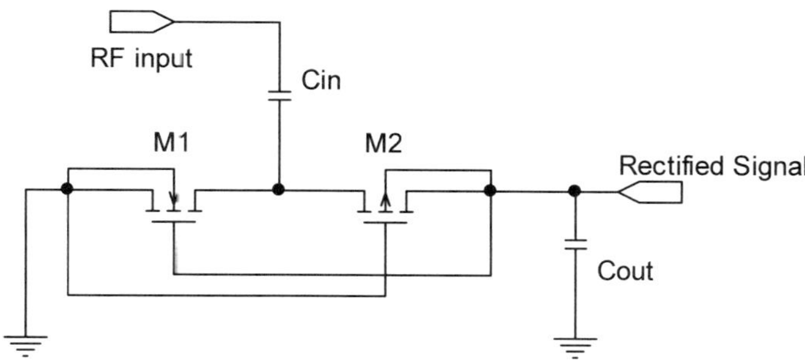


**Figure 3.** Self-$V_{th}$-Cancelation CMOS rectifier Circuit.

Another rectifier is the "four-transistor-cell" CMOS rectifier, which outperforms CMOS diode-based rectifiers, even when static $V_{th}$ cancelation technique is used to reduce the turn-on voltage of the diodes. In this configuration, the on-resistance of the CMOS transistors is decreased by increasing gate-source voltage $V_{GS}$ and reverse leakage is reduced by reversing the polarity of $V_{DS}$ in the cross-coupled structures. Fig. 4 illustrates an example of "four-transistor-cell" rectifier.

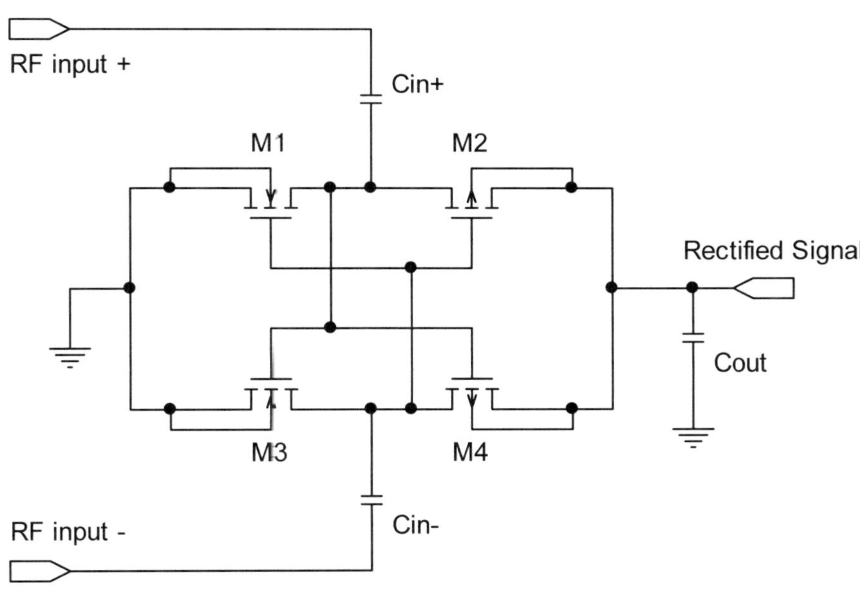


**Figure 4.** CMOS Four-Transistor-Cell Rectifier (Differential-Drive CMOS Rectifier).

The drawback of the four-transistor-cell topology is that it does not perform well when the received RF power is in the range of few μW. This problem is more pronounced when the tag is implemented in low-cost CMOS technologies, where the threshold voltage of NMOS and PMOS transistors lays in range o few hundred mV. There is the possibility that the transistors may not turn-on completely and the rectifier efficiency can be severely impaired.

The use of Schottky Barrier diodes in conventional Dickson rectifiers were considered as an attractive solution as a consequence of Schottky lower forward voltage drop and fast switching speed . Although, this kind of device is not readily supported in almost all CMOS technologies it is possible to be done with few mask flow changes. This chapter will show that procedure on a low-cost CMOS technology.

Fig. 5 shows the basic concept regarding a conventional Dickson rectifier with SBDs.

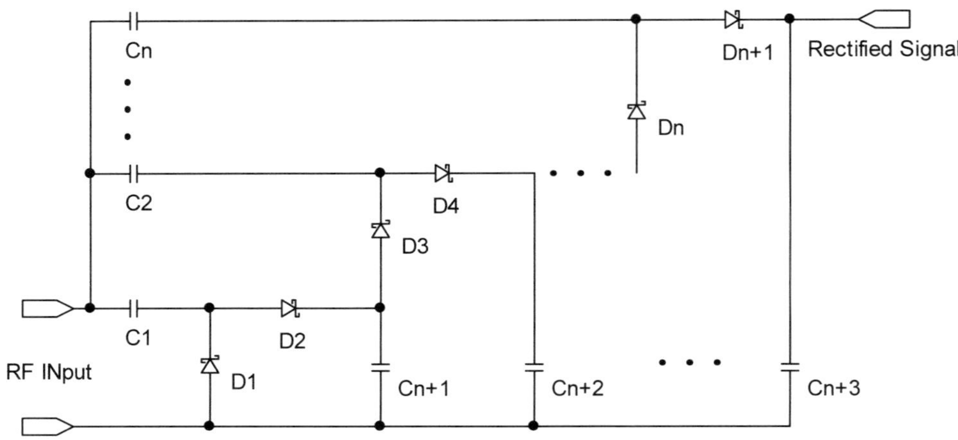


**Figure 5.** Basic Dickson Rectifier Circuit with SBD.

## 3. Silicon based Schottky Barrier Diode (SBD)

The Metal-Semiconductor contact (also called as Schottky Barrier Diode) has some features that allow its use in high frequency applications and systems that must operate at low voltage levels. These features are, basically, the low level of minority charge accumulation during commutation, which leads to high switching speeds and the low voltage drop between its terminals. Low turn on voltage, fast recovery time and low junction capacitance are advantages that SBD offer over other types of PN diodes. These are the main reasons that SBD are so popular in RF applications. Fig. 6 shows the energy band diagram for this kind of contact at thermal equilibrium. In this work, since we have used TSMC process, the metal is aluminium and the semiconductor is N-type, moderately doped, obtained by N Well diffusion (Janan et al, 2006), (Rainee and Philip, 2003) (Avenin, 1996).

As can be seen, there is a build in contact potential $V_{bi}$ expressed by:

$$V_{bi} = \phi_{BN} - \frac{kT}{q} ln\left(\frac{N_C}{N_D}\right) \tag{6}$$

where $kT/q$ is the thermal voltage (25.9mV at T=300K), $N_C$ is the effective state density (constant for a given temperature) in the conduction band, $N_D$ is the donor doping level and $\phi_{BN}$ is maximum height of the potential barrier (Streetman, 1980).

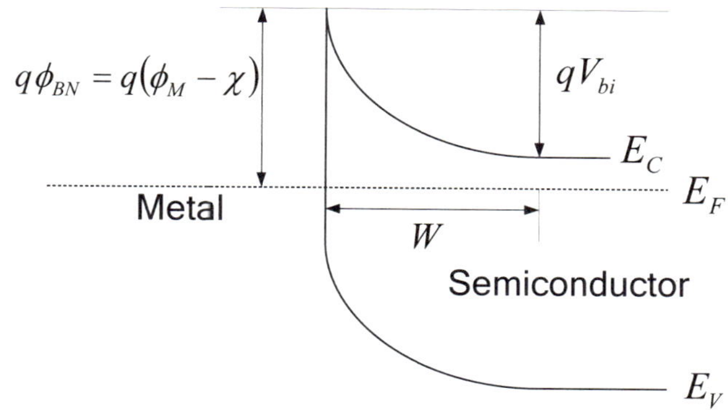


**Figure 6.** Energy Band Diagram for a Metal-Semiconductor Contact.

Eq. (6) shows that the built in voltage $V_{bi}$ can be reduced if a moderate to low doping semiconductor is used. Considering ideal values for metal work function ($\phi_M \approx 4.28V$) and semiconductor electron affinity ($\chi \approx 4V$), the barrier $\phi_{BN}$ can be as low as 280mV. Considering, yet, eq. (6), the built in voltage $V_{bi}$ can be further reduced by controlling the doping level $N_D$.

It must be necessary to evaluate the doping concentration $N_D$ in order to use eq. (6) to obtain *Vbi*. For this procedure a C-V curve for a Metal-Insulator-Semiconductor (MIS capacitor)) structure is used. Fig 7 and Fig. 8 show a typical MIS capacitor (with N type semiconductor) and a C-V curve, respectively.

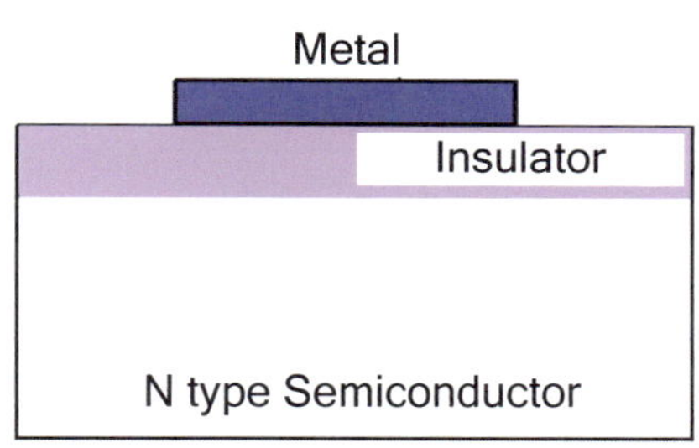


**Figure 7.** Metal-Insulator-Semiconductor (MIS) Capacitor.

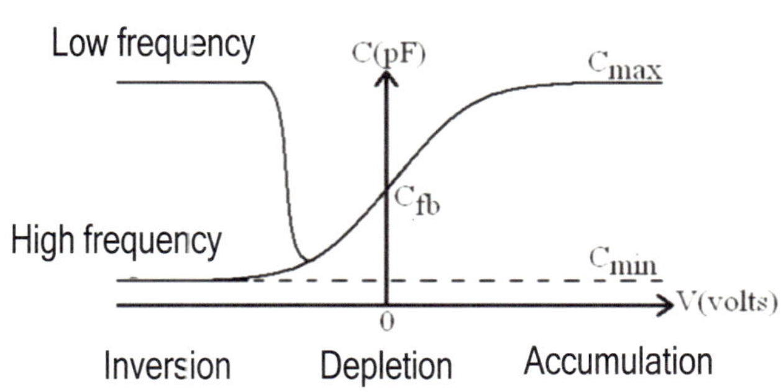


**Figure 8.** MIS C-V Curve.

The C-V curve can be obtained by simulating a PMOS transistor with TSMC model parameters as indicated in Fig. 9.

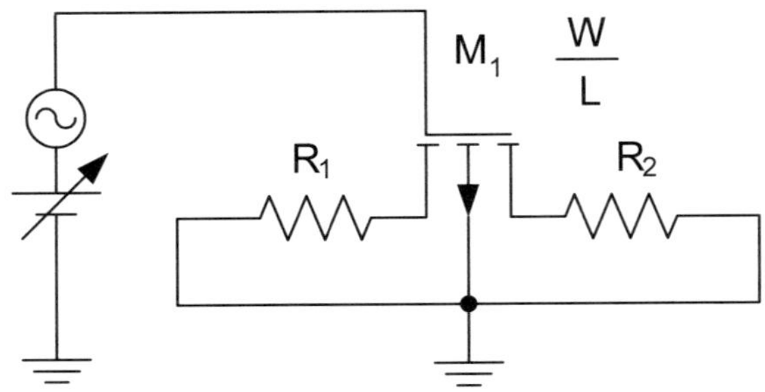


**Figure 9.** PMOS Transistor used to Plot C-V Curve.

In this simulation, resistors R1 and R2 are very large in order to restrict the action of PMOS in the channel area. The DC source is swept from negative to positive voltage values, to validate all regions of operation of the MOS capacitor formed by the gate, insulator and channel. The AC source can be set into low or high frequencies; therefore, it is possible to obtain the C-V curve behaviour as illustrated in Fig. 4.

The capacitor area (A) is determined by the geometric aspect W and L of the PMOS transistor.

The following equations are used to extract the doping concentration $N_D$ in a recursive way:

$$W_D = \left( \frac{C_{max}}{C_{min}} - 1 \right) \frac{\varepsilon_0 \varepsilon_S A}{C_{max}} \tag{7}$$

$$N_D = \frac{4 \varepsilon_S \phi_F}{q W_D^2} \tag{8}$$

$$\phi_F = \frac{kT}{q} ln \left( \frac{N_D}{n_i} \right) \tag{9}$$

where $W_D$ is the depth of depletion region formed in the contact, $\varepsilon_0$ and $\varepsilon_S$ are the vacuum and silicon dielectric permittivity, respectively, $A$ the contact area (considering a parallel plate capacitor).

The I-V characteristic of the Metal-Semiconductor structure is similar to a $P^+N$ junction. In the forward bias mode (metal connected to positive voltage and semiconductor connected to ground), the device turns on at voltages as low as 0.28V. The Metal-Semiconductor structure offers large current density due to the smaller built-in potential as well as the nature of thermion-emission compared to $P^+N$ diffusion. Also at Metal-Semiconductor interface there is the image-force-induced lowering phenomenon of the barrier energy for charge carrier emission, in the presence of an electric field. To understand this phenomenon, consider an electron, in vacuum and at a distance from a metal surface. A positive charge will be induced on the metal at a distance -a from the surface resulting in an attractive force between them. This force is known as the force of the image and has associated with it an image potential energy which corresponds to the potential energy of an electron at a distance a from the metal. When an external field is applied, together these two energy components have the effect of lowering the Schottky barrier. Thus at high fields, the Schottky barrier is considerably lowered. According to the thermo-emission proposed by (Sze, 1981), the forward I-V characteristics can be represented by:

$$I_D = I_S exp\left(-\frac{q\phi_{BN}}{kT}\right)\left[exp\left(-\frac{q\phi_{BN}}{kT}\right)-1\right] \tag{10}$$

where $I_S$ is the saturation current, $\phi_{BN}$ is the Schottky barrier height, $q$ is unit charge, $k$ is boltzmann constant and $T$ is the absolute temperature. When the reverse bias is applied to the Schottky structure, the electrons are depleted at the semiconductor side. As the reverse voltage increases, breakdown similar to PN-junction can happen in the Metal-Semiconductor device. The reverse biased I-V curve of our Schottky diode exhibits "soft" breakdown characteristics, with breakdown voltage at approximately 5V.

## 4. SBD implementation in low-cost CMOS technologies

In the fabrication of Schottky Barrier Diodes there are two fundamentals arrangements of structures. It can be a conventional structure that is formed only by the overlap of the metal over semiconductor or in a finger configuration that optimize (decrease) the series resistance of the device. Guard rings are linked to these devices and overlap all the SBD structure to avoid latch-up and to separate the SBD from the others tag circuits that performs analog and/or digital functions.

This item aims to investigate the Schottky configuration with fingers for applications in high frequency in order to improve the efficiency of power conversion. It will be described the changes in the masking process of a low-cost CMOS technology, particularly, the 0.35μm channel length TSMC (Taiwan Semiconductor Manufacturing Company) process. The procedures outlined here can be applied to other similar technologies.

The layer pattern shown in Fig. 10 will be used in the process sequence.

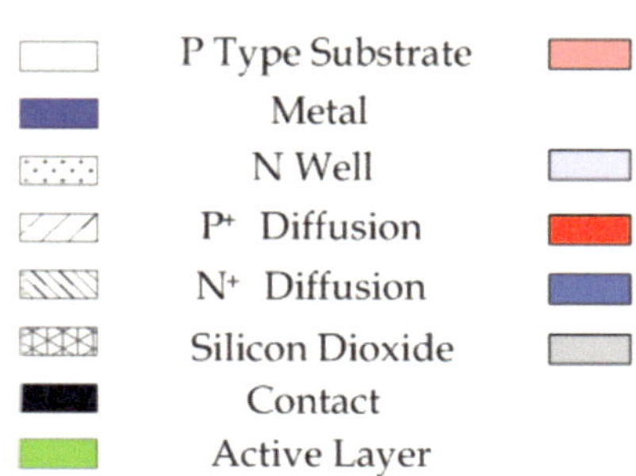


**Figure 10.** Layer Pattern.

It will be shown the development of a multifinger SBD, since it offers better electrical characteristics. Fig. 11 illustrates a simple view of a two fingers device.

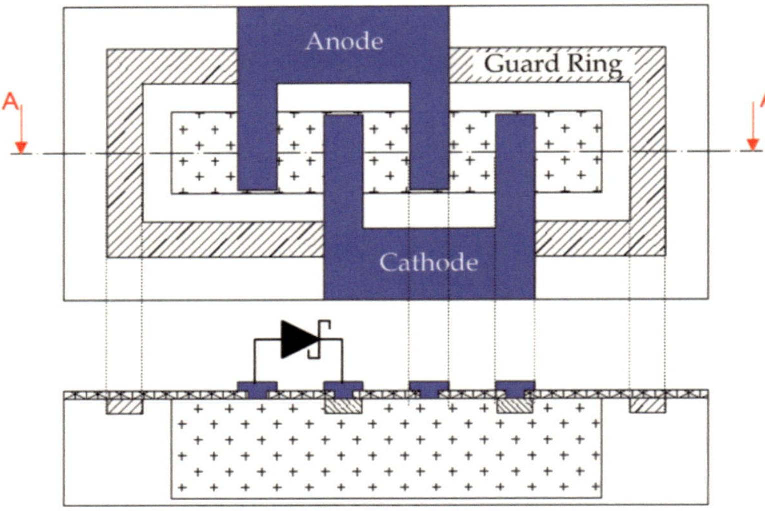


**Figure 11.** Two Finger SBD Structure.

Observe that the anode corresponds to the Metal-Semiconductor contact whereas the cathode corresponds to the ohmic contact. The SBD process in a standard CMOS is presented in the following figures. Fig. 12 (a) and (b) illustrates the P type silicon (substrate) and the oxide grown (actually silicon dioxide, $SiO_2$), respectively.

(a)

(b)

**Figure 12.** The P type wafer and the Oxide Grown.

After silicon oxide growth, an Nwell (#42) mask is used to make an N type well. The mask dimensions determine the diode finger maximum size. After this step, a new layer of silicon oxide is made. Figure 13 (a) and (b) shows those steps.

(a)

(b)

**Figure 13.** (a) N well in a P type wafer, (b) N well in a P type wafer after silicon oxide re-growth

The next step is the ACTIVE (#43) mask, responsible to determine the regions where P+ type materials are diffused. They correspond to the guard ring surrounding the SBD device, as shown in Fig. 14.

**Figure 14.** Guard ring get with P+ diffusion.

Next, the NPLUS (#45) mask is used for ohmic contact, i.e, N+ diffusion over an N type well. This contact will form the diode cathode. The number of contacts made at this stage is directly linked to the amount of diode fingers. In this step it is also open a hole in the oxide (via) over the N type well to form the diode anode (mask #48). Fig. 15 (a) and (b) show those steps.

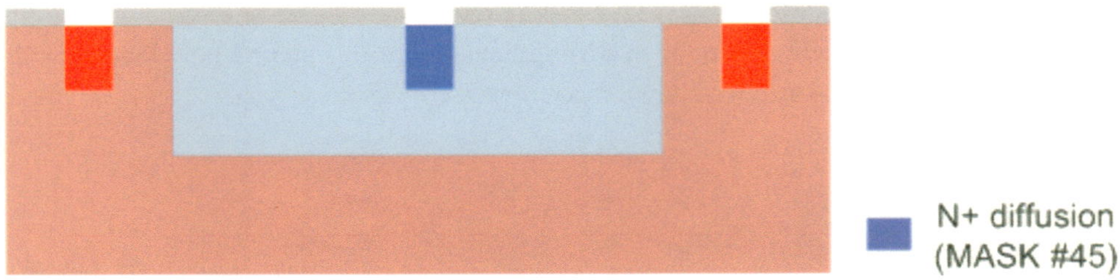


(a)

(b)

**Figure 15.** (a) Hole over N+ (cathode) and P+ (guard ring) diffusion. (b) Via over n type well to form diode anode.

It is necessary to deposit a conductor material in order to access the Schottky cathode, anode and guard ring. Mask METAL1 (#49) is used to define contact regions. That step is shown in Fig 16.

**Figure 16.** Metal definition for contacts in diode.

Finally, the VIA (#50) and METAL2 (#51) masks are used to access the metal layer that contacts the anode, cathode a guard ring. In summary, the following sequence of masks were used:

Mask NWELL (#42)

Mask ACTIVE (#43)

Mask NPLUS (#45)

Mask CONTACT (#25)

Mask METAL1 (#49)

Mask VIA (#50)

Mask METAL2 (#51)

Fig. 17 (a) shows the final layout (similar to Fig. 7) and Figure 17 (b) shows the photo of a SBD.

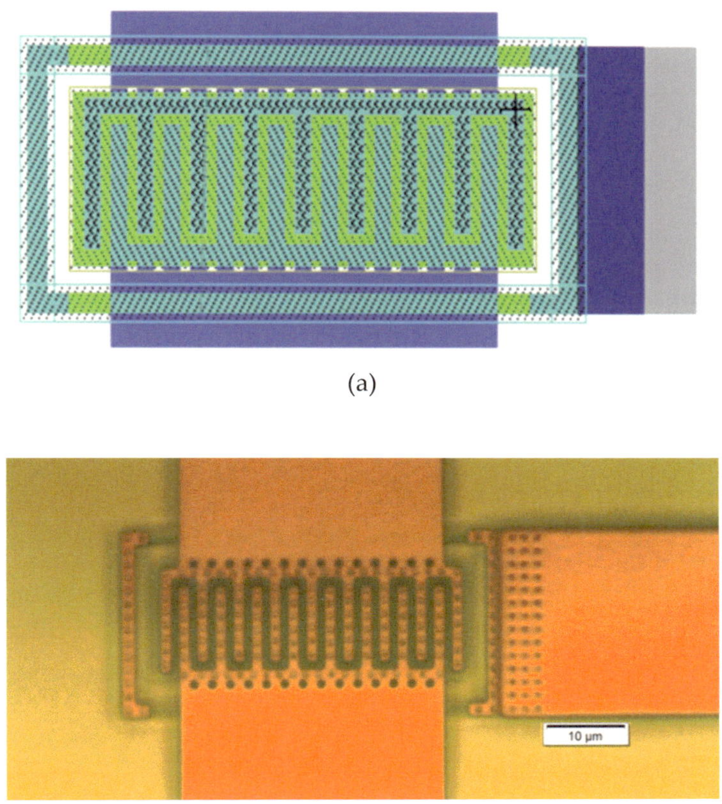


(a)

(b)

**Figure 17.** (a) SBD layout and (b) SBD photo.

Each mask used to form the SBD is shown in Fig. 18. The mask sequence must be seen from bottom up.

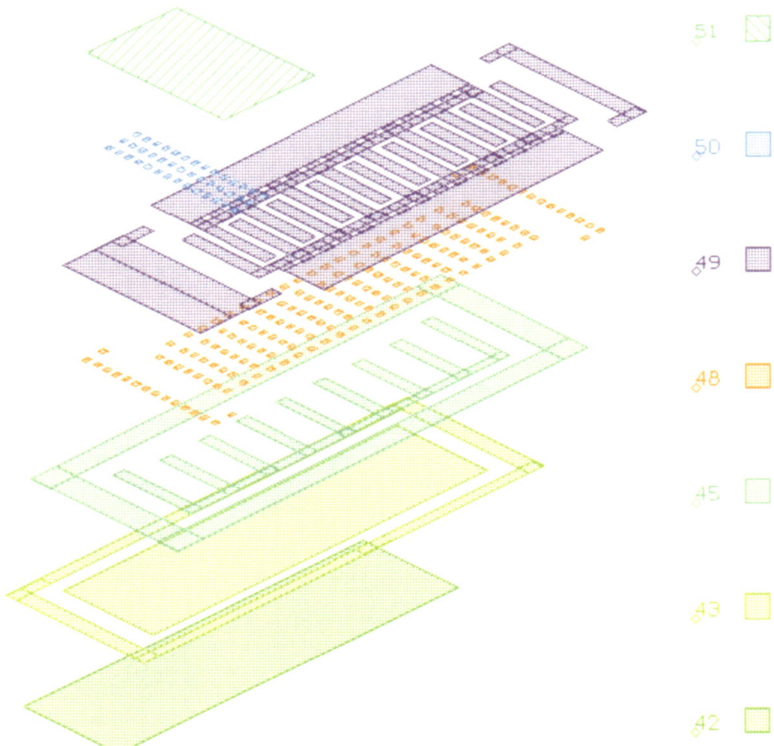


**Figure 18.** SBD masks in a Standard CMOS process

## 5. SBD Small-Signal Model

The most important difference between Schottky and PN structures is the lack of junction capacitance that significantly reduces the electrons recovery time. From the previous explanations, it is now possible to construct the equivalent small signal circuit model of the SBD, as shown in the Fig. 19.

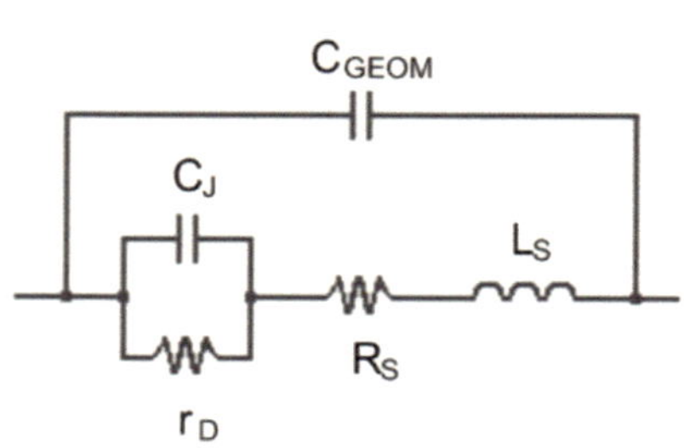


**Figure 19.** Small-signal SBD equivalent circuit.

In this equivalent circuit, capacitance ($C_{GEOM}$) arises from the fingers device geometry and exhibits the parasite capacitance between the two ports interdigitating fingers of Schottky diode. This capacitance can be found between 0.1 to 1pF.

Resistance $r_d$ and a capacitance $C_J$ are both from the depletion region, equated, respectively, by:

$$r_D = \frac{dV}{dI} \tag{11}$$

and

$$C_J = A\left[\frac{qN_D\varepsilon_s}{2\left(V_{bi} - V\right)}\right]^{1/2} \tag{12}$$

where $q$ is the electric charge and the $V$ is the voltage applied across the SBD.

Particularly, for a zero bias condition, i. e. V=0, equation (12) is stated as:

$$C_J(0) = A\left[\frac{qN_D\varepsilon_s}{2\left(\phi_B - V_t\right)}\right]^{1/2} \tag{13}$$

Resistor $r_d$ is, in fact, an incremental value and can be extracted from the forward bias Schottky I-V curve in a region before the degradation imposed by series resistance $R_S$. As a high speed device, the Schottky diode presents a low diffusion capacitance in the forward bias condition too (Philippe, 2002).

It is important to notice the parameter A (junction area) present in the equations (12) and (13). This parameter corresponds to the anode fingers area inside the N well viewed from top, as depicted by Fig. 20.

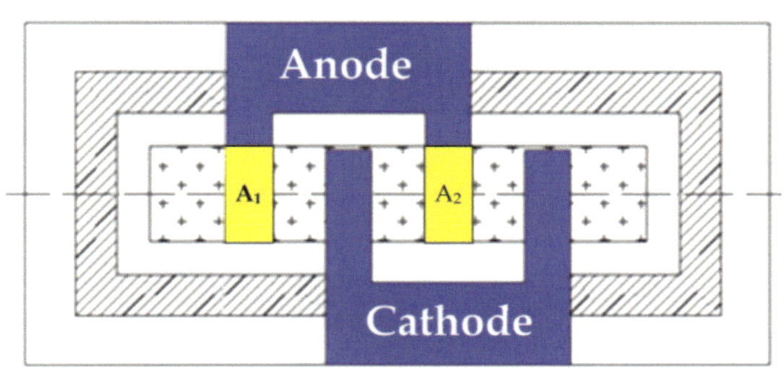


**Figure 20.** The Parameter A (area).

As can be seen A is the sum of all areas ($A_1$+$A_2$+…$A_n$) corresponding to $n$ anode fingers that are inside the N well. The cathode fingers area are not taken into account for junction capacitance as they are associated to ohmic contacts.

Finishing the model, the series resistance ($R_s$) represents the ohmic contacts and the neutral region of the semiconductor resistance. It is, typically, in the range tens of ohms (10 to 200Ω). Parasitic serial inductance ($L_s$) can be as low as 0.01nH and influences the device when operating at extremely high frequencies (GHz range). The SBD fabricated in standard CMOS process have the advantages such as low serial resistance and low parasite capacitance.

## 6. Measured results

The SBDs were diffused in three different versions; with 5 fingers, 10 fingers and 15 fingers. Fig. 21 shows the prototyped chip where it can be observed the various test layout patterns.

Table 1 shows the main calculated small-signal parameters from a set of DC measurements. The presented values are from an average of 40 samples. Those parameters can be used to optimize the final geometry of the SBD.

| | $r_D$ [Ω] | $C_J(0)$ [pF] |
|---|---|---|
| 5 fingers | 227 | 0.4 |
| 10 fingers | 103 | 0.8 |
| 15 fingers | 79 | 1.2 |

**Table 1.** SBD small-Signal parameters.

Fig. 22 shows the IV characteristic for the three diffused SBD. The curves represent an average value for 40 samples. For low level currents, as it is the case of implantable devices, the SBD turn-on voltage is in the range of 200 to 300mV. It is in accordance with eq. (3), considering typical values.

**Figure 21.** Prototyped chip .

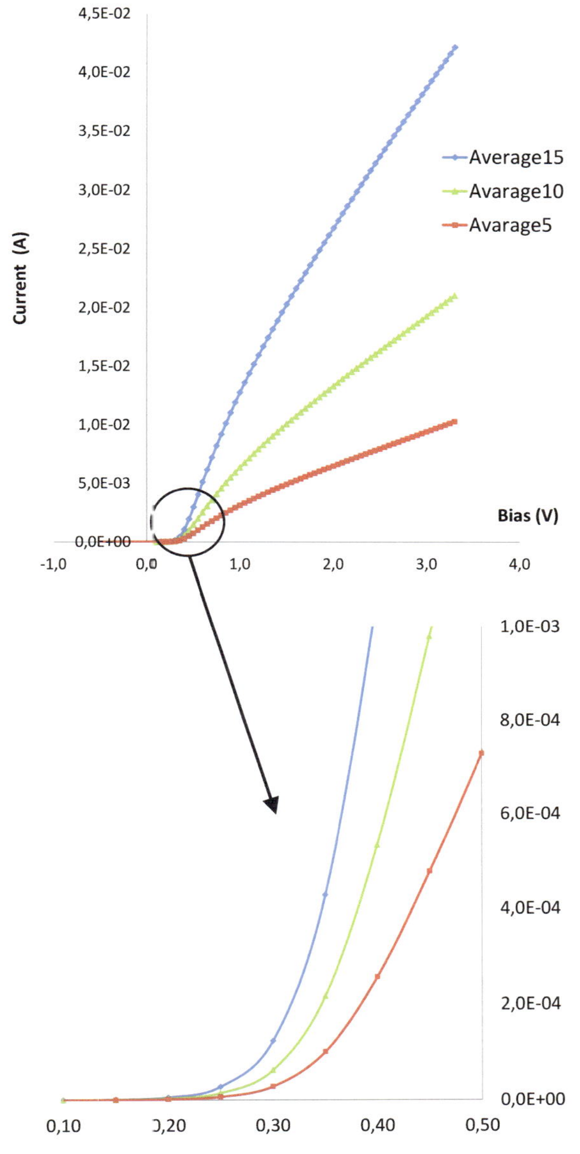


**Figure 22.** SBD IV characteristic.

The main goal at this point is to validate the fabrication process. As can be observed, it is possible to fabricate this kind of device in a standard CMOS technology, and it can be optimized through its geometric aspects.

Notice that this device is part of a more complex system. An improvement on AC-DC conversation efficiency can provide may allow the integration of the entire circuit, which can be even implanted. Nowadays, there are many important biomedical applications under research and development that depend on implanted systems, such as:

- A chip used to measure the glucose level.
- A chip to be used to evaluate the oxygen level.
- A chip to measure the concentration of creatine in the blood, which is used as the main indicator of renal function.
- A chip to indicate the presence of cancerous proteins in the blood.
- A chip used to store personal date and medical record, since blood type to patient history. In case of an emergency the chip can save lives since it reduces the time to obtain blood type, allergies, chronicle illnesses and provide all medical records.

## Author details

David Sebastiao Cabral, Robson Luiz Moreno, Tales Cleber Pimenta,
Leonardo Breseghello Zoccal and Paulo Cesar Crepaldi
*Universidade Federal de Itajuba, Brasil*

## 7. References

Averin, S.V., (1996) Fast-Response Photo-detectors with a Large Active Area, Based on Schottky-Barrier Semiconductor Structure, Kvantovaya Electronika, vol. 23(3), 284, (1996).

Brandl, M. et al, (2005) Low-Cost Wireless Transponder System for Industrial and Biomedical Applications, Information, Communications and Signal Processing, 2005 Fifth International Conference on, 06-09 Dec. 2005, pp. 1444-1447.

Hashemi, S. S., Sawan, M. and Savaria, Y., (2012) A High-Efficiency Low-Voltage CMOS Rectifier for Harvesting Neergy in Implantable Devices, IEEE Transactions on Biomedical Circuits and Systems, vol. PP, Issue 99, 2012, pp. 1-10.

Janam K. et al, (2006) Novel SPICE Macro Modeling for an Integrated Si Schottky Barrier Diode, Gallium Arsenide and Other Semiconductor Application Symposium, 2005, EGAAS 2005. 3-4 oct, pp. 409-412.

Kotani, K and Takashi, Ito, (2009) High Efficiency CMOS Rectifier Circuits for UHF RFIDs Using Vth Cancellation Techniques, ASIC, 2009. ASICON '09. IEEE 8th International Conference on, 20-23 Oct. 2009, pp. 549 – 552.

Philippe, P., El-Kamali, W. and Pauker, V., (2002) Physical Equivalent Circuit Model for Planar Schottky Varactor Diode, Microwave Theory and Techniques: Jorunals, IEEE Transactions Volume 36, ISSue 2, August 2002 pp. 250 - 255.

Pradier, A. et al, (2005) Rigorous Evaluation of Specific Absorption Rate (SAR) Induced in a Multilayer Biological Structure" Wireless Technology, 2005. The European Conference on, 3-4 Oct. 2005, pp. 197-200.

Rainee N. S. and Philip G. N. (2003) Intermodulation-Distortion Performance of Silicon–Carbide Schottky-Barrier RF Mixer Diodes, Microwave Theory and Techniques: Jorunals, IEEE Transactions Volume 51, Issue 2, February 2003, pp. 669 - 672.

Streetman, B., (1980), Solid State Eletronic Devices, Vol.2, pp. 185-190 (1980).

Sze, S. M., (1981) Metal-Semiconductor Contacts, in Physics of Semiconductor Devices, (Publishers: J Wiley & Sons, Singapore), 2nd Edition 1981, pp. 250 - 254

Chapter 7

# Implantable Biomedical Devices

Alireza Zabihian, M.H. Maghami, Farzad Asgarian and Amir M. Sodagar

Additional information is available at the end of the chapter

http://dx.doi.org/10.5772/50336

## 1. Introduction

Almost a decade after the invention of the first semiconductor transistor in 1948, it took around a decade for the revolutionary technology to evolve from producing single devices to the integration of a few transistors as the first *integrated circuit* in 1958. Since then, integrated circuits have been in continuous progress for more than half a century as predicted by the well-known *Moore's law*. While integrated circuits still continue their progress with the same exponential pace, it is almost a decade that a new branch of science and technology has emerged, known as *integrated microsystems*. This can be taken as the natural technological evolution from individual circuit chips and non-circuit modules, e.g., microelectromechanical systems (MEMS) devices, and subsequently to complete systems in small physical dimensions and with light weight. Integrated microsystems have opened windows of hope to providing efficient solutions to some of the problems that have not been resolvable by any other means so far.

Among the many kinds of microsystems being developed for a wide variety of applications, *implantable biomedical microsystems* are of increasing interest to both medical and engineering communities. This is mainly because of the capabilities such devices are expected to provide on the medical side, and also the technical challenges available on the engineering side. Examples of biomedical implants are pacemakers, cochlear implants, visual prostheses, neural recording microsystems, and deep brain stimulators.

This chapter provides an introduction to visual prostheses and intra-cortical neural recording devices. These are, indeed, two types of implantable biomedical microsystems, which are on the forefront of research.

## 2. Neural recording microsystems

Nowadays, several neural recording approaches, *e.g.*, electro-encephalography (EEG) and magnetic resonance imaging (MRI), are widely used as successful medical diagnostic

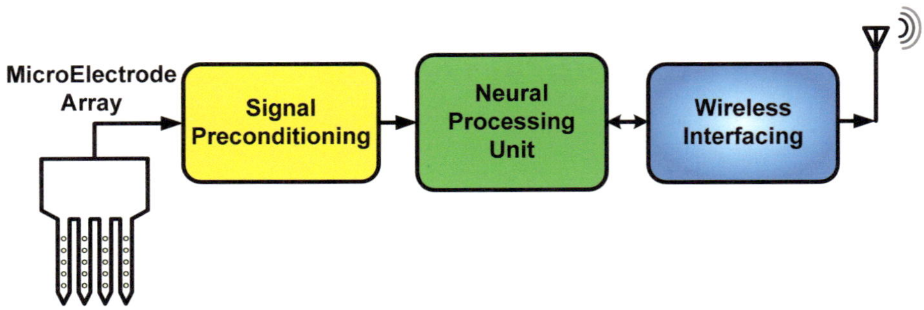


**Figure 1.** Simplified block diagram of a typical implantable neural recording microsystem

methods. What makes these approaches attractive is the fact that they are non-invasive, meaning that they do not make any harm to the subject. These methods, however, are capable of reporting averaged neural activities in the brain. In some branches of advanced research, for instance in medical sciences, cognitive sciences, and in brain-machine interfacing, researchers and scientists need to record neural activities with much higher spatial resolution than what the aforementioned non-invasive approaches are capable of providing. This section reviews general aspects of extracellular neural recording microdevices designed to intra-cortically record neural activities with rather high spatial resolution. Development of such devices is indeed an interesting example of multi-disciplinary research as it brings together several different specialties, such as electrical engineering, microfabrication technology, material sciences, chemical engineering, signal processing, and neuroscience.

As illustrated in the simplified block diagram of Figure 1, an implantable neural recording microsystem generally comprises one or more recording probes, a signal preconditioning module, a neural processing unit, and a wireless interfacing module.

## 2.1. Analog signal preconditioning (analog front-end)

In intra-cortical neural recording, electrical signals sensed by recording probes (also known as electrode arrays or microelectrode arrays (MEAs) when recording multiple channels) contain two different types of neural information: *Action Potentials* (APs) and *Local Field Potentials* (LFPs). Action potentials represent the firings of individual neurons, while local field potentials exhibit averaged synaptic activities of the mass of neurons in vicinity of electrode arrays. The former contains frequencies from 100 Hz to around 10 kHz with up to hundreds of μV of amplitude [1], and the latter contains frequencies from 0.01 Hz to around 200 Hz with amplitudes sometimes as large as a few mV [2].

The main task of a neural signal preconditioning module is the amplification of weak neural signals as well as filtering out frequencies beyond the bandwidth of interest. This is usually done using a preamplifier followed by or combined with a bandpass filter. In some cases, both gain and cut-off frequencies of the signal preconditioning module are either programmable or at least tunable.

### 2.1.1. Neural amplifier design parameters

As an important part of the signal preconditioning module, neural amplifiers need to be designed carefully. This is because they significantly contribute to the quality of the signals recorded in terms of the strength of the neural activities recorded and also their signal-to-noise ratio. As a result, neural amplifiers are designed with high enough mid-band gain and low input-referred noise. Considering the fact that in high-density neural recording per-channel amplifiers are used, it is of crucial importance to design these amplifiers with low power consumption and small silicon area. Key design parameters for neural amplifiers are therefore briefly reviewed as follows:

- **Noise**
  In intra-cortical extracellular neural recording peak-to-peak amplitude of action potentials at the input of the signal preconditioning module is in the order of tens to hundreds of microVolts. As a result, input-referred noise of neural amplifiers for this type of recording is typically kept below 5-30 μV [3].
  Input-referred noise of a neural amplifier has two main components: *thermal* noise and *flicker* noise. The former is caused by recording electrodes and amplifier transistors, and the latter is caused by existing amplifier transistors. The thermal noise component can be reduced by choosing larger transconductance for the transistors used at the input of the neural amplifier. In low-frequency applications such as neural recording, extra care should be taken to keep the flicker noise low. This is because flicker noise significantly increases at low frequencies. There are two techniques used to reduce the contribution of the flicker noise component in the input-referred noise. As a device-level technique, *pMOS* transistors with considerably large channel area are used as the amplifier input transistors. As a circuit-level technique, *Chopper* technique is used to eliminate both the offset of the amplifier and the flicker noise component, which are both of low-frequency nature [4]. To implement this technique an auxiliary amplifier and a few integrated capacitors are needed, which makes it difficult to achieve low flicker noise, low power consumption, and small silicon area occupation at the same time.

- **Silicon area**
  As a general prerequisite for being implantable, neural amplifiers need to be small in physical dimensions. This consideration becomes much more important when designing implantable microsystems to record tens to hundreds (and even thousands) of neural signals in parallel. A neural amplifier is therefore expected to consume small chip area and contain no off-chip components.

- **Power**
  For a neural amplifier, consuming as low power as possible is of importance from two standpoints. First, affordable power budget for the operation of implantable microsystems are limited, whether they are battery operated or telemetry powered. Secondly, from a biological point of view, the heat generated by the circuits that dissipate rather large power can potentially cause damage to the neighboring living

tissues [5]. However, there exists a sever trade-off between the noise of a circuit and its power consumption. In other words, for a specific level of noise, power consumption of a neural amplifier cannot be reduced as much as the circuit designer wishes.

- **NEF**
  *Noise Efficiency Factor* (NEF) is a Figure of merit that expresses how well the trade-off between the power consumption and the input-referred noise level is considered in the design of a circuit [6]. For a neural amplifier, NEF is given as:

$$NEF = V_{ni.rms}\sqrt{\frac{2I_{tot}}{\pi \cdot U_T \cdot 4kT \cdot BW}}$$

  where $V_{ni,rms}$ is the input referred noise, $I_{tot}$ is the total current the amplifier draws from the power supply, $U_T$ is the thermal voltage (KT/q), and BW is the bandwidth of the amplifier. Achieving small values for the NEF of a circuit means that the circuit has been designed efficiently in terms of obtaining low input-referred noise and consuming small power.

- **Input offset voltage**
  To exhibit ideal operation, differential amplifiers need to be designed and implemented symmetrically, both in topology and from the standpoint of the components they contain. This is, of course, the ideal case, which is never expected to happen in the real world, and neural amplifiers are not exceptions. In reality, asymmetric implementation and operation of such amplifiers causes a slight shift in the input-output transfer characteristics of the amplifier, which is modeled as the *offset voltage*.

- **Output voltage swing**
  Output voltage swing of a neural amplifier needs to be as wide as possible in order to allow for the proceeding signal processing to be performed more precisely. This issue becomes more critical as the microfabrication technology is being continually scaled down, resulting in smaller supply voltages, and demanding for the employment of low-voltage circuit design techniques in order to provide enough room for the amplified neural signal to swing.

- **Cut-off frequency**
  Frequency contents of action potentials in a typical intra-cortically recorded neural signal is spread from 100 Hz to around 10 KHz, while that of local field potentials is usually located in the sub-Hz up to a few tens of Hz. Neural amplifiers are designed with a low cut-off frequency of below 1 Hz or around 100 Hz depending on whether LFPs are to be amplified or not. Upper cut-off frequency for a neural amplifier is usually set somewhere between 7 KHz and 10 KHz.

- **CMRR**
  To discriminate between the signal of interest and the non-useful common-mode components of the input signal, (*e.g.*, certain kinds of motion artifacts, noise components induced at the input, and low-frequency variations resulted from probe-

tissue electrochemical interactions) neural amplifiers usually need to have high *common-mode rejection ratio (CMRR)*.

- **PSRR**
  As explained before, input signal to neural amplifiers is very weak in amplitude, typically in the order of tens to hundreds of microVolts. On the other hand, implantable neural recording microsystems are usually powered via power telemetry. As a result, the supply voltage in such systems is susceptible to some voltage ripples and even fluctuations, which can easily be significantly larger than the input signal. Hence, it is of crucial importance for neural amplifiers to have a high *power-supply rejection ratio (PSRR)* in order to suppress supply voltage variations while amplifying the input neural signal by a rather large gain.

### *2.1.2. Different types of neural amplifiers*

It is because of the key role they play in the quality of signals recorded that a wide variety of techniques have been employed for the design of neural amplifiers. Hence, neural amplifiers can be categorized in different ways:

From the standpoint of *system-level architecture*, neural amplifiers can be classified into *feedback amplifiers* and *open-loop amplifiers*. Negative feedback is usually used in the design of amplifiers in order to benefit from some (or all) of the following advantages:

- desensitization of the closed-loop gain against variations of open-loop circuit parameters,
- improvement of the impedance seen into the input and output ports of the amplifier,
- improvement in the bandwidth of the amplifier, and
- improvement in the linearity of the amplifier.

The designer should, however, be aware of the undesired impact of the feedback used on the stability of the amplifier. As a common solution for this problem, there are frequency compensation techniques that are used to stabilize the closed-loop amplifier as desired [7].

According to their *circuit-level architecture*, neural amplifiers also differ in the number of amplifying stages. Typically, a mid-band gain of about 40 dB to 60 dB, and a bandwidth of sub-Hz to 10 KHz are expected for a neural amplifier. Although sometimes a single-stage amplifier is a good choice but because of limited output voltage swing of cascode amplifiers and the lack of programmability of gain and bandwidth in a single-stage amplifier, there is a tendency to use two- or multi-stage amplifiers. One of the best choices for state-of-the-art neural amplifiers is to use a *Low-Noise Amplifier* (LNA) in the first stage, and a second stage to achieve the required gain and bandwidth adjustment. If necessary, a third stage can be used to achieve programmable gain for the neural amplifier [8].

The *signaling approach* used in the design of the amplifier can classify neural amplifiers into *single-ended amplifiers* and *differential amplifiers*. Because of the benefits of differential circuits such as input common-mode DC voltage adjustment, the input stage of the most of neural amplifiers is implemented differentially. But because of not necessity of very wide dynamic range for the neural amplifiers, although the fully-differential amplifiers have advantages such as twice output voltage swing, twice SNR, more linearity and higher CMRR and PSRR in comparison to their single-ended counterparts, but because of requirement of common-mode feedback loop and more power consumption, so the best choice for neural amplification applications is single-ended configuration.

From the *time-domain continuity* point of view, neural amplifiers are categorized into *continuous-time amplifiers* and *discrete-time amplifiers*. The switched-capacitor circuits are often introduced as discrete-time circuits. The most important advantages of switched-capacitor neural amplifiers in comparison to their continuous-time counterparts are, more accurate and adjustable frequency response, and wider dynamic range. In contrast, these circuits are slower at the same power and more silicon area occupier.

Also, *user-controllability* on the specifications of the amplifier (e.g., gain and bandwidth) can be used to classify neural amplifiers *programmable/tunable amplifiers* and *regular amplifiers.*

- Bandwidth Adjustment
  - Amplifiers with RC Filters

    The most common way of bandwidth adjustment for neural amplifiers is the use of resistor and capacitor to realize the filter. However, to achieve sub-Hz lower cut-off frequencies, very large resistors (*R > 10 GΩ*) are needed. Of course, this amount of resistance is achievable using diode-connected transistors, but not very linear. The Figure 2 shows the most common and simple single-stage feedback neural amplifier using an *Operational Transconductance Amplifier* (OTA), integrated resistors, and integrated capacitors. The voltage gain for this amplifier can be given as follows [9].

$$\frac{V_{out}}{V_{in}^{+}-V_{in}^{-}}=\frac{C_1}{C_2}\cdot\frac{1-sC_2/G_m}{\left(\frac{1}{sR_2C_2}+1\right)\left(s\frac{C_LC_1}{G_mC_2}1\right)}=A_M\frac{1-s/\left(2\pi f_z\right)}{\left(\frac{2\pi f_L}{s}+1\right)\left(\frac{s}{2\pi f_H}+1\right)}$$

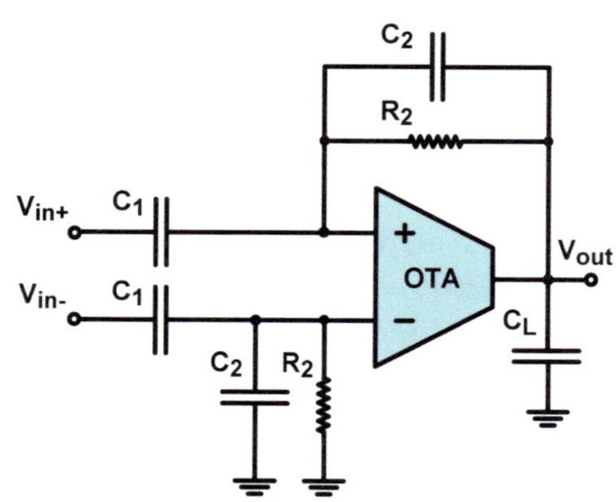


**Figure 2.** A simple single-stage neural amplifier with RC filter

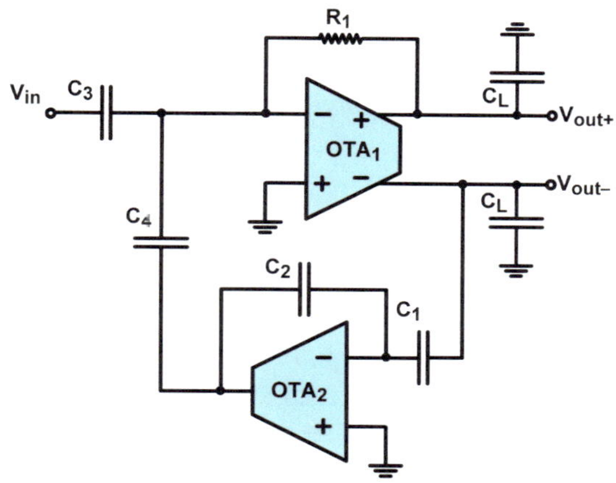


**Figure 3.** A single-stage neural amplifier with feedback filter

| | BW (Hz) | Gain (dB) | NEF | $V_{ni,rms}$ (μV) | Fully Diff. | # of Stages | Supply (V) | Power (μW) | Tech. (μm) |
|---|---|---|---|---|---|---|---|---|---|
| **Harrison 2003, [9]** | 0.025 – 7.2k | 39.5 | 4 | 2.2 | No | 1 | 5 | 80 | 1.5 |
| **Mohseni 2004, [11]** | 50 – 9.1k | 39.3 | 19.4 | 7.8 | No | 2 | 3 | 115 | 1.5 |
| **Heer 2006, [12]** | 10 – 100k | 20 | 8.1 | 5.9 | Yes | 1 | 5 | 160 | 0.6 |
| **Wu 2006, [13]** | 0.003 – 245 | 40.2 | 3.8 | 2.7 | No | 1 | 1 | 2.3 | 0.35 |
| **Denison 2007, [14]** | 0.5 – 250 | 45.5 | 4.9 | 0.93 | No | 1 | 1.8 | 2.16 | 0.8 |
| **Yin 2007, [15]** | 0.015 – 4k | 42.5 | 4.9 | 3.6 | Yes | 1 | 3.4 | 27.2 | 1.5 |
| **Wattanapanitch 2007, [16]** | 45 – 5.3k | 40.9 | 2.7 | 3.1 | No | 2 | 2.8 | 7.56 | 0.5 |
| **Lee 2008, [17]** | 16 – 5.3k | 40 | NA | 5.29 | No | 1 | 1.8 | 9 | 0.18 |
| **Yazicioglu 2008, [A18]** | 0.5 – 100 | 48 | 4.1 | 0.59 | Yes | 2 | 3 | 6.9 | 0.5 |
| **Mollazadeh 2009, [19]** | 94 – 8.2k | 39.6 | 2.9 | 1.94 | Yes | 2 | 3.3 | 79.2 | 0.5 |
| **Yeager 2009, [20]** | 0.5 – 5.9k | 39 | 4 | 4.4 | No | 2 | 1.8 | 5.94 | 0.5 |
| **Zhao 2009, [10]** | 13 – 8.9k | 46 | 3.1 | 5.7 | Yes | 1 | 3 | 6 | 0.35 |
| **Shahrokhi 2010, [21]** | 10 – 5k | 33 | 5.55 | 6.1 | Yes | 2 | 3 | 8.4 | 0.35 |
| **Rezaee-Dehsorkh 2011, [8]** | 300 – 10k | 57.5 | 2.4 | 3 | No | 3 | 1.8 | 20.8 | 0.18 |

**Table 1.** Comparison of different neural amplifiers specifications

A sample of this amplifier can be found in [9] with a midband gain of 39.5dB, while occupying 0.16 $mm^2$ of silicon area in a 1.5-μm CMOS Technology, and consuming 80 μW of power from a 5-V supply. The input referred noise for that amplifier is about 2.2 $\mu V_{rms}$.

- Amplifiers with Feedback Filters
  One of the big problems of neural amplifiers with RC filters is the generating a big time constant to achieve sub-Hz lower cut-off frequency. To solve this problem, the lower cut-off frequency can be generated using the upper cut-off frequency of an auxiliary amplifier in the feedback path. One of these types of neural amplifiers has been presented in [10] which can be seen in the Figure 3. This amplifier has a midband gain of 46 dB, and bandwidth of 13 Hz to 8.9 KHz. It consumes about 6 μW of power from a 3-V supply. The input referred noise for this amplifier is about 5.7 $\mu V_{rms}$.

At the end, a specifications table of neural amplifiers from literature is presented for the comparison.

## 2.2. Architectures for multichannel neural recording microsystems

Advances in neuroscience and clinical applications demand for simultaneous recording of neural potentials from a numerous amount of electrodes in the cortex in integrated manner with low power and low noise. According to different neural recording microsystems reported in the literature, the architecture of the systems can be categorized based on several main parameters. The most significant difference between the neural recording microsystems is related to their recording mode. In general, it can be separated in two different categories: the *Monitoring* mode, and the *Scan* mode [22]. In the monitoring mode, the signals sensed from microelectrode array are passed through the neural signal preconditioning part (neural amplifier) and in the same form (or their compressed form) are modulated and prepared to be transmitted to the world of the outside of the implant.

Considering the need to know neural information from numerous channels and also the shortage of telemetry power for microsystems, and since monitoring of the neural signals is a power-and-area-hungry method of recording, so someone can send just the useful neural information to the outside. In contrast to neuroscientific research, where the study of exact wave form of the neural signals is important, in prosthetic applications just knowing of the occurrence rate of the neural spikes is sufficient [22]. In scan mode, just the existence of neural spikes is detected and the addresses of channels with detected spikes on them are sent to the outside of the microsystem.

The type of wireless transmission is depended upon the type of signal processing on the amplified and filtered out neural signals, whether analog or digital. In some of microsystems the signal processing is done in the analog domain to be sent in the same domain using an analog transmitter. The most important advantages of analog transmitter are lower energy consumption and less implementation complexity. The most commonly-used analog modulation scheme to design the *analog transmission* is *Frequency Modulation*

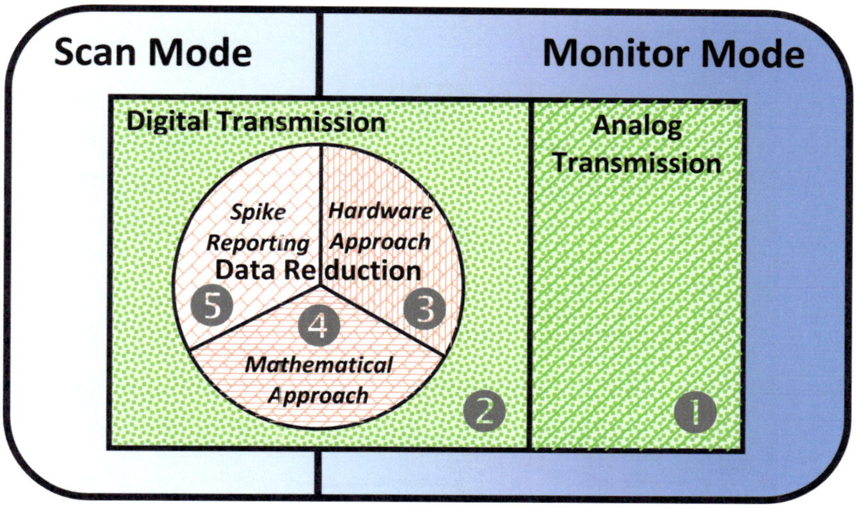


**Figure 4.** The general scope of architectures for multichannel neural recording microsystems

(FM) that is easily implantable. In contrast, the most important advantages of *digital transmission* are higher noise margin, detection and correction of errors, and easy synchronization between transmitter and receiver [23]. These parameters have returned the choice of designers to digital transceivers.

Ideally, it is desired an infinite accuracy for the recording and transmission implant system. Although this accuracy exists intrinsically in analog transmission systems, but considering the problem of noisy transmission, the equivalent accuracy, from the beginning of the system to the end, is not unlimited. Hence, digital transmission systems with appropriate accuracy are used. But aforementioned simple digital monitoring architectures are not useful when the number of recording channels exceeds. Therefore, according to the literature, three different techniques are introduced as *Data Reduction techniques* for implantable microsystem design: *spike reporting*, *mathematical approaches*, and *hardware approaches*. Hence, one of the other ways of categorizing the architectures for multichannel neural recording microsystems is to use or not to use the data reduction techniques. Figure 4 shows the general scope of categorizing the architectures for multichannel neural recording microsystems. So, there are five different architectures that are discussed in the following. However, it should be noticed that one of the other ways of division of these architectures is the choice of *Time-Domain Multiplexing* (TDM) or *Frequency-Domain Multiplexing* (FDM) to simultaneous recording from all the neural channels.

### *2.2.1. Monitor mode, analog transmission, without data reduction*

In this architecture, after simultaneous per-channel passing of neural signals of all the recording channels from signal preconditioning part, neural samples on parallel channels using either time-domain multiplexing or frequency-domain multiplexing are converted to series samples in analog domain. The prepared analog samples are then transmitted using

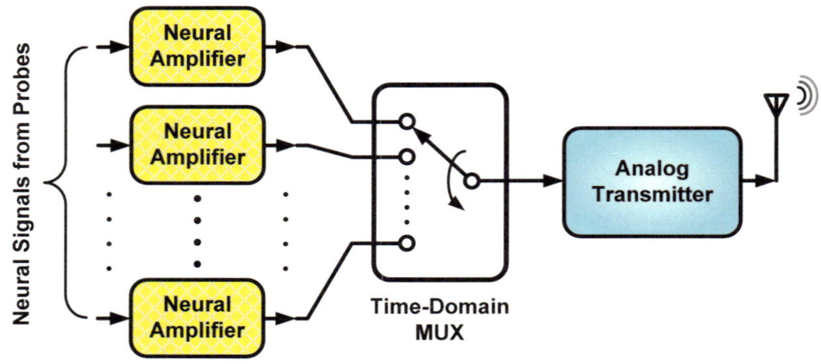


**Figure 5.** Monitor mode, analog transmission, without data reduction architecture with TDM

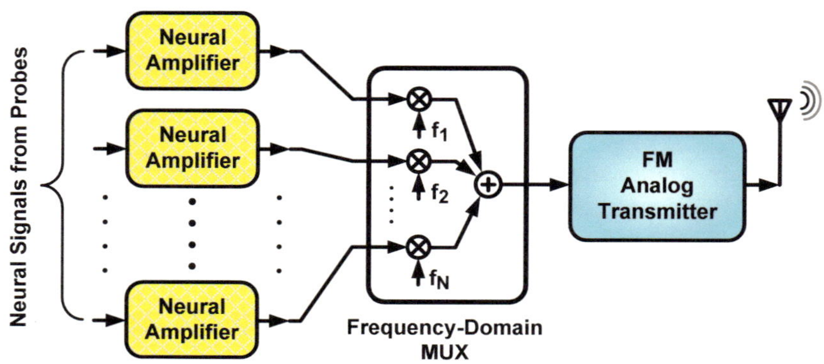


**Figure 6.** Monitor mode, analog transmission, without data reduction architecture with FDM

an analog transmitter (usually with FM modulation). One of the most important advantages of this kind of transmitters is low power consumption. However, here, the environment noise is very destructive. Figure 5 shows such an architecture using time-domain multiplexing. A sample of such an architecture was presented in 2005 for a 8-channel wireless FM neural recording microsystem [24].

But as previously mentioned, another technique to record all the neural channels simultaneously is frequency-domain multiplexing. For the first time, such a multichannel neural recording system was presented in [25]. Figure 6 depicts the mentioned architecture. The most important advantage of such an architecture over its TDM counterpart is its capability to recording from many more neural channels. But, of course, care should be taken in design and implementation of such architecture to avoid frequency interference.

### *2.2.2. Monitor mode, digital transmission, without data reduction*

The difference between this architecture and the previous one is in the way of transmission, i.e., digital versus analog. Considering the advantages of digital transmission over analog one, after signal preconditioning, multiplexing in analog domain, the prepared samples are converted to digital words. Then, these words along with parity bits and synchronization pulses are converted from parallel to serial form, and the prepared bit stream is then delivered to a digital transmitter. Figure 7 shows such a digital monitor architecture. The resolution of the quantization in neural recording systems is typically chosen to be 6 – 10 bits, and the sampling rate of the data converter is typically considered to be about production of 20 – 30 kS/s (twice to three times the Nyquist rate of neural signals) by the number of neural channels. A sample of this architecture is presented in [26].

Noting the low accuracy of multiplexing in analog domain, another possible change to the mentioned architecture can be as to use per-channel analog to digital converters for every neural channel before multiplexing and then to multiplex in digital domain. In this way the sampling rate of any ADC can be as low as 20 – 30 kS/s. Such an architecture (Figure 8) with delta-sigma ADCs is presented in [19], in which the ADCs' resolution and sampling rate are 7 bits and 20 KHz, respectively.

If we dedicate one ADC to every neural channel, then a big problem occurs if the number of channels exceeds. This big problem is large amount of power dissipation and great occupied silicon area related to all of the ADCs. To solve this problem, an approach was proposed by the authors in 2009 regarding the use of delta-sigma modulators instead of a complete ADC

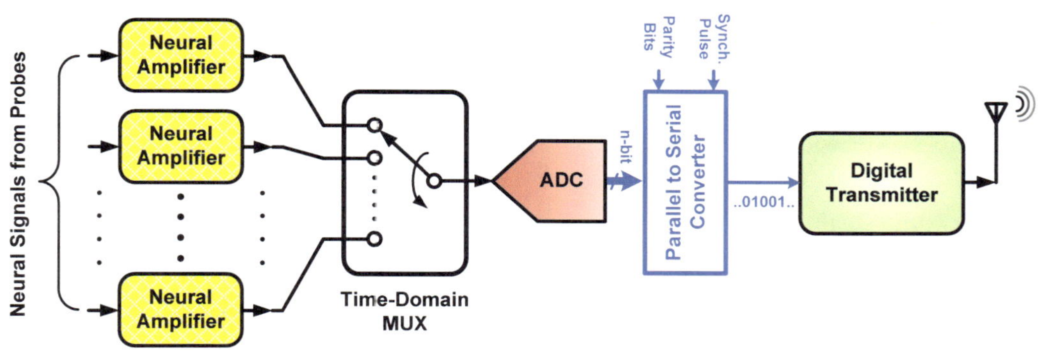


**Figure 7.** Monitor mode, digital transmission, without data reduction architecture

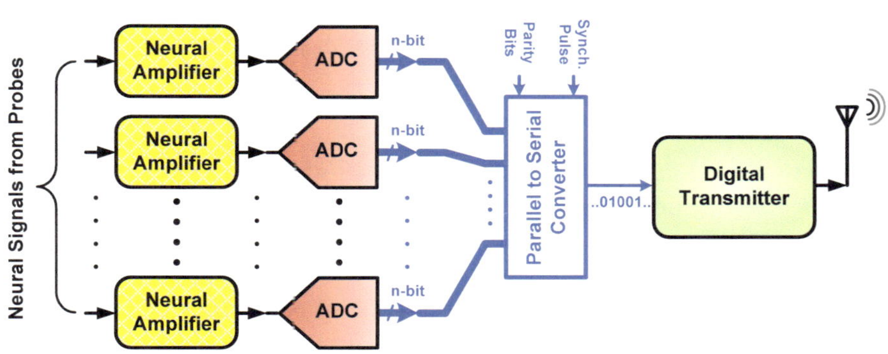


**Figure 8.** Monitor mode, digital transmission, without data reduction architecture with per-channel ADCs

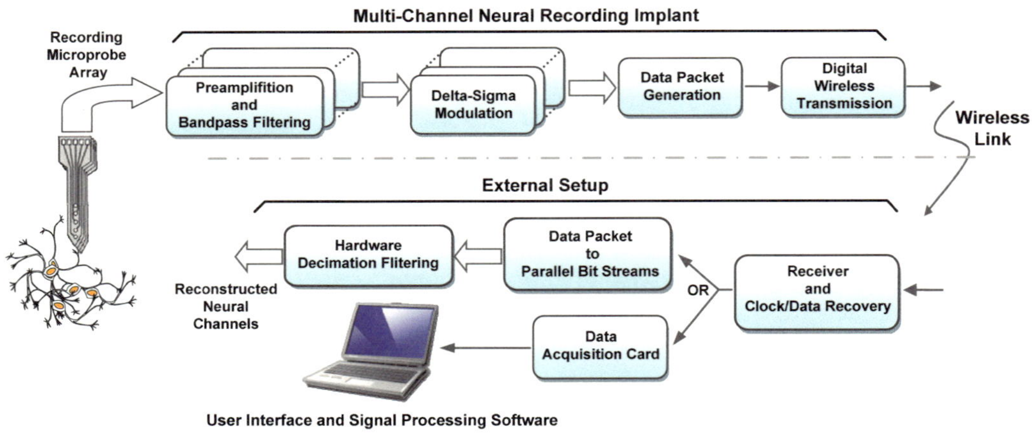


**Figure 9.** Monitor mode, digital transmission, without data reduction architecture based on delta-sigma modulators

in every channel [27]. In this method, the architecture of the ADC is indeed a delta-sigma one but with the difference that delta-sigma modulators are implemented in implant unit and the remained part of a delta-sigma ADC, i.e. decimation filtering, is implemented in the external unit (Figure 9). In this way, a large amount of power and silicon area is saved in the implant side. An 8-channel system is designed and laid-out in a 0.5-μm CMOS Technology. Post layout simulations showed a power consumption about 16.5 μW for every neural recording channel. The recording bandwidth was set to be 6.25 KHz and quantization resolution was considered to be about 8 bits.

### 2.2.3. *Monitor mode, digital transmission, hardware approach data reduction*

One of the other architectures that have been recently published promises the multichannel neural recording using Anti-Logarithmic ADCs [28]. The significant difference between this architecture and the architecture discussed in the previous section is in the type of ADC. It has been showed that, nonlinear (exponential) quantization of neural signals can be very more effective than the linear type and reduces the physical bits of the data converter comparing to its linear counterpart. This architecture is shown in Figure 10.

### 2.2.4. *Monitor mode, digital transmission, mathematical approach data reduction*

It can easily extract the useful information from neural signal using a data compressor based on *Wavelet Transform* or other useful discrete transforms. According to Figure 11, another architecture for multichannel neural recording microsystems can be realized. A 64-channel neural data compressor based on *Walsh-Hadamard Transform* is presented in [29] with a compression factor of 72. But a more efficient 64-channel neural data compressor based on *Discrete Haar-Wavelet Transform* is presented in [30] with a compression factor of 112, in which has been claimed that has a more simpler circuit in comparison with the work in [29]. Anyway, data compressor approach is a power-and-area-hungry one.

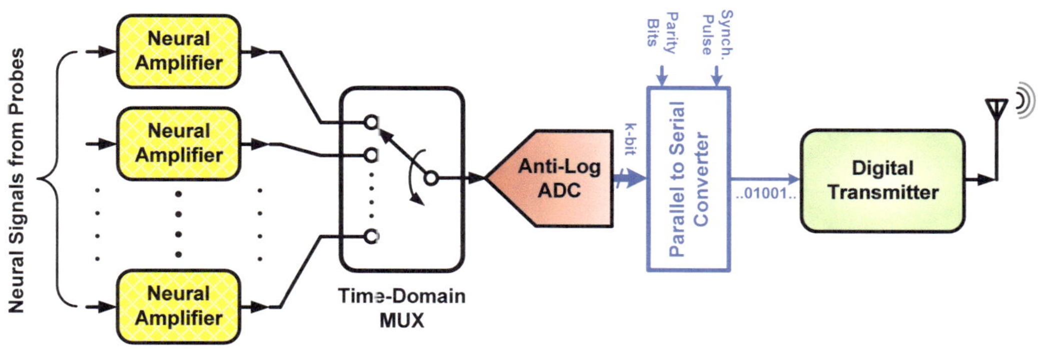


**Figure 10.** Monitor mode, digital transmission, hardware approach data reduction architecture

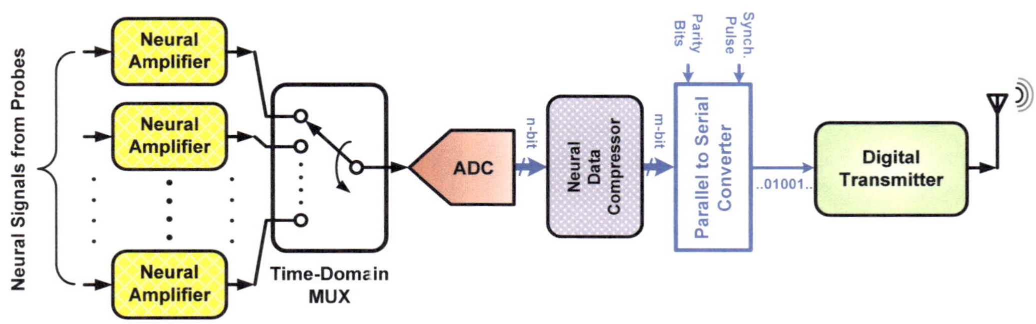


**Figure 11.** Monitor mode, digital transmission, mathematical approach data reduction architecture

### *2.2.5. Scan mode, digital transmission, spike reporting data reduction*

When the number of neural recording channels exceeds (greater than 16 channels), monitor mode of recording is not very practical. Instead of monitoring of neural signals, the system can easily detect the neural spikes on every channel using per-channel spike detectors and then reports the existence of a spike on a channel. The spike detection can be accomplished using one of the three methods: hard thresholding, detection based on spike's features, or detection based on nonlinear energy operator. Such architecture is shown in Figure 12. In

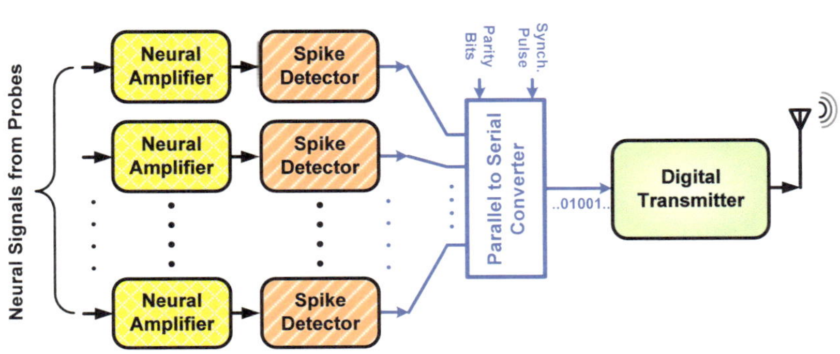


**Figure 12.** Monitor mode, digital transmission, spike reporting data reduction architecture

this architecture after signal preconditioning and spike detection, all the parallel data is converted to a bit stream along with parity bits and synchronization pulses and is then delivered to the digital transmitter. A sample of this architecture for a 100-channel neural recording microsystem is presented in [31] where the spike detectors are simple comparators with adjustable threshold level.

## 3. Visual prostheses

Human vision is known to be one of the highly sophisticated sensory systems could be found in the nature. When looking into someone's eyes, several parts of visual system can be easily seen. A black-looking aperture, **the pupil,** that allows light to enter the eye. A colored circular muscle, **the iris,** which controls the size of the pupil so that more or less light is allowed to enter the eye. A transparent external surface, **the cornea,** that covers both the pupil and the iris. The cornea is the first and most powerful lens of the optical system of the eye and allows, together with **the crystalline lens** the production of a sharp image at the back of the eye. The back of the eye is lined with a layer called the retina. The retina is a membrane containing photoreceptor nerve cells. The image information from over 100 million photoreceptor cells is pre-processed in subsequent layers of retinal cells, and then transported to the next parts of the visual system by the optic nerve comprising around 1.2 million fibers [32]. Failure in the operation of any part of the visual system, illustrated in Fig. 13, can potentially cause blindness. Aside from approached such as cell regrowth using stem cells and semiconductor photodetector arrays, implantable visual prostheses have exhibited successful performance through electrical stimulation [33]. The goal of artificial vision systems, also known as visual prostheses, is to artificially produce a visual perception in individuals with profound loss of vision. The visual prosthesis technology relies on patients having a developed visual cortex and they need have been able to see in the past for this device to be of benefit to them.

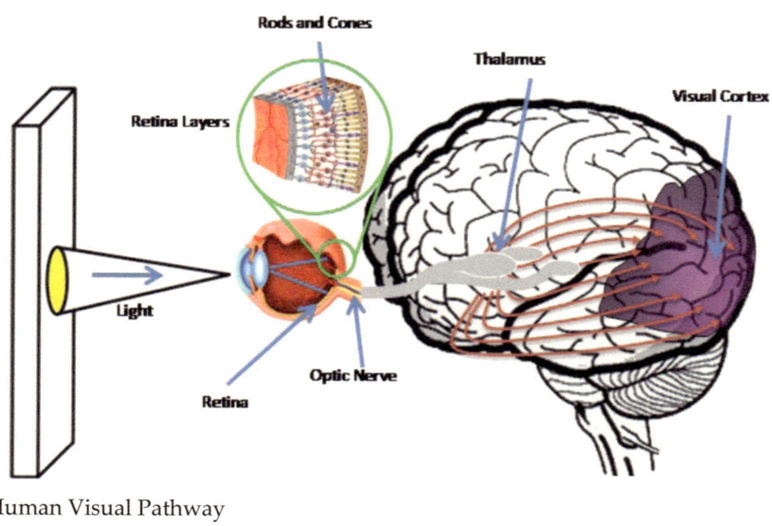


**Figure 13.** Human Visual Pathway

According to the World Health Organization (WHO), population of the blind is estimated 38 million in 1990 worldwide, extrapolated 45 million in 1996 and projected to be 76 million in 2020. The important fact is that almost 80% of the blind suffer needlessly and their blindness could be prevented or treated [34]. The most common causes of adult visual impairment include Age-related Macular Degeneration (AMD), Retinitis Pigmentosa (RP), and diabetic retinopathy, all occurring in the retina. AMD is caused by a combination of genetics and environmental and other individual factors, and is characterized by progressive loss of central vision. RP affects the rod cells first and then the cone cells. Rod and cone cells are used in night vision and ambient daylight levels, respectively. Early symptoms of this retinal degeneration include night blindness and increasing loss of peripheral vision leading to complete blindness [35]. Existing treatments can perhaps slow the progress of these diseases, and no cure is available. However, recent use of molecular genetic strategies has provided some restoration of vision in dogs and humans with RP [36].

In the following sub-sections, general block diagram of a visual prosthesis will be presented. Main building blocks of a typical visual prosthesis system will then be introduced and some of the associated design aspects and challenges in both circuit and system levels will be studied. Furthermore, latest achievements in the visual prosthesis being developed at the Research Laboratory for Integrated Circuits and Systems (ICAS), K.N. Toosi University of Technology, Tehran, Iran, will be reviewed.

### 3.1. General design

Depending on the part of the visual system that fails to function, a visual prosthesis is designed to bypass the failing parts and deliver the image information to the rest of the natural visual system that works perfectly. Hence, several approaches are taken to restore vision to the blind, which can be categorized into: retinal (including epi-retinal and sub-retinal) approaches, optic nerve stimulation, and cortical approaches.

In epi-retinal prostheses, the prosthetic device is attached to the inner retinal surface. The sub-retinal approach involves implanting an electrode array between the bipolar and retinal pigment epithelium. In this case, the rest of the system can be placed out of the eyeball. In both epi-retinal and sub-retinal methods, healthy retinal neurons are electrically stimulated, which bypass the damaged photoreceptors thereby creating visual excitation [37,38].

The optic nerve, which is about 1–2 mm in diameter, serves as a compact conduit for all the information in the visual scene. This means that electrical stimulation of a small area of the optic nerve would be expected to activate a large segment of the visual field. To stimulate the optic nerve, a cuff electrode encircles the optic nerve. Since the electrodes are on the outside of a very densely packed nerve (1.2 million fibers within the nerve), focal stimulation and detailed perception are difficult to achieve [39].

Without taking so many technological, surgical, and cognitive challenges into consideration, stimulation of the visual cortex seems to be capable of restoring vision for the blinds of different types, including those suffering from damages to both retina and optic nerve.

However, for those who are eligible to use retinal prostheses or optic nerve stimulation, stimulation of the visual cortex might not be the first preference. The surgical risk to a patient with an otherwise healthy brain may be higher for visual cortex prostheses. Also, bypassing the visual pathway demands more complicated signal processing by the prosthesis to make up for the non-negligible part of the natural image processing that is missed [40].

Figure 14 shows a generalized architecture for the visual prostheses of different kinds being developed by several groups around the globe [37-41]. Despite so many differences between how these systems are implemented, they are all common in the fact that they capture images from the external world and after some processing, deliver the processed image information to the healthy part of the visual system that is still functional. Successful stimulation of the visual system can lead to the perception of spots of light, referred to as *phosphenes*, in the visual field of the patient [42]. Although unlikely to recreate perfect vision, artificial vision systems may evoke enough phosphene perception to perform every-day tasks such as navigation, recognition, and reading.

According to the simplified block diagram shown in Fig. 14, a visual prosthesis system, in general, comprises several blocks: A video camera, which can be worn on eyeglasses, captures images from the vision field of the patient in the external world. After some external video preprocessing, performed to extract the main useful information from the recorded images and hence to reduce the amount of data, the resulting image information is prepared for wireless transmission. Processed image information along with some stimulation specifications are then transmitted to an implantable module. After the retrieval of the received data, an embedded processor sends digital information to a stimulation back-end, which is in charge of generating analog electrical pulses. Usually, a flexible cable conveys these electrical outputs to an electrode array that interfaces to the target tissue.

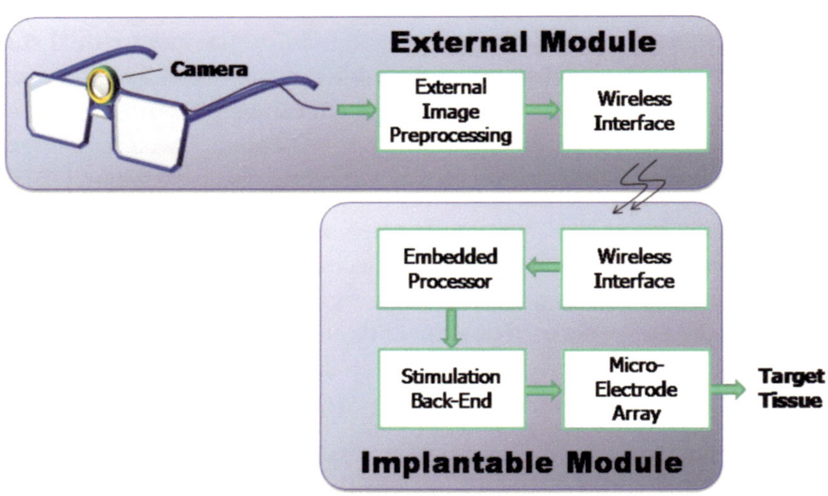


**Figure 14.** General architecture for a visual prosthesis system

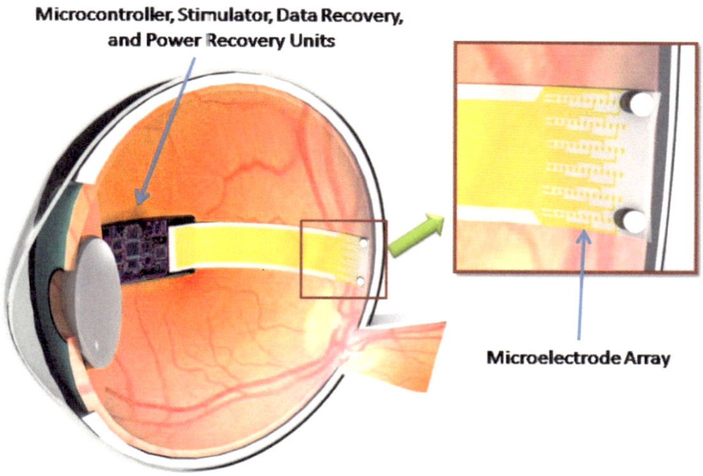


**Figure 15.** Illustration of the ICAS epi-retinal implant

The external unit is usually powered using batteries, while the implanted electronics receive power wirelessly. In an ideal case, all the electronic circuit blocks are integrated on the same platform. Figure 15 shows an illustration of the visual prosthesis being developed at the ICAS laboratory, in which all the implantable electronics are integrated on a micromachined silicon platform. This platform needs to be packaged and sealed in order to prevent any interaction between the electronic parts and the neighboring living tissues and biological fluids. Moreover, non-electronic parts, such as the coils used for inductive power and data telemetry, the microelectrode array (MEA), and the cable connecting the MEA to the electronics package need to be either made from biocompatible materials or at least encapsulated with biocompatible films.

To develop a fully functional visual prosthesis, in addition to the development of the electronics hardware required for this purpose, engineers need to collaborate with specialists in clinical and surgical issues to form a multidisciplinary team. In addition to making decisions on main issues such as surgical and implantation procedures, the medical research team also works on the selection of appropriate types of lab animals, assess and monitor issues related to the health and normal behavior of the subjects pre- and post-implantation, and on the design and development of clinical tests to assess the efficacy of the operation of the implant. In summary, to develop a visual prosthesis system for chronic operation, close collaboration between specialists in both engineering and medical disciplines is inevitable.

## 3.2. External video processing unit

Considering the fact that the implantable module is preferred to be realized with small physical size and operate with low power dissipation, any attempt to reduce the complexity and power consumption is welcomed in the design and implementation of the implant. For this reason, complex image processing tasks are usually performed right after capturing video information on the wearable external module where physical size and supplying electric power are not big concerns.

For video capture, different image-acquisition devices are used in visual prosthesis systems such as charge-coupled devices (CCDs) and complementary metal-oxide semiconductor (CMOS) cameras. Figure 16 shows two CMOS camera modules used as the external video capture device by the ICAS visual prosthesis team [43, 44]. The first generation (Gen.-1) video capture setup, shown in Fig. 16.a, was implemented on the CMUCAM3 module comprising the OV6660 CMOS image sensor. Input and output image sizes are 128 × 128 and 32 × 32 pixels, respectively, and output frame rate is 8.3 images per second. For the second generation (Gen.-2) external video capture device, the MINI2440 board with the OV9660 image sensor was used (Fig. 16.b). For this version, input image size is 256 × 256 pixels, output image size is 32 × 32, and output frame rate is 15 images per second. These are wearable hardware that can be used in dynamic tests to evaluate image processing algorithms used in research prototypes and also in real visual prostheses.

To efficiently utilize the limited bandwidth available for the wireless transfer of the captured images on one hand, and to simplify the tasks the embedded controller is expected to do, some image processing is performed on the external module. Edge detection and image quality enhancement, zoom, contrast and brightness adjustment are considered to be realized on the external side [45-47]. Taking into account limitations in the fabrication of MEAs, two image processing modules were developed in the ICAS visual prosthesis project, each comprising three major tasks: image reduction, extraction of basic features, and result remedy.

In order to assess and evaluate the efficacy of the image processing methods used, a bank of a variety of images, frequently seen in everyday life, was prepared. This includes in-door and out-door images, real pictures taken from the external world and synthesized images such as handwritings and signatures. For the Gen.-1 external module, images were reduced in resolution and color information and processed based on image histogram classification [43]. The proposed algorithm and other well-known approaches such as Canny's method [48], importance map [49] and hard-thresholding [50] were applied to exemplars of the

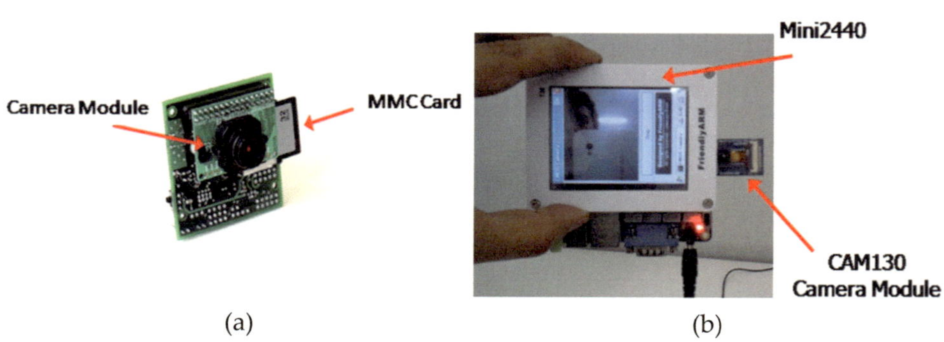


**Figure 16.** Hardware used by ICAS visual prosthesis team (a) First generation, (b) Second generation

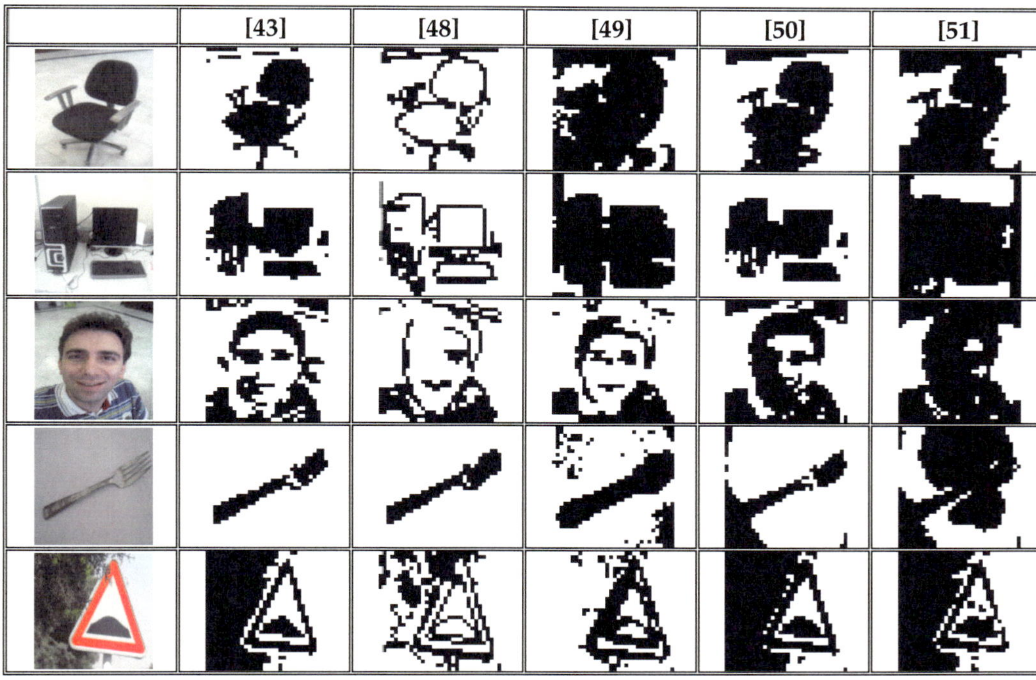


**Figure 17.** Comparison between the first image processing algorithm proposed by ICAS visual prosthesis team and the output of some well-known approaches [43]

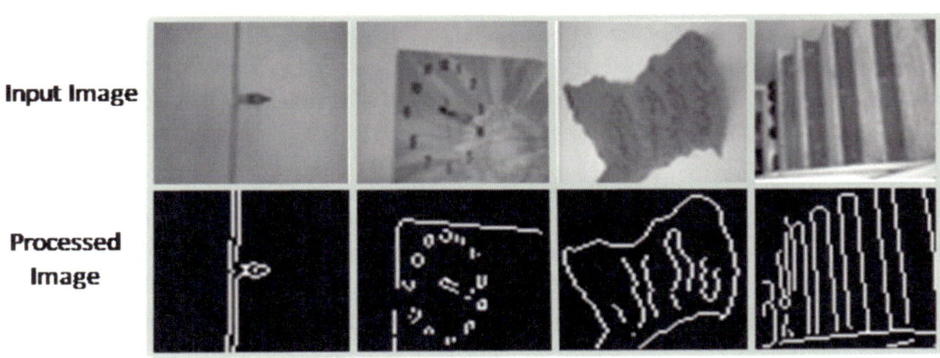


**Figure 18.** Output results of the developed hardware for the second generation of external module of ICAS visual prosthesis team [44]

picture classes in the bank (Fig. 17). The results were then evaluated using questionnaires filled out by a group of randomly selected people.

The algorithm used for external image preprocessing in the Gen.-2 setup was based on the Discrete Cosine Transform (DCT) [52] and Gabor filter [53]. The DCT determines image frequency and sets the frequency for the Gabor filter. Gabor edge detector is like the natural edge detection that is performed in the human visual system. This algorithm was implemented on the MINI2440 board. Output image dimensions were 32 × 32. Figure 18 shows the output results obtained from the developed hardware for the second generation of ICAS visual prosthesis team.

## 3.3. Implant modules

### *3.3.1 Embedded control unit*

Similar to almost any other implantable microstimulating systems, a visual prosthesis sends the incoming data from external module to a stimulation back-end to be delivered to the target tissue by a centralized controller embedded in the system. The controller is in charge of both administering the implant operation and generating stimulation commands/data to be converted to analog stimulation pulses in the stimulation back-end. As these controllers are designed to be implanted in the body, they need to be realized with small physical dimensions, have a limited power budget mainly to comply with living tissue safety standards and limited amount of power transferred to the implant part, and can utilize a limited bandwidth for data telemetry according to frequency allocation regulations. This is why all of the research groups including ICAS visual prosthesis team involved in the design of visual prostheses prefer to design their own special-purpose controller [54-56] rather than an off-the-shelf commercially-available general-purpose controller.

From a functional point of view, the entire visual prosthesis system needs to provide high enough image resolution for acceptable visual perception for the patient. The system also needs to operate fast enough to stimulate the visual system with acceptable stimulation rate for a real-time flicker-free video stream. There are other concerns, however, in the system level that contribute in how the system will be integrated. For instance, it is important to have low number of interconnects between the controller and the stimulation back-end, especially when the system is designed with a high-resolution electrode array. This means that the controller needs to interface with the stimulation back-end in a serial fashion rather than in parallel form.

As an example of a special-purpose microcontroller dedicated to visual prosthesis, the following paragraphs reports on the design of ICAS embedded controller. This controller receives three types of data packets carrying a mode packet and the associated data, and is capable of generating a variety of stimulation signals according to the definition of the received data. Figure 19 shows the block diagram of the ICAS controller designed with a hardwired architecture for small silicon area and power consumption, and fast operation [56]. The data exchange block receives the incoming information in the form of serial data packets along with a synchronized clock signal from the wireless interface block. This block checks the format and contents of the data packets and returns an error message to the extra-ocular module as required. The received data packets may convey either configuration or image information. Configuration parameters are stored in the config. register bank. The image memory is considered to temporarily store the pixelized image information. Corresponding stimulation details for each pixel of the image are then generated in the stimulation generation engine. Stimulation details in the form of packaged commands and data (stimulation packets) are finally framed in the outgoing packet generator in order to be sent to the stimulation back-end.

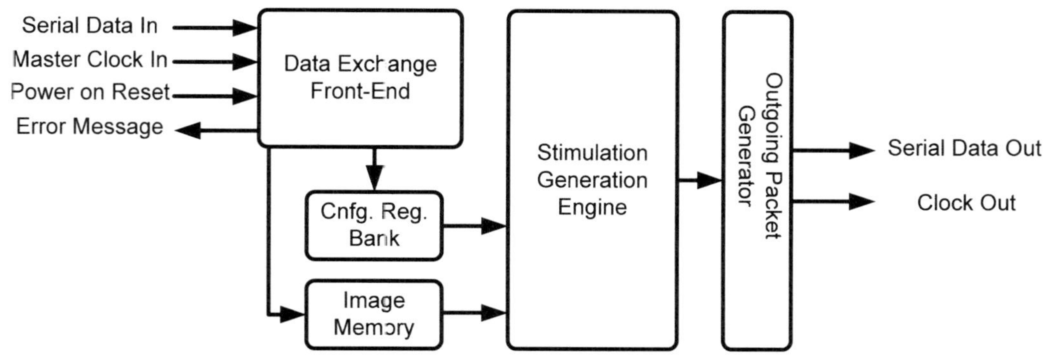


**Figure 19.** Block diagram of the controller designed by ICAS visual prosthesis team

The controller designed by ICAS visual prosthesis team supports the generation of biphasic stimulation pulses (refer to section 3.3.2) in the form of both single pulses and pulse trains. Stimulation packets, sent from the controller to the stimulation back-end, define stimulation pulse amplitudes and timings. This includes amplitudes and pulse widths for both anodic and cathodic phases, an inter-phase delay, and an inter-pulse delay for the pulse train stimulation. The controller returns a data packet containing an error message to the external setup in the case of detecting error in the incoming data packets. The pixelized image sent to the controller are in the form of black and white, number of pixels are 16×16 and input frame rate is 15 frames per second.

The designed controller can be programmed to operate in one of the following three possible operating modes:

- Setup mode, in which the parameters required for the main operation of the system (e.g., stimulation pulse profile) are transferred from the external setup to the controller.
- Image mode, considered for receiving information associated with the image captured externally.
- Site discharge mode, envisioned for connecting the electrodes to the ground. This is to discharge the tissue being stimulated every once in a while in order to prevent tissue damage caused by charge accumulation.

For the controller to operate in either one of the three operating modes introduced above, a set of 10-bit packets is sent from the external setup to the controller. Each 'packet set' starts with a 'START' packet, which is a predefined combination of 0's and 1's (1010101010). A 'MODE' packet (MP) then follows to indicate in what operating mode the controller is to be put. Depending on the type of the packet set received, the next packets are accordingly determined, as shown in Figure 20. A packet set is finally terminated with an 'END' packet. In the case of detecting errors in the incoming packets, the controller generates an error message and sends it to the external setup. To comply with the interconnect challenge, pointed out in the previous section, data communication between the controller and both the external setup and the stimulation back-end is performed in a serial fashion.

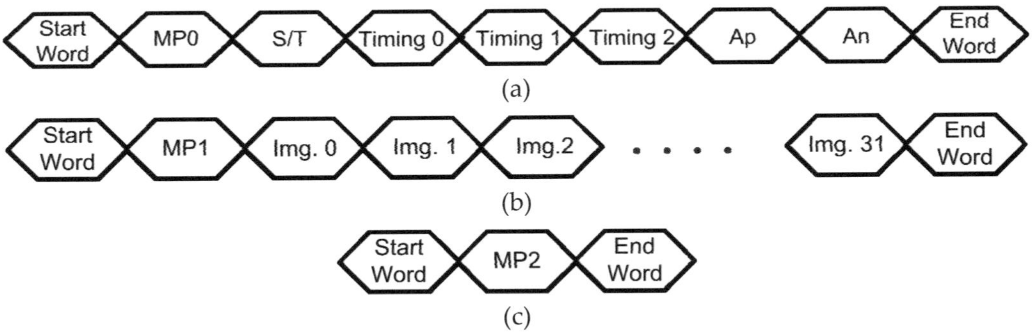


**Figure 20.** Format of the data packets (a) Configuration data packets, (b) Image data packets, and (c) Discharge data packets

| Parameters | Specifications/Values | Parameters | Specifications/Values |
|---|---|---|---|
| **Master clock freq.** | 1 MHz | No. of pulse repetition (pulse train) | 31 times per stimulation |
| **No. of pins** | 5 input pins, 3 output pins | Pulse repetition freq. | 0.14 - 9.8 KHz |
| **Incoming bit rate** | 10.5 Kbps @ 30 fps | Stim. phases width | Anodic 34 – 2018 μs<br>Cathodic 34 - 2018 μs<br>Interphase delay 0 - 994 μs |
| **Outgoing bit rate** | 65.2 × n* Kbps @ 30 fps | Stim. Phases resolution | 34 μs |
| **No. of stim channels** | 16 × 16 | Anodic and Cathodic amplitude resolution | 8 bit |

*n = number of pulse repetition in train strategy

**Table 2.** Designed Controller Specifications

To verify the functionality of the controller, it was implemented on XC2S200. The controller was tested in different operating conditions, including Setup, Image, and Site discharge modes. Serial incoming packet sets were sent to the controller to either program or operate the controller. Functional specifications of the controller are summarized in Table 2. It is worth noting that, at a master clock frequency of 1MHz, the controller is fast enough to support stimulation rate of as high as 30 fps for 256 stimulation sites with a time resolution of 34 μs for biphasic stimulation pulse generation.

### *3.3.2. Stimulation circuitry*

Stimulation circuitry also known as microstimulator is another implant module in visual prosthesis and is in charge of generating and delivering electrical stimulation pulses to the target tissue. Figure 21 shows a generic block level diagram of the components of a

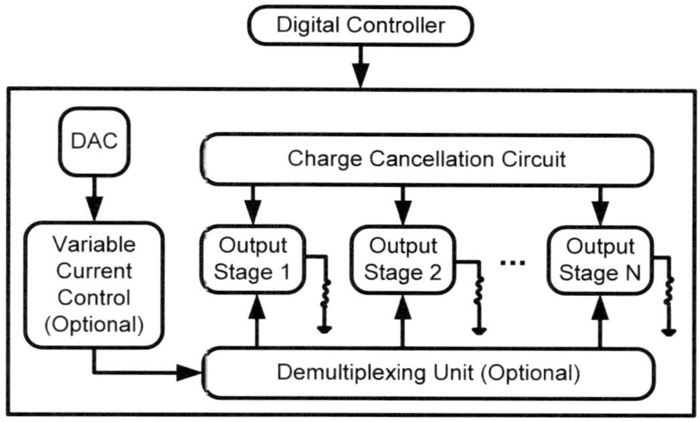


**Figure 21.** A generic block diagram of a microstimulator

microstimulator. The serial data which is wirelessly received and recovered by the data telemetry system, and the clock required for synchronization serve as inputs for the system. A digital controller controls the various blocks of the microstimulator to avoid any conflicts such as discharging while stimulating.

The amplitude of the current generators is controlled by an array of digital-to-analog converters (DAC) allowing digital control of the amplitude of current pulses. The pulse width of each stimulus is controlled by the stimulation sequencer according to the data received. Other parameters such as interphase interval, and stimulation period are also controlled by this block. Along with providing stimulation parameters for an individual stimulus generator, the stimulation sequencer also controls the order of stimulation between different electrodes.

The outputs of the stimulus generators can be designed to pass through a demultiplexer which connects to the electrode array. In this case, the demultiplexer allows one output of the stimulus generator to serve more than one electrode by connecting the output to one of the many electrodes which form a demultiplexed group. This method allows only one electrode in demultiplexed group to stimulate the tissue and thus reduce the flexibility of any-time-any-electrode stimulation but reduces the number of current generators. The stimulus gain controller which is also optional in designing a microstimulator adjusts the gain of the stimulus generator thereby adjusting the full scale (maximum) current generated for each demultiplexed group [57].

Electrical stimulation of excitable cells is generally performed in three forms: 1) voltage-controlled stimulation (VCS), 2) current-controlled stimulation (ICS), and 3) charge-controlled stimulation (QCS), in which voltage, current and electrical charge controlled by switched-capacitor array is applied to the target tissue, respectively. A main drawback of VCS approach is that the current passing through the tissue is highly dependent on the electrode or tissue impedance. Therefore, the charge delivered to the tissue is not well controlled. The VCS form is suitable for power-efficient circuits. The disadvantage of QCS method is large chip-area occupied due to many used capacitors. In ICS form of electrical stimulation, the desired stimulus current passes through the tissue regardless of the tissue impedance. Using this approach with a high-output-impedance output stage for a microstimulator results in better control over the stimulus current and also safer stimulation [58, 59].

There are two general stimulus current waveforms used in neural stimulation: 1) monophasic pulse and 2) biphasic pulse. Monophasic stimulation causes charge accumulation at the electrode-tissue interface and leads to tissue damages. In charge balanced biphasic stimulation, each pulse is followed by a pulse of reverse polarity and results in no residual charge on the electrode and prevents tissue damages. Thus, it is safer and is preferred to monophasic stimulation. Biphasic stimulation is widely used in the neural stimulators and is shown in Fig. 22(a) in the case of rectangular stimulation waveform. The interphase delay $T_d$ separates the opposite phases and thus, they don't reverse the physiological effects of each other. While the circuit is designed to produce charge balanced biphasic pulses, systematic mismatches in circuit design which cannot be avoided, and mismatch between anodic and cathodic current pulses due to manufacturing deviations, would most certainly be present and cause a small but finite charge storage at stimulation sites. Also other unintended sources such as leakage from an adjacent stimulation sites over a period of time may result in buildup of electric charge. The charge cancellation circuitry is activated periodically to perform this discharging process by connecting the electrodes to the common ground potential.

Historically the rectangular waveform has been the choice for the current or voltage pulses employed in neural stimulators [33-40, 57]. But, stimulation efficiency is an important consideration in the stimulation parameters of implantable neural stimulators. There exist some nonrectangular pulse shapes which can results more charge per unit transformed from surface area of the electrode to the target tissue. Some waveform shapes including rectangular, rising exponential, decaying exponential, and rising ramp are shown in Fig. 22(b). Some studies exist in the literature, analyzing the effects of waveform shape and duration on the charge, power, and energy efficiency of neural stimulation [60, 61]. As it proved by the researchers, no waveform was simultaneously energy-, charge-, and power-optimal, and differences in efficiency among waveform shapes varied with pulse width [61].

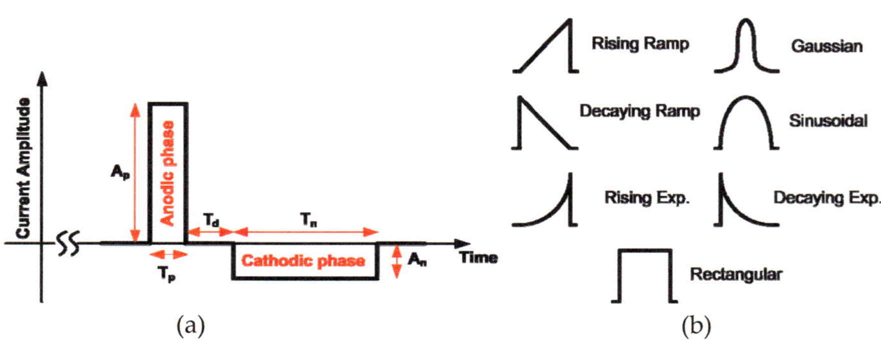


**Figure 22.** (a) Diagram of biphasic current pulse, (b) Different types of stimulating pulses

So, an important factor in designing a microstimulator is related to the application and signal pulse widths. Some researchers have developed appropriate circuits to generate nonrectangular waveforms according to their applications [62].

### 3.3.3. *Microelectrode arrays (MEAs)*

The advent of MEAs more than twenty years ago led to a steady advancement in the development of neural interfaces and neuroscience research. Today advanced microsystems are available for implantation into different organs of body that have multiple electrode sites and are chronically implantable [24, 31]. The packaged electronic circuits containing current drivers in implanted microsystem are connected with enough vias to recording/stimulating MEAs. Typically, a ribbon cable is used with conducting lines for an interconnect from package to electrodes and the flexible cable and MEA are formed in a single process.

The electrode sites are typically made of a conducting metal deposited on a silicon-based substrate. MEAs are usually insulated by a passivation layer, leaving the electrode sites and bonding pads exposed to the target tissue and remaining electronics, respectively [63]. Silicon microelectrodes show good biocompatibility and have the advantage of being compatible with CMOS-based on-chip signal conditioning circuitry [64]. The main problem in silicon-based microelectrodes is that the silicon substrate is mechanically rigid and brittle; therefore if the electrode moves spontaneously, it may cause severe damage in tissue. Therefore, for accommodation for movement, a flexible electrode is highly operational in implantable MEAs.

The main approach for flexible electrodes is polyimide based electrode which has drawn widespread attention [65]. In 1992, Boppart presented a first flexible electrode and used it to measure evoked potentials in brain slices [66]. The research in this field then followed in more advanced designs by Humayun and Weiland's visual prosthesis team in dual-metal-layer processes [67, 68]. Recently, another approach for flexible implantable electrode has been presented using ITO/PET (Indium Tin Oxide/PolyEthylene Terephthalate) by ICAS visual prosthesis group [69]. Among the flexible electrodes, ITO/PET electrode combines good biocompatibility, proper mechanical characteristics, high dielectric strength and is appropriate for microfabrication. The transparency of ITO/PET sheets is in the range of 75 – 80% and they have a measured sheet resistance of about 45 Ω/square. The electrodes can recover to their original shape after rolling or folding as shown in Fig. 23(a). A retinal implantable stimulation electrode has been fabricated with ITO on PET substrate in [69]. Although ITO is very biocompatible, it has relatively high impedance in contrast with other conductors like gold, therefore a layer of gold was evaporated on electrode sites for reducing electrode tissue interface impedance [69]. To passivate the electrode array and ensuring biocompatibility, the electrodes were coated by an insulating polymer, SU-8. This polymer was chosen in this work because of its excellent lithographic properties and also being biocompatible and flexible.

ICAS retinal prosthesis stimulation electrodes, microfabricated on the ITO substrate, consist of 72 (12 × 6) stimulation sites with 100 μm diameter both with circular and rectangular

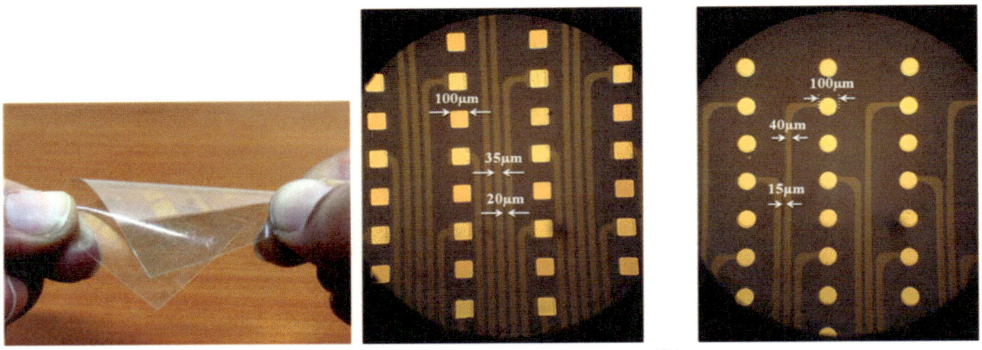


(a) (b)

**Figure 23.** (a) The electrode can be folded and rolled and still maintains the original shape, (b) Stimulation sites of visual prosthesis electrode array taken by electron microscope

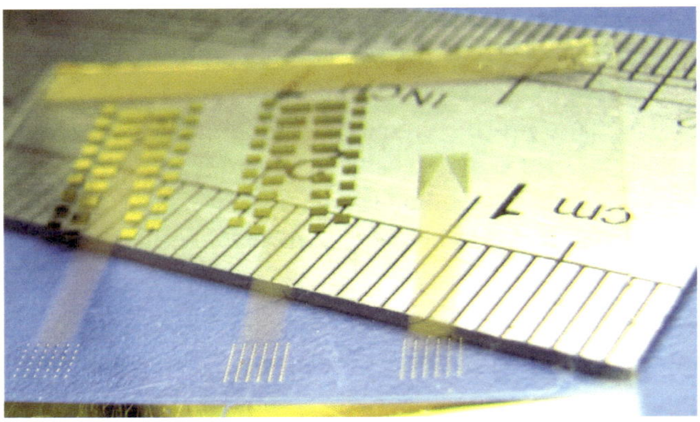

**Figure 24.** Fabricated biomimetic electrodes array contains of 72 sites with 100-µm diameter. The stimulation sites and bonding pads have been coated with gold. (2.47 mm × 2.8 mm)

exposing sites as shown in Fig. 23(b). The fabricated microelectrode arrays are shown in Fig. 24. Stimulation sites and bonding pads were coated with gold and other areas were covered by SU-8 polymer. The whole exposing area of the fabricated microelectrode is 2.47 mm × 2.8 mm, appropriate to be implanted in human eye.

## 4. Wireless telemetry

Wireless telemetry has become an inseparable part of high-performance implantable biomedical devices especially neural recording microsystems and visual prostheses. This is mainly due to the fact that use of wires increases the risk of infection, and also in most applications it is desirable to minimize the size of the implant. In order to benefit from a completely wireless system, the designed wireless interface should be capable of both receiving data from the implant, and sending power and data to the implant. Therefore, on the implant side, the wireless interface is typically consisted of a rectifier and voltage regulator (*power telemetry*), data receiver (*forward telemetry*), and data transmitter (*reverse telemetry*). In depth discussions of wireless telemetry are presented in [70] by the authors. Hence, in this section we briefly review some of the important principles and methods in this field.

Requirements and design constrains for both power and data telemetry are dependent to the application. For example, a multi-channel neural recording system can be designed with around 10-mW power consumption, while a retinal implant may consumes more than 100 mW. Furthermore, position of the implant in body determines the maximum size of the wireless interface. In data transfer, speed of forward telemetry is of great importance in applications where large amount of stimulation data is transmitted continuously to the implant, e.g., visual prostheses and cochlear implants. On the other hand, a high-data-rate reverse telemetry is needed in neural recording microsystems and *brain machine interfaces* (BMIs) for sending recorded signals to external host with minimum delay.

Traditionally, wireless interfaces are based on inductive links, which are composed of two closely-coupled coils with a few millimeters of living tissue in between. These coils are usually tuned to the same resonant frequency to maximize the power transfer efficiency. Wire wound coils and *printed spiral coils* (PSC) are two common types of coils used in biomedical implants. Generally, there are two approaches for implementing a completely wireless microsystem. In the classical approach, only one wireless link is used for power and data telemetry, and data is modulated on the power carrier. Efficient power transfer needs high-Q coils, while for high-speed data transfer low-Q coils are mostly favored. Due to these conflicting requirements, there is a trend towards multiple carrier (multiband) links, where separate links are considered for power and data. The main advantage of this approach is that each link can be optimized individually. However, it should be mentioned that in multiband links there are notable interferences between different carrier signals, which should be reduced by using appropriate techniques such as various geometries and orientations of data coils presented in [71].

In order to optimize the power transfer efficiency and power delivered to the load, a 3-coil power link (with one additional coil on the implant side) has been proposed in [72]. The main idea behind this method is transforming the load impedance to the optimal impedance needed at the primary coil [72]. In forward data telemetry, by designing the link specifically for *binary phase-shift keying* (BPSK) modulation [73], and selecting one of the BPSK demodulators reported in [74-77], data rates as high as the carrier frequency can be achieved. For reverse telemetry, *pulse harmonic modulation* (PHM) [78], or low-power *ultra wide band* (UWB) transmitters [79] can be used to provide data rates in the range of a few Mbps.

Recently, employing capacitive links for implantable biomedical applications was studied in [80, 81]. The idea of capacitive coupling has been already used for inter-chip data communication [82] and power transfer [83], and also for sensing biomedical signals [84, 85]. In this approach a capacitor is formed between two parallel plates, one implanted and the other one attached to the outer part of the skin. The dielectric of this capacitor is mostly the body tissue between the plates. A detailed model of this type of capacitance and the complete capacitive link can be found in [81]. One of the most important advantages of the capacitive coupling over its inductive counterparts is the high-pass nature of the link. As a result, high voltage transfer ratios can be achieved even when the transmitted signal contains wide range of harmonics, like digital data and BPSK signals [81].

Besides size constrains, number/type of wireless links, power transfer efficiencies, and high data rates, one of the most important issues in wireless telemetry is power dissipation in human body. These power dissipations may result in excessive temperature rise in biological tissues, which can even lead to tissue damages. Therefore, in designing all wireless interfaces, the amount of absorbed *radio frequency* (RF) energy has to be evaluated and compared with the human safety levels, which are usually expressed in terms of *specific absorption rate* (SAR) in the standard [86]. Nowadays, SAR calculations can be performed by most of electromagnetic simulators (e.g., SEMCAD X by SPEAG and CST Microwave Studio), and using high-resolution *three-dimensional* (3-D) human body models [87, 88].

## Author details

Alireza Zabihian, M.H. Maghami, Farzad Asgarian and Amir M. Sodagar
*Integrated Circuits & Systems (ICAS) Lab., Department of Electrical & Computer Eng., K. N. Toosi University of Technology, Iran*

## Acknowledgement

The authors would like to thanks M.A Shahzeidi, A. Shaker, H. Salehi, L. Saadati-fard, A. Akhavian, S. Farahmand, and A. Sheikholeslami for their help and support.

## 5. References

[1] Metting van Rijin A.C., Peper A, and Grimbergen C.A. (1986) High-quality recording of bioelectric events, Med. & Biol Eng.& Comput., 29: 1035-1044.
[2] Andersen R.A., Musallam S., and Pesaran B. (2004) Selecting the signals for a brain machine interface, Curr. Opn. Neurobiol., 14: 720–726.
[3] Charles C.T. (2003) Electrical Components for a Fully Implantable Neural Recording System, M.S. Thesis, the University of Utah.
[4] Kester W., Bryant J., Jung W. (1999) Amplifiers for Signal Conditioning, Practical Design Techniques for Sensor Signal.
[5] Seese T.M., Harasaki H., Saidel G.M., and Davies C.R. (1998) Characterization of tissue morphology, angiogenesis, and temperature in the adaptive response of muscle tissue to chronic heating, Lab. Invest., 78: 1553–1562.
[6] Steyaert M. and Sansen W., (1987) A micropower low-noise monolithic instrumentation amplifier formedical purposes, IEEE J. Solid-State Circuits, 22: 1163–1168.
[7] Gray P.R., Hurst P., Lewis S., and Meyer R. (2001) Analysis and Design of Analog Integrated Circuits,4$^{th}$ ed. NewYork:Wiley.

[8] Rezaee-Dehsorkh H., Ravanshad N., Lotfi R., Mafinezhad K., Sodagar A.M., (2011) Analysis and Design of Tunable Amplifiers for Implantable Neural Recording Applications, IEEE J. on Emerg. and Selected Topics in Circ. and Syst., 1: 546-556.

[9] Harrison R. and Charles C. (2003) A low-power low-noise CMOS amplifier for neural recording applications, IEEE J. Solid-State Circuits, 38: 958–965.

[10] Zhao W., Li H., Zhang Y. (2009) A Low-Noise Integrated Bioamplifier with Active DC Offset Suppression, IEEE Conf. on Biomed. Circuits and Syst, 5–8.

[11] Mosheni P. and Najafi K. (2004) A fully integrated neural recording amplifier with DC input stabilization, IEEE Trans. Biomed. Eng., 51: 832–837.

[12] Heer F., Hafzovic S., Franks W., Blau A., Ziegler C., and Hierlemann A. (2006) CMOS microelectrode array for bidirectional interaction with neuronal networks, IEEE J. Solid-State Circuits, 41: 1620–1629.

[13] Wu H. and Xu Y.P. (2006) A 1V 2.3 μw biomedical signal acquisition IC, Proc. IEEE Int. Conf. Digest Tech. Papers, 119–128.

[14] Denison T., et.al. (2007) A 2.2 μW94 94nV/√Hz Chopper-stabilized instrumentation amplifier for EEG detection in chronic implants, Proc. IEEE Int. Solid-State Circuits Conf. Dig. Tech. Papers, 162–163.

[15] Yin M., and Ghovanloo M. (2007) A low-noise preamplifier with adjustable gain and bandwidth for biopotential recording applications, Proc. IEEE Int. Symp. Circuits and Systems, 321–324.

[16] Wattanapanitch W., Fee M., and Sarpeshkar R. (2007) An energy-efficient micropower neural recording amplifier, IEEE Trans. Biomed. Circuits Syst., 1: 136–147.

[17] Lee J., Rhew H., Kipke D., and Flynn M. (2008) A 64 channel programmable closed-loop deep brain stimulator with 8 channel neural amplifier and logarithmic ADC, Proc. IEEE Symp. VLSI Circuits, 76–77.

[18] Yazicioglu R.F., Merken P., Puers R., and Hoof C.V. (2008) A 200μw Eight-channel EEG acquisition ASIC for ambulatory EEG systems, IEEE J. Solid-State Circuits, 43: 3025–3038.

[19] Mollazadeh M., Murari K., Cauwenberghs G., and Thakor N. (2009) Micropower CMOS integrated low-noise amplification, filtering, and digitization of multimodal neuropotentials, IEEE Trans. Biomed. Circuits Syst., 3: 1–10.

[20] Yeager D.J., et. al, (2009) NeuralWISP: A Wirelessly Powered Neural Interface With 1-m Range, IEEE Transactions on Biomedical Circuits and Systems, 3: 379-387.

[21] Shahrokhi F., et.al. (2010) The 128-Channel Fully Differential Digital Integrated Neural Recording and Stimulation Interface, IEEE Transactions on Biomedical Circuits and Systems, 4: 149-161.

[22] Wise K.D., Sodagar A.M., Yao Y., Gulari M.N., Perlin G.E., and Najafi K., (2008) Microelectrodes, Microelectronics, and Implantable Neural Microsystems, Proceedings of the IEEE, 96: 1174-1202.

[23] Sudakshina K. (2010) Analog and Digital Communications, Pearson Education India.

[24] Mohseni P., Najafi K. (2005) A Battery-Powered 8-Channel Wireless FM IC for Biopotential Recording Applications, in Proc. IEEE Int. Solid-State Circuits Conf. Dig. Tech. Papers, 560-561.

[25] Rajabi-Tavakkol A., Sodagar A.M., Refan M.H. (2010) New Architecture for Wireless Implantable Neural Recording Microsystems Based on Frequency-Division Multiplexing, Proc. Annu. Int. IEEE Eng. Med. Biol. Conf. (EMBC), 6449-6452.
[26] Dagtekin M., Lie W., Bashirullah R. (2001) A Multichannel Chopper Modulated Neural Recording System, Proc. Annu. Int. IEEE Eng. Med. Biol. Conf. (EMBC), 757-760.
[27] Zabihian A., Sodagar A.M. (2009) A New Architecture for Multi-Channel Neural Recording Microsystems Based on Delta-Sigma Modulation," IEEE Conf. on Biomed. Circuits and Syst., 81-84.
[28] Akhavian, A., Judy, M. and Sodagar, A.M. (2012) Anti-Logarithmic Quantization for Data Reduction in Multi-Channel Intra-Cortical Neural Recording Implants, accepted for presentation at the IEEE-EMBS International Conference on Biomedical and Health Informatics.
[29] Hosseini-Nejad H., Sodagar A.M., Lotfizad M. (2011) Data Reduction Based on Walsh-Hadamard Transform for Implantable Neural Recording Microsystems", IEEE CAS-FEST Workshop on Brain-Machine/Brain-Computer Interfaces (BMI/BCI).
[30] Shaeri, M.A., Sodagar, A.M. and Abrishami-Moghaddam, H. (2011) A 64-Channel Neural Signal Processor/Compressor Based on Haar Wavelet Transform, Proc Annual IEEE Engineering in Medicine and Biology Society Conference (EMBC), 6409-6412.
[31] Harrison, R.R., Watkins, P.T., Kier, R.J., Lovejoy, R.O., Black, D.J., Greger, B. and Solzbacher, F. (2007) A Low-Power Integrated Circuit for a Wireless 100-Electrode Neural Recording System," IEEE Jour. of Solid-State Circ., 42: 123-133.
[32] Forrester J.V., Dick A.D., Mc Menamin P.G., Lee W.R. (2002) the Eye: Basic Sciences in Practice, London: Harcourt Publishers.
[33] Weiland J.D., Humayun M.S. (2008) Visual Prosthesis, Proceedings of the IEEE, 96: 1076-1084.
[34] World Health Organization website, available at http://www.who.int/blindness/causes/magnitude/en/ (Accessed August 2011).
[35] Margalit E., Sadda S.R. (2003) Retinal and Optic Nerve Diseases, 27: 963–974.
[36] Maguire A.M., Simonelli F., Pierce E.A., Pugh E.N., Mingozzi F., Bennicelli J., Banfi S., Marshall K.A., Testa F., Surace E.M., Rossi S., Lyubarsky A., Arruda V.R., Konkle B., Stone E., Sun J., Jacobs J., Dell'Osso L., Hertle R., Ma J.-X., Redmond T.M., Zhu X., Hauck B., Zelenaia O., Shindler K.S., Maguire M.G., Wright J.F., Volpe N.J., McDonnell J.W., Auricchio A., High K.A., Bennett J. (2008) Safety and Efficacy of Gene Transfer for Leber's Congenital Amaurosis, The New England Journal of Medicine, 358: 2240–2248.
[37] Chen K., Yang Z., Hoang L., Weiland J.D., Humayun M.S., Liu W. (2010) An Integrated 256-Channel Epiretinal Prosthesis, IEEE Journal of Solid-State Circuits, 45: 1946-1956.
[38] Shire D.B., Kelly S.K., Chen J., Doyle P., Gingerich M.D., Cogan S.F., Drohan W.A., Mendoza O., Theogarajan L., Wyatt J.L., Rizzo J.F. (2009) Development and Implantation of a Minimally Invasive Wireless Subretinal Neurostimulator, IEEE Transaction on Biomedical Engineering, 56: 2502-2511.
[39] Chai X., Li L., Wu K., Zhou C., Cao P., Ren Q. (2008) C-Sight Visual Prosthesis for the Blind, IEEE Engineering in Medicine and Biology Magazine, 27: 20-28.

[40] Coulombe J., Sawan M., Gervais J.-F. (2007) A Highly Flexible System for Microstimulation of the Visual Cortex: Design and Implementation, IEEE Transaction on Biomedical Circuits and Systems, 1: 258–269.

[41] Zrenner E., Bartz-Schmidt K.U., Benav H., Besch D., Bruckmann A., Gabel V., Gekeler F., Greppmaier U., Harscher A., Kibbel S., Koch J., Kusnyerik A., Peters T., Stingl K., Sachs H., Stett A., Szurman P., Wilhelm B., Wilke R. (2010) Subretinal Electronic Chips Allow Blind Patients to Read Letters and Combine Them to Words, Proceedings of Royal Society, 278: 1489–1497.

[42] Margalit E., Maia M., Weiland J. D., Greenberg R. J., Fujii G. Y., Torres G. , Piyathaisere D.V., O'Hearn T.M., Liu W., Lazzi G., Dagnelie G., Scribner D.A., de Juan D., Humayun M.S. (2002) Retinal Prosthesis for the Blind, Journal of Survey of Ophthalmology, 47: 335–356.

[43] Shahzeidi M. A. (2010) Video Image Capturing, Processing and Preparation for an Implantable Visual Prosthesis, MSc Dissertation, K.N. Toosi University of Technology.

[44] Shaker A. (2011) Image Capture and Processing to be Used in Visual Prostheses, M.Sc. Dissertation, Shahid Rajaee Teacher Training University.

[45] Boyle J. (2005) Improving Perception from Electronic Visual Prostheses, PhD Dissertation, Queensland University of Technology.

[46] Russ J. (1999) The Image Processing Handbook, Florida USA: CRC Press, pp. 242-247.

[47] Levine M. (1985) Vision in Man and Machine, New York: McGraw-Hill.

[48] Cha K., Horch K., Normann R., (1992) Mobility Performance with a Pixelized Vision System, Vision Research, 32: 1367-1372.

[49] Parikh N., Itti L., Weiland J.D. (2010) Saliency-Based Image Processing for Retinal Prostheses, Journal of Neural Engineering, 7: 1-10.

[50] Liu W., Fink W., Tarbell M., Sivaprakasam M. (2005) Image Processing and Interface for Retinal Visual Prostheses, Proceedings of IEEE International Symposium on Circuits and Systems (ISCAS), 3: 2927- 2930.

[51] Boyle J.R., Maeder A.J. (2008) Region-of-Interest Processing for Electronic Visual Prostheses", Journal of Electronic Imaging, 17: 1-12.

[52] Dowling J., Maeder A., Boles W. (2004) Mobility Enhancement and Assessment for a Visual prosthesis, Proceedings of SPIE Medical Imaging, 780-791.

[53] C. Liu, H. Wechsler (2002) Gabor Feature Based Classification Using the Enhanced Fisher Linear Discriminant Model for Face Recognition, IEEE Transactions on Image Processing, 11: 270-275.

[54] Chen K., Liu W. (2009) Highly Programmable Digital Controller for High-Density Epi-Retinal Prosthesis, Proceedings of 31st Annual International Conference of the IEEE EMBS, 1592-1595.

[55] Talukder M.I., Siy P., Auner G.W. (2008) High Resolution Implantable Microsystem and Probe Design for Retinal Prosthesis, The Open Ophthalmology Journal, 2: 77-90.

[56] Salehi H., Sodagar A.M. (2012) Design of an Application-Specific Controller for a Visual Prosthesis, Proceedings of IEEE International Caribbean Conference on Devices, Circuits, and Systems, 1-4.

[57] Sivaprakasam M., Liu W., Wang G., Weiland J.D., Humayun M.S. (2005) Architecture Tradeoffs in High-Density Microstimulators for Retinal Prosthesis, IEEE Transactions on Circuits and Systems I, 52: 2629-2641.

[58] Ghovanloo M. (2006) Switched-Capacitor Based Implantable Low-Power Wireless Microstimulating Systems, Proceedings of IEEE International Symposium on Circuits and Systems (ISCAS), 2197–2200.

[59] Simpson J., Ghovanloo M. (2007) An Experimental Study of Voltage, Current, and Charge Controlled Stimulation Front-End Circuitry, Proceedings of IEEE International Symposium on Circuits and Systems (ISCAS), 325–328.

[60] Jezernik S., Morari M. (2005) Energy-Optimal Electrical Excitation of Nerve Fibers, IEEE Transactions on Biomedical Engineering, 52: 740–743.

[61] Wongsarnpigoon A., Woock J. P., Grill W.M. (2010) Efficiency Analysis of Waveform Shape for Electrical Excitation of Nerve Fibers, IEEE Transactions on Neural Systems and Rehabilitation Engineering, 18: 319-328.

[62] Ethier S., Sawan M. (2011) Exponential Current Pulse Generation for Efficient Very High- Impedance Multisite Stimulation, IEEE Transactions on Biomedical Circuits and Systems, 5: 30-38.

[63] Selvakumaran J., Keddie J.L., Ewins D.J., Hughes M.P. (2007) Protein Adsorption on Materials for Recording Sites on Implantable Microelectrodes, Journal of Material Science, Materials in Medicine, 19: 143-151.

[64] Metz S., Oppliger F., Holzer R., Buisson B., Bertrand D., Renaud P. (2000) Fabrication and Test of Implantable Thin-Film Electrodes for Stimulation and Recording of Biological Signals, Proceedings of 1st Annual International IEEE EMBS Special Topic Conference on Microtechnologies in Medicine & Biology, 619-623.

[65] Rizzo J., Tombran-Tink J., Barnstable C.J. (2007) Visual Prosthesis and Ophthalmic Devices: New Hope in Sight, Totowa, NJ: Humana Press Inc., pp. 125-128.

[66] Boppart S.A., Wheeler B.C., Wallace C.S. (1992) A Flexible Perforated Microelectrode Array for Extended Neural Recordings, IEEE Transactions on Biomedical Engineering, 39: 37-42.

[67] Rodger D.C., Fong A.J., Li W., Ameri H., Lavrov I., Zhong H., Saati S., Menon P., Meng E., Burdick J.W., Roy R.R., Edgerton V.R., Weiland J.D., Humayun M.S., Tai Y.-C. (2007) High-Density Flexible Parylene-Based Multielectrode Arrays for Retinal and Spinal Cord Stimulation, Proceedings of IEEE Conference on Solid-State Sensors, Actuators and Microsystems, 1385-1388.

[68] Weiland J.D., Humayun M.S., Eckhardt H., Ufer S., Laude L., Basinger B., Tai Y.-C. (2009) A Comparison of Retinal Prosthesis Electrode Array Substrate Materials, Proceedings of 31st Annual International Conference of the IEEE EMBS, 4140-4143.

[69] Ahani A., Saadati-Fard L., Sodagar A.M., Boroumad F.A. (2011) Flexible PET/ITO electrode array for implantable biomedical applications, Proceedings of Annual International Conference of the IEEE EMBS, 2878-2881.

[70] Asgarian F., Sodagar A.M. (2011) Wireless Telemetry for Implantable Biomedical Microsystems. In: Laskovski A.N., editor, Biomedical Engineering, Trends in Electronics, Communications and Software, Rijeka: InTech, pp. 21-44. Available at:

http://www.intechopen.com/books/biomedical-engineering-trends-in-electronics-communications-and-software/wireless-telemetry-for-implantable-biomedical-microsystems (Accessed 2012 July 12).

[71] Jow U.-M., Ghovanloo M. (2010) Optimization of Data Coils in a Multiband Wireless Link for Neuroprosthetic Implantable Devices, IEEE Transaction on Biomedical Circuits and Systems, 4: 301–310.

[72] Kiani M., Jow U.-M., Ghovanloo M. (2011) Design and Optimization of a 3-Coil Inductive Link for Efficient Wireless Power Transmission, IEEE Transaction on Biomedical Circuits and Systems, 5: 579–591.

[73] Simard G., Sawan M., Massicotte D. (2010) High-Speed OQPSK and Efficient Power Transfer Through Inductive Link for Biomedical Implants, IEEE Transaction on Biomedical Circuits and Systems, 4: 192–200.

[74] Gong C.-S.A., Shiue M.-T., Yao K.-W., Chen T.-Y. (2008) Low-Power and Area-Efficient PSK Demodulator for Wirelessly Powered Implantable Command Receivers, Electronics Letters, 44: 841-842.

[75] Asgarian F., Sodagar A.M. (2009) A High-Data-Rate Low-Power BPSK Demodulator and Clock Recovery Circuit for Implantable Biomedical Devices, Proceedings of 4th International IEEE/EMBS Conference on Neural Engineering, 407-410.

[76] Asgarian F., Sodagar A.M. (2009) A Low-Power Noncoherent BPSK Demodulator and Clock Recovery Circuit for High-Data-Rate Biomedical Applications, Proceedings of 31st Annual International Conference of the IEEE EMBS, 4840-4843.

[77] Asgarian F., Sodagar A.M. (2010) A Carrier Frequency Independent BPSK Demodulator with 100% Data-Rate-to-Carrier-Frequency Ratio, Proceedings of IEEE Biomedical Circuits and Systems Conference (BioCAS), 29-32.

[78] Inanlou F., Ghovanloo M. (2011) Wideband Near-Field Data Transmission Using Pulse Harmonic Modulation, IEEE Transaction on Circuits and Systems-I, 58: 186-195.

[79] Chae M.S., Yang Z., Yuce M.R., Liu M. (2009) A 128-Channel 6 mW Wireless Neural Recording IC with Spike Feature Extraction and UWB Transmitter, IEEE Transaction on Neural and Rehabilitation Engineering, 17: 312-321.

[80] Sodagar A.M., Amiri P. (2009) Capacitive Coupling for Power and Data Telemetry to Implantable Biomedical Microsystems, Proceedings of the 2009 IEEE International Neural Engineering Conference., 411-414.

[81] Takhti M., Asgarian F., Sodagar A.M. (2011) Modeling of a Capacitive Link for Data Telemetry to Biomedical Implants, Proceedings of IEEE Biomedical Circuits and Systems Conference (BioCAS), 181-184.

[82] Fazzi A., Canegallo R., Ciccarelli L., Magagni L., Natali F., Jung E., Rolandi P.L., Guerrieri R. (2008) 3-D Capacitive Interconnections with Mono and Bi-Directional Capabilities, IEEE Journal of Solid-State Circuits (JSSC), 43: 275-284.

[83] Culurciello E., Andreou A.G. (2006) Capacitive Inter-Chip Data and Power Transfer for 3-D VLSI, IEEE Transaction on Circuits and Systems-II, 53: 1348-1352.

[84] Svard D., Cichocki A., Alvandpour A. (2010) Design and Evaluation of a Capacitively Coupled Sensor Readout Circuit Toward Contact-less ECG and EEG, Proceedings of IEEE Biomedical Circuits and Systems Conference (BioCAS), 302-305.

[85] Chi Y.M., Maier C., Cauwenberghs G. (2011) An Integrated Low-Noise High-input Impedance Front-end for Capacitive Non-contact Physiological and BCI Sensor Systems, presented at 2011 IEEE CAS-FEST workshop on Brain-machine/Brain-computer Interfaces, Rio de Janeiro, May 2011.

[86] IEEE Standard C95.1-2005. IEEE Standards for Safety Levels with Respect to Human Exposure to Radio Frequency Electromagnetic Fields, 3 KHz to 300 GHz.

# Chapter 8

# Biomedical Instrumentation to Analyze Pupillary Responses in White-Chromatic Stimulation and Its Influence on Diagnosis and Surgical Evaluation

Ernesto Suaste Gómez and Anabel S. Sánchez Sánchez

Additional information is available at the end of the chapter

http://dx.doi.org/10.5772/48704

## 1. Introduction

The pupil is an important element for image perception helping in the focus of parallel rays inside of the eye on the macula and because of its autonomic innervations had been studied in many scientific areas [1-11]. The pupil diameter has been measured with different methods and luminance conditions. Characteristics of pupil diameter like peak velocity contraction, maximum contraction time, amplitude and more [9] have been studied under white light conditions [12] and darkness. Authors have mentioned latency time does not change with age from 14 to 45 years old [3].

Experiments with flicker chromatic lights of equal and different luminance levels have been done; specifically using blue, green and red stimulus [13-16]. Kimura E. and Young R. studied pupil responses to 6 wavelengths [17]. Rodríguez D. and Suaste E. analyzed pupil responses from 400 to 600 nm [18]. Video techniques or image based methods called Video-oculography (VOG), have been employed in the study of pupillary responses [3,8,10,12,14,18,19] with capture ranges of 20, 25 and 102.4 Hz [3,10,12] and pupilometers [17]. High speed video-oculography (HSV) [5, 20] is a technique used in eye tracking systems [21], the study of mice speed movements [22], nistagmus analysis [23], and for pupil dynamic analysis with white light. Another application of VOG had been the objective perimetry as a new proposed method that does not require the opinion of the subject in study using pupillary response.

On the other hand, the World Health Organization describes that 314 millions of people have a visual incapacity, 45 million are blind and 90% live in developing countries, being cataract and refractive errors the principal causes of treatable blindness. During the searching by to resolve cataract blindness, Scientifics have been developed techniques of cataract extraction and many kinds of Intraocular Lens (IOL) with the purpose of giving transparency and flexibility as a natural lens for the eye. IOL could be only for a vision (monofocal), two visions (bifocal) or multiple visions (multifocal). IOL are a method of correcting cataract and refractive errors (from moderate to high) [24]. Speaking of refractive errors and their correction, IOL represent the next step in the refractive surgery. Authors have explained the importance of considering pupil size when an IOL will be or have been implanted [25-27]. Others authors have spoken about visual effects and complications as results from IOL implantation [28-30].

The purpose of this chapter is to show the biomedical instrumentation based on two VOG techniques used to study pupillary responses as well as to describe a useful methodology in order to determine pupillary dynamic evoked by chromatic stimuli plus a white stimulus, using High Speed Video-oculography (HSV) and image eye processing. The mentioned evaluation is applied to know pupillary responses in healthy subjects and in subjects with an implant of IOL (multifocal) which are called pseudophakics.

## 2. Instrumentation and methodology

### 2.1. Introduction

In the late 40´s, researchers used cameras to record eye movements of pilots [31]. But until the 70´s the eye monitoring based on video began. Eye monitoring systems have been classified in two categories: invasive and active against non-invasive and passive. Passive eye monitoring is popular by being non-intrusive [19]. Techniques as electrooculography, electromyography, infrared-oculography and VOG, have been used to monitoring and tracking eye lid, pupillary responses and gaze direction [32]. The VOG is classified as passive eye monitoring because it is non-intrusive. In the next paragraphs is going to be described VOG employed in some preliminary experiments.

### 2.2. Video-oculography

A reference scale is collocated on the lower eyelid of the left eye to convert pixels to millimeters. It is shown in Figure 1.

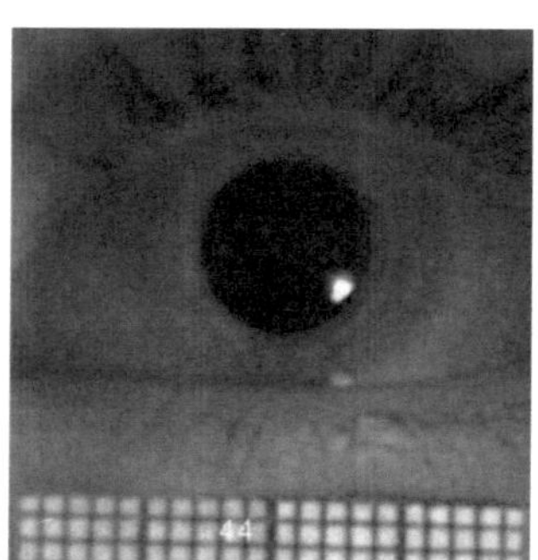

**Figure 1.** Reference in millimeters scale. Pupillary area in this picture is of 34.686 mm$^2$.

The chromatic stimulus is projected on right eye while left eye is being recorded. Eyes can be stimulated with 4 wavelengths inside of the visible spectrum plus a white stimulus. The duration of the stimulus is 6 seconds; 155 fps (frame) are captured per second approximately, which means that pupil measurements were taken each 7ms (time between photos). Eye images are recorded inside of a dark room with infrared light (IRL $\lambda$=900 nm) which is placed at 10 cm from the left eye temporal side. HSV starts with darkness adaptation of 10 min and then the first stimulus was projected. The stimuli sequence is red, blue, green, yellow and white. Five minutes of darkness adaptation between stimuli are necessary for pupil expansion. The HSV is performed from 7:00 to 10:00 hours. IRL is deactivated if there is not recording. In order to avoid gaze deviation, the subject is being sat on a height adjustable seat and his head is placed on chinrest. Camera and IRL are collocated on an elevation table. See Figure 2. All this allowed for specific adaptations, for subject comfort during the HSV. In Figure 3 is showed a series of pupillary pictures from high speed chromatic video-oculography.

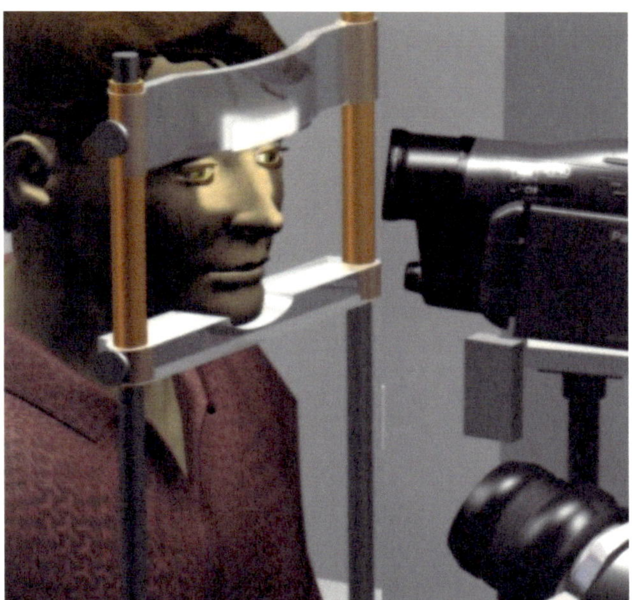

**Figure 2.** The VOG image represents medical center where HSV was performed. Chromatic stimulus was projected to right eye while left eye was filmed and the video was recorded in a computer.

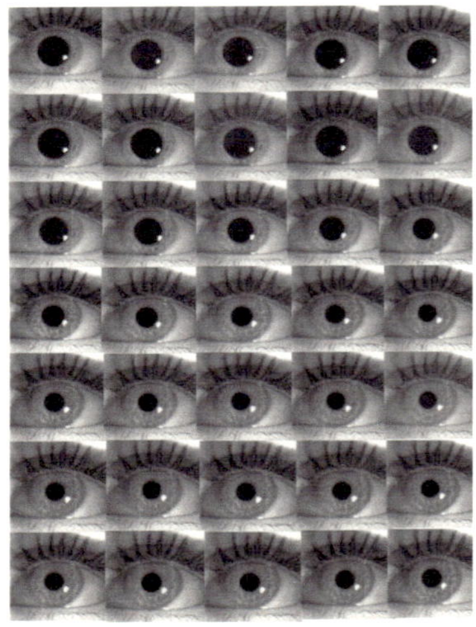

**Figure 3.** It is illustrating a series of pupillary pictures obtained from high speed chromatic video-oculography

### *2.1.1 Cameras*

The next paragraphs are going to describe the cameras used to evaluate pupillary responses in the applications forward in the text, in two categories of VOG. The main difference between them is the number of frames per second. Commercial video cameras (NTSC format) with CCD and CMOS sensors give generally 50 o 60 fps. A little bit number gives 120 fps [33].

#### *2.1.1.1. SONY camera*

A CCD SONY video color camera, DCR-SR42 model is employed in conventional VOG, with 500 lines of horizontal resolution and peak velocity of capture of 30 fps. This camera has a night shot, option which let film using IR illumination. See Figure 4.

#### *2.1.1.2. DALSA HIGH-SPEED video-camera*

A DALSA monochromatic camera, CA-D6-0256W-ECEW model, has a shooting range up to 929 fps and 260x260 pixels of resolution; it gives possibility of taking approximately a frame each second. Pictures could be kept in BMP, JPG, etc formats. See Figure 4.

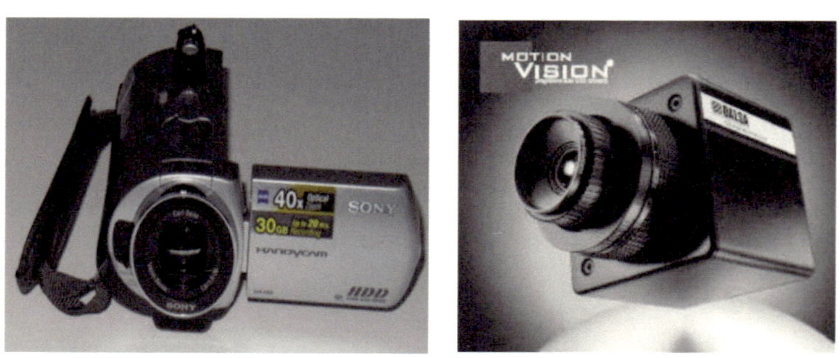


**Figure 4.** SONY camera (left, own elaboration) and DALSA camera (right, Dalsa camera user´s manual).

### *2.1.2. Stimuli*

These stimuli included the two chromatic-opponent-cone axes, a red–green (L–M) axis and a blue–yellow [S _ (L + M)] axis. Four chromatic stimuli plus white are used in these experiments but they could be changed according to the purpose in other studies. Each one is characterized by measuring it's reflectance spectrum; it will be helpful when pupillary responses will be analyzed. Previous studies can be considered in this aspect [13-18].

The luminance level is measured with a Light Photometer IL 400 A. The fotometer sensor is collocated in front of the stimulus where the eye will be, in order to know luminance in that precisely place. Luminance levels are regulated adjusting the input voltage to the light source to each stimulus. See Figure 5. The reflectance spectrum was measured with a spectrometer OSM-400-UV/VIS in order to know the wavelength components in each stimulus [34]. Thirty-six reflectance spectrums were taken from each stimulus, they were averaged and plotted. Stimuli were indicated according their principal component. See Figure 6.

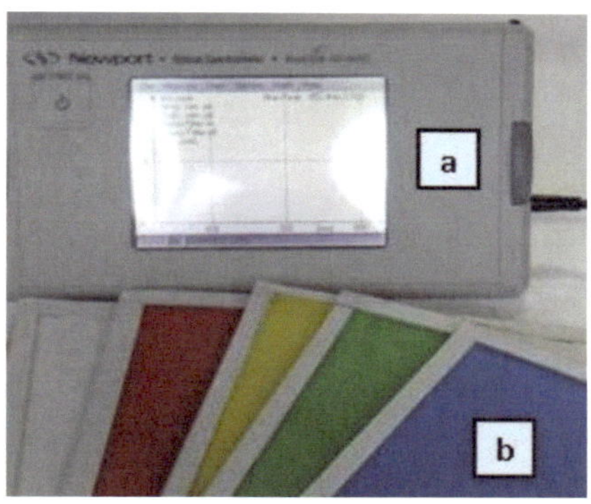


**Figure 5.** a) Spectrometer OSM-400-UV/VIS and b) Stimuli.

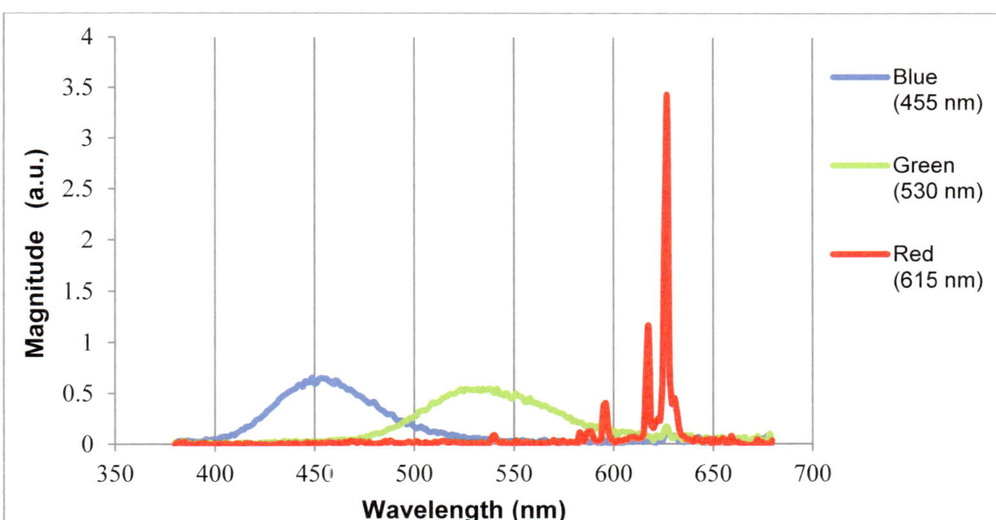


**Figure 6.** Examples of reflectance spectrums.

## 2.2. Objective perimetry

The perimetry is another test where is possible to use VOG. Perimetry is a helpfulness test, in diagnosing ocular diseases as glaucoma or blindness areas, analyzing the visual field. Perimetry has been classified as: Static and Kinetic. Static, keeps an immobile stimulus in a visual field position, and increases progressively its luminance until the subject not be able to detect it. Kinetic, moves the stimulus along visual field. Here is described the objective perimetry as an application of VOG. The design is based on the Goldmann perimeter dimensions [35]. The light source is a stroboscopic lamp and the targets are based on fiber optic with a diameter of 1 mm, controlled by a computer system. The projection of dims targets is based on fiber optics which permits to perform test in colors, in all the areas of the visual field. A VOG system is used for monitoring and recording the pupil constriction. This system consists of an SONY camera and a PC equipped. After pupillary images are processed and analyzed. It is possible to use together at Evoked Visual Potentials (EVP), electro-oculography and electro-retinography with the aim of to observe cerebral activity when the pupil is stimulated and know alterations in the visual pathway [36]. An example of it, it is showed in Figure 7.

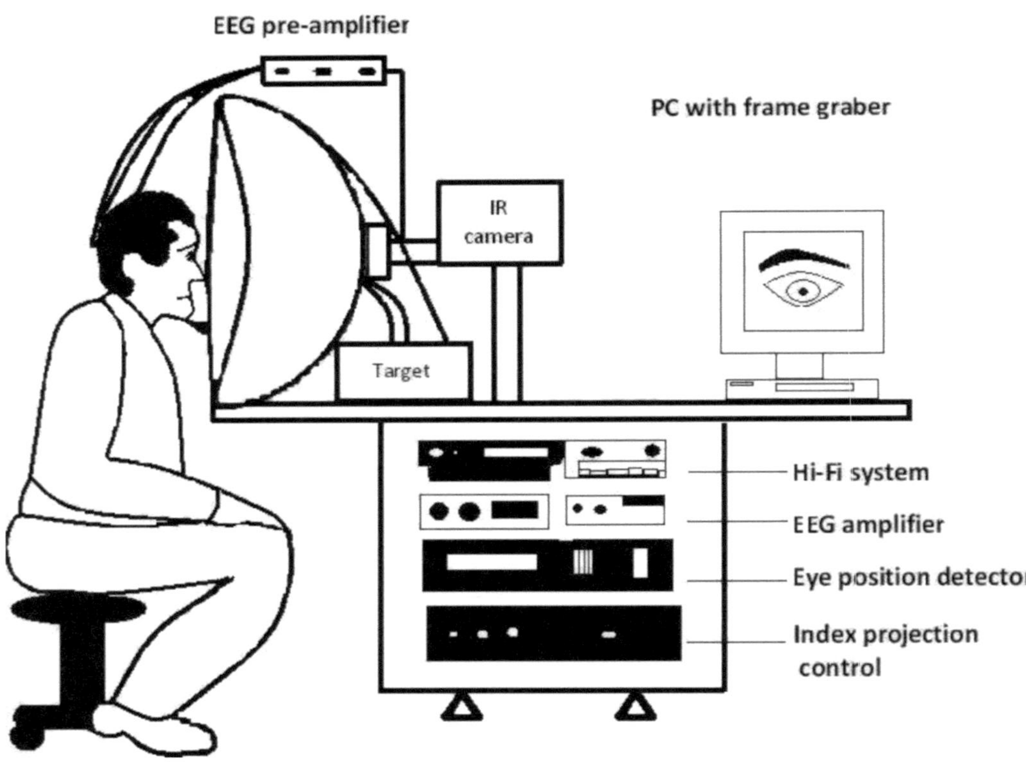


**Figure 7.** It shows objective perimetry and EVP.

### 2.3. Image processing and statistical analysis

This procedure can be done in any programming language of your choice (MATLAB, C Language, etc). The aim of this stage is to identify pupillary areas in each picture. A graph is illustrating the points on the line selected to observe the pupil dynamic is shown in Figure 8. Variations in pupillary areas of the left eye while the stimulus is projected on the right eye are shown in Figure 8a. Pupil parameters are determined from HSV as follows: Area at the beginning (BA), area at latency time (LA), latency time (LT was taken as Barbur J *et al* described the point at which the trace first departed from the baseline), maximum contraction area (MCA shows time at which pupil area comes to its maximum contraction area), time of maximum contraction (TMC refers to period of time measured from the stimulus beginning at the moment when pupil comes to its peak velocity value) and pupil area from 0 to 5 seconds. The first derivate was calculated from the typical graph in order to obtain values as Peak velocity contraction (PVC presents value of maximum velocity during the pupil responses in each stimulus) and time of peak velocity contraction (TPVC). An example of the last two values is presented in Figure 8b.

Images are processed in a Vision Builder AI 3.5 using graphical programming. First a calibration was performed in order to convert pixels to millimeters. Filters were used to highlight the area of interest in the image sequence. Intensity variations were decreased, noise was eliminated and outlines were identified. Steps of image processing are described in Figure 9.

In this context, dates obtained from images can be analyzed for are used statistical analysis. The statistical analysis can be done in any software of your preference depending on the purpose of each experiment. Below, Mean Difference (F test) and Analysis Of Variance (ANOVA) are used to get the necessary comparisons among groups; and, in addition the measures known as average and standard deviation. These statistical analyses are applied in the next section in this chapter.

## 3. Applications of pupillary evaluations and results

### 3.1. Introduction

In this section there are described many applications of Conventional and High-speed VOG, in diagnosis and postsurgical eye applications. These studies were approved by Bioethical Committee for Research in Humans from Center of Research and Advanced Studies (CINVESTAV). Subjects were informed about the project and they signed in their agreement as it is established in the Helsinki Declaration. For that, it is necessary to apply a preview subject's evaluation with the purpose of having a homogenous sample. Tests are applied to volunteers in order to select the sample group: visual acuity, static retinoscopy, D15, and ophthalmoscopy. D15 test was applied to all subjects in order to exclude subjects with color perception problems. Static retinoscopy was done with a Welch Allyen 18240 NY USA under scotopic conditions. Ophthalmoscopy direct was performed with a Welch Allyen ophthalmoscope 11735 NY USA model, without mydriatic application under scotopic conditions. In the next experimental applications HSV was done as it was described before. Subjects with IOL, were facilitated by **Ophthalmologic Hospital Nuestra Señora de la Luz,** Mexico City.

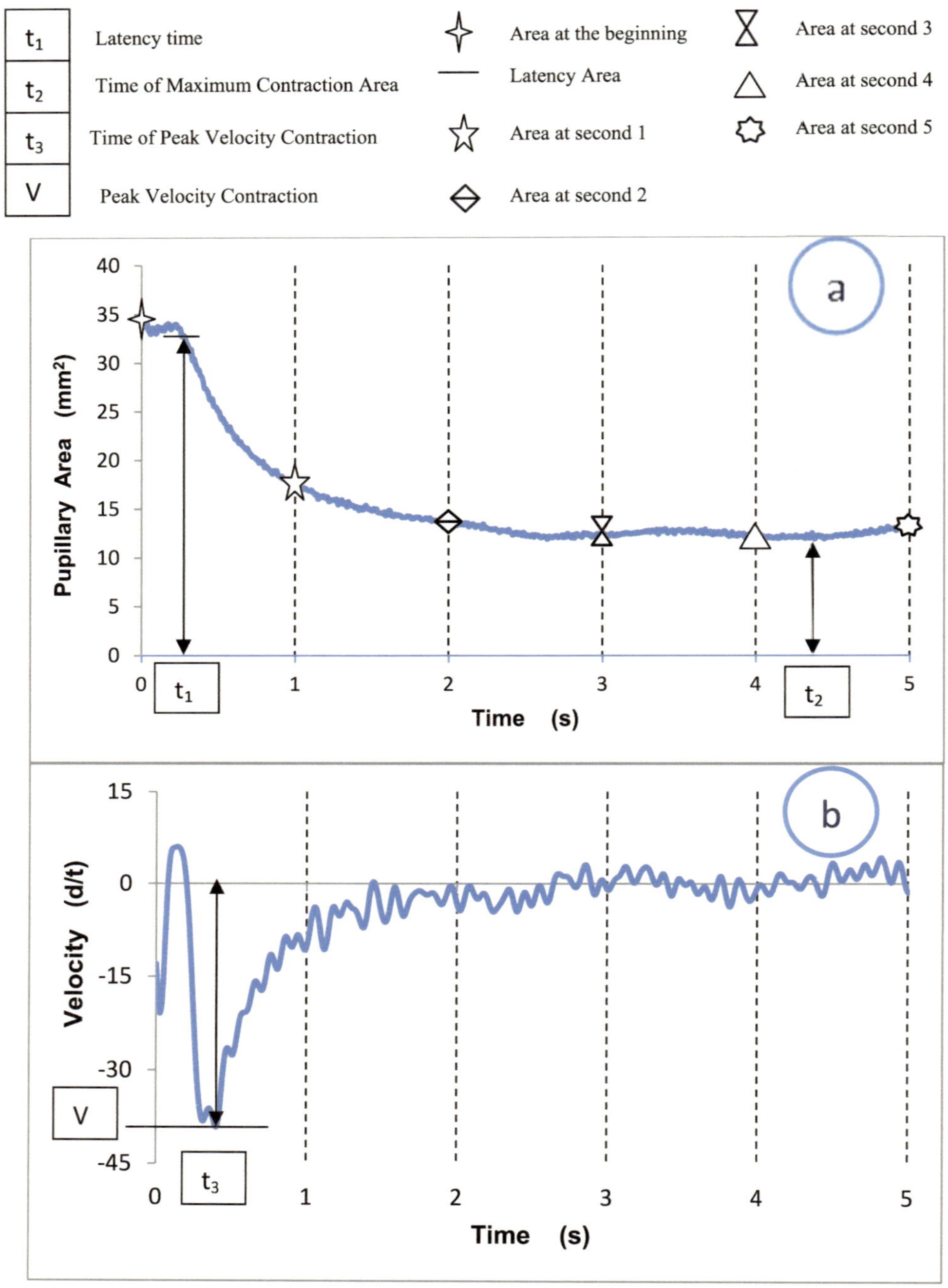


**Figure 8.** a) A typical pupillary response and b) It is first derivate. Where d=mm² and t = ms.

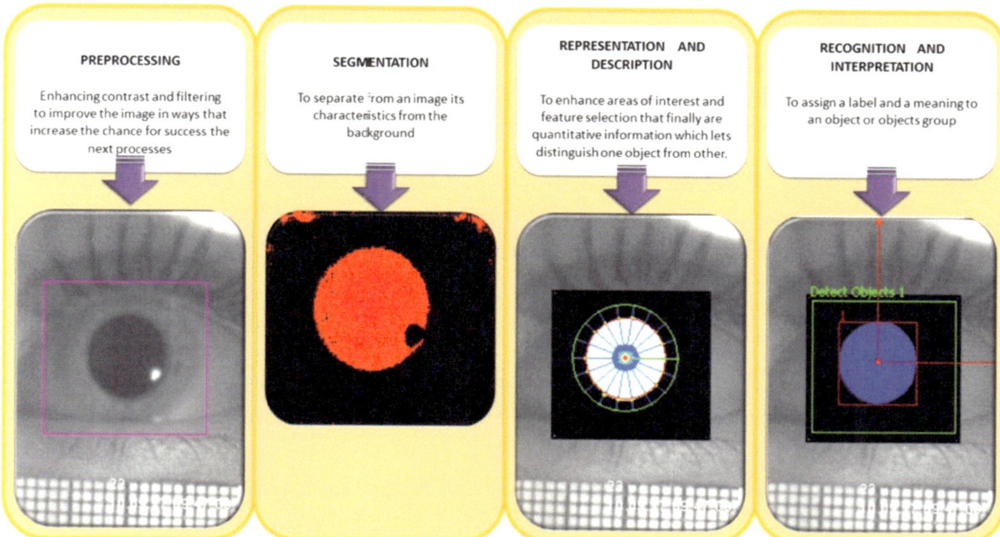


**Figure 9.** Steps of Image Processing are described in the top image.

## 3.2. HSV to measure pupillary latency evoked by isoluminant chromatic stimuli

One important characteristic of Pupillary response is latency (LT), which is defined as the time since the stimulus starts until the pupillary begins its contraction. The aim of this study was to determinate LT in response to 4 chromatic stimuli, they were Blue (455 nm), Green (530 nm), Yellow (570 nm), Red (615 nm) plus white employing HSV and image processing in 7 healthy subjects. Latency measures corresponding to each subject are presented in Figure 10.

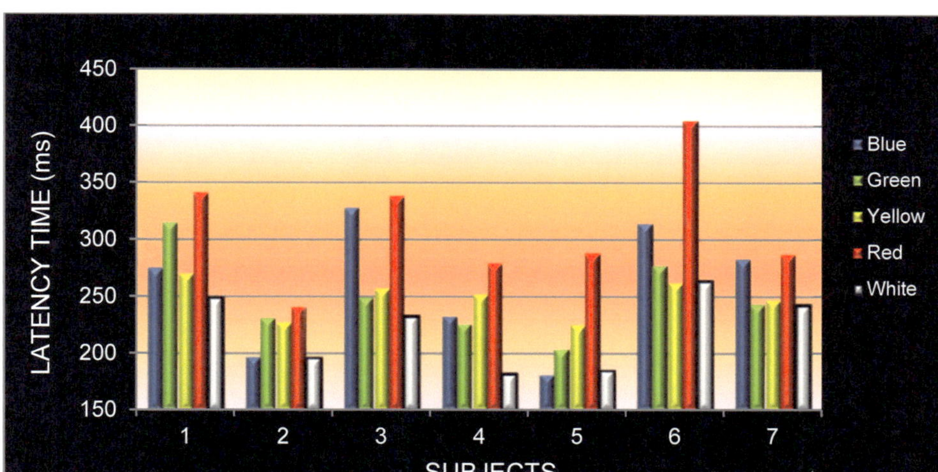


**Figure 10.** Six of seven subjects had the longest times in red. Five of seven subjects showed the shortest times in white. Mean latency in Red stimulus shows larger latency than blue, green, yellow and white.

Statistical analysis: ANOVA test was done among stimuli, considering $\alpha=0.05$, ANOVA $p=0.0075$ which means that at the least one latency time mean is statistically different to the others. And Means comparisons with difference were: red VS blue $p=0.026$; red VS green $p=0.0099$; red VS yellow $p=0.0091$, red VS white $p=4.04$ E-4.

Considering the written above, Bos J. E. describes latency can be a reliable parameter to detect nervous dysfunctions, while the difference between the beginning moment and the maximum velocity can be used to determine muscle diseases [6].

### 3.3. Analysis of pupillary areas at second 3 in response to isoluminant chromatic stimuli with HS-VOG

Pupillary responses from 7 healthy subjects were obtained. Images were processed and it is chosen the pupillary area presented in the third second (since it is considered steady state) of each stimulus to 7 subjects. Areas were plotted in Figure 11; each stimulus is called by its main wavelength component that has been obtained from Reflectance Spectrum. They were Blue (455 nm), Green (530 nm), Yellow (570 nm), Red (615 nm) and lastly white. A luminance level for comfortable reading [37] was chosen, 29 cd/m².

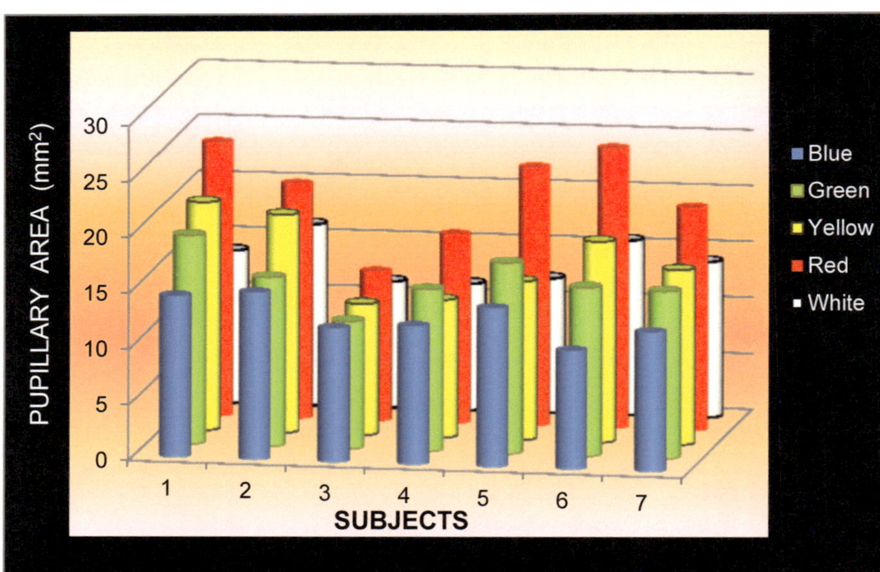


**Figure 11.** It describes areas corresponding to steady state presented in each color by each subject. As it is possible to observe, red responses are the biggest and the smallest without consider white stimulus are in blue. Observing all stimuli, in white 4 of 7 subjects presented the smallest areas in stable state (comparing all).

### 3.4. Conventional video-oculography to evaluate dynamic visual acuity to subjects with intraocular lens implant as a treatment for high refractive errors

Dynamic visual acuity (DVA) is defined as the eye capacity to distinguish details in relative movement conditions between object and subject. DVA have been less studied than Static Visual Acuity (SVA) [38]. In 1985 "The Committee on Vision of the National Research Council" suggested DVA evaluation for car drivers, pilots and sport people [39]. A high refractive error (HRE) is a condition in which parallel rays of light do not focus on retina resulting as blurred vision. Also, glasses in this days; LASER surgery and IOL are used as treatment of HRE. DVA has been studied in its relation with saccadic movements [40]; with an objective method using pupillary responses [41] patented on 2009 [42] and in different luminance levels comparing subjects with monofocal IOL versus multifocal IOL [43].In this experiment is described a VOG application to evaluate DVA in subjects with IOL implant as treatment of HRE. DVA is done before and after IOL implant. Subject is positioned to 3.10 m in front an optotype used as stimulus (optotype were adjusted considering Lovie-Baley card) on a chinrest in order to avoid head movements. Optotype are showed until the maximum measured is obtained from DVA, in an angle of 20º on a curve white screen using a projector in a galvanometer controller by a function generator. It starts with the biggest optotype projection to 0.1 Hz, increasing frequency in steps of 0.1 Hz, until the letter becomes blurred. After, it is showed the second optotype, and the procedure is repeated until the smallest letter that the subject can see. The luminance level on the projection screen is 0.3 cd/m2 and on the optotype is 23.6 cd/m2. Figure 12 shows VOG in DVA. While optotype are projected, VOG is done. When the test finishes, VOG is analyzed in order to know the frequency in which subjects could not see the optotype.

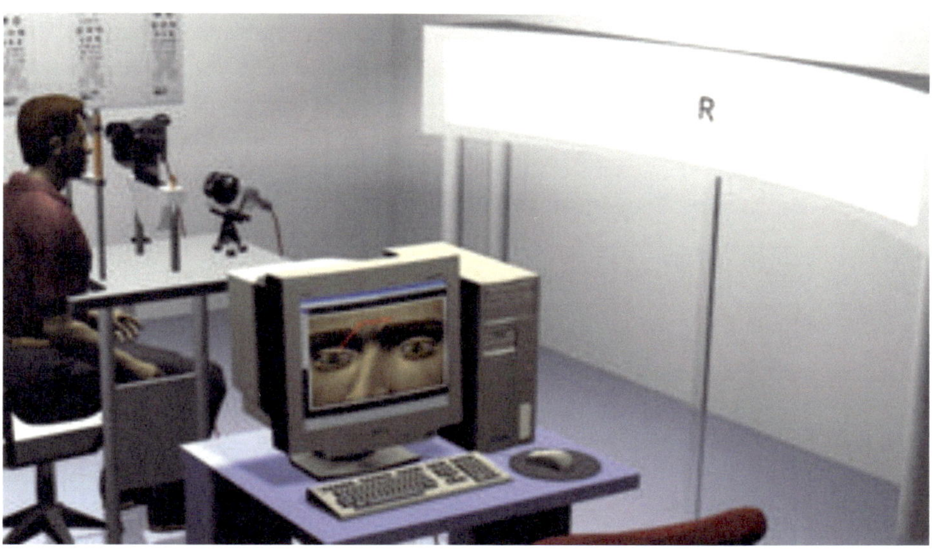


**Figure 12.** Video-Oculography used in DVA. It describes the subject position, Video camera matched to a PC to record the video, optotype and screen of projection.

It is explained to the subject that a letter is going to be projected in front of him/her, which will be in movement from left to right and right to left increasing velocity. The subject in study should indicate when he/she could not be able to see the projected optotype, pushing a button, keeping his head static.

Frequency values in Hz from DVA of two voluntaries, PRE (before) and POST (after) implant are showed in Table 1.

| | PRE | | POST | |
|---|---|---|---|---|
| LETTER | S1 | S2 | S1 | S2 |
| N | 0.9 | 0.9 | 1.2 | 1 |
| R | 0.9 | 0.8 | 0.9 | 1 |
| D | 1 | 0.8 | 0.9 | 0.9 |
| C | - | - | 0.8 | 0.9 |
| O | - | - | 0.8 | 0.8 |
| K | - | - | 0.8 | - |

**Table 1.** Frequency values (Hz) of DVA. An increment of frequencies is observed in subjects 1 and 2 (S1 and S2 respectively).

## 3.5. High-speed VOG applied in a Comparative study between IOL and health eyes

The pupil size has been studied in healthy people [18] and in people with IOL [24, 44] implant; finding that it increases the camp depth and improves near and middle vision, after cataract extraction surgery. The next VOG application has the aim to compare pupillary parameters as: LT, PVC, TPVC and to know if they are related with age or the luminance levels. Two groups are compared: Young-healthy subjects (YS) and IOL Older-subjects (IOL-OS). The luminance (white stimuli) used was 171.31 cd/m$^2$ for YS and 55.16 cd/m$^2$ for OS. Images were captured with HSV methodology as it had been described above. Once eye images were captured, they were processed with a graphic program (Vision Builder AI V3.5), from which the pupil areas were obtained about be statistically compared between groups. See Figure 13 and Figure 14.

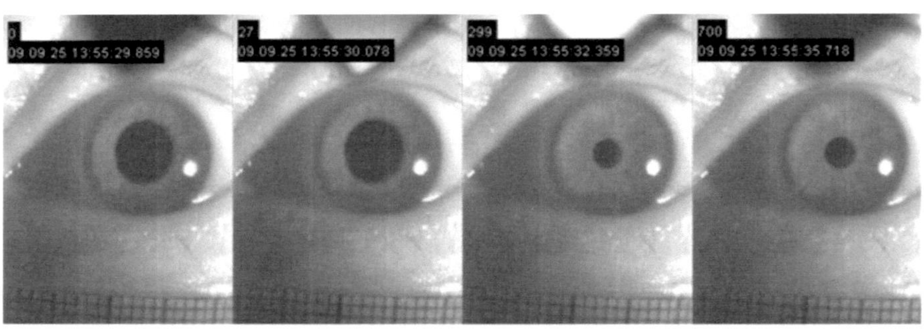

**Figure 13.** A sequence of images obtained by the high speed camera DALSA, left to right: beginning area, latency area, maximum contraction area and steady state area.

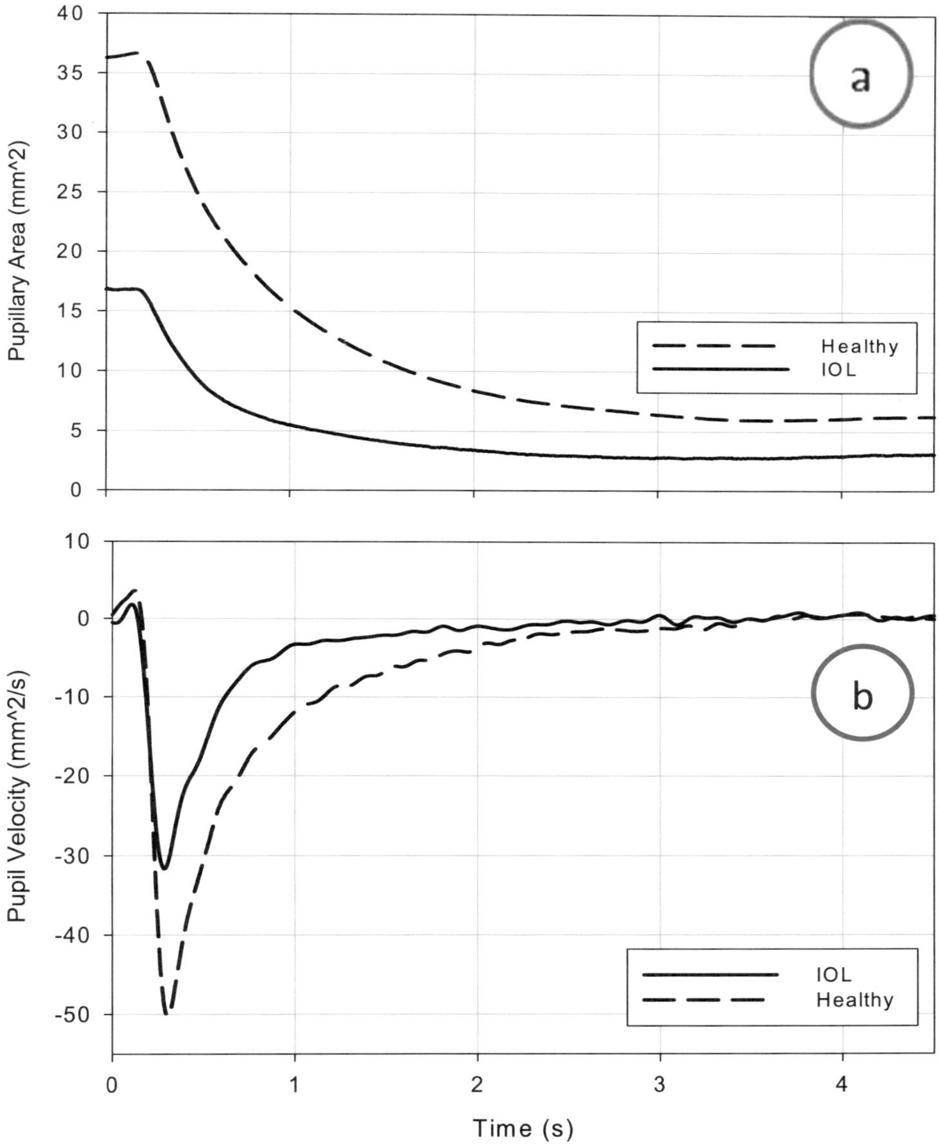


**Figure 14.** a) Curves of pupillary responses from IOL and healthy eyes respectively, b) Pupillary velocity. These curves correspond at average for each one of the groups.

Measures obtained from groups are described in the Tables 2 and Table 3. Those are LT, PVC, TPVC and the age and area (at 3rd second) of each subject are added. The statistical analysis was done in sigma plot V10, with the aim of knowing if they present a significant relation with one or some of them.

| Eye | LT (ms) | PVC (mm²/s) | TPVC (ms) | Age | Area (mm²) |
|---|---|---|---|---|---|
| 1 | 125,38 | -27,15 | 267,47 | 75 | 9,22 |
| 2 | 183,89 | -40,69 | 242,39 | 66 | 19,81 |
| 3 | 200,60 | -20,06 | 300,90 | 58 | 11,47 |
| 4 | 167,17 | -44,56 | 267,47 | 74 | 22,95 |
| 5 | 167,17 | -25,67 | 284,19 | 62 | 9,05 |
| 6 | 125,38 | -31,52 | 334,34 | 65 | 13,44 |
| x | 161,60 | -31,61 | 282,79 | 67 | 14 |
| S | 30,67 | 9,36 | 31,90 | 6,68 | 5,78 |

**Table 2.** It shows the pupil characteristics evaluated in this HSV application for IOL-ES eyes. Where **x** is the average and **s** is the standard deviation corresponding at each characteristic of the group.

| Eye | LT (ms) | PVC(mm²/s) | TPVC (ms) | Age | Area (mm²) |
|---|---|---|---|---|---|
| 1 | 209,2 | -45,80 | 298,11 | 19 | 37,66 |
| 2 | 251,04 | -63,45 | 321,645 | 21 | 34,4 |
| 3 | 188,28 | -48,74 | 303,34 | 22 | 33,54 |
| 4 | 203,97 | -39,41 | 316,415 | 22 | 32,75 |
| 5 | 177,82 | -57,21 | 295,495 | 22 | 29,01 |
| 6 | 214,43 | -48,28 | 303,34 | 24 | 27,85 |
| x | 207,46 | -50,48 | 306,39 | 21,67 | 32,54 |
| s | 25,34 | 8,56 | 10,38 | 163 | 3,61 |

**Table 3.** It shows the pupil characteristics evaluated in this HSV application for YS. Where **x** is the average and **s** the standard deviation corresponding at each characteristic of the group.

All averages were smaller in the IOL group. From **t** paired test $\alpha$=0.05%. The latency (contraction time) p=0.02122, the PVC p=0.01838 and TPVC p=0.3763. Although the luminance levels used and the age between groups were different, it does not exist a significant statistically difference in latency and maximum contraction velocity (Figure 14) between groups. At the same time, the results indicated that age and IOL do not affect statistically on them, however, the TPVC, is far from it [45].

This experiment describes that it is possible to establish differences and similarities between healthy subjects and subjects with an ocular and/or systemic diseases.

### 3.6. ANOVA to analyze pupillary variations in pseudophakic eyes, in response to chromatic stimuli during steady state

Authors have studied visual performance under mesopic and photopic conditions [46], and have defined which IOL provides better contrast sensitivity in diabetic subjects [47-49] On the other hand, studies of pupillary responses have been done in health and diabetic subjects [18,50]. Also ANOVA test is a helpful tool in optometric studies [51-52].

In this study, all subjects have multifocal IOL implant (AcrySof ReSTOR), normal chromatic vision and are older than 50 years old. The pseudophakic eyes have been classified in two groups considering their health systemic characteristics: in hypertension group (HTA) and healthy subjects (HS). Each group is formed by 4 subjects. The statistical test used was ANOVA in order to analyze oscillations of pupillary areas, obtained from pseudophakic eyes employing HSV during steady state (from second 3 to second 5.4). A total of 2288 eye images were analyzed in Vision Builder, 286 from each subject. Pupillary pictures of a Healthy subject and a HTA subject are in Figure 15. Averages obtained by group are showed in Figure 16.

ANOVA test was done from 2288 measures of areas. Results from average, standard deviation and ANOVA test (p values) are described in Tables 4, 5, 6 and 7. Average areas obtained per group to each stimulus are described in Table 4.

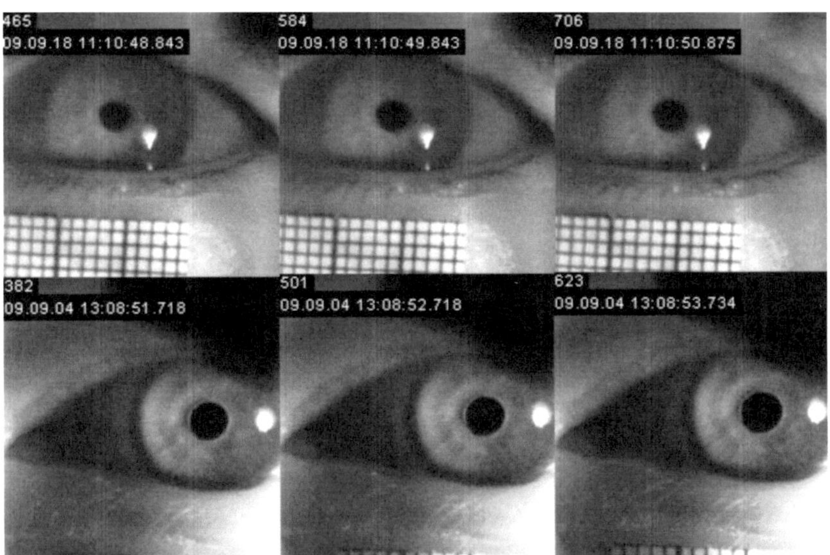


**Figure 15.** At the top, pictures of a HS subject. At the bottom pictures of a HTA subject. Pupillary responses, second 3, 4 and 5 (from left to right). A millimeter scale is observed used to convert pixels to mm during image procession process.

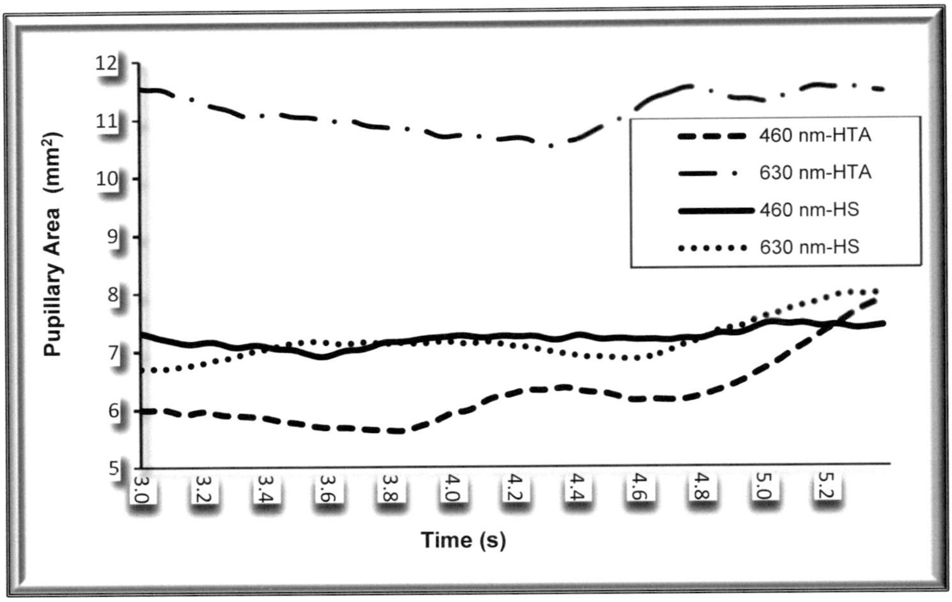


**Figure 16.** It shows average pupillary areas by group, during steady state (from second 3 to second 5.4) in eyes with MIOL implant.

| | 460 nm | 630 nm |
|---|---|---|
| HTA | 6.22 | 11.08 |
| HS | 7.21 | 7.17 |

**Table 4.** It describes averages areas per group in mm².

| | 460 nm | 630 nm |
|---|---|---|
| HTA | 0.54 | 0.32 |
| HS | 0.13 | 0.33 |

**Table 5.** It shows standards deviations per group.

| | HTA | HS |
|---|---|---|
| 460 nm VS 630 nm | 1.84 E-18 | 2.98 E-51 |

**Table 6.** It describes P values of ANOVA with $\alpha$= 0.05%, in comparison between wavelengths.

| | 460 nm | 630 nm |
|---|---|---|
| HTA VS HS | 4.5 E-101 | 0.43 |

**Table 7.** It shows P values of ANOVA with $\alpha$= 0.05%, in comparison between health state.

Based on the results, HTA presents more variation in 460 nm than 630 nm, in pupillary areas during stable state, although pupillary areas of HTA in 630 nm are the biggest; against case in HS Also, the comparative study inside of 460 nm suggests more variation from HTA subjects in contrast to HS. At the same time, was obtained the sum of energy corresponding to all components of frequency components of Fourier, from pupillary responses, to each group. Values of energy are described in Table 8. Frequency Fourier components are described in Figure 15.

| | 460 nm | 630 nm |
|---|---|---|
| **HTA** | 2.147 | 1.964 |
| **HS** | 0.834 | 1.196 |

**Table 8.** Frequency components of Fourier (total sum).

Results obtained from frequency components of Fourier, are in agreement with the results obtained in ANOVA test. Fourier components were obtained from dates that are showed in Figure 17. Observing Figure 16 and Figure 17; Figure 16, shows, bigger average areas in HTA subjects to 630 nm than the other three groups. Figure 17, shows frequency components of major magnitude in 460 nm by HTA subjects; this is related with the results of Table 5 and Table 8 where bigger values are observed in HTA subjects to 460 nm. HTA group has more variation in oscillations (Table 5) and energy content in 460 nm (Table 8).

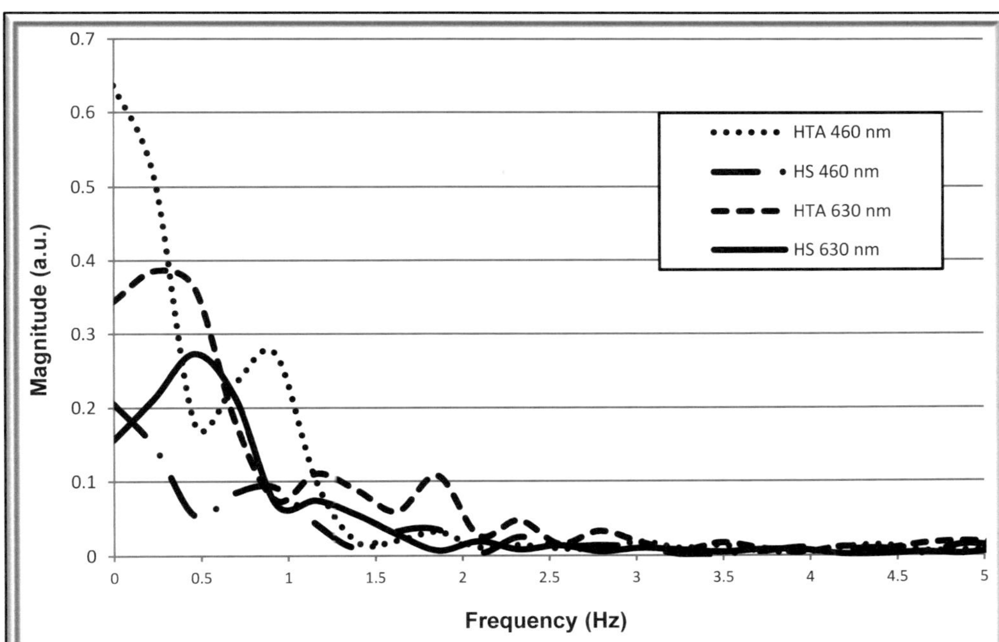


**Figure 17.** Fourier frequency components by group (averages from Figure 16).

### 3.7. Conventional VOG to observe pupillary responses in sickness and healthy people

Another application of conventional VOG, inside of our laboratory is to evaluate pupillary dynamic in the visual spectrum in subjects with diabetes mellitus type 2, poisoning on lead Pd and healthy people. Results of it evaluation are described in Figure 18. It was patented on 2009 [53].

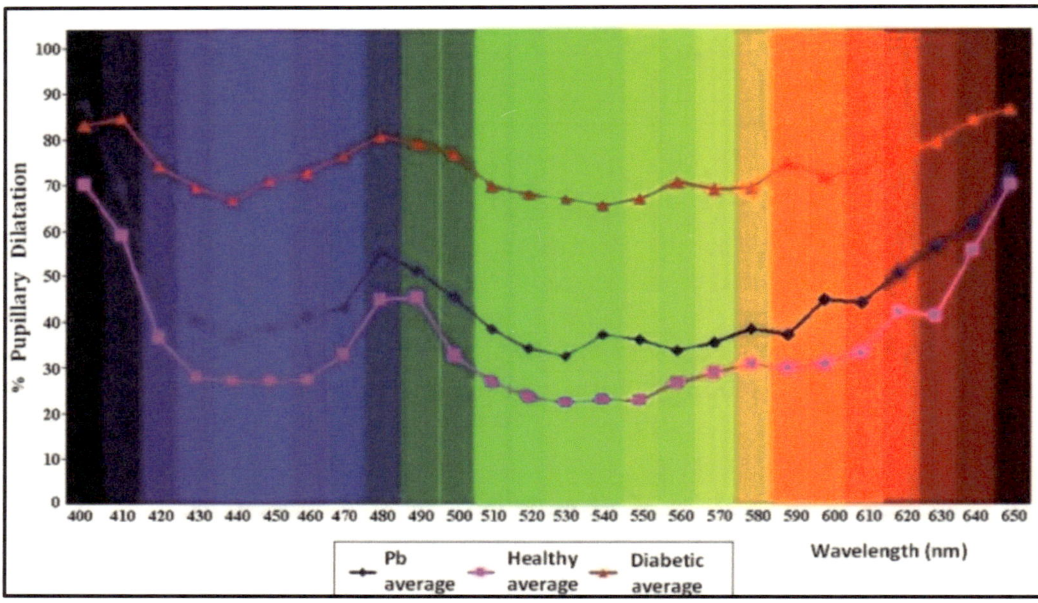


**Figure 18.** Pupillary dilatation in three different types of subjects.

## 4. Conclusions

As described above, it is possible to observe that the biomedical instrumentation proposed in this chapter has an important contribution in diagnosis of systemic diseases as well as in therapeutically and surgical applications. Also, the methodology proposed is a powerful tool, employing VOG techniques in pupillary evaluations and its application; in order to know both eye physiologic conditions and systemic health situation. Using this methodology, with high speed video-oculography as a tool to film a prolonged chromatic stimuli and white; it is possible to determinate details in the pupillary responses and its derivates.

The HSV with chromatic stimuli can help in diagnosis, treatment and care of subjects with systemic diseases, also with/without IOL implant. Besides this, HSV let to know changes in pupillary responses until each millisecons. At the same time; allows knowing differences among pupillary responses to chromatic stimuli and white stimulus by eye image processing, which can be standardized considering the parameters exposed in Figure 8, in healthy subjects and later compared in subjects with some systemic diseases or surgical ocular procedure. Added to these, applications of ANOVA test and Frequency components of Fourier let to analyze pupillary responses in a more complete form.

Therefore VOG techniques plus the methodology proposed plus statistical and Frequency Fourier analysis let to know differences between healthy and with IOL people, as was observed in the above examples. It was in the subjects that were tested with different colors and luminance levels.

While, conventional VOG lets to know frequency changes in DVA. In this aspect, it is necessary to do more measures in healthy and sick subjects. An application of VOG in perimetry is going to be explained in a posterior written because of it let to observe brain activity through pupillary reflex in an objective form.

## Author details

Ernesto Suaste Gómez and Anabel S. Sánchez Sánchez
*Centro de Investigación y de Estudios Avanzados del Instituto Politécnico Nacional, México*

## Acknowledgement

To **National Council of Science and Technology** of Mexico, through the grant project number 141194.

## 5. References

[1] Lennie P. (1981). The physiological basis of variations in visual latency. Vision Res. 21:815-824.
[2] Stark L., Sherman PM (1957). A servoanalytic study of consensual pupil reflex to light. J Neurophysiology 20:17-26.
[3] Kasthurirangan S., Glasser A. (2006). Age related changes in the characteristics of the near pupil response. Vision Res. 46:1393-1403.
[4] MacLachlan C., Howland HC (2002). Normal values and standard deviations for pupil diameter and interpupillary distance in subjects aged 1 month to 19 years. Ophthalmic Physiol Opt. 22:175-182.
[5] Hachol A., Szczepanowska-Nowak W., Kasprzak H., et al (2007). Measurement of pupil reactivity using fast pupillometry. Physiol Meas. 28:61-72.
[6] Bos J. E (1998). Clinical quantitative pupillometry. Neuro-ophthalmol. 8:299-305.
[7] Donnelly WJ, Roorda A. (2003). Optimal pupil size in the human eye for axial resolution. J Opt Soc Am. 20:2010-2015.
[8] Hakerem G., Lidsky A. (1961). Pupillary reactions to sequences of light and dark pulses. Ann. N.Y. Acad. Sci. 156:951-958.
[9] Bitsios P., Prettyman R., Szabadi E. (1996). Changes in autonomic function with age: a study of pupillary kinetics in healthy young and old people. Age Ageing 25:432-438.

[10] Winn B., Whitaker D., Elliott DB, Phillips NJ (1994). Factors affecting light-adapted pupil size in normal human subjects. Invest Ophth and Vis Sci. 35:1132-1137.
[11] Campbell F. W., Gubish R.W.(1966). Optical quality of the human eye. J. Physiol. 186:558-578.
[12] Bos J. E. (1991). Detection of the pupil constriction latency. Med Biol Eng Comput. 529-34.
[13] Kohn M., Clynes M. (1969). Color dynamic of the pupil. Ann N. Y. Acad. Sci. 156:1-20.
[14] Sobaszek A., Nowak W., Hachol A., Moron Z. (2010). Measurement of the eye pupil response to light stimuli with regulated waveform, wavelength and photopic level. J Phys: Conference Series 238:1-9.
[15] Drew P., Sayres R., Watanabe K., Shimojo S. (2001). Pupillary response to chromatic flicker. Exp Brain Res. 136:256-262.
[16] Banks M., Munsinger H. (1974). Pupillometric measurement of difference spectra for three color receptors in an adult and a four-year-old. Vision Res. 4:813-817.
[17] Kimura E., Young R. S. L. (1995). Nature of the pupillary responses evoked by chromatic flashes on a white background. Vision Res. 35:897-906.
[18] Rodríguez D., Zuñiga A., Suaste E. (2005). Pupillary responses to chromatic stimuli in spectrum from 400 nm to 650nm in steady state. Rev Mex Fis. 51:365-370.
[19] Hammoud R. I. (2008). Passive eye monitoring. Algorithms, applications and experiments. Springer, pp. 1-14.
[20] Villamar L., Suaste E. (2008). High velocity videoculography to determination of the pupil dynamic. Tenth Mexican Symposium on Medical Physics. Am Institute of Phys 276-279.
[21] Duchowski A. (2007). Eye tracking methodology. Theory and practice. Second edition. Springer, pp. 49-59.
[22] Skatani T., Isa T. (2004). PC-based high speed video-oculography for measuring rapid eye movements in mice. Neurosci. Res. 49:123-131.
[23] Iijima A., Minamitani H., Ishikawa N. (2001). Image analysis of quick phase eye movements in nystagmus with high-speed video system. Med Biol Eng Comput. 39:2-7.
[24] Morris G. M., Nordan L. T.(2004). Phakic intraocular lenses. Optics and photonics news 26-31.
[25] Artigas J. M., Meneso J. L., Peris C., Adelina F., Díaz-Llopis M. (2007). Image quality with multifocal intraocular lenses and the effect of pupil size. Comparison of refractive and hybrid refractive-diffractive designs. J Cataract Refract Surg. 33:2111-2117.
[26] Alfonso J. F., Fernández-Vega L., Baamonde M. B., Montés-Mico R. (2007). Correlation of pupil size with visual acuity and contrast sensitivity after implantation of an apodized diffractive intraocular lens. J Cataract Refract Surg. 33:430-438.
[27] Alió J. L., Schimchak P., Montés-Micó R., Galal A. (2005). Retinal image quality after microincision intraocular lens implantation. J Cataract Refract Surg. 31:1557-1560.
[28] Lam S., Beck R. W., Hall D. (1989). Creighton J. B., Atonic pupil after cataract surgery. Ophthalmology 96:589-590.

[29] Fellner P., Vidic B., Ramkisson Y., Fu R. D., El-Shabrawi Y., Ardojmand N. (2005). Pupil ovalization after phakic intraocular lens implantation is associated with sectorial iris hypoperfusion. Arch Ophthalmol. 123:1061-1065.

[30] Elgohary MA., Beckingsale AB. (2006). Effect of illumination on visual function after monofocal and multifocal intraocular lens implantation. Eye 20:144-149.

[31] Argue R., Boardman M., Doyle J., Hickey G. (2004). Building a low-cost device to track eye movement. Technical report, Faculty of Computer Science, Dalhousie University, December.

[32] Lo Castro F. (2008). Class I infrared eye blinking detector. Sensors and actuators A: Physical. 148:388-394.

[33] Villamar M. Luis (2011). Form and pupillary dynamic evaluation for clinic diagnosis through a new analysis method based in high-speed video-oculography. CINVESTAV.

[34] Malacara J. L. (2002). The nature color. SIE PRESS Bellingham. Washington 1.

[35] Anderson Dr. (1987). Perimetry with and without automation C. M. Mosby Co.

[36] Suaste E., Palmira R., Solis L. (1997). Fiber optics and video-oculography associated with pupillary responses and visual evoked potentials for objective perimetry. J. Clin. Eng. 22:308-315.

[37] Artigas J. M., Capilla P., Felipe A., Pujol J. (1995). Physiological Optic. Psychophysical of vision. Mc Graw Hill, Inter, pp. 55.

[38] Quevedo L., Aznar-Casanova J., Merindano J. (2010). Una tarea para evaluar la agudeza visual dinámica y una valoración de la estabilidad de sus mediciones. Psicología 31:109–128.

[39] Committee on Vision of the National Research Council. Emergent techniques for assessment of visual performance. (1985). National academy Press, Washington.

[40] Komura Y., Aoki K., Yoshigi H., et al. (2008). The relationship between dynamic visual acuity and sacadic eye movement. Hum. Perform. Meas. 5:23–30.

[41] Zuñiga A, Suaste E. (2002). Objective Method to evaluate dynamic visual acuity using pupillary responses. Rev Mex Ing Biomédica 22:109-115.

[42] Suaste Gómez E. (2009). Instrument to evaluate visual acuity using pupillary responses. Mexican patent Nº 267510, by The Mexican Institute of Industrial Property (IMPI).

[43] Williamson W., Poirier L., Coulon P., et al. (1994). Compared optical performances of multifocal and monofocal intraocular lenses (contrast sensitivity and dynamic visual acuity). Br. J. Ophthalmology 78:249-251.

[44] José F. Alfonso, Luis F. Vega, Baamonde M. B., Montés-Micó R. (2007). Correlation of pupil size with visual acuity and contrast sensitivity after implantation of an apodized diffractive intraocular lens. J Cataract Refract Surgery 33, 430-438.

[45] Villamar L., Sánchez A., Suaste E. (2010). Methodology to determinate pupillary responses based in high speed videoculography in clinical eye applications. AIP Conf Proc 1:162-165.

[46] Montés-Mico R., España E., Bueno I., Neil Charman W., Menezo J. L. (2004). Visual performance with multifocal intraocular lens. Am. Acad. Ophtahlmology. 1:85-96.

[47] Rodríguez-Galietero A., Montés-Micó R., Muñoz G., Albarrán-Diego C. (2005). Blue-light filtering intraocular lens in patients with diabetes: Contrast sensitivity and chromatic discrimination, J Cataract Refract Surg. 31:2088–2092.
[48] Kardon R., Anderson S., Damarjian T., Grace E., Stone E., Kawasaki A. (2009). Chromatic Pupil Responses. Ophthalmology 116:1564–1573.
[49] Kardon R., Anderson S.,, Damarjian T., Grace E., Stone E., Kawasaki A. (2011). Chromatic Pupillometry in Patients with Retinitis Pigmentosa. Ophthalmology 118:376–381.
[50] Suaste E., Sánchez A., Villamar L., Terán O. (2010). High velocity video-oculography to measuring the pupil size in pseudophakic people with multifocal intraocular lens. PAHCE Lima Perú 15-19.
[51] Armstrong R., Eperjesi F., Gilmartin B. (2002). The application of analysis of varianza (ANOVA) to different experimental designs in optometry. Ophthal. Physiol. Opt. 22:248-256.
[52] Armstrong R., Slade S., Eperjesi F. (2000). An introduction to analysis of variance (ANOVA) with special reference to data from clinical experiments in optometry. Ophthal. Physiol. Opt. 20:235-241.
[53] Suaste E. (2009). Pupilocromatógrafo. Mexican patent Nº 267507, by The Mexican Institute of Industrial Property (IMPI).

Chapter 9

# Design and Development of Biomedical and Surgical Instruments in Biomedical Applications

Jeremy (Zheng) Li

Additional information is available at the end of the chapter

http://dx.doi.org/10.5772/48462

## 1. Introduction

The breakthrough in biomedical and surgical instrument research follows the advances of newly developed biomedical technologies, improved composite materials, and renovated manufacturing methodologies. These new biomedical and surgical instruments allow physician to perform complex biomedical treatments and surgical operations with better medical quality. Some more complicated biomedical treatments including microsurgery and endoscopic surgery can be performed through precisely controlled biomedical instruments [1]. The newly explored nontoxic, durable and anti-corrosion materials were developed to keep biomedical and surgical instruments from corrosion due to blood contamination and instrumental sterilization. The modern production techniques help to manufacture cost-effective biomedical instruments and newly developed biomedical technology brings improvement on human life quality [2].

Design and development of biomedical instruments combine engineering principle and techniques with biomedical technology to minimize the unsolved gap between engineering and surgery and apply technical design methodology and engineering problem solving skills to improve medical diagnosis, biomedical treatment, and surgical operations [3]. The researches in biomedical and surgical instruments are involved in interdisciplinary fields including biomedical instrument design, biomechanics in mechanical engineering, biomaterials in chemical engineering, and bio-sensing and bioinstrumentation in electrical engineering. The state-of-the-art instrumental development should be documented to procure and trace biomedical instrumental innovation accordingly for continuous improvement. The multi-disciplinary team effort from physicians, engineers, researchers, and biomedical professionals is required to develop ultimate biomedical product market release accordantly [4]. The crosslink studies of engineering fundamentals, technical disciplines, human anatomy and physiology are preferred in biomedical and surgical instrument design and development. The biomedical and surgical instruments can be applied to many different medical fields, such as organ or tissue probing, occluding, clamping, suturing, ligation, and incising. Since users might not be engineering specialists and improper use of biomedical and surgical instruments can cause alignment problems, the instructed and biomedical protocols should be strictly obeyed and related technical trainings are needed. The biomedical instruments should be kept clean to prevent blood and tissues from hardening since the blood and hardened tissues can be easily trapped in the gap between organ surface and surgical instruments [5]. The patients should be followed up to determine if the biomedical and surgical instruments have been properly used and standard surgical procedures have been applied.

The US biomedical industry is leading worldwide researches in biomedical and surgical instrument development. About 21,000 US companies with over 175,000 employees have been involved in biomedical instrument production [6]. Design and development of biomedical and surgical instruments require advanced techniques implemented to develop special biomedical technology to compete challenging produce market. Since the biomedical and surgical instrument market is high technology oriented, quality competitive and price sensitive, the biomedical and surgical instrument development should be adjusted and controlled for its quality, functionality, manufacturing cost, feasibility, performance, and safety.

There are some common surgical systems in current market. The first surgical system has adjacent surgical preparation and recovery areas [7]. This surgical system has large surgical area with adjacent surgical preparation and recovery areas after operation. The surgical system equipped with biomedical instruments, anesthetic equipment, monitoring equipment, and suture apparatus. The second surgical system has endoscopic biomedical treatment and surgical system [8]. This endoscopic biomedical treatment and surgical system has been supplied to hospitals, nursing homes, and outpatient surgery care centers. This system is widely used in surgical repairing procedures. It also provides computer generated surgical reports to document and track all patient's repairing reports. The third surgical system equips the robotic-assisted biomedical treatment and surgical system [9]. This robotic-assisted biomedical treatment and surgical system can perform remote-controlled biomedical treatment and surgical operation. It consists of the electromechanical instrument with electronic circuit designed as part of computer-controlled sensing system. This robot-controlled biomedical treatment and surgical system can be applied to many complicated patient's medical curing procedures. The fourth surgical system contains biomedical treatment and surgical system for neurosurgical procedure [10]. This neurosurgical system is driven by robotic arm to placing the surgical units. It can quickly hold and place the surgical tools with sensing signal feedback and 3-D endoscope to view and control the biomedical treatment and surgical process.

This chapter focuses on current research, design and development of biomedical instruments in medical treatment and surgical applications by introducing minimally invasive medical treatment and surgical methodology. The newly designed biomedical and surgical instruments can efficiently protect surgical wound during surgery and speed up the operation healing process. The new biomedical and surgical instrument design aids improved body ergonomic design, better driving mechanism, durable functionality, safe performance, and further cost-saving in instrumental production. The computer-aided design, 3-D solid modeling, instrumental motion analysis, and computational simulation have been applied to design and develop these new minimally invasive biomedical and surgical instruments. The computer-aided modeling and simulation results on newly developed biomedical and surgical instruments by using CAD software and structure analysis on instrumental mechanism by applying FEA software are included in this chapter. It can benefit new instrumental design and analysis in geometry, kinematics, dynamics, and visual limitation to assist physician in medical treatment and surgical operation. The experimental testing on prototypes of these newly developed biomedical and surgical instruments have also been included in this chapter to compare with computer-aided design and simulation to verify the credibility of these new biomedical instrument designs.

In general, the connection between new surgical instrument design, CAD and kinematic modeling, simulation and testing, and invasiveness of surgical instrument is as follows: First make conceptual instrument design. Then use CAD software to make 3-D solid modeling and verify kinematic motion by Pro/Mechanism to make sure that all components function properly and there is no part interferences in system assembly. The computer-aided simulation can determine if all systematic functioning parameters are properly defined and selected to provide optimized instrumental performance. The prototype testing is used to verify the instrumental function and compare with results from computer-aided modeling and simulation.

## 2. Computer-aided design, modeling and simulation

The 3-D solid modeling and simulation on these new biomedical and surgical equipments are based on its designed geometry and volumetric weeping boundary. The kinematics and dynamics of newly designed precision mechanism can be simulated and modeled as an open-loop or closed-loop joint chain with rigid features linked to each other in a series patterns. The kinematical analysis of instrumental structure can provide an analytic methodology to define and simulate the moving mechanism. The 3-D modeling and motion analysis on these multilink systems in kinematical and dynamical simulations allow researchers and professionals performing fundamental study and instrumental conceptual verification in biomedical instrumental design and development stage. The instrumental performance can be improved by systematic design control on kinematical and dynamic parameters. The potential impact of system assembly deviation and production errors can be determined per geometric dimensioning and tolerance (GD&T) analysis. All these instrumental analysis and computer-aided simulation can improve biomedical and surgical instrument performance to prevent patient's body from being damaging in biomedical treatment and surgical operation. For example, in newly developed surgiclip instruments, the surgiclip distal move can be well controlled to avoid surgiclip dropping from moving channels, operational force to fully close surgiclip is lower than conventional surgical instruments because of new mechanism design, and eliminate the incident of unexpected closure of surgiclip when biomedical instruments are not properly handled by physician. Also the production and manufacturing cost of these newly developed biomedical and surgical instruments can be reduced due to loose dimensional tolerance control on instrumental components because of this new instrumental mechanism design.

## 2.1. New endo accessible biomedical instrument

Figs. 1 and 2 show the front and rear views of new endoscopic accessible biomedical instrument.

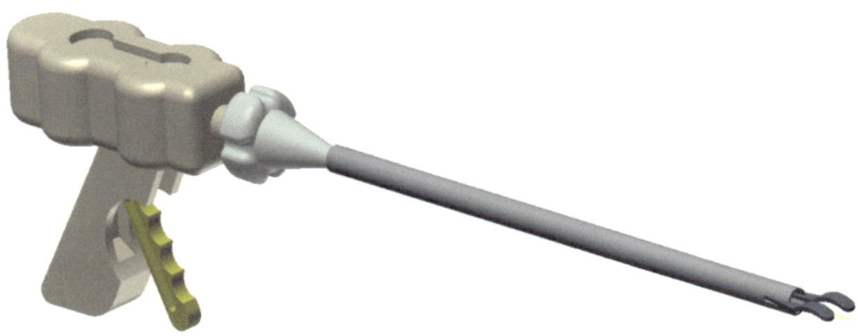

**Figure 1.** Front view of new endoscopic accessible biomedical instrument

**Figure 2.** Rear view of new endoscopic accessible biomedical instrument

Fig. 3 displays the internal driving mechanism of this new endoscopic accessible biomedical instrument.

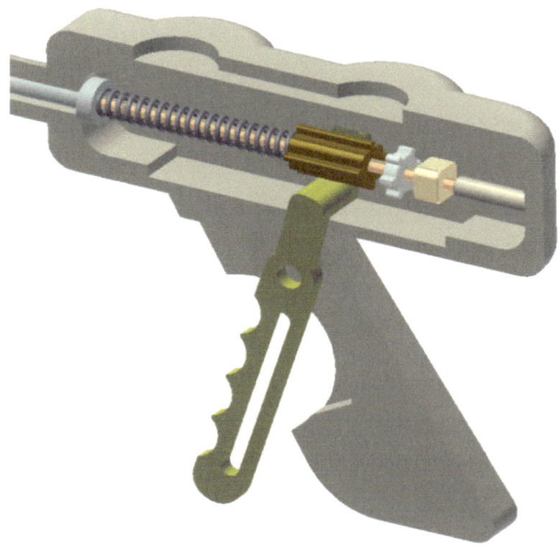

**Figure 3.** Internal driving mechanism of new endoscopic accessible biomedical instrument

The computer aided kinematic simulation has been performed on this new endoscopic accessible biomedical instrument with result shown in Fig. 4.

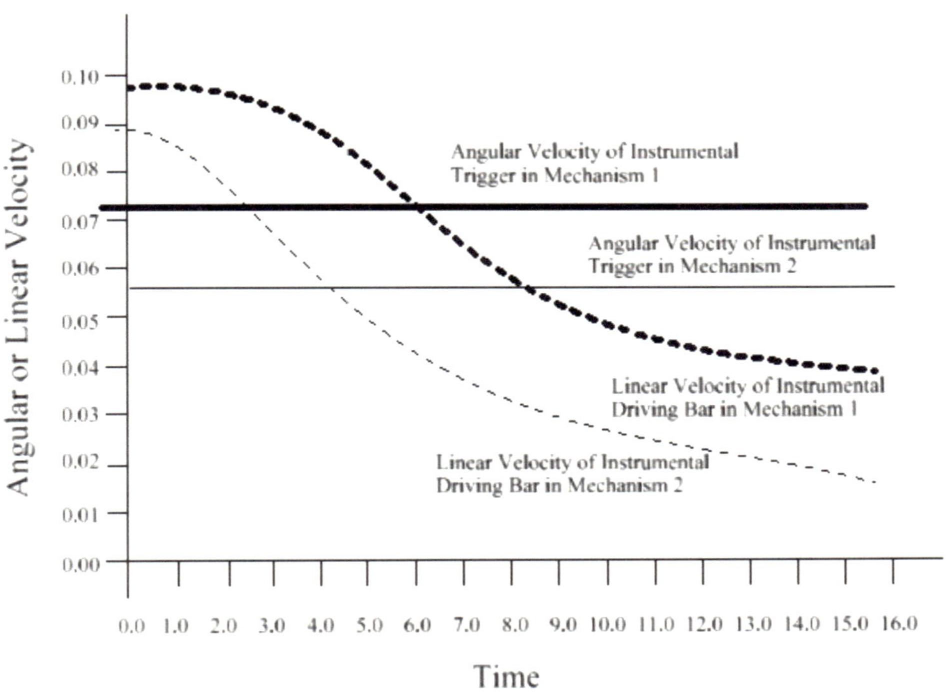


**Figure 4.** Angular or linear velocity vs. time in endoscopic accessible biomedical instrument

The mechanical advantage (MA) of this new instrument can be determined based on above computational simulation.

$$MA = (VR) * 2.212 = (.04788 / .03732) * 2.212 = 2.838 \quad (1)$$

Here VR is the ratio between linear speed of surgiclip driver and angular speed of instrumental handle and number 2.212 is geometric factor of instrumental driving mechanism depending on internal lever system setup. The above result indicates that, when 20 lbf forces are required to fully close biomedical surgiclip, the physician only need put 3.522 lbf that is less than the normal spec of 4 lbf in surgical operation procedure. This will benefit physician in their medical procedures. The computational simulation of this new endoscopic accessible biomedical instrument is also compared with prototype testing shown in Table 1.

| Handle Closure Angle (degree) | Closure Force Measured (lbf) |
|---|---|
| 5 | 2.455 |
| 10 | 2.646 |
| 15 | 2.875 |
| 20 | 3.184 |
| 25 | 3.318 |
| 30 | 3.535 |

**Table 1.** Prototype testing on this new endoscopic biomedical instrument

The force gauge, microscope, and camera measuring system are used to measure the closure force and handle closure angles. In each increment of handle rotation, the required operational force value up to the maximum closure force can be read from force gauge. The prototype testing indicated that the maximum closure force is 3.535 lbf at handle closure angle of 30°. This testing result is very close to the force of 3.522 from computer aided simulation which verifies the feasible functionality of this new endoscopic biomedical instrument. To compare with recently used surgical instruments, this newly developed surgical instrument has several good features: (1). No surgiclip drop-off incident found (2). The operation force is lower than existing instrument (3). Manufacturing cost on this new instrument design might be reduced due to less tolerance control required in components and assembly. Also less closure force is important since it can ease surgical operation and prevent surgeon's hands from fatigue in daily surgical processes.

## 2.2. New open accessible biomedical instrument

Figs. 5, 6 and 7 show the front, rear, and front tip views of newly developed open accessible biomedical instrument.

**Figure 5.** Front view of new open accessible biomedical instrument

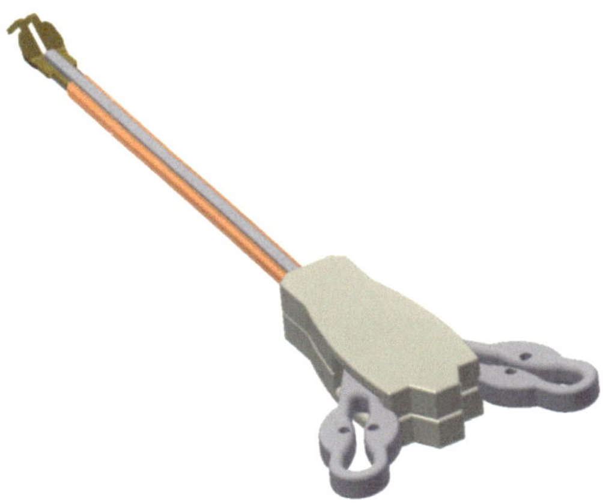

**Figure 6.** Rear view of new open accessible biomedical instrument

Fig. 8 shows the internal driving mechanism of newly developed open accessible biomedical instrument.

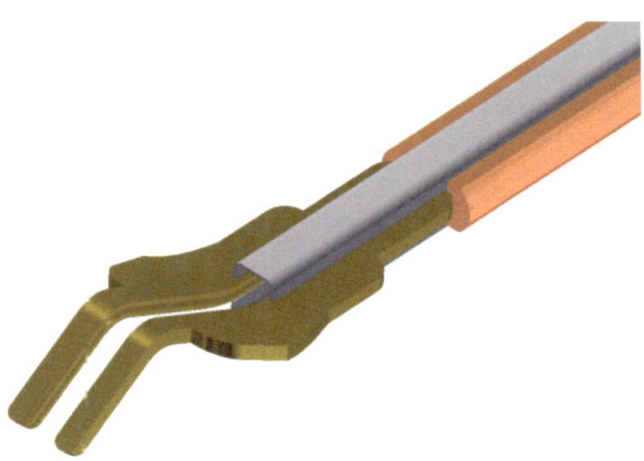

**Figure 7.** Front tip of new open accessible biomedical instrument

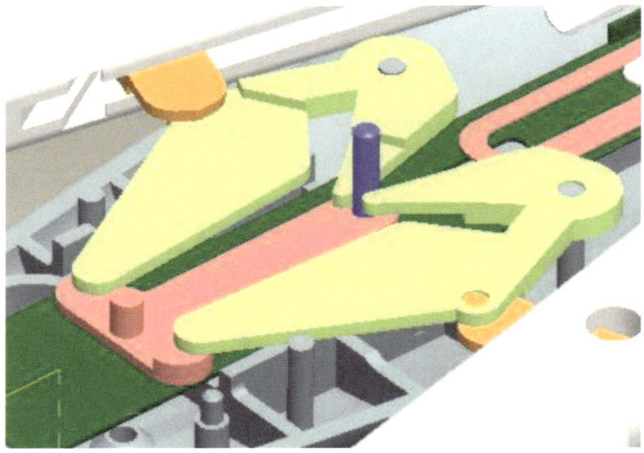

**Figure 8.** Internal driving mechanism of new open accessible biomedical instrument

The computational modeling and simulation are used to determine kinematic function on driving mechanism in this newly developed open accessible biomedical instrument. The simulation result is presented in Fig. 9.

The results from above computer aided modeling and simulation are used to determine the mechanical advantage (MA) of this new open accessible biomedical instrument.

$$MA = (VR) * 2.245 = (.04812 / .0367) * 2.245 = 2.944 \qquad (2)$$

| Trigger Rotation Angle (degree) | Operation Force Measured (lbf) |
|---|---|
| 5 | 2.248 |
| 10 | 2.535 |
| 15 | 2.788 |
| 20 | 3.025 |
| 25 | 3.405 |

**Table 2.** Prototype testing on this new open biomedical instrument

Here VR is the ratio between linear speed of surgiclip driver and angular speed of instrumental handle and number 2.245 is geometric factor of instrumental driving mechanism depending on internal lever system setup. Based on above simulated result, the physician only requires applying 3.397 lbf forces if 20 lbf are required to fully form biomedical open surgiclip. Since this force is less than regular spec of 4 lbf in surgical operation procedure, it will ease physician in performing medical procedures. To verify this computational methodology, the prototype testing is performed on this new open accessible biomedical instrument and the tested result is shown in Table 2.

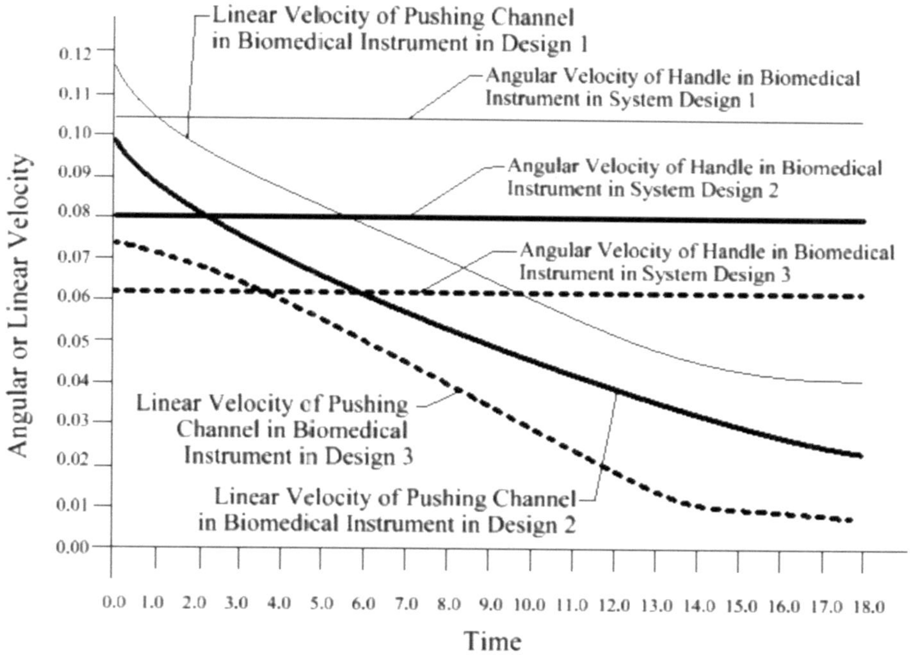


**Figure 9.** Angular or linear velocity vs. time in open accessible biomedical instrument

The force gauge, microscope, and camera measuring system are used to measure the closure force and handle closure angles. In each increment of handle rotation, the required operational force value up to the maximum closure force can be read from force gauge. The prototype experiment shows that the maximum operation force is 3.405 lbf at trigger rotation angle of 25°. The experiment presents very close result to the 3.397 lbf closure forces obtained from computer aided modeling and simulation. Both results verify the credibility of this new open biomedical instrument design. To compare with recently used surgical instruments, this newly developed surgical instrument has several good features: (1). No surgiclip drop-off incident found (2). The operation force is lower than existing instrument (3). Manufacturing cost on this new instrument design might be reduced due to less tolerance control required in components and assembly. Also less closure force is important since it can ease surgical operation and prevent surgeon's hands from fatigue in daily surgical processes.

## 3. Conclusion

The design and development of biomedical instrument are introduced in this chapter to benefit readers in learning of fundamental design methodology, biomedical engineering technique, and biomedical instrumental technology. Two new biomedical instruments developed by author are also included for detail explanation in this research field. Both computer aided modeling / simulation and prototype testing demonstrate the reliable function of these two new biomedical instruments with better ergonomic design, no surgiclip drop-off incident, reduced manufacturing cost, increased mechanical advantage, and improved unit performance. Future improvement will include further simplifying the internal driving mechanism, strengthening the instrumental driving mechanism in case dealing with thick tissues, and continuously performing stress analysis on different instrumental components for optimized design.

## Author details

Jeremy (Zheng) Li
*School of Engineering, University of Bridgeport, USA*

## 4. References

[1] Sun, W., Starly, B., Nam, J. & Darling, A., 2005, "Bio-CAD Modeling and Its Application in Computer-Aided Tissue Engineering", *Journal of Computer-Aided Design*, Vol. 37, pp. 1097-1114.

[2] Barrett, W. & Garber, S., 2003, "Surgical smoke—A review of the literature", *Journal of Surgery Endoscope*, Vol. 17, pp. 979-985.

[3] Starly, B., Fang, Z., Sun, W. & Regli, W. 2005, "Three-Dimensional Reconstruction for Medical-CAD Modeling", *Journal of Computer-Aided Design and Application*, Vol. 2, pp. 431-438.

[4] Cheng A., Chiu, P., Chan, P. & Lam, S., 2004, "Endoscopic Hemostasis for Bleeding Gastric Strormal Tumors by Application of Hemoclip", *Journal of Laparoendoscopic & Advanced Surgical techniques*, Vol. 14, pp 69-171.

[5] Piatt, J., Starly, B., Faerber, E. & Sun, W., 2006, "Application of Computer-Aided Design Methods in Craniofacial Reconstructive Surgery Using Image-Guidance System", *Journal of Neurosurgery*, Vol.104, pp. 64-67.

[6] Connie, G., Chiu, N., & Nguyen, S., 2011, "Single-incision laparoscopic appendectomy Using conventional instruments: an initial experience using a novel technique", *Journal of Surgical Endoscopy*, Vol. 25, pp. 1153-1159.

[7] Lin, H., Lo, W., Cheng, Y. & Peng, C., 2007, "Endoscopic Hemoclip Versus Triclip Placement in Patients with High Risk Peptic Ulcer Bleed", *Journal of Gastroenterol,* Vol. 102, pp. 539-543.

[8] Evans, P., Starly, B. & Sun, W., 2006, "Computer-Aided Tissue Engineering for Design and Evaluation of Lumbar-Spine Arthroplasty", *Journal of Computer-Aided Design and Application*, Vol. 3, pp. 771-778.

[9] Kassam, A., Thomas, A., Snyderman, C., Carrau, R., Gaedner, P., Mintz, A., & Kanaan, H., 2007, "Fully endoscopic expanded endonasal approach treating skull base lesions in pediatric patients", *Journal of Neurosurgery*, Vol. 106, pp. 75-86.

[10] Laufer, L., Anand, V. & Schwartz, T., 2007, "Endoscopic, endonasal extended ranssphenoidal, transplanum transtuberculum approach for resection of suprasellar lesions", *Journal of Neurosurgery*, Vol. 106, pp. 400-406.

Section 3

# Biomedical Diagnostics and Sensorics

Chapter 10

# Applications of Metrotomography in Biomedical Engineering

Radovan Hudák, Jozef Živčák and Richard L. Magin

Additional information is available at the end of the chapter

http://dx.doi.org/10.5772/50713

## 1. Introduction

More than one hundred years ago X-ray technology started its triumphal procession when Wilhelm Conrad Roentgen discovered a new kind of radiation in his laboratory in Wuerzburg, Germany in the year 1895. Up to this moment most of the developments in X-ray technologies and computed tomography have been focused on special medical applications. Eighty years later computer tomography (CT) was first tested, and it has since become a powerful tool well-accepted in industrial applications. Today industrial CT is central to innovations in material testing and geometry analysis, and to the development of high-tech quality-control devices and industrial and medical tools [13].

Besides the challenge to optimize the CT systems hardware, performance and capabilities, the biggest challenge at this moment is to process, in a reasonable amount of time, the huge amounts of data resulting from today's CT scanners.

The result of a CT scan displays the sample or object as a three-dimensional image composed of so called voxels [1]. Each voxel has a gray value that represents the local X-ray absorption density. The resolution of this three dimensional (3D) imaging system is given in part by the number of voxels in the 3D image, which in turn is given by the number of pixels in the detector. By using sub-pixel respectively sub voxel interpolation, the effective resolution can be increased. Using techniques derived from 2D image processing, 3D voxel images are evaluated to arrive at dimensional measurements for the scanned samples or objects. This approach is especially advantageous because the 3D image reproduces the complete sample or object, including both outer and inner measurement features. Ultimately the user needs to know whether the sample or object under inspection meets his tolerance requirements and whether or not his measurement device can answer this question. In addition, reproducibility and operator independence are important criteria for the shop-floor deployment of a measurement tool.

Industrial CT uses a series of 2-dimensional (2D) projections taken at specific intervals around the entire sample. Basically any type of industrial CT system uses three principal components: an X-ray tube, an X-ray detector, and a rotational stage. Everything is enclosed within a radiation-shielding steel/lead/steel cabinet that typically ranges between four and 10 feet cubed. This allows use of the system in a public environment without any additional safety concerns. Micro computed tomography (micro-CT) is primarily the same as standard CT except it uses a micro focus tube instead of a traditional tube. A micro-CT scan yields resolutions in microns because the focal spot of a micro focus tube is only a few microns in size. For comparison, micro-CT resolution is about 100 times better than the best CAT scan in the medical field. And there are now nano focus tubes available with a focal spot less than one micrometer in size for the very precise measurement needed mostly for material inspection.

In biomedical applications, micro-computed tomography scanners can function as scaled-down (i.e., mini) clinical CT scanners. They provide a 3D image of most, if not all, of the torso of a mouse scaled proportionally to a human CT image at a resolution of 50–100 μm. Micro-CT scanners, on the other hand, can image specimens the size of intact rodent organs at spatial resolutions from cellular (20 μm) down to subcellular dimensions (e.g. 1 μm). Micro-CT scanners fill the resolution-hiatus between microscope imaging, which resolves individual cells in thin sections of tissue, and mini-CT imaging of intact volumes.

High quality industrial X-ray detectors used for CT are typically a new generation of an amorphous silicon flat panel area detector. They offer very high sensitivity, resolution and bit depth. The resulting 2D X-ray images are very clear and the contrast is unparalleled. A modern high-end CT scan consists of taking several 2D X ray images around the object, preferably covering 360 degrees (complete rotation). CT systems typically acquire between 360 images (one image every degree) or 3600 images (one image every 0.1 degree) depending on the desired final resolution. Each image is between three to 10 megapixels, averaged and filtered to reduce noise. The 2D digital images taken during this step are saved directly into a single folder used in the next step of the CT process [4].

Once the acquisition process of the CT scan is completed, CT calibration and CT reconstruction algorithms are used to reconstruct the 3D CT volume. These 3D images are made of voxels (three-dimensional pixels), and with the use of visualization software, the 3D volume can be manipulated in real time. Because of this it is possible to slice through anywhere inside an object to inspect and look for defects, to take accurate measurements, to reconstruct a surface model, and so forth. Industrial CT technology is improving very quickly. Years ago a few single CT slices would take hours to generate. Now it is possible to reconstruct in just seconds complete 3D models with billions of voxels. This opens the door for numerous new applications like 3D reverse engineering, rapid prototyping, 3D metrology and more. In that regard, industrial CT has become a very competitive technology for 3D scanning. The principal benefit of using 3D CT for scanning or digitization is to get a complete model of an object, both external and internal surfaces, without destroying it.

One of the new systems available today is Metrotom (Carl Zeiss, Germany) which offers new applications in the area of biomedical engineering, in addition to its industrial applications

## 2. Materials and methods

Metrotomography presented by the Metrotom device (Fig. 1) uses X-ray technology based on a simple principle: an x-ray source illuminates an object with electro-magnetic beams – the x-ray beams. The beams meet on a detector surface and are recorded in varying degrees of intensity, depending on the thickness of the material and its absorption characteristics.

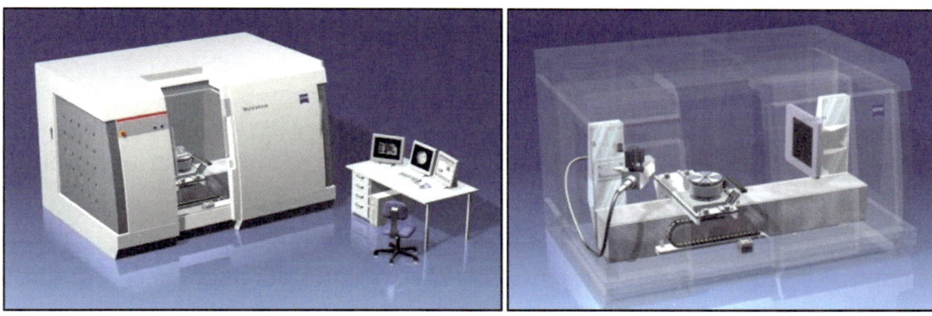

**Figure 1.** Metrotom (Carl Zeiss, Germany) and X-ray sensor.

The result is a two-dimensional gray-scale image. However, this image is only meaningful for visual inspection when shown as a cross section. Metrotom rotates the component 360° around its own axis, producing a 3D image of the interior of the sample or object.

Metrotom has a measuring volume of 300 mm x 300 mm x 300 mm. The ability to perform a quantitative metrotomograph analysis of a material depends on the principle of cumulative material thicknesses. It is possible to metrotomograph plastics, for example, up to a thickness of 250 mm, and light metal alloys such as aluminum or magnesium up to a thickness of 120 mm. It is even possible to perform a tomograph on steel up to a thickness of 10 mm. This thickness is sufficient to provide a qualitative material analysis up to a resolution of 50 mm.

### 2.1. Mathematical model of X-ray CT transmission

The reconstruction of three-dimensional objects such as the simple key shown in Figure 2 by the metrotomography is based upon using X-ray computed tomography (x-ray CT) to acquire complete information on the distribution of material in each object. The underlying physics and mathematics of this process will be briefly described in this section. More information on these principles can be found in the technical literature (14, 15).

The X-ray photon density that emerges when a narrow bean of monochromatic X-rays with energy E (Joules) and intensity $I_0$ (Joules/sec-cm$^2$), passes through a homogeneous material of density $\eta$ (g/cm$^3$) and atomic number Z can be expressed as:

$$I(x) = I_0 exp[-\beta(\eta, Z, E)x] = I_0 exp[-\beta_0 x] \quad (1)$$

where $\beta_0$ is the X-ray attenuation coefficient (1/cm). If we further assume for an inhomogeneous material that the attenuation coefficient is a space varying function, and the material can be represented by thin slabs, then adding up (or integrating the attenuation in each slab) we find that in one dimension the total attenuation by the material from x=0 to x=L is given by:

$$I(x = L) = I_0 exp\left[-\int_0^L \beta(x)\, dx\right] \quad (2)$$

Further, if we now scan the X-ray beam across the material in the y-direction we obtain an intensity profile for the object as:

$$I(y) = I_0 exp\left[-\int_0^L \beta(x, y) dx\right] \quad (3)$$

In X-ray CT imaging the X-ray source and detection equipment is designed to collect such intensity profiles over cross sections of three-dimensional objects. Each slice of the object presents a two-dimensional X-ray attenuation map –β(x,y) – to the beam with a thickness defined by the dimensions of the detector.

We need to keep track of the relationship between the fixed, laboratory frame of reference for the object (x,y) and the rotating frame of reference for the X-ray system (x′,y′), which is a function of the rotation angle θ is given by the simple matrix equation:

$$\begin{bmatrix} x' \\ y' \end{bmatrix} = \begin{bmatrix} x \cos\theta & y \sin\theta \\ -x \sin\theta & y \cos\theta \end{bmatrix} \quad (4)$$

Then, as illustrated in Figure 2, a simple plot of the X-ray intensity as the X-ray beam scans across the key as the angle θ can be written as:

$$I_\theta(x') = I_0 exp\left(-\int_{y'=A}^{y'=B} \beta(x, y) dy'\right) \quad (5)$$

The detected data then consists of many two-dimensional scans or projections, $P_\theta(x')$, each taken at a different angle (see Figure 2):

$$P_0(x' = p) = -ln\left\{\frac{I_0(x'=p)}{I_O}\right\} = \int_{Line\ AB} \beta(x, y)\, dy' \quad (6)$$

By rotating this projection through 180 degrees we collect information on the absorption of X-rays from all angles.

Finally, the overall relationship between the projection of the absorbed X-ray intensity is contained in the complete integration over the physical extent of the object. This representation has the mathematical form of the Radon transformation (16, 17):

$$P_\theta(x') = \iint_{Object} \beta(x, y)\delta(x' - p) dxdy \equiv R(p, \theta)[\beta(x, y)] \quad (7)$$

Inversion of the Radon transform, by simple back projection or some form of algebraic reconstruction gives the needed information, the cross section of the X-ray absorption β(x,y).

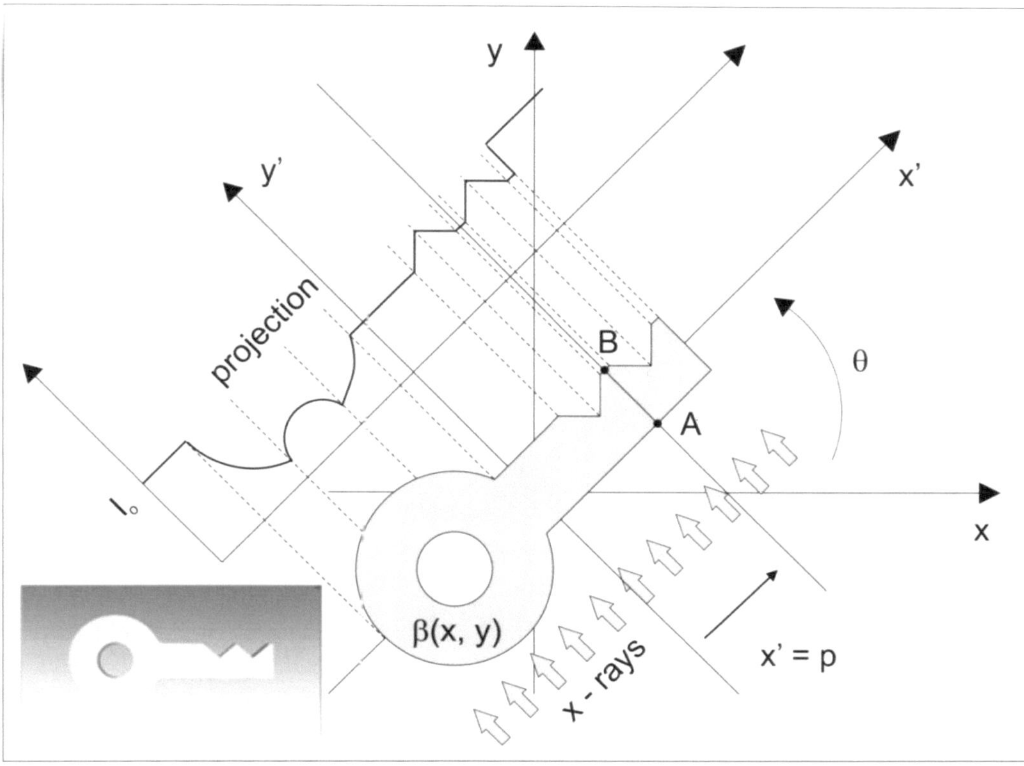


**Figure 2.** X-ray beam intensity profile of a key with X-ray attenuation β(x, y) along the x' axis for the viewing angle θ. From the profile the projection $P_\theta$ (x') can be constructed as a formal Radon transform.

The metrotomography procedure provides testing technology with a complete range of evaluation possibilities, from assembly inspection to damage analysis, including inspection of materials, porosity analyses and conventional defect checks, as well. At a glance, metrotomography now clearly shows the defects in areas where previously an inspection was not possible at all, or possible only using the time-consuming and costly cross section.

Workpiece data recorded using the metrotomography procedure can be applied to all areas of quality assurance and can be evaluated against the traditional metrology, as well as reverse engineering applications and comparison of geometrics.

Metrotomography uses a software environment called Calypso. Every metrotomographed component (whether a standard geometry or freeform surfaces) can be extensively evaluated using Calypso to perform the following steps: reading the features and orientation from the drawing and specifying a measurement strategy, generating a CNC measurement plan based on the computed STL or CAD data, entering and aligning the CAD model with the CT data, starting a new CNC measurement plan and evaluating the protocol.

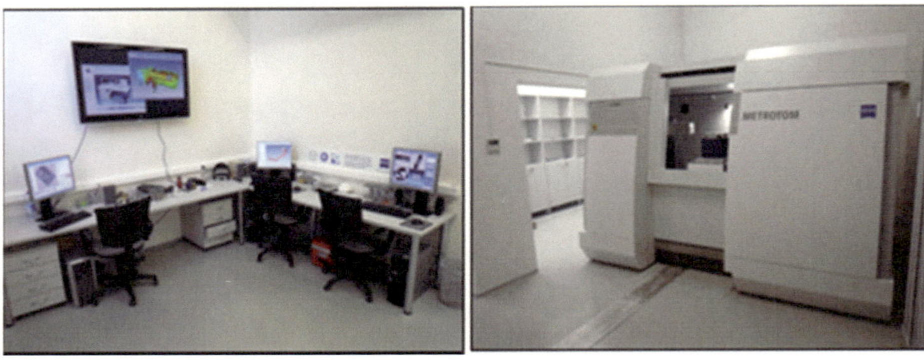

**Figure 3.** Technology Center of Computed Tomography, Department of Biomedical Engineering, and Measurement, Technical University in Kosice.

Industrial CT hardware and software at the Department of Biomedical Engineering and Measurement at the Technical University of Košice is shown above (Fig. 3.).

The industrial CT's reverse engineering capability is the quickest and the best solution, particularly when no CAD data exists for a component. When the evaluated workpiece (e.g. cube) is tomographed, a point cloud is computed from the resulting 3D model. Splines and knots are generated via reverse engineering. A complete CAD model, which can be displayed in all standard formats, is available at the end of the process. The duration of this process is approximately 1 hour.

For comparison of geometries, standard data formats such as IGES, STL, VIDA and STEP can be easily compared using a 3D model generated with the Metrotomography procedure. The plan/actual comparison work (e.g. a damper bearing evaluation) is described in the following steps: scanning the CAD design data of the bearing, entering the point cloud of the bearing from the metrotomograph, aligning the data sets with each other and displaying the measurement deviations in a color map. Fig. 4 shows Metrotom's measurement of the multidirectional valve, depicting the reverse engineering function of Metrotom, the material inspection, and the metrological possibilities of the scanner and software.

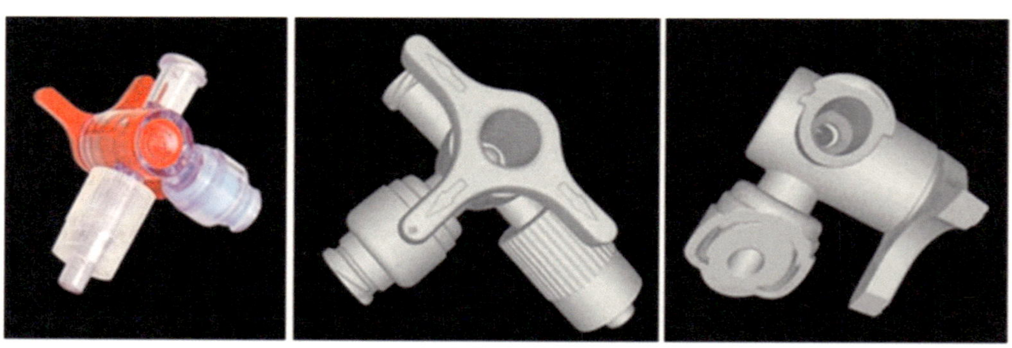

**Figure 4.** CAD models of the multidirectional valve – presentation of the reverse engineering.

Step by step, an X-ray scan rotates around the object being measured. From the X-ray, the position of each voxel is calculated. According to the density of material, each voxel has a value from the gray scale in the range from 0 to 65535. This allows separation between the object itself and other low density materials, such as air or support materials. The 3D point cloud makes it possible to see the component from different directions, and to evaluate not only the surface of the model but also the inner environment in cross-sections.

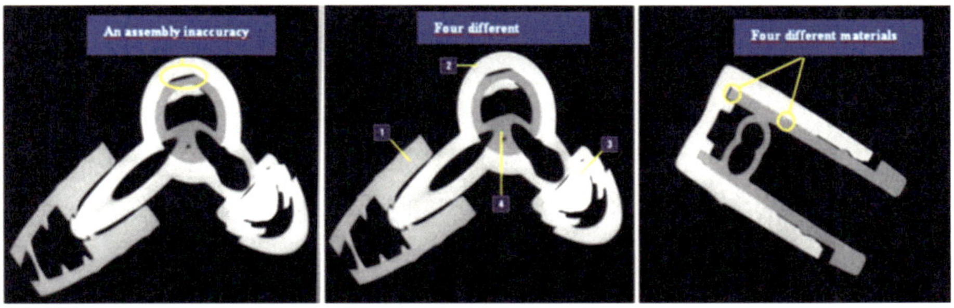


**Figure 5.** An analysis of the constructional junctions in multidirectional valve.

Figure 5 presents the inspection function of metrotomography. An advantage of this method is the possibility of inspecting constructed junctions in assembled work pieces for contact surfaces analysis, quality control, and detection of foreign materials or air spaces.

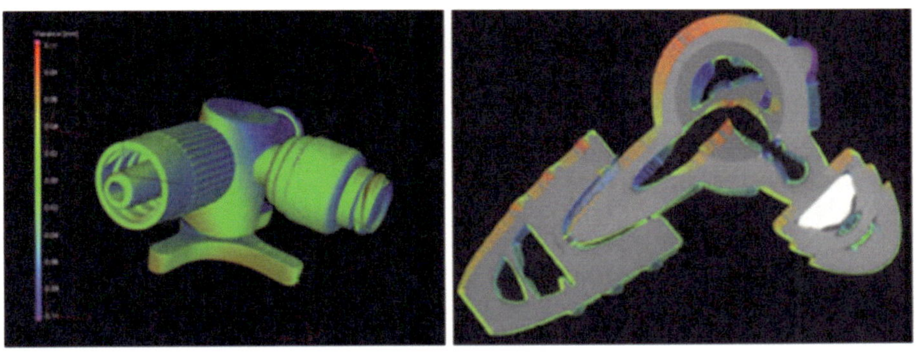

**Figure 6.** Geometry deviations analysis of the multidirectional valve.

The Metrotom measures with relatively high accuracy. Calypso software (Carl Zeiss, Germany) allows an evaluation of each obtained component. Comparing the CAD model (Fig. 6, 7), which is created with nominal geometry and dimensions, with metrotomograph's model, it is possible to generate a view of geometric deviations. Calypso also offers an evaluation of length parameters, angles and geometry, and position deviations.

Carl Zeiss used metrotomography to scan an epithetic hand, foot and plastic skull (Figure 8). These objects were selected to evaluate the kind of plastic materials frequently used in the practice of medicine and in biomedical engineering research. Wooden materials and the metallic parts of the skull were investigated to check the Metrotom's capabilities versus those of an industrial CT.

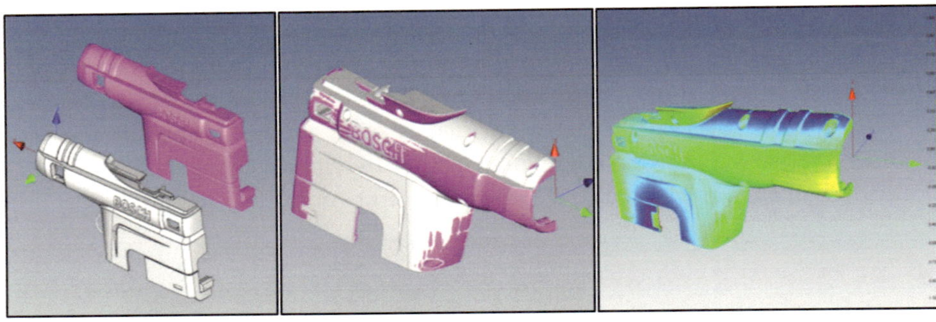

**Figure 7.** CAD model (left) with CT data and evaluation of geometry deviations with default toleration field (middle and right).

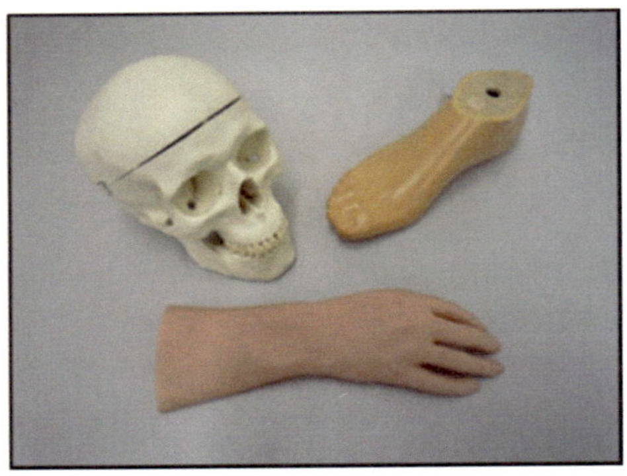

**Figure 8.** Samples from the field of biomedical engineering evaluated by metrotomography (epithesis and plastic human skull).

## 3. Results of measurement

The products of biomedical engineering research or research in prosthetics and orthotics (Fig.8) were scanned by an industrial CT machine and investigated using different software applications. This initial study shows the functions and possibilities of industrial CT and software applications (Calypso and VG Studio Max).

Software VG Studio Max (Volume Graphics, Germany) is a tool which accepts a visualization of obtained data and applies the following analysis: geometric analysis (2D & 3D dimensioning, actual/nominal comparison, actual/actual comparison, wall thickness analysis and extraction of STL surface from a point cloud), and material analysis (detection of defects, inclusions detection and possibility of material distribution and position in composite material).

VG Studio Max, as well as other related applications, offers useful tools and methods for data visualization. The point cloud makes it possible to separate, by grey color intensity, the different density of materials and resultant inner material detection (Fig. 9). Within the artificial foot are visible reinforcing materials and inner structures and holes for foot assembly.

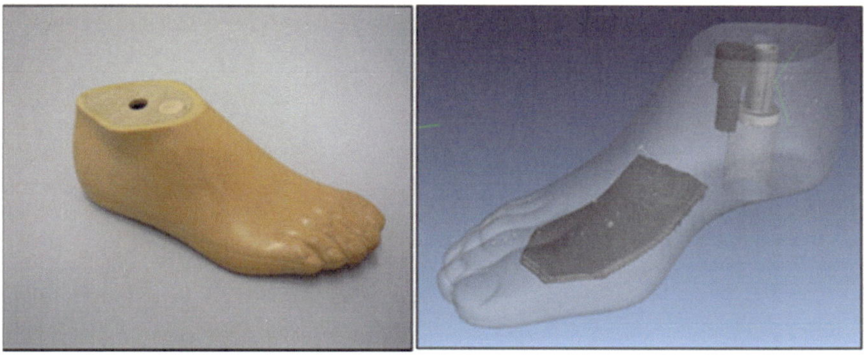

**Figure 9.** Epithetic foot and obtained 3D model (visible transparency of lower density material – soft surface plastic and wood).

With the greater translucency and the lower density of the foot's skin-colored plastic cover material, problematic air spaces (originating at the plastic casting) are getting more apparent. VG Studio Max enables detection of material inhomogeneity often presented by air cavities. By use of histogram function in the relation with an air cavity geometry it is possible to assess the exact position of the cavity.

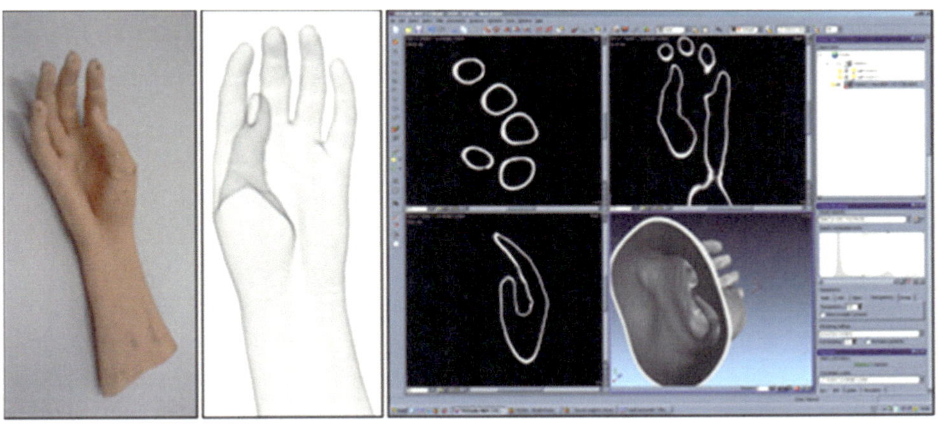

**Figure 10.** Epithetic hand glove (left), its X-ray scan (middle) and an environment of the VG-Studio Max software with three cross-sections and 3D view of rendered model of the glove.

Approximately 900 X-ray scans were captured by single steps during one revolution of the measured object around the vertical axis. Subsequently, the 3D model was processed (Fig. 10, middle), which allows non-destructive cross-sectional analysis (Fig. 11). The right side of Figure 9 shows the window of VG Studio Max 2.0. In four windows, it is possible to visualize the 3D view of the rendered model and the epithetic glove cross-sections in perpendicular views.

The software enables easy use of the measure features, e.g. a glove wall thickness. The histogram in the right lower corner of the window gives information about number and types of used materials, and the different densities in the observed object.

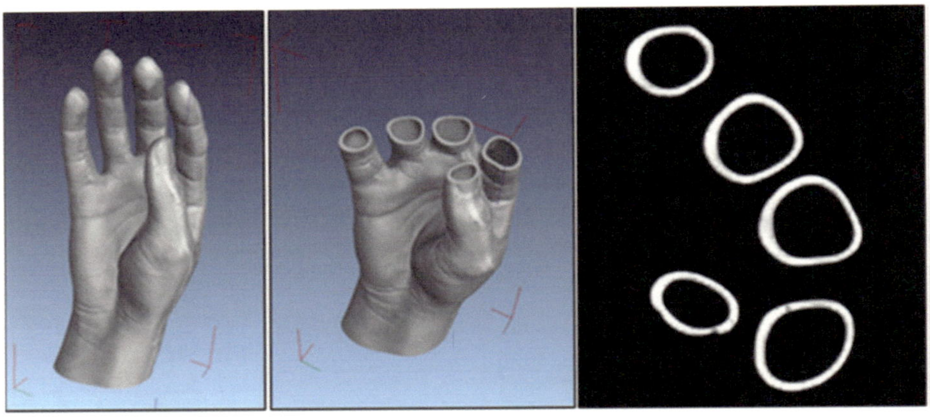

**Figure 11.** Rendered 3D model created by point cloud grid (left), cross-section of the 3D model in an arbitrary direction and cross-section of the glove model in one of the three views.

The VG Studio Max animation consists of multiple overflights around the object or crossing the object in an optional direction. Data can be loaded into the generally-supported STL format and further processed for reverse engineering or rapid prototyping/manufacturing.

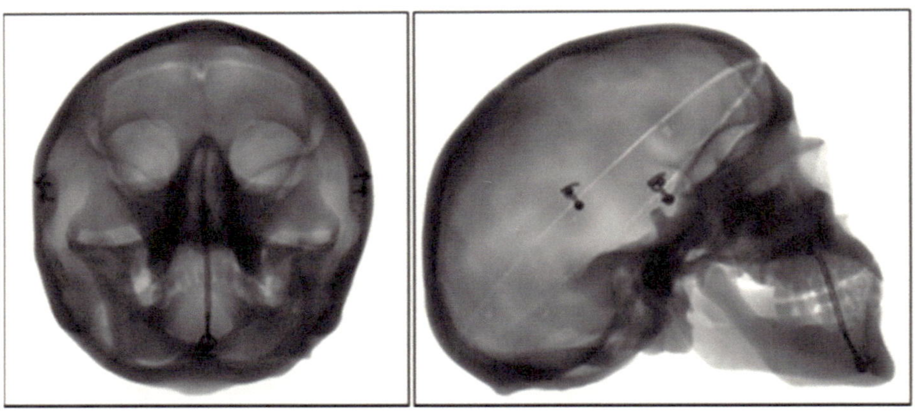

**Figure 12.** Two views of skull X-rays.

Different grey scales in the presented scans (Fig. 12) are caused by reduction of X-ray energy detected by an X-ray detector. This represents higher material thickness where the X-ray is passing through (skull borders) or higher material density (springs and clasps).

The skull model as shown in Fig. 13 contains two types of material: metallic springs and clasps, and a plastic skull. When there is a large disparity between the density of different materials, other selected materials may remain hidden (e.g. only metallic parts are visible).

Technology center of computed tomography at Technical university of Kosice supports many kinds of research. Biomedical research and research in prosthetics and orthotics are important supported areas. Tomography can be used for various evaluations, most commonly, for the digitalization of objects with very complicated shapes. In biomedical engineering, many objects have surfaces so complex, that they are not measurable by any other methods of digitalization. Touching probes, lasers or optic scanners cannot reach areas which are mostly hidden. With CT scanners, 100% of the information about an object's shape can be accessed. For example human teeth (Fig. 14) or animal skulls (Fig. 15) can be digitized. VGStudio Max software can extract from surface points via the STL model. STL is universal triangular model which can be imported to every CAD/CAE/FEM/RP software for further processing.

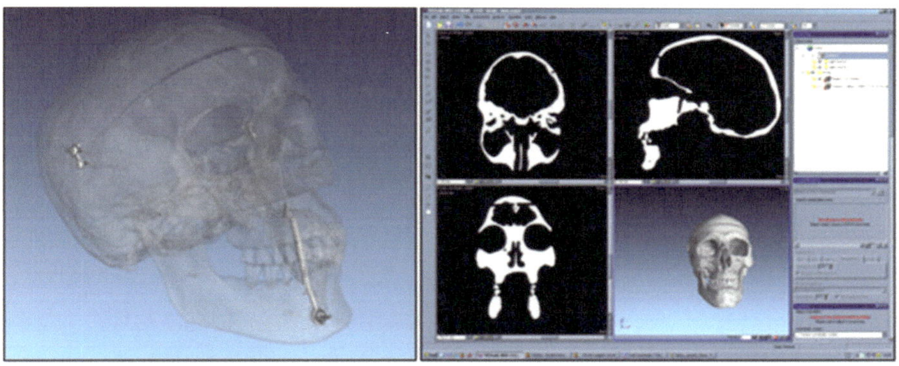

**Figure 13.** Skull translucency shows the metallic components of the assembly (left); a window with control tools of the VG-Studio Max software (right).

With CAD software, parameterization is possible, or perhaps the design of a supplement for a scanned object. In FEM (Finite element method) software, the stress/strain analysis can be performed. The STL model is ideal for Rapid Prototyping. With a 3D printer, a plastic or even metal copy of a real object can be made. Fig. 15 presents the results of the digitalization and printing of animal skulls. The bottom picture shows the original monkey skull and the printed copy of the monkey skull. More can be found about the rapid creation of copies of complex-shaped objects in other publication from several authors [10].

Orthosis design also requires very complicated plastic objects, difficult to digitalize with any other scanning technology. Examples of the digitalization of orthosis for hands made from low temperature thermoplastics (LTTP) are pictured in Fig. 16. With the obtained data it is possible to do further analysis of curvature, for example, or a stress/strain analysis, etc.

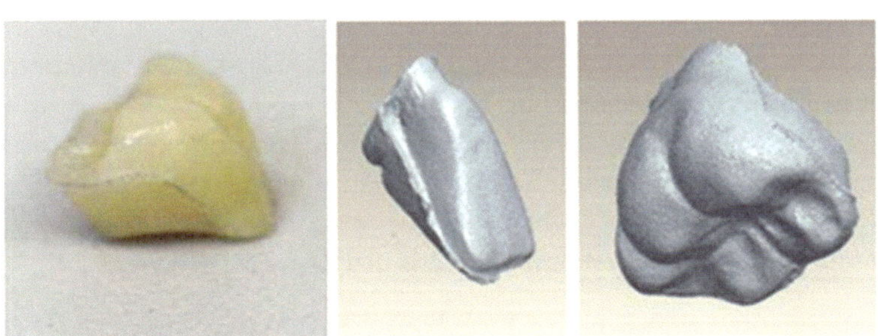

**Figure 14.** STL format of human teeth (middle and right).

**Figure 15.** Skulls of animals (top) and of monkey's skull printed with 3D printer (bottom left).

X-ray is kind of radiation that penetrates through objects, providing information not only about the surface of object, but also about its inner volume. After reconstruction of the point cloud, the inside of the object is visible using virtual cross-sections without destroying real object, or separating materials with different density.

Metrotom 1500 with maximum power of x-ray source 250 W is ideal for plastic parts and light metal alloys. Also metals with higher density can be scanned with Metrotom 1500, but wall thickness of the sample or object is limited. An STL model of metal dental bracket provides a nice example of digitalization for dental clinic (Fig. 17). The maximum dimension of this bracket is 3 mm. With so small an object, a point cloud makes it possible to achieve resolution of around 9μm. However, the resolution of sub-voxeling process can be increased. Small objects can be magnified more than bigger ones, because they are placed closer to the x-ray source. The size of the projection is zoomed many times, and so the size of the voxel (volume pixel) of the final point cloud is just a few micrometers.

An inspection of the inner structure of a pork femur is shown in Figure 18. The difference in gray-values depends on the density of the material. The air around the bone is black because of its lower density. The outer structure of the bone has a higher density, so the color of the pixels in this area is light gray. The density of the bone can be seen to change considerably from the outer surface to the inner volume in the cross- section picture.

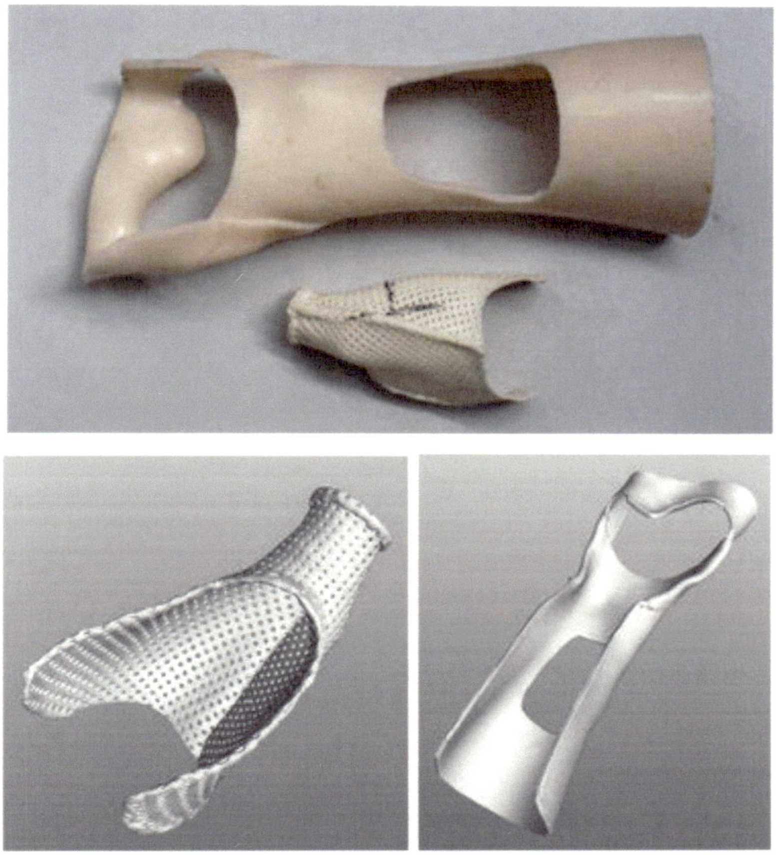

**Figure 16.** Plastic orthesis (top) and their point clouds (bottom).

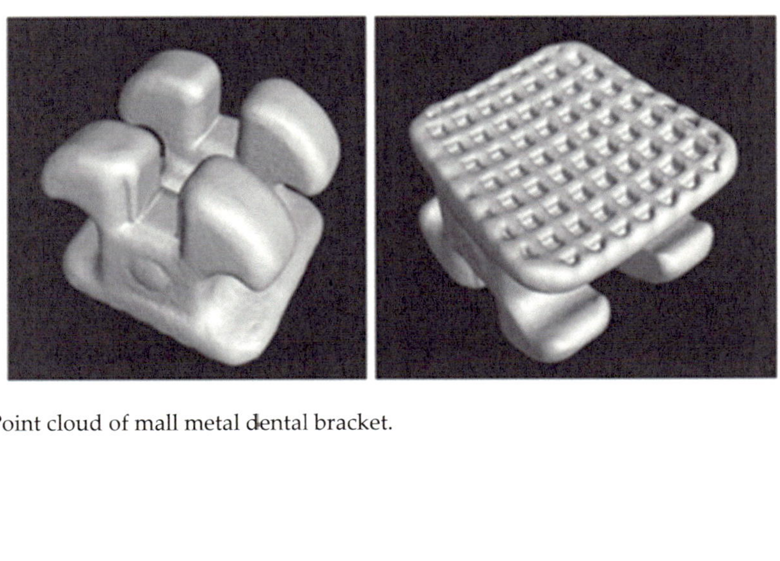

**Figure 17.** Point cloud of mall metal dental bracket.

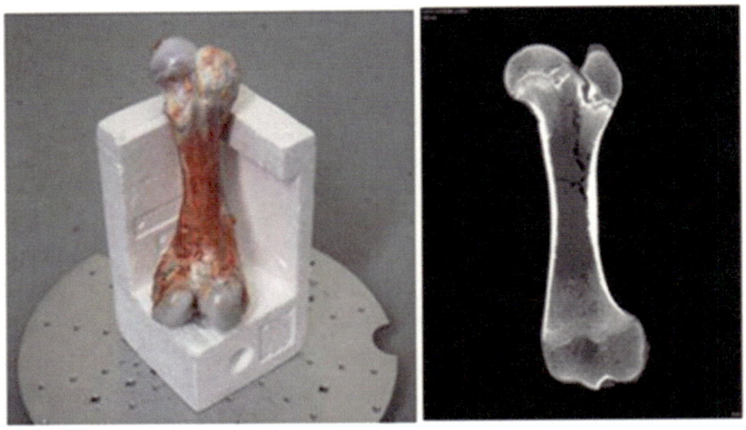

**Figure 18.** Pork femur (left) and its virtual cross-section (right).

Other research at our laboratory used CT technology in a porosity analysis of human bone (Fig. 19). The research measured the amount of solid material in two human demineralised bone matrices, before and after one of them was cultivated with mesenchymal stem cells (MSC) for two weeks. After this cultivation, the amount of solid material in the cultivated bone increased dramatically. The porosity of selected regions in each sample was calculated and compared. Results of research can be found in the authors' publication [6].

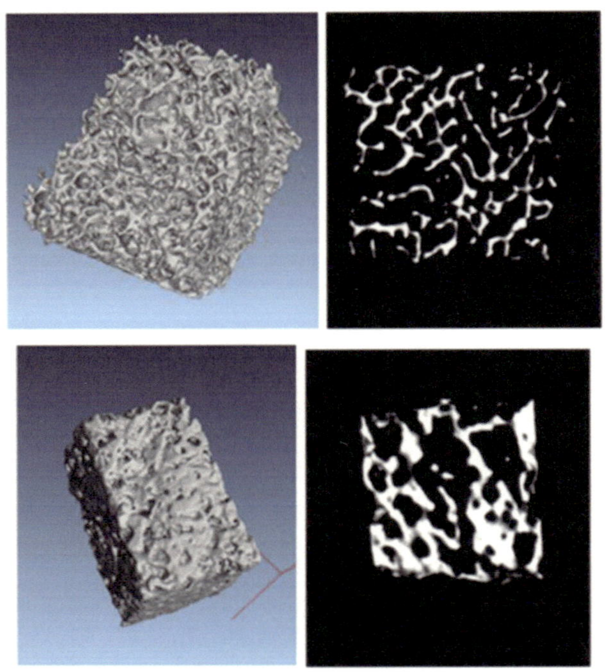

**Figure 19.** Demineralised human bone matrix without hMSCs (top) and demineralised human bone matrix with hMSCs after two weeks of cultivation (bottom).

Industrial tomography offers biomedical researchers the advantages of nondestructive testing and a precise view of inner structure. But it is also a tool capable of sharply accurate data reconstruction and very precise geometrical measurements. For example, Figure 20 presents a spherical form of a used acetabular component that was measured with Calypso software. With Calypso, researchers can evaluate characteristics of objects and make a protocols or graphical presentations of results. Graphical interpretation of form deviations in a magnified, used acetabular component are presented in Figure 19. Deviations have been filtered to eliminate scratches on the spherical surface.

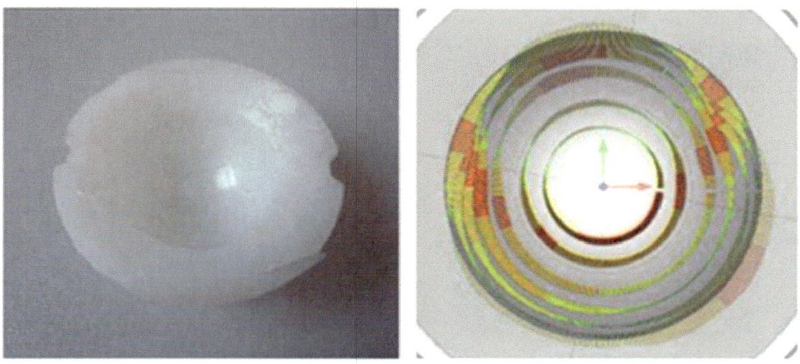

**Figure 20.** Used acetabular component (left) and form deviations on spherical surface (right).

The quality of the reconstructed point cloud and accuracy of measured data depends markedly on the density and the cumulative wall thickness of a scanned object. Because of that, materials with lower density are more suitable for scanning. Titanium, in comparison with other metals like steel or copper, has a relatively low density, and so small components made from titanium are measurable without restrictions.

One of the latest projects supported here is the digitalization of titanium dental implants. Analyses of material homogeneity, porosity, assembly quality and geometry were performed on four different implants (Figure 21). With digitalized data, appropriate modifications are made to the implants and the new modified dental implants are printed with the rapid prototyping technology.

## 4. Example of the use of tomography in biomedicine

A CT scan of the patient's head was obtained via medical CT in a clinical environment. For further reconstruction and implant design, the optimal density of the imaging is less than 1 mm. Medical screenings are stored in normalized format DICOM (Digital Imaging and Communication in Medicine). Because nowadays there are several generations of DICOM format, adapted software applications, such as MIMICS and 3MATIC (from Materialise, Belgium), are available.

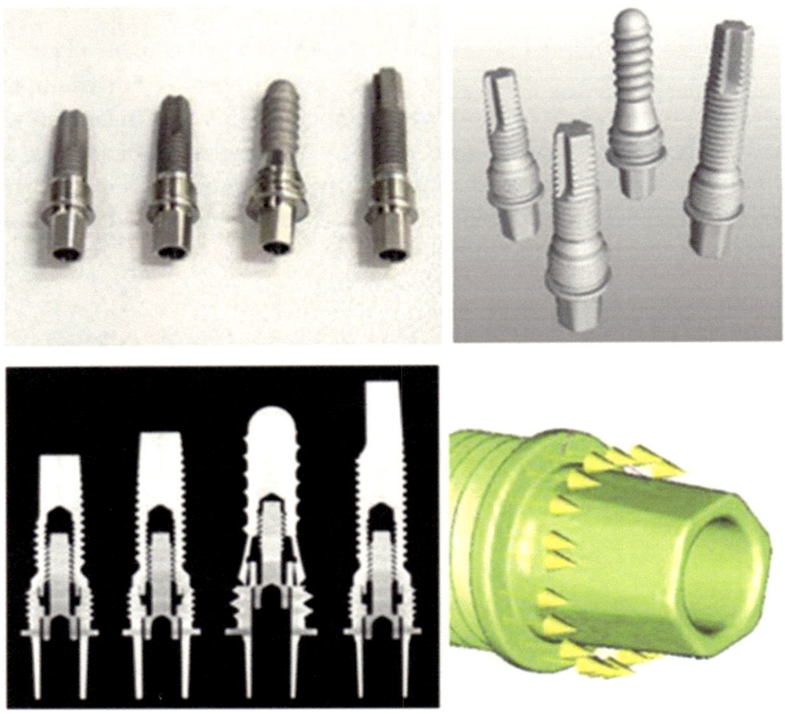

**Figure 21.** Four dental implants (top left), rendered point cloud (top right), cross-section of point cloud (bottom left) and detail to STL file imported to metrology software Calypso.

MIMICS software is used for transformation of the DICOM format into the 3D model. In general, the DICOM format is a series of slices – screens located one above the other – representing the complete model. A single shade of grayscale represents tissues with several different densities (Fig. 22).

It is necessary to separate soft and hard tissues to distinguish bone tissue from other human tissues. The MIMICS software contains a "mask tool", that the operator can use to achieve this effect. For the final model to represent only the requested areas, colors are modified by contrast and brightness level. In some cases, it is more effective to convert soft tissues to 3D, as well. For instance, in cranial implants the design of the implant has to follow brain tissue precisely to avoid creating pressure. After the mask is released, software creates the 3D model.

The 3D model is created as a point cloud that has its own surface structure. Often, the point cloud uses software tools to clean the surface of noise and other tissue burrs. For this cleaning the user's knowledge of anatomy is important, to avoid omitting significant areas that can affect final implant design. With the surface cleaned, the model is prepared for further processing. It is saved in MCS format. The software can also read bitmap pictures or jpegs, as well as the DICOM format. For those using older formats of DICOM, it is necessary to perform manual setup of the resolution (Fig. 23).

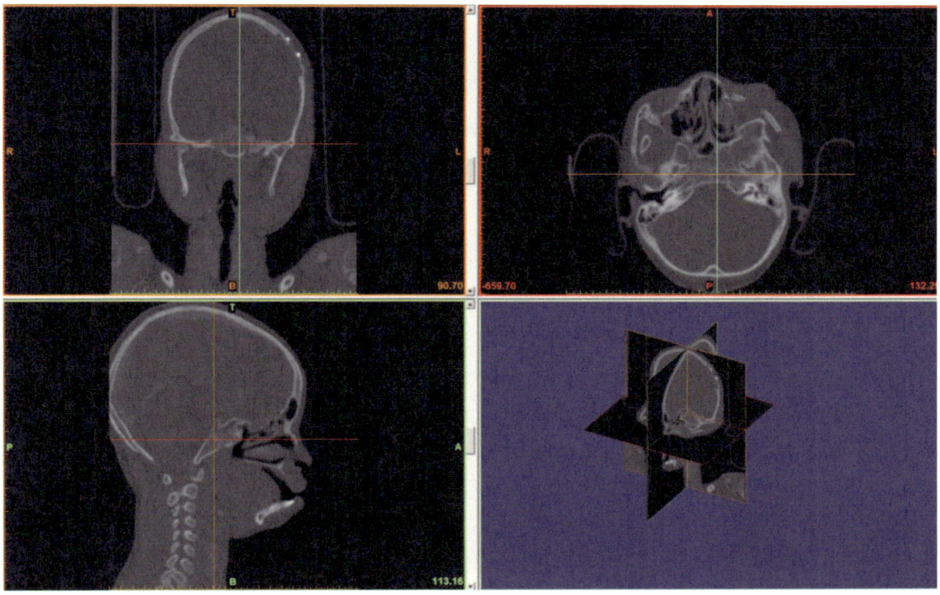

**Figure 22.** Mimics software environment.

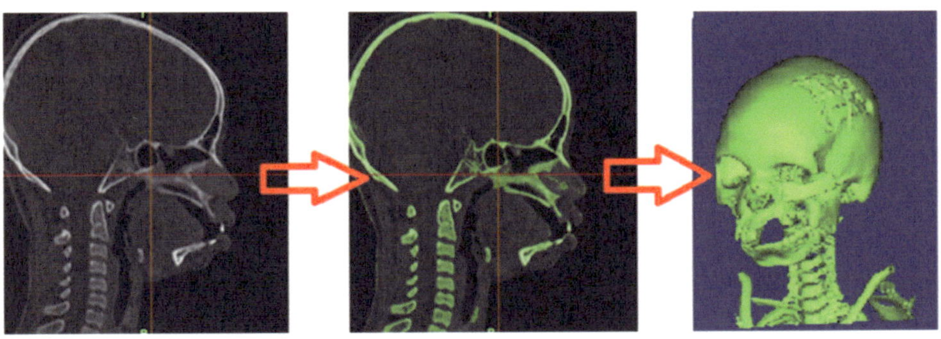

**Figure 23.** Steps of creation of 3D model form DICOM format (CT).

## 4.1. Adaptation of 3D model and implant design

The 3MATIC (Materialise, Belgium) application software allows the transformation of an uncounted 3D model into a series of polygons.

The size of the triangles represents the precision and the quality of the model – the more triangles, the smoother the surface of the model (Fig. 24). At the start of the process, the steps to optimize the triangles are performed. Next, the steps necessary to link the chosen type of implant and its localization are performed. In the case of a damaged jawbone, over-material was surgically removed to prevent it from interfering with the implant. At this step, consulting the surgery is required to verify the contact points/areas for the final application of the implant.

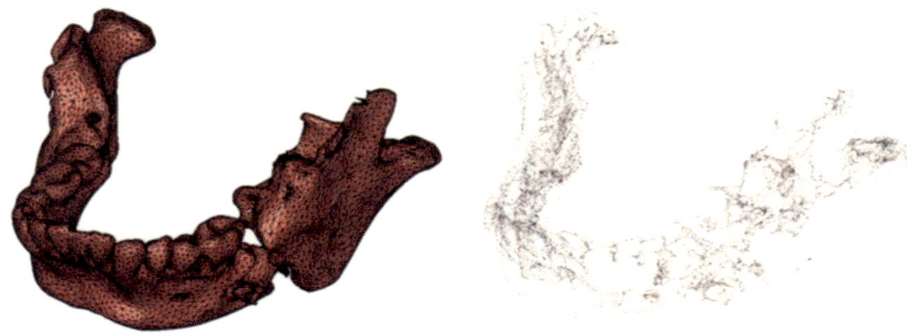

**Figure 24.** Model represented by mesh.

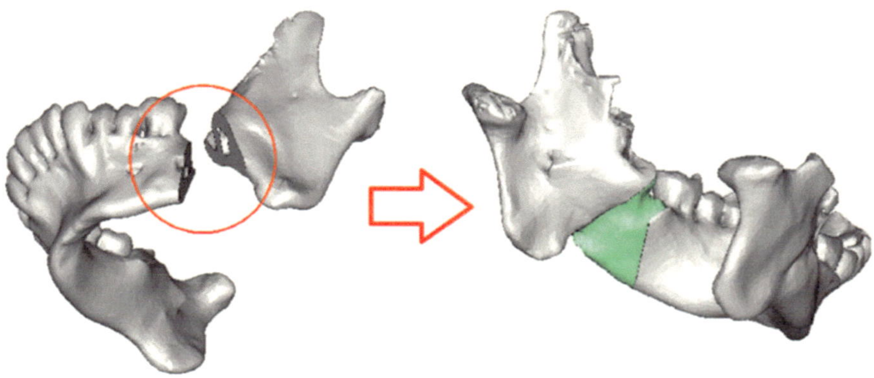

**Figure 25.** Damaged area and implant replacement.

The missing part of the model is reconstructed based on the present quality of the bone tissue. Here, the bone-like geometry was obtained by industrial CT (Metrotom 1500, Carl Zeiss, Germany). It is important that the complex geometry of the surface does not affect the physiological function of the jaw. Of course, the replacement must by morphologically similar to the missing part: differences in the size of the implant can completely change the ratios of the jawbone, leading to abnormal changes in the joint. Such changes affect other parameters in maxillofacial area, potentially causing a pathologic effect on the complete system. After modeling the replacement, analysis of the bone wall structure thickness must be performed. This step is important to create holes and interfaces needed to fix the implant to the bone (Fig. 25). Openings are designed individually and must be positioned so that they cannot affect important anatomic points, like vessels or nerves. The number of the openings should be limited to the minimum number required to fix the implant robustly to the bone. For better interface contact between the implant and the bone, the structure of the implant is made with predefined porosity (Fig. 26). That allows healthy bone to grow through the implant and stabilize it in position. Such stabilization is expected because the jawbone, as part of a live human articular system, is routinely exposed to mechanical stresses.

Afterwards, it is important to repair texture errors, like overhanging triangles, unwanted holes, etc. These errors can affect the surface relief of the final design. At this point, the implant is ready for production.

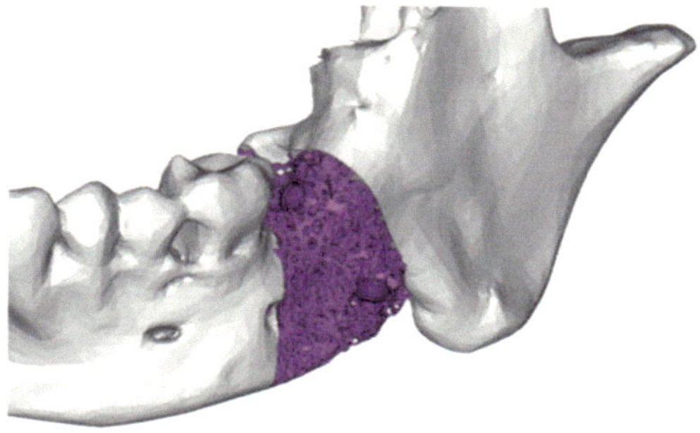

**Figure 26.** Creation of porous implant.

## 5. Conclusions

This study shows the possibilities and the limits of industrial CT when it is used for different biomedical applications. Wherever better resolution of output data is required, wherever the size of an analyzed object is problematic, there is a place for micro CT technology. Data obtained by metrotomography are usable in many biomedical applications, including material structure and homogeneity analysis, the inspection of the assembly of medical aids or devices, the evaluation of geometry deviations, quality control in medical production and reverse engineering. After acquisition of a digital point cloud, there are software tools that can enable different metrological or material analyses, and provide added value in biomedical research and development.

## Author details

Radovan Hudák and Jozef Živčák
*Technical University of Kosice, Faculty of Mechanical Engineering, Department of Biomedical Engineering and Measurement, Kosice, Slovakia*

Richard L. Magin
*University of Illinois at Chicago, Department of Bioengineering, Chicago, IL, USA*

## Acknowledgement

This contribution is the result of the project: Creation and promotion of technologies in diagnostics of components and junctions with computed tomography (ITMS: 26220220038) supported by the Research & Development Operational Programme funded by the ERDF and the project: Research of New Diagnostic Methods in Invasive Implantology (MSSR-3625/2010-11) supported by Ministry of Education, Science, Research and Sport of the Slovak Republic.

## 6. References

[1] Ritman, E. L.: Micro-Computed Tomography—Current Status And Developments, Annual Review of Biomedical Engineering, Vol. 6: 185-208, August 2004.

[2] Lettenbauer, H., Georgi, B. and Weiß, D.: Means to Verify the Accuracy of CT Systems for Metrology Applications (In the Absence of Established International Standards),

DIR 2007 - International Symposium on Digital industrial Radiology and Computed Tomography, June 25-27, 2007, Lyon, France.
[3] Lee, Y. S, Seon, J. K., Shin, V. I., Kim, G. and Jeon, M.: Anatomical evaluation of CT-MRI combined femoral model, BioMedical Engineering OnLine 2008, 7:6 doi:10.1186/1475-925X-7-6.
[4] Noel, J.: Advantages of CT in 3D Scanning of Industrial Sample or objects, 3D Scanning Technologies Magazine., Vol. 1, No. 3, 18 — December 2008.
[5] Andreu, J. P. and Rinnhofer, A.: Modeling Knot Geometry in Norway Spruce from Industrial CT Images, Springer-Verlag Berlin Heidelberg, SCIA 2003, LNCS 2749, pp. 786–791, 2003.
[6] Gromošová, S., Rosocha, J., Živčák, J., Hudák, R., Kneppo, P.: New modular semiautomatic system for preparation of the demineralized bone matrix for clinical transplantation. In: World Congress on Medical Physics and Biomedical Engineering – WC 2006: Imaging the future medicine: August 27 - September 1, 2006 COEX Seoul, Korea. Heidelberg: SpringerLink, 2006. 4 p. ISBN 978-3-540-36841-0.
[7] Toporcer, T., Grendel, T., Vidinský, B., Gál, P., Sabo, J., Hudák, R.: Mechanical properties of skin wounds after atropa belladonna application in rats. In: Journal of Metals, Materials and Minerals. vol. 16, no. 1 (2006), p. 25-29. ISSN 0857-6149
[8] Hutníková, L., Hudák, R., Živčák, J.: Scoliosis severity diagnostics: the new application for automatic X-ray image analysis, In: Infusing Research and Knowledge in South East Europe: 3rd Annual South-East European Doctoral Student Conference : Thessaloniky, 26-27 June, 2008, ISBN 978-960-89629-7-2, ISSN 1791-3578.
[9] Gal, P., Kilik, R., Spakova, T., Pataky, S., Sabo, J., Pomfy, M., Longauer, F., Hudak, R.: He-Ne laser irradiation accelerates inflammatory phase and epithelization of skin wound healing in rats. In: Biologia. roč. 60, č. 6 (2005), s. 691-696. ISSN 0006-3088.
[10] Cierniak R.: X-Ray Computed Tomography in BiomedicalEngineering. Springer London, 2011, ISBN 978-0-85729-026-7.
[11] Gajdos I., Katuch P.: Complex approach to the reverse engineering techniques. Scientific Papers of University of Rzeszow : Zeszyty Naukowe Politechniki Rzeszowskiej : Mechanika z. 80. No. 273, 2010, p. 81-86. - ISSN 0209-2689.
[12] Wagner J.: Contribution to the design optimization of electromechanical actuators of mechatronics systems, In: Metalurgija/Metallurgy, Vol.49, 2010, No 2, pp.600 – 603, ISSN 0543-5846.
[13] Penhaker, M., Darebnikova, M., Cerny, M. Sensor network for measurement and analysis on medical devices quality control,In proceedings 1st International Conference on e-Technologies and Networks for Development, ICeND 2011, Communications in Computer and Information Science, 171 CCIS, pp. 182-196. Springer,3 August 2011 through 5 August 2011,Dar Es Salaam,ISSN: 18650929,ISBN: 9783642227288,DOI: 10.1007/978-3-642-22729-5_16ABBREVIATED SOURCE TITLE: Commun. Comput. Info. Sci.
[14] Nadine Barrie Smith, Andrew Webb, "Introduction to Medical Imaging: Physics, Engineering and Clinical Applications" Cambridge University Press, Cambridge, UK, 2010.
[15] Paul Suetens, "Fundamentals of Medical Imaging" (2nd ed), Cambridge University Press, Cambridge, UK, 2009.
[16] Stanley R Deans, "The Radon Transform and Some of Its Applications, Dover, Mineola, NY, 2007.
[17] Gabor T Herman, 'Fundamentals of Computerized Tomography: Image Reconstruction from Projections (2nd ed), Springer, NY.

Chapter 11

# Fiber Optic–Based Pressure Sensing Surface for Skin Health Management in Prosthetic and Rehabilitation Interventions

Dimitris Tsiokos, George T. Kanellos,
George Papaioannou and Stavros Pissadakis

Additional information is available at the end of the chapter

http://dx.doi.org/10.5772/50574

## 1. Introduction

### 1.1. Background and motive

The work presented here responds to the high-prevalence of pressure ulcers and the need for better diagnostic, treatment and prevention practices in the clinic. Factors in pressure ulcer development are classified as intrinsic (e.g. disuse muscle antrophy due to motor paralysis or impaired/absent sensation due to sensory paralysis) or extrinsic (e.g. applied pressure due to external loading to soft tissues, shear due to poor posture and/or poor support materials, or other adverse microenvironment at support interface due to raised temperature, sweating, incontinence, infection). Pressure ulcers are localized areas of tissue breakdown in skin and/or underlying tissues [1], [2]. They can occur in all situations where subjects are subjected to sustained mechanical loads, but are particularly common in those who are bedridden, wheelchair bound or wearing a prosthesis or orthosis. The ulcers are painful, difficult to treat, and represent a burden to the community in terms of healthcare and finances. Consequently, the pressure ulcer problem affects the quality of life of many young and elderly individuals.

It has become apparent that a complete pressure management system integrated with the medical intervention is required in order to measure and redistribute pressure at the human machine interface and prevent the development of pressure ulcer. In this respect, the rapidly evolving field of optical fiber sensing seems to hold a strong potential for providing effective solutions towards accurately measuring and monitoring pressure, strain and shear between the human skin and the support surface [3], [5]. Sensing by means of light offers a number of advantages when utilizing the appropriate fiber sensor configuration, since light propagation is highly sensitive to external forces and perturbations yielding real-time measurements with almost negligible hysteresis [6]-[8]. In addition, optical fibre sensors provide immunity to electromagnetic interference, high sensitivity, small size and low weight, passiveness, resistance to harsh environments, multiplexing capabilities and possibility to parallelize the readout. Equally important is that optical fiber based pressure sensors can in principle confront with true medical requirements as real time data acquisition, high sensing resolution and increased dynamic range. These fiber sensing properties have turned photonic sensing technology into more versatile and often more reliable than its electronic counterparts and have been already identified and utilized in a number of applications in diverse fields. Structural health monitoring, automotive industry, oil and gas extraction, aeronautics and aerospace, robotics, healthcare, etc. have already adopted fiber sensor configurations in several crucial sensing functionalities, but unfortunately only minor attempts have been pursued towards synergizing the field of photonic sensing with biomechanics, orthopaedics and rehabilitation [9]-[11].

Being fully aware of this new technological sensor toolkit, our work is born out of the need for readdressing a number of traditional challenges in support surfaces and prosthetics by taking advantage of, and effectively integrating recently available technological advances that offer the opportunity to tackle previously unresolved problems. That is, integrate knowledge in photonic sensing with rehabilitation engineering and biomechanics in order to address the unanswered question of pressure ulcer development in the human-machine interfaces of biomedical interventions.

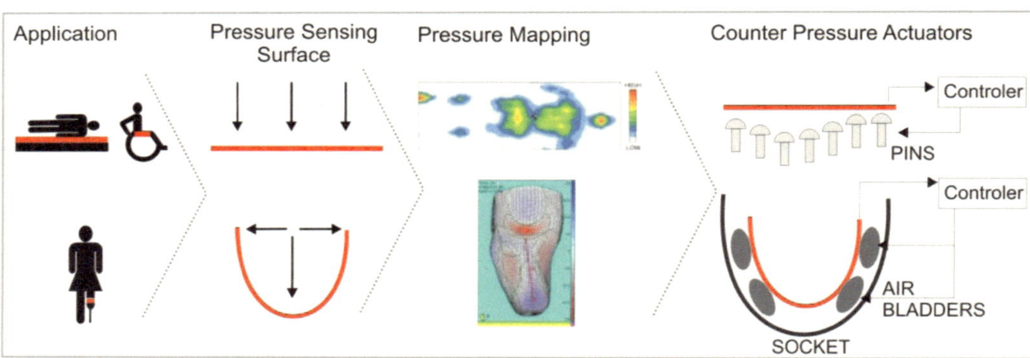


**Figure 1.** Schematic of the pressure management system proposed for both cases of bed/seating system sensing surface (top row) and lower extremity prosthetic socket sensing surface (bottom row). The first step involves the measurement of the pressure loads across the sensing surface, then generate pressure maps that define pressure distribution and finally drive counter pressure actuators to redistribute pressure across the surface for pressure relief.

The pressure sensing system that we are describing in this chapter aims to be embedded in a pressure management expert system that is presented in fig. 1. Specifically, in order to maintain skin health at areas of the skin that prolonged pressure loads are applied, a pressure tension relief is introduced in order to redistribute pressure and relief any excessive pressure or tension applied on the skin by means of a sensor matrix and counter pressure controllers and actuators. The pressure management system can be customized to be applied in medical beds or seating systems (wheelchair) and prosthetic sockets in lower extremity prosthetic interventions as depicted in fig. 1. A dynamic control system of supporting pins for the bed and seating system or air bladders for the prosthetic socket will anticipate with the help of feedback of fiber optic pressure sensors, points of high pressure at the human-machine interface (HMI) and will locally decrease pressure in the material at those locations before those pressure thresholds are reached in real time. Pressure redistribution protects tissues against prolonged and excessive epidermal pressure developed in the HMI. This will in turn prevent the onset or deterioration of pressure ulcers.

To this end, we are reporting on the development of a flexible 2D optical fiber-based pressure sensing surface suitable for human machine interfaces in biomedical and rehabilitation applications. The sensor comprises of highly-sensitive Fiber Bragg Grating elements embedded in a thin polymer sheet to form a 2x2 $cm^2$ sensing pad with a minimal thickness of 2.5mm, while it is easily expandable in order to be used as a building block for larger surface sensors. The fabricated pad sensor was combined with a low physical dimension commercially available interrogation unit to enhance the portability features of the complete sensing system. Sensor mechanical properties allow for matching human skin behavior, while its operational performance exhibited a maximum fractional pressure sensitivity of 12 $MPa^{-1}$ with a spatial resolution of 1x1$cm^2$ and demonstrates no hysteresis and real time operation. In parallel, in order to maximize sensing surface durability while maintaining functional properties we conducted mechanical tests in three different case studies through which we identified the optimized fabrication properties (thickness, fiber positioning depth, fiber type) of the sensing surface.

More specifically, the chapter is organized in five different sections. The rest of the first section describes the state-of-the-art in pressure sensing technologies while the FBG sensor presented in this chapter will be briefly benchmarked against currently available technologies. Section 2 presents the principle of operation of the proposed pressure sensing scheme. The development of the optical fiber 2-D pressure sensing pad takes advantage of the highly sensitive 1-D Fiber Bragg Grating (FBG)-based array structures, which are arranged in a 2-dimensional sensing surface. Section 3 will describe the experimental proof of concept of the concept presented in Section 2 and the results obtained in the experiment. Section 4 presents a sensor optimization study that was performed in order to optimize the sensor operational features versus its mechanical and structural properties. We have identified the basic fabrication parameters that will enhance sensor pads rigidity and durability to guarantee the sensor pads reliability. These parameters are: optical fiber grating optimum inscription characteristics, optical fiber type (hydrogenated/non-hydrogenated fiber), depth of fiber embodiment in the polymer (hosting) material and thickness of the polymer sheet. We have performed a thorough analysis of these parameters and the results will be presented and discussed in this section. Section 5 will describe in more detail the application perspective of the developed sensor. The targeted technological applications will be discussed including medical beds, wheelchairs and lower extremity below-the-knee prosthetic sockets while the required characteristics and specifications of the sensing surface per application will be highlighted. Finally Section 6 will describe the summary of the chapter and the conclusions obtained.

### 1.2. State-of-the-art in pressure sensing technology

Efforts to prevent pressure ulcer development are plagued with inconsistencies and a general lack of best practice guidelines. For instance, repositioning patients in medical beds is still the most common approach used in an attempt to prevent the development of pressure ulcers, but additional measures are diverse. The monitoring of magnitude and timing of all the extrinsic parameters requires a mere quantitative assessment of the pressure profile at a given time. Information of the potentially ever-changing multidirectional loading patterns in real time is still an unresolved HMI sensing issue.

The variety of research transducers for pressure measurements are classified based on their operation principle [12]-[15], [16], [17] as fluid-filled sensors [18], pneumatic sensors, diaphragm deflection strain gauge [19], cantilever/beam strain gauge, MEMS and printed circuit sheet sensors [18]-[25]. The most commonly used, in- vivo clinical pressure sensors (capacitive, piezoelectric, ink-film based) are the Tekscan (Boston, MA), the Xsensor (Calgary, Canada), Schönefeld, (Germany), the Vista medical (Winnipeg, Canada), the Rincoe Socket Fitting System and the Novel (Munich, Germany) [20]-[32] (see table 1). Industrial equivalents include "Bodyfitter" by Sensor Products (Madison, NJ), ElekSen (Iver Heath Bucks, UK), Pressure Profile Systems Inc. (Los Angeles, CA). The underlying technology of these products is basically the measurement of a certain material's conductivity as it changes with pressure [33]. However, these sensors possess many disadvantages such as accuracy, hysteresis, signal drift, the response to curvature, spatial resolution and temperature sensitivity [20]-[32]. An ideal system should be able to monitor real interfacial stresses continuously, solve the associated data acquisition and conditioning issues, and allow placement at the assistive device interface without significant obstruction to the original boundary conditions. These sensors are conditioned for low pressure and short-term applications, and are therefore not addressing sensor creep. So for the consistency of results (i.e. drift compensation) a post processing of the raw data is always recommended but not available in current products. This rather laborious process is associated with the known variances of particular sensing elements and must be simplified if these instruments reach the clinical field. In addition to that, it seems almost impossible to calibrate and monitor in real time electrical, piezoresistive and capacitive systems for conditions where the sensor carrier is bended, stretched or bulged [13], [15]. A study [34] found that the Tekscan system overshoot readings that were applied in areas smaller than 4 $cm^2$, showed substantial hysteresis (+20%), drift and creep (19), but still is preferred by clinicians for its real time display capabilities and resolution. Other studies compared commercial systems for accuracy and repeatability (Talley pressure electropneumatic Evaluator-Talley Medical, UK, DIPE-Next Generation CA, US [13]-[15], [33], Force Sensing Array, FSA-Vista Medical, Canada) and reported problems with accuracy, repeatability, speed, data presentation, pronounced hysteresis (+14-25%) and significant creep (12%) [33]. They were also shown to underestimate the force applied on a small contact area (less than 4 cm$^2$). In all of these evaluations one common observation was the inability of the sensors to comply with large radii of curvature and surfaces with very complicated geometry. Sensor protrusion into the skin was another notable limitation since it caused erroneously high measurements in these latter studies.

To summarize the above analysis, it becomes obvious that there is currently no system that manages simultaneously micro-controlling of pressure management and higher-level ergonomic adaptations in a real time dynamic environment in the arena of pressure management devices. With respect to the sensing elements adopted so far, severe limitations in pressure ulcer diagnosis can be attributed to poor sensor accuracy, consistency (sensor drift and hysteresis) and calibration reliability. These factors are also mainly responsible for the absence of a reliable sensing system that will be able to report real time measurements of the potentially ever-changing multidirectional loading patterns in human/machine interface issues.

### *1.2.1. Optical fiber pressure sensors*

Limited work has been done in the field of healthcare towards synergizing photonic sensing with biomechanics, orthopaedics and rehabilitation applications. Within these attempts, a FBG-based pressure sensor has been demonstrated in the design of a high-resolution optical fiber manometry catheter [35]. On the other hand, fiber optic surface sensing structures for health-care pressure measurements have not yet been adequately addressed. To this end, a 2D fiber-sensing configuration was presented by Chu-Yu Huang et al. [36], where a 2D mesh of simple optical fibers embedded in a silicon-polymer material was used to assess shoe insole pressure, exhibiting however low sensitivity.

Efforts in fabricating a 2D fiber sensing configuration with increased sensitivity are also currently being deployed in [37]. The measurement of mechanical quantities using optical fibers and Bragg grating (FBG) sensors as considered here relates to forces that act transversely upon the optical fiber cladding. A variety of sensing mechanisms that convert either a transverse line load, a hydrostatic pressure (in case of a bare optical fiber) or a transverse load (on an embedded optical fiber) into an optical quantity that can be encoded in the Bragg peak wavelength of a FBG reflection signal have been proposed.

A first method hosts the FBG in a mechanically asymmetric birefringent optical fiber. The mechanical load is then directly encoded in the spectral separation of the two Bragg reflection wavelengths returned by the FBG. The most straightforward implementation of a mechanically asymmetric birefringent optical fiber is the side-hole fiber (with elliptical core) first demonstrated by Xie et al. in 1986 [38]. In 2007, Jewart et al. demonstrated the Bragg grating sensing characteristics of a side-hole fiber with large airholes [39]. The high transverse line load sensitivity of 176 pm/(N/mm) that was reported for the peak separation shows that optimizing the transverse sensitivity of optical fibers is possible with an adapted cross-section. Despite its high sensitivity to transverse loading, this sensor starts to work after a certain non-zero transverse line load while it does not allow achieving a high birefringence without significantly increasing their temperature sensitivity. Dedicated microstructured optical fibers (MOF) provide a solution to those difficulties. The experimental results published so far indicate that the sensitivity to temperature in highly birefringent MOFs strongly depends on the fiber geometry and can be up to 3 orders of magnitudes lower than in standard elliptical core fibers [40]-[44]. However, the sensitivities obtained with these MOF are still not sufficient in view of the required pressure measurement resolutions imposed by HMI demanding applications in medical mattresses and prosthetic sockets.

| | X Sensor | FSA | Tekscan | Talley | Pressure | Novel | FBG-based |
|---|---|---|---|---|---|---|---|
| Principle of operation | Capacitive | Piezo-resistive | Resistive | Electro-pneumatic | Pneumatic | Capacitive | OPTICAL |
| System | Seat Mattress | Seat, Back, Bed, In shoe, Orthotists | Seat, In shoe, Dental | Individual sensor | Individual sensor | Seat, Foot, Specialst e.g. bike seat hand | Matress, whellchair, seat, socket |
| Sensor size (mm) | Seat 12.5x12.5 Hi-res 2.7x2.7 | Bed 19x50 Foot 9x16 | Foot 5x5 | 100 mm round 28 mm round | 25 or 62.5 | 2.7x2.7 min 31x47 max | 1000x1000 |
| Sample rate | Up to 70,000 Sensors s-1 | 3,072 sensors s-1 | 316,800 sensors s-1 | N/A | N/A | Up to 20000 sensors s-1 | Real-time |
| Range (mmHg) | 0-220 | Bed 0-200 Foot 0-1500 | Seat 0-200/1,000 Foot 0-7500 | 20-300 | 0-125 | Bed 0-200 Foot 0-1,800 | At least 3000 |
| No of sensors | Seat 2304 Bed 10,240 Hi-res 65K | Up to 32x32 | Over 2,000 | 1 | 1 | Up to 2,304 | 4 or 8 |
| Quoted Accuracy | 10% or 10 mmHg | 10% | Clin. ± 3% Lab. ± 1% | ± 2% | ±3 mmHg | Typically ±5% | Unknown |
| Output device | Computer | Computer | Computer | Handheld digital gauge | Handheld digital gauge | Computer | Interrogator |

**Table 1.** Comparison of commercially available interface pressure measuring systems vs the targeted proposed sensing scheme

## 2. Proposed pressure sensing concept

In this section, we describe the development of a 2D optical FBG-based pressure sensing surface that combines the advantages of the FBG-array sensors with novel, elastic and flexible Polydimethyl-siloxane (PDMS) polymer material to provide a light-weight, compliant and flexible 2D pressure sensing surface. The sensor comprises of highly-sensitive Fiber Bragg Grating elements embedded in a thin polymer sheet to form a 2x2 $cm^2$ sensing pad with a minimal thickness of 2.5mm, while it is easily expandable in order to be used as a building block for larger scale sensors. The sensor's enhanced performance exhibited a maximum fractional pressure sensitivity of 12 $MPa^{-1}$ with a spatial resolution of 1x1$cm^2$ while it demonstrated no hysteresis and real time operation. The mechanical properties of this pad sensor makes it very unobtrusive while they allow for wrapping, embedding or attaching the sensor to irregular shapes and geometries, offering enhanced response to curvature. The fabricated pad sensor was combined with a low physical dimension commercially available interrogation unit interrogation unit [47] to enhance the portability features of the complete sensing system. The physical and operational characteristics of the presented pad sensor and particularly its high sensitivity in low absolute pressure values, its high spatial resolution and unobtrusive characteristics combined with potential portability are ideally suited for biomedical applications including amputee sockets, shoe sensors, wearable sensors, wheelchair seating-system sensors, hospital-bed monitoring sensors and other ergonomics sensors.

The development of the optical fiber 2-D pressure sensing pad takes advantage of the highly sensitive 1-D FBG-based array structures, which are arranged in foils as shown in Fig. 2(a) to form a 2-dimensional sensing surface. The foiled optical fiber sensor elements are embedded in a thin silicon polymer material to form an elastic sensing sheet. Based on the intensity modulation caused Bragg wavelength shifting, induced by the bending of the embedded fibers, a map of displacement or force over an area is generated. The pressure is obtained from the force applied on each sensing point divided by its effective area. Multiplexed FBG array configurations are used to address applications that require multipoint monitoring of the applied external forces, where every respective FBG element comprises a single point of measurement. As shown in Fig. 2(a), longitudinal spacing d of the FBGs defines the axial spatial resolution of the linear sensor.

The 2D surface sensing is obtained by proper arrangement of FBG arrays in 2D structures, as shown in Fig. 2(a), built on a flexible and stretchable silicon-polymer Polydimethyl-siloxane (PDMS) sheet. PDMS is suitable for sensing applications to match ideal skin behavior, since it is flexible, stretchable/elastic and with controllable viscosity and hardness. This pad can be wrapped around, embedded in, attached and anchored to irregularly shaped and/or moving objects or bodies and allows quasi-distributed sensing of mechanical quantities such as deformation, pressure, stress or strain along the entire surface. 2D spatial resolution is now defined by the fiber axial sensor distribution d and the spacing of optical fibers D. The presented 2D pressure sensor concept may be arranged as a uniform large scale surface (Fig. 2(a)), or may be implemented as an assembly of small scale building blocks that are properly interconnected, as shown Fig.2(b). The second approach gives the advantage of increased sensor shape flexibility while decreasing manufacturing complexity, that comes however at the expense of increased connectorisation and surface sensing discontinuities. In the present communication, we report on the implementation and evaluation of a 2x2 $cm^2$ sensing surface serving as a building block for larger scale sensors [48].

WDM interrogation method allows for multiplexed sensor networks as each is assigned a given "slice" of the input broad-band light spectrum. We make use of a novel interrogation unit [47] that features miniaturized properties, such as a weight of 150g , power consumption of <0.25 W and physical dimensions in the order of cm (LxWxD; 7x4.6x1.8 cm) while exhibiting a maximum operational frequency of 2.5 kHz for both wavelength shift and FBG central wavelength power loss measurements, an operational dynamic range of 32nm with 5pm resolution, to highlight the potential of implementing a fully portable highly sensitive sensing system.

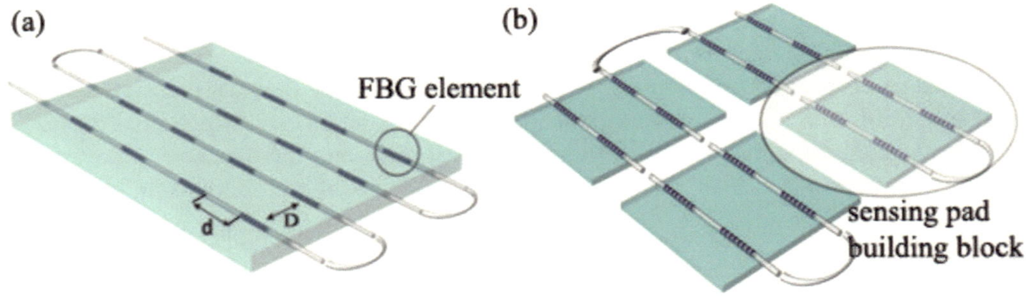


**Figure 2.** a) PDMS 2D sensing surface with FBG-array optical sensing elements b) elementary 2D sensors used as building blocks for large scale surface sensors

## 3. Experimental demonstration

### 3.1. Experimental setup

A fundamental four element (2x2) FBG-based sensing surface of Fig. 2(b) is implemented by intersecting 2 rows of optical fiber patchcords, each bearing an array of 2 FBG acrylate coated sensors. The length of each FBG sensing element is 5mm and their longitudinal spacing d is fixed to 5mm, while optical fibers are spaced D=1cm, leading to a total sensing area of 2x2 $cm^2$. The optical fiber sensors are embedded in the PDMS material with a nominal elasticity of E=650 kPa (Young's Modulus) so as to produce an elastic sheet of 2.5 mm thickness exhibiting a maximum allowable bend radius of 20 mm. When optical fibers are embedded into the elastic PDMS material, the effective material properties of the fiber reinforced composite (i.e. homogenized average properties which can be measured experimentally) can be assumed to be linear anisotropic if deformation is small and both materials are within the linear region. Full characterization of the effective material properties of the heterogeneous composite structure can be addressed using a series of static FEA solutions [49].

For the fabrication of the sensing pad we used acrylic sheets with etched molds and holders for the optical fibers, as shown in Fig. 3a. A CO laser system (laser beam μm) was used to etch 250 μm depth fiber trenches on 2.5-mm-thick acrylic boards. The optical fibers were assembled on the acrylic top board to create the composite optical FBG sensor. Then a PDMS elastomer (RTV 615 silicone elastomer made by Momentive) mixture was prepared by mixing the copolymer with a curing agent (10:1 ratio). The produced PDMS was poured into the mold, and the composite was placed in vacuum for 24 h to remove any air sensors was completely cured. The PDMS-based sensing pad was finally lifted away from the acrylate board after it was cured. The optical part of the experimental setup is depicted in Fig. 3(b). A Superluminescent-LED source was used to power the FBG elements of the sensing pad, while an optical coupler fed the back-reflected light to the Ibsen I-MON 80 D interrogation unit. A NI DAC card installed in a PC was used to read the extracted data.

In order to evaluate the sensor performance, a series of vertical load tests were conducted throughout the total surface of the pad sensor using a gauge test stage. A Material Tester system, the MTS 858 Mini Bionix II, was used to apply vertical force and displacement to the prototype sensor through a force gauge with a pin-head of 1cm$^2$ (fig.5a) and a universal motion controller. The resolution of the applied displacement stage was 1μm with a force gauge resolution of 10 mN.

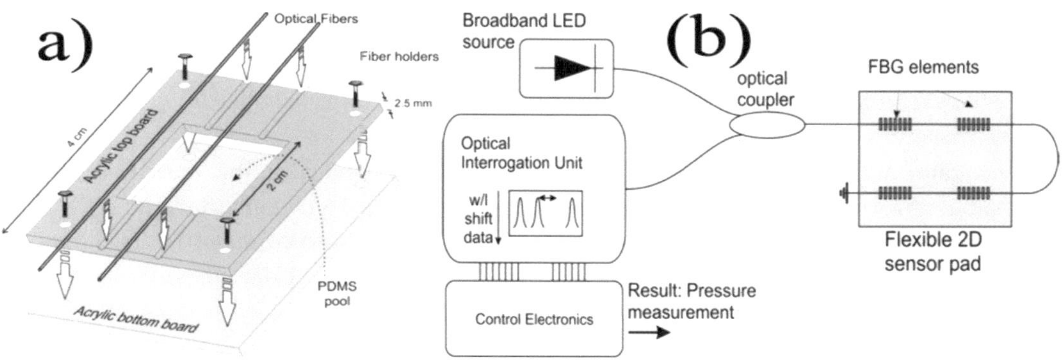


**Figure 3.** a) Schematic description of the fabrication procedure for the 2x2 FBG element sensor b) experimental setup of the optical circuitry

### 3.2. Results

Figure 4(a) shows the power spectrum for all four FBGs before (blue line) and after (red line) a load was applied to FBG 3. In the blue spectrum, each peak represents the corresponding centre (Bragg) wavelength of each FBG element (4 in total) when no forces are applied. The FBG wavelengths are spaced 2nm apart, while the total wavelength range of the 2x2 sensing pad is 8nm as shown in Fig. 4(a). Each Bragg wavelength peak represents a single pressure monitoring point exhibiting a FWHM bandwidth of 0.5 nm with sidelobe suppression greater than 17dB. When vertical force or displacement is applied to a FBG element, its Bragg wavelength is shifted. In our experiment the sensor was placed on a metal table with stable temperature, to isolate the sensor from temperature variations. Temperature independent operation can be also obtained by employing an additional FBG sensor that will be responsible solely for temperature sensing without being affected by pressure. More specifically, as the proposed 2x2 pressure sensor is intended for Human-Machine interface systems in biomedical applications, sensor temperature variations will result to roughly the same wavelength shift to all FBGs. This common wavelength shift can be perceived as an offset to the pressure induced resonance shifting, which in turn can be quantified by means of the additional FBG sensor that should be located outside the pressing area acting as the temperature reference sensor. Once this offset has been quantified, sensing pad temperature calibration can then be obtained by removing this offset from the pressure-induced wavelength shift measurements.

The red spectrum of Fig 4(a) depicts the power spectrum of the four FBG sensor elements when 400μm of vertical displacement corresponding to 5N force was applied to FBG3. As shown, the force applied to FBG3 produced a shift of 0.4 nm to the central wavelength of FBG3 while small variations in the FBG 2 and 4 spectrums are due to the crosstalk between the 2nm spaced FBG channels and their sidelobes overlapping.

The wavelength shift of FBG3 corresponds to 5.188x10-3 $MPa^{-1}$ fractional pressure sensitivity. From the same graph, a power-loss of more than 60% was measured for the central wavelength of FBG3 corresponding to a power loss fractional pressure sensitivity of 12 $MPa^{-1}$. The power-loss method significantly increases the sensor sensitivity due to the autocorrelation function between the FBG filter envelope and the detection filter of the interrogator CCD pixel. However, increased sensitivity comes at the cost of restricted dynamic range, limiting the wavelength shifting tolerance of our method to the FWHM of the FBG power spectrum. A conventional wavelength shift measurement method may be applied for larger pressure values that correspond to increased wavelength shifts.

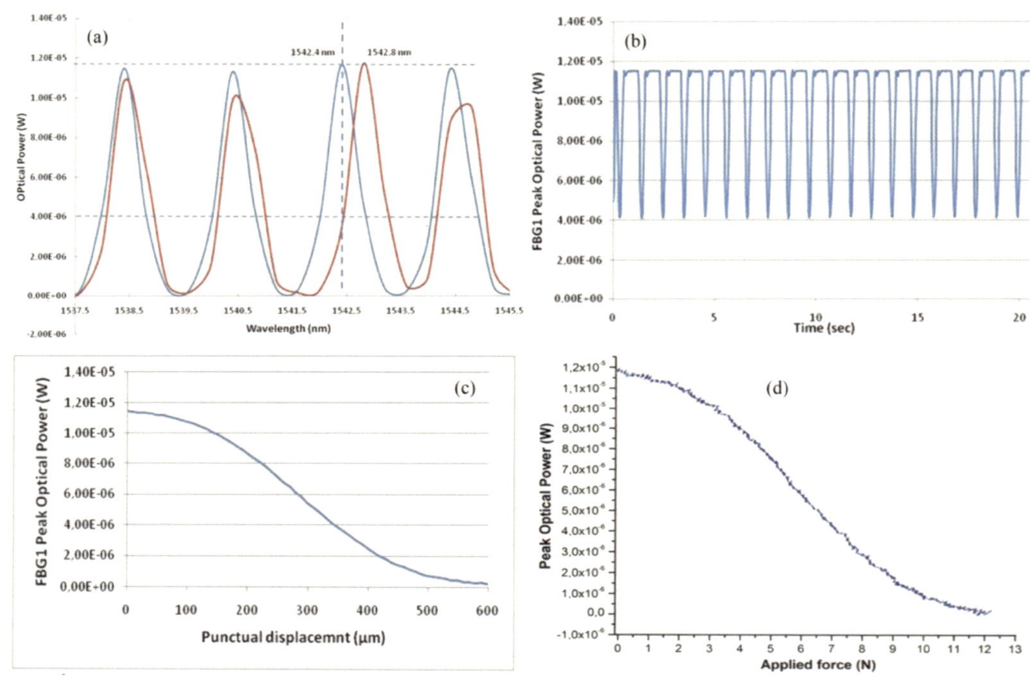


**Figure 4.** (a) Power spectrum for the 4-FBG sensor: blue line: without any axial load, red line: vertical displacement applied to FBG3. A wavelength shift occurs b) Cyclic loading test: Power loss trace for FBG1 for 400μm vibrating displacement applied c) Power loss vs vertical displacement for FBG1 (Ramp measurement) d) Power loss vs force for FBG1

In order to evaluate the measurement repeatability capability of the sensing pad, we conducted vertical load tests for each FBG element using a 1 $cm^2$ –head pin in a cyclic pattern. Specifically, we repeatedly tested the sensor by using a vibrating pin to apply a vertical maximum displacement of 400μm to FBG1 at 10Hz, corresponding to 5N force or 50 KPa of pressure.

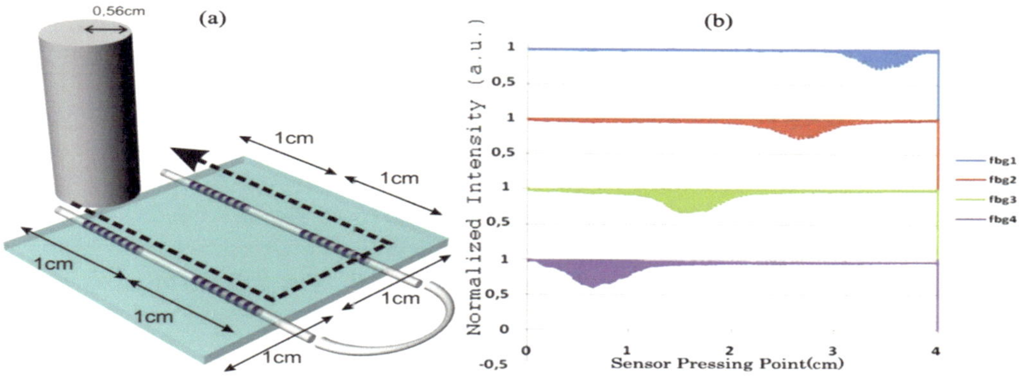


**Figure 5.** a) Schematic of 2x2 sensor and sliding under the pin b) Simultaneous measurement of 4 FBG normalized intensities vs the position of the pin.

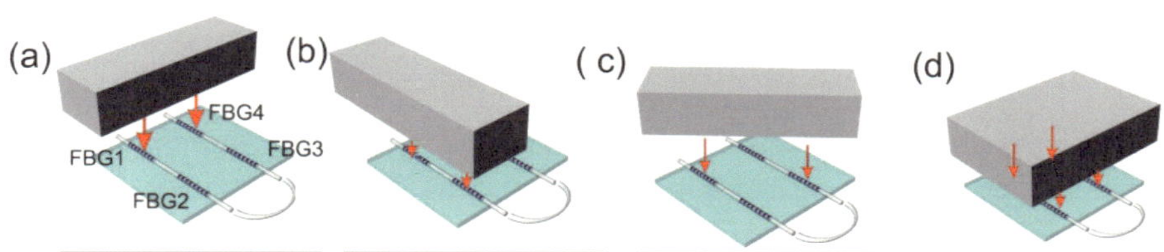


| Panel | FBG1 | FBG4 | FBG2 | FBG3 |
|---|---|---|---|---|
| (a) | 1% | 5% | 95% | 97% |
| (b) | 11% | 99% | 0% | 95% |
| (c) | 19% | 90% | 87,5% | 25% |
| (d) | 0% | 1% | 2,2% | 1,2% |

**Figure 6.** a) Schematic of 2x2 sensor and sliding under the pin b) Simultaneous measurement of 4 FBG normalized intensities vs the position of the pin.

Figure 4(b) shows the optical power measurements versus time for FBG1 Bragg wavelength obtained by means of an optical photodiode. Power loss sensitivity of 60% is confirmed for every duty cycle of the vibrating pin. The graph demonstrates the fast response of the sensing system to the cyclic force pattern applied with negligible hysteresis. A short dumped oscillation of the optical power appears at the end of every wave cycle on the graph. Due to its adhesive and visco-elastic characteristics, the PDMS is locally pulled upwards by the pin beyond the PDMS surface level whenever (i.e. every 1 sec) the pin returns to its starting position. When the PDMS detaches from the pin, it returns to its resting position through a damped oscillation. The oscillation translates into stress oscillation of the corresponding FBG and eventually appears as an optical power oscillation at the end of every cycle of the graph shown in Figure 4(b). Ramp measurements with step increment of vertical displacement were also performed to identify the FBG sensors' dynamic range using the power loss method. Figure 4(c) depicts the Bragg wavelength peak power of FBG1 versus displacement and the corresponding force (Fig. 4(d)). Step increment of displacement was set to 10 μm with overall ramp duration of 1sec. Figures 4(c,d) reveal a dynamic range of 600μm displacement, 10 N of force or 100kPa of pressure and a near-linear sensitivity of 10% power loss per 1N (10 kPa). Similar results were obtained for each of the four FBG elements.

Sensing elements for distributed pressure sensing systems have to operate independently. In particular, 1:1 mapping of each pressure reading to the corresponding point under pressure, will avoid complex mathematical post-processing of the results. To verify the independent operation of each FBG sensing element in our configuration, we slid the 2x2 fiber optic sensing pad in a circular manner under a vibrating pin with 1 cm2-rounded head, as shown in Fig. 5(a). The pin vibrated at a frequency of 10 Hz and a peak-to-peak vertical displacement of 250 μm. We simultaneously measured the peak power of each FBG Bragg wavelength and the result is depicted in Fig. 5(b). The horizontal axis of Fig. 5(b) refers to the relative pressing point in cm as the pin moves over the FBGs, while normalized intensity values are used for the FBG Bragg wavelengths to compensate for the different mean optical powers between the two fiber optic patch-cords. The result clearly shows independent operation of each FBG sensor within the 1cm fiber axial length, while the spatial resolution of the FBG sensing elements is calculated to as low as 1 $cm^2$.

In order to study the fiber-based sensor operation under more realistic conditions, we tested the sensor in multipoint operation using a rectangular metal bar with 1cm edge to press all possible 2-point combinations and a metal plate with a surface larger than the total sensor to press all four sensing points. The metal patterns were set to vibrate at a frequency of 10 Hz and for a peak-to-peak displacement of 600μm, driving the sensing elements to their operational limits. Figure 6 (a),(b),(c),(d) depict some of these cases along with the tables indicating the percentage of optical power received for each FBG wavelength at the moment of maximum displacement. In Fig. 6 (a),(b),(d), small variations in the indicated FBG power losses are due to the slightly different response of each FBG. Fig. 6(c) shows that aside from FBGs 1 and 3, small power losses occur in FBGs 2 and 4 due to unwanted partial overlapping between the 1cm metal bar and the latter FBGs. However, clear identification of the multipoint pattern is still allowed. Finally, it should be noted that while the fiber deformation mechanism for the pin-based experiments relies on fiber bending, in Fig. 6(d) the axial extension of the FBGs is due to the Poisson effect material expansion of the PDMS that exhibits a Poisson ratio nominal value of 0.5.

## 4. Sensor optimization - Comparative studies

### 4.1. Purpose of the case study

With this work we aim to bring optical fiber sensing closer to their deployment in rehabilitation applications, such as medical beds, wheelchairs and amputee sockets. The developed polymer material pressure sensor pads with embedded FBG elements have to confront with true medical requirements as real time data acquisition, high sensing resolution and increased dynamic range but also requiring a number of fabrication, packaging, manufacturing and operational challenges underlined by the large diversity of the patients to be treated (human factor) and the increased variability of patients' real life conditions. Specifically for the medical mattress bed and wheelchair application, sensor pads applied on the human–machine interface surface must withstand excessive instant stresses that occur by the patients spontaneous movements. As such, the rigidity of the sensors employed and their permanent damage threshold should far exceed their operational limits, in order to guarantee their sustainability. In this paper, we identify the basic manufacturing parameters that will enhance sensor pads rigidity and durability to guarantee the sensor pads reliability. These parameters are: optical fiber grating optimum inscription characteristics [50], optical fiber type, depth of fiber embodiment in the polymer material and thickness of the polymer sheet [45]. We have also performed a thorough analysis of these parameters and the results are presented and discussed here. We concluded that optimum sensor pad layout that enhances durability and preserves required sensitivity is fiber embodiment at the polymer center with thickness 3mm [51].

## 4.2. The specimens

The main fabrication parameters that affect the FBG rigidity and durability are the depth of fiber embodiment in the polymer material, the thickness of the polymer sheet and fiber type and grating inscription method.

Hydrogenation of the optical fibre minimizes the inscription time, but also severely limits the strength of the fibre. In this article we perform comparative tests between hydrogenated and non hydrogenated fibers to study their durability behavior. Commercial, standard-NA, Ge-doped enhanced photosensitivity –non-hydrogenated fibres were used. This choice was carried out with respect to the laser sources available and the photosensitivity they induce. Furthermore, suitable choice of the laser wavelength defines the grating inscription time and energy accumulation in the optical fibre body. Between the 248 and 193 nm nanosecond excimer laser ultraviolet sources, it was proved that by using 193 nm laser radiation, strong Bragg reflectors can be straightforwardly inscribed in commercially available standard NA germanosilicate fibres. 193nm excimer laser radiation excites structural and electronic defects lying near the band-gap of the germanosilicate core, rendering the inscription process dependent upon several types of pre-existing defects, while allowing high inscription yield [52][53].

| **Specifications** | **SMF 28e** | **GF1B** |
|---|---|---|
| **Second Mode Cut-off** | ≤1260 nm | 1260 ± 100 nm |
| **Bend loss @ 1550 (100 turns)** | 0.03 dB (50 mm mandrel radius) | 0.09 dB (25 mm mandrel radius) |
| **NA** | 0.14 | 0.13 |
| **Proof Test Level** | ≥ 100 kpsi (0.7 GPa) | ≥ 100 kpsi (0.7 GPa) |
| **Operating Temperature** | - 60 °C to +85°C | - 55 °C to +85°C |
| **Coating Material** | UV Cured, Dual Acrylate | UV Cured, Dual Acrylate |
| **Price** | 0.2 € per metre | 4 € per metre |

**Table 2.** Specification and cost data for the smf 28e and gf1b fibres considered

Commercially available photosensitive optical fibres were reviewed, while considering cost parameters, photosensitivity behaviour, splicing losses, mechanical properties and laboratory handling. In such an investigation these fibres were exposed using a variety of laser wavelengths and exposure conditions for illustrating the optimum Bragg grating recording envelope with respect to mechanical strength and grating spectral characteristics.

After considering the data of Table 2, we concluded that two fibres should be further investigated: SMF-28e (drawn by Corning Inc.) and GF1B (drawn by Nufern) [50]. Specification and cost data for those two fibres appear in Table 2.

For the inscription of the FBGs the phase mask technique was used employing an ArF excimer laser emitting at 193nm. A versatile experimental set up was developed for maintaining high robustness and stability over long exposure periods. A custom made phase mask holder and a tension gauge system allow the straightforward recording of concatenated Bragg gratings of different periods and strengths, over different spatial positions in a single optical fibre. Further equipment is currently embedded into the setup for gaining the capability to perform grating apodization. Table 3 summarizes the specifications of the developed FBG. Both fiber type FBG sensors have been embedded in a series of polymer sheet specimens in order to allow the mechanical behavior studies versus two key manufacturing parameters: thickness of the polymer sheet and fiber embodiment depth.

Specifically, specimens employing polydimethyl-siloxane (PDMS) RTV-615 polymer material were fabricated with their thickness ranging from 2mm to 3mm. The two fiber types FBG sensors are embedded in the middle of the PDMS sheet for each specimen (Fig. 7.b). Measurements of the two fiber types on the same sensor pad configuration will provide a first comparison study for the two types of fabricated FBG. Measurements will be taken using the wavelength shift method around the FBG sensor at positions 1cm away from the sensor and the sensors will be driven to their permanent damage limits.

| **Characteristics** | **SMF28e** | **GF1B** |
|---|---|---|
| **FBG Length** | 2 mm | 2mm |
| **Energy density** | 166 $mJ/cm^2$ | 166 $mJ/cm^2$ |
| **Laser frequency** | 40 Hz | 40 Hz |
| **Inscription time** | 25 min | 2min 40 sec |
| **Accumulated fluence** | 597.6 K $J/cm^2$ | 63.7 K $J/cm^2$ |
| **FBG strength** | 10.23 dB | 10.45 |
| **Side lobe suppression (non optimized set-up)** | 5 dB | 5 dB |

**Table 3.** FBG specifications for both fiber types

The effect of fiber embodiment depth in the PDMS towards the mechanical and operational characteristics of the sensor pads is studied using specimens of Fig. 7.a. The specimens exhibit thickness of 2mm and 3mm while the two fiber sensors where of the same type. The fibers are embedded one in the mid-depth of the PDMS and the second is positioned close to the PDMS surface (400μm). This configuration will allow for characterizing the sensors behavior when sensors are embedded in the top/bottom surface of PDMS.

The sensor pads fabrication procedure employs specially designed metal plates or acrylic boards where the optical fibers are positioned to create the composite optical FBG sensor. PDMS elastomer (RTV 615 silicone elastomer made by Momentive) mixture is prepared by mixing the copolymer with a curing agent (10:1 ratio). The mixture is placed in a vacuum system to remove any air bubbles that have been formed during mixing. The produced PDMS is poured into the mold, and the composite is placed in vacuum for 24 h until the PDMS sheet with the embedded FBG sensors was completely cured. Fig. 7(d) depicts a photograph of the sensor.

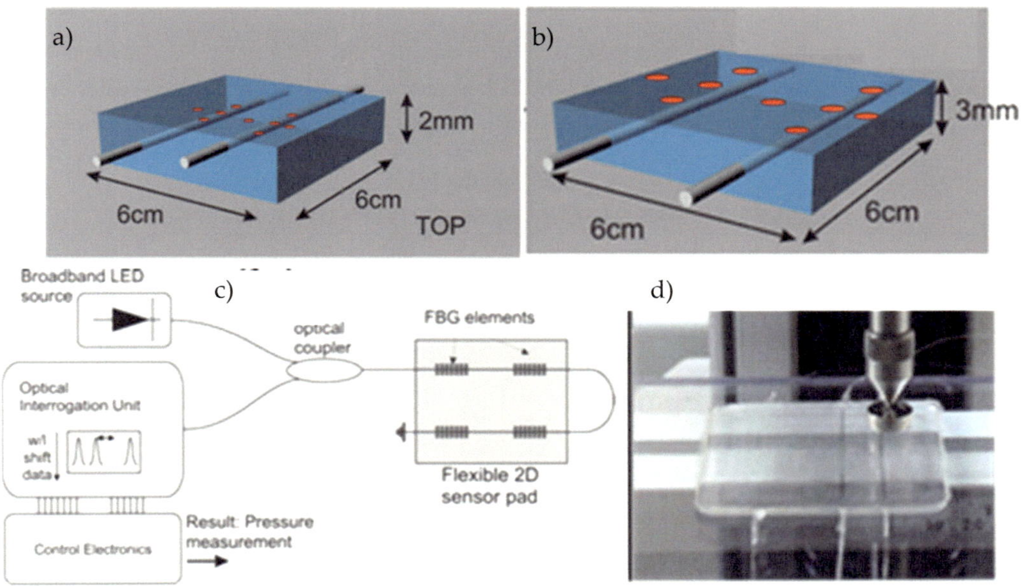


**Figure 7.** a) Fiber embodiment depth study specimens b) thickness study specimens c) optical part of experimental setup d) photo of specimen under test

### 4.3. Experimental setup

The optical part of the experimental setup is similar to the one used in the first experiment in Section 2 as depicted in Fig. 7(c). A Superluminescent-LED source is used to power the FBG elements of the sensing pad, while an optical coupler fed the back-reflected light to the AOS interrogation unit. In order to evaluate the sensor performance, a series of vertical load tests were conducted using a gauge test stage. A Material Tester system, the Mcmesin i5, was used to apply vertical force and displacement to the prototype sensor through a force gauge with a pin-head of 1cm$^2$ (Fig. 7(d)). A conical pin is pressing a 1cm$^2$ round metal plate with rounded edges to guarantee homogeneous pressure distribution.

### 4.4. Comparative studies' results

In this section we present the results for the three different case studies (embodiment depth, thickness and fiber type) with respect to FBG sensors sensitivity and their dynamic range of ultimate damage point.

### 4.4.1. *Fiber embodiment depth study*

Figure 8 presents the results obtained for hydrogenated SMF-28 fiber FBG sensors when embedded in a 2mm thick PDMS sheet in the center and top position of the cross-section. The results reveal a 50% increased sensitivity and a 40% increased durability for the FBG positioned in the center of the PDMS layer.

### 4.4.2. *Thickness study*

Figure 9 presents the results obtained for hydrogenated SMF-28 fiber FBG sensors when embedded in 2mm and 3mm thick PDMS sheets respectively. Again an increased sensitivity of 50% and a marginal increase of durability are evident for the thicker (3mm) sensor pad.

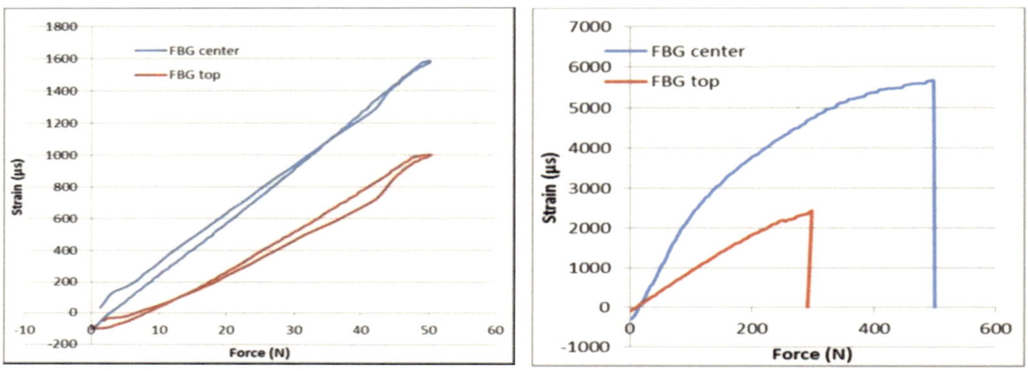


(a) (b)

**Figure 8.** 2mm specimen a) FBG center/top sensitivity graph for b) FBG center/top dynamic range

### 4.4.3. *Fiber type study*

The aforementioned results show that the optimum configuration for thickness/embodiment depth is when FBGs are embedded in the center of a 3mm thick PDMS sheet. Figure 10 presents the results obtained for hydrogenated SMF-28 fiber FBG sensors and non-hydrogenated GF1B fiber FBG respectively for this optimum configuration. We notice a 20% increased sensitivity for the hydrogenated fiber but with a 40% decrease in dynamic range when compared to the non-hydrogenated fiber.

To summarize the case studies, we have identified the basic manufacturing parameters that enhance the sensor pads rigidity and durability to guarantee their reliability in biomedical applications such as medical beds, wheelchairs and amputee sockets. We have performed an analysis of the fabrication parameters and concluded that the optimum sensor pad layout that enhances durability and preserves required sensitivity is fiber embodiment at the polymer center with thickness of 3mm non-hydrogenated fiber.

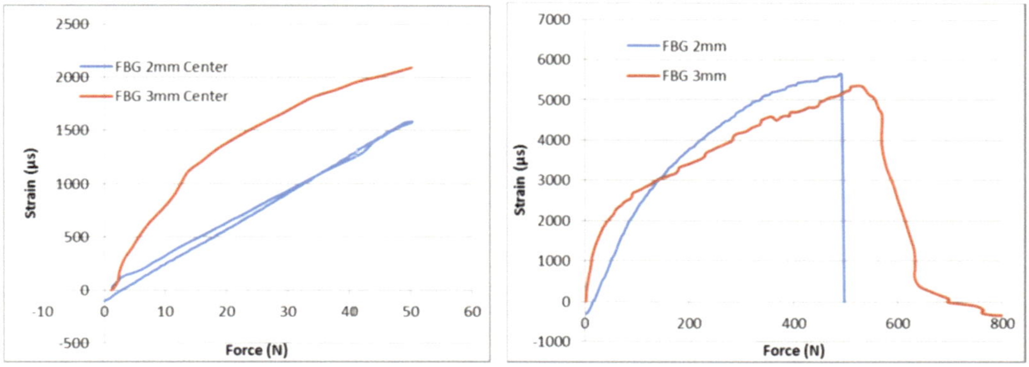


(a) (b)

**Figure 9.** 2mm specimen a) FBG center/top sensitivity graph for b) FBG center/top dynamic range

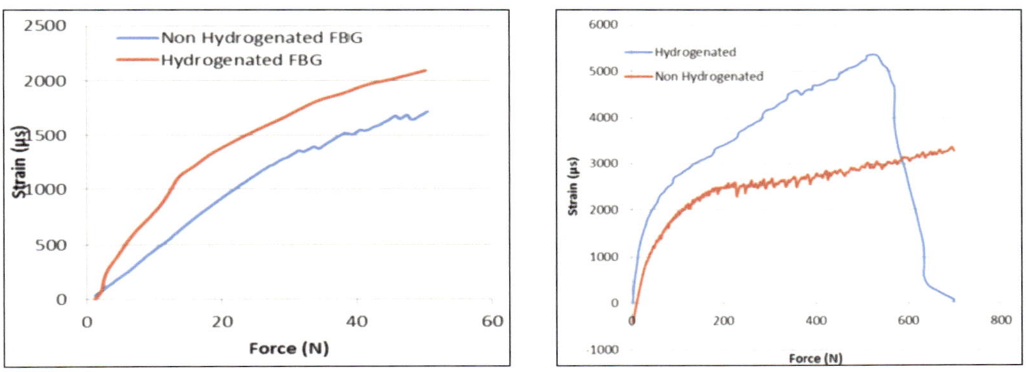


(a) (b)

**Figure 10.** 3mm specimen a) Hydrogenated/non hydrogenated fiber sensitivity graph for b) dynamic range

# 5. Application perspective studies

## 5.1. Pressure monitoring requirements in prosthetics

An assistive device with unresolved sensing challenges is the prosthetic socket. There are well over 32 million amputees in the world, nearly 60% of which being trans-tibial (19.2 million), 75% of which (14.4 million) are complaining of discomfort or significant reduction of autonomy and mobility mainly due to poor socket fit and the resulting development of pressure ulcers (WHO 2010 world report [33]). Project SMARTSocket (SMARTSocket: FP7-PEOPLE- IAPP Grant agreement 251649) deals with the comprehensive understanding and quantification of the differences between two socket interventions (Elevated Vacuum -EV vs Total Surface bearing-TSB-A), leading to some important conclusions:

Given the up to date depth of this investigation (80 patients) several interesting findings were reported: (1) A new socket-stump assessment method revealed for the first time the magnitude of true shear occurring within the socket in dynamic activities (jumping-running, pivoting); (2) max skin deformation did not correlate with max loading rates during strenuous activities; Maximum stump sliding-slippage reached levels of up to 15 cm (aver. 8± 7cm) while max residual bone pistoning reached values of 19 cm (aver. 12± 7cm) [65]-[71]. Stump skin deformations exceeded 20% of resting length and translated to skin stretching of up to 5± 4cm in average depending on the stump area (distal-proximal). Most interestingly strenuous activities revealed stump localized maximal accelerations exceeding 3Gs (39.8 m/s2 for running) suggesting very high previously unrecorded localized force gradients.

In addition, in a series of recent studies [33], [54]-[64] direct pressure was measured with an appropriately instrumented socket that showed interface pressures to approximately 415 kPa and resultant shear stresses to approximately 65kPa [55], [56]. As a reference, peak pressure on the stump during walking typically range from 700 to 870 kPa pressure [58] and peak shear stresses from 24 to 70kPa. Shear management was out of the scope of this study; however shear values were measured for further kinematics and biomechanics analysis.

## 5.2. Pressure monitoring requirements in medical beds and seating systems

Project IASiS (FP 7-SME-Grant Agreement 232479) responded to a pan-European Pressure ulcer survey showing prevalence higher than 25% in bedridden and wheelchair bound patients [33], [2] IASiS addressed pressure ulcer incidence and treatment by developing and demonstrating an Intelligent Adaptable Surface envisaged to be capable of redistributing the pressure applied on the skin in bedridden patients or wheelchair users. This adaptable mechanism comprises of self-shaping actuator-driven elements and is responsible for relieving pressure in a timely manner according to the information received by the sensing modules. The IASiS sensors were designed to detect the magnitude of pressure events, and feed it back to the active controllers of the hospital bed/seat surface. The most important result from the clinical trials in IASiS (benchmarked also against the literature) was some more definite operational boundaries for the sensor. The interface pressures on different types of hospital bed mattresses or specialty beds were: 62-107±15mmHg (8.3-14.3kPa) for the areas of Sacrum when semi-recumbent, backrest at 45%; 6-156±22mmHg (8.1-20.8kPa) at the trochander when side lying, hips and knees at 60 degrees; 107-213±17mmHg (14.3-28.4 KPa) on the heels in supine lying; and 60-146±12mmHg (8-19.5 kPa) in the inchial tuberocities when sitting on 10cm standard cushion.

## 5.3. Sensors per application

Table 4 represents the full sensor specifications tree. Specifically the table summarizes the outcomes of research projects and studies regarding the targeted characteristics of a pressure sensor in order to comply with the requirements of three rehabilitation interventions. It becomes apparent that the most demanding application both in terms of dynamic range as well as flexibility and sampling rate is the prosthetic socket. That is due to its deployment by the patient in every day activities including highly strenuous actions. In the contrary the medical bed is more demanding in sensitivity and that is due to the micro loading dynamics developed in the long run at the skin-mattress interface of a bed-ridden patient.

| Functionality, Type of activity to be detected | **Limited motion, low speed-low load, large duration events** | **Moderate relative motion, speed, moderate loading and medium duration events** | **High relative motion, high speed, impact type loading, small duration events** |
|---|---|---|---|
| **Clinical Application** | **Specialty Hospital Bed Acute Rehab** | **Wheelchair Seats** | **Amputee Sockets (Highly Strenuous Activities)** |
| Full Scale output Pressure (kPa) | Pressure: 0-40kPa | Pressure: 0-300kPa | Pressure: 0-1MPa |
| Accuracy | Pressure: <10 Pa | Pressure: <1 kPa | Pressure: <1 KPa |
| Unit sensor size | $2cm^2$ | $1cm^2$ | $1cm^2$ |
| Thickness | <4mm | <5mm | <5mm |
| Flexibility (Bending radius) | 4cm | 2cm | 2cm |
| Sensitivity | Pressure: 5 Pa | Pressure: 10 Pa | Pressure: 10 Pa |
| Sampling rate | >15Hz | >50Hz | >400Hz |
| Hysteresis | Negligible | Negligible | Negligible |

**Table 4.** The sensor specification tree per application and functionality versus characteristics and operational ranges.

## 6. Conclusion

The embodiment of FBG inscripted optical fibers in polymer 2D surfaces allows for functional and durable pressure sensor configurations meeting specific requirements claimed by specific rehabilitation interventions at the human machine interface. We have developed an optical fiber based 2D pressure sensor exhibiting a high sensitivity of 10% optical power loss per 10kPa pressure and a high spatial resolution of $1cm^2$. The sensing elements have a real-time response and demonstrated no hysteresis as the cyclic measurements demonstrated, while their operation is independent, yielding a 1:1 correlation of each FBG sensor indication to the respective sensing point without the need of data post-processing and allowing for easy pressure pattern identification in multi-point operation. The presented 2x2 $cm^2$ sensing surface is easily expandable and can be used as a building block for larger scale sensors depending on the application. The mechanical properties of the presented sensor pad allow for embedding or attaching the sensor to irregular shapes and geometries, offering enhanced response to curvature while the low physical dimension commercially available interrogation unit enhances the portability features of the complete sensing system. The sensor's minimal thickness, make it very unobtrusive, with minimal interference on the measurement interface. These attractive physical and operational characteristics are ideally suited for biomedical applications in biomechanics, rehabilitation and orthotics such as amputee sockets and wheelchair/hospital bed -system sensors. In addition, we have identified the basic manufacturing parameters that enhance the sensor pads rigidity and durability to guarantee their reliability in the abovementioned biomedical applications Comparative studies showed that the optimum sensor pad layout that enhances durability and preserves required sensitivity is fibre embodiment at the polymer centre with thickness of 3mm non-hydrogenated fibre. Finally we have identified and categorized the specifications of the developed sensing surface that will meet the requirements imposed by the specific applications.

## Author details

Dimitris Tsiokos and George T. Kanellos
*Informatics and Telematics Institute, Center for Research and Technology Hellas, Thessaloniki, Greece*

George Papaioannou
*S.S.F. Safe Smart Fabric Adaptable Surface Ltd, Nicosia, Cyprus*

Stavros Pissadakis
*Institute of Electronic Structure and Laser, Foundation for Research and Technology Hellas, Heraklion, Greece*

## Acknowledgement

The work presented here was partially supported by EU-FP7-SME-2008-1, No 232479,– IASiS and SMARTSocket: FP7-PEOPLE- IAPP Grant agreement 251649.

## 7. References

[1] American Pressure Ulcer Advisory Panel (1998). Pressure ulcer Prevalence, cost and risk assessment: consensus development conference statement. Decubitus 2:24-8

[2] Pezzin, L.E., Dillingham, T.R., Mackenzie, E.J., Ephraim, P. and Rossbach, P., (2004). "Use and satisfaction with prosthetic limb devices and related services". Arch Phys Med Rehabil, May, 85(5),pp. 723-9.

[3] Petrovic, S.J., Dobb, H., Mezentsev, K.V., Kalli, K.M., IEEE, , Webb, J.D.M., IEEE, and Bennion, I.M., (2007). "Sensitivity of LPGs in PCFs Fabricated by an Electric Arc to Temperature, Strain, and External Refractive Index". Journal of lightwave technology, 25(5).

[4] Murphy, P.R., James, W.S. and Tatam, P.R., (2007). "Multiplexing of Fiber-Optic Long-Period Grating-Based Interferometric Sensors". Journal of lightwave technology, March, 25(3).

[5] Mignani, G.A. and Baldini, F., (1997). "Fibre-optic sensors in health care". Phys. Med. Biol. , 42,pp. 967-979.

[6] Mignani, G.A. and Baldini, F., (1996). "Biomedical sensors using optical fibres". Rep. Prog. Phys, 59,pp. 1-28.

[7] Huang, C.Y., Wang, W.C., Wu, W.J. and Ledoux, R.W., (2007). "Composite Optical Bend Loss Sensor for Pressure and Shear Measurement". IEEE SENSORS JOURNAL, 7(11).

[8] Kim, S.H. and Lee, J.J., (2003). "Phase-Shifted Transmission/Reflection-Type Hybrid Extrinsic Fabry–Pérot Interferometric Optical Fiber Sensors". Journal of lightwave technology, March, 21(3),pp. 797.

[9] Geernaert, T., Luyckx, G., Voet, E., Nasilowski, T., Chah, K., Becker, M., Bartelt, H., Urbanczyk, W., Wojcik, J., De Waele, W., Degrieck, J., Terryn, H., Berghmans, F. and Thienpont, H., (2009). "Transversal Load Sensing With Fiber Bragg Gratings in Microstructured Optical Fibers". IEEE Photonics Technology Letters, 1 January, 21,pp. 6-8.

[10] Kanellos, T.G., Mitrogiannis, C., Nianios, G., Pleros, N. and Papaioannou , G., (2009). "High spatial resolution FBG-array based strain sensor". Proceedings of the International Commission for Optics (ICO) Topical Meeting on "Emerging Trends and Novel Materials in Photonics", Delphi, Greece, October 7-9.

[11] Gusarov, A., Chojetzki, C., Mckenzie, I., Thienpont, H. and Berghmans, F., (2008). "Effect of the fiber coating on the radiation sensitivity of type IFBGs". IEEE Photonics Technol. Lett, 20,pp. 1802-1804.

[12] Pressure sensors: selection and applications by DUANE TANDESKE. (Edt).MARCEL DEKKER Inc., New York(1990) ISBN 0-8247-83-65-4.

[13] Sensors in Biomedical Applications Fundamentals technology and applications: Gabor HarsaNyi CRC press (2000) ISBN 1-566760885-3.

[14] Handbook of Modern Sensors 3rd Edition. Jacob Fraden (Edt): Springer (2003) ISBN-10: 0-387-00750-4

[15] Sensors and actuators in mechatronics Andrzej M. Pawlak. CRC- Taylor and Francis( 2007) ISBN-10: 0-8493-9013-3

[16] Cork, R. (2007): XSENSOR technology: a pressure imaging overview. Sensor Review, vol. 27 pp. 24-28.

[17] Van Drongelen, S., Van der Woude, L. H., Janssen, T. W., Angenot, E. L., Chadwick, E. K. and Veeger, D. H. (2005): Mechanical load on the upper extremity during wheelchair activities. Arch Phys Med Rehabil, vol. 86(6), Jun, pp. 1214-1220.

[18] Appoldt, F.A., Bennett, L. and Contini, R., (1969). "Socket pressure as a function of pressure transducer protrusion". Bulletin of Prosthetics Research, Spring,pp. 236-249.

[19] Sanders, J.E. and Daly, C.H., (1993). "Measurement of stresses in the three orthogonal directions at the residual limb-prosthetic socket interface". IEEE Trans Rehabil Eng 1(2),pp. 79-85.

[20] Convery, P. and Buis, A.W., (1998). "Conventional patellar-tendon-bearing (PTB) socket/stump interface dynamic pressure distributions recorded during the prosthetic stance phase of gait of a trans-tibial amputee". Prosthet Orthot Int, Dec, 22(3),pp. 193-8.

[21] Convery, P. and Buis, A.W., (1999). "Socket/stump interface dynamic pressure distribution recorded during the prosthetic stance phase of gait of a trans-tibial amputee wearing a hydrocast socket". Prosthet Orthot Int, Aug, 23(2),pp. 107-112.

[22] Engsberg, J.R., Springer, M.J.N. and Harder, J.A., (1992). "Quantifying interface pressure in below-knee-amputee socket". Journal Association of Children's Prosthetic-Orthotic Clinics 27(3),pp. 81-88.

[23] Houston, V.L., Mason, C.P., LaBlanc, K.P., Beatties, A.C., Garbarini, M.A. and Lorenze, E.J., (1994). "Preliminary results with the DVA-Tekscan BK prosthetic socket/residual limb stress measurement system". Proceedings of the Proceedings of 20th Annual Meeting American Academy of Orthotist and Prosthetist, Nashville, TN,pp. 8-9.

[24] Sanders, J.E., Daly, C.H. and Burgess, E.M., (1993). "Clinical measurement of normal and shear stresses on a trans-tibial stump: characteristics of wave-form shapes during walking". Prosthet Orthot Int, Apr, 17(1),pp. 38-48.

[25] Zhang, M., Turner-Smith, A.R., Tanner, A. and Roberts, V.C., (1996). "Frictional action at residual limb/prosthetic socket interface". Med Eng Phys, 18(3),pp. 207-214.

[26] Polliack, A.A., Landsberger, S., McNeil, D.R., Sieh, R.C., Craig, D.D. and Ayyappa, E., (1999). "Socket measurement systems perform under pressure". Jounal of Biomechanics, June,pp. 71-80.

[27] Polliack, A.A., Sieh, R.C., Craig, D.D., Landsberger, S., McNeil, D.R. and Ayyappa, E., (2000). "Scientific validation of two commercial pressure sensor systems for prosthetic socket fit". Prosthet Orthot Int, Apr, 24(1),pp. 63-73.

[28] Brimacombe, J.M., Anglin, C., Hodgson, A.J. and Wilson, D.R., (2005). "Validation of Calibration Techniques for TEKSCAN Pressure Sensors." Proceedings of the XXth ISB Congress - 29th ASB Annual Meeting, Cleveland, Ohio, July 31st-August 5th.

[29] Cork, R., (2007). "XSENSOR technology: a pressure imaging overview". Sensor Review, 27(1),pp. 24-28.

[30] Hadcock, L., Stevenson, J., Morin, E., Bryant, T., Reed, S., Abdoli, M. and Tasker, T., (2007). "Pressure Measurement Applications for Humans". Queen's University, Fergenbaum Mitchell School of Rehabilitation Queen's University, Kingston, Ontario.

[31] Papaioannou, G., Protopappas, V.C., Glaros, C., Morres, I. and Tsopelas, P., (2005). "Tekscan pressure sensor equilibration and conditioning". Proceedings of the 3rd European Medical & Biological Engineering Conference, Prague, Czech republic, November 20-25, 2005.

[32] Pramanik, C., Saha, H. and Gangopadhyay, U., (2006). "Design optimization of a high performance silicon MEMS piezoresistive pressure sensor for biomedical applications,". Journal of Micromechanics and Microengineering, 16,pp. 2060-2066.

[33] Bader D. Et., al. (2010) Pressure ulcer Research. Current and Future Perspectives. (eds) Springer Verlag Berlin ISBN-13 978-3-642-06404-3.

[34] 22Papaioannou, G., Protopappas, C.V., Tsopelas, P., Mitrogiannis, C., Nianios, G. and Tashman, S., (2008), "A new Method for pressure sensor Equilibration and conditioning" Br. Journal of Biomotricity, 2(3), pp. 176-195.

[35] J. W. Arkwright, N. G. Blenman, I. D. Underhill, and S. A. Maunder, M. M. Szczesniak, P. G. Dinning, and I. J. Cook, "In-vivo demonstration of a high resolution optical fiber manometry catheter for diagnosis of gastrointestinal motility disorders", Opt. Express, Vol. 17, No. 6, 16 March 2009, pp. 4500-4506

[36] Chu-Yu Huang, Wei-Chih Wang, Member, IEEE, Wen-Jong Wu, and William R. Ledoux "Composite Optical Bend Loss Sensor for Pressure and Shear Measurement", IEEE Sensors Journal, VOL. 7, NO. 11, pp. 1554-1565, 2007

[37] Francis Berghmans, "Photonic skins for optical sensing: highlights of the PHOSPHOS project", in Optical Fiber Sensor Congference - OFS-20, Technical Digest (CD) (Optical Society of America, 2009), paper OF101 08.

[38] H. M. Xie, Ph. Dabkiewicz, R. Ulrich, and K. Okamoto. Side-hole fiber for fiber-optic pressure sensing. Opt. Lett., 11:333–335, 1986.

[39] C. Jewart, K. P. Chen, B. McMillen, M. M. Bails, S. P. Levitan, J. Canning, and I. V. Avdeev. Sensitivity enhancement of fiber bragg gratings to transverse stress by using microstructural fibers. Optics letters, 31(15):2260–2262, 2006.

[40] T. Martynkien, M. Szpulak, and W. Urbanczyk. Modeling and measurement of temperature sensitivity in birefringent photonic crystal holey fibers. Appl. Opt., 44:7780–7788, 2005.

[41] W. J. Bock and W. Urbanczyk. Measurements of sensitivity of birefringent holey fiber to temperature, elongation, and hydrostatic pressure. In Proc. of the 21st IEEE-Instrumentation and Measurement Technology Conference, volume 2, pages 1228–1232, Como, Italy, 2004.

[42] D. Kim and J. U. Kang. Sagnac loop interferometer based on polarization maintaining photonic crystal fiber with reduced temperature sensitivity. Opt. Express, 12:4490–4495, 2004.

[43] CH. L. Zhao, X. Yang, Ch. Lu, W. Jin, and M.S. Demokan. Temperatureinsensitive interferometer using a highly birefringent photonic crystal fiber loop mirror. IEEE Photon. Tech. Lett., 16:2535–2537, 2004.

[44] T. Martynkien, G. Statkiewicz, M. Szpulak, J. Olszewski, G. Golojuch,W. Urbanczyk, J.Wojcik, P. Mergo, M. Makara, T. Nasilowski, F. Berghmans, and H. Thienpont. Measurements of polarimetric sensitivity to temperature in birefringent holey fibers. Meas. Sci. Technol., 18:3055–3060, 2007.

[45] G. T. Kanellos, G. Papaioannou, D. Tsiokos, C. Mitrogiannis, G. Nianios, and N. Pleros, "Two dimensional polymer-embedded quasi-distributed FBG pressure sensor for biomedical applications," Opt. Express 18, pp. 179-186, 2010.

[46] C. Yan, E. Ferraris, T. Geernaert, F. Berghmans, D. Reynaerts, Development of flexible pressure sensing polymer foils based on embedded fibre Bragg grating sensors, Procedia Engineering, Volume 5, Eurosensor XXIV Conference, Eurosensor XXIV Conference, pp. 272-275, 2010.

[47] http://www.ibsen.dk/products/im/I-MON-80D-Interrogation-monitor

[48] G. T. Kanellos, G. Papaioannou, D. Tsiokos, C. Mitrogiannis, G. Nianios, and N. Pleros, "Two dimensional polymer-embedded quasi-distributed FBG pressure sensor for biomedical applications," Opt Express 18, 179-186 (2010).

[49] C. Jewart, K. Chen, B. McMillen, M. Bails, S. Levitan, J. Canning and I. Avdeev, "Sensitivity enhancement of fiber Bragg gratings to transverse stress by using microstructural fibers," Optics Letters, V. 31, No. 15, pp. 2260-2262 (2006).

[50] S. Pissadakis and M. Konstantaki, "Photosensitivity of germanosilicate fibers using 213nm, picosecond Nd : YAG radiation," Opt Express 13, 2605-2610 (2005).

[51] Kanellos, G.T.; Tsiokos, D.; Pleros, N.; G. Papaioannou, Childs, P.; Pissadakis, S.; "Enhanced durability FBG-based sensor pads for biomedical applications as human-machine interface surfaces", BioPhotonics, 2011 International Workshop on, 8-10 June 2011, page(s): 1 – 3, Parma, Italy.

[52] Albert, B. Malo, K. O. Hill, F. Bilodeau, D. C. Johnson, and S. Theriault, "Comparison of One-Photon and 2-Photon Effects in the Photosensitivity of Germanium-Doped Silica Optical Fibers Exposed to Intense Arf Excimer-Laser Pulses," Appl Phys Lett 67, 3529-3531 (1995).

[53] J. Albert, K. O. Hill, D. C. Johnson, F. Bilodeau, S. J. Mihailov, N. F. Borrelli, and J. Amin, "Bragg gratings in defect-free germanium-doped optical fibers," Opt Lett 24, 1266-1268 (1999).

[54] Sonk WA, et.al., (1970) Effect of liner materials on interface pressure in below knee prosthesis. Arch Phys Med Rehabil 51:666-669.

[55] Pollick AA, et.al., (2002) Laboratory and clinical tests of a proptotype pressure sensor for clinical ssessment of prosthetic socket fit (prost Ortht Int 26:23-34.
[56] Sanders JE., (1995) Interface mechanics in external prosthetics: review of interface stress measurement techniques. Med Biol. Eng Vomput 33:509-516.
[57] Lowe LB., et.al., Suction-socket pressure in lower extremity prosthesis. J Niomech. 1:247-257.
[58] Armstrong DG. Et. al. (1998) Is there a critical level of plantar foot pressure to identify patients at risk for neuropathic foot ulceration? J Foot Ankle Surg 37:303-307.
[59] Hosein R., et.al., (2000) A study of in-shoe plantar shear in normals. Clin. Biomech 15:46-53.
[60] Appoldt FA., et.al., (1998) stump-socket pressure in lower extremity prosthesis. J biomech 1:247-257.
[61] Sanders JE. et. al., (1998)Effects of alignment changes on stance phase pressures and shear stresses on trans-tibial amputees: measurements from 13 transducer sites IEEE trans Rehab Eng 6:21-31.
[62] Naylor PDF (1955) Experimental friction blisters BR J Dermat 67:327-342.
[63] Pearson JR., et.al., (1973) Pressures in critical regions of the below knee patellar tendon bearing prosthesis. Bull Prosth Res 10-19:52-76.
[64] Burgess EM, et.al., (1977) /a study of interface pressures in the below knee prosthesis (physiological suspension: and interim report). Bull Prosthe res 10-28:58-70.
[65] Papaioannou, G.,Tsiokos D., Fiedler G., Kanelos G.T., Mitrogiannis, C., Avdeev I., Wood J. and McKinney R. (2010). "Dynamic radiography imaging as a tool in the design and validation of a novel intelligent amputee socket", J.M.R.S. Tavares and R.M.N. Jorge (eds.), Computational Vision and Medical Image Processing: Recent Trends, Computational Methods in Applied Sciences 19, DOI 10.1007/978-94-007-0011-6 5,_c Springer Science+Business Media B.V. 2011.
[66] Papaioannou, G., Mitrogiannis, C., Nianios, G. and Fiedler, G., (2010). "Assessment of amputee socket-stump-residual bone kinematics of strenuous activities using Dynamic Roentgen Stereogrammetric Analysis". Journal of Biomechanics; 43(2010) 871-878.
[67] Papaioannou, G., Nianios, G., Mitrogiannis, C. and Fiedler, G., (2010). "Assessment of internal and external prosthesis kinematics during strenuous activities using Dynamic Roentgen Stereophotogrammetric Analysis". Journal of Prosthetics and Orthotics, 22:1-15.
[68] Papaioannou, G., Fiedler, G., Mitrogiannis, and C. Nianios, G., (2010). "In-vivo velocity and acceleration characteristics of trans-tibial amputee socket-stump interaction during strenuous activities", Journal of Rehabilitation Research, ACCEPTED March 2010.
[69] Papaioannou, G., Fiedler, G., Mitrogiannis, C., Nianios, G., (2010). "Amputee skin deformation maps using Dynamic Roentgen Stereogrammetric imaging". Computational Vision and Medical Image Processing, ISBN: 978-0-415-57041-1. CRC Press: pp. 236-247.
[70] George Papaioannou, Christos Mitrogiannis, George Nianios and Goeran Fiedler. "Assessment of Vacuum-assisted trans-tibial amputee socket dynamics" (2010), International Journal for Computational Vision and Biomechanics, 8(3), pp.271-284.
[71] Papaioannou, G., Mitrogiannis, C., Nianios, G. and Fiedler, G., (2009). "Tracking high speed arthrokinematics using a new and high resolution Biplane Dynamic Roentgen Stereogrammetric method". International Journal of Imaging, 2:(A09) pp. 66-85.

Chapter 12

# Quantum Dots in Biomedical Research

Adriana Fontes, Rafael Bezerra de Lira,
Maria Aparecida Barreto Lopes Seabra, Thiago Gomes da Silva,
Antônio Gomes de Castro Neto and Beate Saegesser Santos

Additional information is available at the end of the chapter

http://dx.doi.org/10.5772/50214

## 1. Introduction

Quantum dots (QDs) are colloidal semiconductor nanocrystals which have unique optical properties due to their three dimensional quantum confinement regime. The quantum confinement may be explained as follows: in a semiconductor bulk material the valence and conduction band are separated by a band gap (Eg). After light absorption, an electron ($e^-$) can be excited from the valence band to the conduction band, leaving a hole ($h^+$) in the valence band. When the electron returns to the valence band, fluorescence is emitted. During the small time scale of the light absorption the $e^-$ and $h^+$ perceive one another and do not move so independently due to Coulomb attraction (Brus, 1984). The $e^-$- $h^+$ pair may be observed as an Hydrogen-like species called exciton and the distance between them is called the exciton Bohr radius ($a_B$). When the three dimensions of the semiconductor material are reduced to few nanometers and the particles become smaller than the Bohr radius, one can say that they are in quantum confinement regimen and in this situation these nanoparticles are named quantum dots (QDs). For example, the exciton Bohr radius of CdS and CdSe bulk materials presents a size of $a_B$ = 3 to 5 nm.

In this way, QDs can be defined as colloidal particles made of semiconductor materials with diameters ranging typically from 2 to 10 nm. The semiconductor particle (named "core") is usually coated by a layer of another semiconductor material (named "shell") which in general has a greater band gap than the band gap of the core rendering excellent optical properties. The QDs' core is responsible for the fundamental optical properties (i.e. light absorption and emission) and the shell is used to passivate the surface of the core with the goal to improve its optical properties and reduce chemical attack. The shell separates physically the optically active core from its surrounding medium (Dabbousi *et al.*, 1997; Santos *et al.*, 2008a) as depicted in Figure 1. As a consequence, the nanoparticles' optical properties become less sensitivity to changes induced, for example, by the presence of oxygen or pH in the local environment. At the same time, the shell reduces the number of surface dangling bonds, which can act as trap states for electrons and minimize the QDs fluorescence efficiency.

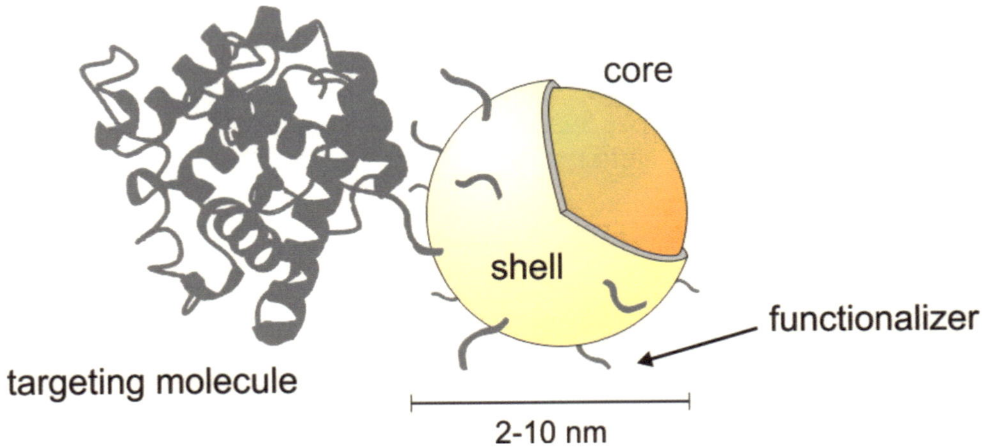


**Figure 1.** A schematic representation of a functionalized core-shell quantum dot bound to a biomolecule.

For biomedical purposes, in which fluorescence in the visible region is usually required, both core and shell are composed of elements from the II B and VI A groups of the Periodic Table. The major examples are CdSe/ZnS, CdTe/CdS and ZnSe/ZnS QDs (Dabbousi *et al.*, 1997; Santos *et al.*, 2008a). Most QDs crystallize either in the cubic zinc blend or in the hexagonal wurtzite type structure (Yeh *et al.*, 1992).

In nanosized regime many QDs' physico-chemical properties are different from those of the same bulk materials. Since QDs are fluorescent nanoparticles, an example of these changes is the shift of the emission color according to the particle size. In this case, QDs made from the same material, but with different sizes, can present fluorescence light emission in different spectral regions (from the ultraviolet to the infrared light) as represented in Figure 2. This is a consequence of QDs energy level discretization and also of the QDs band gap energy changes according to their size. After absorption, electrons come back to valence band and QDs emission is proportional to the band gap energy. As smaller the QDs are, the higher is the band gap energy and more towards to the blue end is the emission (since the energy is inversely proportional to the wavelength of the light).

Another observed feature for these systems is that the QDs' absorption bands are broad and extend up to the UV region, as observed in Figure 3 (A). The first peak (located at greater wavelength) represents an exciton formed by transitions between discrete states. The width of the first absorption band is related to the size dispersion of the nanoparticles and can give us information about the QDs' average size and nanoparticles concentration (Santos *et al.*, 2008a). On the other hand, the width of the emission spectrum is related to the presence of crystal defects which result in discreet electronic states between the conduction and the valence band. These new electronic states displace the emission towards to the red and broaden the emission band and is related to the passivation shell.

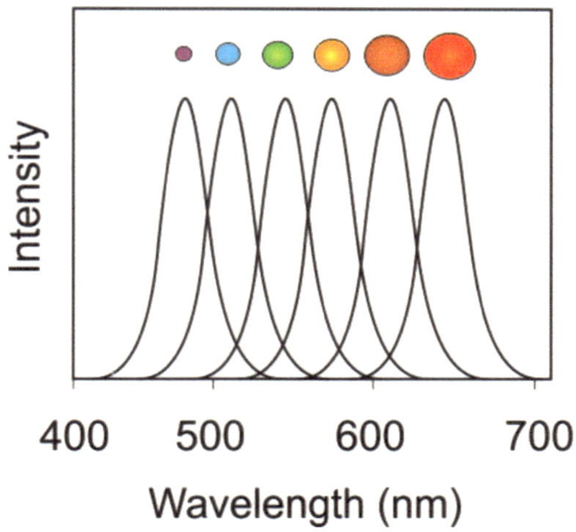


**Figure 2.** Emission spectra as a function of size for the same quantum dot material. The colored spheres represent the size decrease of the particles.

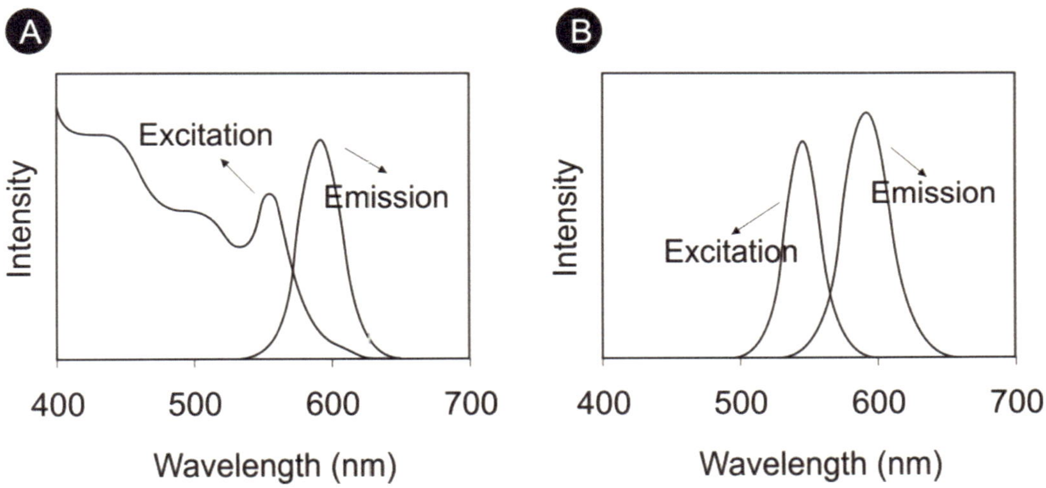


**Figure 3.** Characteristic absorption and emission band profile of (A) QDs colloidal suspension (A) and (B) a typical organic fluorophore (B).

The QDs' physico-chemical properties have offered considerable advantages and complementary characteristics over the conventional fluorescent dyes. Besides the size tunable emission discussed before, compared to organic fluorophores, the major advantages offered by QDs are:

1. A broad absorption band (Fig. 3A), allowing a flexible cross section for multiphoton microscopy and as well as for Fluorescence Energy Transfer (FRET) processes (Fig. 3A and B compare the characteristic absorption and emission band profiles of QDs and organic fluorophores).
2. An active surface for chemical conjugation. QDs can be conjugated to a variety of proteins or antibodies and become inorganic-biological hybrids nanoparticles that

combine characteristics of both materials, that is, the fluorescence properties of QDs with the biochemical functions of the attached biomolecules (Fig. 1).

3. High resistance to photobleaching: the most important advantage of QDs over organic dyes allowing long term observation of these fluorescent nano-probes.

Colloidal QDs can be synthesized in organic or aqueous medium. When compared to organometallic routes, water-based QDs syntheses are cheaper, less toxic and intrinsically biocompatible to applications in biomedical fields (Santos *et al.*, 2008a). The colloidal synthesis generally involves several consecutive stages: (i) nucleation from an initially homogeneous solution, (ii) growth of the preformed crystal nuclei into isolated particles, reaching the desired size from the reaction mixture and (iii) post preparative treatments, such as colloidal purification, size precipitation and UV light exposure.

During the colloidal synthesis QDs end up coated by organic or inorganic molecules (called surfactants or stabilizers), which keep the nanocrystals away from each other preventing agglomeration and precipitation (Brus, 1984; Santos *et al.*, 2008a) (Figure 1). In some cases, as for CdTe QDs for example, the surfactant molecules may also act as precursors of the passivation shell (Menezes *et al.*, 2005). For the direct aqueous synthetic procedures the main classes of organic molecules used as surfactants are alkyl-thiol molecules such as mercaptopropionic acid - MPA, mercaptoacetic acid - MAA and mercaptosuccinic acid – MSA, Dihydrolipoic acid – DHLA, cysteine – CYS, cysteamine – CYSAM and different mercaptodithiols. The carboxyl, thiol or amine terminals of these molecules can be used as chemical bridges to conjugate biomolecules (such as proteins and biopolymers) which confer more specificity for biological applications. The chemical binding of such biomolecules to the surface of the QDs is a process defined as bioconjugation. It can be accomplished by simple adsorption (of stabilizing agent such as: MPA, MSA or cysteine) to the biomolecule or by covalent attachment. Currently, bioconjugation occurs between carboxyl-amine (through EDC and Sulfo-NHS) groups, amine-amine (by glutaraldehyde), disulfide bonds and streptavidin-biotin interactions (Goldman *et al.*, 2002).

For the non-aqueous synthetic routes, nucleation and growth of QDs occur in the solution phase in the presence of organic surfactant molecules, which dynamically adhere to the surface of growing crystals. Typical surfactants include long-chain carboxylic and phosphonic acids (e.g., oleic acid and *n*-octadecylphosphonic acid), alkanethiols (e.g., dodecanethiol), alkyl phosphines, alkylphosphine oxides (classical examples are trioctylphosphine, TOP, and trioctylphosphine oxide, TOPO), and alkylamines such as hexadecylamine (Yin & Alivisatos, 2005). In order to be applied to biological systems as active fluorophores these nanocrystals must be extracted from the organic phase to an aqueous phase. An alternative method of dispersing non-aqueous QDs is to form a hydrophilic coating that carries along with it a layer of hydration consisting of hydrogen-bonded water molecules. This often is accomplished by using hydroxyl bearing polymers or Polyethylene glycol (PEG) modifications. These also prevent aggregation due to the high energy needed to remove the bound water layer.

# 2. Applications of quantum dots in biomedical sciences

Since the first mention in the literature, in 1998, QDs have been studied extensively and the applications of these fluorescent nanocrystals range from imaging fixed and live cells all the way to fluoroimmunoassays rendering innovative diagnostic methodologies (Bruchez Jr. *et al.*, 1998; Chan & Nie, 1998). QDs have been used in many different studies, such as a probe in DNA hybridization, in receptor mediated endocytosis, monitoring of parasite metabolism and visualization of tissue and cellular structures in real time. Due to their photostability and low cytotoxicity the QDs are starting to be used as fluorophores for *in vivo* applications, but there is still a great discussion about their safe use. When injected in the initial stage of embryonic development of *Xenopus embrios*, for instance, the QDs demonstrated to be stable, non-toxic and resistant to photobleaching (Dubertret *et al.*, 2002). This experiment also showed its potential in monitoring the development and cellular differentiation processes that occur during embryogenesis. The use of QDs as fluorophores is important for the real time diagnosis of tumors. Preliminary experiments with QDs emitting in the near infrared conducted in animals have shown promising results in the sensitive detection of cancerous tumors and *in vivo* systems (Cai *et al.*, 2006; Gao *et al.*, 2010). The prospects of the applications of QDs, especially those free of heavy metals such as zinc based QDs, make them even more promising for its current use in the near future. Moreover, cells labeled with QDs can be injected in small animals and the fluorescence can be used to follow a particular pathway in the organism, such as the carcinogenesis process, helping to understand the process and discover new kinds of treatments (Noh *et al.*, 2008).

## 2.1. Quantum dots as fluorophores for imaging and detection purposes

### *2.1.1. Non-specific labeling*

The staining of a biological sample can occur even when the reporting probe is not designed to interact with a specific molecule. Untargeted labeling of the probe with the (biological) material is defined as a *non-specific interaction*, and can be usually mediated by hydrophobic and/or electrostatic interactions between the surface molecules of the particles with molecules in suspension or on the anchoring surface such as cellular plasma membrane or even by internalization process (Biju *et al.*, 2010).

In the past years, when the use of QDs in biomedical research was still at the beginning, passive labeling (simple staining of biological samples) was of great interest since researchers aimed to study the probe itself as a potential dye. In such applications, labeling could give information about bioavailability and more importantly about the optical properties of these nanoparticles in biological conditions. It has been shown that the simple incubation with a biological specimen may have the potential to stain it, revealing its structural features or even their biological behavior. We observed this feature for instance in the non-targeted glutaraldehyde-capped $CdS/Cd(OH)_2$ QDs staining of different neural cell lines, normal and cancerous cells (Santos *et al.*, 2008b) as demonstrated in the staining pattern observed in Figure 4 (A – D). For these systems the unrestricted labeling/internalization allows the identification of minor details of the cellular architecture, such as cell-cell contacts, axons and intracellular organelles, as shown on the images of Fig. 4A and Fig. 4B. Moreover, these QDs are taken up at different rates depending on cellular stage as for normal glial or glioblastoma cells (Farias *et al.*, 2006) – Figures 4C and 4D, respectively. Therefore, passive labeling can be a useful strategy when one aims to label the whole biological sample or to study differences in the behavior of normal *versus* cancer cells in diagnostic purposes.

### 2.1.2. *Internalization of quantum dots by live cells*

In general, the binding of non-targeted particles with living cells results in internalization of the particles. This process may be accomplished by different routes, which depend either on the particle properties (size, shape, surface functionalization, surface charge and the combination of these properties) or on the cell type (i.e. lineage, metabolic state, cell cycle stage, normal or cancerous cells). The first assumption was that the main internalization process resulted from endocytosis. One of the first reports to show that internalization of these nanoparticles occurs by endocytosis was described by Jaiswal *et al.* (Jaiswal *et al.*, 2003), where human cancer (HeLa) cells and *Dictyostelium discoideum* amoeba cells internalize negatively-charged DHLA-capped QDs, a process inhibited by low temperature treatment and co-localized with endosome markers.

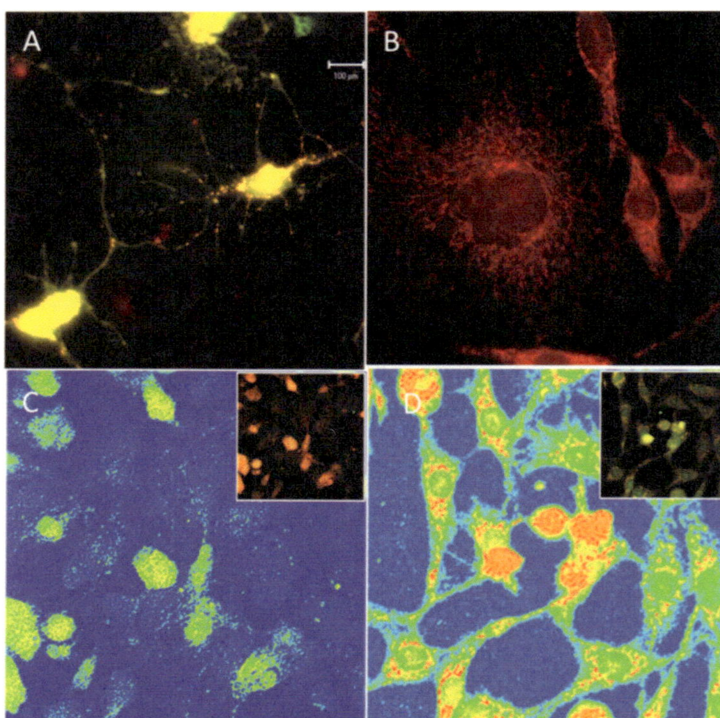


**Figure 4.** Non-targeted glutaraldehyde-capped CdS/Cd$(OH)_2$ labeling of live neuron live cells (A) and live glioblastoma cells (B). It is possible to observe the cell body and axons in living neurons and intravesicular structures in glioblastomas. Intensity map images of glial (C) and glioblastomas (D) incubated for three minutes with these QDs. Insets are the corresponding fluorescence images. (Santos *et al.*, 2008a).

Molecule specific endocytosis is known as receptor-mediated endocytosis which are clathrin or caveolae-mediated endocytosis, or clathrin/caveolae independent endocytosis. It is probably the major pathway where QDs are uptaken by cells. It seems that lipid rafts localized within the plasma membrane plays an important role in the QDs uptake as well. These rafts provide a support for the assembly of many receptors, adaptors as well as proteins involved in a signaling complex such as caveolae and clathrin. (Nichols, 2003a; Nichols 2003b)

In 2011, Maysinger and collaborators synthesized QDs with almost the same hydrodynamic size (between 8-10 nm) and functionalized with different short ligands such as cysteine, cysteamine, dihydrolipoic acid and mercaptopropionic acid (Al-Hajaj *et al*, 2011). These QDs were tested in human embryonic kidney cells (Hek 293) and human heptocellular carcinoma cells (Hep G2) in order to achieve information about these QDs uptake and elimination. They showed that most of the QDs with the same size but different surface properties were uptaken through lipid raft-mediated endocytosis with the contribution of the XAG transport system (responsible for the carrier-mediated Na(+)-independent transport of anionic amino acids such as glutamate and aspartate across the plasma membrane of cells) which takes up cysteine, glutamate and aspartate. The contribution of a P-glycoprotein transporter on QD efflux was also demonstrated during the experiments. Figure 5 shows the hypotheses about QDs internalization and elimination.

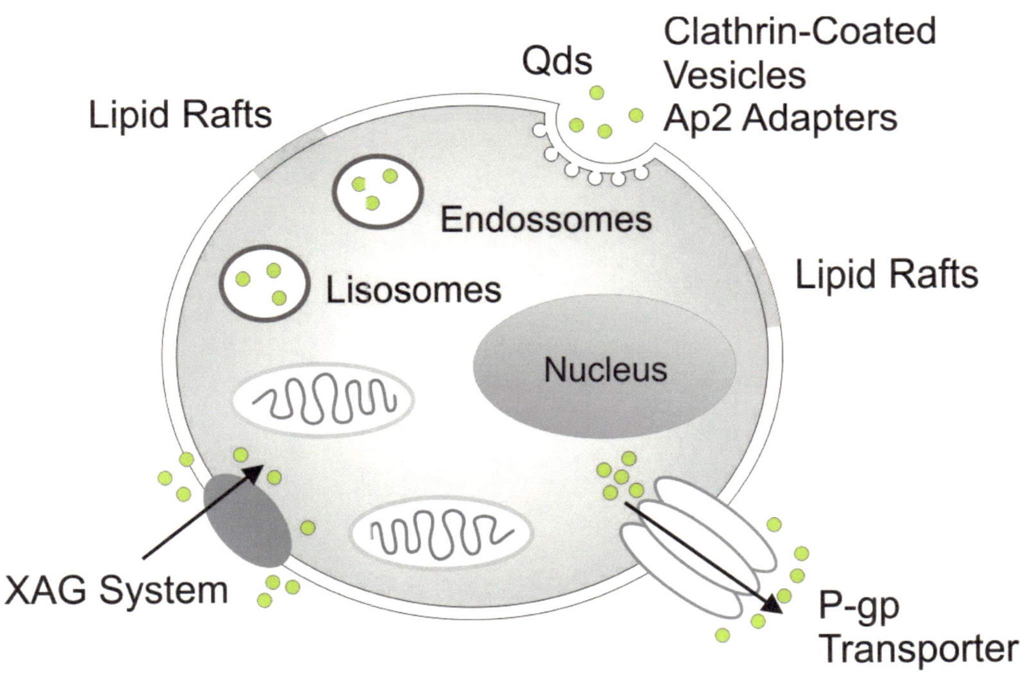


**Figure 5.** Representation of all the cell signaling mechanisms Studied by using QDs (Al-Hajaj *et al*, 2011).

These results corroborated with those obtained from Chan's (Jiang *et al.*, 2008), where they showed the size dependent internalization of particles using both pathways clathrin- and caveolae- mediated endocytosis. It has been shown that particles with a diameter of d = 40 -

50 nm are endocytosed more efficiently than those larger or smaller (Jiang *et al.*, 2008). Sizes also dictates the final location of the particles (i.e. cytosol, nucleus), being able or not to cross their natural cellular barriers (Williams *et al.*, 2009), which is on the other hand cell-type dependent (Williams *et al.*, 2009).

However, QDs internalization by cells not only depends on their size. Although size is an important parameter, charge is thought as one of the most important parameter controlling cell-QD interactions (Conroy *et al.*, 2008). An interesting finding of charge-mediated internalization and interactions with intracellular structures was found by Conroy et. al. (Conroy *et al.*, 2008), who demonstrated that these carboxyl-coated (negative) QDs but not amine-coated (positive) are able to enter macrophage-like cells and bound nuclear structures rich in the positive histone proteins. In fact, such interactions were sufficiently strong to change QDs' optical and colloidal properties even in cell-free conditions (Conroy *et al.*, 2008).

Lira *et al* have recently shown that even in the same cell population, carboxyl-coated QDs have differential access to intracellular compartments and when they reach the nucleus, they actually bind nuclear/nucleolar structures, as shown in Figure 6 for permeabilized human-derived peripheral blood cells (Lira *et al.*, 2012). Figure 6 shows that the intracellular localization of these carboxyl-QDs for same cell population may differ from cell to cell. Depending on the cell, QDs could or not reach the nucleus (square 1 and 2, respectively). As will be discussed, the surface charge plays a critical role on such interactions. Although the internalization efficiency is significantly higher for positively-charged materials due to the

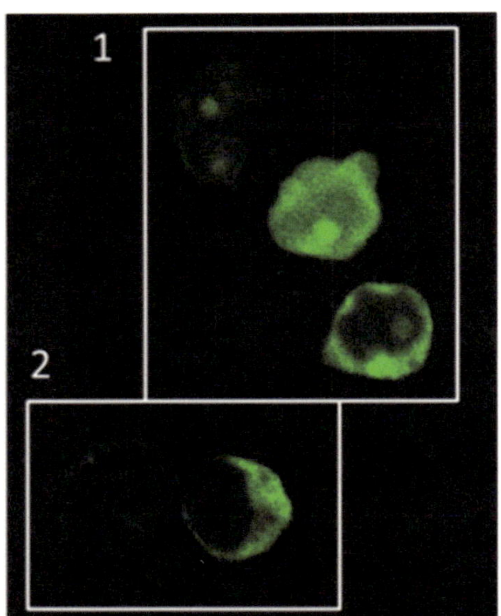


**Figure 6.** Non-specific labeling of fixed peripheral blood mononuclear cells. The image shows an optical field where CdTe/CdS QDs can reach only the cytoplasm (square 2) or can cross the nuclear membrane and reach the nucleus (square 1). In the nucleus, these nanoparticles bind with high affinity nuclear structures such as nucleoli (Lira *et al.*, 2012).

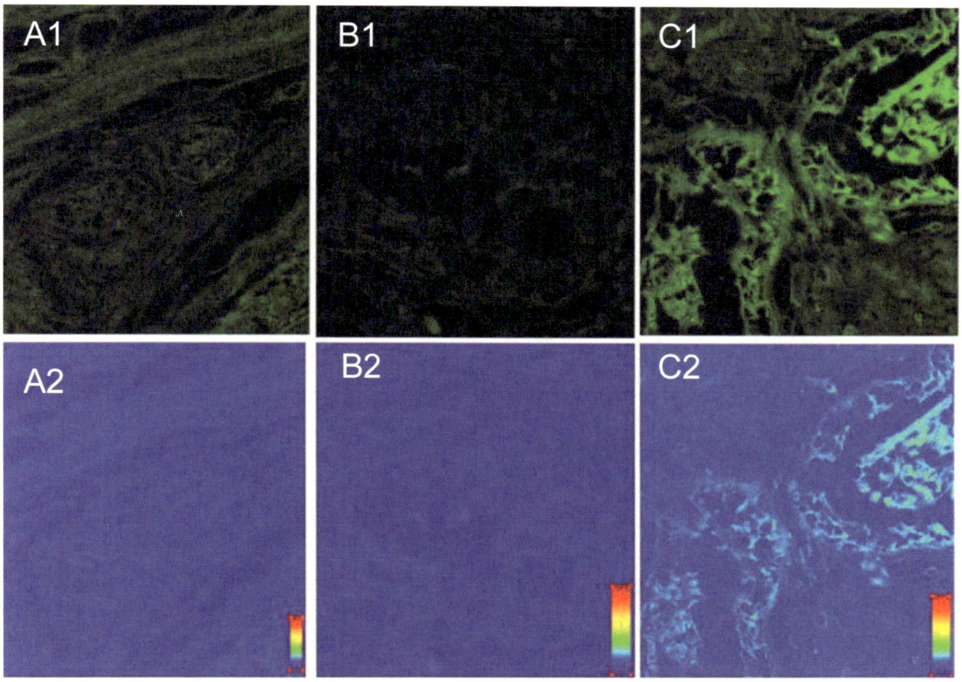


**Figure 7.** Human mammary tissue diagnosed as Fibroadenoma (Fib). (A1) Fib treated with Evan's Blue solution (EB); (B1) Fib incubated with QDs diluted in EB (QD-FIB-EB); (C1) Fib incubated with QD-Con-A conjugate diluted in EB (QD-Con-A-FIB-EB). A2, B2 and C2 are the intensity maps of A1, B1 and C1, respectively. The bright pattern observed in (1c) is related to regions of high glucose/mannose expression in the tissue (Santos *et al.*, 2006).

interactions with the negative cell surface, it is believed that cationic sites on the negatively charged cell surface can mediate the interaction of negative nanomaterials (Ghinea *et al.*, 2009) eventually leading to internalization by cells.

### *2.1.3. Some examples of specific labeling*

The capacity of QDs for specific labeling cells and tissues depends on the bioconjugation. Santos *et al.*, for example, reported the use of $CdS/Cd(OH)_2$ QDs functionalized with glutaraldehyde and conjugated to concanavalin-A (Con-A) lectin (Santos *et al.*, 2006) to investigate cell alterations regarding carbohydrate profile in human mammary tissues diagnosed as fibroadenoma (benigne tumor). Con-A lectin is a protein which binds specifically to glucose/mannose residues expressed in the plasma membrane. Figure 7 shows the QD-Con-A more expressive staining of mammary tissue diagnosed with Fibroadenoma

Con-A was used also in another work for cellular labeling of *Candida albicans* with CdTe/CdS QDs conjugated or not to Con-A (Kato *et al.*, 2012). Fluorescence microscopy analysis of the yeast cells showed that the non-functionalized QDs do not label *C. albicans* cells, however for the QD conjugated to Con-A the cells showed a fluorescence profile indicating that the cell wall was preferentially marked.

In another work of the same group it was also used $CdS/Cd(OH)_2$ QDs functionalized with glutaraldehyde as efficient fluorescent labels for living human red blood cells (Santos *et al.*, 2008a), the aim of this investigation was to determine the antigen-A expression in subgroups of group A erythrocytes.

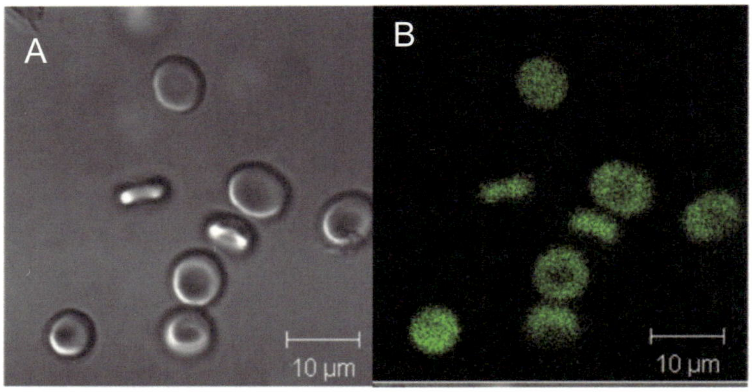


**Figure 8.** Microscopic confocal images obtained for QDs/anti-A marking living A+ erythrocytes. A is the DIC observation of the marked red blood cells and (B) is the marking pattern when excited at 488 nm (Santos *et al.*, 2008a).

### *2.1.4. Quantum dots for intracellular delivery*

QDs can be used as a probe for monitoring protein dynamics in live cells, allowing the study of their traffic down to a single molecule (Pinaud *et al.*, 2010), taking advantages of the most striking properties as a fluorescent probe, which is long term imaging for prolonged periods of time (Courty *et al.*, 2006). However, traffic of molecular dynamics, especially in live cells, are almost exclusively carried out for surface molecules – membrane proteins, accessible by the external side of the cells. This limitation arise mainly due to the incapacity of water dispersed QDs to cross the lipid bilayers by simple diffusion (only few works report tracking of intracellular molecules) (Chen & Gerion, 2004).

a. Physical methods

The physical methods to deliver aqueous compounds into cells are of special interest since the precise control over the cell (extent of delivery over the population) and the amount of materials can be reached in most cases. These are mainly based on microinjection and electroporation. In fact these two traditional and well recognized methods are among the most efficient methods to deliver QDs into cells. The electroporation is based on the application of one or more strong electrical pulses, which is thought to create localized pores in the membrane bilayer for enhancing its permeability – Figure 9A. Using electroporation, Chen and Gerion delivered QDs into HeLa cells (Chen & Gerion, 2004). The QDs were able to be recognized by the cellular machinery and enter the cell nucleus in living cells, although in a fraction of the total number of cells and as agglomerated particles. In fact, nanoparticle aggregates of up to 500 nm have been reported to be produced later after the application of electric pulses, even for protein-conjugated QDs. However, if agglomeration does not matter, as in the case of simple cell labeling, electroporation can be well suited. In fact, cells filled with QDs after electroporation can be readily seen in living mice for cell tracking purposes (Yoo *et al.*, 2010).

Figure 9 shows schematic representations of the most common strategies for intracellular delivery of membrane-impermeable materials. Figure 9A and B represent physical processes while Fig. 9C and D are chemical methods. In electroporation, cells are exposed to an electric field and a single or multiple pulses are applied, creating pores that allow the passage of materials to the cell interior. In the microinjection (Figure 9B), a micropipette delivers precise amounts of fluids inside any compartment of the cells. In Fig. 9C, the conjugation of QDs with Cell Penetrating Peptides (CPPs) (discussed later) can deliver them into cells by direct membrane entrance (as shown in the scheme of Figure 9C) or by endocytosis. Also by endocytosis, polycation-coated QDs (green spheres) trigger "proton-sponge effect", (discussed later) releasing endo/lysosomal content into the cytosol. In Figure 9D, binding of negative cargos to lipoplex systems results in endocystosis likely due to charge interactions with negative plasma membrane. After internalization, charge neutralization seems to release the cargo from the lipid system.

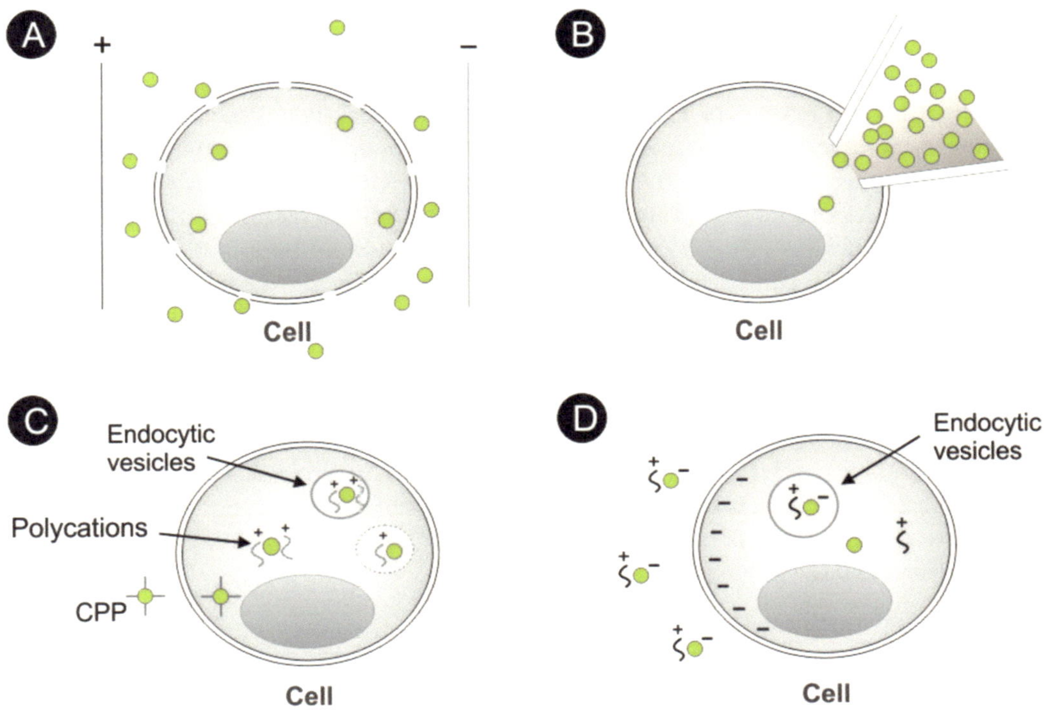


**Figure 9.** Schematic representations of four types of processes used in the internalization of QDs: electroporation (A); microinjection (B); CPP and polycation-mediated internalization (C) and lipoplex mediated process (D).

Another physical method for intracellular delivery of membrane impermeable materials is microinjection. This technique is based on the insertion of precise volumes inside an aqueous compartment (such a cell) by micropipettes – Figure 9B. Since the first attempts of using QDs as fluorescent probes, microinjection is recognized as a potent method to insert these particles in intracellular media. One example of the application of microinjection it is the use of micelle-capped QDs as an agent to follow the development of tissues derived from a single cell in living *Xenopus embrios* after transfection (Dubertret *et al.*, 2002) or dynamics changes during the vasculature development in Zebrafish (Rieger *et al.*, 2005).

Although their recognized efficiency, both methods suffer from some drawbacks. Electroporation not only cause QDs to aggregate, but may seriously compromise cellular viability. On the other hand, microinjection is technically and costly demanding, requiring specialized equipment and, as a serial technique it has poor statistical significance.

b. Chemical methods

Chemical approaches represent a wealthy range of strategies for intracellular delivery of membrane impermeable materials, and include covering cargos' surface or couple/bind them to a vehicle, promoting the labels enter into cytoplasm of a large number of cells simultaneously in a straightforward way. Moreover, it can actually be used in living animals - the methods described above can only be used in such applications in very specific conditions.

Many methods to allow QDs to reach the cell cytosol are based on the conjugation of surface of nanoparticles to interact or to be recognized by cells until they reach the cytoplasm by different means. One of the most effective chemical methods for nanoparticle delivery into cells is the conjugation with Cell Penetrating Peptides (CPPs). A number of publications report such a class of molecules for this purpose, in which the mechanism of cell entry is similar to endocytosis (Thorén *et al.*, 2004) rather than direct bypass through the lipid bilayer, although the consensus for the real pathway is still controversial. If trafficked into cells by endocytosis, these QDs bioconjugates need to be released from endo/lysosomal compartments to reach their targets (if such target is some intracellular organelles, for example).

A wide range of molecules can be conjugated to QDs' surface to be specifically delivered to cells (toxins, sugars, polymers and so on); however most of them lead to receptor-mediated endocytosis, which predominantly result in entrapment into endocytic vesicles. For this reason, we will not address here intracellular delivery of QDs by molecules which do not explicitly release these particles freely in cytosol.

Other chemical modifications can result in intracellular release after nanoparticle endocytosis rather than simple membrane permeation – as proposed for CPPs. One of such approaches is to cover QDs' surface with osmotic active polymers such as polyethyleneimine. After endocytosis, such polycations are capable of sequestering protons by $H^+$-pumps in the endo/lysosomal membrane, which in turn force the entrance of $Cl^-$ ions and water to balance osmotic effects (this is the reason why this approach is called the "proton-sponge effect"). As a consequence, it leads vesicle rupture and releases endocytosed materials into the cell cytosol. Using this approach, Yezhelyev *et al.* delivered siRNA conjugated-QDs to breast cancer cells (Yezhelyev *et al.*, 2008). The functionality of the system was showed by a remarked reduction in cyclophilin B protein expression after gene silencing. One similar approach is the osmotic lysis, where endo/lysosomal vesicles are also ruptured, now by submitting cells to hypotonic solutions. In fact, it was the method used to track for the first time an intracellular protein in living cells using QDs (Courty *et al.*, 2006) where kinesin from *Drosophila* were delivered and tracked in HeLa cells. Lately, Nelson *et al.* reported a detailed study on the movement of Myosin Va (a molecular motor which tracks over actin filaments) inside COS-7 cells (Nelson *et al.*, 2009). However, lysosome lysis might be harmful to cells as some acidic proteins such as proteases are released in the cytosol, which may degrade the constituents in there.

c. Quantum dots encapsulation

Quantum Dots can be entrapped in a vehicle for its delivery instead of being conjugated to transporter molecules, a strategy that can be also suited for intracellular delivery after endocytic uptake. It is quite advantageous because it allows the conjugation of targeting moieties (i.e. antibodies, ligands) on the surface of the nanoparticles, which was otherwise occupied by the targeting transporter molecules (as in the case of CPPs peptides and polymers). Moreover, it can avoid the rupture of acidic intracellular vesicles, which has the tendency to cause cytotoxicity effects. The encapsulating vehicles can be classified in two major groups, named polymeric and lipid delivering systems. QDs were encapsulated in functionalized polymeric poly(lactic-co-glycolic acid) (PLGA) nanospheres and delivered into the cell cytosol after endocytosis of the complex (Kim *et al.*, 2008). After preferential endocytosis of antibody-coated polymer nanospheres into ErbB2 over expressing cancer cells, the polymer were degraded in the acidic intracellular compartments releasing the bioconjugated QDs, which in turn could reach and label intracellular structures such as mitochondria and actin filaments.

Another approach is using micelles. An advantage of encapsulating QDs in lipid micelles relies on the small size of the resulting probe, up to 25 nm (Carion *et al.*, 2007). Taking advantages on the physical-chemical and photostability of these QD-containing micelles, the group who reported this system for the first time could track cell lineage developments in live *Xenopus embrios* (Dubertret *et al.*, 2002). This breakthrough report was one of the first reports on the use of QDs for in vivo imaging.

Among the vehicles composed of lipids, probably the most popular is liposomes (Valenzuela, 2007; Al-Jamal & Kostarelos, 2007). Liposomes are lipid vesicles containing one (or more) lipid bilayer(s) enclosuring an aqueous compartment and that can entrap hydrophilic and/or hydrophobic materials during its formation (Valenzuela, 2007). As in the case of micelles (or any other encapsulation system), their interaction with biological species depends on the physical-chemical properties, which can be fine-tuned. In fact, Yang *et al.* (Yang *et al.*, 2009) encapsulated water aqueous CdTe QDs in folate-conjugated liposomes and showed that these vesicles can be directed to folate-overexpressing cancer cells and be monitored by QDs fluorescence. The resulting system is resistant to optical and chemical degradation, with lower toxic effects.

QDs can also be delivered to cells by commercial cationic liposomes, the lipofection system (Fig. 9D). Lipoplex are positively-charged lipidic vesicles (mainly liposomes) able to bind negative particles, including oligonucleotides and QDs, which mediate charge interactions with cells, leading to endocytosis of the resulting system and eventually the release of cargos inside the cell. In such an application, Yoo *et al.* (Yoo *et al.*, 2008) reported for the first time the use of these lipid vesicles as QD vehicles for protein tracking inside living cells. In contrast to earlier works, their bioconjugated QDs could escape from cellular vesicles and reach the cytosol, where they could be used to track the movements of actin, kinesin and tubulin proteins. Although the mechanism of endossomal release of materials delivered by cationic liposomes is not known, it is believed that charges play important roles in membrane destabilization, which could explain the successfully applications of such liposomes. However cytosolic release is not the main fate of delivered moieties in most applications of cationic liposomes, as exemplified above. It is important to note that lipofection delivery is not based on encapsulation; it is rather based on electrostatic interactions with negatively-charged cargos.

## 2.2. Quantum dots as probes in other bioassays

An increasing interest in using QDs as more than passive/active labels is reflected by the great number of published data in the literature in the past decade. There is a growing research community that recognizes that the fluorescent QDs may be extensively applied as a central component of nano-probes (Algar & Krull, 2008). We may classify among all the suggested applications the following: Fluorescence Resonance Energy Transfer (FRET) for bioassays, optical biosensors and Photodynamic Therapy (PDT).

In all these applications, the QDs act as scaffolds for the assembly of biomolecular probes while its fluorescence is modulated by biorecognition events. In the particular case of FRET-QDs studies, a broad absorption band combined with a size-tunable fluorescence and larger physical size (when compared to conventional dyes) allow: (i) optimization of the spectral overlap with any potential FRET acceptor; (ii) excitation at a wavelength far from the acceptor absorption peak (minimizing acceptor direct excitation); QDs can be excited over a range of wavelengths in the blue-ultraviolet region of the spectrum to allow minimization of the direct excitation of acceptors and (iii) the ability to assemble multiple acceptors around a QD core to increase the overall FRET efficiency (Algar & Krull, 2008; Bakalova *et al.*, 2004; Juzenasa *et al.*, 2008; Medintz & Mattoussi, 2009; Tekdas *et al.*, 2012). The use of fluorescence resonance energy transfer (FRET) as a mechanism of tuning QDs' fluorescence is particularly advantageous and due to their high photostability QDs are ideal donors (Algar & Krull, 2008; Bakalova *et al.*, 2004; Medintz & Mattoussi, 2009). Moreover, the potentially high quantum yield of QDs helps to maximize Förster distances, while the narrow emission can be tuned to optimize spectral overlap and reduce crosstalk between donor and acceptor (Algar & Krull, 2008; Medintz & Mattoussi, 2009).

The great potential of FRET-QDs applications may be exemplified by several reports. For instance, Stringer *et al.* developed a biosensor that is able to detect troponin I to diagnose early injuries of cardiac muscles (Stringer *et al.*, 2008) and also to detect small amounts of nitrated ceruloplasmin (a significant biomarker for cardiovascular disease, lung cancer, and stress response to smoking) (Pyo & Yoo, 2012). Another interesting application is described by Krull *et al.* which performed solid-phase hybridization assays aiming multiplexed nucleic acid diagnostics using QDs as donors in FRET processes (Algar & Krull, 2008; Medintz & Mattoussi, 2009). They developed multiplexed assays using immobilized QDs as both FRET donors and scaffolds for the immobilization of oligonucleotides probes, where the association of fluorescent acceptor dyes with sequence-specific hybridization events provided the basis for transduction. QD donors were paired with one or more acceptor dyes, and the ratios of QD fluorescence and FRET-sensitized acceptor fluorescence provided an analytical signal. The basic idea is depicted in Figure 10.

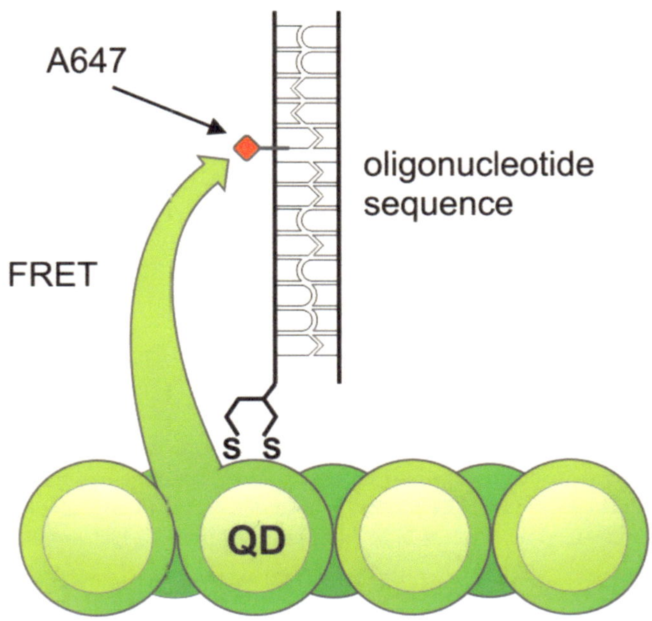


**Figure 10.** Schematic representation of a FRET process. Immobilized QDs are derivatized with dithiol-terminated probe oligonucleotides and under light excitation the QDs are envolved in the emission of the Alexa Fluor 647 dye bound to a determined oligonucleotides sequence (Algar & Krull, 2008; Medintz & Mattoussi, 2009).

QDs may also play a critical role as energy acceptors in bioluminescence resonance energy transfer (BRET) processes, with a bioluminescent protein as the energy donor. BRET resembles FRET in many aspects except that it does not require external light source for the donor excitation. The broad excitation spectra and large Stokes shift of QDs allow them to be excited by nearly all the bioluminescent proteins in BRET assemblies. Feasibility of QDs as the BRET acceptor for a mutant of Renilla luciferase (Luc8 with improved chemical stability and light efficiency) has been recently realized both *in vitro* and *in vivo* (Samia *et al.*, 2006).

More recently QDs have also been applied in photodynamic therapy (PDT) related processes (Juzenasa *et al.*, 2008). This could be done due to the combination of the unique optical properties of these nanostructured systems with their active chemical surfaces. PDT

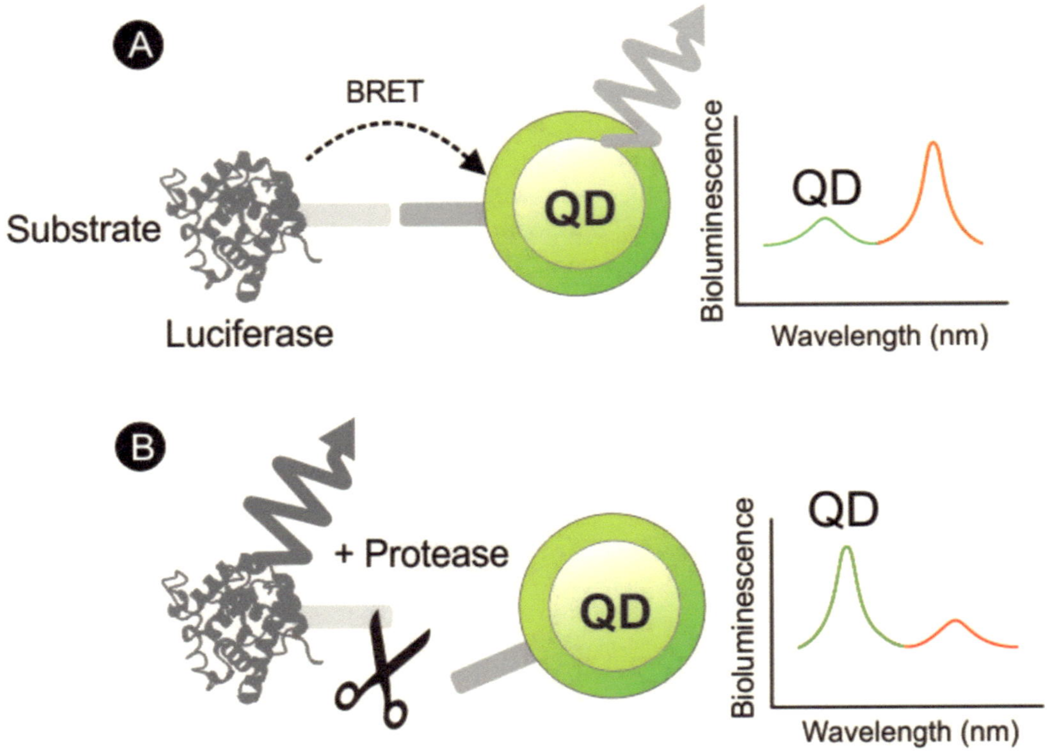


**Figure 11.** Schematic representation of BRET-QDs sensor applied to detect protease activity. In this assembly QD and luciferase protein are closely linked together through a peptide substrate. In process (A) QD fluorescence induced by the BRET process is observed and in the presence of a protease (B) the BRET process is disrupted leading to a loss of bioluminescence-induced QD emission (Xia & Rao, 2009).

causes cell death (by necrosis or apoptosis) when singlet oxygen and other reactive species of oxygen (ROS) are produced while photosensitizers are stimulated by light. In PDT studies QDs may work as energy donors for traditional photosensitizers or interacting directly with molecular oxygen by mechanisms of energy transfers to generate singlet oxygen as described in Figure 12. PDT based QDs have been used both for treatment of skin lesions and for the treatment of skin cancers (Xia & Rao, 2009). QDs conjugated with Pc4, a known photosensitizing protein, were excited at 488 nm and by energy transfer mechanisms the protein was excited indirectly, emitting at 680 nm. In other words, the QDs, when excited, emit in a wavelength which excites the protein (Xia & Rao, 2009).

## 3. Some drawbacks of quantum dots

Non-specific interactions are a common phenomenon on the application of biological probes. Besides some benefits, these interactions are commonly a negative feature. An incomplete conjugation may result in residual non-conjugated QDs in the same colloidal suspension which can bind or interact non-specifically with the biological system and interfere in the desired results interfering in the specificity of the original applications.

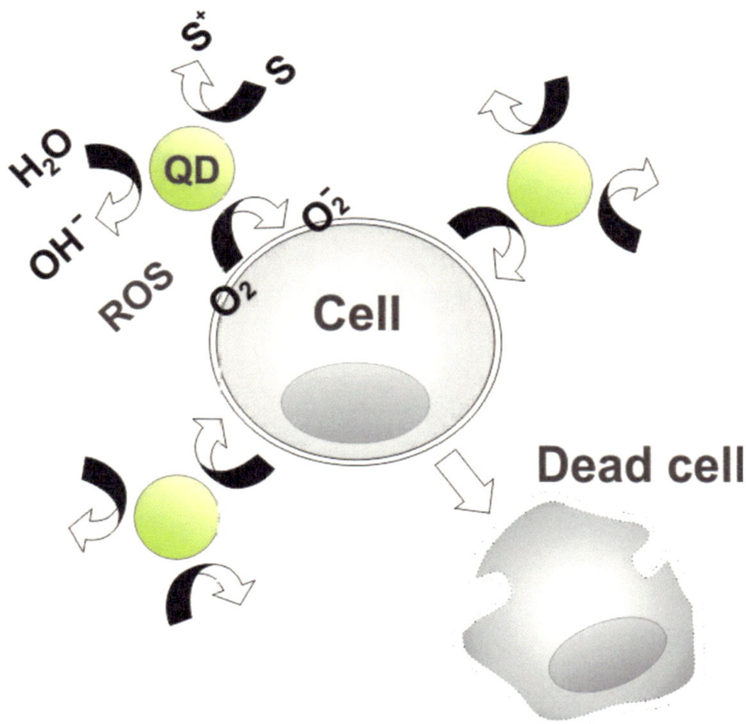


**Figure 12.** The basic process in the production of ROS species in cell PDT using QDs as producers of $O_2^{\cdot-}$.

The most common strategy to overcome non-specific labelling relies in covering the QDs surface with polar polymer molecules, such as polyethylene glycol (PEG). This is because such polymers are biologically "inert" and hinder electrostatic interactions of nanoparticle surface against cell surface or molecules in suspension Pegylated nanoparticles are therefore less prone to aggregation (that is, much more stable) and virtually binding-free. Moreover, they can allow further conjugation with functional biomolecules, include proteins and antibodies (Hezinger *et al.*, 2007; Medintz *et al.*, 2005). Pegylated bioconjugated QDs are then able to bind specifically their targets, being stable and virtually free of non-specific interactions. Pegylation, however, is not universally inert. We have demonstrated that PEG-coated CdS/Cd(OH)$_2$ QDs are able to bind live parasites cells, triggering endocytosis by specialized endocytic pathways such as those using the flagellar pocket (Chaves *et al.*, 2008).

Understanding the interactions of nanoparticles and biological specimens, specially cells, is of great interest since one can therefore modulate specific cellular processes. Unrestricted interactions of any kind of materials, including QDs, have the potential to be toxic, especially at higher concentration and/or with enhanced adsorption/internalization. Beyond the changes over cell function, more evident effects are prone to be caused by QDs, including cellular ones such: (i) changes in cell morphology (Chang *et al.*, 2009), (ii) oxidative stress (Lovrić, *et al.*, 2005), (iii) release of heavy metal compounds (Kirchner *et al.*, 2005) and (iv) genetic and epigenetic damage (Choi *et al.*, 2008), as well as local inflammation in live rats, as we have recently reported.

## 4. General conclusions

QDs have broad and strong one-photon absorption, narrow and symmetric size-tunable fluorescence bands, and a great resistance to photobleaching, making them an attractive alternative to molecular fluorophores in imaging applications and bioanalytical chemistry assays. This Chapter discusses some current applications of QDs as well as presents some drawbacks that still remain. Taken together, all these findings show that a deeper understanding of the mechanisms underlying QDs-biological systems interactions is helpful in the way that researchers can avoid side effects and improve the quality of labeling of QDs for diagnostics and therapeutic purposes.

## Author details

Adriana Fontes, Rafael Bezerra de Lira, Maria Aparecida Barreto Lopes Seabra,
Thiago Gomes da Silva, Antônio Gomes de Castro Neto and Beate Saegesser Santos
*Biomedical Nanotechnology research group of the Universidade Federal de Pernambuco,
Recife, Pernambuco, Brazil*

## Acknowledgement

The authors are grateful to CAPES, CNPq, FACEPE, HEMOPE, L'óreal, Brazilian Academy of Sciences and UNESCO. This work is also linked to the National Institute of Photonics (INCT-INFO). The authors also wish to thank Pedro Barroca for the schematic drawings.

## 5. References

Algar, W. R.; Krull, U. J. (2008) Quantum Dots as Donors in Fluorescence Resonance Energy Transfer for the Bioanalysis of Nucleic Acids, Proteins, and Other Biological Molecules. Anal. Bioanal. Chem., Vol. 391, pp. 1609-1618.

Algar, W. R.; Tavares, A. J.; Krull, U. J. (2010) Beyond Labels: A Review of the Application of Quantum Dots as Integrated Components of Assays, Bioprobes, and Biosensors Utilizing Optical Transduction. Anal. Chim. Acta, Vol. 673, pp. 1-25.

Al-Hajaj, N.A., Moquin, A., Neibert, K.D., Soliman, G.N., Winnik, F.M., Maysinger, D. (2011) Short Ligands affect Modes of QD uptake and elimination in Human Cells. ACS Nano, Vol.6, pp.4909-4918.

Al-Jamal, W. T.; Kostarelos, K. (2007) Liposome-nanoparticle hybrids for multimodal diagnostic and therapeutic applications. Nanomedicine, Vol. 2, pp. 85-98.

Bakalova, R.; Ohba, H.; Zhelev, Z.; Ishikawa, M.; Baba, Y. (2004) Quantum dots as photosensitizers? Nature Biotechnology, Vol. 22, pp. 1360-1361.

Biju, V.; Itoh, T.; Ishikawa, M. (2010) Delivering quantum dots to cells: bioconjugated quantum dots for targeted and nonspecific extracellular and intracellular imaging. Chem. Soc. Rev., Vol. 39, pp. 3031–3056.

Brus, L. E. (1984). Electron–electron and electron–hole interactions in small semiconductor crystallites–the size dependence of the lowest excited electronic state. Journal of Chemical Physics, Vol. 80, pp. 4403–4409.

Cai, W.; Shin D.-W.; Chen, K.; Gheysens, O.; Cao. Q; Wang, S. X.; Gambhir; S. S. Chen, X. (2006) Peptide-Labeled Near-Infrared Quantum Dots for Imaging Tumor Vasculature in Living Subjects. Nano Lett., Vol. 6, pp 669–676.

Carion, O.; Mahler, B.; Pons, T.; Dubertret, B. (2007) Synthesis, encapsulation, purification and coupling of single quantum dots in phospholipid micelles for their use in cellular and in vivo imaging. Nature Protocols, Vol. 2, pp. 2383-2390.

Chang, S. Q.; Dai, Y. D.; Kang, B.; Hana, W.; Mao, L.; Chen, D. (2009) UV-enhanced cytotoxicity of thiol-capped CdTe quantum dots in human pancreatic carcinoma cells. Toxicology Letters, Vol. 188, pp. 104–111

Chaves, C. R.; Fontes, A.; Farias, P. M. A.; Santos, B. S.; Menezes, F. D.; Ferreira, R. C.; Cesar, C. L.; Galembeck, A.; Figueiredo, R. C. B. Q. (2008) Application of core–shell PEGylated CdS/$Cd(OH)_2$ quantum dots as biolabels of Trypanosoma cruzi parasites. Applied Surface Science, Vol. 255, pp. 728-730.

Chen, F.; Gerion, D. (2004) Fluorescent CdSe/ZnS Nanocrystal-Peptide Conjugates for Long-term, Nontoxic Imaging and Nuclear Targeting in Living Cells. Nano Letters, Vol. 4, pp. 1827-1832.

Choi, A. O.; Brown, S. E.; Szyf, M.; Maysinger, D. (2008) Quantum dot-induced epigenetic and genotoxic changes in human breast cancer cells. J Mol Med, Vol. 86, pp. 291-302.

Conroy, J.; Byrne, S. J.; Gun'ko, Y. K.; Rakovich, Y. P.; Donegan, J. F.; Davies, A.; Kelleher, D.; Volkov, V., (2008) CdTe Nanoparticles Display Tropism to Core Histones and Histone-Rich Cell Organelles. Small, Vol. 4, pp. 2006-2015.

Courty, S.; Luccardini, C.; Bellaiche, Y.; Cappello, G.; Dahan, M. (2006) Tracking Individual Kinesin Motors in Living Cells Using Single Quantum-Dot Imaging. Nano Letters. Vol. 6, pp. 1491-1495.

Dabbousi, B. O.; Rodriguez, V. J ; Mikulec, F. V.; Heine, J. R.; Mattoussi, H.; Ober, R. (1997). (CdSe) ZnS core-shell quantum dots: synthesis and characterization of a size series of highly luminescent nanocrystallites. Journal of Physical Chemistry B, Vol. 101, pp. 9463–9475.

Dubertret, B.; Skourides, P.; Norris, D. J.; Noireaux, V.; Brivanlou, A. H.; Libchaber, A. (2002) In Vivo Imaging of Quantum Dots Encapsulated in Phospholipid Micelles. Science, Vol. 298, pp. 1759-1762.

Farias, P. M. A.; Santos, B. S.; Menezes, F. D.; Ferreira, R.; Fontes, A.; Carvalho H. F.; Romão L.; Moura-Neto, V.; Amaral, J. C. O. F.; Cesar, C. L.; Figueiredo, R. C. B. Q.; Lorenzato, F. R. B. (2006) Quantum dots as fluorescent bio-labels in cancer diagnostic. Phys. Stat. Sol. (C), Vol. 3, pp. 4001–4008.

Gao, J.; Chen, X.; Cheng, Z. (2010) Near-infrared quantum dots as optical probes for tumor imaging. Curr. Top Med Chem., Vol. 10, pp. 1147-1157.

Ghinea, N; Simionescu, N. (1985) Anionized and Cationized Hemeundecapeptides as Probes for Cell Surface Charge and Permeability Studies: Differentiated Labeling of Endothelial Plasmalemmal Vesicles. The Journal Of Cell Biology Volume, Vol. 100, pp. 606-612.

Goldman, E. R.; Anderson, G. P.; Tran, P. T.; Mattoussi, H.; Charles, P. T.; Mauro, J. M. (2002) Conjugation of Luminescent Quantum Dots with Antibodies Using an Engineered Adaptor Protein To Provide New Reagents for Fluoroimmunoassays. Anal. Chem., Vol. 74, pp. 841-847.

Jaiswal, J. K.; Matoussi, H.; Mauro, J. M.; Simon, S.; (2003). Long-Term Multiple Color Imaging Of Live Cells Using Quantum Dot Bioconjugates. Nature Biotechnology, Vol. 21, pp. 47-51.

Jiang, W.; Kim, Y.; Rutka, S. B. J. T.; Chan, W. C. W. (2008) Nanoparticle-mediated cellular response is size-dependent. Nature Nanotechnology, Vol. 3, pp. 145-150.

Juzenas, P.; Chen, W.; Sun, Y. P.; Coelho, M. A. N.; Generalov, R.; Generalova, N.; Christensen, I. L. (2008) Quantum dots and nanoparticles for photodynamic and radiation therapies of cancer. Advanced Drug Delivery Reviews, Vol .60, pp. 1600-1614.

Kato, I. T.; Santos, C. C.; Benetti, E.; Tenorio, D. P. L. A.; Cabral Filho, P. E.; Sabino, C. P.; Fontes, A.; Santos, B. S.; Prates, R. A.; Ribeiro, M. S. CdTe/CdS-MPA quantum dots as fluorescent probes to label yeast cells: synthesis, characterization and conjugation with Concanavalin A. (2012) Photonics West, San Francisco. Proceedings of SPIE - Colloidal Nanocrystals for Biomedical Applications VII, Vol. 8232, pp. 82320D.

Kim, B. Y. S.; Jiang, W.; Oreopoulos, J; Yip, C. M.; Rutka, J. T.; Chan, W. C. W. (2008) Biodegradable Quantum Dot Nanocomposites Enable Live Cell Labeling and Imaging of Cytoplasmic Targets. Nano Letters, Vol. 8, pp. 3887-3892.

Kirchner, C.; Liedl, T.; Pellegrino, S. K. T.; Javier, A. M.; Gaub, H. E.; Stölzle, S.; Fertig, N.; Parak, W. J. (2005) Cytotoxicity of Colloidal CdSe and CdSe/ZnS Nanoparticles. Nano Letters, Vol. 5, pp. 331-338

Lira, R. B.; Cavalcanti, M. B.; Seabra, M. A. B. L.; Silva, D. C. N.; Amaral, A. J.; Santos, B. S.; Fontes, A. (2012) Non-specific interactions of CdTe/Cds Quantum Dots with human blood mononuclear cells. Micron, Vol. 43, pp. 621-626.

Liu, W.; Howarth, M.; Greytak, A. B.; Zheng, Y.; Nocera, D. G.; Ting, A. Y.; Bawendi, M. G. (2008) Compact Biocompatible Quantum Dots Functionalized for Cellular Imaging. J. Am. Chem. Soc., Vol. 130, pp. 1274-1284.

Liu. W.; Zhang, S.; Wang, L.; Qu, C.; Zhang, C.; Hong, L.; Yuan, L.; Huang, Z.; Wang, Z.; Liu, S.; Jiang, G. (2011) CdSe Quantum Dot (QD)-Induced Morphological and Functional Impairments to Liver in Mice. PLoS ONE, Vol. 6, e24406. doi:10.1371/journal.pone.0024406.

Lovrić, J.; Bazzi, H. S.; Cuie, Y.; Fortin, G. R. A; Winnik, F. M.; Maysinger, D. (2005) Differences in subcellular distribution and toxicity of green and red emitting CdTe quantum dots. J Mol Med, Vol. 83, pp. 377-385.

Ma-Hock, L.; Brill, S.; Wohlleben, W.; Farias, P. M. A.; Chaves, C. R.; Tenório, D. P. L. A.; Fontes, A.; Santos, B. S.; Landsiedel, R.; Strauss, V.; Treumann, S.; van Ravenzwaay, B. (2012) Short term inhalation toxicity of a liquid aerosol of $CdS/Cd(OH)_2$ core shell quantum dots in male Wistar rats. Toxicology Letters, Vol. 208, pp. 115-124.

Medintz, I. L.; Mattoussi, H. (200) Quantum Dot-Based Resonance Energy Transfer and Its Growing Application in Biology. Phys. Chem. Chem. Phys., Vol. 11, pp. 17-45.

Medintz, I. L.; T. Uyeda, H.; Goldman, E. R.; Mattoussi, H. (2005) Quantum dot bioconjugates for imaging, labelling and sensing. Nature Materials, Vol. 4, pp. 435-446.

Menezes, F. D. de; Brasil Jr., A. G.; Moreira, W. L.; Barbosa, L. C.; Cesar, C. L.; Ferreira, R. C. de; Farias, P. M. A. de; Santos, B. S. (2005). CdTe/CdS core shell quantum dots for photonic applications, Microelectronics Journal, Vol. 36, pp. 989–991.

Nelson, S.R.; Ali, M.Y.; Trybus, K.M.; Warshaw, D.M. (2009) Random walk of processive, quantum dot-labeled myosin Va molecules within the actin cortex of COS-7 cells. Biophys J., Vol. 97, pp. 509-518.

Nichols, B. J. (2003a). Caveosomes and endocytosis of lipid rafts. J. Cell Sci., Vol. 116, pp. 4707-4714.

Nichols, B. J. (2003b). GM1-containing lipid rafts are depleted within clathrin-coated pits. Curr. Biol., Vol. 13, pp. 686-690.

Noh, Y.-W.; Lim, Y. T.; Chung, B. H. (2008) Noninvasive imaging of dendritic cell migration into lymph nodes using near-infrared fluorescent semiconductor nanocrystals. The FASEB Journal , Vol. 22, pp. 3908-3918.

Pinaud F.; Clarke S.; Sittner, A.; Dahan, M. (2010) Probing cellular events, one quantum dot at a time. Nature Methods, Vol. 7, pp. 275–285.

Pyo, D., Yoo, J. (2012) New Trends in Fluorescence Immunochromatography. J. Immunoassay and Immunochemistry, Vol. 33, pp. 203-222.

Rieger, S.; Kulkarni, R. P.; Darcy, D.; Fraser S. E.; Koster, R. W. (2005) Quantum Dots Are Powerful Multipurpose Vital Labeling Agents in Zebrafish Embryos. Developmental Dynamics, Vol. 234 pp. 670-681.

Samia, A. C. S.; Dayal, S.; Clemens, B. (2006) Quantum Dot-based Energy Transfer: Perspectives and Potential for Applications in Photodynamic Therapy. Photochemistry and Photobiology, Vol. 82, pp. 617-625.

Santos, B. S., Farias, P. M. A. ; Fontes, A. . Semiconductor Quantum Dots for Biological Applications. In: Mohamed Henine (Editor Chefe). (Org.). Handbook of Self Assembled Semiconductor Nanostructures Novel Devices in Photonics and Electronics. Amsterdam: Elsevier, 2008a, p. 773-798.

Santos, B. S.; Farias, P. M. A.; Menezes, F. D.; Brasil Jr, A. G.; Fontes, A.; Romão, L.; Amaral, J. O.; Moura-Neto, V.; Tenório, D. P. L. A.; Cesar, C. L.; Barbosa, L. C.; Ferreira, R. (2008b) New highly fluorescent biolabels based on II–VI semiconductor hybrid organic–inorganic nanostructures for bioimaging. Applied Surface Science, Vol. 255, pp. 790–792.

Santos, B. S.; Farias, P. M. A. ; Menezes, F. D. ; Ferreira, R. C.; Alves Junior, S.; Figueiredo, R. C. B. Q.; Carvalho Junior, L. B.; Beltrão, E. I. C. (2006) CdS-Cd$(OH)_2$ core shell quantum dots functionalized with Concanavalin A lectin for recognition of mammary tumors. Physica Status Solidi. C, Conferences and Critical Reviews, Vol. 3, pp. 4017-4022.

Stringer, R. C.; Hoehn, D.; Grant, S. A. (2008) Quantum Dot-Based Biosensor for Detection of Human Cardiac Troponin I Using a Liquid-Core Waveguide. Sensors Journal, IEEE, Vol. 8, pp. 295–300.

Tekdas, D. A.; Durmus, M.; Yanıka, H.; Ahsen V., (2012) Photodynamic therapy potential of thiol-stabilized CdTe quantum dot-group 3Aphthalocyanine conjugates (QD-Pc)

Spectrochim Acta Part A: Molecular and Biomolecular Spectroscopy, Vol. 93, pp. 313–320

Valenzuela, S., Liposome techniques for synthesis of biomimetic lipid membranes in Ferrari, M.; Martin, D. (Eds). Nanobiotechnology of biomimetic membranes, , New York: Springer, 2008 p. 75-87.

Verma, A.; Stellacci, F. (2010) Effect of Surface Properties on Nanoparticle–Cell Interactions. Small, Vol. 6, pp. 12-21.

Williams, Y.; Sukhanova, A.; Nowostawska, M.; Davies, A. M.; Mitchell, S.; Oleinikov, V.; Gun'ko, Y.; Nabiev, I.; Kelleher, D.; Volkov, Y. (2009) Probing Cell-Type-Specific Intracellular Nanoscale Barriers Using Size-Tuned Quantum Dots. Small, Vol. 5, pp. 2581-2588.

Xia, Z., Rao, J. (2009) Biosensing and imaging based on bioluminescence resonance energy transfer. Current Opinion in Biotechnology, Vol. 20, pp. 1–8.

Yang, C., Ding, N.; Xu, Y.; Qu, X.; Zhang, J.; Zhao, C.; Hong, L.; Lu, Y.; Xiang, G. (2009) Folate receptor-targeted quantum dot liposomes as fluorescence probes. Journal of Drug Targeting, Vol. 17, pp. 502–511.

Yeh, C. Y.; Lu, Z. W.; Froyen, S.; Zunger, A. (1992). Zinc-blende-wurtzite polytypism in semiconductors. Physical Review B, Vol. 46, pp. 10086–10097.

Yezhelyev, M. V.; QI, L.; O'Regan, R. M.; Nie, S.; Gao, X. (2008) Proton-Sponge Coated Quantum Dots for siRNA Delivery and Intracellular Imaging. J. Am. Chem. Soc., Vol. 130, pp. 9006–9012.

Yin, Y.; Alivisatos, A. P. (2005) Colloidal nanocrystal synthesis and the organic–inorganic interface. Nature, Vol. 437, pp. 664-670.

Yoo, J. S.; Won, N.; Kim, H. B.; Bang, J.; Kim, S.; Ahn, S.; Soh, K. S. (2010) In vivo imaging of cancer cells with electroporation of quantum dots and multispectral imaging. Journal of Applied Physics, Vol. 107, pp. 124702-124710.

Yoo, J.; Kambara, T.; Gonda, K.; Higuchi, H. (2008) Intracellular imaging of targeted proteins labeled with quantum dots. Experimental Cell Research, Vol. 314, pp. 3563-3569.

# Chapter 13

# Forced Oscillation Technique in the Detection of Smoking-Induced Respiratory Changes

Alvaro Camilo Dias Faria, Karla Kristine Dames da Silva,
Gerusa Marítmo da Costa, Agnaldo José Lopes and Pedro Lopes de Melo

Additional information is available at the end of the chapter

http://dx.doi.org/10.5772/48408

## 1. Introduction

Chronic obstructive pulmonary disease (COPD) is a major public health problem with high and increasing prevalence (Gold 2011). According to WHO estimates, 80 million people have moderate to severe COPD (WHO, 2012). There is general agreement in the literature that it is necessary to develop new accurate and noninvasive tests of lung function (Enright and Crapo, 2000; Kaminsky and Irvin, 2001; Polkey et al.., 2004). In the particular case of COPD, the National Heart Lung and Blood Institute recently recommended that research on new technologies to improve the non-invasive testing of lung function in this disease should be a priority (Croxton et al., 2002).

The Forced Oscillation Technique (FOT) offers a simple and detailed approach to investigating the mechanical properties of the respiratory system. This method characterizes the respiratory impedance and its two components, respiratory system resistance (Rrs) and reactance (Xrs). These parameters are usually measured at various frequencies using small pressure oscillations superimposed at the mouth during spontaneous breathing. The method is simple and requires only passive co-operation and no forced expiratory maneuvers. Another important advantage, particularly in pathophysiological research, is that FOT can be used to provide information on the mechanical characteristics of the respiratory system that is complementary to the information provided by spirometry (Navajas and Farré, 2001; Macleod and Birch, 2001; Oostveen et al., 2003; Bates et al., 2011; Kaczka and Dellacà 2011). This technique has the potential to greatly increase our knowledge regarding the pathophysiology of smoking, as well as to help in the clinical diagnosis of early smoking-induced respiratory alterations and COPD (Faria et al., 2009; Faria et al., 2010; Silva et al., 2011; Postma et al., 2012; Amaral et al., 2012).

This chapter discusses the history and current state of the art of FOT for detecting smoking-induced respiratory diseases. We focus on how FOT has emerged as a powerful method not only to extract clinically relevant information but also to provide insight into the mechanisms responsible for smoking-induced respiratory diseases. The main topics covered by this review will be as follows:

- First, we present a short overview of COPD in section 2;
- Section 3 provides a brief description of FOT for basic clinical assessment. Here, we describe the interpretation of the FOT parameters and the potential and limitations of this technique;
- The main results presented in the literature concerning the diagnosis of the effects of smoking and COPD using multi-frequency and single-frequency FOT methods are described in section 4;
- Section 5 presents and discusses new results concerning the evaluation of diagnostic accuracy in patients classified by the GOLD (2011) stage;
- In section 6, we highlight important future directions for this research field. We discuss the high potential of FOT in telemedicine, the use of FOT to evaluate changes in the complexity of the respiratory system, and the use of FOT parameters in clinical decision support systems based on machine learning;

We conclude by examining the current use of FOT as a diagnostic tool in smoking-induced respiratory diseases and suggesting further studies needed to achieve its full potential in routine clinical use.

## 2. Short review of Chronic Obstructive Pulmonary Disease

COPD is a preventable and treatable disease, characterized by airflow limitation, which is partially reversible (GOLD, 2011).. The limitation is often progressive and is associated with an abnormal inflammatory response of the lungs to noxious particles or gases, especially cigarette smoke (GOLD, 2011). COPD increases in prevalence and mortality worldwide each year, causing enormous socio-economic damage. Estimates by the World Health Organization (WHO) suggest that approximately 65 million people have moderate to severe COPD. Worldwide, more than 3 million people died of COPD in 2005, which corresponded to 5% of all deaths worldwide (WHO, 2012). In 2002, the disease was the fifth leading cause of death worldwide. The total deaths from COPD are projected to increase by 30% over the next 10 years unless urgent measures are taken to reduce the underlying risk factors, particularly tobacco use. Estimates indicate that by 2030, COPD may become the third leading cause of death worldwide (WHO, 2012).

The complex pathophysiological behavior of COPD is characterized by the presence of chronic bronchitis, obstructive bronchiolitis and emphysema (GOLD, 2011). The disease process is directly related to an amplified inflammatory response of the lungs, triggering the destruction of the lung parenchyma and the consequent disruption of defense mechanisms and normal repair. Such changes are responsible for airflow limitation and air trapping, observed in various stages of the disease (GOLD, 2011). Pathological changes occur in four different regions of the lung: larger caliber airway, peripheral airways, lung parenchyma and pulmonary vasculature (ATS/ERS, 2004, GOLD, 2011). In larger caliber airways, structural changes occur in the goblet cells and submucosal glands, causing mucus hypersecretion and squamous metaplasia, as shown in Figure 1 (ATS/ERS, 2004, GOLD, 2011).

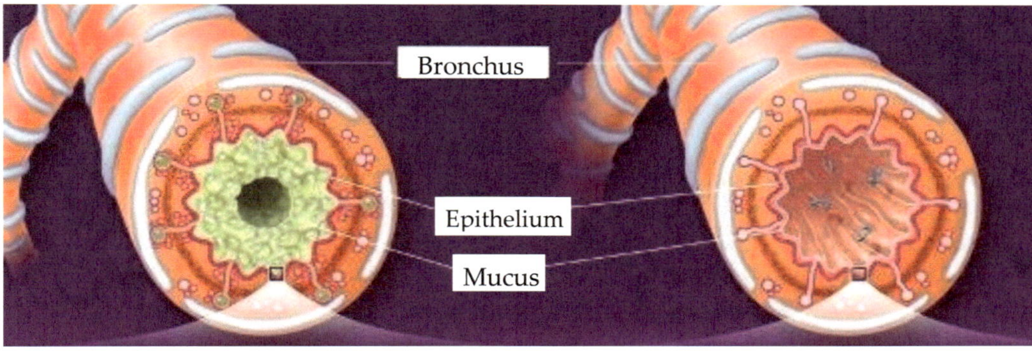


**Figure 1.** Normal bronchus (right). On the left, a bronchus depicting the inflammatory process due to COPD (Source: http://www.nlm.nih.gov/ images/ency/fullsize/19377.jpg).

In peripheral airways (<2 mm diameter), we observed thickening of the airway wall, peribronchial fibrosis, exudate, narrowing of the airways (obstructive bronchiolitis) and increased inflammatory response. In the lung parenchyma, the structural changes involve the destruction of the alveolar wall, the apoptosis of epithelial cells and emphysema (Figure 2) (ATS/ERS, 2004, GOLD, 2011).

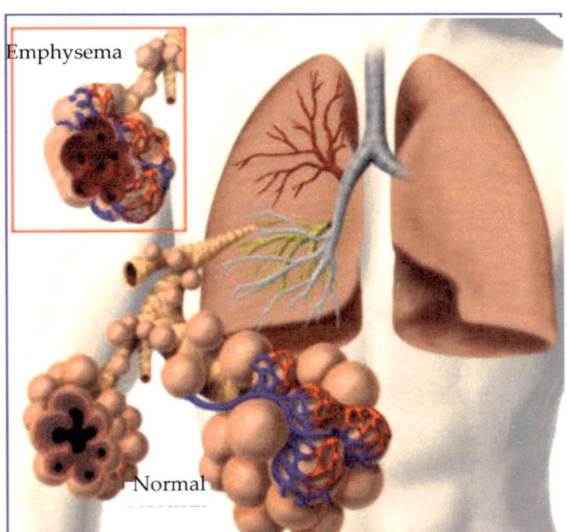


**Figure 2.** Illustration of an alveolar emphysema (highlighted). Destruction of lung parenchyma and vasculature. (Source: http://www.nlm.nih.gov/ images/ency/fullsize/19377.jpg).

The main characteristic of COPD is airflow obstruction, which is not fully reversible. Spirometry is the gold standard technique used to assess this obstruction, and the parameters obtained for these analyses are derived from forced expiratory maneuvers

(ATS/ERS, 2005). However, the modifications to respiratory mechanics are not always detected by this test (Coe et al. 1989). Moreover, some patients are not able to reliably perform spirometry, as the methods require good subject co-operation and maximal effort (Crapo et al., 2003). Whole-body plethysmography features a more complex method in which the individual must remain isolated from the external environment, breathing spontaneously within a hermetically sealed box (ATS/ERS, 2005). The advantage of this method is the opportunity to obtain important variables related to lung mechanics, especially the residual volume and functional residual capacity (ATS/ERS, 2005). The main disadvantage is the maintenance of individuals in a closed environment, which can generate claustrophobic reactions. Recommendations for research in COPD (Croxton et al., 2002) include the need for improved noninvasive mechanical tests of lung function. In this context, FOT was suggested by Crapo et al. (2003) as an attractive alternative for diagnosing obstruction in COPD, as it requires little patient effort and cooperation. A brief description of this technique is provided in the next section.

## 3. Forced oscillation basics

Since the FOT methodology was introduced in the mid-1950s (DuBois et al., 1956), numerous variants of the FOT have been developed. This short review is focused on the use of FOT in the clinical diagnostic of COPD, addressing only the most basic concepts, and the reader is referred for more detailed information to other review and monograph articles (Peslin and Fredberg, 1986; Navajas and Farré, 2001; Macleod and Birch, 2001; Oostveen et al., 2003; Marchal and Hall, 2010; Bates et al., 2011; Kaczka and Dellacà 2011).

### 3.1. Measurement principle

Subjecting a physical system to forced oscillations is a very general approach to the investigation of its structure and other properties (Ljung, 1987). Its application to respiratory mechanics was first proposed by DuBois and co-workers (1956). This method consists of applying small sinusoidal pressure variations to stimulate the respiratory system at frequencies higher than the normal breathing frequency and measuring the flow response. The basic instrumentation used to evaluate respiratory impedance by FOT is described in Figure 3.

An electric signal is produced in the impedance analyzer and applied to a loudspeaker that converts it to a corresponding pressure waveform. Usually, this pressure signal presents an amplitude of approximately 2 cm $H_2O$ (peak-to-peak). This signal is directed to the airway opening of the patient, which is connected *via* a mouthpiece to the set-up. The airflow (V′) is measured using a pneumotacograph (PNT in Figure 1), and the pressure (P) is measured at the airway input of the patient. The resulting signals are amplified, filtered and digitized in the impedance analyzer. Then, the respiratory impedance (Zrs) is calculated using the fast Fourier transform (FFT) of these signals (1):

$$Zrs(f) = \frac{FFT(P)}{FFT(V`)} \tag{1}$$

In practice, the sinusoidal pressure excitations are superimposed on the subject's spontaneous breathing. To enable spontaneous breathing by the patient, the system allows the individual to breathe comfortably during the experiment through a tube (Bias tube in the Figure 3) that operates predominantly as a pneumatic inertance element. This inertance provides a low-impedance path to the atmosphere for the low frequencies associated with the breathing process, while imposing high impedances to the high frequencies produced by the loudspeaker. A pneumatic resistor may also be used for this purpose. To renew the air breathed by the individual, the system also includes a bias flow (Figure 3) of approximately 0.2 l/s near the subject's mouth.

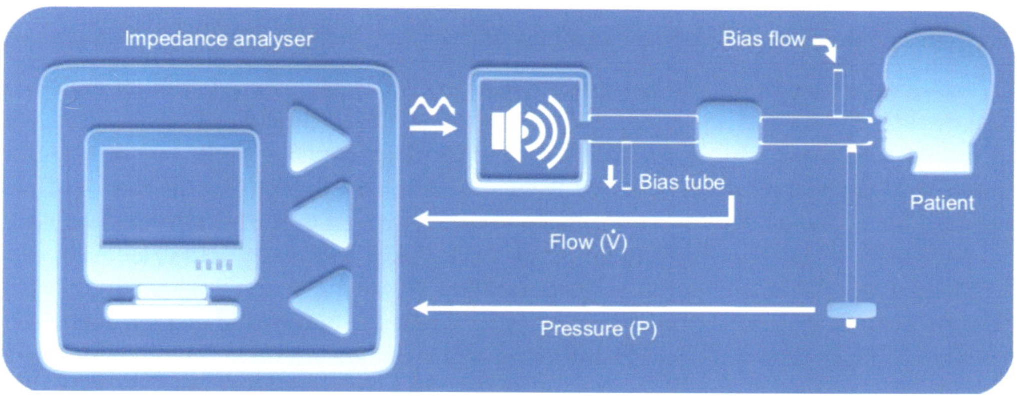


**Figure 3.** Basic schematic arrangement of forced oscillation respiratory impedance measurement.

To perform the FOT analysis, the volunteer remains seated, keeping the head in a normal position and breathing spontaneously through a mouthpiece. During the measurements, the subjects firmly support their cheeks and mouth floor using both hands, and a nose clip is worn. This method allows the evaluation of the "respiratory input impedance". Applying the oscillating pressure across the chest wall and measuring the oscillatory flow downstream at the mouth allows us to estimate the "transfer impedance". The respiratory input impedance is much more widely used clinically and is the focus of this work. The interested reader may find detailed information on "transfer impedance" in previous works (Mac Leod and Birch, 2001; Oostveen et al., 2003).

## 3.2. Devices

FOT analysis can use oscillations on a single (mono) frequency or more than one (multi) frequency test signals. Each implementation has its advantages and disadvantages. Analyses using a single frequency are suitable for instantaneous assessment of the total impedance, making it possible to identify the rapid changes in impedance associated with changes in airway caliber during the respiratory cycle.

However, tests using several frequencies are slower, with results that reflect the average behavior of the respiratory system over several cycles. Multifrequency instruments usually include a frequency range of approximately 4–32 Hz. The advantage in this case lies in a much more detailed analysis that provides indices associated with the total resistance and reactance in several frequencies. The original multi-frequency FOT method focused on two forms of forcing: a forced white noise signal (Michaelson et al., 1975) and an impulse waveform applied at the mouth (Landser et al., 1976). We now know that an impulse is the least reliable and desirable excitation waveform to apply for system identification because of signal-to-noise limitations over the bandwidth of interest (La Prad et al., 2008; Pintelon and Schoukens, 2001). The highest possible signal-to-noise ratio is produced using pseudorandom noise (Macleod and Birch, 2001; Oostveen et al., 2003; Bates et al., 2011), which is a periodic signal designed specifically to include only a designated set of desired frequency components, each represented by a precisely defined amplitude and phase.

FOT based on a pseudorandom noise signal has been validated over a period of more than three decades (Mac Leod and Birch, 2001). Importantly, FOT should not be confused with the more recently introduced technique of Impulse Oscillometry (IOS). IOS differs from classical FOT in the data processing and the parameters used to interpret the raw data (Mac Leod and Birch, 2001; Hellinckx et al., 2001). Several technical and clinical validation issues also remain to be assessed for IOS techniques (MacLeod and Birch, 2001; Hellinckx et al. 2001; Ritz et al., 2002). Although the signal used in IOS has the practical advantage of being relatively easy to generate, it has significant disadvantages in terms of energy distribution (Bates et al., 2011). From a system identification point of view, the impulse excitation signal used in IOS is a much worse excitation signal than the multisine used in FOT. This difference is associated with a worse crest factor in the impulse signal (La Prad et al., 2008; Pintelon and Schoukens, 2001). This characteristic introduces concerns associated mainly with the following points (Mac Leod and Birch, 2001): (a) whether energy transfer during impulse excitation is sufficient (especially ~ 5 Hz), (b) the tendency of impulses to induce non-linear flow effects, (c) the possibility of reflex responses to impulses and (d) possible shear effects occurring at the locus of the airway wall.

### 3.3. Limitations

As for other techniques of functional assessment, the limitations of FOT and its consequences must be recognized. An important source of errors is related to the process of spontaneous breathing of the patient, which introduces both random and systematic errors. These errors are reduced by using excitation frequencies at least 10 times higher than those present in the spontaneous ventilation process and with appropriate acceptance criteria (Mac Leod and Birch, 2001; Oostveen et al., 2003; Melo et al., 2000). The errors may be easily evaluated using the coherence function ($\gamma^2$) between the pressure and airflow signals. The coherence function is the equivalent in the frequency domain of a correlation coefficient in the time domain. A perfect coherence (1.00) describes no influence of the respiratory signal in the results and may be obtained performing the exams in apnea conditions. In practice, the patient ventilates during the exam. The respiratory influence increases with the amplitude and frequency of the ventilation (irregular breathing or acute hyperventilation), introducing proportional reductions in the coherence function. A minimal coherence value of 0.9 is usually considered adequate (Mac Leod and Birch, 2001; Faria et al., 2010). Any time the coherence computed for any of the studied frequencies is smaller than this threshold, the maneuver may not be considered valid, and the examination needs to be repeated.

The compliance of the soft tissues of the upper airways, including the cheeks, comprises a mechanical impedance placed in parallel with the respiratory system. The resulting effect of this placement is to reduce the impedance measured in relation to its actual value. This effect is more pronounced in the presence of high impedances, as is the case for highly obstructive COPD patients. In practice, this drawback is minimized by asking the patient to firmly support their cheeks and mouth floor (Navajas and Farré 2001, Oostveen et al., 2003). Artifacts can also occur if the glottis is closed or if the seal around the mouthpiece is lost during testing. Swallowing or an improper seal with the nose clip during the measurement are reasons to discard the measurement. Most of these events can easily be detected in the flow signal.

## 3.4. Interpretation of the results

FOT characterizes the module of the respiratory impedance (Zrs), which is associated with respiratory system resistance (Rrs) and reactance (Xrs) as described in equation (2):

$$\mathrm{Zrs} = \sqrt{\mathrm{Rrs}^2 + \mathrm{Xrs}^2} \tag{2}$$

The Zrs is related to the total mechanical load provided by the respiratory system, including the resistive and reactive properties of the lung and chest wall. A convenient way to represent the behavior of the impedance tests employs the description of the resistive and reactive properties of the respiratory system, allowing a direct correlation with the mechanical properties involved.

### *3.4.1. Multi-frequency*

Usually, the results obtained in multi-frequency systems are described for each studied frequency in the whole range evaluated, as demonstrated in Figure 4A. The Rrs measured by FOT describes the total resistance of the respiratory system, including both frictional losses during the airflow process (similar to airway resistance measurements in plethysmography) and the resistance related to lung and chest wall tissue. There is no consensus in the literature concerning the parameters used in the interpretation of these curves. Some groups use simple resistance values, describing the total resistance in the specified frequency, whereas other groups use an analysis of linear regression in the frequency range between 4 and 16 Hz (Figure 4A).

This analysis is used to obtain the intercept resistance (R0) and the slope of the resistive component of the impedance (S). These parameters are associated with the total resistance of the respiratory system (Lorino et al., 1997) and with the respiratory system's non-homogeneity (Peslin et al., 1991; Pride, 1992), respectively. Using the same frequency range, the mean resistance (Rm), a parameter commonly related to airway caliber, is also calculated (Macleod D, Birch M, 2001).

The Xrs is directly related to the energy storage by the components of the respiratory system. These components are the dynamic compliance and the inertance. The dynamic compliance is composed of the thoracic gas compression, the lung and bronchial wall compliances, the compliance of the chest wall/abdomen compartment and the compliance of the soft tissues of the mouth, cheeks and pharynx (upper airway). On the other hand, the respiratory inertance includes the mass of the central airway gas and the tissue inertance. While the lower frequency portion of the Xrs curve is dominated by the effects of the dynamic compliance (negative values in Figure 2B), the higher frequencies are dominated by the effects of inertance (positive values in Figure 4B). In the case where the effects of compliance and inertance are equal, Xrs becomes zero, and resonance occurs (resonant frequency - fr in Figure 4B).

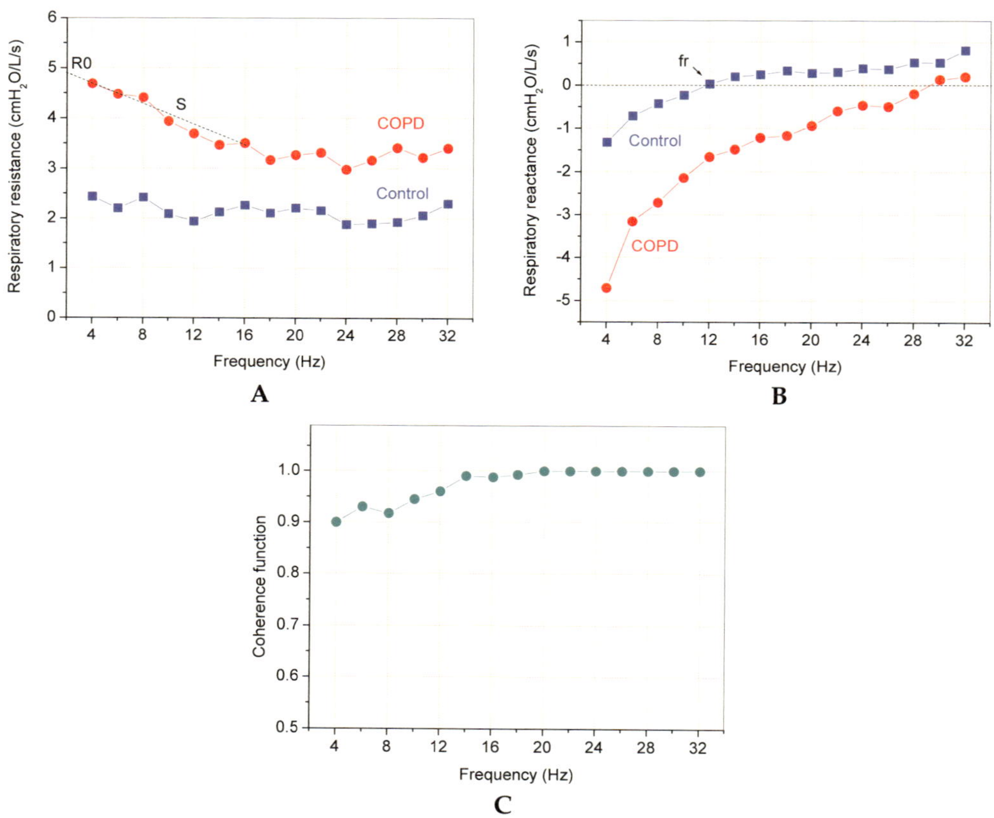


**Figure 4.** Examples of results for the resistance (A), reactance (B) and coherence function (C) obtained in normal subjects and in patients with COPD. The analysis used to obtain the intercept resistance (R0) and the slope of the resistive component of the respiratory impedance (S) is described in the text.

There is a consensus in the literature concerning the behavior of respiratory input impedance in normal subjects and patients. In general, normal individuals show resistances with nearly constant values (Figure 4A). The reactance at low frequencies is negative due to system compliance, displaying an increasing value up to a null at approximately 8 Hz (resonant frequency). From this point, the reactance becomes positive, dominated by the inertial properties of the system (Figure 4B). Patients generally exhibit higher levels of resistance, decreasing with increasing frequency (Figure 4A). The magnitude of the reactance at low frequencies is greater because of reduced compliance, and the resonant frequency is generally higher. Figure 4B illustrates the behavior described.

Figure 4C shows experimental results demonstrating the typical behavior of the coherence function. Note the decrease in the coherence function in the region of low frequencies, which is associated with interference due to the harmonics derived from the spontaneous breathing process.

### *3.4.2. Mono-frequency*

The use of multi-frequency or mono-frequency FOT depends on the desired application. Multi-frequency is preferred in studies exploring the patterns or mechanisms of the frequency dependence of Zrs in health and disease. In contrast, single-frequency is used in the study of relatively rapid changes in Zrs, such as the changes observed during the respiratory cycle (Dellacà et al., 2004), deglutition apnea (Souza et al., 2008), deep inspiration (Slats et al. 2007), and the evaluation of airway patency in sleep apnea (Badia et al., 1998; Lemes et al., 2003). Figure 5 shows representative examples of the typical morphology of the airflow and impedance signals obtained in a control (A) and a COPD (B) individual. Notice the difference in the impedance scales.

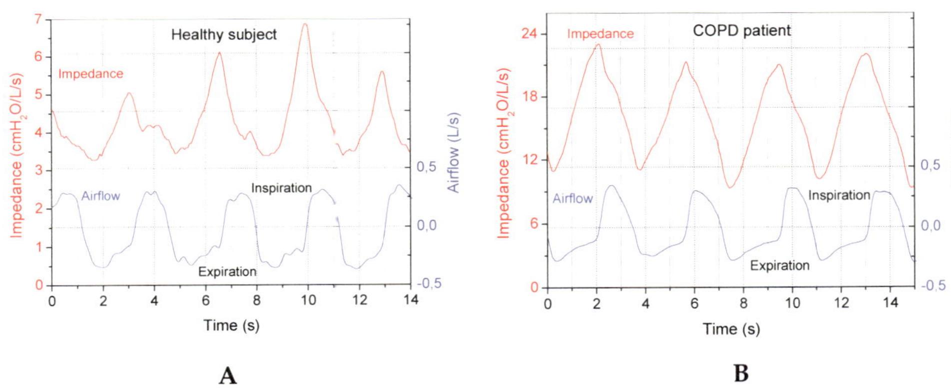


**Figure 5.** Typical airflow and respiratory impedance observed in normal subjects (A) and COPD individuals (B). Notice the difference in the impedance scales.

A characteristic feature of COPD is that Zrs is often very different between inspiration and expiration, in contrast to the situation in normal subjects (Dellaca et al., 2007; Bates et al., 2011). These characteristics may be observed in Figure 5. Note the smaller difference between inspiration and expiration in the normal subject (Figure 5A) and the higher values of expiratory impedance in the COPD patient (Figure 5B).

The parameters used to interpret raw single-frequency FOT data depend slightly on the research group (Dellacà et al. 2004; Johnson et al. 2005; Dellacà et al. 2010; Silva et al., 2011). In general, Zrs and its components (Rrs, Xrs) are considered as the mean values during inspiration (Zi, Ri, Xi) and expiration (Ze, Re, Xe), the difference between Xi and the mean Xe (ΔXrs) has been used as an index of expiratory flow limitation (Dellacà et al. 2004). In previous studies from our group (Silva et al., 2011), the mechanical alterations during different phases of the respiratory cycle were characterized using the following parameters:

- The mean respiratory impedance (Zm), calculated for the complete exam;
- The mean impedance during the inspiration cycles (Zi);
- The mean impedance during the expiration cycles (Ze);
- The mean impedance at the beginning of inspiration (Zbi);
- The mean impedance at the beginning of expiration (Zbe);
- The mean peak-to-peak impedance (Zpp), the difference between Zbe and Zbi;
- The mean change in the impedance (ΔZrs), the difference between Ze and Zi.

This analysis has been successfully applied in our laboratory in the diagnosis of respiratory changes in advanced COPD patients. These results, together with other studies aiming to diagnose the abnormal effects of smoking and COPD using multi and mono-frequency FOT, are described in the next section.

## 4. Main results presented in the literature concerning the diagnosis of the effects of smoking and Chronic Obstructive Pulmonary Disease

FOT has been applied by a number of investigators to obtain a detailed analysis of the respiratory mechanics in smokers compared with non-smokers and former smokers. COPD was also studied. This section focuses on a historically organized review of the main works dedicated to the diagnosis of abnormal changes in respiratory mechanics due to smoking. It is important to point out that FOT has also allowed other important advances in COPD, associated, for example, with the study of animal models (Bates et al., 2011), mechanical ventilation (Navajas and Farré, 2001) and pharmacological response (Woulers et al., 1992).

### 4.1. The first studies in the 1960s and 1970s

Grimby et al. (1968) investigated 15 patients with varying degrees of obstructive lung disease (11 COPD) using oscillations of 3, 5, 7 and 9 Hz. The authors observed frequency dependence of both resistance and compliance, which were interpreted as effects of the uneven distribution of the mechanical properties in the lungs. It was concluded that measurements of total respiratory resistance by the FOT appear to be as useful for assessing abnormalities in airway resistance as the plethysmographic or esophageal pressure techniques. In the 1970s, a random noise pressure wave was used in the classical work of Michaelson et al. (1975) to investigate 10 normal subjects, 5 smokers, and 5 patients with COPD. The authors observed small differences between normal subjects and smokers. These two groups behaved approximately like a second-order system. In COPD, however, the phase angle was more negative at all frequencies, and the resonant frequency was between 15 and 29 Hz. In addition, the behavior of Zr deviated markedly from the second-order behavior observed in normal subjects. Kjeldgaard et al. (1976) studied a group of non-smokers (n = 10) and two groups of smokers, the first without respiratory symptoms (n = 14) and with an average of 20 pack-years and a second group of smokers with respiratory disease (n = 6) and with an average of 48 pack-years. A significant increase in the resistance values measured at 3 Hz and dependence of the resistance on frequency (S) was observed between the control group and the group of smokers without symptoms and between the control group and the group of smokers with the disease. Hayes et al. (1979) compared the respiratory function of 12 nonsmokers, 15 young smokers (mean age 29.9 years) and 8 patients with COPD. The authors observed a non-significant increase of resistance in the smokers compared with the control group and a significant increase in the group of patients. In the resistive curve, there was a rise in values in the COPD group compared with the control group throughout the frequency range. A greater dependence of the resistance values on the frequency was observed in COPD patients. The authors also reported a reduction of dynamic compliance between the control group and the group of smokers and between the control group and the group of patients with COPD. However, these changes were only statistically significant when comparing the control group with the group of patients. The increase in fr was significant when comparing the control group and the smokers, as well as in the comparison of the control group with the patients. These changes were obtained in the reactance curve, in which the values were more negative in the curve of patients compared with the control group. The authors suggested that the difference is associated with lower compliance and a less homogeneous respiratory system.

## 4.2. Studies performed in the 1980s

The development of digital computers, methods of signal analysis based on the FFT and accurate sensors contributed to the development of sophisticated instrumentation (Delavault et al., 1980; Farré et al., 1986; Farré et al., 1989; Franken et al., 1985; Pelle et al., 1986), which allowed the expansion of this research area. In the early 1980s, Peslin et al. (1981) studied the impedance of smokers and former smokers compared with a control group. A non-significant increase of resistance was observed in ex-smokers and a significant increase was observed in smokers. Unlike the peak flows, the FOT indexes were not correlated with cigarette smoking expressed in pack-years, indicating that FOT would not be able to detect early changes in the airways caused by smoking. Landser et al. (1982) showed a small increase in the values of the resistance curve when comparing smokers with nonsmokers and concluded that FOT had little sensitivity in detecting the effects of smoking on lung function. Brochard et al. (1987) studied the effect of smoking on the lung function of workers in a gas industry. They observed no significant increases of R0 and fr when comparing the control group with the group of ex-smokers and smokers. Cauberghs and Woestjine (1989) analyzed the behavior of Rrs and Xrs in 16 subjects with obstructive diseases (asthma and COPD) and with different degrees of airway obstruction. The authors noted that Rrs showed higher values and more negative Xrs values with increasing obstruction. A significant increase in fr was observed. Coe et al. (1989) evaluated the effects of smoking on lung function in young and older individuals. The authors observed increased resistance (of 6 Hz) and fr when comparing all non-smokers with all smokers. The subjects were subsequently classified into groups aged 32-44 years (24 pack-years) and between 45-64 years (24 pack-years). No significant changes were observed in the comparisons in the younger group. On the other hand, significant changes were observed in comparing resistance and fr in subjects over 45 years.

### 4.3. Studies performed in the 1990s

Initially, Van Noord et al. (1991) studied individuals with asthma, chronic bronchitis and emphysema, comparing the parameters of FOT, spirometry and plethysmography. The authors' conclusion was that the FOT parameters were more sensitive in classifying these individuals. Pasker et al. (1996) also assessed lung function in different groups of individuals with and without respiratory disorders using FOT and spirometry. In the group of patients with obstructive diseases (asthma, chronic bronchitis and emphysema), changes were found in the values of the resistance and reactance of the respiratory system. The authors emphasized that the data from the impedance measurements by FOT are complementary to that obtained from spirometry.

### 4.4. Studies in the 21st century

The developments in the twenty-first century begin with Yang and Yang (2002). These researchers evaluated the lung function of 180 non-smokers, 109 smokers with 18.8 mean pack-years and 82 ex-smokers with 20.3 mean pack-years. They found resistance significantly increased in the group of smokers compared with nonsmokers. No significant changes were found when comparing nonsmokers and former smokers. Janssens et al. (2001) observed that Obstructive Lung Disease (OLD) is highly prevalent in elderly subjects but markedly under-diagnosed, which may be associated with the fact that only 40-50% of hospitalized elderly patients are able to adequately perform spirometric tests. These authors evaluated the diagnostic value of the FOT for identifying OLD in an acute-care geriatric hospital. Significant correlations were found between spirometric and Zrs measurements. The Zrs parameters yielding the best sensibility and specificity for detecting OLD were fr (Se=76%; Sp=78%) and R0 (Se=76%; Sp=74%). Seventy-six percent of the patients were correctly classified as having OLD or not. The authors concluded that FOT could contribute to the diagnosis of OLD in elderly hospitalized patients. In a later work assessing the high potential for FOT in this age range, Guo et al. (2005) investigated the diagnosis of obstructive lung disease in older patients. These authors studied 97 subjects, 48 normal subjects (control group) and 49 patients who were assessed by FOT, the interrupter technique (IT) and spirometry. The authors aimed to compare the performance of FOT and IT in the diagnosis of elderly patients with abnormal flow-volume curves and bronchodilator response. There was significant correlation between the FOT indices and FEV1 and FEV1/FVC. Furthermore, FOT precisely identified 81.4% of cases of obstruction, with Se of 78% and Sp of 85%. The fr and R0 were the parameters with better sensitivity (Se) and specificity (Sp). The authors concluded that FOT presents better performance than IT in the evaluation of bronchial obstruction in elderly subjects (Guo et al. 2005). Di Mango et al. (2006) compared healthy subjects (n = 21) with a group of COPD classified according to the degree of airway obstruction (mild, n=16; moderate, n=23; and severe, n=40) to evaluate the clinical potential of FOT in detecting changes in the respiratory mechanics in these patients. The COPD Rrs curves were significantly higher than for the control group. The increased obstruction caused an increase in total resistance, especially at lower frequencies, resulting in a dependence of the resistance on frequency. The Xrs became more negative with obstruction, with the most marked changes in the lower frequencies. All resistance values showed significant changes with the degree of obstruction ($p<0.0001$). The mean values of R0 and Rm increased significantly when the groups of normal and COPD patients with mild obstruction were compared. S decreased significantly, but there was no difference between the control and COPD with mild obstruction. All parameters showed significant changes in the reactive parameters ($p<0.006$). It was shown that by increasing the degree of obstruction, Rrs increased, and Xrs become more negative. Interestingly, the resistance showed significant changes in the initial condition of obstruction, whereas in the later stages, the reactive parameters were most sensitive. This behavior is consistent with the mixed pattern usually developed in the later stages of COPD. Dellacà et al. (2004) used FOT at 5 Hz to detect expiratory flow limitation (EFL) in 15 subjects with COPD. This work studied the Zrs parameters along the ventilation cycle and compared them with the gold standard method, esophageal balloon manometry. According to the authors, the parameter that best described the EFL was ΔXrs (difference between mean inspiratory and expiratory Xrs), with Se=95% and Sp=98%. This work established that ΔXrs values ≥ 2.8 cmH2O are characteristic of EFL. The authors also correlated higher values of ΔXrs with a more advanced stage of the disease. In a later study from the same group, Dellacà et al. (2006) studied the EFL through monofrequency FOT (5 Hz) in patients with COPD and restrictive ventilatory disease. Nasal continuous positive airway pressure (CPAP) was used at different levels to evaluate the reduction of the EFL (0, 4, 8 and 12 cmH2O). The ΔXrs was able to correctly classify 94.8% of breaths as flow-limited or not, producing a 95% sensitivity and specificity of 98%. The authors suggested that the identification of EFL by FOT can modulate the level of CPAP titration to correct the EFL, eliminating unnecessary hemodynamic effects and inspiratory muscle overload due to increased lung volume (Dellacà et al. 2006). More recently, this group (Dellacà et al. 2007) compared FOT (5 Hz) with the technique of negative expiratory pressure (NEP) in the evaluation of the EFL. The authors found ΔXrs sensitivity and specificity values of 93% and 91%, respectively. It was reported that both techniques are effective for detecting EFL, although they employ different methodologies. They pointed out that FOT has the advantage of allowing a quantitative measurement of the phenomenon of EFL. The study conducted by Johnson et al. (2007) examined the ability of single-frequency FOT (5 Hz) to detect longitudinal changes during an exacerbation of COPD compared with spirometry, gas exchange, symptoms and a quality of life questionnaire. Thirty-nine subjects with COPD were analyzed. FOT parameters were positively correlated with changes in symptoms and quality of life, representing objective measurements to document the exacerbation. Slats et al. (2007) analyzed by FOT at 8 Hz the effect of deep inspiration in Rrs of individuals with asthma and COPD compared with a control group. In asthmatic patients, a direct relationship was found between the number of inflammatory cells and the bronchodilator effect of deep inspiration, resulting in reduced resistance of the respiratory system. In subjects with COPD, this relationship was not clearly observed, possibly due to the absolute loss of alveolar septa, leading to a reduction of the effect of parenchymal interdependence. This mechanism was probably related to fewer bronchodilations by deep breaths in COPD patients. The authors assume that this loss in ability to reduce respiratory resistance by deep inspiration is due to structural damage of the airways or lung parenchyma in COPD. These results indicated that, in both asthma and COPD, the mechanisms of bronchodilation by deep inspiration are changed. However, this change occurs by different pathophysiological mechanisms, most easily identified by monofrequency FOT in asthma (Slats et al. 2007). Faria et al. (2009) investigated if FOT would be able to detect the early effects of smoking. To this end, pulmonary function was assessed by FOT and spirometry in a group of smokers (n=28) and in a group of nonsmokers (n=28). A small, non-significant reduction was observed of the spirometric parameters, which were still at normal levels. In contrast, the FOT parameters (R0, fr and Zrs) increased, and more negative values in Xm and a more reduced Cdyn were observed. The Rrs curves showed higher values in smokers than in nonsmokers. In the Xrs curves, the values for the smokers were more negative. The clinical potential of FOT was evaluated by calculating the area under the ROC curve (AUC) (Swets, 1988). This analysis showed that R0, Cdyn, and Zrs offered accuracies equal or greater than 75%, indicating that these parameters can be useful in identifying early changes due to smoking. Interestingly, comparing the AUCs obtained among oscillometric and spirometric parameters, it was observed that the accuracy was significantly higher for the FOT parameters (Figure 6, Table 1). These results suggested that FOT might be more sensitive than spirometry to detect early changes due to smoking. They also suggest that FOT could be a useful tool in screening smokers who will develop respiratory disease resulting from changes induced by smoking. If this hypothesis is confirmed in a wider number of subjects, FOT may offer the possibility of demonstrating abnormalities during a phase at which pathological changes are still potentially reversible, helping to prevent the development of COPD. Continuing this research, Faria et al. (2010) compared the diagnostic accuracy of the FOT and spirometric parameters in groups with different degrees of tobacco consumption. One hundred and seventy subjects were divided into five groups according to the number of pack-years smoked: four groups of smokers classified as <20, 20-39, 40-59, and >60 pack-years and a control group. The early adverse effects of smoking in the group with < 20 pack-years were adequately detected by FOT parameters.

In this group, the comparisons of the ROC curves showed significantly better diagnostic accuracy ($p<0.01$) for the FOT parameters. On the other hand, in the groups of 20-39, 40-59, and > 60 pack-years, the diagnostic performance of the FOT was similar to that observed with spirometry. This study provided additional evidence that the FOT parameters are able to detect early smoking-induced respiratory involvement when pathologic changes are still potentially reversible (<20 pack-years). These findings also suggest that FOT presents a similar sensitivity to that presented by spirometry in detecting more advanced changes (20-39, 40-59, and >60 pack-years). Ionescu et al. (2010) compared healthy and COPD groups by applying constant-phase models (Bates et al. 2011) to FOT data within the range 4-48 Hz.

Changes in respiratory mechanics from healthy COPD patients were observed with four- and five-parameter constant-phase models. Tissue damping (p<<0.01), tissue elastance (p<0.02) and tissue hysteresivity (p<<0.01) provided significant separation between healthy and COPD groups. The authors concluded that the identified model values are sensitive to variations between healthy and COPD lungs. In a recent work from our group, Silva et al. (2011) used the parameters described in section 3.4.2 to evaluate the diagnostic potential of mono-frequency FOT in patients with severe COPD. The respiratory impedances were always significantly higher in COPD patients than in the control group (Figure 7; Zm, Zbi, Zi, Zbe and Ze; p<0.001). Similar comparisons revealed that Zpp (p<0.001) and ΔZrs (p<0.005) were also significantly increased in patients with COPD. It was observed that the respiratory impedance did not change significantly during the respiratory cycle in the control group (Figure 7; ANOVA, p=ns). Conversely, considering the cycle from the beginning of the inspiratory phase to the end of the expiratory phase, the Zrs values were significantly increased in the COPD group (ANOVA, p<0.005). COPD patients presented Ze significantly higher than Zi (p<0.001) and Zbe significantly higher than Zbi (p<0.001).

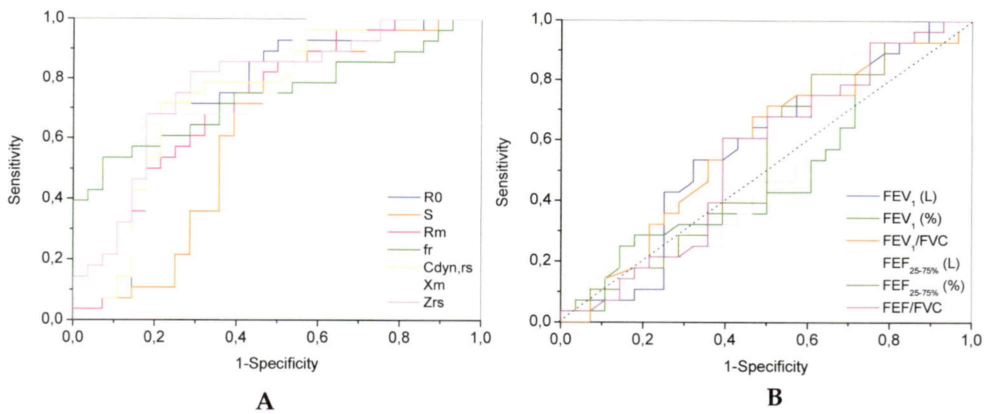


**Figure 6.** Receiver operating characteristic (ROC) curves for FOT (A) and spirometric parameters (B). The comparisons of these curves are described in Table 1.

According to the literature, ROC curves with AUCs between 0.50 and 0.70 indicate low diagnostic accuracy, AUCs between 0.70 and 0.90 indicate moderate diagnostic accuracy, and AUCs between 0.90 and 1.00 indicate high diagnostic accuracy (Swets et al. 2008; Golpe et al. 1999). An AUC > 0.80 is usually considered to be adequate for clinical use (Swets et al. 2008; Golpe et al. 1999). Taking these values into consideration, it was observed that Zm, Zi, Ze, Zbi, Zbe and Zpp represented highly accurate measurements. However, ΔZrs values do not attain adequate values for clinical use. Ze was the most suitable for correctly identifying the effects of COPD, with an AUC of 0.976, Se of 100% and a Sp of 90%. These promising results are consistent with the physiology involved (Silva et al. 2011) and suggest that the Zrs observed in different phases of the respiratory cycle may be useful in the detection of COPD. It is important to point out that the description of sensitivity, specificity and accuracy is dependent on the population studied and that the cited work was conducted in patients with severe airway obstruction. Studies in patients with mild and moderate airflow obstruction are still necessary to confirm this hypothesis. The role of FOT in the identification of "choke-points", where flow limitation occurs, was highlighted by Bates et al. (2011). Timmins et al. (2012) recently used single breath nitrogen washout and computerized tomography to study the relationship between airflow obstruction, emphysema extent and small-airways function in COPD. Single-frequency FOT (6 Hz) was also used to quantify EFL. The authors investigated 26 subjects with COPD and observed that the severity of COPD and of airflow obstruction are probably independently predicted by both small-airways disease and emphysema extent. Garcia et al. (2012) recently suggested that FOT is a promising solution for the problem of small-airways assessment and that FOT may represent a more sensitive test for early lung damage in smokers than the $FEV_1$.

| | $FEV_1$ *(L)* | $FEV_1$ (%) | $FEV_1$/FVC (%) | $FEF_{25-75\%}$ (L) | $FEF_{25-75\%}$ (%) | FEF/FVC (%) |
|---|---|---|---|---|---|---|
| R0 ($cmH_2O/L/s$) | 0.17±0.08* | 0.25±0.10* | 0.16±0.10 | 0.21±0.09* | 0.21±0.10* | 0.19±0.10 |
| **S** ($cmH_2O/L/s^2$) | 0.04±0.09 | 0.12±0.10 | 0.03±0.10 | 0.09±0.10 | 0.08±0.10 | 0.07±0.10 |
| Rm ($cmH_2O/L/s$) | 0.14±0.08 | 0.22±0.10* | 0.13±0.10 | 0.18±0.09* | 0.18±0.10 | 0.16±0.10 |
| fr (Hz) | 0.16±0.08* | 0.24±0.09** | 0.15±0.09 | 0.21±0.08* | 0.20±0.09* | 0.19±0.09* |
| Xm ($cmH_2O/L/s$) | 0.16±0.09 | 0.24±0.09** | 0.15±0.09 | 0.21±0.09* | 0.20±0.09* | 0.19±0.09* |
| Crs,dyn ($L/cmH_2O$) | 0.17±0.07* | 0.25±0.09** | 0.16±0.09 | 0.21±0.08** | 0.21±0.09* | 0.19±0.10* |
| Z4Hz ($cmH_2O/L/s$) | 0.21±0.08* | 0.29±0.10** | 0.20±0.10* | 0.25±0.09** | 0.25±0.10* | 0.23±0.10* |

**Table 1.** Differences and statistical significance in the diagnostic performances of FOT and spirometric parameters, calculated by the difference between AUCs. Positive values denote higher values of AUC in the FOT parameters. * $p<0.05$; ** $p<0.01$.

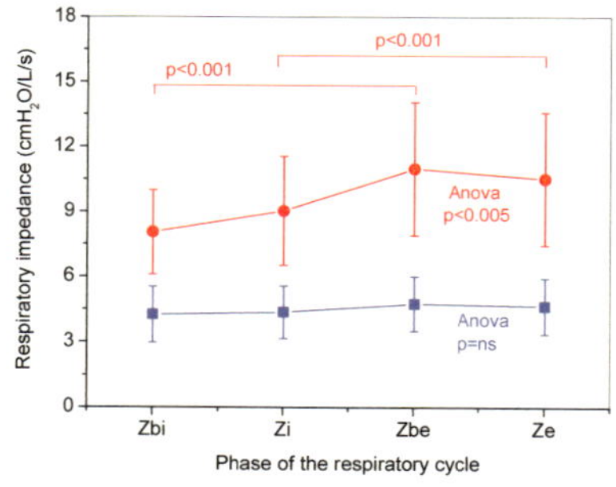


**Figure 7.** Mean Zrs values during the ventilatory cycle in COPD (red lines) and healthy subjects (blue lines). Adapted from Silva et al. 2011.

## 5. Diagnostic accuracy in patients classified by the GOLD

This section presents new results concerning the evaluation of the diagnostic accuracy of multi-frequency FOT in patients classified by the GOLD stage (GOLD, 2011). As far as we are aware, although it is a relevant technical and clinical question, there are no data in the literature concerning these evaluations.

### 5.1. Patients and methods

The study was performed in a control group formed by twenty healthy subjects and seventy-five outpatients with COPD, who were classified by spirometry according to the degree of airway obstruction as mild (n=20), moderate (n=20), severe (n=20), and very severe groups (n=15). According to GOLD orientation, these measurements were performed after the use of bronchodilator medication (GOLD, 2011). Bronchodilator administration was performed by means of the inhalation of four puffs of albuterol, each containing 100 μg, at 1-min intervals, using a spacer mouthpiece. The total dose administered was 400 μg. The exams were performed after 15 min of the bronchodilator administration. This study was approved by the Ethics Committee of the State University of Rio de Janeiro. Informed consent was obtained from all volunteers before inclusion in the study. The instrumentation and the measurement protocol used are described in section 3. The general characteristics of the evaluated subjects are given in Table 2. Volunteers in all five groups were comparable in age, weight and height, showing no statistically significant differences. In general, the spirometric parameters were highest in normal subjects and lowest in very severe patients, with the mild, moderate and severe subjects in between.

| | control | COPD | | | | p value |
|---|---|---|---|---|---|---|
| | (n=20) | I (n=20) | II (n=20) | III (n=20) | IV (n=15) | |
| Age (year) | 59.2 ± 14.4 | 54.8 ± 11.5 | 65.9 ± 9.6 | 66.0 ± 7.8 | 67.2 ± 8.9 | ns |
| Height (cm) | 159.5 ± 8.1 | 161.4 ± 7.3 | 165.0 ± 6.8 | 166.2 ± 9.0 | 159.9 ± 14.2 | ns |
| Weight (kg) | 63.0 ± 10.2 | 59.9 ± 8.9 | 59.4 ± 13.1 | 59.8 ± 12.5 | 57.7 ± 14.2 | ns |
| $FEV_1$ (L) | 2.5 ± 0.7 | 2.2 ± 0.5 | 1.6 ± 0.4 | 1.1 ± 0.2 | 0.7 ± 0.2 | <0.0001 |
| $FEF_1$ (%) | 106.5 ± 19.8 | 89.1 ± 13.9 | 63.4 ± 8.3 | 41.6 ± 4.1 | 27.8 ± 6.9 | <0.0001 |
| $VEF_1$/FVC | 85.8 ± 5.2 | 65.5 ± 5.5 | 51.9 ± 9.4 | 39.1 ± 8.2 | 35.8 ± 8.3 | <0.0001 |

**Table 2.** Biometric and spirometric characteristics of the investigated subjects. Ns: non-significant.

### 5.2. Results

The mean Rrs and Xrs curves for the different COPD classifications are shown in Figure 8. The increment in airway obstruction caused an increase in total resistance, mainly at the lower frequencies (4-16 Hz) and not at the higher ones, and resulted in a frequency-dependent Rrs. The mean Xrs decreased in proportion to the degree of airway obstruction, becoming more marked at lower frequencies, which resulted in an increase in the resonant frequency.

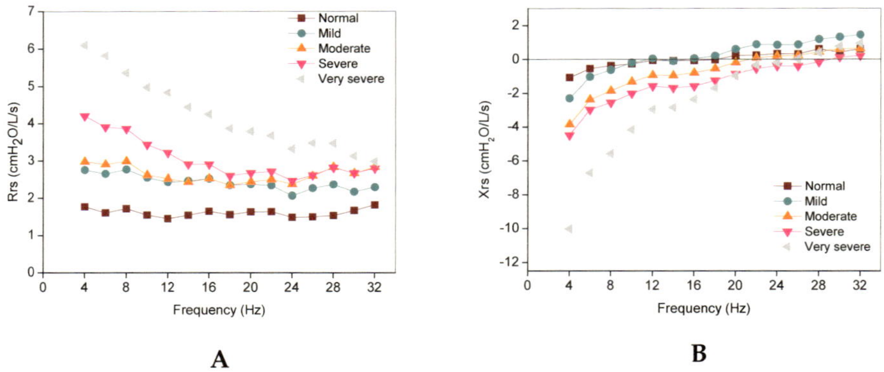


**Figure 8.** Mean values of resistance (A) and reactance (B) as a function of frequency in the control group and the different groups of COPD subjects.

Figure 9 shows the alterations of the resistive properties with advancing airway obstruction. All resistive and reactive parameters presented statistically significant differences ($p<0.0001$).

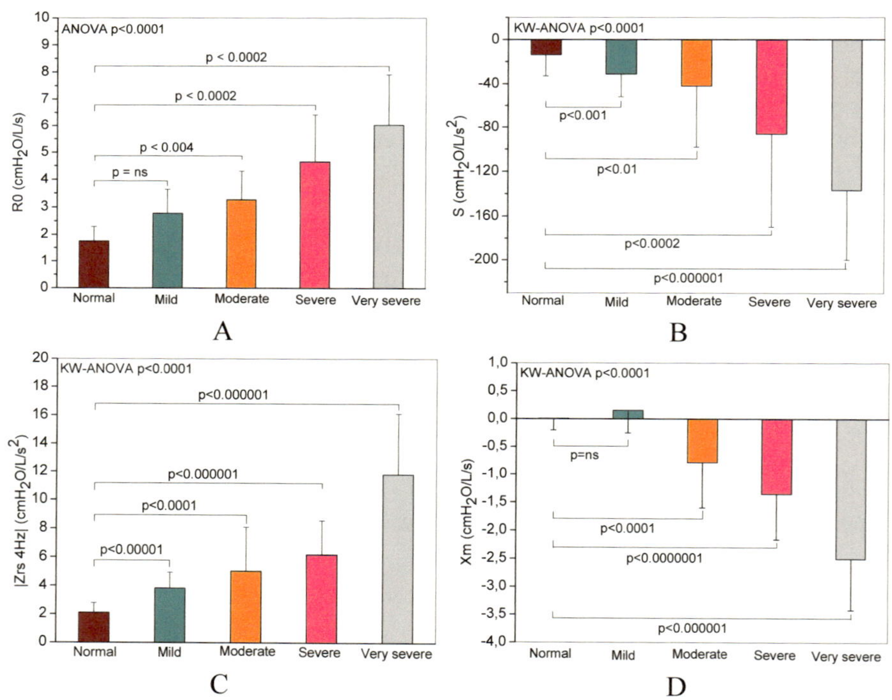


**Figure 9.** Changes in total respiratory resistance (R0; A), the slope of the resistive component of the respiratory impedance (S; B), mean respiratory reactance (Xm, C), and impedance modulus in 4 Hz ( |Zrs4Hz |; D) in control and COPD patients according to bronchial obstruction severity evaluated by the GOLD (2011) criteria.

The results of the evaluation of the clinical potential of the studied FOT indices are illustrated in the ROC curve presented in Figure 10. A complete description of the values of Se, Sp, area under the curve and the cut-off points is given in Table 3.

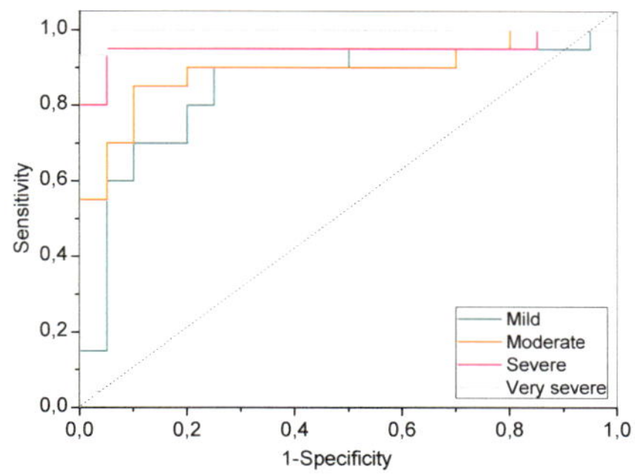


**Figure 10.** Receiver operating characteristic (ROC) curves for R0 obtained by comparing the control group and groups of COPD patients classified according to the GOLD (2011) criteria. Derived parameters are described in Table 3.

| | AUC | | | | Sensitivity (%) | | | | Specificity (%) | | | | Cut-off point | | | |
|---|---|---|---|---|---|---|---|---|---|---|---|---|---|---|---|---|
| | A | B | C | D | A | B | C | D | A | B | C | D | A | B | C | D |
| R0 ($cmH_2O/L/s$) | 0.85 | 0.89 | 0.95 | 1.00 | 90.0 | 85.0 | 95.0 | 100.0 | 75.0 | 90.0 | 95.0 | 95.0 | 1.91 | 2.14 | 2.53 | 2.53 |
| S ($cmH_2O/L/s^2$) | 0.81 | 0.74 | 0.85 | 0.99 | 75.0 | 65.0 | 80.0 | 100.0 | 90.0 | 95.0 | 95.0 | 95.0 | -26.32 | -37.52 | -49.58 | -41.18 |
| Xm ($cmH_2O/L/s$) | 0.61 | 0.89 | 1.00 | 1.00 | 50.0 | 75.0 | 95.0 | 100.0 | 85.0 | 95.0 | 100.0 | 100.0 | 0.16 | 0.28 | 0.47 | 1.52 |
| \|Zrs4Hz\| ($cmH_2O/L/s$) | 0.91 | 0.90 | 0.95 | 1.00 | 95.0 | 85.0 | 90.0 | 100.0 | 75.0 | 95.0 | 100.0 | 100.0 | 2.35 | 2.92 | 3.92 | 3.92 |

**Table 3.** Values of area under the curve (AUC), sensitivity (Se) and specificity (Sp) for the optimal cut-off points for the FOT indices in COPD patients presenting mild (A), moderate (B), severe (C) and very severe (D) airway obstruction. AUC: area under curve.

## 5.3. Respiratory impedance curves and derived parameters

Figure 8A shows that, in healthy subjects, the mean Rrs was approximately 2 $cmH_2O/L/s$ in the frequency range of 4-32 Hz. The mean Rrs is greater in patients with COPD than in healthy subjects, due mainly to a reduction in the airway lumen, which results in increased resistance to flow. The increase in R0 clearly identified these changes (Figure 9A). There is also an increase in the dependence of Rrs on frequency, as illustrated in Figures 8A and 9B. *X*rs tends to be more negative in COPD than in normal individuals at all frequencies (Figures 8B and 9D). The value |Zrs4Hz| is related to the total mechanical load of the respiratory system. Therefore, it may be associated with fatigue and breathlessness, which are important symptoms in predicting quality of life in COPD patients (GOLD, 2011). The changes in the resistive and elastic properties of COPD patients resulted in significant increases in |Zrs4Hz| (Figure 9C). The results described in Figures 8 and 9 are in agreement with the previous results described in section 4, providing additional evidence that FOT provides parameters that are consistent with the pathophysiological fundamentals involved in COPD.

### 5.4. FOT as a diagnostic test: sensitivity and specificity of FOT indices

ROC curves were developed in the 1950s to evaluate radio signals contaminated by noise. It was later observed that these curves are very useful in medical decision-making. These curves describe the probability of true-negative (specificity) versus the probability of false-positive (1-sensitivity) for various decision criteria. In this context, the larger the area under the curve (AUC), the more valid is considered the diagnostic test in comparison with the gold standard. As noted previously, some authors suggest that an area under the ROC curve >0.70 is considered adequate (Goedhart et al., 2005), while others (Swets et al., 2008; Golpe et al., 1999) consider 0.8 to be a good cut-off value for a useful discriminator for clinical use. According to the literature, ROC curves with AUCs between 0.90 and 1.00 indicate high diagnostic accuracy (Swets, 1988; Golpe et al., 1999). In the present analysis, we considered 0.8 to be the minimum value of the AUC for adequate diagnostic accuracy. As expected, the AUC increased with increasing respiratory changes (Figures 8, 9 and 10, Table 2). The smallest diagnostic value of the FOT parameters is presented in patients with mild airway obstruction. It is interesting to note that, even in this adverse situation, R0 and S were able to obtain adequate values of AUC. On the other hand, Xm did not reach adequate values for clinical use. Among all the studied parameters, |Zrs4Hz| was the best, showing a high diagnostic accuracy (AUC=0.91) with a Se of 95% and a Sp of 75% (Table 3). Adequate (R0, Xm) and highly accurate (|Zrs4Hz|) values of AUC were observed considering patients with moderate airway obstruction. The abnormal respiratory mechanics in COPD patients with severe airway obstruction were identified with high diagnostic accuracy by all of the studied FOT parameters (Table 3). Finally, all of the studied parameters provided an almost perfect diagnosis of patients in the group with very severe obstruction.

## 6. Some future directions

### 6.1. Clinical decision support systems based on machine learning algorithms to assist in the diagnosis of Chronic Obstructive Pulmonary Disease by forced oscillation

In the context of a diagnosis framework, the interpretation of resistance and reactance curves and of the derived parameters measured by the FOT require training and experience, and they represent a difficult task for the untrained pulmonologist. Methods based on machine learning (ML) have been widely used to develop classifiers. These systems can extract information from different classes of signals after having been trained to perform this specific task by learning from examples. This possibility raises the question of whether an ML-based approach to the analysis of FOT data can provide an efficient method to recognize COPD. In fact, only a few recent studies have addressed this question (Barruá et al., 2004; Barruá et al., 2005; Meratz et al., 2008). However, the cited studies used an Impulse

Oscillation System, which has differences from classical FOT, including data processing and the parameters used to interpret raw data (Mac Leod and Birch, 2001; Hellinkx et al., 2001; Ritz et al., 2002). Thus, to further elucidate this question, our group has investigated the development of a clinical decision support system based on ML algorithms to facilitate the diagnostic of COPD using FOT measurements. The first study was conducted using Artificial Neural Networks (ANN). The system was developed based on the results obtained in 15 normal subjects and 15 COPD patients (Amaral et al., 2010). Two training strategies and the performance of the resulting networks were evaluated by analyzing the diagnosis Se, Sp and accuracy. The proposed classifiers presented adequate performance (Se, Sp and accuracy>0.9), both in the total FOT parameters analyzed and in the reduced sets of FOT parameters. This result indicates that the ANN-based classifiers can help to facilitate the diagnosis of COPD by FOT (Amaral et al., 2010). On the basis of these promising results in the continuation of this work (Amaral et al., 2011), the methods described below were also investigated:

- Neuro-fuzzy classification (CNF);
- Linear Bayes Normal Classifier (LBNC);
- K Nearest Neighbor (KNN);
- Decision Tree (DT);
- Support Vectors Machines (SVM).

This second study included the examinations of 25 normal subjects and 25 patients with COPD. The training strategies of the ANN used previously were reevaluated, and new strategies were investigated. The performances of the resulting six classification algorithms were also analyzed for the determination of Se, Sp and diagnostic accuracy. The classifiers based on ANN, KNN and SVM presented the best performance, reaching values that allow a very accurate clinical diagnosis (Se≥87%, Sp ≥ 94% and AUC≥0.95), both in the total FOT parameters and in reduced sets of FOT parameters. Among all of the studied classifiers, the best performance was presented by KNN-based analysis (Se, Sp and accuracy = 1.00). This result was obtained using all parameters. The high accuracy obtained proved the feasibility of developing a system to support clinical decisions based on machine learning algorithms to simplify the diagnosis of COPD by FOT. More specifically, it shows that the best classifiers for this task are those based on RNA, KNN and SVM (Amaral et al., 2011).

## 6.2. Forced oscillation in telemedicine

The high prevalence of chronic respiratory diseases has led to an increasing demand for assistance services in recent years. This increase has introduced a gradual rise in the admission of patients (Murray and Lopez, 1997), increasing the financial burden. In addition, several COPD patients have difficulty accessing traditional health services due to the severe limitations that are associated with the disease in its advanced stages. To minimize these problems, health services using home care and telemedicine have been developed (Guo and Moulder, 2000; Demiris, 2004). Recently, the European Commission on Telemedicine (Commission of the European Communities, 2008) highlighted the potential of telehealth in the management of COPD and the pressing need for quality research in this field.

The ability of the FOT to measure respiratory impedance during spontaneous breathing could be useful for unsupervised monitoring of airway obstruction, resulting in great benefits to patients with COPD. However, the implementation of telemedicine services using FOT depends on the development of a dedicated instrument and protocol. Rigau et al. (2002) were the first to describe a portable FOT system for home care applications. The system allowed the online computation of Rrs and Xrs and of reliability indices at 5 Hz. The device was compared with a conventional FOT system using signals from 14 patients with chronic respiratory disease, showing results that virtually coincided with the ones computed with the reference conventional FOT system.

More recently, Dellacà et al. (2010) developed a FOT device for the home monitoring of Zrs, which transmits the data through the Internet. Its accuracy, stability and reliability were evaluated in a pilot study measuring the Zrs in the unsupervised self-measurements of five healthy subjects and 36 consecutive daily home measurements in one healthy subject and one COPD patient. The results of this pilot study demonstrate that unsupervised home monitoring of Zrs using the FOT yields accurate and reproducible data.

Telemedicine services using FOT hold the promise of improving the understanding and management of COPD and its exacerbation. They would also allow online interaction between the patient at home and the health provider, optimizing the follow-up monitoring of the disease and adjusting the treatment accordingly. Another contribution of this research would be to allow a daily monitoring of the variability in airway obstruction in patients with COPD. This possibility may provide new insights into the dynamics of the COPD airway obstruction, as described in the next section.

## 6.3. Contribution of forced oscillation to systems medicine and complexity measurements

Reductionism has been the predominant paradigm in the science of clinical medicine since Descartes and the Renaissance (Ahn et al., 2006). Although reductionism has been responsible for tremendous successes in modern medicine, there are indications that the approach has limitations, mainly when applied to chronic, complex diseases, such as COPD. Complex biological systems cannot be predicted by the sum of their parts alone, and an alternative and complementary explanation must be sought. One alternative explanation that has received much recent attention in respiratory medicine is the systems perspective (Kaminsky et al. 2011; Suki et al., 2011; Suki and Bates 2011; Frey et al., 2011) Rather than dividing a complex problem into its component parts, the systems perspective investigates the composite characteristics of a problem and evaluates the problem using computational and mathematical tools. Given the lung's highly complex structure and function, a systems biology approach to understanding the lung has been suggested as an ideal application of the systems perspective (Kaminsky et al., 2011).

In the particular case of respiratory physiology, it is now well recognized that respiratory functions often show signs of complexity, including fractal (Glenny, 2011; Nelson et al., 1990; Thamrin et al., 2010) and emergent (Glenny, 2011; Kaczka et al., 2011; Suki and Bates,

2011; Suki et al., 2011; Macklem, 2005) behavior. Other important characteristics include long-range fractal correlations (Frey et al., 2005) and power law distributions of the time series (Frey et al., 1998; Suki, 2002). These characteristics can contain useful and clinically relevant information (Thamrin and Stern, 2010), because complexity appears to be lost in the presence of an illness. Goldberger (Goldberger, 1997; Goldberger et al., 2002) proposed that the increased regularity of signals represents a 'decomplexification' characteristic of illness. According to this hypothesis, health is characterized by 'organized variability,' and disease is defined by decomplexification, increased regularity and a reduction in variability. In a more recent work, Vaillancourt and Newell (2002) proposed that disease may manifest with abnormally increased or decreased complexity.

Therefore, interest in using fluctuation analysis to characterize respiratory patterns has become widespread over the past five years (Frey et al., 2011; Thamrin and Stern, 2010; Veiga et al., 2011). Using these methods, Frey and colleagues (2005) investigated the use of the day-to-day fluctuations in peak expiratory flow (PEF) over 6 months in patients with chronic asthma to determine whether the future risk of exacerbation could be predicted from fluctuations in PEF. In a later study, Thamrin et al. (2009) showed that long-range correlations in daily PEF measurements were useful in predicting long-term treatment response. A telemedicine system based on forced oscillation associated with fluctuation analysis has the potential to provide valuable risk predictors on an individual basis that could help in evaluating treatment efficacy or disease control in COPD.

Fluctuation analysis has also the potential to contribute to the classification of COPD patients. Muskulus et al. (2010) recently investigated the hypothesis that short-term variability in respiratory impedance during continuous tidal breathing may distinguish COPD and asthma. These authors observed that stochastic approaches were not able to provide a clear discrimination. On the other hand, they were able to reliably distinguish COPD patients based on the data coming from a deterministic nonlinear system and using nonlinear time series analysis. This result suggests that the dynamics of the respiratory impedance provide relevant clinical information that may contribute to the differential diagnosis between COPD and asthma.

There are clear indications that the combination of reductionism and complex systems methodologies constitutes a powerful integrative approach to scientific research and clinical medicine. The unique ability of FOT to provide easy, noninvasive and detailed respiratory function data may offer a central contribution by allowing easy daily monitoring and by obtaining the large databases necessary for robust analysis.

## 7. Conclusions

This chapter initially provided a brief overview of COPD, FOT and their data interpretation. This was followed by a historical review that described the maturation of this method over the past five decades as a useful complement to spirometry in the diagnosis of smoking-induced respiratory changes. In addition to these previous studies, new results were presented concerning the diagnosis of COPD patients with different degrees of airway obstruction. These results, together with the results described in the historical review, provided clear evidence supporting the use of FOT as a versatile clinical tool, able to contribute to COPD prevention and diagnosis. However, routine clinical use of FOT has yet to gain full acceptance. Interest in the approach is growing and shows considerable promise, especially for detecting respiratory changes due to smoking in the initial stages and for implementing telemedicine services. However, realizing this promise remains a work in progress. It relies on the development of patient-friendly portable systems for screening smokers and for home-care, and on an appropriate mathematical description of lung mechanics. It is also necessary to overcome a number of challenging practical problems related to validation studies in a great number of subjects and developments in sophisticated mathematical methods for the interpretation of the dynamics of long impedance time series. The future of FOT as a diagnostic tool for smoking-related respiratory abnormalities is thus highly linked to the interdisciplinary work of engineers, physicians, mathematicians and physiologists.

## Author details

Alvaro Camilo Dias Faria, Karla Kristine Dames da Silva and Gerusa Marítmo da Costa
*Biomedical Instrumentation Laboratory,*
*Institute of Biology and Faculty of Engineering, Rio de Janeiro, Brazil*

Agnaldo José Lopes
*Pulmonary Function Laboratory, Faculty of Medical Sciences, Rio de Janeiro, Brazil*

Pedro Lopes de Melo
*Biomedical Instrumentation Laboratory,*
*Institute of Biology and Faculty of Engineering, Rio de Janeiro, Brazil*
*Clinical and Experimental Research Laboratory in Vascular Biology,*
*Institute of Biology, Rio de Janeiro, Brazil*

## Acknowledgement

The authors would like to thank the Brazilian Council of Research and Development (CNPq), the Rio de Janeiro State Foundation for Research (FAPERJ), and the Rio de Janeiro State University – PROCIÊNCIA Program for research grants.

## 8. References

Ahn AC, Tewari M, Poon CS, Phillips RS. The limits of reductionism in medicine: could systems biology offer an alternative? *PLoS Med* 3(6):e208, 2006.

Amaral, JLM, Faria, ACD, Lopes, AJ, Jansen, JM, Melo, PL. (2010). Automatic Identification of Chronic Obstructive Pulmonary Disease Based on Forced Oscillation Measurements and Artificial Neural Networks. *Proceedings of the 32nd Annual International Conference of the IEEE EMBS*, ISBN: 978-1-4244-4123-5, Buenos Aires, Argentina, August-September 2010.

Amaral, JL, Lopes, AJ, Jansen, JM, Faria, AC, Melo, PL. (2011). Machine learning algorithms and forced oscillation measurements applied to the automatic identification of chronic obstructive pulmonary disease. *Comput Methods Programs Biomed*, Vol. 105, No. 3, pp. 183-93, ISSN: 0169-2607.

American Thoracic Society/European Respiratory Society. (Oct 2004). Standards for diagnosis and management of patients with COPD. Available from: http://www.ers-education.org/pages/default.aspx?id=725.

Badia, JR, Farré, R, Montserrat, JM, Ballester, E, Hernández, L, Rotger, M, Rodriguez-Roisin, R, Navajas, D. (1998). Forced oscillation technique for the evaluation of severe sleep apnoea/hypopnoea syndrome: a pilot study. *Eur Respir J*, Vol. 11, pp. 1128-34, ISSN: 1399-3003.

Bates JHT, Irvin CG, Farré R, Hantos Z (2011). Oscillation Mechanics of the Respiratory System. *Compr Physiol*, vol. 1: pp. 1233-1272, ISSN: 9780470650714 0470650710.

Barúa, M, Nazeran, H, Nava, P, Granda, V, Diong, B. (2004). Classification of Pulmonary Diseases Based on Impulse Oscillometric Measurements of Lung Function Using Neural Networks. *Proceedings of the 26th Annual International Conference of the IEEE EMBS*, ISBN: 0-7803-8439-3, San Francisco, CA, USA September 2004.

Barúa, M, Nazeran, H, Nava, P, Diong, B, Goldman, M. (2005). Classification of Impulse Oscillometric Patterns of Lung Function in Asthmatic Children using Artificial Neural Networks. *Proceedings of the 27th Annual International Conference of the IEEE EMBS*, ISBN: 0-7803-8741-4, Shanghai, China, September 2005.

Boser, SR, Park, H, Perry, SF, Menache, MG, Green, FH. (2005). Fractal geometry of airway remodeling in human asthma. *Am J Respir Crit Care Med*, Vol. 172, pp. 817-823, ISSN: 1535-4970.

Brochard, L, Pelle, G, De Palmas, J, Brochard, P, Carre, A, Lorino, H, Half, A. (1987). Density and Frequency Dependence of Resistance in Early Airway Obstruction. *Am Rev Resp Dis*, Vol. 135, pp. 579-594, ISSN: 0003-0805.

Burrows, B, Knudson, RJ, Cline, MG, Lebowitz, MD. (1977). Quantitative Relationships between cigarette smoking and ventilatory function. *Am Rev Respir Dis*, Vol. 115, pp. 195-205, ISSN: 0003-0805.

Cauberghs, M, Van de Woestijne, KP. (1989). Effect of upper airway shunt and series properties on respiratory impedance measurements. *J Appl Physiol*, Vol. 66, No. 5, pp. 2274-2279, ISSN: 1522-1601.

Coe, CI, Watson, A, Joyce, H, Pride, NB. (1989). Effects of smoking on changes in respiratory resistance with increasing age. *Clin Sci*, Vol. 76, pp. 487-494, ISSN: 1470-8736.

Commission of the European Communities (Nov 4 2008), Communication from the Commission to the European Parliament, the Council, the European Economic and Social Committee and the Committee of the Regions on telemedicine for the benefit of patients, healthcare systems and society, In: *http://eur-lex.europa.eu/*, Available from: http://eur-lex.europa.eu/LexUriServ/LexUriServ.do?uri=COM:2008:0689:FIN:EN:PDF.

Crapo, RO, Jensen, RL, Hargreave, FE. (2003). Airway inflammation in COPD: physiological outcome measures and induced sputum. *Eur Respir J*, Vol. 21, Suppl. 41, pp. 19s-28s, ISSN: 1399-3003.

Croxton, TL, Weinmann, GG, Senior, RM, Hoidal, JR. (2002) Future research directions in chronic obstructive pulmonary disease. *Am J Respir Crit Care Med*, Vol. 165, pp. 838–844, ISSN: 1535-4970.

Dellacà, RL, Santus, P, Aliverti, A, Stevenson, N, Centanni, S, Macklem, PT, Pedotti, A, Calverley, PMA. (2004). Detection of expiratory flow limitation in COPD using the forced oscillation technique. *Eur Respir J*, Vo. 23, pp. 232-240, ISSN: 1399-3003.

Dellacà, RL, Rotger, M, Aliverti, A, Navajas, D, Pedotti, A, Farre, R. (2006). Noninvasive detection of expiratory flow limitation in COPD patients during nasal CPAP. *Eur Respir J*, Vol. 27, pp. 983-991, ISSN: 1399-3003.

Dellacà, RL, Duffy, N, Pompilio, PP, Aliverti, A, Koulouris, NG, Pedotti, A, Calverley, PM. (2007). Expiratory flow limitation detected by forced oscillation and negative expiratory pressure. *Eur Respir J*, Vol. 29, pp. 363-374, ISSN: 1399-3003.

Dellacà, RL, Gobbi, A, Pastena, M, Pedotti, A, Celli, B. (2010). Home monitoring of within-breath respiratory mechanics by a simple and automatic forced oscillation technique device. *Physiol Meas*, Vol. 31, No. 4, pp. N11-24, ISSN: 1361-6579.

Delavault, E, Saumon, G, Georges, R. (1980). Identification of transducer defect in respiratory impedance measurements by forced randon noise, correction of experimental data. *Resp. Physiol.*, vol. 40, pp. 107-117, ISSN: 1569-9048.

Demiris, G. (2004). Electronic home healthcare: concepts and challenges. Int J Electronic Healthcare, Vol. 1, No. 1, pp. 4-16, ISSN: 1741-8461.

Di Mango, AMGT, Lopes, AJ, Jansen, JM, Melo, PL. (2006). Changes in respiratory mechanics with increasing degrees of airway obstruction in COPD: Detection by Forced Oscillation Technique. *Resp Med*, Vol. 100, pp. 399-410, ISSN: 0954-6111.

Dubois, AB, Brody, AW, Lewis, DH, Burgess, BF Jr. (1956). Oscillation mechanics of lungs and chest in man. *J Appl Physiol*, Vol. 8, pp. 587-594, ISSN: 1522-1601.

Enright, PL, Crapo, RM. (2000). Controversies in the use of spirometry for early recognition and diagnosis of chronic obstructive pulmonary disease in cigarette smokers. *Clinics in Chest Medicine*: Chronic obstructive pulmonary disease 2000, 21(4): 645-652, ISSN: 0272-5231.

Faria, ACD, Lopes, AL, Jansen, JM, Lopes, PL. (2009). Evaluating the Forced Oscillation Technique in the Detection of Early Smoking-induced Respiratory Changes. *BioMed Eng Online*, Vol. 8, pp. 22, ISSN: 1475-925X.

Faria, ACD, Costa, AA, Lopes, AJ, Jansen, JM, Melo, PL. (2010). Forced oscillation technique in the detection of smoking-induced respiratory alterations: diagnostic accuracy and comparison with spirometry. *Clinics*, Vol. 65, No. 12, pp. 1295-1304, ISSN: 1807-5932.

Farré, R, Ferrer, M, Rotger, M, Torres, A, Navajas, D. (1998). Respiratory mechanics in ventilated COPD patients: Forced oscillation versus occlusion techniques. *Eur Respir J*, Vol. 12, pp. 170-176, ISSN: 1399-3003.

Farré, R, Gavela, E, Rotger, M, Ferrer, M, Roca, J, Navajas, D. (2000). Noninvasive assessment of respiratory resistance in severe chronic respiratory patients with nasal CPAP. *Eur Respir J*, Vol. 15, pp. 314-319, ISSN: 1399-3003.

Farré, R, Navajas, D, Rotger, M. (1986). Optical method for determining the frequency response of pressure measurement systems in respiratory mechanics. *Med & Biol Eng & Comput*, Vol. 24, pp. 78-82, ISSN: 0140-0118.

Farré, R, Peslin, R, Navajas, D, Gallina, C, SUKI, B. (1989). Analisys of the dynamic characteristics of pressure transducers for studying respiratory mechanics at high frequencies. *Med & Biol Eng & Comput*, Vol. 27, pp. 531-537, ISSN: 0140-0118.

Franken, H, Caubergs, M, Ringelhann, A, Clément, J, Woestijne, KP. (1985). Forced oscillation technique: comparison of two devices. *J Appl Physiol*, Vol. 59, No. 5, pp. 1654-1659, ISSN: 1522-1601.

Frey, U, Silverman, M, Barabasi, AL, Suki, B. (1998). Irregularities and power law distributions in the breathing pattern in preterm and term infants. *J Appl Physiol*, Vol. 85, pp. 789-797, ISSN: 1522-1601.

Frey, U, Brodbeck, T, Majumdar, A, Taylor, DR, Town, GI, Silverman, M, Suki, B. (2005). Risk of severe asthma episodes predicted from fluctuation analysis of airway function. *Nature*, Vol. 438, pp. 667–670, ISSN: 0028-0836.

Frey, U, Maksym, GN, Suki, B. (2011). Temporal Complexity in Clinical Manifestations of Lung Disease. *J Appl Physiol*, Vol. 110, No. 6, pp. 1723-31, ISSN: 1522-1601.

Garcia, G, Perez, T, Verbanck, S. (2012). Functional measurements of the peripheral airways in COPD. *Rev Mal Respir*, Vol. 29, No. 2, pp. 319-27, ISSN: 0761-8425.

Glenny, RW. (2011). Emergence of matched airway and vascular trees from fractal rules. *J Appl Physiol*, Vol. 110, No. 4, pp. 1119-29, ISSN: 1522-1601.

Goedhart, DM, Zanen, P, Kerstjens, HAM, Lammers, JWJ. (2005). Discriminating asthma and COPD based on bronchodilator data: an improvement of the methods. *Physiol Meas*, Vol. 26, pp. 1115-1123, ISSN: 1361-6579.

GOLD - Global initiative for chronic obstructive lung disease. (2011): Global strategy for the diagnosis, management and prevention of Chronic Obstructive Pulmonary Disease – Revised 20111, In: *www.goldcopd.org*, Accessed June 1, 2011, Available from: < http://www.goldcopd.org/uploads/users/files/GOLD_Report_2011_Feb21.pdf>.

Goldberger, AL. (1997). Fractal variability versus pathologic periodicity: complexity loss and stereotypy in disease. *Perspect Biol Med*, Vol. 40, pp. 543-561, ISSN: 1529-8795.

Goldberger, AL, Amaral, LA, Hausdorff, JM, Ivanov, P, Peng, CK, Stanley, HE. (2002). Fractal dynamics in physiology: alterations with disease and aging. *Proc Natl Acad Sci USA*, Vol. 99, Suppl. 1, pp. 2466–2472, ISSN: 1091-6490.

Golpe, R, Jimenéz, A, Carpizo, R, Cifrian, JM. (1999). Utility of home oximetry as a screening test for patients with moderate and severe symptoms of obstructive sleep apnea. Sleep, Vol. 22, No. 7, pp. 932-937, ISSN: 1550-9109.

Grimby, G, Takishima, T, Graham, W, Macklem, P, Mead, J. (1968). Frequency dependence of flow resistance in patients with obstructive lung disease. J Clin Invest, Vol. 47, pp. 1455-1465, ISSN: 1558-8238.

Guo, Z, Moulder, JC. (2000). An internet based telemedicine system. *Proceedings of the IEEE EMBS International Conference*, ISBN: 0-7803-6449-X, Arlington, VA, USA, November 2000.

Guo, YF, Sun, TY, Hermann, F, Janssens, JP. (2005). Comparison or airway resistance measurements by the forced oscillation technique and the interrupter technique for detecting chronic obstructive pulmonary disease in elderly patients. *Chin Med J*, Vol. 118, pp. 1921-24, ISSN: 0366-6999.

Hayes, DA, Pimmel, RL, Fullton, JM, Bromberg, PA. (1979). Detection of Respiratory Mechanical Dysfunction by Forced Randon Noise Impedance Parameters. *Am Rev Resp Dis*, Vol. 120: pp. 1095-1099, ISSN: 0003-0805.

Hellinckx, J, Cauberghs, M, De Boeck, K, Demedts, M. (2001). Evaluation of impulse oscillation system: comparison with forced oscillation technique and body plethysmography. *Eur Respir J*, Vol. 18, pp. 564-70, ISSN: 1399-3003.

Ionescu, C, Derom, E, De Keyser, R. (2010). Assessment of respiratory mechanical properties with constant-phase models in healthy and COPD lungs. *Comput Methods Programs Biomed*, Vol. 97, No. 1, pp. 78-85, ISSN: 0169-2607.

Janssens, JP, Nguyen, MC, Herrmann, FR, Michel, JP. (2001). Diagostic value of respiratory impedance measurements in elderly subjects. *Respir Med*, Vol. 95, No. 5, pp. 415-22, ISSN: 0954-6111.

Johnson, MK, Birch, M, Carter, R. (2005). Use of reactance to estimate transpulmonary resistance. *Eur Resp J*, Vol. 25, No. 6, pp. 1061-1069, ISSN: ISSN: 1399-3003.

Johnson, MK, Birch, M, Carter, R, Kinsella, J, Stevenson, RD. (2007). Measurement of physiological recovery from exacerbation of chronic obstructive pulmonary disease using within-breath forced oscillometry. *Thorax*, Vol. 62, No. 4, pp. 299-306, ISSN: 1468-3296.

Kaczka, DW, Ingenito, EP, Body, SC, Duffy, SE, Mentzer, SJ, DeCamp, MM, Lutchen, KR. (2001). Inspiratory lung impedance in COPD: Effects of PEEP and immediate impact of lung volume reduction surgery. *J Appl Physiol*, Vol. 90, pp. 1833-1841, ISSN: 1522-1601.

Kaczka, DW, Lutchen, KR, Hantos, Z. (2011). Emergent behavior of regional heterogeneity in the lung and its effects on respiratory impedance. *J Appl Physiol*, Vol. 110, No. 5, pp. 1473-1481, ISSN: 1522-1601.

Kaczka, DW, Dellacá, RL. (2011). Oscillation Mechanics of the Respiratory System: Applications to Lung Disease. *Critical Reviews™ in Biomedical Engineering*, Vol. 39, No. 4, pp. 337–359, ISSN: 0278-940X.

Kaminsky, DA, Irvin, CG. (2001) New insights from lung function. *Curr Opin Allergy Clin Immunol,* Vol. 1, pp. 205-209, ISSN: 1473-6322.

Kaminsky DA, Irvin, CG, Sterk, PJ. (2011). Complex Systems in Pulmonary Medicine: A Systems Biology Approach to Lung Disease. *J Appl Physiol*, Vol. 110, No. 6, pp. 1716-1722, ISSN: 1522-1601.

Kjeldgaard, JM, Hyde, RW, Speers, DM, Reichert, WW. (1976). Frequency dependence of total respiratory resistance in early airway disease. *Am Rev Resp Dis*, Vol. 114, pp. 501-508, ISSN: 0003-0805.

LaPrad, AS, Lutchen, KR. (2008). Respiratory impedance measurements for assessment of lung mechanics: Focus on asthma. *Respir Physiol Neurobiol*, Vol. 163, pp. 64-73, ISSN: 1569-9048.

Lándsér, FJ. Nagels, J, Demedts, M, Billiet, L, Woestijne, KP. (1976). A new method to determine frequency characteristics of the respiratory system. *J Appl Physiol*, Vol. 41, No. 1, pp. 101 – 106, ISSN: 1522-1601.

Làndsér, FJ, Clément, J, Van de Woestijne, KP. (1982). Normal values of Total Respiratory Resistance and Reactance Determined by Forced Oscillations: Influence of Smoking. *Chest*, Vol. 81, No. 5, pp. 586-590, ISSN: 1931-3543.

Lemes, LNA, Melo, PL. (2003). Forced Oscillation Technique in the sleep apnea/hypopnea syndrome: identification of respiratory events and nasal continuous positive airway pressure titration. *Physiological Measurement*, Vol. 24, No. 1, pp.11-26, ISSN: 1361-6579.

Ljung, L. (1987). *System identification: Theory for the user*. (First Edition), Prentice-Hall Inc.,ISBN: 0-13-881640-9, Londres.

Lorino, AM, Zerah, F, Marinette, A, Harf, A, Lorino, H. (1997). Respiratory resistive impedance in obstructive patients: linear regression analysis *vs* viscoelastic modeling. *Eur Respir J*, Vol.10, pp. 150-155, ISSN: 1399-3003.

Macklem, PT. (2005). Complexity and respiration: a matter of life and death, In: *Physiologic basis of respiratory disease*, Hamid Q, Shannon J, Martin J, editors, pp. (605-609), Hamilton, ON, Canada, BC Decker, Retrieved from <http://web.squ.edu.om/med-Lib/MED_CD/E_CDs/Physiology%20basis%20of%20Respiratory%20Disease/startme.pdf.

Macleod, D, Birch, M. (2001). Respiratory input impedance measurements: forced oscillation methods. *Med Biol Eng Comput*, Vol. 39, pp. 505-516, ISSN: 0140-0118.

Marchal, F, Hall, GL. (2010). Forced oscillation technique. *Eur Respir*, Vol. 47, pp. 121-136, ISSN: 1399-3003.

Melo PL, Werneck MM, Giannella-Neto A. (2000). A new impedance spectrometer for scientific and clinical studies of the respiratory system. *Rev Sci Instrum*, Vol. 71, pp. 2867-2872, ISSN: 1089-7623.

Meraz, E, Nazeran, H, Goldman, M, Nava, P, Diong, B. (2008). Impulse Oscillometric Features of Lung Function: Towards Computer-Aided Classification of Respiratory Diseases in Children. *Preceedings of the 30th Annual International IEEE EMBS Conference*, ISBN: 978-1-4244-1815-2, Vancouver, British Columbia, Canada, August 2008.

Michaelson, ED, Grassman, ED, Peters, WR. (1975). Pulmonary mechanics by spectral analysis of forced random noise. *J Clin Invest*, Vol. 56, No. 5, pp. 1210-30, ISSN: 0021-9738.

Murray, CJL, Lopez A. (1997). Global mortality, disability, and the contribution of risk factors: Global Burden of Disease Study. *Lancet*, Vol. 349, pp. 1436-1442, ISSN: 0140-6736.

Muskulus, M, Slats, AM, Sterk, PJ, Verduyn-Lunel, S. (2010). Fluctuations and determinism of respiratory impedance in asthma and chronic obstructive pulmonary disease. *J Appl Physiol*, Vol. 109, No. 6, pp. 1582-91, ISSN: 1522-1601.

Navajas, D, Farré, R. (2001). Forced oscillation assessment of respiratory mechanics in ventilated patients. *Critical Care*, Vol. 5, pp. 3–9, ISSN: 1364-8535.

Navajas, D, Farré, R. (2001). Forced oscillation technique: from theory to clinical applications. *Monaldi Arch Chest Dis*, Vol. 56, No. 6, pp. 55-562, ISSN: 1122-0643.

Nelson, TR, West, BJ, Goldberger, AL. (1990). The fractal lung: universal and species-related scaling patterns. *Experientia*, Vol. 46, pp. 251–254, 1990, ISSN: 0014-4754.

Oostveen, E, MacLeod, D, Lorino, H, Farré, R, Hantos, Z, Desager, K, Marchal, F. (2003). The forced oscillation technique in clinical practice: Methodology, recommendations and future developments. *Eur Respir J*, Vol. 22, pp. 1026-1041, ISSN: 1399-3003.

Pasker, HG, Schepers, R, Clément, J, Van De Woestijne, KP. (1996). Total respiratory measured by means of the forced oscillation technique in subjects with and without respiratory complaints. *Eur Respir J*, Vol. 9, pp.131-139, ISSN: 1399-3003.

Peslin, R, Hannhart, B, Pino, J. (1981). Mechanical Impedance of The Chest in Smokers and Non-smokers. *Bull Europ Physiopath Resp*, Vol. 17, pp. 93-115, ISSN: 0395-3890.

Peslin, R, Fredberg JJ. (1986). Oscillation mechanics of the respiratory system. In: *Handbook of physiology*, Vol. 3, part I. Am. Physiol. Soc., (First Edition), Bethesda, Maryland, sect. 3.

Peslin, R, Marchal, F, Duvivier, C, Ying, Y, Gallina, C. (1991). Evaluation of a modified head generator for respiratory impedance measurements. *Eur Respir Rev*, Vol. 1, No. 3, pp. 140-145, ISSN: 1600-0617.

Pride, NB. (1992) Forced oscillation technique for measuring mechanical properties of the respiratory system. *Thorax*, Vol. 47, pp. 317-320, ISSN: 1468-3296.

Pelle, G, Lorino, AM, Mariette, C, Harf, A. (1986). Microcomputer-based system to calculate respiratory impedance from forced randon noise data. *Med & Biol Eng & Comput*, Vol. 24, pp. 541-544, ISSN: 0140-0118.

Postma, DS, Brusselle, G, Bush, A, Holloway, JW. (2012). I have taken my umbrella, so of course it does not rain. *Thorax*, Vol. 67, No. 1, pp. 88-9, ISSN: 1468-3296.

Pintelon, R, Schoukens, J. (2001). *System Identification: A Frequency Domain Approach*. IEEE Press, (First Edition), ISBN: 0780360001, Piscataway, NJ.

Polkey, MI, Farré, R, Dinh-Xuan, AT. (2004). Respiratory monitoring: revisiting classical physiological principles with new tools. *Eur Resp J*, Vol. 24, pp. 718-719, ISSN: 1399-3003.

Rigau, J, Farre´, R, Roca, J, Marco, S, Herms, A, Navajas, D. (2002). A portable forced oscillation device for respiratory home Monitoring. *Eur Respir J*, Vol. 19, pp. 146–150, ISSN: 1399-3003.

Ritz, T, Dahme, B, Dubois, AB, Folgering, H, Fritz, GK, Harver, A, Kotses, H, Lehrer, PM, Ring, C, Steptoe, A, van de Woestijnek, KP. (2002). Guidelines for mechanical lung function measurements in psychophysiology. *Psychophysiology,* Vol. 39, pp. 546–567, ISSN: 1469-8986.

Silva, KKD, Lopes, AJ, Jansen, JM, Melo, PL. (2011). Within Total inspiratory and expiratory impedance in patients with severe chronic obstructive pulmonary disease. *Clinics*, Vol. 66, No. 12, pp. 2085-2091, ISSN: 1807-5932.

Slats, AM, Janssen, K, van Schadewijk, A, van der Plas, DT, Schot, R, van den Aardweg, JG, de Jongste, JC, Hiemstra, PS, Mauad, T, Rabe, KF, Sterk, PJ. (2007). Bronchial inflammation and airway responses to deep inspiration in asthma and chronic obstructive pulmonary disease. *Am J Respir Crit Care Med*, Vol. 15, No. 176(2), pp. 121-8, ISSN: 1535-4970.

Souza, CS, Mesquita Jr, JA, Melo, PL. (2008). A novel system using the forced Oscillations Technique for the biomechanical analysis of swallowing. *Technology and Health Care*, Vol. 16, No. 5, pp. 331-341, ISSN: 0928-7329.

Suki, B. (2002). Fluctuations and power laws in pulmonary physiology. *Am J Respir Crit Care Med*, Vol. 166, pp. 133–137, ISSN: 1535-4970.

Suki, B, Bates, JH. (2011). Emergent behavior in lung structure and function. *J Appl Physiol*, Vol. 110, No. 4, pp. 1109-10, ISSN: 1522-1601.

Suki, B, Bates, JH. (2011). Lung tissue mechanics as an emergent phenomenon. *J Appl Physiol*, Vol. 110, No. 4, pp. 1111-1118, ISSN: 1522-1601.

Suki, B, Bates, JHT, Frey, U. (2011). Complexity and Emergent Phenomena, In: *Comprehensive Physiology*, Wiley, pp. 995-1029, Retrieved from < http://www.comprehensivephysiology.com/WileyCDA/CompPhysArticle/refId-c100022.html> .

Swets, JA. (1988). Measuring the accuracy of diagnostic systems. *Science*, Vol. 240, pp. 1285–1293, ISSN: 1095-9203.

Thamrin, C, Stern, G, Strippoli, M, Kuehni, C, Suki, B, Taylor, D, Frey, U. (2009). Fluctuation analysis of lung function as a predictor of long-term response to beta agonists. *Eur Respir J*, Vol. 33, pp. 486-493, ISSN: 1399-3003.

Thamrin, C, Stern, G. (2010). New methods: what do they tell us? Fluctuation analysis of lung function. *Eur Respir Mon*, Vol. 47, pp. 310–324, ISSN 1025-448x.

Thamrin, C, Stern, G, Frey, U. (2010). Fractals for physicians. *Paediatr Respir Rev*, Vol. 11, No. 2, pp. 123-31, ISSN: 1526-0542.

Timmins, SC, Diba, C, Farrow, CE, Schoeffel, RE, Berend, N, Salome, CM, King, GG. (2012). The relationship between airflow obstructions, emphysema extent and small airways function in COPD. *Chest*, in press, ISSN: 1931-3543.

Vaillancourt, DE, Newell, KM. (2002). Changing complexity in human behavior and physiology through aging and disease. *Neurobiol Aging*, Vol. 23, No. 1, pp. 1-11, ISSN: 0197-4580.

Van Noord, JA, Clément, J, Van de Woestijne, KP, Demedts, M. (1991). Total Respiratory Resistanse and Reactance in Patients with Asthma, Chronic Bronchitis and Emphysema. *Am Rev Resp Dis*, Vol. 143: pp. 922-927, ISSN: 0003-0805.

Veiga, J, Lopes, AJ, Jansen, JM, Melo, PL. (2011). Airflow pattern complexity and airway obstruction in asthma. *J Appl Physiol*, Vol. 111, No. 2, pp. 412-419, ISSN: 1522-1601.

WHO - World Health Organization. (March 2012). Burden of COPD. Available form: <http:// http://www.who.int/respiratory/copd/burden/en/>.

Wouters, EF, Lándsér, FJ, Polko, AH, Visser, BF. (1992). Impedance measurement during air and helium-oxygen breathing before and after salbutamol in COPD patients. *Clin Exp Pharmacol Physiol*, Vol. 19, No. 2, pp. 95-101, ISSN: 1440-1681.

Yang, SC, Yang, SP. (2002). Bronchial Responsiveness and Lung Function Related to Cigarette Smoking and Smoking Cessation. *Chang Gung Med J*, Vol. 25, pp. 645-655, ISSN: 2072-0939.

Section 4

# Medical Electronics and Signal Processing

Chapter 14

# Low-Voltage, Low-Power $V_t$ Independent Voltage Reference for Bio-Implants

Paulo Cesar Crepaldi, Tales Cleber Pimenta,
Robson Luiz Moreno and Leonardo Breseghello Zoccal

Additional information is available at the end of the chapter

http://dx.doi.org/10.5772/39231

## 1. Introduction

Microelectronics has become a powerful tool of electronic systems for biomedical applications. In recent years, integrated circuits are being fabricated with large densities and endowed with intelligence. The reliability of these systems has been increasing and the costs have been reducing. The interaction between medicine and technology, as it is the case of microelectronics and biosensor materials, allows the development of diagnosing devices capable of monitoring pathogens and diseases. The design of sensors, signal conditioners and processing units aim to place the whole system in the patient or, even more desirable, implanted, where it becomes a Lab-on-Chip and/or a Point-of-Care device (Colomer-Farrarons et al., 2009). Once an implanted device becomes part of a biological data acquisition system, it must meet important constraints, such as reduced size, low power consumption and the possibility of being powered by an RF link, thus operating as a passive RFID tag (Landt. J, 2005).

The low power restriction is extremely important to the patient safety in order to avoid local heating and consequently possible tissue damage. It also limits the power of RF transmitter that can, as well, induce dangerous electromagnetic fields – EMF (large current density in the body tissue surrounding the implant). The EMF risks can be extended to the implanted device itself such as malfunction (undesirable lack of action, erroneous action and hazardous action) and even, permanent damage.

The focus of this chapter is to discuss the implementation of a CMOS voltage reference and the boundary conditions, including the use of a low cost CMOS process (0.35 TSMC for instance), low-voltage low-power operation and simple circuit topology.

## 2. Typical implanted device as a smart biological sensor

A typical CMOS front-end architecture for an in-vivo Biomedical Implanted Device – BID is shown in Figure 1. The system consists, basically, of the sensitive biological element, the transducer or detector element and its associate electronics and signal processing, and the RF link to establish a communication with the external unit. The combination of the implanted device, the local wireless link and a communication network results in a Wireless Biosensor Network (WBSN) (Guennoun, et al., 2008).

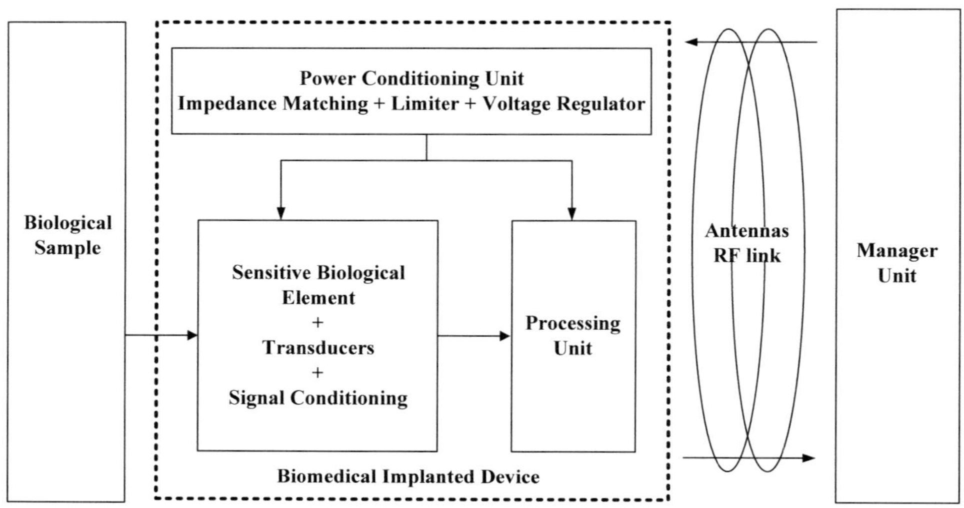


**Figure 1.** Typical Implanted Biomedical Device acting as a RFID Tag.

Linear systems based on semiconductor devices demand a stable power supply voltage for proper operation. Fluctuations on the input line voltage, load current and temperature variations may cause the circuit to deviate from its optimum operation bias point and even loose its linearity. Therefore, the power supply topology must assure minimum impacts on the linearity under those variations (Crepaldi et al., 2010). The impact of temperature variations in implantable devices is minimized once the body temperature is kept stable at approximately 37°C by an efficient biological feedback system (Mackowiak et al., 1992). Even in the presence of a disease or during a surgery proceeding, the body temperature suffers from just a few Celsius degrees variation.

As can be seen on Figure 1, a Voltage Regulator is part of the power conditioning unit. It is responsible to provide a stable voltage to the sensors/transducers and their associated electronics.

The classic topologies designed to provide stable power supply voltage are the linear and the switched voltage regulators. Switched regulators present a complex topology, mainly due to its control systems, and generally require more power consumption and larger silicon area than linear ones. Additionally they generate more noise at the regulated output due to its inerently switching operation (Rincon-Mora & Allen, 1998).

The low-dropout (LDO) voltage regulator is one of the most popular power converter used in power management and it is extremelly suitable for implanted systems. This kind of regulator requires a voltage reference circuit with a good Process-Voltage-Temperature (PVT) tolerance, generally achieved by Bandgap references. There are alternative circuits capable of obtaining low-voltage and high-accuracy, nevertheless some of those approaches may require components not readily available in CMOS technology and may require additional fabrications steps. Bandgap references based on weak inversion operation are a promising trend in biomedical applications (Roknsharifi et al., 2001; Magnelli et al., 2011). Since the reference is intended to be used in an implanted device, the temperature range is narrow and therefore it is not taken into account. The reference voltage Power Supply Rejection Ratio (PSRR) and process dependence are the main concerns.

## 3. Voltage reference

Figure 2 shows the voltage reference suitable for umplented devices. Transistors $M_1$ and $M_2$ form the composite structure (Ferreira & Pimenta, 2006). This kind of arragement represents the key feature for low-voltage operation, and along with low current operation (in the range of nA), the circuit provides low power operation. The voltage reference is obtained at $M_2$ drain and it corresponds to its $V_{DS}$ voltage. The current $I_D$ is be fixed at tenths of nA in order to reduce the total power consumption, as stated. Also, it is desirable to have the power supply reduced to a minimum, respecting, however, the corner process.

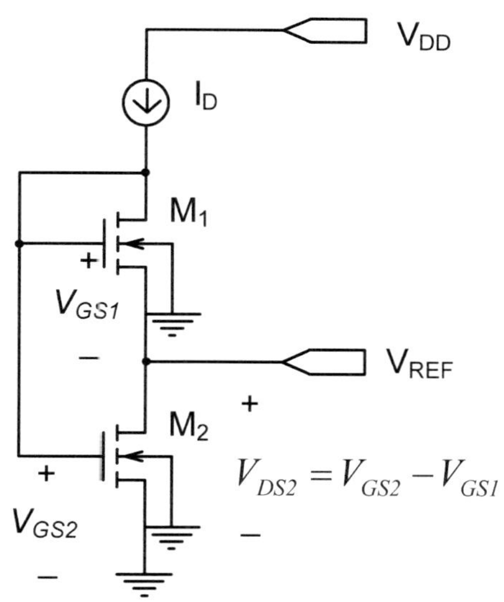


**Figure 2.** Voltage Reference Basic Topology.

If the MOS transistors are biased in the sub-threshold region, the drain current is given by equation (1). This current is based on the channel diffusion current referred to voltage source. It is a consensus formulation among EKV, ACM and BSIM3v3 models. $I_S$ is the weak inversion characteristic current, $T$ is the absolute temperature, $n$ is the slope factor in weak inversion (typically 1.3), $k$ is the Boltzmann constant, $(W/L)$ is the transitor geometric aspect ratio, $V_{TH}$ is the threshold voltage and $q$ is the charge of the electron.

$$I_{DS} = I_S\left(\frac{W}{L}\right)exp\left(\frac{V_{GS}-V_{TH}}{\frac{nkT}{q}}\right)\left[1-exp\left(-\frac{V_{DS}}{\frac{kT}{q}}\right)\right] \tag{1}$$

Considering transistor $M_2$ operating in the saturation region, equation (1) can be simplified for $V_{DS}$ values that are larger than the thermal equivalent voltage $(kT/q)$. At body temperature, approximately 310K, $(kT/q)$ can be set to 26.7mV, so for an 80mV at $V_{DS}$ (3 times larger) the (*1-exp*) term in equation (1) can be neglected and the drain current is expressed as:

$$I_{DS} = I_S\left(\frac{W}{L}\right)exp\left(\frac{V_{GS}-V_{TH}}{\frac{nkT}{q}}\right); \quad V_{DS} \geq 3\frac{kT}{q} \approx 80mV@T = 310K \tag{2}$$

The current $I_S$ is the same for transistors $M_1$ and $M_2$ since it is a function of process parameters. $V_{REF}$ is obtained by considering that $M_1$ and $M_2$ drain currents ($I_{DS}$) are also equal.

$$\frac{I_{DS}(M1)}{I_{DS}(M2)} = \frac{I_S\left(\frac{W}{L}\right)_{M1} exp\left(\frac{V_{GS1}-V_{TH1}}{\frac{nkT}{q}}\right)}{I_S\left(\frac{W}{L}\right)_{M2} exp\left(\frac{V_{GS2}-V_{TH2}}{\frac{nkT}{q}}\right)} = 1 \tag{3}$$

By inspection of Figure 2 it is possible to establish a relationship between the drain source voltage of M2 and the gate voltages of M1 and M2, given as:

$$V_{DS2} = V_{GS2} - V_{GS1} \tag{4}$$

By substituting (4) into (3), $V_{DS2}$ is given as:

$$V_{DS2} = \frac{nkT}{q} ln\left[\frac{\left(\frac{W}{L}\right)_{M1}}{\left(\frac{W}{L}\right)_{M2}}\right] - V_{TH1} + V_{TH2} \tag{5}$$

Transistor $M_2$ has a nominal threshold voltage ($V_{TH0}$) but $M_1$ suffer from body effect and, consequently, its threshold voltage should be adjusted by:

$$V_{TH1} = V_{TH0} + \gamma\left(\sqrt{2\Phi_F + V_{SB}} - \sqrt{2\Phi_F}\right) \tag{6}$$

where $\gamma$ is the body factor coefficient and $2\Phi_F$ (≈600mV) is the Fermi potential. Notice that $V_{SB}$ (bulk-source potential) is equal to $M_2$ drain source voltage or, in other words, it is equal to $V_{REF}$. The following approximation (Burington, 1973). can be used, if $(V_{REF})^2 << (2\Phi_F)^2$.

$$\begin{aligned} \sqrt{a+x} &= \sqrt{a} + \frac{x}{2\sqrt{a}}; \quad a^2 >> x^2 \\ \sqrt{2\Phi_F + V_{REF}} &= \sqrt{2\Phi_F} + \frac{V_{REF}}{2\sqrt{2\Phi_F}}; \quad V_{REF}{}^2 << (2\Phi_F)^2 \end{aligned} \tag{7}$$

By combining (5), (6) and (7), the reference voltage is given as:

$$V_{REF} = \frac{n\frac{kT}{q} ln\left[\frac{\left(W/L\right)_{M1}}{\left(W/L\right)_{M2}}\right]}{1 + \frac{\gamma}{2\sqrt{2\Phi_F}}} \tag{8}$$

Considering that (Tsividis, 1999):

$$1 + \frac{\gamma}{2\sqrt{2\Phi_F}} = n \tag{9}$$

The resulting equation for the reference voltage is:

$$V_{REF} = \frac{kT}{q} ln\left[\frac{\left(W/L\right)_{M1}}{\left(W/L\right)_{M2}}\right] \tag{10}$$

As can be observed, the reference voltage does not depend on MOS transistors threshold voltages and its value is adjusted by the geometric aspect ratio between the M1 and M2. The threshold voltage is largely affected by process variations (corners). For instance, in TSMC 0.35μm technology, the 3σ deviation from typical conditions can be as large as 20%.

Furthermore, the operation in the subthreshold region (or weak inversion) provides promotes an additional feature for the circuit, which is the low-voltage and low-power topology (Bero & Nyathi, 2006; Nomani et al., 2010; Ueno et al., 2006).

### 3.1. $V_{REF}$ range values

The minimum $V_{REF}$ value is determined by the approximation that leads to eq. (2). The maximum value is determined by the approximation that leads to eq. (7) and Table I shows the relative error at different values of $V_{REF}$.

| $V_{REF}$ [mV] | $\sqrt{2\Phi_F + V_{REF}}$ | $\sqrt{2\Phi_F} + \frac{V_{REF}}{2\sqrt{2\Phi_F}}$ | Relative Error (%) |
|---|---|---|---|
| 80 | 0.825 | 0.826 | 0.196 |
| 100 | 0.837 | 0.839 | 0.297 |
| 120 | 0.849 | 0.852 | 0.416 |
| 140 | 0.860 | 0.865 | 0.550 |
| 160 | 0.872 | 0.878 | 0.699 |

**Table 1.** $V_{REF}$ Relative Error for eq. (7) approximation.

For this project, it is adopted 100mV for $V_{REF}$. This value is larger than $3(kT/q)$ and represents an error of less than 0.5%, as stated in Table I. Besides, it is an "exact" value to be used in the voltage regulator to obtain other reference values.

### 3.2. $V_{REF}$ temperature impact

Although the proposed circuit is intended to be used in a temperature controlled environment, a temperature analysis is performed, and it shows a linear behavior. Although it is an important result, the implanted biomedical system could use any calibration method to compensate the process corners deviations. The temperature behavior of $V_{REF}$ can be found from eq. (11) at the different temperatures $T_0$ and $T$.

$$\frac{V_{REF}(T)}{V_{REF}(T_0)} = \frac{\frac{kT}{q} ln\left[\frac{\left(W/L\right)_{M2}}{\left(W/L\right)_{M1}}\right]}{\frac{kT_0}{q} ln\left[\frac{\left(W/L\right)_{M2}}{\left(W/L\right)_{M1}}\right]} = \frac{T}{T_0} \tag{11}$$

It can be inferred from eq. 11 that the drain-source voltage of M1 presents a PTAT (Proportional to Absolute Temperature) behavior. Fig. 3 shows the simulation of circuit from Fig. 1 over the 35°C to 42°C temperature range, for a 500mV power supply voltage. That temperature range corresponds to limits between surgical procedures (lowered body temperature) or any pathology (fever). The simulation includes the three corners; typical, slow and fast. Additional circuitry, as shown in Fig. 1 (Processing Unit), can be added to provide an analog to digital conversion, where the gain and offset errors can be minimized.

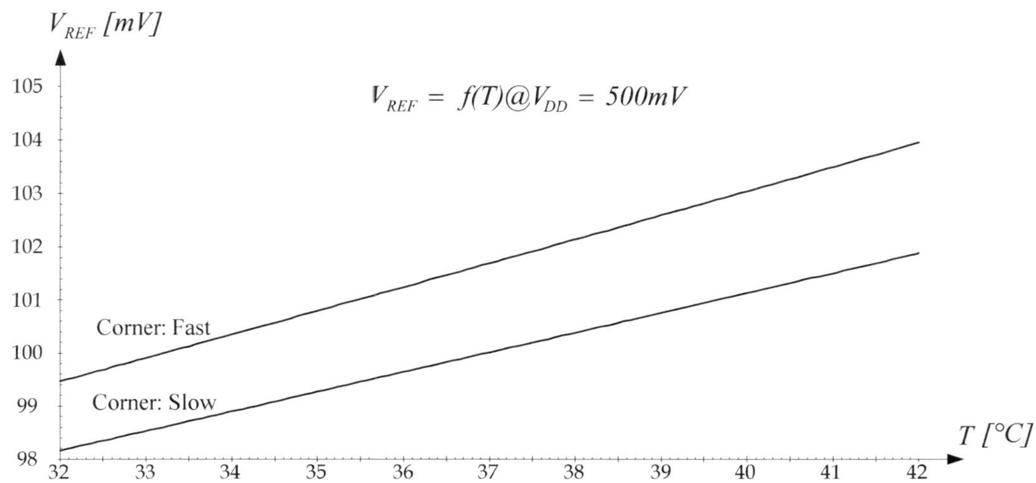


**Figure 3.** Simulation of $V_{REF}$ voltage © $V_{DD}$=0.5V for a clinical temperature range including the fast and slow process corners.

Including this temperature impact, the voltage reference can be stated as having a nominal value of 100mV (typical) with a worst case dispersion of +4% (fast corner) and -1,8% (slow corner). The respective temperature coefficients are 0.35mV/°C (slow corner) and 0.45mV/°C (fast corner).

## 4. The voltage reference circuit implemented with composite transistors

Fig. 4 shows the circuit used to generate the current $I_D$. Transistor M5 is biased by the voltage reference, which it is assumed to be constant, and its drain current ($I_{REF}$) is mirrored by M3-M4. The overall circuit implementation is done by using composite transistors as depicted in Fig. 5. The current $I_D$ is fixed at approximately 15nA. As can be observed, there is a feedback loop M2-M5 that does improve the PSRR of the circuit, as it will be demonstrated by simulation. The use of composite transistors is fundamental to reduce the mismatch between the mirrored currents.

As it is the case of self-biased circuits, it is necessary a startup circuit. It is implemented through transistor $M_{START}$, and capacitors $C_{START1}$ and $C_{START2}$. On power up, an impulsive current will flow and the circuit will be lead to the desired operation point condition. All the transistors aspect ratios are optimized by a set of interactive simulations aiming the target values $I_D$=15nA and $V_{REF}$=100mV, for the typical process parameters.

Transistor M6 is included in the feedback loop to improve the power supply rejection ratio (PSSR) at higher frequencies, as it acts a low pass filter.

Mostly transistors aspect ratios are also refined by interactive simulations. Transistor M2 aspect ratio is assumed to be 50/1 where the channel length of 1μm is adopted to be approximately 3 times the minimum size of 0.35 TSMC process to reduce the short channel effects.

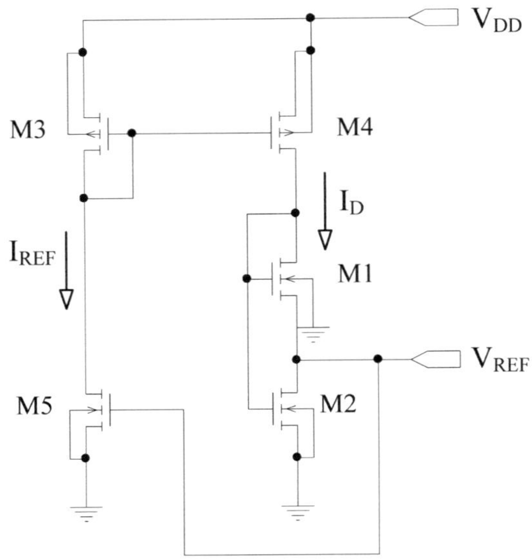


**Figure 4.** $I_D$ current generation by mirroring concept.

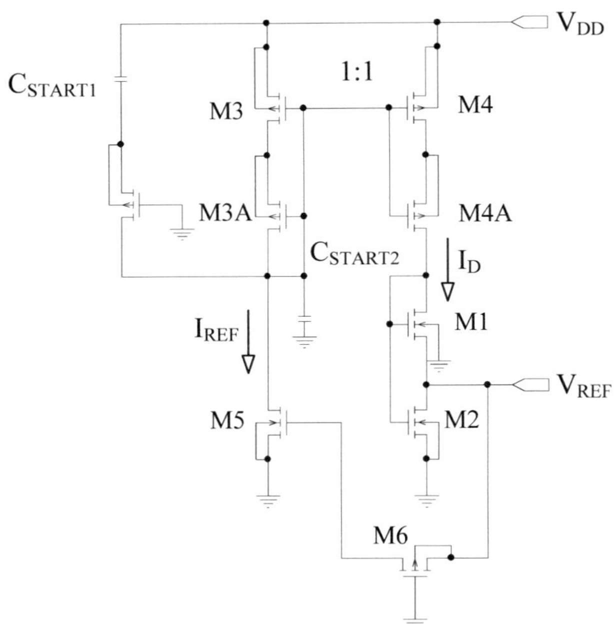


**Figure 5.** Proposed Reference circuit.

# 5. Simulation results

This section presents a set of electrical simulations that validate the main concepts of the voltage reference.

### 5.1. Minimum power supply

As stated early, it is important to keep the whole system operating in the low power condition. Fig. 6 shows the simulation used to investigate the minimum power supply that maintains the circuit proper function. The temperature was kept constant at 37ºC. The three curves are result of typical, slow, and fast PMOS and NMOS parameters of 0.35 TSMC process.

As it can be observed, the supply voltage can be as low as 500mV. Table 2 lists the reference voltage values for some supply voltages and the relative deviation from the nominal (typical) value. The 500mV power supply indicates a worst case deviation of 1.69% at the process corners. This simulation shows an important result since it is in accordance with equation (10), thus indicating an independence of the voltage reference regarding the process corners. Additionally, the use of transistors operating in weak inversion allows power supply voltage reduction to values that characterize low voltage operation.

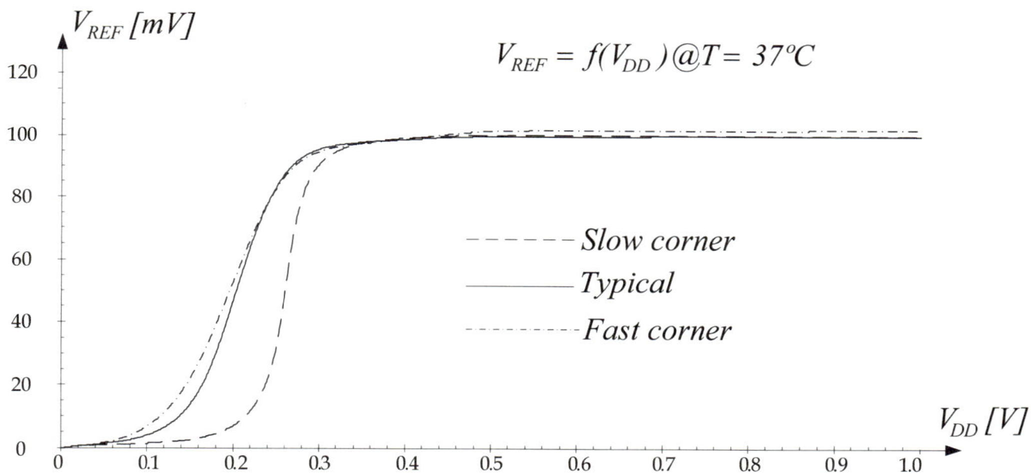


**Figure 6.** Simulation to Evaluate the Minimum Power Supply Voltage.

| | $V_{REF}$ @ T=37ºC (mV) | | | |
|---|---|---|---|---|
| $V_{DD}$ [V] | Slow | Typical | Fast | Deviation (worst case) |
| 0.5 | 100.31 | 99.99 | 101.68 | +1.69% |
| 0.6 | 100.38 | 100.09 | 102.04 | +1.95% |
| 0.7 | 100.39 | 100.11 | 102.10 | +1.99% |
| 0.8 | 100.40 | 100.13 | 102.15 | +2.01% |

**Table 2.** $V_{REF}$ as a Function of $V_{DD}$ for typical values and process corners.

### 5.2. Matching between $I_{REF}$ and $I_D$

The PMOS composite pairs improve the matching between currents $I_{REF}$ and $I_D$. The simulation results on Fig. 7 show the relative error (ER in %) between currents $I_{REF}$ and $I_D$ for the typical and corners process. At a 500mV supply voltage, the worst case is approximately 0.155%. The current matching between $I_{REF}$ and $I_D$ is achieved by the PMOS current mirror due to the higher impedance of the composite structure. This output impedance, for both PMOS pairs, can be stated as:

$$r_O(M3A) = ng_m(M3A)r_O(M3A)r_O(M3) \tag{12}$$

Another point of interest is the fact that the matching between the currents is significant (lower dispersion) from 500mV of power supply, confirming the use of this minimum value.

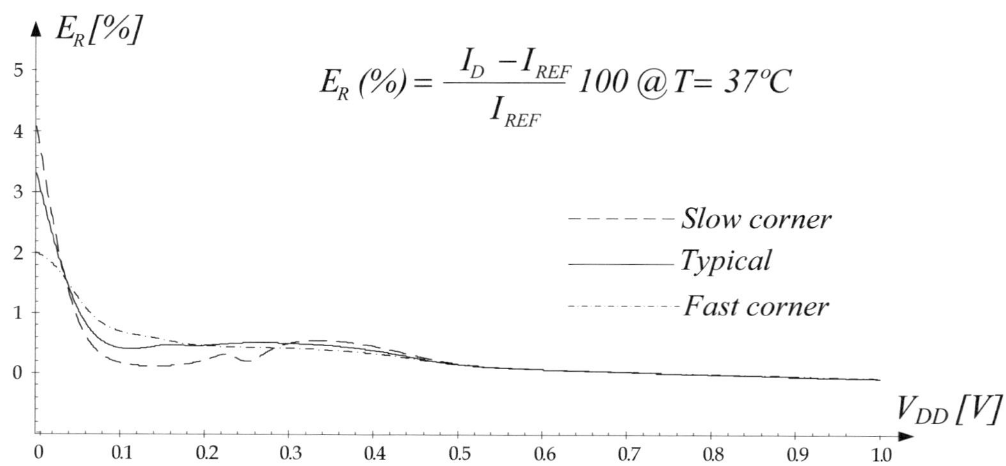


**Figure 7.** Simulation to Evaluate Mismatch Between $I_{REF}$ and $I_D$.

### 5.3. Geometric aspect ratio for transistors M1 and M2

Eq. (10) presents the geometric aspect ratios of transistors M1 and M2, $(W/L)_1$ and $(W/L)_2$, respectively. Therefore, it is possible to evaluate this ideal relationship to achieve the desired target value for the reference voltage. As mentioned previously, it was adopted the minimum channel length L as 1μm to minimize short channel effects.

Consequently it is also necessary to adopt a geometric aspect ratio of transistor M2. The $(W/L)_2$ relationship must be large enough to maintain the $I_D$ current along all the process corners. A simulation of M2 shows that a 50/1 geometric aspect is enough. Therefore, a simulation process is used to investigate the ideal W/L relationship for M1. Fig. 8 shows the simulation of equation (10) considering the $V_{REF}$ as a function of geometric aspect ratios $(W/L)_1$ and $(W/L)_2$. Table 3 resumes the values for the 100mV target value.

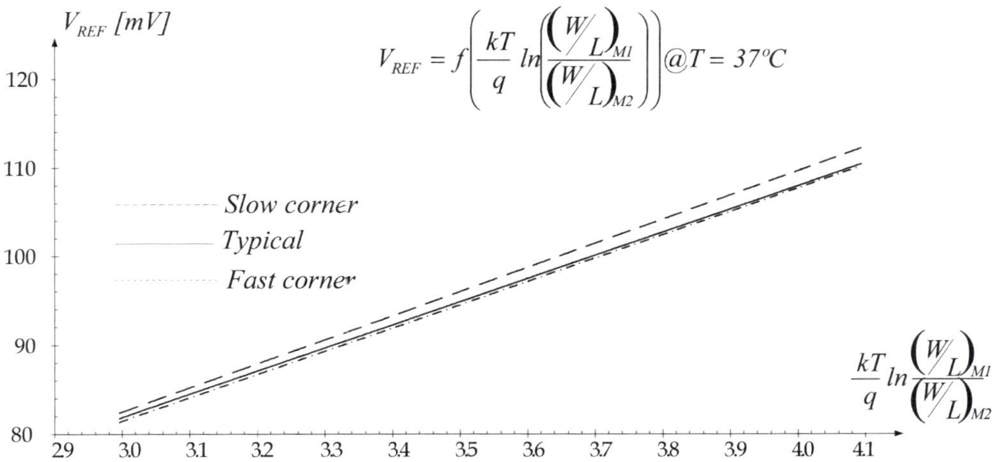


**Figure 8.** Simulation used to Evaluate the Geometric Aspect Ratio of Transistor M1

| $V_{REF}$=100mV@ T=37ºC and $(W/L)_{M2}$=50/1 | | | |
|---|---|---|---|
| | Slow | Typical | Fast |
| $\ln\left[\frac{(W/L)_{M1}}{(W/L)_{M2}}\right]$ | 3.6951 | 3.7069 | 3.6448 |
| $(W/L)_{M1}$ [µm] | 2012.5 | 2036.4 | 1913.7 |
| Equation (10) considering (kT/q)=26.73mV@T=37ºC | | | |
| $\ln\left[\frac{(W/L)_{M1}}{(W/L)_{M2}}\right]$=3.7453 and $(W/L)_{M1}$=2107 [µm] | | | |

**Table 3.** Simulated and Calculated Geometric Aspect Ratio for Transistor M1.

It was adopted, in this work, $(W/L)_1$ =2036/1 as the typical value. Although there is a dispersion of about 9% between the calculated and simulated (W/L) values for the worst case corner (fast), the impact on the reference voltage is minimized by the logarithmic dependence.

## 5.4. Monte Carlo analysis

A set of 5000 runs were performed to evaluate the statistical parameters related to $V_{REF}$. Figs. 9 and Fig. 10 show the simulation result for the reference voltage $V_{REF}$ and the total power dissipation $P_D$. Table 4 presents the main values.

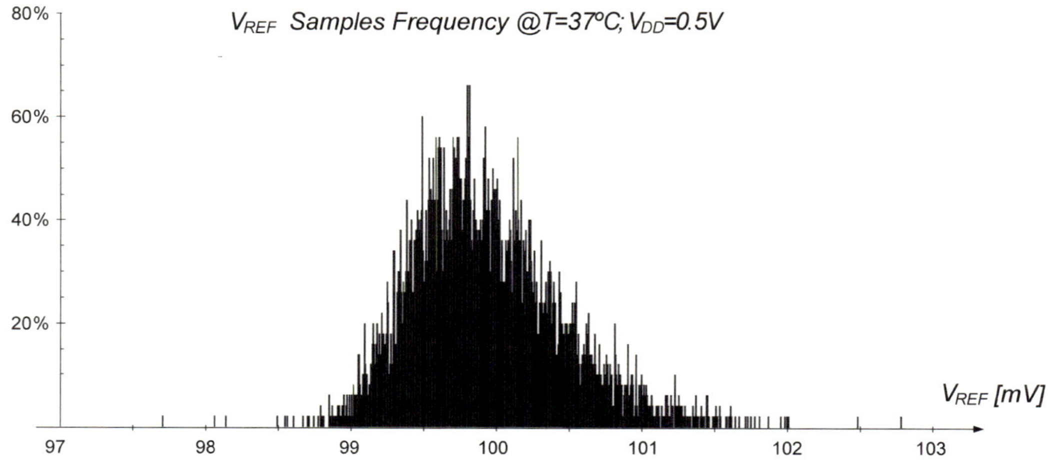


**Figure 9.** Monte Carlo Analysis – $V_{REF}$ percentage samples.

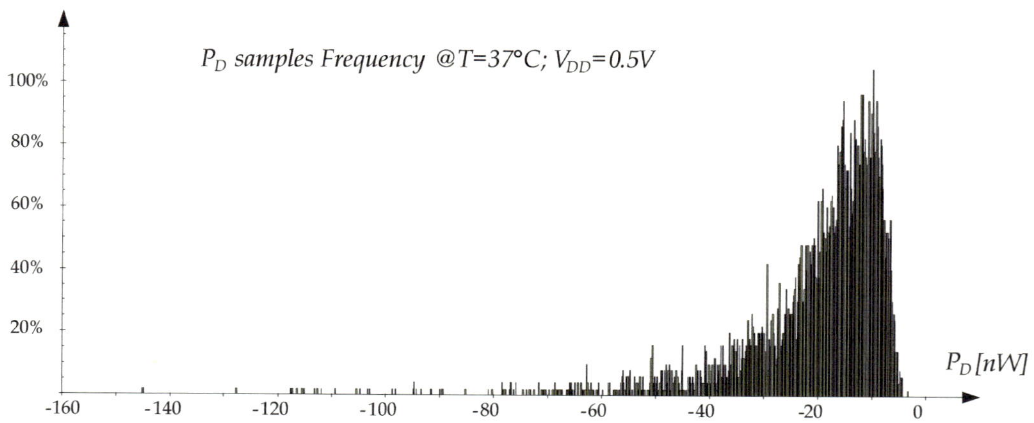


**Figure 10.** Monte Carlo Analysis – $P_D$ percentage samples.

| | $V_{REF}$[mV] | $P_D$ [nW] |
|---|---|---|
| Mean | 99.9 | 16.9 |
| $\sigma$ | 0.503 | 14.6 |
| $3\sigma$ | 1.512 | 43.9 |

**Table 4.** Monte Carlo Analysis @ $V_{DD}$=500mV and T=37°C.

Table 4 shows that the $V_{REF}$ can be expressed as 99.9±1.512mV (±1.5%) for a $3\sigma$ dispersion. This is an important result considering that the process inherently dispersion on Vt is approximately ±20% ($3\sigma$). A total power dissipation in the range of tenths of nW characterizes a low-power operation. The minus signal in the simulation results is due to the simulation algorithm.

## 5.5. Start-Up circuit

As it is the case of a self-polarized circuit, it is necessary a start-up approach to move the circuit operation to the desired condition. In other words, the start-up circuit must lead the main circuit to the desired operating point. This is realized by introducing the additional components $M_{START}$, $C_{START1}$ and $C_{START2}$. Fig. 11 shows the simulation of $M_{START}$ current and $C_{START1}$ voltage as a response to a voltage ramp applied to $V_{DD}$. As the current vanishes to zero, $C_{START1}$ charges toward $V_{DD}$ and the power dissipated in $M_{START}$ tends to zero. The fast and small impulsive current $I_{DS(MSTART)}$ is sufficient to start the whole reference circuit.

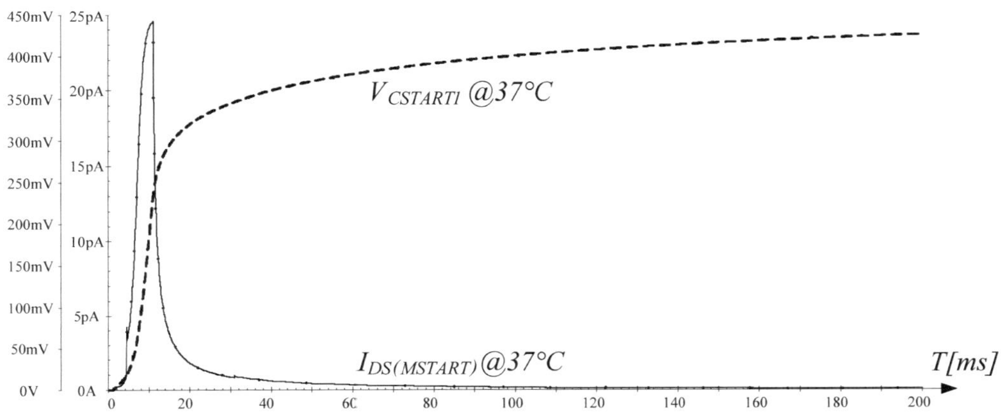


**Figure 11.** Current though $M_{START}$ and $C_{START1}$ voltage.

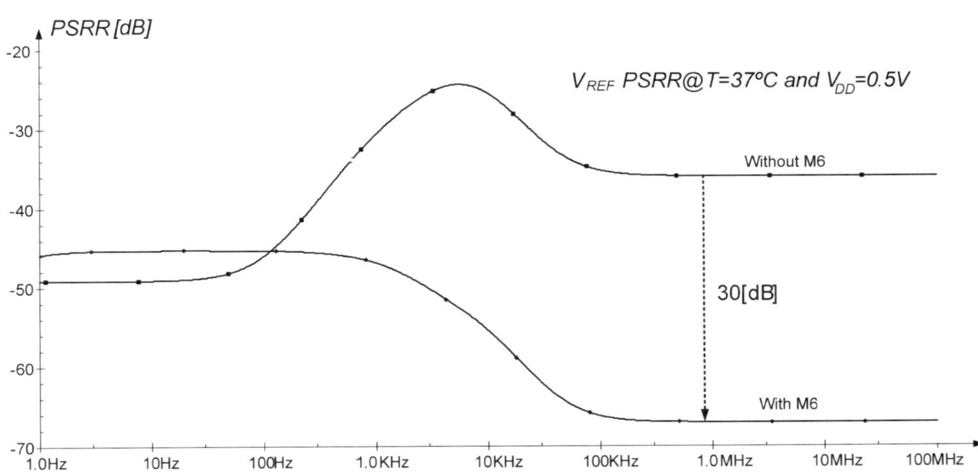


**Figure 12.** PSRR simulation with and without transistor M6.

## 5.6. Power Supply Rejection Ratio (PSRR)

The voltage reference must exhibit a high PSRR, especially at high frequencies since the implanted device will be activated by a Radio Frequency link. The PMOS transistor placed between M2 and M5 acts as a low-pass filter. Fig. 12 shows the PSRR simulation. As it can be observed from the PSRR simulation presented in Fig 12, the PSRR can be 65dB in the MHz frequency range.

## 6. Layout

The proposed circuit was implemented in standard 0.35μm TSMC CMOS process through MOSIS educational program. Table 5 shows the aspect ratios of the all transistors. In this table the factor M represents a multiplier; i. e. the respective transistor is, actually, a parallel association. For instance, transistor M4A is a parallel association of 3 identical transistors with a geometric aspect ratio of 1000/2.

| Transistor | W/L [μm] | M |
|---|---|---|
| M1 | 50/1 | 1 |
| M2 | 2036/1 | 1 |
| M3 | 150/2 | 1 |
| M3A | 1000/2 | 3 |
| M4 | 150/2 | 1 |
| M4A | 1000/2 | 3 |
| M5 | 2500/1 | 5 |
| M6 | 2500/120 | 1 |

**Table 5.** All Transistors Geometric Aspect Ratio.

The capacitors are poly-insulator-poly – PIP structures and the layouts of the NMOS and PMOS transistors were implemented using multifinger common centroid configuration. Besides better matching, this layout technique is less sensitive to process variation (Hastings, 2001; Qiang et al., 2011). The source-bulk connection of the PMOS transistors is possible since the TSMC is an n-well process, and therefore all the PMOS transistors are fabricated in different wells.

Mainly for the design of analog integrated circuits, the layout of two matched components is realized in such a way that they can be divided into identical sections, placed symmetrically in a matrix array.

The common centroid layout using matched components arranged in a matrix array, in identical and symmetrical sections, is essential to reduce or even eliminate the systematic mismatching. The distances between the centroids components are null and so are the mismatching caused by mechanical and temperature stress. For instance, in order to improve the differential pair match in operational amplifiers, these transistors are placed in a cross coupled array. Fig. 13 (a) shows two matched devices, each composed of two segments arranged in an array of two rows and two columns (cross-coupled pair). Resistors are rarely laid out as cross-coupled pairs because the resulting arrays usually have unwieldy aspect ratios. If the matched devices are large enough to segment into more than two pieces, then the cross-coupled pair can be further subdivided as show Fig. 13 (b).

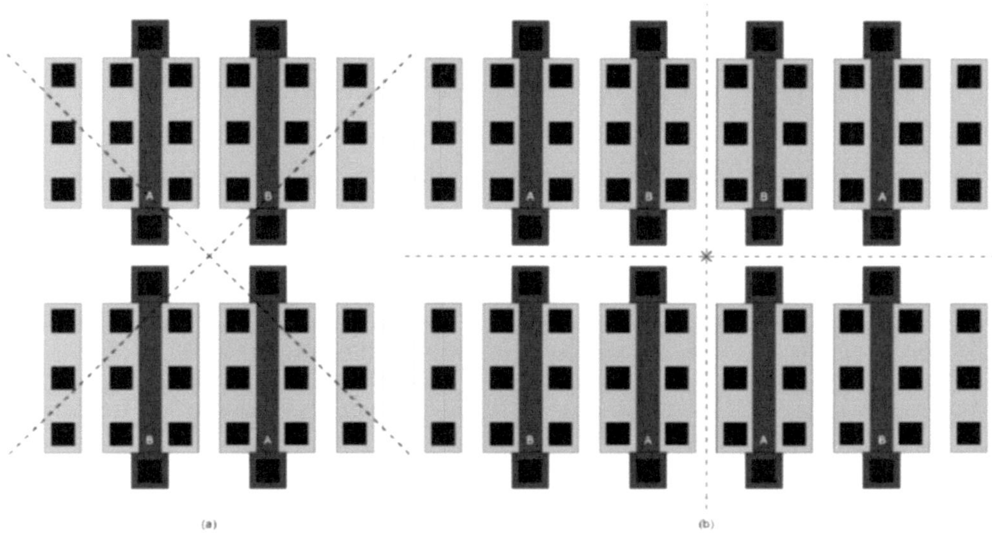

**Figure 13.** Examples of two dimensional common-centroid arrays.

It is recommended that matched components are fabricated near each other, minimizing the mechanical stress. The mechanical stress difference between two matched components is proportional to the abrasive gradient and their distance. For calculations purposes, the location of the component is determined as the average contribution of each section of the component. The resultant location is called centroid of the component. It is important that any symmetric axis crosses the centroid of the device or component

To design components with a centroid layout some rules must be observed:

1. *Coincidence*: The matched devices centroids must be superimposed or as close as possible;
2. *Symmetry*: The component matrix must be symmetrical along the X and Y axes. Ideally, the symmetry must be a consequence of the placement positions of the components and not for the symmetry of each component individually;
3. *Dispersion*: The matrix must exhibit the greatest dispersion level, i.e., each component must be placed with high symmetry along the matrix;
4. *Compression*: The matrix should be as compact as possible, ideally close to a square shape.

A better matching between integrated components reflects in the overall performance of the designed circuit or system. Depending on the matching accuracy, it is possible to consider the following cases:

1. *Minimum*: In the range of ± 1% (representing 6 to 7 bits of resolution). Used for general components in an analog circuit. For instance, current mirrors and biasing circuits;
2. *Moderate*: In the range of ± 0.1% (representing 9 to 10 bits of resolution). Used in bandgap references, operational amplifiers and input stage of voltage comparators. This range is the most appropriate for analog designs.

3. *Severe*: In the range of ± 0.01% (representing 13 to 14 bits of resolution). Used in high precision analog to digital converters (ADCs) and digital to analog converters (DACs). Analog designs using capacitors relations reach this resolution easier than those that use resistors relations.

In the case of a MOS transistor, the process and electrical parameters that have must be taken into account into matching purposes are listed in Table 6.

| Process Parameters | Electrical Parameters |
|---|---|
| Flat band voltage | Drain current |
| Mobility | Gate-Source voltage |
| Substrate Dopant Concentration | Transconductance |
| Chanel length variation | Output resistance |
| Chanel width variation | |
| Short channel effect | |
| Narrow channel effect | |
| Gate oxide thickness | |
| Source/Drain sheet resistance | |

**Table 6.** Process and Electrical Parameters for Component Matching.

## 7. Conclusions

This chapter presented a low-voltage low-power voltage reference for biomedical applications in which the operating temperature is kept almost constant. Besides a simple topology, the proposed circuit has the advantage of low power dissipation, thus avoiding patient tissue damages. The topology offers a low dependence on process corners and high PSRR. Simulation results point to a reference voltage of 100mV with ±1.5% dispersion (3σ) considering typical and corners parameters. The maximum total dissipated power is about 60.8nW (max) and the PSRR is better than 45dB for a frequency range between 1Hz and 100MHz.

Table 7 shows a comparison of this work with other previously reported in the literature.

| | This Work | (Lukaszewicz et.al, 2011) | (Li et al., 2007) |
|---|---|---|---|
| Technology | CMOS 0.35μm | CMOS 65nm | CMOS 0.5μm |
| $V_{DD}$ [V] | 0.5 | 2.6 – 3.63 | 4 - 6 |
| $I_D$ [μA] | 0.12 | 47 | - |
| $V_{REF}$ [mV] | 100 | - | - |
| $I_{REF}$ [μA] | - | 6.45 | 1.612 |
| Area [mm²] | 0.43 | - | 0.026 |
| PSRR [dB] | 65@10MHz | 103@10MHz | 45 |
| Process Sensitivity [%] | ±1.5 | ±3 | ±5.2 |

**Table 7.** Comparison with previous work.

## Author details

Paulo Cesar Crepaldi, Tales Cleber Pimenta,
Robson Luiz Moreno and Leonardo Breseghello Zoccal
*Universidade Federal de Itajuba, Brasil*

## 8. References

Bero, B. & Nyathi, J. (2006). Bulk CMOS Device Optimization for High-Speed and Ultra-Low Power Operations. 49th IEEE International Midwest Symposium on Circuits and Systems, 2006. MWSCAS '06. 6-9 Aug. 2006, pp. 221-225.

Burington, R. S. (1973). Handbook of Mathematical Tables and Formulas. McGraw-Hill Book Company, 5th Edition, 1973.

Colomer-Farrarons, J.; Miribel-Catala, P.; Rodriguez, I. & Samitier, J. (2009). CMOS front-end architecture for In-Vivo biomedical implantable devices. Industrial Electronics, 2009. IECON '09. 35th Annual Conference of IEEE Publication, 3-5 Nov, 2009, pp. 4401 – 4408.

Crepaldi, P.C.; Pimenta, T. C.; Moreno, R. L. & Rodriguez, E. C. (2010) A Linear Voltage Regulator for an Implanted Device Monitoring System. Analog Integrated Circuits and Signal Processing, Vol. 65, Number 1, March 2010, pp. 131-140.

Ferreira, L. H. C. & Pimenta, T. C. (2006). A Weak Inversion Composite MOS Transistor for Ultra-Low-Voltage and Ultra-Low-Power Applications. Proc. 13th Int. Conf. Mixed Design Integ. Circuits Syst., Gdynia, Poland, Jun. 2006.

Guennoun, M.; Zandi, M. &El-Khatib, K. (2008). On the use of Biometrics to Secure Wireless Biosensor Networks. Information and Communication Tecnologies: From Theory to Applications, 2008. ICTTA 2008. 3rd International Conference on Digital Idenfier. 7 – 11 April 2008. pp. 1-5.

Hastings, A. (2001). The Art of Analog Layout, Publisher: Prentice Hall; 2nd edition (July 4, 2005), ISBN-13: 978-0131464100.

Landt. J. (2005). The History of RFID, Potentials, IEEE, Volume 24, Issue 4, Oct – Nov, 2005, pp. 8-11.

Li, W.; Lenain, H. & Y. Xiaoling. (2007). All CMOS Temperature, Supply Voltage and Process Independent Current Reference", 7th International Conference on ASIC, 2007. ASICON '07, 22-25 Oct. 2007, pp. 600-603.

Lukaszewicz, M.; Borejko, T. & Pleskacz, W.A. (2011) A resistorless current reference source for 65 nm CMOS technology with low sensitivity to process, supply voltage and temperature variations. IEEE 14th International Symposium on Design and Diagnostics of Electronic Circuits & Systems (DDECS), 2011, pp. 75 - 79

Mackowiak, P. A.; Wasserman, S. S. & Levine, M. M. (1992). A critical appraisal of 98.6°F, the upper limit of the normal body temperature, and other legacies of Carl Reinhold August Wunderlich. JAMA, volume 268, no. 12, Sept 23/30 1992, pp. 1578-1580.

Magnelli, L.; Crupi, F.; Corsonello, P.; Pace, C. & Iannaccone, G. (2011). A 2.6 nW, 0.45 V Temperature-Compensated Subthreshold CMOS Voltage Reference. IEEE Journal of Solid-State Circuits, Feb 2011, Volume: 46 , Issue: 2, pp. 465-474.

Nomani, W. K.; Anis, M. & Koley, G. (2010). Statistical Approach for Yield Optimization for Minimum Energy Operation in Subthreshold Circuits Considering Variability Issue. IEEE Transactions on Semiconductor Manufacturing, Vol. 23 No. 1, February 2010. Pp. 77-86.

Qiang, M.; Linfu, X.; Yiu-Cheong M. & Young, E. F. Y. (2011). Simultaneous Handling of Symmetry, Common Centroid, and General Placement Constraints. IEEE Transactions on Computer-Aided Design of Integrated Circuits and Systems, Vol. 30, Issue:1, 2011 , pp. 85 – 95.

Rincon-Mora, G. A. & Allen, P. E. (1998). Study and Design of Low Drop-Out Regulators. School of Electrical and Computer Engineering – Georgia.

Roknsharifi, M.; Haider, M.R. & Islam, S.K. (2011). A low-power area efficient voltage reference and data generation unit for inductively powered implant system", Biomedical Wireless Technologies, Networks, and Sensing Systems (BioWireleSS), 2011 IEEE Topical Conference on, Publication Year: 2011, pp: 107 – 110.

Tsividis, Y. P. (1999). Operation and Modeling of the MOS Transistor," Mc-Graw Hill, 1999.

Ueno, K.; Hirose, T.; Asai, T. & Amemiya, Y. (2006). Ultralow-Power Smart Temperature Sensor with Subthreshold CMOS Circuits. 2006 International Symposium on Intelligent Signal Processing and Communication Systems (ISPACS2006) Yonago Convention Center. 12-15 Dec. 2006, pp. 546-549.

Chapter 15

# Evaluation of Maximum Voltage or Maximum Link Distance on Implantable Devices

Paulo Cesar Crepaldi, Tales Cleber Pimenta,
Robson Luiz Moreno and Rômulo Mota Volpato

Additional information is available at the end of the chapter

http://dx.doi.org/10.5772/48648

## 1. Introduction

The current technology allows the implementation of electronic devices under the skin for therapeutic purposes. As a result the wireless technology can be used to monitor some illness and mitigate the patient`s discomfort. As an example, consider the case of diabetes patients that must undergo to daily painful blood collections to monitor the blood sugar levels. Therefore an electronic device capable of measuring the blood sugar level and transmit the result to an external device would greatly improve the quality of life of those patients. Nevertheless, the placement of an implantable device requires a minor surgery.

Once the implantable device is placed in a subject, the battery lifetime and its charge will dictate the system lifespan [1].

Consequently, it could be used the passive target technology, in which the device contains its own energy source. Thus the limitation imposed by batteries would not exist in addition to size reduction to the device. The radio frequency identification – RFID technology fits perfectly into that application.

An important parameter to be analyzed is the operation frequency. The communication frequency between the external reader and the implantable device should suffer the smallest interference due to the human tissue. The frequency of 13.56 MHz offers low attenuation and can be chosen for implantable devices. This chapter discusses the energy transfer from reader to tag by inductive coupling and its limitations. It presents a way to evaluate the target voltage provided by the inductive coupling by using basic circuit theory.

## 2. Basic inductive coupling circuit

Figure 1 shows a typical inductive coupling system. Observe that the system is composed by the reader and the tag. The reader is used to receive data from the tag and also to transfer energy to it.

It is chosen series resonance configuration, as shown in Figure 2, in order to raise the voltage at inductor $L_1$, since voltage in a series resonance inductor is larger than the voltage provided by the source. From basic circuit theory and by observing Figure 3, the impedance seen by the reader is given as:

$$Z = R_1 + (j\omega L_1 - j\frac{1}{\omega C_1}) \tag{1}$$

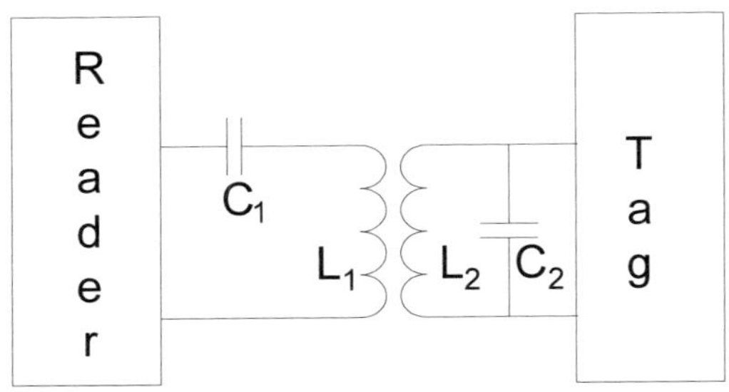


**Figure 1.** Typical inductive coupling system.

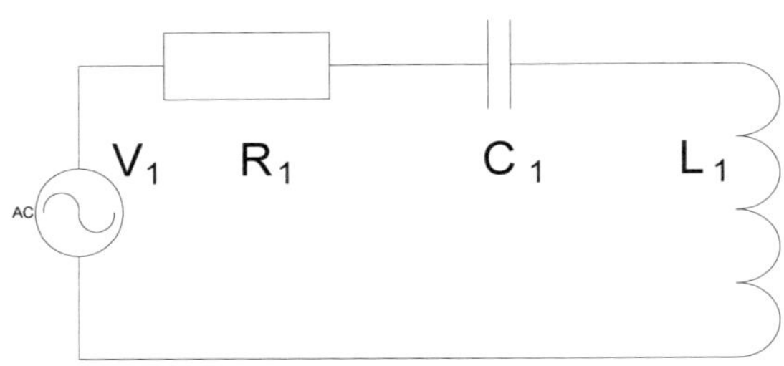


**Figure 2.** Simplified inductive coupling circuit at the reader.

The resonance, for low frequency operation, is given as:

$$\omega L_1 = \frac{1}{\omega C_1}. \tag{2}$$

However impedance Z becomes resistive and equal to $R_1$ that represents the inductor series resistance. Therefore, the reader impedance depends on resistance $R_1$ and voltage the inductor becomes:

$$E_1 = jI\omega L_1 = j\frac{V_1 \varpi L_1}{R_1} = jQV_1. \tag{3}$$

At this point it is important to define the quality factor of the resonant circuit, $Q = wL_1/R_1$. It defines the ratio of stored and dissipated energy in an inductor. It demonstrates that the reader efficiency increases by using series resonance, as summarized by expression (4).

$$|E_1| = |V_1| Q \tag{4}$$

The reader receives data and power by the inductive coupling through $L_1$ and $L_2$. The reader takes advantage of the parallel resonance and high impedance that occurs at frequencies near the resonance. It indicates that, at resonance, the voltage over the *LC* circuit is high and can be used to power up the target. Therefore the inductive coupling allows the use of passive target concept, or self-powering. Nevertheless tuned circuits have multiple resonances that cause a reduction in the energy transfer from reader to target. Thus a better understanding of the influence of resonance circuits may help to determine precisely the supply voltage at the target.

## 3. Concept of inductance

A current flowing in a straight infinite conductor generates a magnetic flow density (or magnetic induction) proportional to the current. That relationship was observed by Biot Savart, as given by (5).

$$\vec{B} = \frac{\mu_0}{4\pi} \int i \frac{d\vec{l} X \vec{a}_r}{|\vec{r}|^2} \tag{5}$$

where:

$d\vec{l}$ represents an elemental piece of conductor,
$\vec{a}_r$ represents the unit directional vector,
$|\vec{r}|^2$ represents the module of distance where the magnetic flow intensity is calculated,
$\mu_0$ is the vacuum permeability constant.

From (5), there will be a magnetic flow area around the conductor. The magnetic flow is given by (6)

$$\phi = \int \vec{B} d\vec{S} \tag{6}$$

where:

$\vec{B}$ - represents the magnetic induction vector,
$d\vec{S}$ - represents the area vector inside the magnetic induction vector.

In that line, the magnetic flow is proportional to the current flowing in the conductor and there is a linear relationship between them, known as inductance, as shown by (7).

$$L\frac{di}{dt}=\frac{d\phi}{dt}\Rightarrow L=\frac{d\phi}{di} \tag{7}$$

The premise of infinite and straight conductor of the Biot Savart law is not obeyed in the construction of inductors, thus the inductance parameter of a component will depend on many factors such as geometric shape, number of coils and resistance of the conductor.

## 4. Concept of mutual inductance

Whenever two inductors are close, the magnetic flow generated by one influences the flow in the other, as indicated in Figure 3.

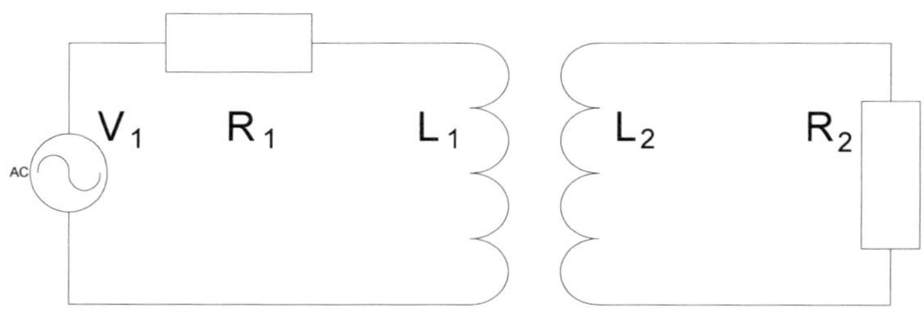


**Figure 3.** Simplified inductive coupling.

Therefore, a time varying current i1 flowing on inductor 1 generates a magnetic flow ϕ21 into inductor 2. The density of magnetic flow that reaches inductor 2 depends on the position and distance between the inductors. Thus mutual inductance is defined as the number of coils of inductor 2 that receives the magnetic flow generated by inductor 1, divided by current i1, as shown by (8).

$$M_{21}=\frac{N_2\phi_{21}}{i_1} \tag{8}$$

where :

1. $N_2$ is the number of coils of inductor 2,
2. $i_1$ is the current on inductor 1,
3. $\phi_{12}$ is the magnetic flow on inductor 2 due to inductor 1,
4. $M$ is mutual inductance between inductors 1 and 2.

If there is any current on inductor 2, the same phenomenon occurs, as given by (9).

$$M_{12}=\frac{N_1\phi_{12}}{i_2} \tag{9}$$

Consider two inductors of length $D$ and sectional areas $A_1$ and $A_2$, much smaller than $D$, number of coils $N_1$ and $N_2$ for inductors 1 and 2, respectively, and placed on the same vertical axis, as shown in Figure 4. As can be observed, inductor 1 is placed inside inductor 2 and they have the same orientation. If it is applied a current into inductor 2, the mutual inductance is given by (9).

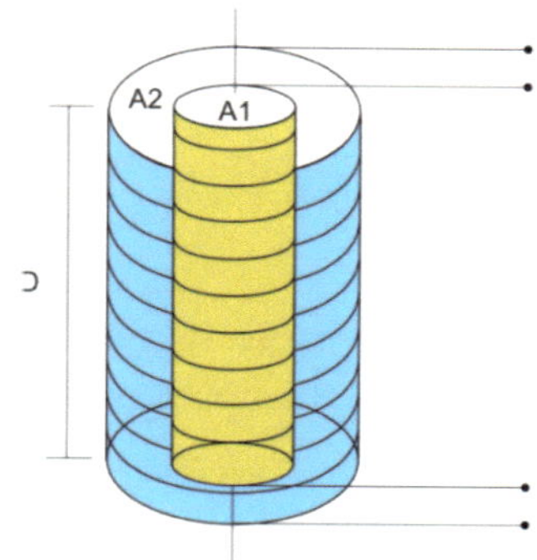


**Figure 4.** Long inductors coupled on the same axis.

If the magnetic field is uniform inside inductor 2, then flow $\phi_{12}$ can be taken as (10).

$$\phi_{12} = B_2 A_1 \tag{10}$$

Expression (10) can be placed into (9), as:

$$M_{12} = \frac{N_1 A_1 B_2}{i_2} \tag{11}$$

By considering that the inductors core is air and the coils are composed of close and simple layers, the Biot e Savart expression can be used, where:

$$B_2 = \frac{\mu_0 N_2 i_2}{d} \tag{12}$$

Thus, by combining (11) and (12):

$$M_{12} = \frac{N_1 N_2 \mu_0 A_1}{d} \tag{13}$$

From the analysis of (13) it can be observed that for the auto inductance, the number of coils is the same, thus the expression becomes:

$$L = \frac{\mu_0 N^2 A}{d} \tag{14}$$

For the inductor, the coupling will be taken in its own area, meaning that they are equal, thus:

$$L_1 = \frac{\mu_0 N_1{}^2 A}{d} \tag{15}$$

$$L_2 = \frac{\mu_0 N_2{}^2 A}{d} \tag{16}$$

By combining (15) and (16), one obtains:

$$M = \frac{\mu_0 A}{d}\sqrt{\frac{L_1 d}{A\mu_0}}\sqrt{\frac{L_2 d}{A\mu_0}} = \sqrt{L_1 L_2} \tag{17}$$

In real case, areas $A_1$ and $A_2$ are not equal, indicating that the magnetic flow is not covered completely by both inductors. Therefore, the coupling factor is reduced, as given by:

$$M = k\sqrt{L_1 L_2} \tag{18}$$

where $k$ is the magnetic coupling factor.

## 5. Inductive coupling with simple resonance

Although we have discussed inductive coupling between reader and target, at resonance, that characterize a double resonance, we can use simple resonance. In this configuration the reader presents just an inductor magnetically coupled to the inductor at the tag. The simplified circuit is shown in Figure 5. Observe the resonant circuit is positioned at the tag. In order to simplify the analysis, consider the circuit in free space. By considering also inductors without loss, the circuit of Figure 5 can be equated by using (2), resulting into (19) and (20).

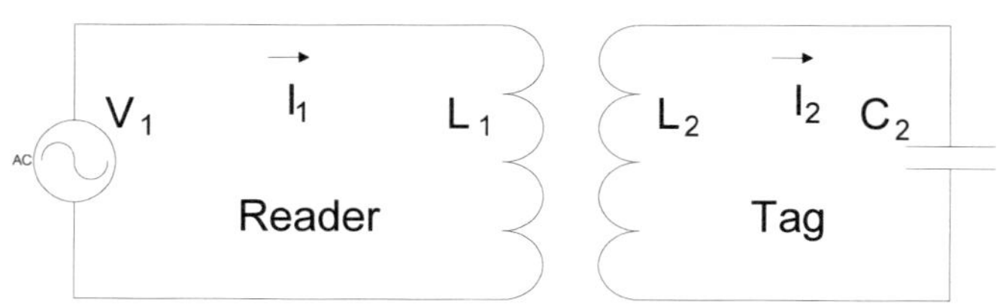


**Figure 5.** Inductive coupling with simple resonance at the tag.

$$V_1 = I_1 j\varpi L_1 - I_2 j\varpi M \tag{19}$$

$$0 = I_2(j\varpi L_2 + \frac{1}{jwC_2}) - I_1 j\varpi M \tag{20}$$

where $M$ is the mutual inductance between inductors $L_1$ and $L_2$.

From (20):

$$I_2 = \frac{I_1 j\varpi M}{j\varpi L_2 + \frac{1}{j\varpi C_2}} \tag{21}$$

By replacing (18) into (21):

$$I_2 = \frac{I_1 j\varpi k\sqrt{L_1L_2}}{j\varpi L_2 + \dfrac{1}{j\varpi C_2}} \tag{22}$$

Now, replacing (22) into (19):

$$V_1 = I_1 j\varpi L_1 - \frac{I_1 j\varpi k\sqrt{L_1L_2}\, j\varpi k\sqrt{L_1L_2}}{j\varpi L_2 + \dfrac{1}{j\varpi C_2}} \tag{23}$$

Thus, the impedance seen by the generator is:

$$Z_1 = \frac{V_1}{I_1} = j\varpi L_1 + \frac{\varpi^2 k^2 L_1 L_2}{j\varpi L_2 + \dfrac{1}{j\varpi C_2}} \tag{24}$$

From the analysis of (24), it can be observed that the inductance seen by the reader is inductance $L_1$ added to impedance $Z_a$ reflected from the target, and represented by:

$$Z_a = \frac{\varpi^2 k^2 L_1 L_2}{j\varpi L_2 + \dfrac{1}{j\varpi C_2}} \tag{25}$$

Therefore, by using the same analysis, the impedance $Z_b$ reflected on inductor $L_2$ is:

$$Z_b = \frac{\varpi^2 k^2 L_1 L_2}{j\varpi L_1} \tag{26}$$

The equivalent circuit reflected at the target is shown in Figure 6.

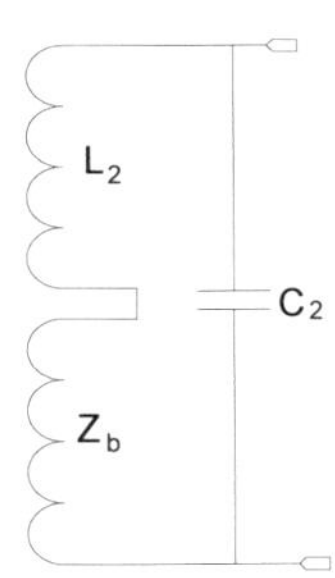


**Figure 6.** Equivalent circuit reflected at the inductor $L_2$.

By considering the equivalent circuit at resonance, then:

$$0 = (j\varpi L_2 + \frac{\varpi^2 k^2 L_1 L_2}{j\varpi L_1} + \frac{1}{j\varpi C_2}) I_2 \quad (27)$$

From the development of (27):

$$0 = j\varpi L_2 (1 - k^2) + \frac{1}{j\varpi C_2} \quad (28)$$

From (28), the resonance frequency is given as:

$$Fo_1 = \frac{1}{2\pi\sqrt{L_2(1-k^2)C_2}} \quad (29)$$

Thus the resonance frequency at the target was modified by the term $r$ given by:

$$r = \frac{1}{\sqrt{1-k^2}} \quad (30)$$

Consequently, the resonant frequency varies according to the coupling factor $k$. Thus, the distance between the inductors and their relative orientation can modify the amount of energy transferred by the inductive coupling. In order to validate equation (29), it was run a Spice simulation with a coupling factor ranging from 0.1 to 0.3, as shown in Figure 7. It can be observed that resonance frequency increases along with the coupling factor. As an initial condition, $L_1$ and $L_2$ were taken as 3,5 μH and capacitor $C_1$ equals to 38 pF. Observe, from Figure 7, that voltage on inductor $L$ increases along with the coupling factor.

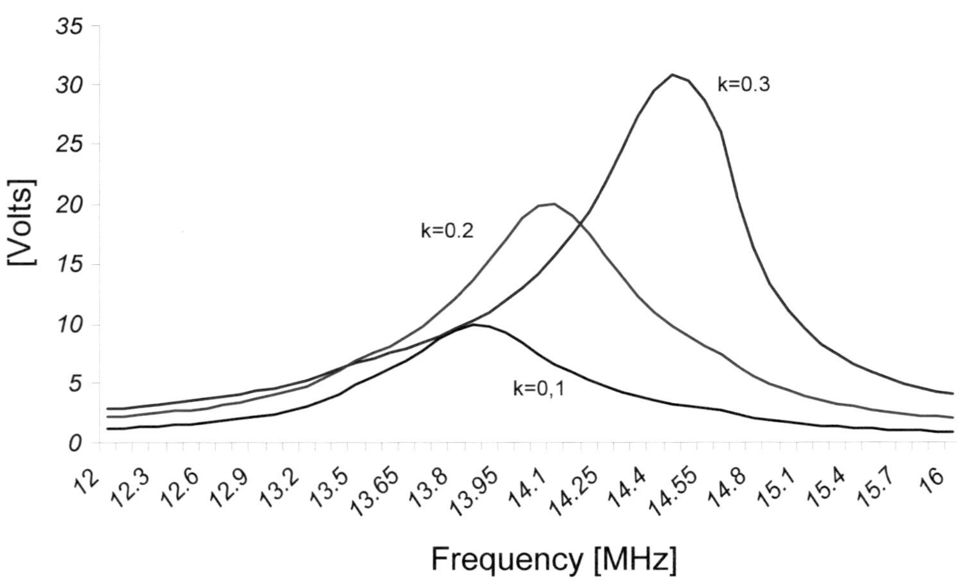


**Figure 7.** Spice simulation of coupling factor.

# 6. Inductive coupling with double resonance

There are two tuned circuits in the double resonance, where the primary is the reader and the secondary is the tag. Figure 8 presents the basic configuration for the double resonance inductive coupling.

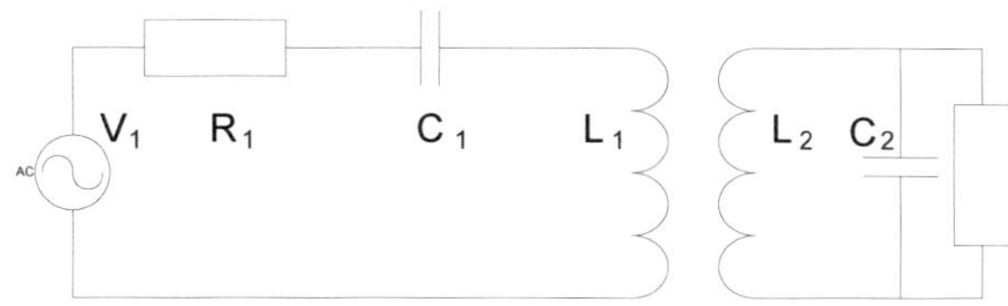


**Figure 8.** Double resonance inductive coupling.

From the analysis of Figure 8 and by considering free space and inductors without loss, then:

$$V_1 = I_1(j\varpi L_1 + \frac{1}{j\varpi C_1}) - I_2 j\varpi M \quad (31)$$

$$0 = I_2(j\varpi L_2 + \frac{1}{j\varpi C2}) - I_1 j\varpi M \quad (32)$$

From (32) it can be obtained that:

$$I_2 = \frac{j\varpi M I_1}{j\varpi L_2 + \frac{1}{j\varpi C_2}} \quad (33)$$

By replacing (33) into (31) one obtains:

$$V_1 = I_1(j\varpi L_1 + \frac{1}{j\varpi C_1}) + \frac{\varpi^2 M^2}{j\varpi L_2 + \frac{1}{j\varpi C_2}}) \quad (34)$$

Therefore, the impedance seen by the generator is:

$$Z = \frac{V_1}{I_1} = (j\varpi L_1 + \frac{1}{j\varpi C_1}) + \frac{\varpi^2 M^2}{(j\varpi L_2 + \frac{1}{j\varpi C_2})} \quad (35)$$

It can be rewritten as:

$$Z = j\left\{\frac{(1 - w^2 L_1 C_1)(1 - w^2 L_2 C_2) + w^4 M^2 C_1 C_2}{w C_1 (1 - w^2 L_2 C_2)}\right\} \quad (36)$$

Expression (36) allows the behavior analysis of the impedance at the generator, as shown in Figure 8. As previously shown, the mutual inductance depends on the coupling factor. Therefore, it can be verified the influence of the coupling factor in the response of a double tuned circuit. It was run a Spice simulation, as shown in Figure 9, where the coupling factor ranged from 0.1 to 0.2, and the frequency varied from 12 to 16 MHz. As an initial condition, $L_1$ and $L_2$ were taken as 3,5 μH and capacitors $C_1$ and $C_2$ are equal to 38 pF. In that case, the resonance frequencies at primary and secondary are equal and it will be taken as an individual resonance.

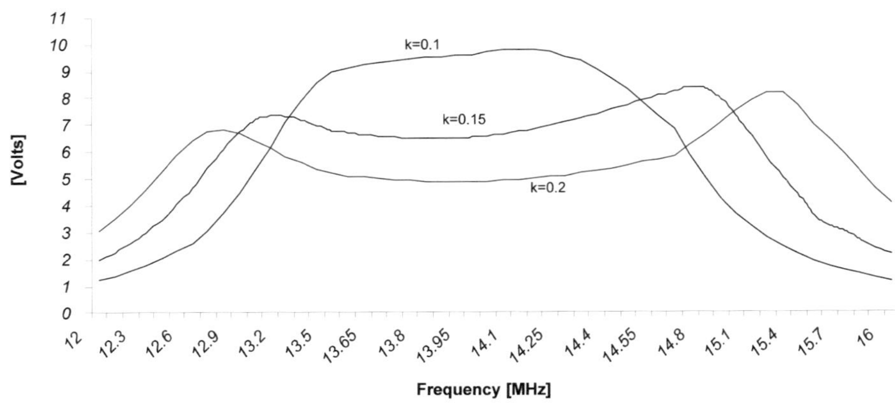


**Figure 9.** Spice simulation of double resonance.

From Figure 9 it can be observed that larger coupling factor causes larger deviation of the resonance frequency from the individual frequency. The energy transfer by RF coupling is directly dependent on the variation of the coupling and consequently dependent on the approaching between reader and tag, in other words orientation of the reader and tag inductances strongly changes the double resonance between reader and tag.

## 7. Mutual inductance measurement method

According to [3] and [4], the mutual inductance between two inductors can be measured. Considering two magnetically coupled inductors, as shown in Figure 10, the inductance seen by the generator is given as:

$$L_s' = L_1 + M_{12} + M_{21} \tag{37}$$

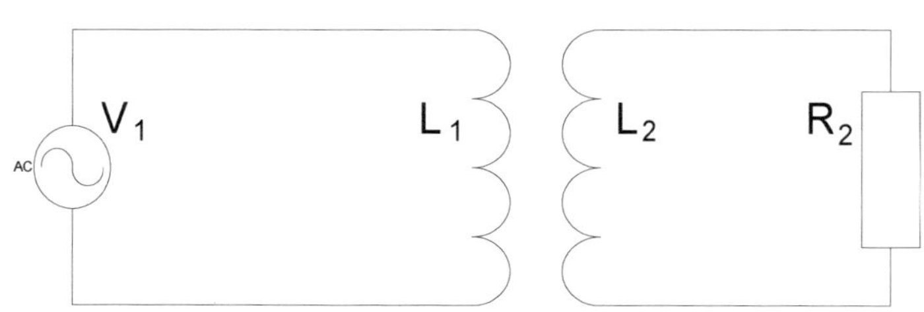


**Figure 10.** Magnetically coupled circuits.

Thus, the inductance seen at the generator terminals is the inductance plus the mutual inductance of inductor 1 over inductor 2, plus the mutual inductance of inductor 2 over inductor 1. Now, considering the series association, as shown in Figure 11, the total inductance is given as:

$$L_s` = L_1 + L_2 + M_{21} + M_{12} \tag{38}$$

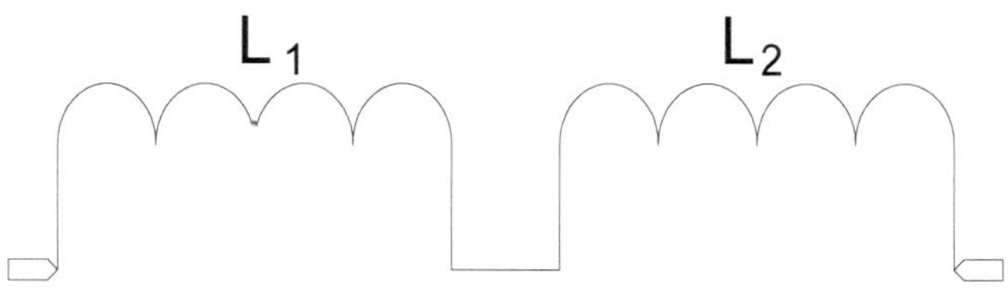


**Figure 11.** Series association of inductors.

If inductances $L_1$ and $L_2$ are associated in series, as shown in Figure 11, the resulting inductance is the sum of the individual inductance and the mutual inductances. If the measurement method is altered, as shown in Figure 12, where one inductor is inverted, the new series inductance is given as:

$$L_s`` = L_1 + L_2 - M_{12} - M_{21} \tag{39}$$

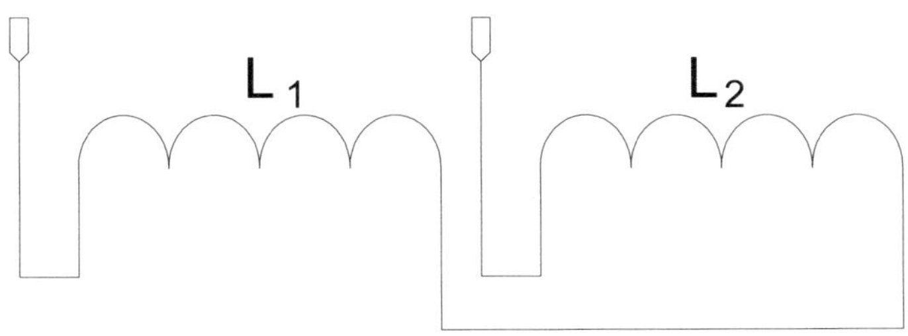


**Figure 12.** Series association of inductors, in which one inductor is inverted.

Now, subtracting $L'$ from $L''$ results:

$$L_1 + L_2 + M_{12} + M_{21} - L_1 - L_2 + M_{12} + M_{21} = L_s` - L_s`` \tag{40}$$

By considering $M_{12} = M_{21} = M$, then:

$$M = \frac{L_s` - L_s``}{4} \tag{41}$$

Once $L_1$ and $L_2$ are known, the coupling factor can be found as:

$$k = \frac{M}{\sqrt{L_1 L_2}} \tag{42}$$

## 8. Model for the energy transfer based on the classic circuit theory

The energy transfer between reader and tag in free space can be modeled using the classic circuit theory. Consider Figure 13 that represents the magnetic coupling between reader and tag.

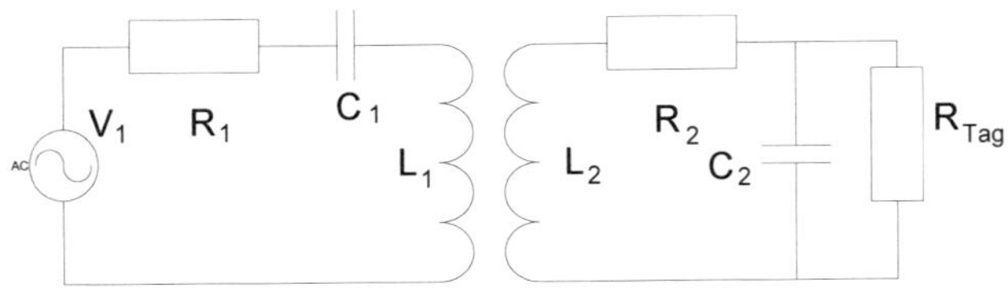


**Figure 13.** Magnetic coupling between reader and tag.

Observe that resistor $R_2$ represents the losses on $L_2$, $R_{tag}$ represents the load at the tag and $R_1$ represents the losses at inductor $L_1$. The analysis can be greatly simplified if the reader circuit can be converted into the series equivalent circuit, since the reader load could be represented as the resistance losses of capacitor $C_2$. Therefore, the quality factor of capacitor $C_2$ can be expressed in terms of its losses resistance, as indicated in Figure 14. The equivalence between series and parallel circuit is granted if the real and imaginary parts are equal, thus:

$$y_p = G_p + j\omega C_p \tag{43}$$

$$R_s = \frac{G_p}{G_p^{\,2} + (\omega C_p)^2} \tag{44}$$

$$C_s = \frac{G_p^{\,2} + (\omega C_p)^2}{\omega^2 C_p} \tag{45}$$

$$G_p = \frac{1}{R_p} \tag{46}$$

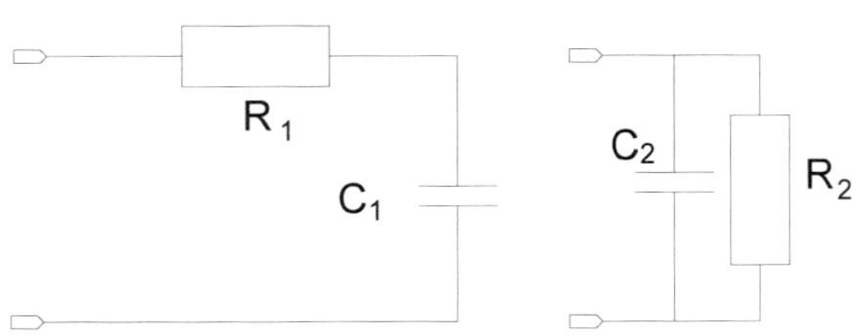


**Figure 14.** Capacitive equivalent circuits.

That approximation allows the conversion of tag load $R_p$ into $R_s$, as given by (44). The approximation is possible since the capacitor presents low losses at the frequency range.

Thus, tag load provides the larger contribution in the energy dissipation in the magnetic coupling between reader and tag.

Observe also that the equivalent capacitor given by (45) is frequency dependent that implies in another source of variation in the resonance frequency at the tag. Based on that premise, the equivalent circuit is shown in Figure 15.

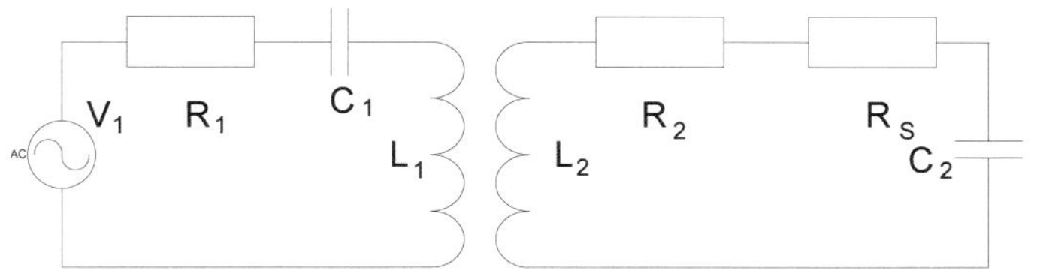


**Figure 15.** Modified equivalent circuit.

The circuit of Figure 15 can be equated as:

$$R_t = R_2 + R_s \tag{47}$$

Thus:

$$V_1 = I_1(R_s + j\omega L_1 + \frac{1}{j\omega C_1}) - I_2 j\omega M \tag{48}$$

where $M$ is the mutual inductance between $L_1$ and $L_2$.

$$0 = -I_1 j\omega M + I_2(R_t + j\omega L_2 + \frac{1}{j\omega C_2}) \tag{49}$$

Combining (48) and (49) results into:

$$V_2 = \frac{V_1 M}{[(\omega M)^2 + (Rt + j\omega L_2 + \frac{1}{j\omega C_2})(R_s + j\omega L_1 + \frac{1}{j\omega C_1})]C_2} \tag{50}$$

It can be observed from (5) the possibility of predicting the voltage at the tag, under free space conditions. Nevertheless, in real application, the tag shall be placed inside a human being, usually in the belly area, in order to measure any biological data. Since pork tissue presents electromagnetic properties similar to human tissue, it will be used in the measurements.

## 9. Comparison between simulated and measured data for free space

It was used the test set up shown in Figure 16, where $L_1$ =1.77 uH and $L_2$ =5.4uH. Observe that the inductors are axially aligned. That orientation was chosen to achieve the best magnetic coupling, considering the ratio between length and diameter of the inductor. The inductors series resistances $R_1$ =1.14Ω and $R_2$ =2.2 Ω (at 13.56 MHz) were obtained using a network analyzer. The experimental measurements and the simulations were conducted considering a generator having a 1V and a 50 Ω internal impedance. The tag load was taken as a 1 kΩ resistor. Table 1 presents the measurement results.

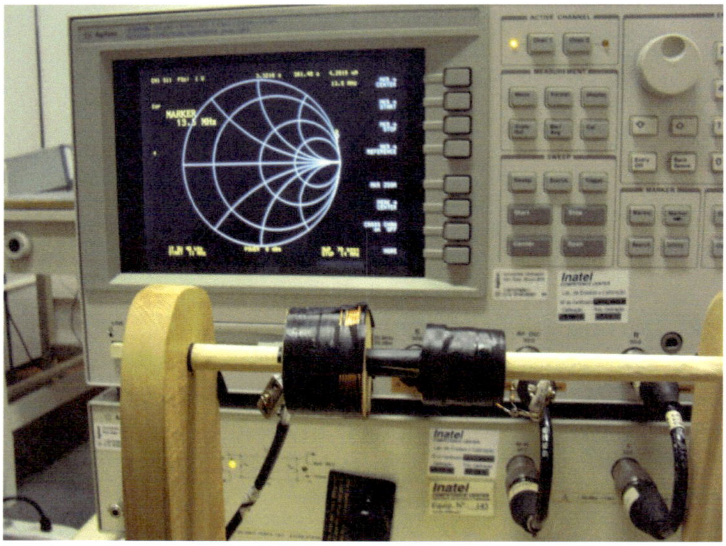


**Figure 16.** Free space measurement test set up.

| Measurement | Distance $L_1$ - $L_2$ | $M$ |
|---|---|---|
| $L'$=10.00uH<br>$L''$=6.33uH | 5mm | 0.917 uH |
| $L'$=9.48uH<br>$L''$=6.71uH | 10mm | 0.692uH |
| $L'$=9.13uH<br>$L''$=7.00uH | 15mm | 0.532uH |
| $L'$=8.74uH<br>$L''$=7.26uH | 20mm | 0.370uH |
| $L'$=8.55uH<br>$L''$=7.40uH | 25mm | 0.287uH |

**Table 1.** Mutual inductance measurements.

It was conducted a set of simulations of equations (44), (45) and (50) for the range of 12 to 16 MHz and the result is shown in Figure 17. It can be observed that the tag voltage is approximately 1V and the resonance frequency varied with the mutual impedance. Thus a variation in the resonance frequency will cause a change in the inductor series resistance. Therefore, in case of frequency deviation at the generator, the resistance losses can change and may alter the measurement data. As a consequence, variable capacitors $C_1$ and $C_2$ were added to adjust the tag voltage level at the same operation frequency. That procedure maintain the inductor characteristics regardless any frequency variation. Table 2 shows a comparison between free space measurement and simulation data.

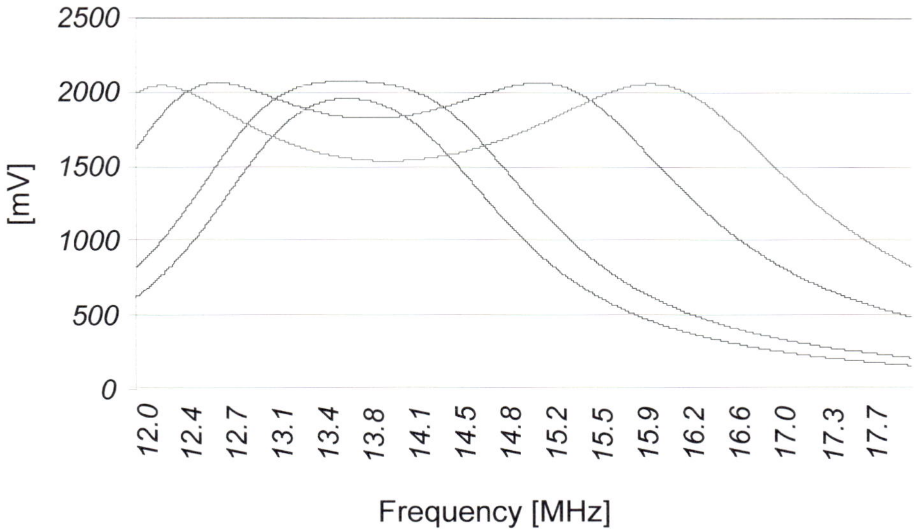


**Figure 17.** MATLAB simulation.

| Distance | Measured | Simulated | *M* |
|---|---|---|---|
| 25mm | 769mV | 1001mV | 0.287uH |
| 20mm | 943mV | 1061mV | 0.370uH |
| 15mm | 1038mV | 1063mV | 0.532uH |
| 10mm | 1026mV | 1055mV | 0.692uH |
| 5mm | 1007mV | 1052mV | 0.917uH |

**Table 2.** Comparison between free space measurement and simulation data.

As it can be observed, there is an error between the measurement and the simulation data, as it is shown in Table 3. Note that the error is smaller than 4.3% for distances smaller than 15mm. The error becomes larger for distance over 15mm, since there is magnetic field scattering due to coil imperfections. The connection cables between generator and reader may cause a magnetic field distribution, thus increasing the error.

| Distance | Error |
|---|---|
| 5mm | -4.3% |
| 10mm | -2.75% |
| 15mm | -2.34% |
| 20mm | -11.12% |
| 25mm | -23.17% |

**Table 3.** Error between measurement and simulation data for free space.

## 10. Comparison between free space and animal tissue

Once the tag voltage for free space is known, it can be compared to implanted conditions, where there is tissue between reader and tag. Figure 18 shows the set up used for the measurements, and Table 4 provides the tag voltage comparison between free space and pork tissue conditions. Since pork tissue presents electromagnetic properties similar to human tissue, it will be used in the measurements.

| Distance | Free Space | Pork Tissue |
|---|---|---|
| 10mm | 1932mV | 1869mV |
| 15mm | 1869mV | 1787mV |
| 20mm | 1671mV | 1549mV |
| 25mm | 1247mV | 1202mV |

**Table 4.** Comparison between free space and pork tissue data.

The generator voltage was raised to approximately 1.94V in order to assure that low voltage measurements are not spoiled by noise. The pork tissue thickness is approximately 10mm. As it can be directly observed form Table 4, the free space data is different form the pork tissue data. The small difference suggests that at 13.56MHz the pork tissue causes s variation in the magnetic permeability as compared to free space. The error between free space and pork tissue data is presented in Table 5. The 5mm measurement was not conducted due to the pork tissue thickness The first measurement, 10mm, was conducted with the reader in direct contact with the pork tissue.

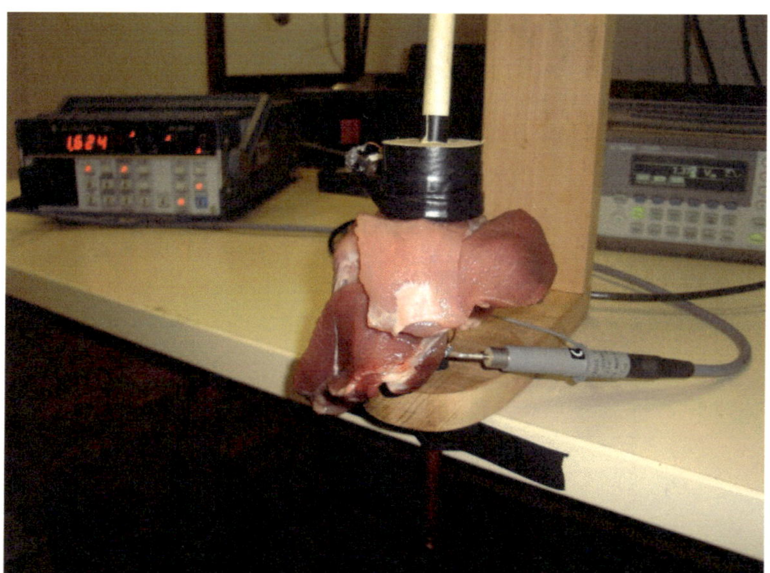

**Figure 18.** Test set up using pork tissue.

| Distance | Error |
|---|---|
| 10mm | -3.26% |
| 15mm | -4.39% |
| 20mm | -7.30% |
| 25mm | -3.61% |

**Table 5.** Error between free space and pork tissue data.

## 11. Conclusions

The classic circuit theory can be used to obtain the tag voltage from the mutual inductance between reader and tag in a RFID system. Therefore, based on the estimate of the mutual inductance between reader and tag, it is possible to estimate voltage at the tag. Nevertheless the main distress is the variation on the resonance frequency due to the mutual inductance, and ultimately, the coupling factor.

Two approximations must be conducted to estimate the tag voltage. The first one is due to the magnetic scattering between reader and tag inductors that becomes more relevant as the distance between them increases. The second approximation is due to the tissue that alters the magnetic permeability and consequently reduces the tag voltage. Thus, by considering the simulation errors and the errors due to the tissue, it is possible to estimate the voltage at the tag. Table 6 presents the compiled errors.

| Distance | Error |
|---|---|
| 10mm | -5.92% |
| 15mm | -6.66% |
| 20mm | -17.60% |
| 25mm | -26.90% |

**Table 6.** Total errors between simulated and measured data.

Therefore, by taking into account both approximations it is possible to estimate the voltage drop at the tag and consequently, the power reduction. Once the power reduction is known, it can be taken into account during the tag circuit design. Consequently, the use of classic theory of magnetically coupled circuits is a simple way to estimate the voltage in implanted devices. Nevertheless additional studies regarding the resonance frequency variation is still required.

## Author details

Paulo Cesar Crepaldi, Tales Cleber Pimenta and Robson Luiz Moreno
*Universidade Federal de Itajuba, Brasil*

Rômulo Mota Volpato
*Inatel Santa Rita do Sapucai, Brasil*

## 12. References

[1] M. M. Ahmadi, G. A. Julien, "A Wireless Implantable Microsytem for Continuous Blood Glucose Moritoring", *IEE Transations on Biomedical and Systems,* Vol 3, No. 3 June 2009 Pag 169-180.

[2] F. Ramos, M. Santana, R. M. Volpato, R. L. Moreno and T. C. Pimenta, "Front –End of an Implantable Medical Device", *Wireless Systems International Meeting,* May 26-28, 2010 Campina Grande , Brazil.

[3] TESLA Q-METRO Model BM 409 *Service manual.*

[4] F. E. Terman, J. M. Pettit, *Electronic Measurements,* MacGraw-Hill 1952.

[5] K. Finkenzeller, *RFID Handbook – Fundamental and Application in Contactless Smart Cards and Identifications,* 2010, John Wiley & Sons.

[6] Mehdi Kiani, Maysam Ghovanloo, "An RFID-Based Closed-Loop Wireless Power Transmission System for Biomedical Applications", *IEEE Transactions on Circuits and Systems—II*: Express Briefs, Vol. 57, No. 4, April 2010.

Chapter 16

# Biomedical Image Signal Processing for Reflection-Based Imaging

Paul Jansz, Steven Richardson,
Graham Wild and Steven Hinckley

Additional information is available at the end of the chapter

http://dx.doi.org/10.5772/50213

## 1. Introduction

Optical coherence tomography (OCT), ultrasound and other reflection based biomedical imaging technologies involve image signal processing that is primarily a filtering, digitizing and summing process so that the tissue cross-section can be visualized. In particular, in OCT, a series of adjacent one dimensional *in-vivo* axial interferograms (A-scan) are summed to form a two dimensional (B-scan) reflection map or reflectogram. Further graphical combinations can add adjacent B-scan together to form three dimensional C-scans. A physician can make a subjective interpretation and evaluation from the B and/or C-scans that may lead to actions impacting on the patient's prognosis. More objective information can be obtained by using backwards fitting models (BFM) that fit tissue characteristics, including layer depth and reflectivity, to imaged tissue A-scans, returning values that are not significantly different to the actual values.

BFMs can be either primarily deterministic or stochastic. One example of the latter is a genetic algorithm model (GAM). In this chapter, a GAM is characterised for its degree of precision and accuracy to retrieve the depth and reflectivity profile of a simulated A-scan of a virtual tissue model with defined tissue layer depths and layer refractive indicies. This stochastic model intrinsically evolves successively more precise and accurate generations of solutions, in accordance with certain software defined specific and random selection control parameters. This chapter presents a characterisation of the dependence of the accuracy and precision of the estimated layer depths and reflectivities, returned by this version of the GAM, on the number of generations, and the values of the GAM's selection-control parameters.

# 2. Theory

## 2.1. Optical coherence tomography

Optical coherence tomography (OCT) is a medical imaging technique that is fundamentally an application of low coherence interferometry (Drexler *et al* 2008), (Fercher 1996), (Izatt *et al* 1997). In OCT, a low coherent near infrared source is used to generate a reflection intensity map of the tissues cross section. An OCT scan can be 1 to 3 mm deep (Friebel *et al* 2009), depending on the tissue type and the optical properties of the light source, specifically the wavelength and intensity. Using a conventional solid state broadband light source, the axial resolution is typically 1 to 10 micrometers, depending on the bandwidth, central wavelength (Drexler *et al* 2008) and the sources Fourier envelope shape (Adie 2007) (Rossetti *et al* 2005) (Shidlovski 2008). Four key elements impact on the OCT detector signal: the light source, the optical delay line (ODL), type of interferometer used and the sample characteristics.

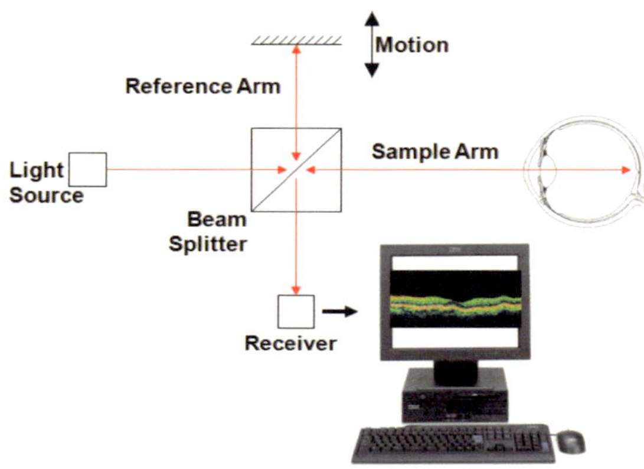


**Figure 1.** Operating principle of a Michelson interferometer type OCT system.

The light source is low-coherent in that it has a broad frequency bandwidth. All the light frequencies interfere with each other resulting in a self modulated light source where the width of the individual peak in the time domain is proportional to the image axial resolution, measured by the coherence length ($L_c$) of the source (Eq. (1)) divided by the average tissue refractive index. The $L_c$ can be determined from the spectral characteristics of the source using,

$$L_C = \frac{\ln 4.\lambda_0^2}{\pi \Delta \lambda}, \qquad (1)$$

where $\lambda_0$ is the source central wavelength, and $\Delta\lambda$ is the spectral Full Width at Half Maximum (FWHM) of the power spectrum, assuming it has a Gaussian spectral profile. Typical OCT sources have $\lambda_0$ at 840 nm and 1320 nm, with $\Delta\lambda$ equal to 60 nm. From Equation (1), these values give coherence lengths of 5.2 µm and 12.8 µm, respectively.

Because the inverse Fourier Transform of a perfectly Gaussian spectrum in the frequency domain is itself a Gaussian in the time domain, a perfectly Gaussian spectrum will have one peak and no repeated peaks; ideal for stratified samples. The less Gaussian the source spectrum in the frequency domain, the more frequently that peaks appear in the time domain. A Michelson or Mach Zehnder interferometer can then be used to manipulate the introduced light to acquire an interference pattern of the multi-layered sample's reflected beam and the reflected reference ODL beam at the detector (Fig. 1).

## 2.2. The forward model

The use of a Matlab OCT circuit simulation model to produce interferogram A-scans from a defined Gaussian spectral light source for a user defined stratified sample has been previously used to characterise typical OCT light sources (Jansz *et al* 2012) and optical delay lines (Jansz *et al* 2011). With this forwards model, backward fitting models (BFM) can now be tested to retro-fit certain sample parameters. These parameters for the present BFM version are sample layer thicknesses and reflectivities.

### *2.2.1. The source*

Suppose that a light source emits a continuous distribution of wavelengths whose amplitude is a function of the wavelength. That is, $A = A(\lambda)$. For example, if the light source is modelled as a spectrum of continuous wavelengths, with a Gaussian spectral shape defined by the peak amplitude ($A_0$), the peak wavelength ($\lambda_0$), and the spectral bandwidth, FWHM ($\Delta\lambda$), we have,

$$A(\lambda) = A_0 Exp\left( \frac{-\ln(16)(\lambda - \lambda_0)^2}{(\Delta\lambda)^2} \right), \tag{2}$$

with the laser power given by,

$$P = A_0 \Delta\lambda \sqrt{\frac{\pi}{\ln(16)}} \tag{3}$$

### *2.2.2. Light amplitude in the interferometer*

The distribution of wavelengths is first passed through a 50% mirror, with half of the light reflected ($R$), and half transmitted ($T$). The result is a reflected and transmitted wave with amplitude distributions,

$$A_R(\lambda) = A_T(\lambda) = \frac{A(\lambda)}{\sqrt{2}}. \tag{4}$$

Once the original light source is split, it becomes important to keep track of the distance travelled by each wave, as any difference will be associated with a phase shift, and therefore a change in the interference pattern. The transmitted wave, considered to be the sample arm of the interferometer, travels to a multi-layered surface consisting of $n$ partially reflecting interfaces, the phantom structure to be imaged. The transmitted wave goes through transmission and reflection at each interface. Upon returning from the multi-layered interface, the transmitted wave is reflected by the 50% mirror to the detector. The total distance travelled by the transmitted wave which reflects off the interface of the multi-layered structure is denoted $d_i$ for $i = 1,2,\ldots,n$. The thickness $\Delta d_i$ of the $i^{th}$ layer in the sample (i.e. the distance between the $i^{th}$ and $(i+1)^{th}$ interface) is then given by

$$\Delta d_i = \frac{d_{i+1} - d_i}{2}, \quad i = 1,2,\ldots,n-1 \tag{5}$$

The reflectivity of the interface is denoted by $r_i$ for $i = 1,2,\ldots,n$. We have assumed that the contribution of waves which are reflected off multiple interfaces within the multi-layered structure is negligible. Therefore it makes sense to decompose the detected component of the transmitted wave into $n$ parts corresponding to each of the reflecting surfaces. Hence, we have,

$$A_T(\lambda)_i = \begin{cases} \dfrac{A(\lambda)}{2}\sqrt{r_1}, & i = 1 \\ \dfrac{A(\lambda)}{2}\sqrt{r_i}\prod_{j=1}^{i-1}\left(1 - r_j\right), & i = 2,3,\ldots,n \end{cases} \tag{6}$$

The reflected wave, considered to be the reference arm of the interferometer, travels from the 50% mirror to another reflector which is moved incrementally (i.e. no Doppler effect) before being reflected back through the 50% mirror (transmitted) to a detector. The total distance travelled by the reflected wave is denoted $d_{n+1}$. Note that a shift of the moving reflector by an amount $\delta$ will result in an increase in the total distance travelled by the reflected wave of $2\delta$. We will denote the reflectivity of the reference arm mirror by $r_{n+1}$ (although typically $r_{n+1} = 1$). The final amplitude distribution of the reflected wave is,

$$A_R(\lambda) = \frac{A(\lambda)}{2}\sqrt{r_{n+1}}. \tag{7}$$

In the interest of notational convenience, let us define a reflectivity factor,

$$RF_i = \begin{cases} \sqrt{r_1}, & i = 1 \\ \sqrt{r_i}\prod_{j=1}^{i-1}\left(1 - r_j\right), & i = 2,3,\ldots,n. \\ \sqrt{r_{n+1}}, & i = n+1 \end{cases} \tag{8}$$

Then the amplitudes of the transmitted and reflected waves can be expressed as,

$$\begin{aligned} A_T(\lambda)_i &= \frac{A(\lambda)}{2} RF_i, \quad i = 1,2,\ldots,n \\ A_R(\lambda) &= \frac{A(\lambda)}{2} RF_{n+1}. \end{aligned} \tag{9}$$

### 2.2.3. Light wave interference in the interferometer

Having defined expressions for the amplitudes of the interfering waves, we now consider the interference of these waves. Without loss of generality, we can represent all waves using a sine function with origin at the detector. The expression for the reflected wave is,

$$y_R(\lambda,x,t) = A_R(\lambda)\sin\left(\frac{2\pi}{\lambda}(x + d_{n+1} - ct)\right), \tag{10}$$

while for the (originally) transmitted components we have,

$$y_T(\lambda,x,t)_i = A_T(\lambda)\sin\left(\frac{2\pi}{\lambda}(x + d_i - ct) + \phi_i\pi\right), \quad i = 1,2,\ldots,n, \tag{11}$$

where $\phi_i$ is a phase shift indicator function given by,

$$\phi_i = \begin{cases} 1, & n_{i-1} < n_i \\ 0, & n_{i-1} > n_i \end{cases}, \quad i = 1,2,\ldots,n, \tag{12}$$

where $n_i$ denotes the refractive index of the $i^{th}$ layer of the sample (not to be confused with the number of layers in the sample $n$). Note that $n_0$ denotes the refractive index of the medium in front of the sample. Note also that $\phi_{n+1} = 1$.

For the sake of simplifying notation, let us denote,

$$\omega = \frac{2\pi}{\lambda}(x - ct), \tag{13}$$

$$\theta_i = \frac{2\pi d_i}{\lambda} + \phi_i\pi, \quad i = 1,2,\ldots,n. \tag{14}$$

Then we can write,

$$y_R(\lambda,\omega) = A_R(\lambda)\sin(\omega + \theta_{n+1}) \tag{15}$$

$$y_T(\lambda,\omega)_i = A_T(\lambda)\sin(\omega + \theta_i), \quad i = 1,2,\ldots,n \tag{16}$$

The resultant wave arriving at the detector is therefore given by,

$$\begin{aligned} Y(\lambda,\omega) &= y_R(\lambda,\omega) + \sum_{i=1}^{n} y_T(\lambda,\omega)_i \\ &= \sum_{i=1}^{n+1} \frac{A(\lambda)}{2} RF_i \sin(\omega + \theta_i) \\ &= \sum_{i=1}^{n+1} \frac{A(\lambda)}{2} RF_i \left[\sin(\omega)\cos(\theta_i) + \cos(\omega)\sin(\theta_i)\right] \\ &= C_1 \sin(\omega) + C_2 \cos(\omega) \\ &= \sqrt{C_1^2 + C_2^2}\,\sin\left(\omega + a\tan\left(\frac{C_2}{C_1}\right)\right) \end{aligned} \tag{17}$$

where,

$$C_1 = \sum_{i=1}^{n+1} \frac{A(\lambda)}{2} RF_i \cos(\theta_i)$$
$$C_2 = \sum_{i=1}^{n+1} \frac{A(\lambda)}{2} RF_i \sin(\theta_i) \tag{18}$$

It follows that the amplitude of the resultant wave is given by,

$$Amplitude(\lambda) = \sqrt{C_1^{\,2} + C_2^{\,2}}, \tag{19}$$

and hence that the total intensity of detected light over all wavelengths is given by,

$$I = \int_{-\infty}^{\infty} \left[ C_1^{\,2} + C_2^{\,2} \right] d\lambda. \tag{20}$$

Equation (20) can be expressed in a more convenient form by simplifying the integrand as follows,

$$\begin{aligned}
C_1^{\,2} + C_2^{\,2} &= \left( \sum_{i=1}^{n+1} \frac{A(\lambda)}{2} RF_i \cos(\theta_i) \right)^2 + \left( \sum_{i=1}^{n+1} \frac{A(\lambda)}{2} RF_i \sin(\theta_i) \right)^2 \\
&= \frac{A(\lambda)^2}{4} \left[ \begin{aligned} &\sum_{i=1}^{n+1} RF_i^2 \cos^2(\theta_i) + 2\sum_{i=1}^{n} \sum_{j=i+1}^{n+1} RF_i RF_j \cos(\theta_i)\cos(\theta_j) \\ &+ \sum_{i=1}^{n+1} RF_i^2 \sin^2(\theta_i) + 2\sum_{i=1}^{n} \sum_{j=i+1}^{n+1} RF_i RF_j \sin(\theta_i)\sin(\theta_j) \end{aligned} \right] \\
&= \frac{A(\lambda)^2}{4} \left[ \sum_{i=1}^{n+1} RF_i^2 + 2\sum_{i=1}^{n} \sum_{j=i+1}^{n+1} RF_i RF_j \cos(\theta_i - \theta_j) \right]
\end{aligned} \tag{21}$$

$$\begin{aligned}
&= \frac{A(\lambda)^2}{4} \left[ \sum_{i=1}^{n+1} RF_i^2 + 2\sum_{i=1}^{n} \sum_{j=i+1}^{n} RF_i RF_j \cos(\theta_i - \theta_j) + 2\sum_{i=1}^{n} RF_i RF_{n+1} \cos(\theta_i - \theta_{n+1}) \right] \\
&= \frac{A(\lambda)^2}{4} \left[ \begin{aligned} &\sum_{i=1}^{n+1} RF_i^2 + 2\sum_{i=1}^{n} \sum_{j=i+1}^{n} RF_i RF_j \cos\left( \frac{2\pi}{\lambda}(d_i - d_j) + \pi(\phi_i - \phi_j) \right) \\ &\qquad + 2\sum_{i=1}^{n} RF_i RF_{n+1} \cos\left( \frac{2\pi}{\lambda}(d_i - d_{n+1}) + \pi(\phi_i - \phi_{n+1}) \right) \end{aligned} \right] \\
&= \frac{A(\lambda)^2}{4} \left[ \begin{aligned} &\sum_{i=1}^{n+1} RF_i^2 + 2\sum_{i=1}^{n} \sum_{j=i+1}^{n} RF_i RF_j (-1)^{\phi_i + \phi_j} \cos\left( \frac{2\pi}{\lambda}(d_i - d_j) \right) \\ &\qquad + 2\sum_{i=1}^{n} RF_i RF_{n+1} (-1)^{\phi_i + 1} \cos\left( \frac{2\pi}{\lambda}(d_i - d_{n+1}) \right) \end{aligned} \right]
\end{aligned}$$

Hence, the intensity I at the detector can be expressed as,

$$I = B_0 + \sum_{i=1}^{n} B_i F\left(d_i - d_{n+1}\right), \tag{22}$$

where,

$$B_0 = \frac{1}{4}\int_{-\infty}^{\infty} A(\lambda)^2 \, d\lambda \sum_{i=1}^{n+1} RF_i^2 + \frac{1}{2}\sum_{i=1}^{n-1}\sum_{j=i+1}^{n} RF_i RF_j (-1)^{\phi_i+\phi_j} F\left(d_i - d_j\right), \tag{23}$$

$$B_i = \frac{1}{2} RF_i RF_{n+1} (-1)^{\phi_i+1} \tag{24}$$

$$F(x) = \int_{-\infty}^{\infty} A(\lambda)^2 \cos\left(\frac{2\pi x}{\lambda}\right) d\lambda \tag{25}$$

Note that if $A(\lambda)$ is given by equation (2) then,

$$B_0 = \frac{A_0^{\,2}\Delta\lambda}{4}\sqrt{\frac{\pi}{2\ln(16)}} \sum_{i=1}^{n+1} RF_i^2 + \frac{1}{2}\sum_{i=1}^{n-1}\sum_{j=i+1}^{n} RF_i RF_j (-1)^{\phi_i+\phi_j} F\left(d_i - d_j\right) \tag{26}$$

The expression given in equation (22) separates the intensity into a constant offset component $B_0$ (i.e. constant for a specific sample structure with fixed distances $d_1, d_2, \ldots, d_n$ and reflectivity's $r_1, r_2, \ldots, r_n$), and an interference component for each of the layers given by $B_i F(d_i - d_{n+1})$. The coefficient $B_i$ contains only information relating to layer reflectivity's, while the function $F(d_i - d_{n+1})$ contains the information related to the layer distances.

### 2.2.4. *Demonstrating the forwards model functionality*

We have demonstrated the use of the forwards model in characterising various OCT optical delay lines (ODLs) as well as typical OCT light sources.

#### 2.2.4.1. *Optical delay line simulations*

The simulation produced A-scans of a typical moving optical delay line (ODL), as well as a stepped stationary ODL. For the former, the model generated typical A-scans using a Gaussian spectral light source. However, the model showed that there was not enough definition of layer peaks in the A-scan for the stationary stepped ODL. To overcome this, the model showed that the light in the ODL need to be modulated in the light source axis by an amount equal to the source wavelength (Jansz *et al* 2011).

#### 2.2.4.2. *Characterising simulated light sources*

The typical OCT light source is a super luminescent light emitting diode (SLD). It is preferred as its spectral shape is Gaussian. The inverse Fourier transform of a Gaussian spectrum in the frequency domain is a single peak Gaussian in the time domain, ideal for multi layer interferometry. Simulated single and multiple SLD light sources were used to characterise A-scans of virtual samples. They demonstrated particular artefacts such as side lobes, whose intensity decreased as the sources central wavelengths moved closer together. Equation (1) was also verified by the simulation demonstrating that broader bandwidth sources generated thinner A-scan peaks (Jansz *et al* 2012).

## 2.3. The backward fitting model (BFM) - genetic algorithm approach

We will now propose a method for determining the reflectivity's and distances $\{(r_i, d_i)\}_{i=1}^{n}$ of each layer in a sample structure, given a discrete set of $M$ observations of intensity at known reference arm distances, $O = \{(I^j, d_{n+1}{}^j)\}_{j=1}^{M}$. It will be assumed that the intensity observations will be made at local maxima of $I$; at least one observation is made for $d_{n+1}$ such that $|d_i - d_{n+1}| > 1.5\Delta\lambda$ for all $i = 1,2,\ldots,n$; the reference arm distances are indexed such that $d_{n+1}^j < d_{n+1}^{j+1}$ for $j = 1,2,\ldots,M-1$; and the sample layers are separated by at least $\Delta\lambda$ to ensure minimal layer interference effects.

### 2.3.1. *BFM – genetic algorithm method*

The problem of reverse fitting an interferogram to a set of $M$ observations $O = \{(I^j, d_{n+1}^j)\}_{j=1}^{M}$ can be formulated as a least squares problem:

$$\min_{s \in S} LS(s) := \min_{s \in S} \sum_{j=1}^{M} \left( I^j - B_0 - \sum_{i=1}^{n} |B_i| \tilde{F}\left(d_i - d_{n+1}{}^j\right) \right)^2 \tag{27}$$

where the solution space $S = \{s = (B_0, |B_1|, \ldots, |B_n|, d_1, d_2, \ldots, d_n) : s \in \Re \times (0,0.5)^n \times \Re^n\}$, and the function $\tilde{F}(x)$ is the cubic-spline interpolant of the local maxima of F(x). Since this is a non-linear optimization problem there is no obvious systematic/efficient approach to obtaining a solution, so instead we will utilize a meta-heuristic genetic algorithm approach to try to identify a 'near optimal' solution.

The basic idea behind a genetic algorithm is as follows (Hillier and Lieberman 2005):

1. Define an initial population $S^0$ of solutions, and evaluate the objective function (equation 27) for each member of the population.
2. Select out the less optimal solutions from population $S^0$ (i.e. those which have a large objective value). Randomly 'breed' the remaining solutions to obtain a new solution population $S^1$. The optimal solutions from which the new solutions are bred are called 'parents', while the new solutions are called 'children'.
3. Repeat step 2 until a pre-defined termination criterion is satisfied.

By continually selecting out the optimal solutions and 'breeding' these to give more optimal solutions, the selected solution set evolves towards a near optimal solution i.e. it evolves towards the specific sample parameter values producing the interferogram, produced by the forwards model. One testable assertion in this mathematically stochastic paradygm, is that, for an optimal solution to be achieved, diversity needs to be maintained in the population at all iterations. This may be achieved in a number of ways. In this approach, two methods will be employed:

1. By introducing a mutation rate in which child solutions randomly inherit a feature not possessed by either parent.
2. The independent addition of new members which were not bred from the initial population.

### *2.3.2. BFM – The genetic algorithm*

Initialise: Specify values for the following parameters:

- The size of the solution population ***P***.
- The non-negative integers ***P*₁, *P*₂, *P*₃**, which respectively define the number of best solutions retained for the next population, the number of solutions randomly selected from the worst solutions for inclusion in the next population, and the number of new solutions bred from the solutions retained from the current population. Note that ***P*₁, *P*₂, *P*₃**, must be chosen such that $P_1 + P_2 + P_3 \leq P$.
- The maximum number of algorithm cycles or generations, ***N***.
- The termination tolerance $\varepsilon$ .
- The mutation rate ***MR*** %

Following are the steps required to perform the algorithm:

**Step 1.** Identify all observations $O'$ which are locally maximum relative to the other observations in $O$ (i.e. $O' = \left\{\left(I^j, d_{n+1}{}^j\right) : I^j > I^{j-1} \text{ and } I^j > I^{j+1}\right\}$ ). The size of $O'$ (denoted $n'$ ), is the estimated number of layers in the sample. Denote the index set of $O'$ as $J' = \left\{i : \left(I^i, d_{n+1}{}^i\right) \in O'\right\}$ .

**Step 2.** Refine the solution space $S$ as follows:

i. Set the offset value $B_0 = \min I^j$ ;
ii. Note that the location of the layer identified in Step 1 will be such that $d_{i-1} < d_i < d_{i+1}$ for all $i \in J'$ .
Denote the refined solution space $S'$ .

**Step 3.** Randomly generate an initial population $S^0 \subset S'$ of size ***P***, and evaluate ***LS(s)*** for every $s \in S^0$ .

**Step 4.** Use the existing population $S^k$ ( $k \in \{0,1,2,\ldots\}$ ) to generate $S^{k+1}$ as follows:

i. Let $S_1{}^{k+1}$ denote the set consisting of the $P_1$ solutions $s \in S^k$ with the lowest values of ***LS(s)***.
ii. Let $S_2{}^{k+1}$ denote a random sample of $P_2$ solutions from $S^k \setminus S_1{}^{k+1}$ .
iii. Generate /breed a set $S_3{}^{k+1}$ of $P_3$ new solutions. Each element $s \in S_3{}^{k+1}$ is constructed as a convex combination of randomly chosen solutions $s_1, s_2 \in S_1{}^{k+1} \cup S_2{}^{k+1}$

$s = \alpha s_1 + (1-\alpha) s_2$

where $\alpha \in (0,1)$ is a uniform random variable.

A mutation is randomly applied to ***MR*** **%** of the elements of the solution vector ***S***. The mutated element is set to a random value, while ensuring that $s \in S$.

i. Randomly generate/introduce a set $S_4^{k+1}$ of $P - \sum_{i=1}^{3} P_i$ new solutions.

ii. Set $S^{k+1} = \bigcup_{i=1}^{4} S_i^{k+1}$.

**Step 5.** Repeat Step 4 for a fixed number of cycles ***N***, or until there exists a member $s \in S^k$ such that $LS(s) < \varepsilon$, for a pre-specified tolerance $\varepsilon$.

The optimal member of the final population $s = (B_0, |B_1|, \ldots, |B_{n'}|, d_1, d_2, \ldots, d_{n'})$ directly provides the total distance travelled by the laser light off each of the $n'$ layers identified by the algorithm (i.e. $d_1, d_2, \ldots, d_{n'}$ ). The reflectivities of the layers can be obtained recursively as follows:

$$r_1 = \left( \frac{2|B_1|}{RF_{n+1}} \right)^2 \tag{28}$$

$$r_i = \left( \frac{2|B_i|}{RF_{n+1} \prod_{j=1}^{i-1} (1 - r_j)} \right)^2, \quad i = 2,3,\ldots,n' \tag{29}$$

Note: We will never get negative values of the coefficients because we are using the upper envelope function.

# 3. Method

## 3.1. Testing the precision of the genetic algorithm model (GAM)

This characterization of the efficacy of the BFM – Genetic Algorithm compares the spread of the depth and reflectivity of each layer for 2, 3, 4 and 5 layer sample models, for 20, 50, 100, 200, 400 and 800 generations of the GAM. This is in order to gauge the level of precision of the GAM as a function of generation number and number of sample strata. Ideally the precision of the two parameters should remain statistically not significantly different from the actual parameter values for a given layer irrespective of the number of layers in the sample.

The following GAM control variables were used for 2, 3, 4 and 5 strata virtual samples:

- P = 1000 – The total solution population size at the start of each generation.
- P1 = 100 – The number of optimal solutions retained for inclusion in the next generation.

- P2 = 250 – The number of solutions randomly selected from the remaining ranked solutions not in P1, for inclusion in the next generation.
- P3 = 300 – The number of new solutions (children) bred from a convex combination of P1 and P2, for inclusion in the next generation.
- P4 = P – (P1+P2+P3) = 350 – number of extra solutions randomly generated so that the total population quota, P, is achieved for the next generation. This is an implicit variable.
- N= 20, 50, 100, 200, 400, 800.
- Epsilon (ε) = 0.000001 – termination tolerance.
- Mutation rate = 0.01 – for each generation of size P, 1% of P has an introduced mutation.

The thickness was equivalent for each stratum being 100μm. The strata reflectivities used were based on approximate tissue strata refractive indices ($n$), alternating between 1.45 for the first stratum and 1.49, with $n$ of air being 1, above the first stratum. The expected reflectivities for the $i^{th}$ interface can then be calculated from,

$$R_i = \frac{(n_i - n_{i-1})^2}{(n_i + n_{i-1})^2}, \tag{30}$$

given that $i = 1$ refers to the top most stratum ($n_1$) interface with the air ($n_0$). The calculated percentage reflectivities are then 3.37359 for the surface and only 0.0185108 for the lower interfaces. Each generation number is repeated 7 times.

The degree of statistical "equality" of simulated depths to actual strata depths follows from the relative error of the depths introduced by the degree of coherence of the virtual light source. It provides a region of acceptable depths about the actual depths that are experimentally not significantly different from their actual values. The degree of source coherence defines an axial resolution that is measured by the source's coherence length ($L_c$) divided by the tissue refractive index. With the average tissue refractive index of 1.47 and the light source's central wavelength ($\lambda_0$) of 1550 nm and the full-width-half-maximum bandwidth ($\Delta\lambda$) of 40 nm, the $L_c$ is 26.5 μm (equation 1). Hence, the in-tissue resolution is 18.03 μm, which is 9.01 μm either side of the actual depth. It follows then, that the relative error (%) for each strata of depth: 100, 200, 300, 400, 500 μm is 9.01, 4.51, 3.00, 2.25, 1.80%, respectively, using the virtual source's characteristics.

The precision results were compared graphically, with the independent variable as the generation number and the dependent variable a measure of the precision, i.e. the relative 99% confidence interval of the depth and reflectivity, with respect to the average depth and reflectivity, expressed as a percentage. This relative percentage precision was compared as one graph per layer that included each of the two to five layer sample structures. As indicated above, the relative error (%) associated with the source coherence for each layer was included in each of these graphs as an indication of acceptable precision of the simulated depths.

## 3.2. GAM parameter effect on accuracy and precision

This characterization of the efficacy of the BFM – Genetic Algorithm identifies a trend for which combination of GAM control variable magnitudes achieve optimal convergence speed, i.e. the least number of generations that give a satisfactory precision level for the returned parameters, strata depths and reflectivities. The procedure uses the same five strata sample as in the GAM precision section above (3.1) with the following variation of GAM control parameters in table 1.

Three trials of 7 simulations, each for only 20 generations were undertaken. The pooled mean and pooled standard deviation of the 3 trials for depth and reflectivity were calculated. The relative error (%) between these means and the actual depths and reflectivities were compared graphically for each parameter variation. Also compared graphically, were the relative error (%) between the pooled standard deviations and their pooled means, for each depth and its reflectivity. As indicated above, the relative error (%) associated with the source coherence for each layer was included in these graphs as an indication of acceptable accuracy of the simulated depths.

| GAM Parameters | Varying P1 | Varying P2 | Varying P3 | Varying Mutation Rate (MR) |
|---|---|---|---|---|
| P | 1000 | 1000 | 1000 | 1000 |
| P1 | 0, 20,... 800 | 100 | 100 | 400 |
| P2 | 100 | 0, 20,... 800 | 100 | 100 |
| P3 | 100 | 100 | 0, 20,... 800 | 100 |
| Mutation Rate | 0.01 | 0.01 | 0.01 | 0.5, 0.2, 0.1, 0.05, 0.02, 0.01, 0.005, 0.002, 0.001, 0.0005, 0.0002, 0.0001 |
| $\varepsilon$ | 0.0000001 | 0.0000001 | 0.0000001 | 0.0000001 |

**Table 1.** Variation of GAM parameters

# 4. Results, Inferences and Implications

## 4.1. GAM precision

The following section demonstrates the capability of the GAM to provide a precision for layer depth and reflectivity for samples with different number of layers, such that the parameter precisions are not significantly different for any given layer. Results for strata depth precisions is followed by the reflectivity precision results, each demonstrated graphically.

### *4.1.1. GAM strata depth precision*

Fig. 2 shows that, though the GAM precision for each layer depth is dependent on the number of sample layers, all precisions fall within the relative error boundary of the source resolution, i.e. they are all acceptable precision variations. Layer depth precision generally decreases with the increase in the number of layers. The first, more reflective layer, has better precision by more than an order of magnitude, compared to the other layers. This is due to the more prominent peak of the first layer due to its greater reflectivity.

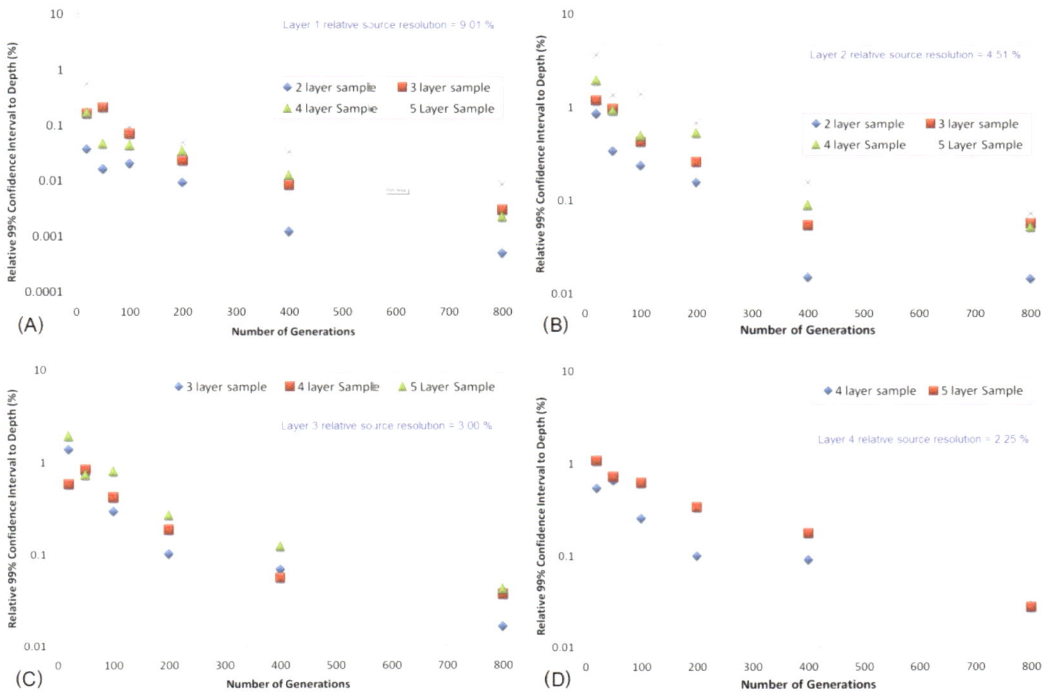


**Figure 2.** The precisions (99% confidence intervals) of the GAM calculated strata depths by number of sample layers and number of GAM generations. The precisions for returned (A) layer 1, (B) layer 2, (C) layer 3, and (D) layer 4 depths, are presented.

#### *4.1.1. GAM layer reflectivity precision*

The reflectivity precision parallels the depth precision trends for each layer (Fig. 3 A – D), though these precisions are significantly less sparse.

### 4.2. GAM control parameter effects on performance

Here we investigate the effect of the four GAM parameters on the accuracy and precision of the calculated layer depths and reflectivities, produced from 20 generations, for a five layer virtual sample. Hence the better the accuracy and precision, the more optimal the GAM parameter. The accuracy was measured by the relative error (%) of the resulting pooled mean depth and pooled mean reflectivity compared to the actual, for three trials each of seven 20 generation GAM cycles. The precision was denoted by the relative standard deviation, being the quotient of the pooled standard deviation to the pooled mean for the three trials, expressed as a percentage.

#### *4.2.1. GAM strata depth accuracy and precision*

It is important to note, that due to time constraints, the GAM accuracy and precision to predict the layer depth has been characterised using a univariate approach.

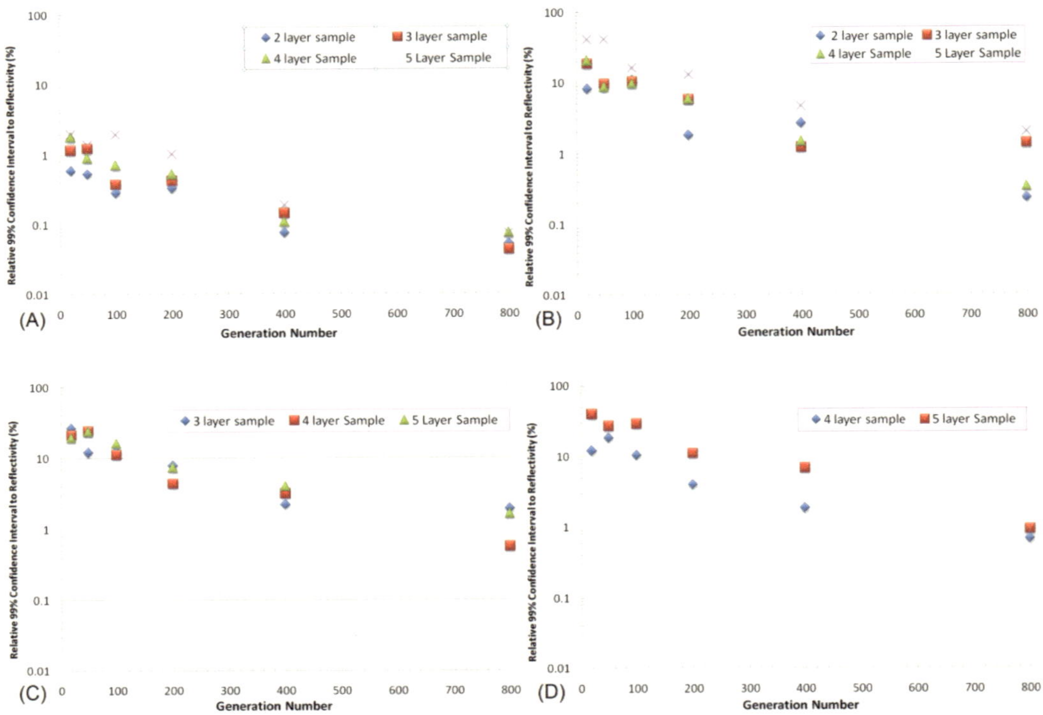


**Figure 3.** The precisions (99% confidence intervals) of the GAM calculated strata reflectivities by number of sample layers and number of GAM generations. Precision for returned (A) layer 1, (B) layer 2, (C) layer 3, and (D) layer 4 reflectivities, is presented.

*4.2.1.1. P1 effect on layer depth*

First P1 is the control parameter that indicates the number of best solutions kept for the next generation. It would then seem probable that maximizing this value would arrive at the solution sooner. From the GAM results of three trials, Fig. 4 contradicts this prediction.

Fig. 4 shows that optimal accuracy and precision is not limited to maximizing P1 but rather that in layer 1, optimality is achieved at lower values of P1, while all other layers are optimized randomly across the P1 spectrum. Fig. 4 shows that the percentage of depth relative errors (DREs) that fall inside the percentage error boundaries of the source's in-tissue resolution for layers 1 to 5 (Fig. 4A to 4E) are 100, 61, 32, 73 and 100% respectively.

Considering layer 1 (Fig. 4A) for the given fixed GAM parameters, for optimal layer 1 depth predictions, P1 needs to be between 100 and 300, with best results below 200. Note also that in this region, the precision is also the greatest, being closest to the null line.

For layer 2 (Fig. 4B), P1 delivers best results 61% sporadically across the 0 to 800 spectrum. A constant dip in the precision (red squares) between 120 and 200 may suggest an optimal region of P1 for predicting layer 2. Also P1 from 340 to 580 shows significant accuracy and precision, with the depth relative error within the relative error boundaries of the source's

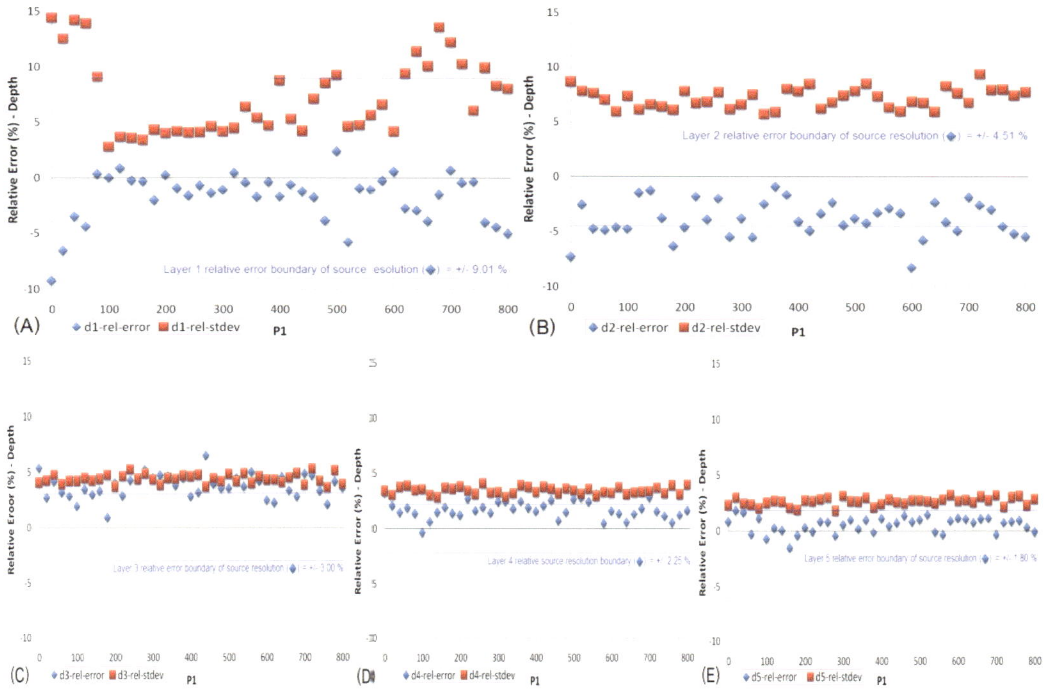


**Figure 4.** Effect of P1 varying on the relative errors and standard deviation errors for (A) layer 1, (B) layer 2, (C) layer 3, (D) layer 4, (E) layer 5 depth GAM calculations. These are the Average values of 3 trials. The other GAM control variables, P2, P3, ε and Mutation rate were fixed at 100, 100, 0.0000001, and 0.01, respectively.

in-tissue resolution. Layer 2 depth is consistently being underestimated, indicated by the negative relative error values (blue diamonds).

Layer 3 has best depth prediction at P1 = 180, while the accuracy and precision values are not separated. For the accuracy to be not significantly different to zero percent, the precision values (red squares) need to be significantly more positive than the absolute value of the accuracy (relative error) values (blue diamonds).

Layer 4 has best results with P1 between 40 and 200, and 600 to 800. Layer 5 has best results with P1 between 120 and 220.

Layer 2 results show the greatest degree of spread with in a corridor, basin or boundary of attraction. This 'basin of attraction' thins as the layer becomes deeper as well as getting progressively more accurate and precise. This difficulty of the GAM to locate the second and third layers is because they falls in the shadow of the much more intense (i.e. more reflective) first layer, while locating the lower layers becomes progressively easier the deeper the GAM searches.

Though the GAM results seem random, their 'basin of attraction' localization imparts a degree of confidence in the reproducibity of the GAM solutions which are reliably attracted to some random data corridor or geometry; for layer 1 a 'wine glass' geometry, layer 2 a wide corridor, and layers 3 – 5, narrow corridors. These regions of 'random' solutions are a product of the interplay between the GAM's stochasticity and its parametric control.

In summary, for the constant values of P2, P3, Mutation rate and tolerance being 100, 100, 0.01 and 0.0000001 respectively, while P1 is best between 100 and 300 for layer 1, there is no particular value of P1 that is best for the other layers. More refined analysis investigating other values of P2, P3, and MR, for this range of P1, is necessary to establish a broader picture of the effects of P1 and its interaction with the other GAM control parameters.

*4.2.1.2. P2 effect on layer depth*

P2 is the control parameter that indicates the number of not-best solutions randomly chosen from the sample set remaining after the P1 set has been chosen, which are kept for the next generation. It would then seem probable that minimizing this value would arrive at the solution sooner. From the GAM results of three trials, Fig. 5 suggests this prediction for the layer depth calculations.

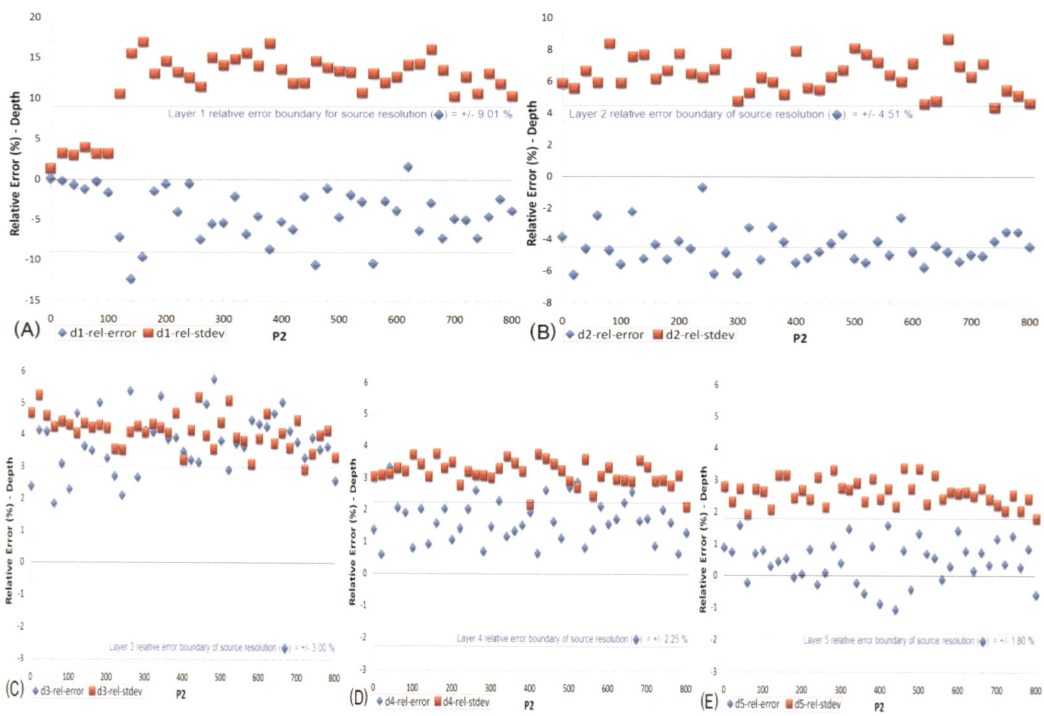


**Figure 5.** Effect of P2 varying on the relative errors and standard deviation errors for (A) layer 1, (B) layer 2, (C) layer 3, (D) layer 4, (E) layer 5 depth GAM calculations. These are the average results of 3 trials. The other GAM control variables, P1, P3, ε and Mutation rate were fixed at 100, 100, 0.0000001, and 0.01, respectively.

Fig. 5 shows that the percentage of depth relative errors (DREs) that fall inside the percentage error boundaries of the source's in-tissue resolution for layers 1 to 5 (Fig. 5A to 5E) are 90, 44, 20, 83 and 100% respectively.

In Fig. 5A, the layer 1 accuracy (blue Diamonds) and precision (Red squares) are best for P2 between 0 and 100, being closer to zero. The precision reduces and accuracy is more random beyond these points. Layer 2 results show less spread of the accuracy and precision than for layer 1. However because the blue error boundary of the source resolution is now half compared to layer 1, ~50% less values fall in the +/- 4.51% acceptability zone. As for the previous section, a 'basin of attraction' for both the accuracy and precision, thins as the layer becomes deeper as well as getting progressively more accurate and precise. Again the difficulty of locating the second layer is noted due to the magnitude of the first layer's signal. This also affects the third layer, for which the accuracy values are now larger than the precision, showing that 34% of the depth estimates are significantly different to the actual layer depth value. This shadowing effect is reduced for the lower layers where the majority of the values are not significantly different to the actual depths, with progressively becoming more accurate and precise.

In summary, for the constant values of P1, P3, Mutation rate and tolerance being 100, 100, 0.01 and 0.0000001 respectively, while P2 is best between 0 and 100 for layer 1, there is no particular value of P2 that is best for the other layers. More refined analysis investigating other values of P1, P3, and MR, for this range of P2, is necessary to establish a more accurate picture of the effects of P2 and its interaction with the other GAM control parameters.

*4.2.1.3. P3 effect on depth*

P3 is the control parameter that indicates the number of children generated by a randomly selected, with replacement, convex combination of P1 and P2. It would then seem probable that neither maximizing or minimizing this value would arrive at a suitable solution sooner. From the GAM results of three trials, Fig. 6 suggests there is no value of P3 that is reproducibly of high accuracy or precision.

Fig. 6 shows that the percentage of depth relative errors (DREs) that fall inside the percentage error boundaries of the source's in-tissue resolution for layers 1 to 5 (Fig. 5A to 5E) are 100, 63, 39, 88 and 100% respectively.

In Fig. 6A, the layer 1 accuracy values (blue Diamonds) are not significantly different to the actual depth. Layer 2 results (Fig. 6B) show more spread of the accuracy and precision than for layer 1, with the depth being under estimated for all values of P3. As for the previous section, a 'basin of attraction' for both the accuracy and precision, thins as the layer becomes deeper as well as getting progressively more accurate and precise. Again due to the magnitude of the first layer's signal, The GAM has difficulty of locating the second and third layers. For the third layer (Fig. 6C) the accuracy values are now larger than the precision, showing that 22% of the depth estimates are significantly different to the actual value. This shadowing effect is reduced for layers 4 (Fig. 6D) and 5 (Fig. 6E); the majority of the values are not significantly different to the actual depths, though layer 3 and 4 values are over estimated. Layer 5's accuracy is demonstrated by symmetry about the zero line, with precision comparable to layer 1.

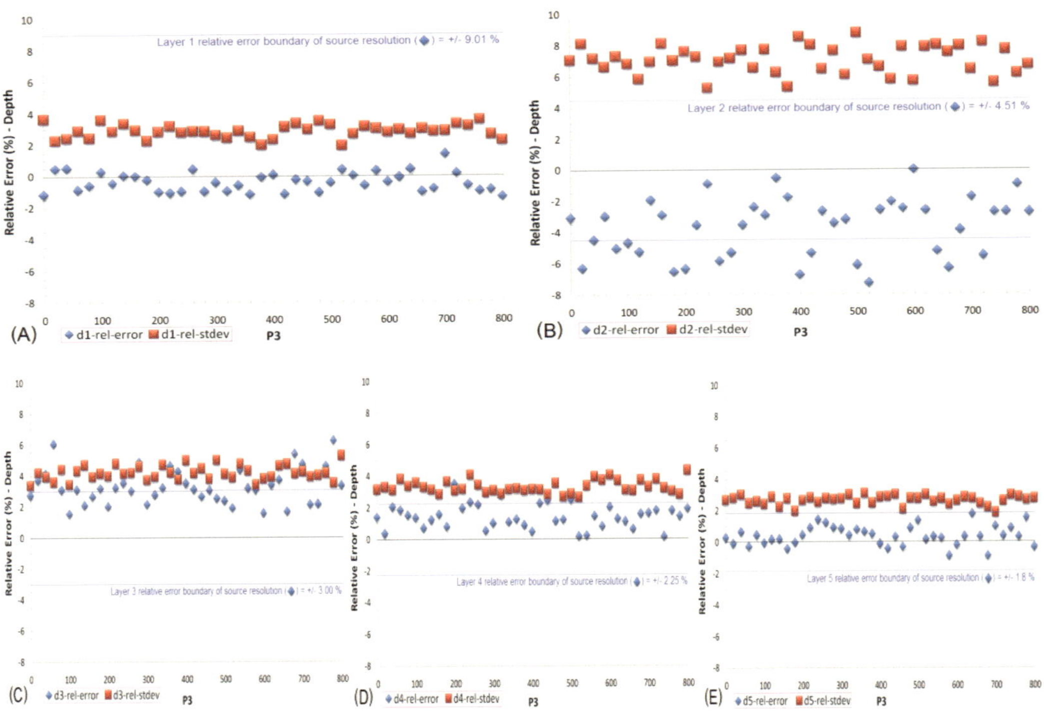


**Figure 6.** Effect of P3 varying on the relative errors and standard deviation errors for (A) layer 1, (B) layer 2, (C) layer 3, (D) layer 4, (E) layer 5 depth GAM calculations. These are the average results of 3 trials. The other GAM control variables, P1, P3, ε and Mutation rate were fixed at 100, 100, 0.0000001, and 0.01, respectively.

In summary, for the constant values of P1, P2, Mutation rate and tolerance being 100, 100, 0.01 and 0.0000001 respectively there is no particular value of P3 that will benefit the GAM accuracy or precision. Further, more refined analysis investigating other values of P1, P2, and MR, for this range of P3, is necessary to establish a broader picture of the effects of P3 and its interaction with the other GAM control parameters.

*4.2.1.4. Mutation rate effect on layer depth*

Mutation rate (MR) is the control parameter that indicates the proportion of each generation of size P, that has (MR x 100) % introduced mutation.

Fig. 7 shows that the percentage of depth relative errors (DREs) that fall inside the percentage error boundaries of the source's in-tissue resolution for layers 1 to 5 (Fig. 5A to 5E) are 100, 50, 0, 50 and 100% respectively.

In Fig. 7A, the layer 1 accuracy values (blue Diamonds) are not significantly different to the actual depth, with a decreasing general trend towards smaller MR, except for a MR of 0.005, which is as accurate as 0.5. Layer 2 relative error results (Fig. 7B) are all under estimated but not significantly different to zero. Again due to the magnitude of the first layer's signal, The GAM has difficulty of locating the second and third layers. For the third layer (Fig. 7C) all the accuracy values fall outside the relative error boundary of the source resolution as well as being over estimated. Also 17% of the values are larger than the precision, implying that these depth estimates are significantly different to the actual value. This shadowing effect is reduced for layers 4 (Fig. 7D) and 5 (Fig. 7E); the majority of the values are not significantly different to the actual depths. Layer 5's accuracy is demonstrated by symmetry about the zero line, with significantly better accuracy and precision than layer 1. As for the previous section, a 'basin of attraction' for both the accuracy and precision, widens as the layer becomes deeper as well as getting progressively more accurate and precise.

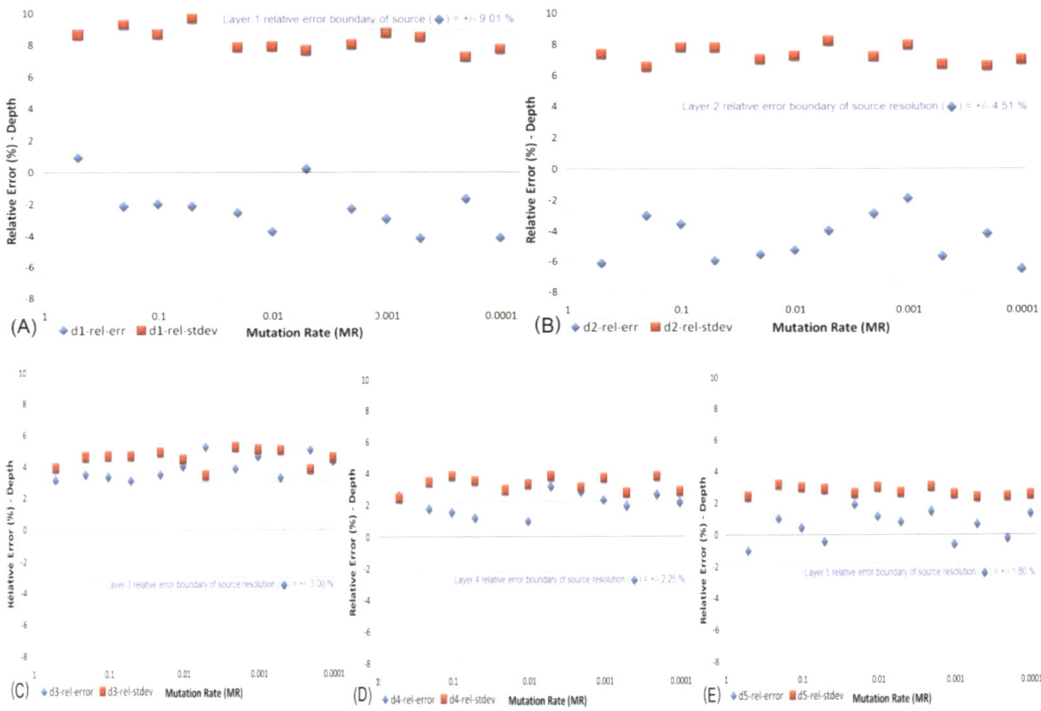


**Figure 7.** Effect of Mutation rate varying on the relative errors and standard deviation errors for (A) layer 1, (B) layer 2, (C) layer 3, (D) layer 4, (E) layer 5 depth GAM calculations. These are the average results of 3 trials. The other GAM control variables, P1, P2, P3 and ε were fixed at 400, 100, 100, and 0.0000001, respectively.

In summary, for the constant values of P1, P2, P3 and tolerance being 400, 100, 100, and 0.0000001 respectively, there is no particular value of MR that will benefit the GAM accuracy or precision for calculating the layer depths. More refined analysis investigating other values of P1, P2, and P3, over this range of MR, is necessary to establish a broader picture of the effects of MR and its interaction effects with the other GAM control parameters on the estimation of layer depth.

### *4.2.2. GAM layer reflectivity accuracy and precision*

It is important to note, that due to time constraints, the GAM accuracy and precision to predict the layer reflectivities has been characterised in only a univariate manner, with each parameter varied singularly, while the other parameters were kept constant, as indicated.

#### *4.2.2.1. P1 effect on layer reflectivity*

First P1 is the control parameter that indicates the number of best solutions kept for the next generation. It would then seem probable that by maximizing this parameter, for each generation, the GAM will converge faster to the actual layer reflectivities.

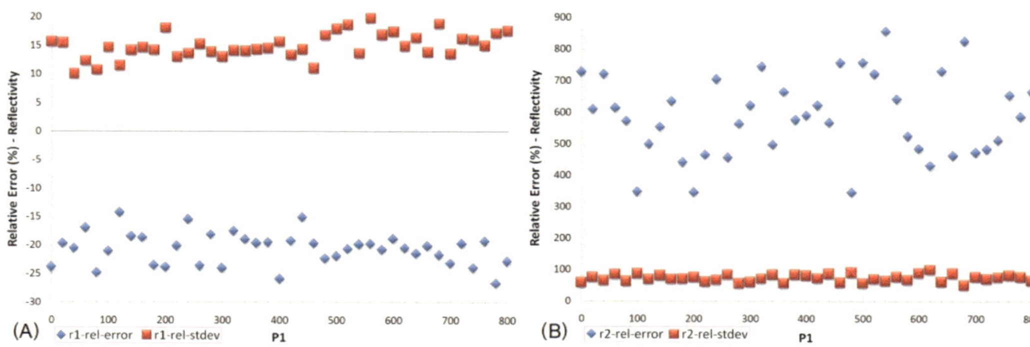


**Figure 8.** Effect of P1 varying on the relative errors and standard deviation errors for (A) layer 1, (B) layer 2 reflectivity GAM calculations. These are the Average values of 3 trials. The other GAM control variables, P2, P3, ε and Mutation rate were fixed at 100, 100, 0.0000001, and 0.01, respectively.

However, the two Fig. 8 graphs demonstrate no relationship between P1 and the accuracy and precision of the calculated reflectivity for varying P1 from 0 to 800, given that the other fixed GAM control parameters, P2, P3, MR and ε, are 100, 100, 0.01 and 0.0000001 respectively. Layer 1 (Fig. 8A) reflectivity is the most accurate and precise, with the other layers demonstrating similar accuracy and precision to that of layer 2 (Fig. 8B). However as the pooled standard deviation precision values (red squares) are less than the absolute relative error values (blue diamonds), i.e. accuracy, for all layers, all reflectivity estimates are significantly different from the actual layer reflectivities. Hence, 20 generations is too small to obtain satisfactory accuracy and precision, even after 3 trials, using this GAM version. Also the level of precision is not satisfactory for layers 3 to 5, being each similar to layer 2 (Fig. 8B).

More refined analysis investigating other values of P2, P3, and MR over this range of P1, is necessary to establish a broader picture of the effects of P1 and its interaction effects with the other GAM control parameters on the estimation of layer reflectivity.

#### *4.2.2.2. P2 effect on layer reflectivity*

P2 is the control parameter that indicates the number of not-best solutions randomly chosen from the sample set remaining after the P1 set has been chosen, which are kept for the next generation. It would then seem probable that minimizing this value would arrive at the solution sooner. From the GAM results of three trials, Fig. 9 suggests this prediction for the layer reflectivity calculations, but only for P2 = 0, for all layers. Layer 3 to 5 results are similar to layer 2 results (Fig. 9B).

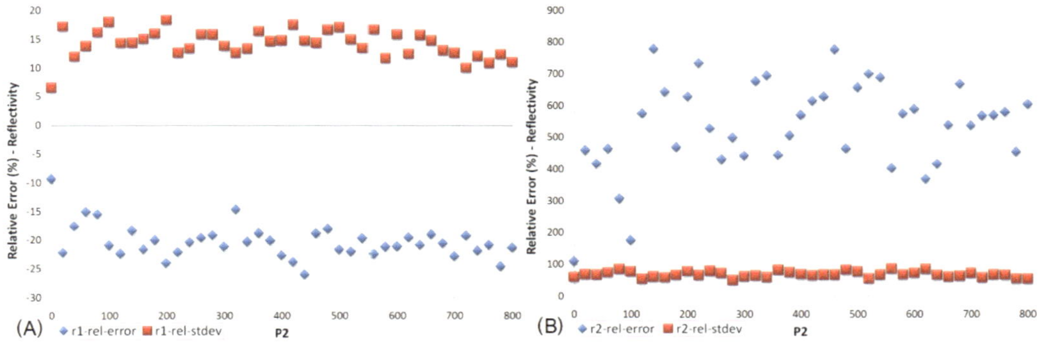


**Figure 9.** Effect of P2 varying on the relative errors and standard deviation errors for (A) layer 1, (B) layer 2 reflectivity GAM calculations These are the Average values of 3 trials. The other GAM control variables, P1, P3, ε and Mutation rate were fixed at 100, 100, 0.0000001, and 0.01, respectively.

Other than P2 = 0, the two Fig. 9 graphs demonstrate no general relationship between P2 and the accuracy and precision of the calculated reflectivity for varying P1 from 0 to 800, given that the other fixed GAM control parameters, P1, P3, MR and ε, are 100, 100, 0.01 and 0.0000001 respectively. Again Layer 1 (Fig. 9A) reflectivity is the most accurate and precise, with the other layers, 3 to 5, demonstrating similar accuracy and precision to that of layer 2 (Fig. 8B). However as the pooled standard deviation precision values (red squares) are less than the absolute relative error values (blue diamonds), i.e. accuracy, for all layers, all reflectivity estimates are significantly different to the actual values. Hence, 20 generations is too low, to obtain satisfactory accuracy and precision, even after 3 trials, with this GAM version.

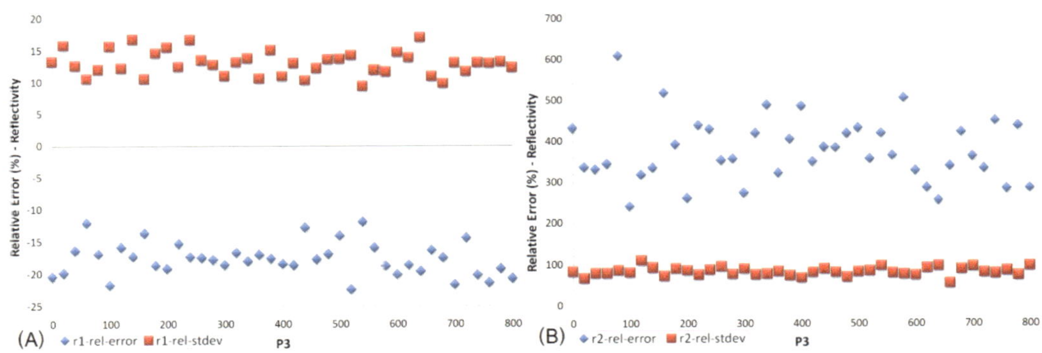


**Figure 10.** Effect of P3 varying on the relative errors and standard deviation errors for (A) layer 1, (B) layer 2 reflectivity GAM calculations. These are the Average values of 3 trials. The other GAM control variables, P1, P2, ε and Mutation rate were fixed at 100, 100, 0.0000001, and 0.01, respectively.

*4.2.2.3. P3 effect on layer reflectivity*

P3 is the control parameter that indicates the number of children generated by a randomly selected, with replacement, convex combination of P1 and P2. It would then seem probable that neither maximizing or minimizing this value would arrive at a suitable solution sooner. From the GAM results of three trials, Fig. 10 suggests there is no value of P3 that is reproducibly of high accuracy or precision for the reflectivity, and all values are significantly different to the actual reflectivities for layers 1 and 2. This also applies to the lower layers as they are similar to layer 2 results (Fig. 10B).

For the same reason that the depth results were best for layer 1, the reflectivity results are best for layer 1 because its reflectivity is orders of magnitude greater than the lower layer reflectivities. Layer 2 results show no relationship at all to P3, with the accuracy values significantly different to 0 %.

*4.2.2.4. Mutation rate effect on layer reflectivity*

Mutation rate (MR) is the control parameter that indicates the proportion of each generation of size P, that has (MR x 100) % introduced mutation.

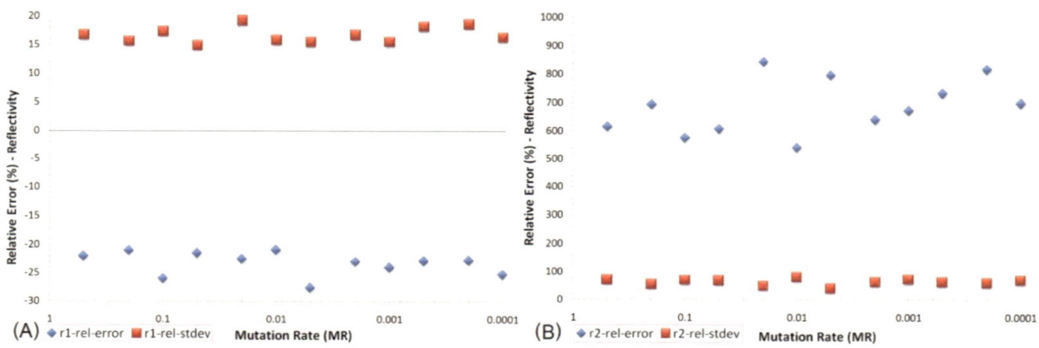


**Figure 11.** Effect of Mutation rate varying on the relative errors and standard deviation errors for (A) layer 1, (B) layer 2 reflectivity GAM calculations. These are the average results of 3 trials. The other GAM control variables, P1, P2, P3 and ε were fixed at 400, 100, 100, and 0.0000001, respectively.

In Fig. 11A, the layer 1 reflectivity accuracy relative error values (blue Diamonds) are significantly different to zero percent. Layer 2 relative errors (Fig. 11B) are all over estimated and significantly different to zero percent, based on the large precision values (red squares). This is also true for the lower layers, 3 to 5. Also the same non-relationship trend of accuracy and precision for layers 3 to 5, is similar to layer 2. Again due to the large first layer's reflectivity and very small reflectivity of the lower layers, this version of the GAM has difficulty of locating the lower layer reflectivities, given only 20 generations of evolution.

In summary, for the constant values of P1, P2, P3 and tolerance being 400, 100, 100, and 0.0000001 respectively, there is no particular value of MR that will benefit the GAM accuracy or precision for calculating the layer reflectivities. More refined analysis investigating other values of P1, P2, and P3, over this range of MR, is necessary to establish a broader picture of the effects of MR and its interaction effects with the other GAM control parameters on the estimation of layer reflectivity.

### *4.2.3. GAM layer depth and reflectivity accuracy and precision summary*

Table 2 summarises the results of the GAM estimates of depth and reflectivity. With the exception of P2, all other parameters show no significant relationship to the relative errors of the GAM estimated depth and reflectivity calculated.

| Layer # (P = 1000) | Optimal Depth | | | | Optimal Reflectivity | | | |
|---|---|---|---|---|---|---|---|---|
| | P1 0 to 800 | P2 0 to 800 | P3 0 to 800 | MR 0.0001 - 0.5 | P1 0 to 800 | P2 0 to 800 | P3 0 to 800 | MR 0.0001 - 0.5 |
| 1 | 100 - 300 | 0-100 | AV | AV | All SD to 0% | 0 | All SD to 0% | All SD to 0% |
| 2 | NSV- 61%(1) | NSV - 44% | NSV - 63% | NSV - 50% | All SD to 0% | 0 | All SD to 0% | All SD to 0% |
| 3 | NSV - 32% | NSV - 20% | NSV - 39% | NSV - 0% | All SD to 0% | 0 | All SD to 0% | All SD to 0% |
| 4 | NSV - 73% | NSV - 83% | NSV - 88% | NSV - 50% | All SD to 0% | 0 | All SD to 0% | All SD to 0% |
| 5 | AV | AV | AV | AV | All SD to 0% | 0 | All SD to 0% | All SD to 0% |

(1) The percentage of results that are within the relative error boundary of the source resolution. NSV = no specific value; AV = all values; SD = significantly different.

**Table 2.** General and relative error results summary

In the case of P2 = 0, the reflectivity accuracy and precision are significantly improved for all layers, while the layer depth accuracy and precision are significantly improved for the first layer. Except for P2 = 0, all other values of P1, P2, P3, and MR return reflectivities that are significantly different to the actual reflectivities as indicated in the Table 2 as "All SD to 0%", meaning that all the values of the control parameter give reflectivities that are significantly different to the actual reflectivity values.

## 5. Discussion

### 5.1. GAM precision

The results have demonstrated that the precision of GAM layer depth estimation worsens for any given layer as the number of layers in the sample increases. This difference in results between different layered samples reduces as the GAM generation number increases. One can now gauge the degree of result reliability with a given A-scan, which indicates number of layers, so that an appropriately long generation number calculation can be undertaken if a sample with a larger number of layers is predicted.

Though the layer depth and reflectivity precision increases with increasing number of generations, so does the time to arrive at a more optimal solution. This increase in time is linear: if one generation takes 1 min, then 800 generations will consume 800 min. Certainly not practical for returning specific layer depths from a B-scan consisting of 600 A-scans, if each A-scan result was generated from 800 GAM generations. Clearly it is necessary to optimize the speed by minimizing the generation number to the point that the relative error of the depth is just within the light source's resolution boundary. Furthermore, The back fitting software's application will be assisting the clinician, by returning depth and reflectivity of points of interest on A-scans in the B-scans, not necessarily all depths and reflectivities of the B-scan.

The reflectivity precision parallels the depth precision trends for each layer (Fig. 3 A – D) because locating the correct depth is enhanced by greater layer reflectivity. Also, the more the layers the more there are peaks in the A-scan for the GAM to locate, requiring more generations to achieve equivalent precision to A-scans with less peaks.

## 5.2. GAM control parameter effects on depth estimation

For all the parameters, P1, P2, P3 and Mutation rate, layer 3 has least accurate results with most or all values falling outside the relative error boundary of the expected source resolution. layer 2 results show the greatest degree of spread with in a corridor, basin or boundary of attraction. This 'basin of attraction' thins as the layer becomes deeper as well as getting progressively more accurate and precise. This difficulty of the GAM to locate the second and third layers is because it falls in the shadow of the much larger (i.e. more reflective) first layer, while locating the lower layers becomes progressively easier the deeper the GAM searches.

The term 'basin of attraction' is used because, for the three trials, each trial produced the same region of graph values without the actual values being the same. This is a product of the interplay between the GAM's stochasticity and its parametric control. This is important to note as it imparts a degree of confidence in the reproducibity of the GAM solutions which are reliably attracted to some random data corridor or geometry. This 'basin of attraction' construct is applicable and evident in all of the GAM depth estimates, because the GAM is a parameter *controlled* stochastic algorithm, and not solely stochastic.

## 5.3. GAM control parameter effects on reflectivity estimation

For all the parameters, P1, P2, P3 and Mutation rate, layer 1 is the most accurate and precise. However all GAM estimated reflectivities are significantly different to the actual values for all five layers. A larger number of evolution generations are needed, using this version of the GAM. This will require either repeating the GAM evolution to run for a much larger number of generations or extrinsically evolving the GAM by altering the software so that it evolves faster, i.e. alter the existing GAM version so that it arrives at suitable accuracy and precision sooner.

### 5.4. Future backwards fitting model research

Further trials with realistic non-Gaussian light sources (Rossetti *et al* 2005), (Shidlovski 2008), (Unterhuber *et al* 2008) that generated A-scans with side lobes and other artefacts, will require the programming of the GAM to detect and disregard such false information, resulting in the return of accurate parameter values. This will involve further extrinsic evolution of the GAM as well as exploring other types of Backwards Fitting Models that though more deterministic may be much faster due to loss of the random element. However further investigation is needed to establish this.

## 6. Conclusion

This chapter has demonstrated that a genetic algorithm approach suggests some success at extracting layer depth and reflectivity values from virtual samples with realistic biological layer depths and refractive indices. The GAM's efficacy has been challenged by these realistically small reflectivities, returning values that are an order of magnitude larger than the actual values. More extensive testing of the GAM using a multivariate approach is needed to fine tune the GAM control parameters to deliver accurate and precise solutions at optimal speed for the least number of generations possible. Further extrinsic evolution of the GAM to extend its application to non Gaussian light sources is envisaged. This will enable the deconvolution of more realistic A-scans. This may provide the opportunity to give a more objective measure of sample layer characteristics to better inform physicians, assisting in their diagnosis and monitoring of particular tissue pathologies.

## Author details

Paul Jansz, Steven Richardson, Graham Wild and Steven Hinckley
*School of Engineering, Edith Cowan University, Australia*

## 7. References

Adie, S.G. (2007) Enhancement of Contrast in Optical Coherence Tomography: New Modes, Methods and Technology, University of Western Australia, PhD Thesis, Chapter 2, 10-12.

Drexler, W., Chen, Y., Aguirre, A., Povazay, B., Unterhuber, A., and Fujimoto, J.G. (2008) Ultrahigh resolution optical coherence tomography. *Optical Coherence Tomography: Technology and Applications*, W. Drexler and J.G. Fugimoto, Eds. Berlin: Springer-Verlag, 239-279.

Fercher, A.F. (1996) Optical coherence tomography, in *Journal of Biomedical Optics*, 1(2), 157-173.

Friebel, M., J. Helfmann, U. Netz, and M. Meinke. (2009) Influence of oxygen saturation on the optical scattering properties of human red blood cells in the spectral range 250 to 2000 nm. *Journal of Biomedical Optics*, 14(3), 034001-1 – 6.

Hillier, F.S., and Lieberman, G.J. (2005), Introduction to operations research, McGraw Hill, New York.

Izatt, J.A., Kulkarni, M.D., Kobayashi, K., Sivak, M.V., Barton, J.K., and Welch, A.J. (1997) Optical Coherence Tomography for Biodiagnostics, *Opt. Photon. News*, 41-47.

Jansz, P.V., Wild, G., Richardson, S., and Hinckley, S. (2011) Simulation of optical delay lines for optical coherence tomography, *Proc. IQEC-CLEOPR ACOFT*, Sydney.

Jansz, P.V., Wild, G., Richardson, S., Hinckley, S. (2012) Low coherence interferometry modelling using combined broadband Gaussian light sources. *Proc. SPIE* 8351 APOS, Sydney.

Rossetti, M., Markus, A., Fiore, A., Occhi, L., and Velez, C. (2005) Quantum dot superluminescent diodes emitting at 1.3µm. *IEEE Photonics Technology Letters*, 17(3), 541-544.

Shidlovski, V.R. (2008) Superluminescent diode light sources for OCT. *Optical Coherence Tomography: Technology and Applications*, W. Drexler and J.G. Fugimoto, Eds. Berlin: Springer-Verlag, 281-299.

Unterhuber, A., Považay, B., Aguirre, A., Chen, Y., Kärtner, F.X., Fujimoto, J.G., and Drexler, W. (2008) Broad bandwidth laser and nonlinear optical light sources for OCT, in *Optical Coherence Tomography: Technology and Applications*, Drexler, W. and Fugimoto, J.G., Eds. Berlin: Springer-Verlag, 301-358.

# Chapter 17

# Wideband Wireless Power Transmission to Enhance Efficiency for Low Input Power for Biomedical Applications

Chin-Lung Yang, Yu-Lin Yang and Chun-Chih Lo

Additional information is available at the end of the chapter

http://dx.doi.org/10.5772/46120

## 1. Introduction

In this chapter, a novel Ultra wideband (UWB) technology is applied in a special aspect for the wireless power transmission (WPT) to achieve a novel wireless wideband powering approach and enhance the power conversion efficiency (PCE) for low average input power. Due to the fact that low transmission power has relatively little impacts and causes relatively slight injury to human bodies, it is one of the essential key technologies in biomedical implant chips and devices. The whole wideband wireless power transmitting and receiving systems are implemented to validate the feasibility of the wireless power transmission system using impulsive waves (wideband power) and the improvement of the conversion efficiency of the rectifier circuitry. This chapter further applies UWB technologies in a special aspect for the transmission of energy rather than messages to achieve a novel wireless impulsive powering approach and enhance the power conversion efficiency for low average input power. The whole impulsive wireless power transmitting and receiving systems are implemented to validate the feasibility of the wireless power transmission using impulsive waves and the improvement of the conversion efficiency of the rectifier circuitry.

UWB technology is important in modern communications systems. Because these devices generally operate in the sub-nanosecond range, designing impulse generator circuitry is particularly challenging. UWB technology has the advantages of low power operation, high data transfer rates, and excellent spatial capacity, making it highly suitable for use in short distance commercial communication systems [Hirt 2003], wireless personal area networks (WPANs), secure communications in military applications, the detection of unexploded ordnance (UXO) and mines, ground penetrating radar (GPR), precision positioning and tracking [Bertoni 1992], collision avoidance for motor vehicles [Hirt 2003], and innovative wireless power transmission applications as presented in this chapter (Yang 2011).

The idea of wireless power transmission was proposed early in 1899 by Nikola Tesla, and William C. Brown demonstrated the microwave-powered helicopter successfully in 1964 [Brown 1965]. Recently, Intel Corporation fulfilled a high power of wireless coupling to power up electrical appliances, 60-Watt bulbs, with the efficiency more than 75% at the distance of 2 meters in 2008. These show the feasibility of the wireless power transmission technologies. Recently, advanced fabrication techniques of the required components such as rectifiers have enabled a reduction in cost and size that has enabled Radio Frequency Identification (RFID) tags. There are two primary means of wirelessly powering transmission depending on whether the power coupling is through the electric or magnetic field. Inductive coupling of the magnetic field has been used broadly in a great many applications in short ranges [Zimmerman 2006] as well as at high efficiency by resonant magnetic coupling [Kurs 2007]. This sort of the techniques is, however, limited by the distance and the size of the coils. The other method, which most combines with antenna, so-called rectenna, couples power via RF electric fields propagating between high gain external and internal antennas. One attractive feature is that using electromagnetic RF wave propagation for wireless power transmission allows the achievement of a smaller scale in a further operating distance. These rectennas can be formed of any kind of antenna such as dipoles, monopoles, Yagi-Uda antennas, microstrip antennas, spiral antennas, parabolic antenna, retrodirective antennas, and even an antenna array [Rodenbeck 2004]. Also, the rectifier can be implemented by a shunt full-wave rectifier, a bridge rectifier, a voltage doubler, and hybrid types.

Recently, WPT technology has become one of the most-growing, high-impact technologies that will revolutionize the world in the recent years. One of the highlight applications can be useful for biomedical devices. The power supply module for biomedical implantable devices is the core technology among them. Conventionally, batteries or wired power transfer will cause the limitations of implanted devices in time and in space; therefore, the wireless power technology applying in biomedical implantable devices will become an urgent matter and an on-going trend. The most critical part of the wireless power transfer technology is its PCE. To develop an efficient wireless power supply system will prolong to expand the applicable scenario and the use of time of the implantable devices. Besides, one of the severe restrictions in biomedical applications is the requirement that the maximum input power must be smaller than the upper bound of the human being safety, such as maximal Specific Absorption Rate (SAR), which disables the common WPT technologies to achieve their optimal efficiency operating conditions. In this chapter, an impulsive power transfer technologies with an impulsive generator circuit is demonstrated to receive sufficient external wireless power supply under low average input power (as illustrated in Figure 1) and convert the wireless power to the output voltage efficiently. We further design and implement an impulsive generator circuit to recharge the electronic devices wirelessly and compare with the traditional continuous wave techniques.

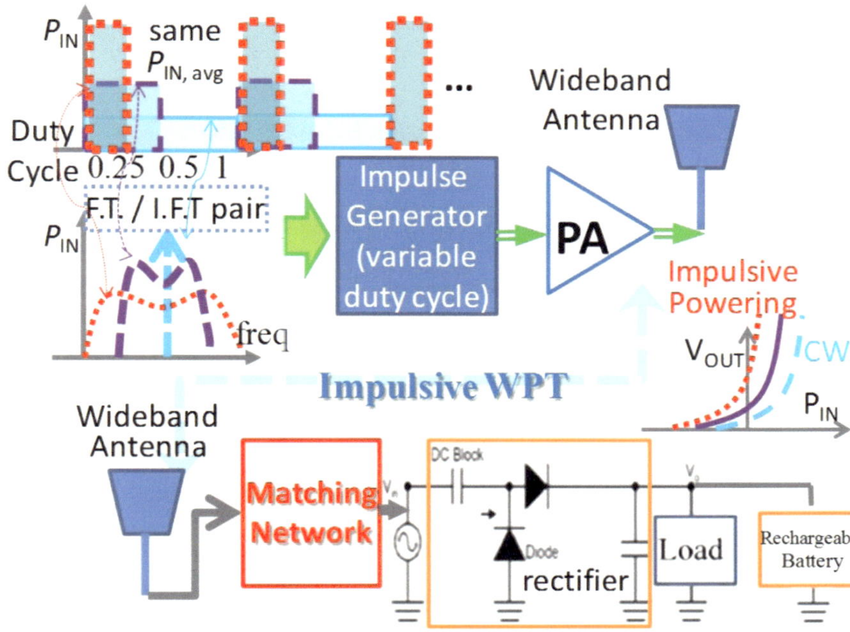


**Figure 1.** Schematic of proposed monocycle pulse generator.

To achieve the optimal conversion efficiency, proper operation condition should be well-controlled such as input power, resistive load, and loading currents to make proper matching network and optimize the rectifier efficiency [Yo 2008]. However, most of these circuits require driving at a high level of input power for its optimal efficiency, which is less preferred in biomedical applications due to the security concern, such as the regulations of SAR according to FCC or International Electrotechnical Commission (IEC). In this chapter, instead of using conventional CW for WPT, we further vary the duty cycles of the pulse waves and form a broadband power transmission system to promote the PCE of the rectifier at its weak power operation conditions.

Several wired and wireless experimental results prove that this technique is quite suitable for low input power transmission which is good for biomedical applications. In order to deliver the UWB power efficiently, a horn antenna with high directivity, large gain, and broad bandwidth acts as the transmit antenna. Also, biomedical environments are set to test the proposed system and a simplified wireless biomedical tissue model is assumed and analysed. The impulsive power generated by the impulse generator is amplified by the UWB power amplifier and then delivered through the horn antenna. The wideband power generated by the impulse generator is amplified by the UWB power amplifier and then delivered through the horn antenna. And the received impulsive power is converted into a direct current (dc) power by the Cockcroft–Walton type voltage-doubler rectifier composed of Schottky diodes to supply the chips or rechargeable batteries. In this chapter, the UWB impulsive wireless transmission systems have been proved to achieve 50% PCE even when the input power of the rectifier is lower than 0 dBm. Due to the fact that low transmission power has relatively little impacts and causes relatively slight injury to human bodies, it is one of the essential key technologies in biomedical implant chips and devices.

## 2. System description of impulsive power transmission

The concept of the varying duty cycle is illustrated in Figure 1, and our testing system is shown in Figure 2. From Figure 1, we try to vary the duty cycle to form wideband power spectrum density (PSD) energy instead of conventional narrowband CW power. As the duty cycle reduces under the constraint of the same average input power, we observe that the output power of the rectifier increases dramatically according to the operation conditions such as pulse periods, resistance loading values, and channel conditions. The reason to gain much more efficiency will be addressed briefly in the following section.

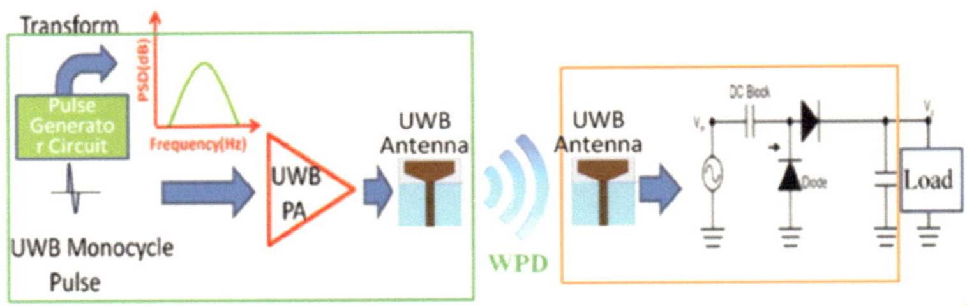


**Figure 2.** The testing system verifies the performance of impulsive wireless power transmission.

In Figure 2, a testing system to verify the output voltage and efficiency of impulsive powering is presented. This system includes an impulse generator circuit, a UWB PA, UWB antennas, and a two-stage rectifier to convert RF power into dc power. An UWB monocycle pulse generator is designed and fabricated by using both a shunt step recovery diode (SRD) and a wideband bipolar junction transistor (BJT), followed by a pulse shaping differentiator. This design will be presented and discussed in details later. The generator produces the extremely narrow impulse width about 290 ps, the ringing level is as low as -21.8 dB, and its measured bandwidth is 200 MHz to 6 GHz (5.8 GHz), whose circuit and performance will be addressed in Section 3. Then, we use an UWB PA to transmit the impulsive power through a pair of UWB antennas. The rectifier is a two-stage voltage doubler to convert the RF power to dc power. The rectifier can be high efficiency after an optimization procedure of careful design of the biasing of the input power and the resistive load, harmonic rejection, and the matching network [Yo 2004]. A similar rectifier circuit is used to examine the performance at a weak input power condition.

The concept of gaining extra output voltages can be explained from the non-linear transfer function of the rectifier which outputs more efficiently at high input power. Observing from the impulsive wave power distribution, the energy is concentrated within the specific pulse duration to enforce a high efficiency of the rectifier. When the pulse is off, the charged capacitor stored the energy and released with a relatively large time constant due to that the diodes are off and the reverse current is small. The analysis model of the PCE of the rectenna conversion efficiency depends on the diode electrical parameters and the circuit losses at dc and the fundamental frequency. The mathematical model of the diode efficiency has been derived for varying input power levels [McSpadden 1998]. In this chapter, we try to build a probability model to evaluate the performance. The impulse power signal $V_{UWB}(t)$ generates a bi-state instant power distribution whose probability cumulative distribution functions (cdf) can be defined as $P_{cdf}(X) = Prob\{P_{instant\ (in\ dBm)} \leq X\}$.

$$P_{cdf,\ UWB}(X) = \begin{cases} 0 & X < 1 - D \\ P_{avg} / D & X \geq 1 - D \end{cases} \quad (1)$$

where X is the random variable of the instant powers in dBm and $D$ is defined as the duty cycle for the impulse wave. Given the rectifier of the 2-stage voltage doubler follows a specific transfer function $V_{out}(t) = H_{rectifier}(P_{in,\ dBm}(t))$ at the moment $t$. This transfer function can be obtained by simulation with the (HSMS-286) Schottky diode precise models [Young 2002] or by measurement after well-matching. Because the exponential increase of the diode current with the growth of the input power biasing, the transfer function $H_{rectifier}(\cdot)$ is found to have the property of convex and increase monotonically and exponentially, which means the average over high $P_{cdf,\ UWB}$ will increase as the high instant $P_{in}$ parts can be heavily weighted. Therefore, the average output voltage can be calculated as the expectation value of the input power according to the transfer function $H_{rectifier}(\cdot)$ and the probability distribution $P_{cdf,\ UWB}$ under the assumption that the Schottky diodes response quickly enough for these instant power variations of impulsive powers. The practical improvement ratios and trends can be estimated empirically varying with the different duty cycle $D$.

$$V_{out}(dc) = E\ \{ H_{rectifier}(P_{in,\ dBm})\} \quad (2)$$

From the experiments of impulsive tests, the output voltage increases significantly as duty cycle $D$ decreases. Although at most of the time the instant power is zero, and yet a small portion of high peak power ($P_{avg}/D$) drives the rectifier with much higher efficiency under the exponential-like curve of $H_{rectifier}(\cdot)$. This implies that non-uniform power distributions can improve the output voltage by using some portion of large instance powers. For instance, the duty cycle reduces, and the instant power rises. Therefore, same average input power will result in higher PCE according to the portion of the high-level power and the peak values of the instant powers.

## 3. Circuit description and design

Pulse signals used in UWB systems are generally Gaussian pulses or monocycle pulses, both of which feature a wideband spectrum. The spectral characteristic of an ideal bipolar monocycle pulse do not include a dc component, and the frequency response is similar to that of a band pass filter. A spectrum with these characteristic provides a number of benefits for the wireless data transmission. Intuitively, an impulsive Gaussian wave can be generated by means of combining different phases Gaussian waves of different delay times. Then, a monocycle pulse is obtained by shaping the network and simple RC differentiator

[Reed 2005]. This is the principle on which pulse generators are generally based. Previous studies on UWB pulse generators are generally classified into four categories: logic gate-based pulses, modified oscillator- based designs [Teshirogi 2005], SRD-based generators as a waveform edge [Protiva 2010] sharpener, and transistor-based generators. In the past, monocycle pulse generators using SRD usually adopted serial connected prototypes, followed by a microstrip line stub with a shorted end.

In [Ma 2007][Han 2005], Han and Nguyen compared a shunt connected SRD with an inductor and serial connected SRD using a short circuited microstrip line stub. They demonstrated that a shunt SRD produces a pulse with less ringing [Ma 2007][Han 2005]. This makes a shunt-mode pulse generator a better choice for samplers. As suggested in [Ma 2007][Han 2005], we adopted a shunt SRD and second-order transient circuit to reduce ringing in our proposed pulse generator. Second-order RLC transient response was developed to produce a Gaussian pulse with reduced ringing, and BJT was used to perform impulse shaping to reduce ringing in the Gaussian wave even further [Han 2002]. For this reason, the monocycle pulse was created after the differentiator. The proposed device was fabricated using discrete components and a BJT. The fabricated pulse generator circuit demonstrated excellent performance in the aspects of pulse width, symmetry, and ringing.

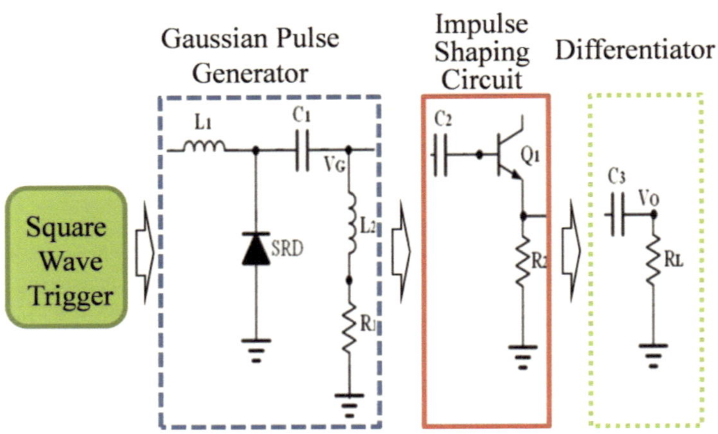


**Figure 3.** Schematic of proposed monocycle pulse generator.

As shown in Figure 3, the circuitry in the proposed monocycle pulse generator is laid out three parts: a Gaussian pulse generator, a pulse shaping circuit, and an RC differentiator. The Gaussian pulse is generated by the SRD accompanied by a second-order RLC transient circuit. Unlike pulses based on active transistors, the SRD requires no extra bias, and functions as a switch with extremely short transition time. The voltage across the serial inductor $L_1$ changes with the time-varying current through $L_1$. The voltage generates an instant, sharp spike at the moment that the shunt SRD switch turns off. The change in voltage on this serial inductor $L_1$ can be calculated from $V(t)=L_1\, di(t)/dt$, where $i(t)$ is the current through $L_1$. Through the second-order transient circuit response of $R_1L_2C_1$, a sub-nanosecond Gaussian pulse can be created. According to Kirchhoff's rules, we obtain:

$$L_1 \frac{di(t)}{dt} = \frac{1}{C_1} \int i(t)dt + L_2 \frac{di(t)}{dt} + R_1 i(t) \tag{3}$$

Let $i(t) = k\, e^{st}$ and substitute it in (3), to obtain:

$$s = -\frac{R_1}{2(L_2 - L_1)} \pm j\sqrt{\frac{1}{(L_2 - L_1)C_1} - \left(\frac{R_1}{2(L_2 - L_1)}\right)^2} \tag{4}$$

$$\equiv -\zeta \pm j\sqrt{w_o^{\,2} - \zeta^2} = s_1, s_2 \tag{5}$$

where $\omega_o$ is the resonant frequency and $\zeta$ is the damping coefficient. The solution is:

$$i(t) = k_1 e^{-s_1 t} + k_2 e^{-s_2 t} \tag{6}$$

According to (5), a change in damping coefficient $\zeta$ can be classified according to three types of second-order transient responses: under-damping ($\zeta<\omega_o$), critical-damping ($\zeta=\omega_o$), and over-damping ($\zeta>\omega_o$). To reduce ringing in the monocycle pulse, the over-damping transient condition was selected as the principle component in the design of the Gaussian pulse (on node $V_G$). A wideband BJT ($Q_1$) and simple RC differentiator were used to convert the Gaussian pulse into a bipolar monocycle pulse. A passive wideband BJT ($Q_1$) was intentionally selected to function as a diode (base-emitter junction) in shaping Gaussian pulses. Additional DC offset is not required due to that the shallow emitter and the narrow base width, a fast transitional behavior of this wideband BJT which operates in the diode mode can be achieved, so a fast transition can be available by using this EB junction diode.

When the Gaussian pulse is on the rising edge, the BJT ($Q_1$), functioning as a diode, turns on to charge the capacitor $C_3$. Conversely, when the Gaussian pulse is on the falling edge, the capacitor $C_3$ provides a reverse bias to the BJT ($Q_1$) to shut down $Q_1$ and discharges through $R_2$. The width of the Gaussian pulse can be further compressed after shaping. Finally, the Gaussian pulse is differentiated into a monocycle pulse through a simple RC differentiator. The simulation results of Gaussian pulse and monocycle pulse waveforms are shown in Figure 4. A pulse width of 280 ps was generated; however, the amplitude was reduced considerably from 1.25V to 0.235V, due to loss in the differentiator. Figure 4(b) is the Fourier transform of the simulated pulse in the frequency domain, implying an ultra-wide bandwidth of nearly 5.7 GHz (220 MHz–5.9 GHz). According to the simulation, the ringing ratio can be further reduced by exploiting its symmetrical waveform. Ringing exists in all practical impulse circuits; however, compensation can be used to reduce the effects of ringing. If positive and negative cycles have precisely the same pulse width and opposite phase ripple, then the ringing can be reduced to the minimal level. Ringing is optimized according to the second-order transient response, the shaping network, and RC differentiator. However, this monocycle pulse still encounters ringing, due mainly to the unbalanced switching transient time of BJT ($Q_1$), noise from fabrication, and tolerances of the component values.

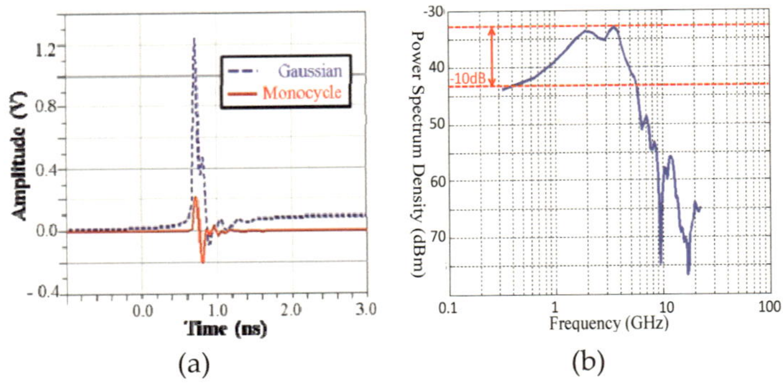


**Figure 4.** (a) Simulated waveforms of the Gaussian pulse and monocycle pulse using over-damping response in time domain; (b) The spectrum of the simulated monocycle pulse.

## 4. Wireless channel model through tissues

A RF-DC rectifier circuit is one of the core techniques in microwave wireless power transmission. Moreover, the PCE is the major parameter for the performance of the rectifier circuit [Yoo 1992]. To achieve the optimal PCE, the wireless power systems need to operate with proper loads and at high input power. However, when such techniques are practically applied in biomedical purposes or implanting systems, there are many limitations such as SAR regulations, the limited space, biomedical compatibility, the transmission distance, and the absorption of the human beings' tissues. Mostly, the received power is very weak in such wireless power transmission applications, so the rectifier cannot achieve high Vout and good PCE. Therefore, it is a crucial issue of promoting the $V_{out}$ and PCE of rectifier at low input power level under a proper consideration of the tissue effects.

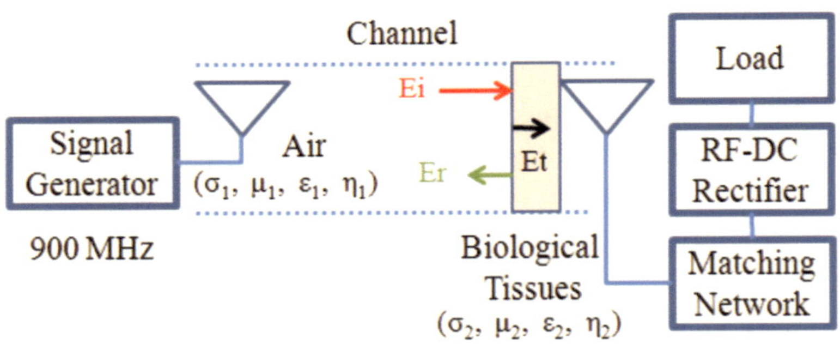


**Figure 5.** System block diagram of wireless power transmission.

For the applications of the wireless power transmission in practical biomedical environments, it is inevitable to deal with many loss factors in wireless channels. In addition to the factors of the free-space path loss (FSPL), standing waves, polarization mismatch of the microwave power, the attenuation in the wireless channels becomes much more complicated under the influences of the biological tissues such as muscle, bone, and fat dielectrics which produces different biological attenuation and the reflection between the interface. This chapter provides a novel technique to improve the $V_{out}$ and PCE at low input power level ($P_{IN}$). We also built up analysis models and design the experiments of the power transmission over different media channels of wired transmission, air transmission and the biological tissues to validate the impulsive wireless power transmission techniques. The influence from the biological tissues is also another main concerned factor in wireless power transmission to address in this chapter.

## 5. Channel model

The channel model of the wireless power transfer system is simply shown in Figure 5. Due to the complexity of the realistic wireless transmission channel, we will create a simple model in this chapter to simplify the loss from the transmission channel without the complicated multipath influences and fading phenomenon. We assume the biological tissues to be muscles, and the main factors of attenuation are considered including FSPL ($L_{path}$), biological tissue loss ($L_{tissue}$), and the reflection loss ($L_{interface}$) over the interface. We can establish the fundamental analysis to estimate the loss of transmission channel as the equations below.

We assume the antenna gain is 0 dBi and the microwave transfers in free space without obstacles nearby to cause reflection or diffraction, so we may apply Friis Formula to estimate the path loss. From (7), we found that as the wavelength decreases, FSPL will increase significantly. The numerical results are shown as Figure 6(a).

$$\mathrm{FSPL} = (\frac{4\pi d}{\lambda})^2 = L_{path} \tag{7}$$

where d is the distance between the transmitter and receiver and $\lambda$ is the wavelength.

We assume the tested muscle as a homogeneous medium. From (8) and (9), the biological tissue loss is determined by the propagation constant and the thickness of tissue. From (10), the propagation constant is determined by frequency, $\sigma$, $\mu$, and $\varepsilon$ of the tissue [Gabriel 1996]. So the biological tissue loss increases as the frequency or the thickness of the tissue increases. The related equations can be analyzed as below.

$$E_x = E_0 e^{-\alpha z} \tag{8}$$

$$L_{tissue} = \frac{E_0 - E_x}{E_0} = 1 - e^{-\alpha z} \tag{9}$$

$$\alpha = R_e(\gamma)\,, \gamma = j\omega\sqrt{\mu\varepsilon}\sqrt{1 - j\frac{\sigma}{\omega\varepsilon}} \tag{10}$$

where $\sigma$ : conductivity, $\gamma$ : propagation constant

$$\mu = \mu_0\mu_r : \text{permeability}, \varepsilon = \varepsilon_0\varepsilon_r : \text{permittivity}$$

Microwave power of different frequencies pass through the media with the different intrinsic impedances causes the different amount of the incident power and reflected power.

This can be calculated by (11). The reflected power tends to decrease as the frequency increases, and it does not vary as much after the frequency is higher than 400 MHz (as shown in Figure 6 (a)).

$$L_{interface} = \Gamma =, \frac{E_r}{E_i} = \frac{\eta_2 - \eta_1}{\eta_2 + \eta_1}, \ \eta = \sqrt{\frac{j\omega\mu}{\sigma + j\omega\varepsilon}} \quad (11)$$

where $\eta$ : intrinsic impedance

Let the distance of the transmitter and the receiver be 60 cm and thickness of the pork be 1 cm. The losses of the wireless channel are mainly composed of $L_{path}$, $L_{tissue}$, and $L_{interface}$. When one of them increases greatly, the channel loss will also increase dramatically. As the Figure 6(a) shows, when the frequency increases, the overall channel loss increases substantially due to the significant increase of FSPL. As the frequency and tissue thickness increase, the loss of biological tissues increases as Figure 6(b) below.

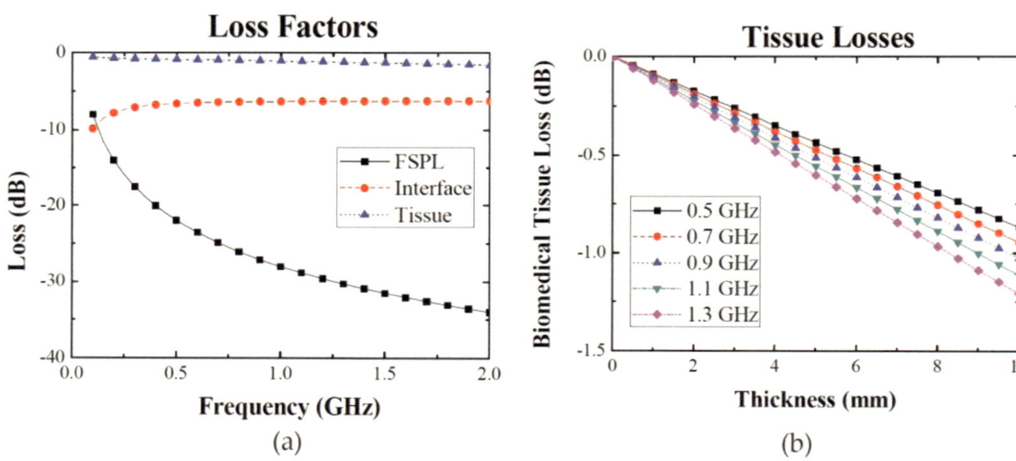


**Figure 6.** (a) The losses in different frequencies; (b) The biomedical tissue loss of different thickness.

To deal with detailed E and H-fields, Poynting vector can be obtained as follows.

$$\begin{aligned} \vec{H}^i &= \sqrt{\frac{j\omega\mu_0\left(j\omega\varepsilon_{1(air)} + \sigma_{1(air)}\right)}{\left(j\omega\mu_0\right)^2}} E_0 e^{-\gamma_{1(air)}z}\hat{y} \\ &= \sqrt{\frac{j\omega\varepsilon_{1(air)} + \sigma_{1(air)}}{j\omega\mu_0}} E_0 e^{-\gamma_{1(air)}z}\hat{y} \end{aligned} \quad (12)$$

The incident wave's H-field ($\vec{H}^i$), the reflection ($\vec{H}^r$), and transmissionas ($\vec{H}^t$) can be expressed as a function of the wave impedance:

$$\vec{H}^i = \hat{y}\frac{E_0}{\eta_{1(air)}}e^{-\gamma_{1(air)}z} \tag{13}$$

$$\vec{H}^r = -\hat{y}\frac{RE_0}{\eta_{1(air)}}e^{-\gamma_{1(air)}z} \quad , \quad \vec{H}^t = \hat{y}\frac{TE_0}{\eta_{2(skin)}}e^{-\gamma_{2(skin)}z} \tag{14}$$

where the transmission coefficients is obtained by

$$T = \frac{2\eta_{2(skin)}}{\eta_{2(skin)} + \eta_{1(air)}} \tag{15}$$

Last, the Poynting vector, which represents the power density in W/m², is given by

$$\vec{S} = \vec{E} \times \vec{H} \Rightarrow |S| = |E||H| \tag{16}$$

Therefore, the incident and reflection power densities at the interface on the air-side and the transmission power density at the interface on the skin-side are:

$$\left|S_{1(air)}{}^i\right| = \frac{E_0{}^2}{\eta_{1(air)}}, \qquad \left|S_{1(air)}{}^r\right| = \frac{\Gamma^2 E_0{}^2}{\eta_{1(air)}}, \qquad S_{2(skin)}{}^t = \frac{T^2 E_0{}^2}{\eta_{2(skin)}} \tag{17}$$

Finally, the ratios of transmission-to-incident power ($P_{t/i}$) and reflection-to-incident power ($P_{r/i}$) are:

$$P_{r/i} = \frac{\left|S_{1(air)}{}^r\right|}{\left|S_{1(air)}{}^i\right|} = \Gamma^2, \qquad P_{t/i} = \frac{\left|S_{2(skin)}{}^t\right|}{\left|S_{1(air)}{}^i\right|} = \frac{T^2\eta_{1(air)}}{\eta_{2(skin)}} \tag{18}$$

## 6. Fabrication and measurement setup

The impulsive wave is amplified with an UWB PA (ZRON-8G) whose bandwidth is 2-8 GHz and its gain is almost constantly 20 dB over this band. Then the power is transmitted and received with a pair of UWB horn whose gain is 10 dBi. The received power is fed into a two-stage voltage doubler as shown in Figure 7. $C_1$ (0.1 pF) is used to filter out the dc component and $C_2$ (1 pF) functions as the ripple and noise filter. The rectifier usually requires to be optimized according to its input power biasing and the resistive load value. However, it is not easy to match to our UWB pulse signals up to 5.8 GHz, so we simply apply the broadband feature of the Schottky diodes to transfer the broadband power, yet this system is not optimal at this stage. The whole receiving circuit is fabricated on the substrate of Rogers RO4003C. We will compare two major performance parameters. One is the conversion efficiency and we try to figure out the optimal operation condition for an UWB powering transmission system. The other is to compare the difference of the input power of the rectifier to generate the same output voltage. That is useful to count how much power is saving for the same output voltage level.

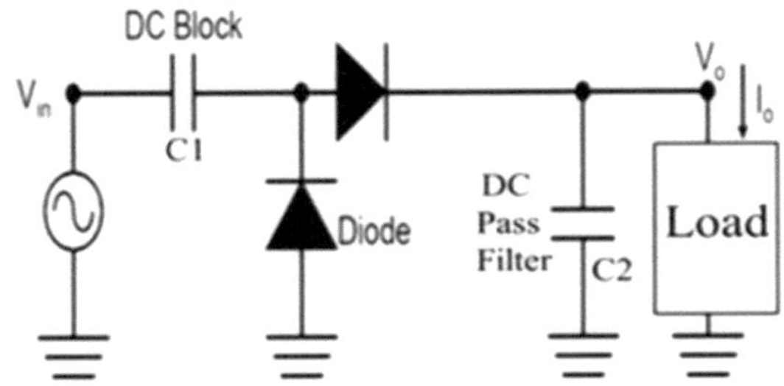


**Figure 7.** The circuit of the voltage doubler for the testing system of impulsive wireless power transmission.

A prototype of this monocycle pulse generator was implemented using discrete components. The substrate of the high frequency circuit was Rogers RO4003C with the dielectric constant of 3.55 and thickness of 32 mil (0.8182 mm). MuRata surface mount devices (SMD) and discrete components of the pulse generator are listed below. The optimized values of the components were $L_1$=3 nH, $L_2$=4.7 nH, $C_1$=$C_2$=3 pF, and $R_1$=$R_2$=150 Ω, based on theoretic simulations and fine tuning in the fabrication process. The driving inductance $L_1$ of the second-order transient circuit was estimated for the initial design using the equations in [Han 2005], and 3 nH, $L_2$, and $R_1$ were selected to ensure over-damping conditions according to the analysis in Section 3. However, the combination of $C_1$ and the equivalent resistance, $R_{eq}$, of $R_1$ and impedance of the BJT resulted in a high-pass filter for the input driving signal. Therefore, $C_1$ may be too small, blocking the generated pulses. In addition, the upper bound of $C_1$ can be estimated by preventing the input clock signal, with a rise time of $t_r$, from slewing; thereby implying $C_1 < t_r / (2.2R_{eq})$. $C_2$ was used to remove the dc component of the impulse and had to be kept small in consideration of the total equivalent capacitance value. Finally, $R_2$ and $C_3$ were fine tuned in ADS simulation to produce a symmetrical waveform. BFG520 BJT (Philips Semiconductor, NXP) was selected for its wideband, extending up to 9 GHz. Metelics MMDB30-0805 SRD with 0.46 pF junction capacitance provided an extremely short transition time of 30 ps.

A testing system of impulsive wireless power transmission is setup to measure its power conversion efficiency and to compare with the traditionally continuous wave WPT systems. The impulse generator is triggered with a 10 MHz square wave with amplitudes of 2, 3, 4, and 5 Vpp, and the generator outputs average power (instant peak power) of -31.0 dBm (2.83 dBm), -27.3 dBm (7.14 dBm), -25.1 dBm (10.10 dBm), and -23.7 dBm (11.86 dBm), respectively. The power is calculated according to equation (19):

$$P_{UWB,\,avg} = \text{The power of a mono} - \text{pulse} / \text{The period of trigger signals} \quad (19)$$

# 7. Results and discussion

## 7.1. Waveform of pulse generator circuit

Figure 8 presents the results of characterizing the waveform of the monocycle pulse. Figure 8(b) is the Fourier Transform of the measured pulse in the frequency domain, implying an ultra-wide bandwidth of 5.2 GHz (900 MHz – 5.1 GHz). The measured and simulated results were closely matched. The width of the output pulse of the generator circuit was approximately 290 ps, and the amplitude was 310 mV (peak-to-peak). The symmetry is evident in the similarities in amplitude and width in the positive and negative cycles of the measured waveform. The monocycle pulse has a highly symmetrical shape. Conversely, when the positive and negative cycles differ in amplitude and width, the pulse width cannot be minimized and the sidelobe ringing increases. This can be dealt with by carefully tuning the differentiator circuit during fabrication. Moreover, this aspect of symmetry can reduce the ringing even further. In the end, the ringing level was reduced to only -21.8 dB. Ringing level is defined as

$$20\log\left[\frac{\text{The peak-to-peak value of ringing}}{\text{The peak-to-peak value of monocycle pulse}}\right] \quad (20)$$

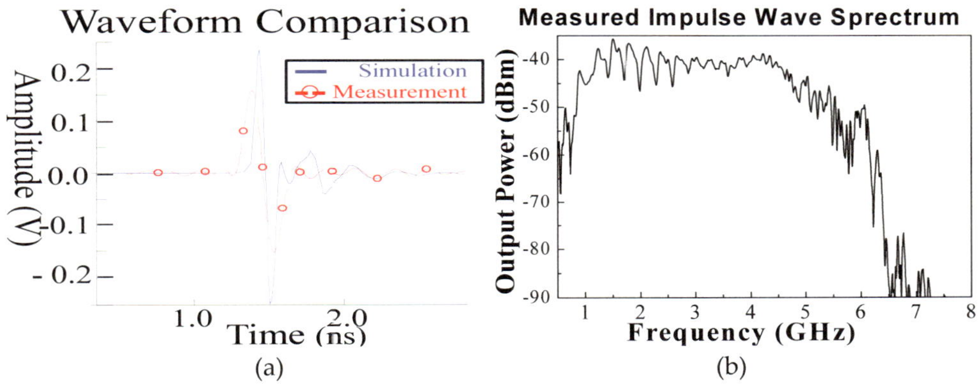


**Figure 8.** (a) Comparison of simulated and measured pulse waveforms; (b) Response of the measured monocycle pulse in frequency domain.

Unlike some generators requiring high frequency sources, we used a 10-MHz or lower square wave signal as a trigger source, applying a high speed digital real-time oscilloscope (Agilent DSO81204B) to measure the pulse in the time domain. Moreover, the frequency range of the input triggered square waves can be very broad. In this study the range was verified to cover 30 Hz to 30 MHz, resulting in stable monocycle pulse waveforms of identical widths with variations in the amplitude of less than 3 %. This implies that a triggering square wave circuit can be simple and does not require a specific frequency range, eliminating the need for a bulky external signal generator.

Figure 9 presents the results of measuring the monocycle pulse waveform using a triggering source of 10 MHz square waves with amplitudes of 2 to 5 V. When the amplitude of the triggering source was increased, the amplitude of the monocycle pulse also increased. The width of the pulse remained unchanged, as shown in Figure 9. The ringing ratio was not amplified, but remained below -21 dB. Maintaining ultra low ringing is beneficial to UWB communication systems. Details of the monocycle pulse are summarized in Table 1. Positive and negative cycles are nearly equal in amplitude and duration, demonstrating a high degree of symmetry.

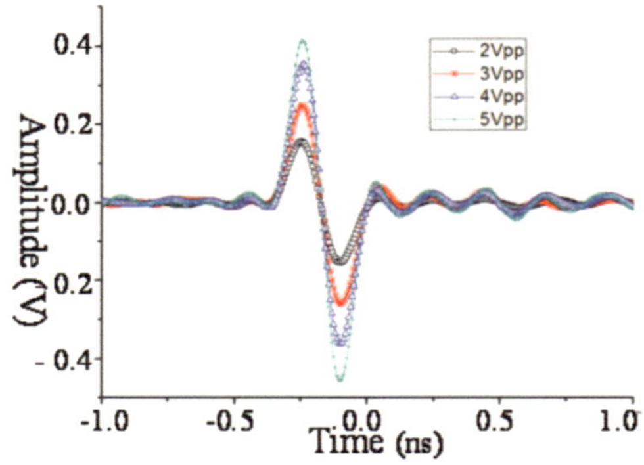


**Figure 9.** Measurement results with variations in triggering amplitude.

| Trigger Square Wave Amplitude ($V_{PP}$) | Output Peak-to-peak Amplitude (mV) | Ringing Level (dB) |
|---|---|---|
| 2 | 320.0 | -21.8 |
| 3 | 509.0 | -21.0 |
| 4 | 716.0 | -21.5 |
| 5 | 876.0 | -22.0 |

**Table 1.** Monocycle Pulse in Relation to Triggering Amplitudes

Table 2 provides a comparison of performance between various monocycle pulse generators fabricated with discrete components that have appeared in recent publications. Each of these devices generates sub-nanosecond pulse waveforms with additional dc bias; however, our proposed hybrid shunt SRD and BJT pulse shaping circuitry requires no dc bias. Moreover, as seen in this table, our design has the advantage of tunable pulse amplitude, ultra low ringing, short pulse width, and excellent symmetry.

| Reference | [Han 2002] | [Lee 2001] | [Miao2006] | **This work** |
|---|---|---|---|---|
| Peak-to-peak Amplitude (mV) | 400 | 700 | 300~600 | **320 ~ 876** |
| Ringing Level (dB) | -17 | -20.9 | -16.9 ~ -16 | **-21.8** |
| Pulse Duration (ps) | 300 | 350 | 200 ~ 400 | **290** |
| Technology | SRD | SRD | CMOS | **SRD/BJT** |

**Table 2.** Comparison of This Work to Other Pulse Generators

## 7.2. Wired transmission verification

We observe the impacts of reducing duty cycles of the impulse waves under same average input power (-10 dBm) on the PCE through a short low loss coaxial cable to remove the wireless channel uncertainties. As the duty cycles reduce, the larger instant power helps to overcome the potential barrier of the rectifier circuits, so the PCE can be improved. However, on the other hand, the wider bandwidth of matching network is required and parts of the power are out of band, so the PCE cannot achieve to its maximum as the duty cycles becomes smaller and smaller. The measured results are shown in Figure 10.

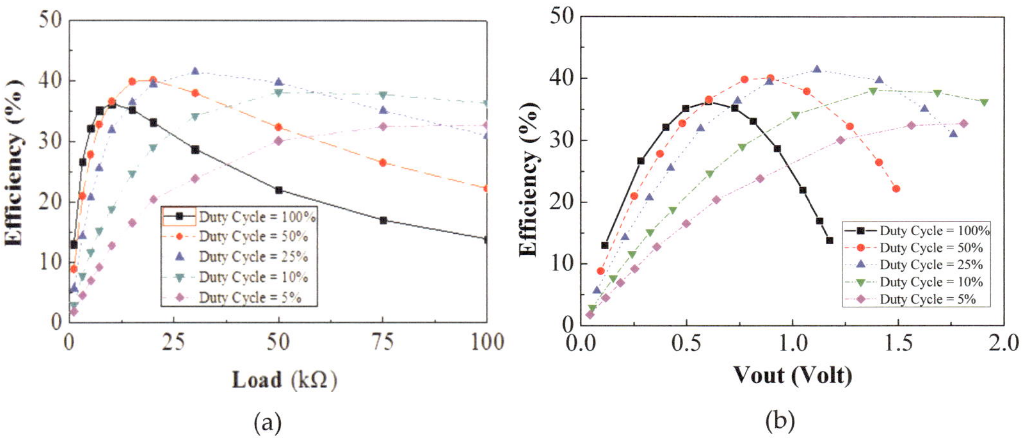


**Figure 10.** (a) The efficiency of different duty cycles and different resistive load under the same average input power. (b) The efficiency of different duty cycles and different Vout under the same average input power.

As the Figure 10(a) shows, the optimal PCE can be achieved when the load is 30 kΩ and the duty cycle is 25%. After that, even though the duty cycle reduces, the PCE starts to decrease instead. Given a 100 kΩ, the maximal PCE can be improved by 22.46% and this is almost twice efficient as the original CW power transmission (16%). The PCE can be ranked in the duty cycles of 10%> 5%> 25%> 50%> 100%. The best PCE can be achieved at duty cycle 10%, not 5%. As the Figure 10(b) shows, the output voltage $V_{out}$ is raised from 1.176 to 1.905 volt. Therefore, one more dimension of freedom is created to meet the optimal PCE and the required $V_{out}$ by varying the duty cycles under specific loading.

## 7.3. The input power gain to obtain same output voltage

To compare the performance of our fabricated impulsive generator for WPT, the circuit is triggered with a 10-MHz square wave from 2 Vpp to 5 Vpp and produces the impulsive power (after a 20 dB PA) from -11 dBm to -3.7 dBm. The output voltages are recorded, and the traditional CW which is optimized reproduces this same output voltage level. The difference of the input power is called saved input power, which implies a better efficiency of the rectifier to output same voltage with less average input power. The results are shown in Table 3. The saved input power of the impulsive powering systems ranges from 1.6 dB to 2.1 dB, which is a worse case. When the trigger source is replaced with a 40 MHz one, the saved input power ranges from 8.4 dB to 10.6 dB.

## 7.4. The optimal Power Conversion Efficiency (PCE)

The fabricated impulsive generator is applied as the power source with the different trigger signals ranging from 10 MHz to 40 MHz to output the different power level ranging from -11 dBm to 13.6 dBm after some adjustment of a -10 dB attenuator and a 20-

dB PA. The output voltage with the 30 kΩ resistive load is shown in Figure 11. We found the $P_{IN}$ for optimal PCE (58%) operation reduces to -2.4 dBm. Compared with traditional CW WPT techniques, high efficiency may be achieved under the operation condition of $P_{IN}$ > 7.5 dBm. This validates our assumption to apply such wideband powering techniques for low input power to generate high output voltage and to enhance the conversion more efficiently.

| To Obtain Same $V_{out}$ (V) | Input Power Required by | | Input Power Saving Ratio (dB) |
|---|---|---|---|
| | Using Impulse (dBm) | Using CW (dBm) | |
| **0.700** | -11.0 | -8.9 | 2.1 |
| **1.207** | -7.3 | -5.5 | 1.8 |
| **1.601** | -5.1 | -3.4 | 1.7 |
| **1.900** | -3.7 | -2.1 | 1.6 |

**Table 3.** The comparison of the input power between impulsive (triggered with a 10 MHz source) and CW with a 12 kΩ load

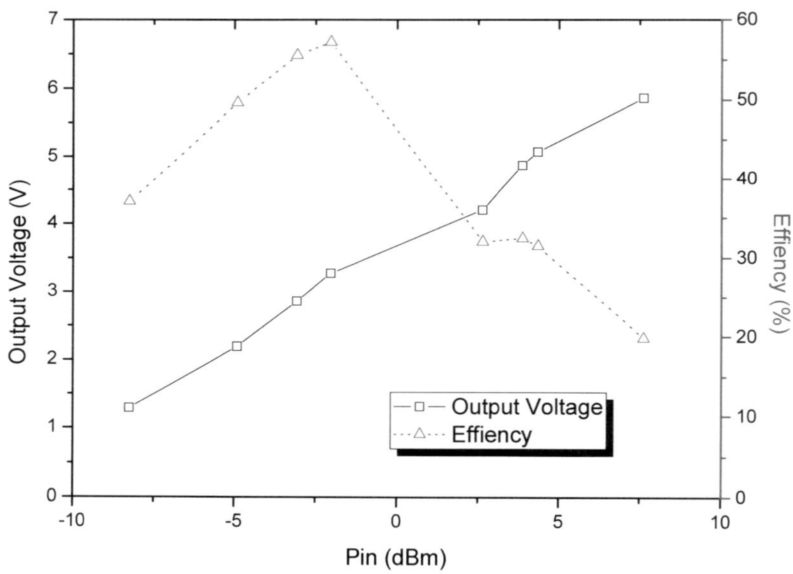


**Figure 11.** The performance of the wideband rechanging for the resistive load of 30 kΩ.

## 7.5. The impulse wireless powering transmission

Last, the impulsive wireless power transmission tests at a distance of 50 cm and 60 cm are performed. The impulsive generator is triggered at 40 MHz square waves and outputs power ranging from -4.8 dBm to 3.9 dBm. The transmission and receipt antennas are using horn antennas of 10 dBi. The results are shown in Table 4. Due to the path loss attenuation, the output voltages are low but are still good for circuits of low power supply of 1.2 V.

| Impulsive Power Trigger with 40 MHz + 20-dB PA (dBm) | $V_{out}$ at Distance of 50 cm (V) | $V_{out}$ at Distance of 60 cm (V) |
|---|---|---|
| -4.8 | 0.336 | 0.262 |
| -0.8 | 0.730 | 0.611 |
| 1.7 | 1.060 | 0.910 |
| 3.9 | 1.250 | 1.100 |

**Table 4.** The performance of output voltage using impulsive wireless power transmission with horn antennas

## 8. Conclusion

In this chapter, a novel impulsive UWB technology is proposed for wireless power transmission, and we designed, fabricated, and validated an improved UWB monocycle pulse generator using a hybrid shunt SRD and wideband BJT. Applying a shunt SRD with a second-order circuit produces a sharp Gaussian pulse, the waveform of which can be converted into monocycle impulse signals after the wideband BJT and RC differentiator. Measurement results closely match those of simulation. The fabricated monocycle pulse generator outputs a symmetrical 290 ps impulse with extremely low ringing (-21.8 dB) triggered by a square wave source across a wide frequency range of 30 Hz to 30 MHz. The proposed impulse generator circuit is well suited to UWB applications with the advantages of simple design, low cost, highly symmetrical impulses, and low ringing.

This novel impulsive generator is applied for wideband wireless power transmission and is verified in experiments. An impulsive generator is designed and fabricated as the experimental testing sources. The measurement results show that the PCE can achieve 50% efficiency by applying the impulsive WPT when the average input power remains below 0 dBm. This novel concept opens a broad angle for the future research of wireless power transmission technologies. In the future, wireless power transmission technologies can be developed in diversifed methods such as wideband power or multiple CW powers.

## Author details

Chin-Lung Yang, Yu-Lin Yang and Chun-Chih Lo
*Department of Electrical Engineering, National Cheng Kung University, Tainan, Taiwan (R.O.C.)*

## 9. References

Bertoni, H. L.; Carin, L.; Felsen, L. B. (1992). *Ultra-wide band short pulse electromagnetic*, New York, Kluwer Publications, (1992).

Brown, W. C.; Mims, J. R.; Heenan, N. I. (1965). An Experiemental Microwave-powered Helicopter, *IRE International Convention Record*, vol. 13, part 5, (Mar. 1965) , pp. 225-235.

Gabriel, S.; Lau, R.W.; Gabriel, C. (1996). The Dielectric Properties of Biological Tissues: III Parametric Models for The Dielectric Spectrum of Tissues, *Physics in Medicine & Biology.*, vol. 41, (1996), pp. 2271–2293.

Han, J.; Nguyen, C. (2002). A new ultra-wideband, ultra-short monocycle pulse generator with reduced ringing, *IEEE Microwave Wireless Compon Lett*, 12 (2002), 206-208.

Han, J.; Nguyen, C. (2005). Coupled-slotline-hybrid sampling mixer integrated with step-recovery-diode pulse generator for UWB applications, *IEEE Trans Microwave Theory Tech*, 53 (2005), 1875-1882.

Hirt, W. (2003). Ultra-wideband radio technology: Overview and future research, *Computer Commun J*. 26 (2003), 46–52.

Kurs, A.; Karalis, A.; Moffatt, R.; Joannopoulos, J. D.; Fisher, P.; Soljačić, M. (2007). Supporting Online Material for Wireless Power Transfer via Strongly Coupled Magnetic Resonances, *Science Magazine*, (June 2007).

Lee, J. S.; Nguyen, C.; Scullion, T. (2001). New uniplanar subnanosecond monocycle pulse generator and transformer for time-domain microwave, *IEEE Trans Microwave Theory Tech*, 49 (2001), 1126-1129.

Ma, T.-G.; Wu, C.-J.; Cheng, P.-K.; Chou, C.-F. (2007). Ultrawideband monocycle pulse generator with dual resistive loaded shunt stubs, *Microwave Opt Technol Lett 23* (2007), 459–462.

McSpadden, J.O.; Lu, F.; Chang, K. (1998). Design and Experiments of a High Conversion Efficiency 5.8-GHz Rectenna, *IEEE Transactions on Microwave Theory and Techniques*, vol. 46, (Dec. 1998), pp.2053-2060.

Miao, M.; Nguyen, C. (2006). On the development of an integrated CMOS-based UWB tunable-pulse transmit module, *IEEE Trans Microwave Theory Tech*, 54 (2006), 3681–3687.

Protiva, P.; Mrkvica, J.; Macháč, J. (2010). A compact step recovery diode subnanosecond pulse generator, *Microwave Opt Technol Lett 52* (2010), Iss.2, 438-440.

Reed, J. H. (2005). *An introduction to ultra wideband communication systems*, Prentice Hall PTR, (2005).

Rodenbeck, C.; Li, M.; Chang, K. (2004). A Phased-array Architecture for Retrodirective Microwave Power Transmission from the Space Solar Power Satellite, *IEEE MTT-S International Microwave Symposium Digest*, vol. 3, (June 2004), pp.1679-1682.

Teshirogi, T.; Saito, S.; Uchino, M.; Ejima, M.; Hamaguchi, K.; Ogawa, H.; Kohno, R. (2005). Residual-carrier-free burst oscillator for automotive UWB radar applications, *Electron Lett* 41 (2005), 535–536.

Yang, C.-L.; Lo, C.-C.; Yang, Y.-L. (2003). Sub-nanosecond Pulse Generators for Impulsive Wireless Power Transmission, *IEEE Transactions on Circuits and Systems II*, (Dec. 2011), pp. 817 - 821.

Yo, T.-C.; Lee, C.-M.; Hsu, C.-M.; Luo, C.-H. (2008). Compact Circularly Polarized Rectenna with Unbalanced Circular Slots, *IEEE Transactions on Antenna and Propagation,* (Mar. 2008), vol. 56, no. 3, pp. 852-886.

Yoo. T.; Chang, K. (1992). Theoretical and Experimental Development of 10 and 35 GHz Rectennas, *IEEE Transactions on Microwave Theory and Techniques*, vol. 40, no. 6, (Jun. 1992), pp.1259-1266.

Young, H. S.; Chang, K. (2002). A High Efficiency Dual Frequency Rectenna for 2.45- and 5.8-GHz Wireless Power Transmission, *IEEE Transactions on Microwave Theory and Techniques*, vol. 50, (July 2002), pp.1784-1789.

Zimmerman, M.; Chaimanonart, D.N.; Young, D. J. (2006). *In Vivo* RF Powering for Advanced Biological Research, *Engineering in Medicine and Biology Society, EMBS 28th Annual International Conference of the IEEE*, (2006), pp. 2506-2509.

# Chapter 18

# A Low Noise Low Power OTA with Adjustable Gain PID Feedback Network for EEG SoC Arrays

Robson Moreno, Tales Pimenta, Paulo Crepaldi, Odilon Dutra,
Gustavo Della Colletta and Leonardo Zoccal

Additional information is available at the end of the chapter

http://dx.doi.org/10.5772/45754

## 1. Introduction

Standard electroencephalogram (EEG) exams are subject to noises and interferences that may mask or corrupt signals and may cause a wrong medical evaluation. The noise from the environment is more relevant for discrete topologies, in which the components are placed far apart from other. That problem is more relevant on the neurological amplifiers, where the signals are in the range of tens of microvolts. Thus, the use of integrated circuits for the neurological signal amplification is essential to reduce that interference.

Additionally, cables used to connect the electrodes placed on the scalp and the amplifiers are also susceptible to interferences since they work as antennas, thus capturing all kind of environmental noises. Therefore the cables should be as short as possible, or even removed to be immune to the environmental interferences.

This chapter presents a circuit topology of a neurological amplifier to be placed directly on top of the electrodes. The proposed implementation offers better tradeoff among power x area x input referred noise than previously works [1] and offers a bandwidth even wider than necessary to accommodate EEG signals, thus providing a tool for further neurological studies.

Other works [2] present better noise efficiency factor (NEF) but at the expense of more complex source-degenerated current mirrors architecture, which makes them more susceptible to process variations.

The main circuit is comprised of a standard folded Cascode operational transconductance amplifier (OTA) and a fully integrated proportional, integral and derivative (PID) feedback network composed by a pMOS pseudo-resistor [3] and small integrated capacitors. The amplification can be adjustable over 5 different discrete values for better fitting the neural amplification to the analog to digital conversion (ADC) stage.

The amplifier topology was validated for ON 0.5 $\mu$m under the MOSIS program. Post layout simulations reveal the amplifier can provide a gain ranging from 34.32 dB to 43.63 dB, and the whole chip dissipates just 26 $\mu$W. The input referred noise is as low as other similar works [1] while requiring a smaller bias current. The circuit takes an area of just 0.134 mm$^2$.

## 2. EEG basic concepts and characteristics

EEG signals have particular characteristics that demand specific instruments to process them properly. The most important and specific characteristic of EEG signals is its small amplitude when measured by devices placed on the patient's scalp. According to the medical literature [4, 5], EEG signals' amplitude vary tipically from 5 to 10 $\mu$V to 500 $\mu$V within a bandwidth of about tens of miliHertz to 100 Hertz. They may present spikes of comparatively high amplitudes at very low frequencies, denoted local field potentials (LFP) that can achieve 1 V to 2 V [6].

Additionally, the EEG signals may suffer variations due to age, as shown in Table 1.

| **Rithm** | **DELTA** | **THETA** | **ALPHA** | **BETA** |
|---|---|---|---|---|
| Frequency Component | < 4 Hz | 4 to 7 Hz | 8 to 13 Hz | > 13 Hz |
| Amplitude | 100 $\mu$V | Child: 20 $\mu$V<br>Adult: 10 $\mu$V | Baby: 20 $\mu$V<br>Child: 75 $\mu$V<br>Adult: 50 $\mu$V | 10 to 20 $\mu$V |
| Main Scalp Area | Front | Temporal | Occipital<br>Pariental | Front |
| Human Condition | Deep Sleep | Sleepy | Relaxed<br>Closed Eyes | Relaxed<br>Openned Eyes |

**Table 1.** EEG Amplitudes Variations.

Those particularities suggest that the acquiring system should be able to provide adjustable gain, so that the physician could adjust the gain in order to obtain the best signal resolution.

Another important fact to consider is acquiring process itself. The acquiring devices may disturb and add others characteristics to the signal, that must be treated correctly by the measurement system, which is performed in this case by the EEG SoC array system.

For instance, the electrodes usually add 1 $V_{DC}$ to 2 $V_{DC}$ offset that must be eliminated. Figure 1 shows the most typical electrodes used on acquiring EEG signals.

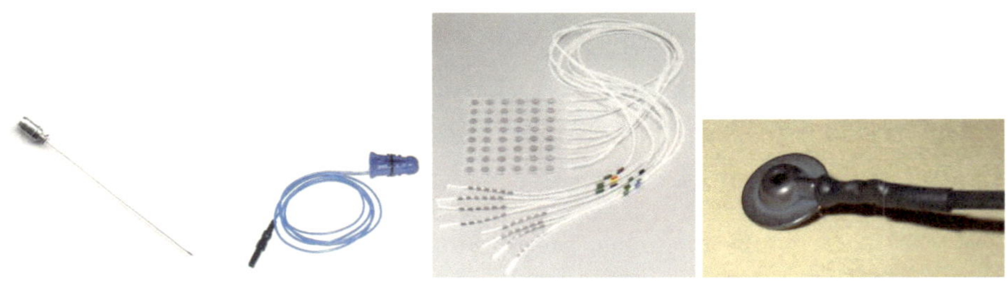

(a) Niddle Electrode. (b) Ear Electrode. (c) Cortical Electrode. (d) Plate Dish Electrode.

**Figure 1.** Example of Electroencephalogram Electrodes.

Therefore the acquiring system must be capable of acquiring the data correctly, by taking into account the signal singularities and avoiding disturbing the measured signal.

The description of the measuring system and the design of the neural amplifier will be presented in the next sections.

## 3. System architecture

This chapter describes the design of a neural amplifier to be used as part of an EEG acquisition system, denoted by EEG system on chip (SoC) array.

As per EEG signal characteristics, it is necessary at least 22 acquisition elements to obtain enough data to properly perform an EEG neurological exam. Figure 2 shows the system architecture.

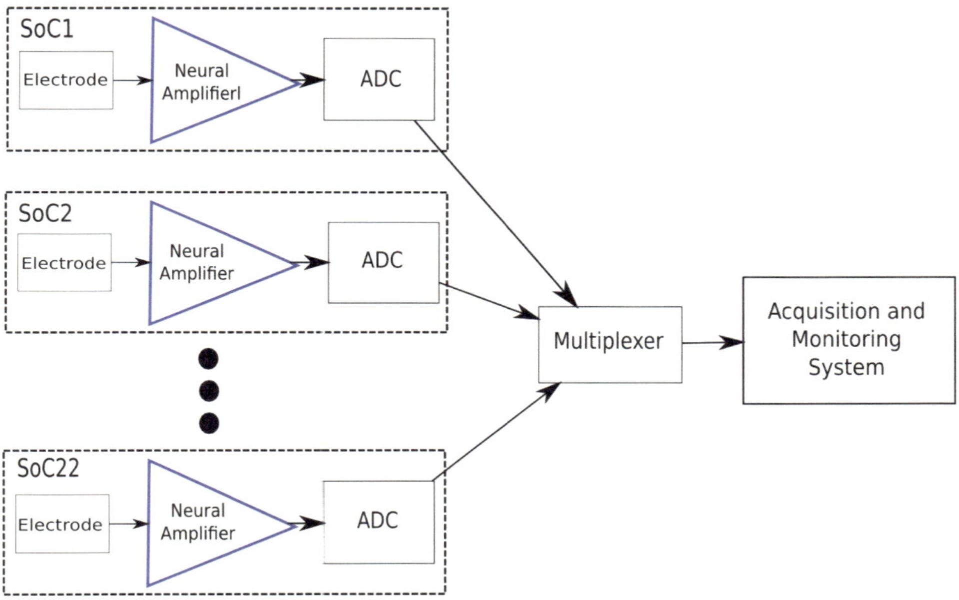


**Figure 2.** EEG Acquistion System Arquitecture.

Each acquiring element of the system is composed by an electrode, a neural amplifier (which is the focus of this work) and an analog to digital converter (ADC). If the amplification and AD conversion is placed on top of the electrode, the signal will be acquired, amplified and converted to digital almost at the same spot, and thus the previously related interferences may be deeply eliminated.

The digital converted signal from each electrode is multiplexed, serialized and then transmitted to the computer.

Figure 3 shows an example of physical implementation, where each small white spot on the blue cap represents an EEG SoC element. The output lines of the EEG SoC elements are input into a single element that multiplexes and transmits the data. The transmission can be performed by fiber optics, wire or even by any wireless procedure.

**Figure 3.** EEG Acquistion System Physical Structure.

## 4. Neural amplifier

The whole amplifier should provide low input referred noise and low power in order to meet the requirements of a neural amplifier for extended EEG applications. Figure 4 shows the basic circuit topology that will be detailed in the next sections.

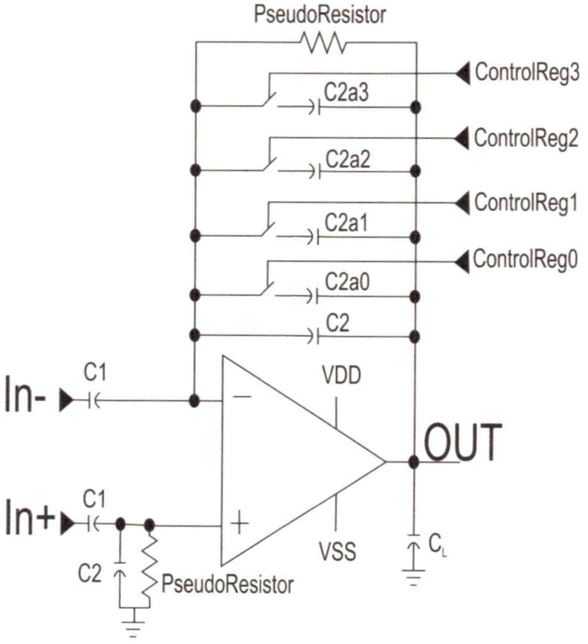


**Figure 4.** Proposed Neural Amplifier.

It also needs to provide an active band pass filter, allowing that signals in very low frequencies (hundreds of miliHertz) up to the proposed 1500 Hertz pass through while being amplified.

That is achieved with the PID feedback network, comprised by the OTA, decoupling capacitors, nMOS switches, pseudo-resistors and integration capacitors, that will be described on the next sections.

The achieved Neural Amplifier closed loop frequency response can be seen in Figure 5. Low and high-cut-off frequencies, as well as gains and input referred noise for each gain option are also compiled in Table 2.

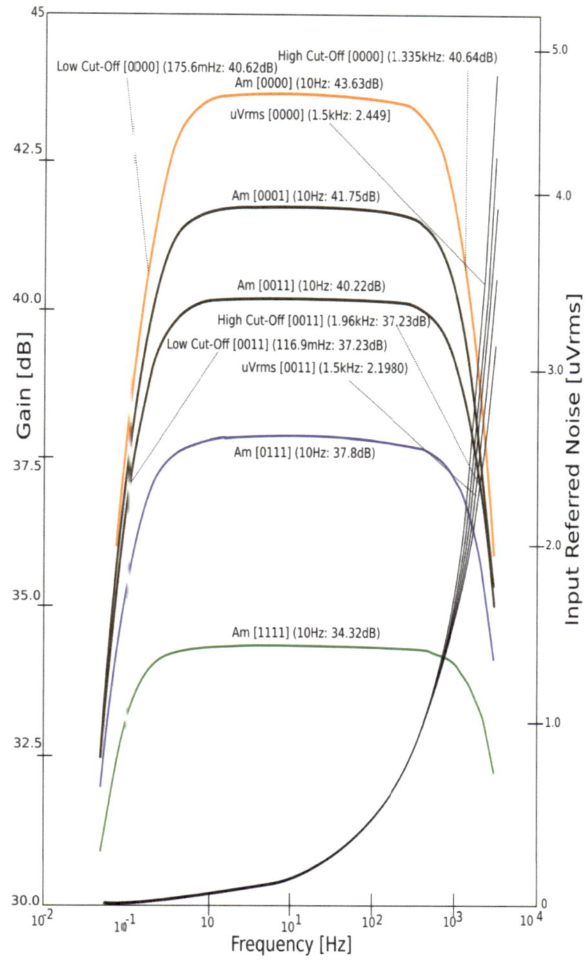


**Figure 5.** Neural Amplifier's Frequency Response.

| | Am (Designed) | Am (Simulated) | Low-CutOff | High-CutOff | Noise @ 1,5[kHz] |
|---|---|---|---|---|---|
| Register | [dB] | [dB] | [mHz] | [kHz] | [$\mu$Vrms] |
| 0000 | 43,52 | 43,63 | 175,6000 | 1,3350 | 2,4490 |
| 0001 | 41,94 | 41,75 | 150,7000 | 1,6435 | 2,2977 |
| 0011 | 40,00 | 40,22 | 116,9000 | 1,9600 | 2,1980 |
| 0111 | 37,50 | 37,80 | 88,2000 | 2,5643 | 2,0080 |
| 1111 | 33,98 | 34,32 | 55,5750 | 3,1000 | 1,9980 |

**Table 2.** Gains and Respective Input Referred Noise for Proposed Neural AMplifier.

## 4.1. PID feedback network with adjustable gain

The feedback network implements a band pass filter while controlling the gain, which can range approximately from 34.3 dB to 43.6 dB as shown in Figure 5. The variable gain is necessary to best fit the signal to the ADC stage, thus avoiding loss of resolution or signal saturation, while keeping the signal as reliable as possible. It also could mean an ADC of fewer bits, and consequently operating at lower frequencies, thus meaning even lower power dissipation. The inputs ControlReg come from digital registers that can be set by the software controlled by a physician, and the values are either $V_{DD}$ or $V_{SS}$ (in this case, $+1.8V$ or $-1.8V$, respectively).

The 4 ControlReg options allow 16 different gain combinations. However, due to capacitor integration concerns, to be presented in the next section, some combinations are not feasible. Therefore Table 2 presents only 5 different combination gains.

The highest gain is achieved with all ControlReg registers set as 0, in other words, just $C_2$ is connected to the network. The lower gain is implemented with all ControlReg registers set to 1, where $C_2$ and all integration capacitors $C_{2aX}$ are connected, as show in Table 2. Any other combination of ControlRegs implements a gain within the range of 43.52 dB to 33.98 dB.

The neural amplifier topology could be modified to reduce the number of gain steps by reducing the number of ControlReg lines, such as 2 or 3 lines.

The midband gain is given by (1):

$$A_M = \frac{C_1}{C_2 + \sum C_{2aX}} \tag{1}$$

where $C_{2aX}$ stands for each integration capacitor connected to the feedback network (controlled by its respective ControlReg switch, with X ranging from 0 to 3. $C_1$, $C_2$ and $C_{2aX}$ are shown in Figure 4.

The bandwidth, for $C_1$ and $C_L \gg C_2 + \sum C_{2aX}$ is given approximately by (2):

$$BW = \frac{g_m}{A_M.C_L} \tag{2}$$

where $g_m$ is the OTA transconductance, $A_M$ is the midband gain, BW is the bandwidth and $C_L$ is the load capacitance [1].

#### 4.1.1. *Integration capacitors*

Integration capacitors $C_2$, $C_{2a0}$, $C_{2a1}$, $C_{2a2}$ and $C_{2a3}$ were taken as 139, 34.8, 34.8, 69.5 and 139 fF, respectively. They were implemented using a matched capacitor matrix [7], as shown in Figure 6, to decrease process variations that could disturb the gain and bandwidth, since it is essential to keep them as accurately as possible. Each individual capacitor provides 34.76 fF. They have equal wide and length dimensions, of 6.6 $\mu$m. By connecting groups of capacitors, it is possible to obtain multiple values.

Capacitor $C_1$ was sized 18 pF and $C_L$ is equal to 15 pF, and the received the same layout care as the integration capacitors. A guard ring made of dummy capacitors surrounds the matrix of capacitors to protect it against incoming noises.

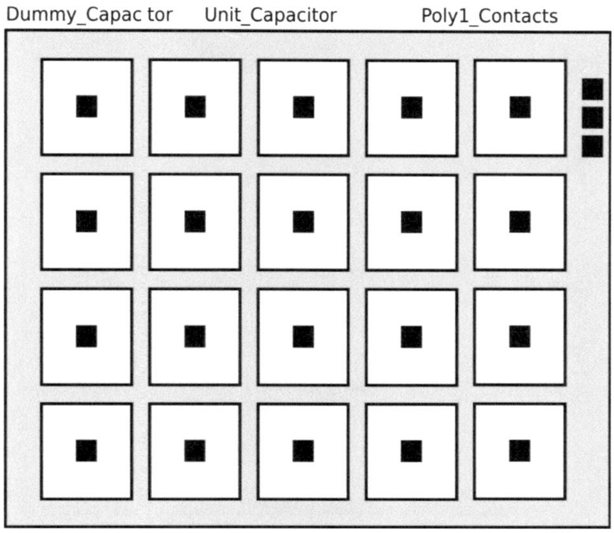


**Figure 6.** Matrix of Matched Capacitors for Integration Capacitors Layout.

*4.1.2. pMOS pseudo-resistor*

The pseudo-resistor presented in Figure 4 is actually composed of 6 diode connected pMOS transistors, as shown in Figure 7. In this topology each transistor was sized 4 $\mu$m x 4 $\mu$m. As described in [3], under positive $V_{GS}$, the parasitic source-well-drain pnp bipolar junction transistor (BJT) is activated, making the devices to act as junction BJT diode, thus providing the resistivity behavior indicated in Figure 8. It can be observed that for $V_{GS}$ close to 0 V the resistance decreases. It is not interesting to our application, since the low-frequency cutoff given by (3) increases for lower values of resistance.

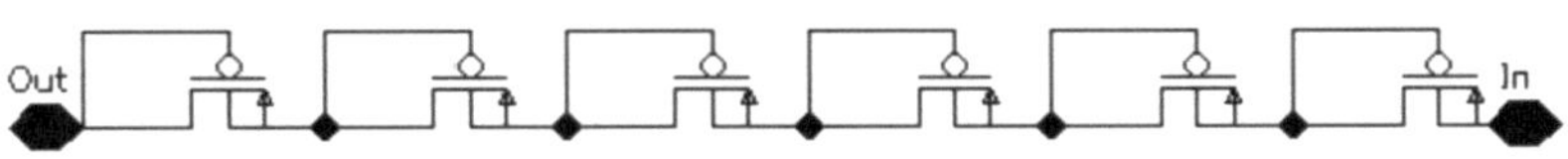


**Figure 7.** pMOS Pseudoresistor Implementation.

$$W_L = \frac{1}{2.R_{PseudoResistor}.C_2} \qquad (3)$$

The cutoff should be as close to zero as possible but at the same time, it should block the DC signals, so that the offset generated by electrodes can be eliminated in order to avoid biasing problems on the OTA differential pair. Therefore the OTA was designed to provide approximately 90 mV of systematic offset to achieve the low cutoff frequency required by the EEG applications, hence keeping capacitance $C_2$ low. It reduces the need of large area to build large integration capacitances, since the pseudo-resistor provides resistance on the order of $10^9$ Ohms for this range of $V_{GS}$. It was chosen the dimension of 4 $\mu$m x 4 $\mu$m for the capacitors to avoid any short channel effects on the feedback network, which could cause unexpected behaviors.

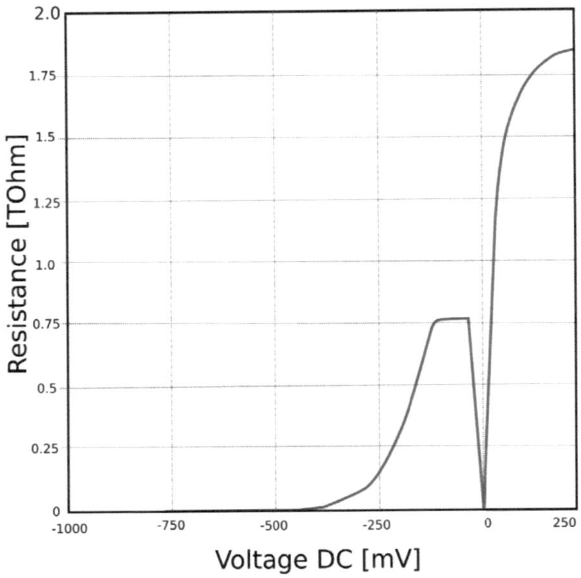


**Figure 8.** PseudoResistor Resistance Behavior.

*4.1.3. Parasitic insensitive nMOS switch*

In order to switch the integrator capacitors of the PID network it was used a topology of nMOS transmission switches [8], as shown in Figure 9. That topology is essential since it substantially minimizes the effects of parasitic on the switching transistors.

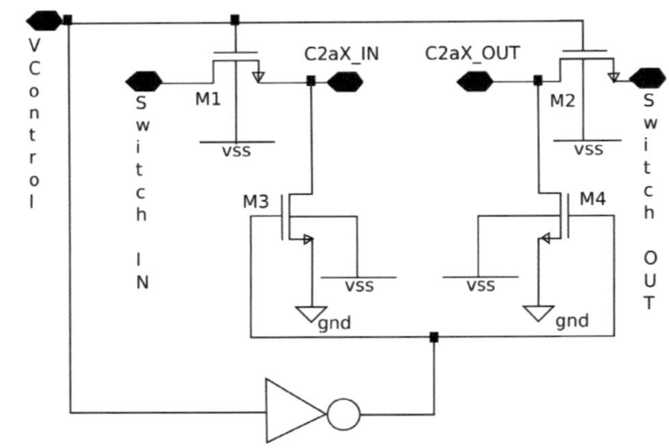


**Figure 9.** nMOS Transmission Switch.

The circuit works switching the integrator capacitor placed between $C_{2aX-IN}$ and $C_{2aX-OUT}$, as indicated in Figure 9. The switched capacitors correspond to each capacitor $C_{2a0}$ to $C_{2a3}$ in Figure 4. As the control register goes high ($V_{DD}$) the signal $V_{Control}$ biases directly transistors $M_1$ and $M_2$, and the switching capacitor is placed on the OTA feedback network while transistors $M_3$ and $M_4$ are kept off. Whenever the control register assumes low level ($V_{SS}$), $M_1$ and $M_2$ are turned off and $M_3$ and $M_4$ are turned on, taking potential GND to the sources of $M_1$ and $M_2$, thus decreasing the effects of parasitic when the feedback branch is not on. All transistors were sized 4 $\mu$m x 2 $\mu$m.

Figure 10 shows the schematic cf the OTA used for the neural signal amplification that can be used in a wide range of applications [1].

## 4.2. OTA design

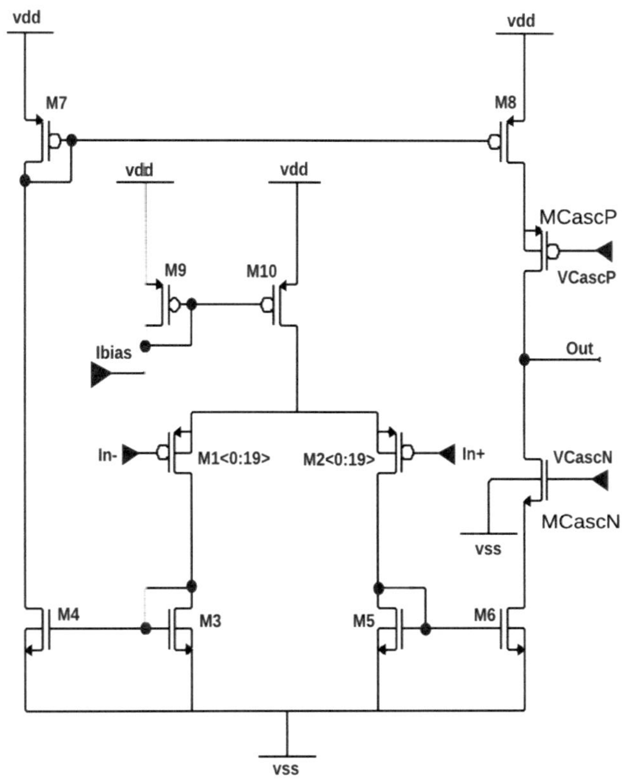


**Figure 10.** OTA Design.

The bias current IBias was set to 3 $\mu$A, so that $M_1$ to $M_8$ drain currents are 1.5 $\mu$A and total bias drained current is 6 $\mu$A.

It was calculated the region of operation for each transistor by calculating the moderate inversion characteristic current IS [9] using equation (4):

$$I_S = \frac{2.\mu.C_{OX}.{U_T}^2}{\kappa}.\frac{W}{L} \tag{4}$$

where $U_T$ is the thermal voltage $\frac{kT}{q}$, and $\kappa$ is the subthreshold gate coupling coefficient which is equivalent to $1/n$ where n denotes the reciprocal of the change in surface potential $\psi_{sa}$ for a change in gate-to-body voltage $V_{GB}$ [1, 9, 10].

Next it was calculated the inversion coefficient, which is given by the transistor drain current divided by moderate inversion characteristic current [1], as (5):

$$IC = \frac{I_D}{I_S} \tag{5}$$

An IC > 10 means the device operates in strong inversion. In case IC < 0.1, it operates in weak inversion. Any IC between those limits means the device is operating in moderate inversion.

In this work, the transconductance $g_m$ of those devices operating in weak and moderate inversion have been modeled by using the EKV model [11], as given by (6):

$$g_m = \frac{\kappa.I_D}{U_T}\cdot\left(\frac{2}{1+\sqrt{1+4.IC}}\right) \tag{6}$$

The strong inversion device modeling is given by (7):

$$g_m = \sqrt{2.I_D.\mu.C_{OX}.\frac{W}{L}} \tag{7}$$

Table 3 summarizes the main data of each device, including its operation region. Devices grouped in the same row in Table 3 have the same size and hence the same region of operation, and same transconductance $g_m$. For simplicity their $g_m$ will be generalized to the first index device (i.e. $g_{m3}$ equals to $g_{m4}$, $g_{m5}$ and $g_{m6}$).

| Devices | $V_{GS}$ [V] | $V_{overdrive}$[V] | IC | W/L | $I_D$ [uA] |
|---|---|---|---|---|---|
| $M_1$, $M_2$ | 0,9033 | 0,0160 | 0,053 | 900 / 2 | 1,500 |
| $M_3$, $M_4$, $M_5$, $M_6$ | 1,3293 | 0,4702 | 43,387 | 10 / 40 | 1,500 |
| $M_7$, $M_8$ | 1,5788 | 0,7197 | 99,008 | 6 / 25 | 1,500 |
| $M_9$, $M_{10}$ | 1,6015 | 0,7142 | 105,609 | 9 / 20 | 3,000 |
| $M_{cascN}$ | 0,9948 | 0,1357 | 3,616 | 12 / 4 | 1,500 |
| $M_{cascP}$ | 1,2945 | 0,4072 | 34,323 | 4.5 / 6.5 | 1,500 |

**Table 3.** OTA's Design Calculated Values

As shown by [1], the input referred thermal noise power for that adopted OTA topology is given by (8):

$$\overline{v^2_{ni,thermal}} = \left[\frac{16.k.T}{3.g_{m1}}\cdot\left(1+2.\frac{g_{m3}}{g_{m1}}+\frac{g_{m7}}{g_{m1}}\right)\right].\Delta f[V^2] \tag{8}$$

It can be observed that in order to minimize the noise, it is necessary to increase $g_{m1}$ and decrease $g_{m3}$ and $g_{m7}$. By proper sizing the differential pair, as shown in Figure 10, it can be guaranteed weak inversion operation. It sets high $g_{m1}$ whereas $g_{m3}$ and $g_{m7}$ are placed into strong inversion, which decreases their $g_m$. Several simulations were conducted to minimize this ratio in order to minimize noise, while keeping the stability of the OTA. By considering the transistors geometry designed and a load capacitance $C_L$ of 15 pF, the OTA provided a 63 degrees phase margin, as shown in Figure 11.

In order to decrease the flicker noise 1/f, which is always a constraint for low frequency applications, it was used a differential pair composed of pMOS transistors, which provide typically, one to two magnitude orders lower than in nMOS devices [9, 12]. The flicker noise is inversely proportional to gate area, so the devices were made as large as possible while keeping it reasonable. The amplifier input referred noise can be related to the OTA input referred-noise [1] by (9):

$$\overline{v^2{}_{ni,amp}} = \left(\frac{C_1 + C_2 + C_{in}}{C_1}\right).\overline{v^2{}_{ni}}[V^2] \tag{9}$$

where $C_1$ and $C_2$ are indicated in Figure 4 and again $C_2$ means the sum of integration capacitors connected to the PID feedback network.

Since $C_{in}$ contributes to a capacitive divider that attenuates the input signal, any increase in $C_{in}$ also increases the input referred noise of the whole amplifier.

#### 4.2.1. Stability criterion

As described in the previous section, the design of the OTA prioritizes the minimum amount of noise generated by increasing the transconductance of the differential pair (denoted by $g_{m1}$) whereas decreasing the transconductance of the current mirrors devices (denoted by $g_{m3}$ and $g_{m7}$). However it can not be done indefinitely due to the risk of losing stability.

For the OTA architecture, the stability criterion is defined as:

$$\frac{g_{m1}}{C_L} \ll \frac{g_{m3}}{C_3} and \frac{g_{m7}}{C_7} \tag{10}$$

where $C_3$ means the capacitance seen by the gate of $M_3$, $C_7$ means the capacitance seen by the gate of $M_7$, $C_L$ is the load capacitance, $\frac{g_{m1}}{C_L}$ denotes the main pole and $\frac{g_{m3}}{C_3}$ and $\frac{g_{m7}}{C_7}$ are secundary poles.

As seen in Figure 11, the OTA was designed to have about 63 degrees of phase margin, ensuring system stability.

### 4.3. Noise Efficiency Factor - NEF

The NEF is one of the most important benchmark for this kind of application. The noise should be minimized while keeping a low power consumption budget. The NEF [11] is given by (11):

$$NEF = V_{ni,rms}.\sqrt{\frac{2.I_{Total}}{\pi.U_T.4kT.BW}} \tag{11}$$

where $V_{ni,rms}$ is the input-referred noise rms voltage, $I_{Total}$ is the total consumed current and BW is the bandwidth, in Hertz.

For better understanding the NEF, it is made a comparison with a bipolar transistor, which is considered not having flicker noise. The NEF of a bipolar transistor is said to be equal 1. All real circuits, although, have a NEF higher than 1.

By replacing (11) for (8), which express the thermal noise for the OTA topology, integrating for the entire bandwidth BW, and assuming $g_{m3}$ e $g_{m7} \ll g_{m1}$ (totally reasonable), then by looking at Table 3, (11) becomes:

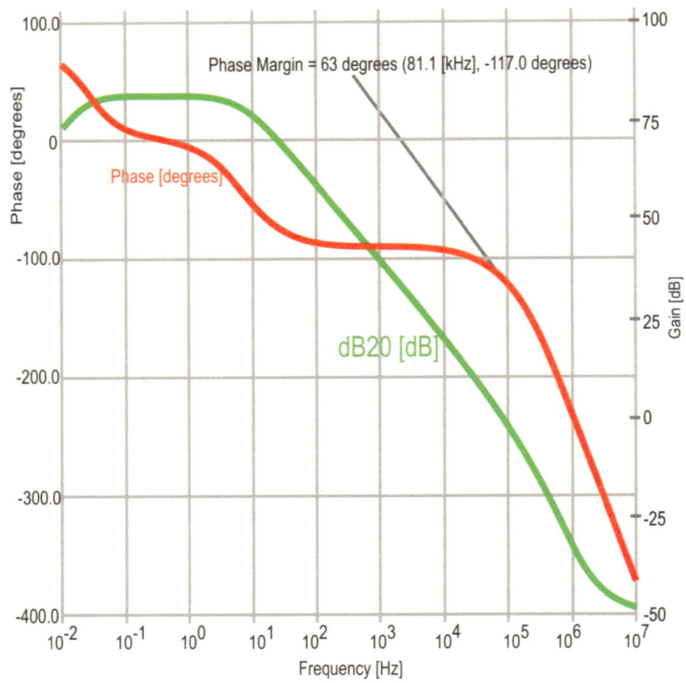


**Figure 11.** OTA Bode Diagram.

$$NEF = \sqrt{\frac{4.I_{Total}}{3.U_T.g_{m1}}} = \sqrt{\frac{16}{3.U_T}.\frac{I_{D1}}{g_{m1}}} \tag{12}$$

where $I_{D1}$ is the drain current through $M_1$ or $M_2$, which is easy to see that it is $\frac{1}{4}$ of $I_{Total}$.

Therefore, it can be concluded that for minimizing NEF, the relative transconductance $g_m$ of the pMOS transistor of the differential pair must be increased. Hence, those devices were sized in such a way to guarantee the operation in saturation - weak inversion since, in that region of operation, the relative transconductance reaches its maximum value of $\frac{\kappa}{U_T}$, as in [1].

Using a more accurate model of thermal noise for the saturation - weak inversion region of operation, as presented in [9], the NEF becomes:

$$NEF = \sqrt{\frac{4}{\kappa.U_T}.\frac{I_{D1}}{g_{m1}}} \tag{13}$$

Finally, assuming a value of $\kappa$ of approximately 0.7, which was calculated for this technology, the NEF can be reduced to (14):

$$NEF = \sqrt{\frac{4}{\kappa^2}} \approx 2,9 \tag{14}$$

That value of 2.9 can be considered the theoretical limit of NEF for the design using ON 0.5 $\mu$m technology.

## 5. Proposed layouts

Figure 12 shows a proposed layout for the OTA. The differential pair devices are designed as 20 parallel devices each one, helping to decrease even more the noise. They are shown at the bottom part. Current mirrors and Cascode devices are placed on the top.

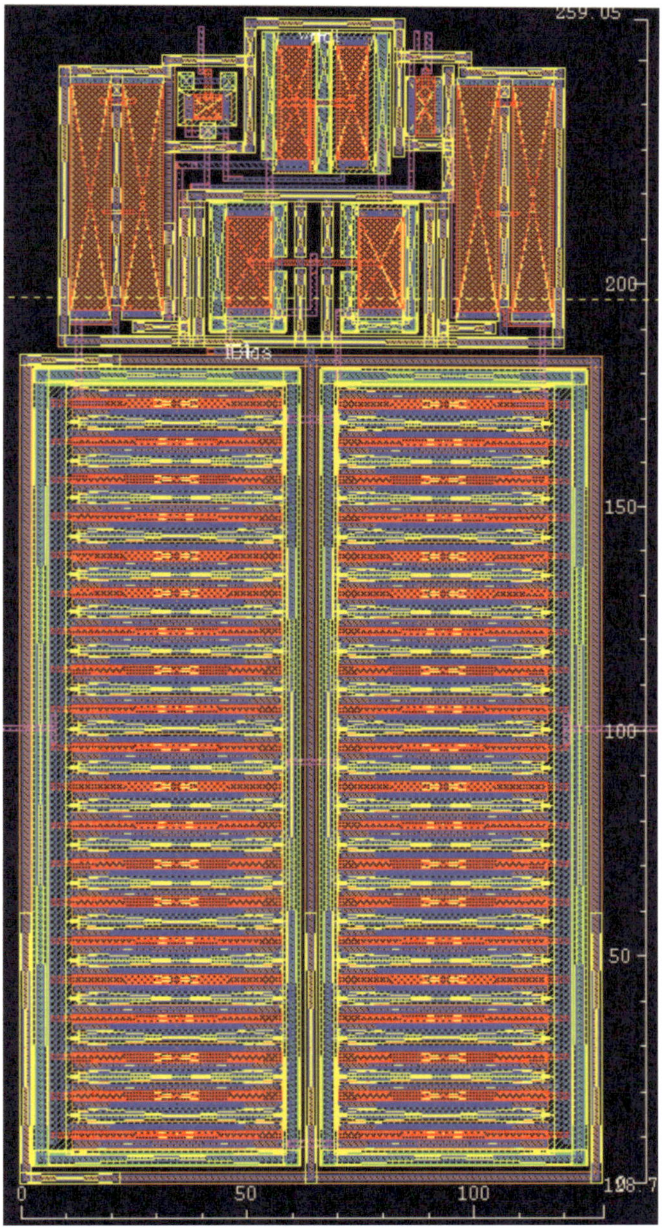


**Figure 12.** OTA Proposed Layout.

Figure 13 shows the proposed implementation of the entire neural amplifier. Decoupling capacitors $C_1$ are implemented aside of the differential pair inputs. All active areas were shielded with a grounded Metal 3 layer. Capacitors $C_2$, pseudo-resistors and nMOS switches are implemented at the top part.

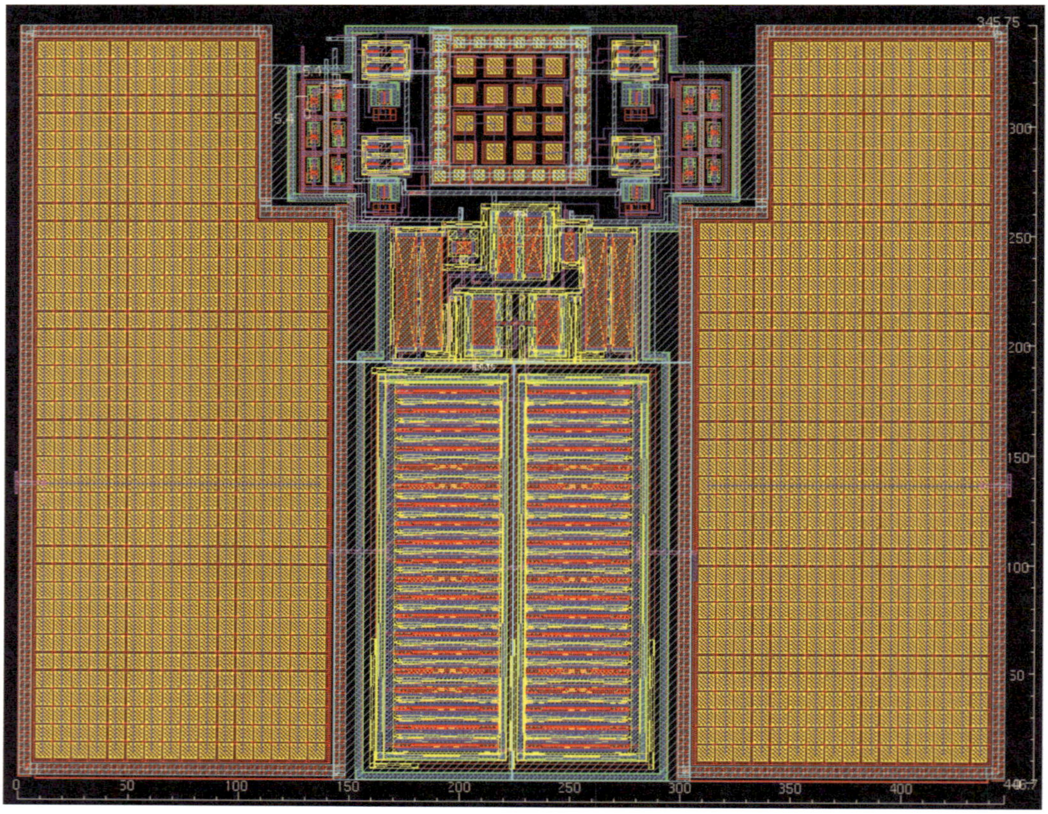


**Figure 13.** Neural Amplifier Proposed Layout.

## 6. Future research

By going through the proccess of designing this neural amplifier, it was realized the need of, basically:

- The neural amplifier must be fabricated and validated;
- Other technologies and diffusion characteristics could be used to evaluate any noise increase;
- Add the sample & hold circuit as well as an ADC;
- Integrate all elements on chip (neural amplifier, sample & hold and ADC);
- Conduct the analysis of disturbances in the analog signal due to noises generated by the digital converter.

## 7. Conclusion

This chapter described the implementation of a neural amplifier in ON 0.5 $\mu$m technology. It consumes only 26 $\mu$W on an $\pm$ 1.8 V power supply. It is comprised of a fully integrated PID feedback network formed by pMOS pseudo-resistors, nom-sensitive nMOS switches and a matrix of matched integration capacitors, capable of amplifying neurological signals on a 1.5 kHz bandwidth.

It also offers the option of choosing the gain among five different discrete values, varying from 43.52 dB to 33.98 db, as described on Table 2. The option of gain controlling is essential. It could mean lesser bits on the ADC converter, so that it could work under lower frequency and consequently dissipating lower power.

The input signal can vary from few $\mu$Vpp to approximately 10 mVpp with total harmonic distortion (THD) lower than 1%, and therefore the amplitude range is much wider than necessary for EEG signals.

The neural amplifier can be part of a fully integrated system on chip (SoC) for a full EEG measurement device, capable of measuring signals in higher frequencies than in standard EEG signals bandwidth. This complete system, an EEG SoC Multichannel Array would also contemplate a sample and hold structure, an ADC converter and a multiplexer for gathering and transmitting the data.

This chapter also presented a compilation of the benchmarks obtained for the neural amplifier, presented in Table 4 along with a comparison to the main references. Since the references, as

| | | **This Work** | **[1]** | |
|---|---|---|---|---|
| | **Technology** | **ON 0.5 $\mu$m** | **Standard 1.5 $\mu$m** | |
| | **Unity [ ]** | **Simulated** | **Simulated** | **Measured** |
| Power Supply Voltage | $\pm$ V | 1,8 | 2,5 | 2,5 |
| Biasing Current | $\mu A$ | 6 | 16 | 16 |
| Gain | dB | 40,22 | 40 | 39,5 |
| Low Cutoff Frequency (40 [dB]) | mHz | 116,9 | 130 | 25 |
| High Cutoff Frequency (40 [dB]) | kHz | 1,96 | 7,5 | 7,2 |
| Input Referred Noise | $\mu V_{rms}$ | 2,1980 | 2,1 | 2,2 |
| NEF | [ ] | 4,55 | 3,8 | 4 |
| THD ($<$ 12.8 mVpp) | % | $< 1$ | - | 1 |
| Dynamic Range (1% THD) | dB | - | - | 69 |
| CMRR $\leq$ 5[kHz] ($>$ than) | dB | 86,32 | 42 | 83 |
| Slew Rate Rise/Fall | $\frac{V}{ms}$ | 100 / 200 | - | - |
| Settling Time Rise/Fall | [$\mu$s] | 60 / 15 | - | - |
| PSRR $\leq$ 5[kHz] ($>$ than) | dB | 75,12 | 42 | 85 |
| CrcssTalk | dB | - | - | -64 |
| Area | $mm^2$ | 0,134 | 0,16 | 0,16 |
| Power | $\mu W$ | 26 | 80 | 80 |
| Phase Margin | $^o$ | 63 | 52 | - |

**Table 4.** Results and Comparison

in [1] did not offer gain control, all benchmarks were calculated taking the 40 dB gain as reference, in order to present similar circumstances.

## Acknowledgments

This work was supported by CAPES, CNPq, MEC and FAPEMIG.

## Author details

Robson Moreno, Tales Pimenta, Paulo Crepaldi, Odilon Dutra, Gustavo Della Colletta and Leonardo Zoccal
*Federal University of Itajuba, Brazil*

## 8. References

[1] R.R. Harrison and C. Charles. A low-power low-noise cmos amplifier for neural recording applications. *Solid-State Circuits, IEEE Journal of*, 38(6):958 – 965, june 2003.
[2] W. Wattanapanitch, M. Fee, and R. Sarpeshkar. An energy-efficient micropower neural recording amplifier. *Biomedical Circuits and Systems, IEEE Transactions on*, 1(2):136 –147, june 2007.
[3] T. Delbruck and C.A. Mead. Adaptive photoreceptor with wide dynamic range. In *Circuits and Systems, 1994. ISCAS '94., 1994 IEEE International Symposium on*, volume 4, pages 339 –342 vol.4, may-2 jun 1994.
[4] John G. Webster. *Medical Instrumentation - Application and Design*. John Wiley & Sons Inc, Sao Paulo, third edition, 1998.
[5] Vera L. S. N. Button. *Instrumentacao Biomedica*. DEB/FEEC Unicamp, Campinas, first edition, 2003.
[6] Sid Deutsch and Alice Deutsch. *Understanding the Nervous System - An Engineering Perspective*. IEEE Press, São Paulo, first edition, 1993.
[7] Alan Hastings. *The Art of Analog Layout*. Prentice Hall, 2001.
[8] David A. Johns and Ken Martin. *Analog Integrated Circuit Design*. John Wiley and Sons, Inc., 1997.
[9] Y. Tsivids. *Operation and Modeling of the MOS Transistor*. McGraw-Hill, second edition, 1998.
[10] N. H. E. Weste and K. Eshraghian. *Principles of CMOS VLSI design*. Addison-Wesley Publishing Company, second edition, 1993.
[11] F. Krummenacher C.C Enz and E. A. Vittoz. An analytical mos transistor model valid in all region of operation and dedicated to low- voltage and low-current applications. *Analog Integrat. Circuits Signal Process.*, 8:83 – 114, 1995.
[12] C.G. Jakobson, I. Bloom, and Y. Nemirovsky. 1/f noise in cmos transistors for analog applications. In *Electrical and Electronics Engineers in Israel, 1996., Nineteenth Convention of*, pages 557 –560, nov 1996.